Mountain Flying Bible, a review, by F. E. Potts

Over the many years I have been flying in Alaska, the unforgiving nature of the weather and terrain has impressed on me one very important lesson: that flying is a thinking man's (or woman's) game. Those who do not, or cannot, think, but instead rely only on the quick reflexes of youth or basic physical skills, have a tendency not to survive for long.

As a result, books by an experienced pro that explain the reasons why it is best to perform a maneuver one way rather than another, or describe in detail the thought processes behind various flight decisions, are, for me, the only ones of real value.

It was therefore with considerable interest that I began to read Sparky Imeson's new book, the Mountain Flying Bible – Sparky has a reputation of being a thoughtful and careful pilot, as well as a highly skilled one, and I was curious to see what he had come up with.

What he came up with is a book so good, so complete and detailed, so "useful" at all experience levels, that I found myself wishing I had it when I started my bush flying career in Alaska back in the early 1960s. While it may not have shortened my learning curve all that much (for true learning is something that needs seasoning over the years to achieve real depth on the subconscious level), there certainly would have been far fewer of those `interesting' moments.

Because of the size constraints placed on book reviews I only have room to touch on a few of the many subjects found in this marvelous book, so the ones I selected are those that follow my particular interests. Other pilots would, of course, select other items, and happily the menu Sparky provides is large.

I very much liked where, in the "Warning-Disclaimer", Sparky notes that the book "represents the current view of the author on the issues discussed as of the date of publication." This is an important point, for it reminds the reader that a pilot's learning process should be continuous over their career, and that as a result their view of the subject will (and should) change with time.

Another lesson provided by Sparky's approach to flying is found on page 3-88, where he tells how he built, out of 2x4s, a device which he placed in a stream so he could, by changing its orientation, better learn to understand how terrain modifies wind flow. This type of thinking, along with experimentation, is typical of the best pilots, for the best pilots seek understanding, and through understanding, learn what is needed to survive.

Certainly the depth of information Sparky provides on the subjects of wind (which needs to be thought of as weather, just like something you can see such as fog), turbulence, mountain wave, the infinite varieties of ice, high-altitude physiology, and basic flight maneuvers, are unsurpassed by any other book I have ever read.

One area of aviation that is often neglected is engine management, the science of controlling power and temperature changes. Nowhere is this more important then in environments where one is dealing with changing altitudes (climbing and descending), or serious cold. These subjects Sparky covers in great detail, and if his suggestions are carefully followed they will, in all probability, markedly increase the TBO of one's engine.

Another important subject Sparky covers in depth is emergency landings. Here he not only covers the usual techniques, but as well the psychological hazards. This section alone is well worth the price of the book, and should be reviewed carefully by all pilots. I personally 'knew' many pilots in Alaska who, had they followed Sparky's advice in this section (especially the psychological factors discussed on page 3-163), would be alive today.

Another nice thing about this book is that Sparky provides many photographs of various mountain landing areas, and these photographs give a good introduction to the subject for they each have a lesson to teach, and the examples are good. Perhaps my favorite is the picture on page 5-62, but then, mountain and bush pilots live in a special world, and are special people.

To sum up, Sparky not only deals in depth on the technical aspects of flying in this book, but, even more importantly from my perspective, he deals with the psychological aspects. And, of course, the sections that specifically deal with his specialty, mountain flying, are unsurpassed. This is not to say that this book has value only to mountain pilots, for that is not the case. This book is one of those that all pilots can learn from (just as it deepened my understanding in many areas), and should be part of every serious pilot's reference library. It is, in all likelihood, the best aviation book written in recent years that focuses on light aircraft. Certainly it is the most useful. I recommend it without reservation.

by *F.E. Potts*, author of

F.E. Potts' Guide to Bush Flying: Concepts and Techniques for the Pro

http://www.fepco.com/

Mountain Flying Bible

By Sparky J. Imeson

Aurora Publications
SAN: 297-5262   ISBN: 1-880568

P.O. Box 573
Jackson, Wyoming 83001-0573

http://www.mountainflying.com

Mountain Flying Bible

By Sparky J. Imeson

Published by:

Aurora Publications
SAN: 297-5262   ISBN: 1-880568

P.O. Box 573
Jackson, Wyoming 83001-0573

All rights reserved. Without limiting the rights under copyright reserved below, no part of this book may be reproduced, stored in or transmitted in any form or by any means (electronic, mechanical, photocopying, recording or otherwise), or by any information storage and retrieval system without the written permission from the author or publisher, except for the inclusion of brief quotations in a review.

 and

are registered trademarks of Mountain Flying, LLC.

Copyright © 1998, 2001 by Sparky J. Imeson
Cover Photo © Kay Cooper
Second Edition, Revised
First printing: November 1998
Printed in the United States of America
August 2001

ISBN 1-880568-89-6 $28.95 Softcover

This book is dedicated, with love, to my mother:
Jennie F. Imeson

To the memory of my father:
Paul C. Imeson

To my best friend, my wife:
W. Gaile Imeson

And to my good friend:
Frank Coppola

Thanks for the unquestioned support, guidance, advice and friendship.

ACKNOWLEDGMENTS

Most of us have heros when learning to fly. My heros, whom I tried to emulate, and who were the most influential on my career were Howard Ballew (deceased), Jack Christopherson (who taught me all about flaps, among other things), Dave Low (deceased), and my father (deceased). When the original *Mountain Flying* was written from 1968 to 1970, these four people offered their assistance.

Throughout the intervening years many others have provided their input as to their thoughts and desires for information to be included in any new edition. This book is not a revised edition of the original or revised editions of *Mountain Flying*. It is a new book that has been rewritten to incorporate most of the requested information. As such, it is much larger than the original, and hopefully, not too encumbering.

The *Mountain Flying Bible* began shortly after the original publication of *Mountain Flying,* with notes hastily written in the margins of the book. Next, sticky notes filled the pages. The advent of the notebook computer was a godsend, making it easy to work in airplanes and motel rooms throughout the U.S., Canada, Mexico, Guatemala, Venezuela and Brazil.

No one could have guessed that the book would grow from 144 pages to 512 pages. Not all of the increase deals directly with mountain flying. For example, there are pilots who do not know the proper procedure for taking a fuel sample (page 1-13). This technique should be used for all flights, not just for mountain flights. But, it is more critical in the mountains where there may not be as many suitable forced-landing areas.

A book-writing project requires input from others. This input may be tangible (like proof reading and suggestions) or intangible and obscure (providing motivation and encouragement). This input has been graciously provided to me by the following:

Frank Coppola, Esq., Englewood, CO; Darren DeLouch, Bonham, TX; Mike Ferguson, Director, Montana Aeronautics; Cliff Heglin, Denver, CO; Gaile Imeson, Harbor City, CA; Jennie F. Imeson, Jackson, WY; Brian D. Jones, Parker, CO; Tom Needham, Jackson, WY; Art Tiddens (deceased), Englewood, CO

The Possum Creek Airstrip COVER PHOTO and photographs on pages 5-59 through 5-61 are by Kay Cooper.

About the Author

Sparky Imeson (his real name) was born and raised in Jackson, Wyoming. He grew up in the mountains near his grandfather's homestead, enjoying hunting, fishing and camping. As a Boy Scout, he was introduced to flying with a 20-minute ride over Cheyenne, Wyo. in a DC-3.

Like others who have been bitten by the "flying bug," Sparky waited for the day when he could "spread his wings." He began flying in July 1966 at Jackson in his father's Piper J-3 and Cessna 205.

Sparky worked as a policeman while attending the University of Wyoming (pre-dental). After being accepted at the University of Oregon dental school, Sparky's father flew from Jackson to Laramie to pick him up for home visits before going to school. Sparky decided he liked flying better than looking in someone's mouth. He attended Herrod School of Aviation, Billings, Montana, to become a professional pilot.

In 1969, as part owner of Imeson Aviation, Inc. at the Jackson Hole Airport, he became alarmed at the number of aircraft accidents attributed to mountain flying. He couldn't find a book on the subject so he sat down and wrote the original *Mountain Flying*.

Sparky has a diverse education in aviation, being directly involved in airplane sales and rentals, fueling, maintenance, flight training, on-demand charter, air ambulance, agricultural aerial application, mosquito spraying, aerobatic training, demo pilot, corporate flying and consulting. He is currently flying the Citation X in California.

Sparky received the FAA Northwest Region Flight Instructor of the Year Award in 1974, 1979 and 1995, for providing effective and creative flight and ground instruction. He was named the 2001 Arizona Safety Counselor of the Year for significant contributions to aviation safety.

He spent one year as editor of *Wings West* Magazine until he discovered editors don't get much of an opportunity to fly.

Of his 18,500+ flight hours, the majority has been in small airplanes in the mountains—which is his first love (after his wife, Gaile, and daughters, Lori, Leanne, Brandy and Jody).

Warning–Disclaimer

This book is provided for informational purposes only. The purpose is to provide education and entertainment for the reader. This book represents the current view of the author on the issues discussed as of the date of publication.

This book is an attempt to collect the information necessary to operate the airplane in the mountains, safely, under various conditions of flight. As a result, it is a subjective view, colored by my own experiences, prejudices and requirements. Most of my flight experience has been in mountain flight operations at high-elevation airports. Since my requirements for flying the mountains may differ from your circumstances, some techniques that have worked well for the author and other mountain pilots, may go beyond your experience level. Without background, education, knowledge, training, practice and experience, some of these procedures and techniques can be very dangerous.

Pilots with a desire to learn the advanced techniques, such as the curved-path takeoff or flying in narrow canyons, should do so only with the help of a knowledgeable and qualified mountain instructor.

The purpose of this book is to provide thought-provoking information in a format of a general guide for ground and flight operations. The book is not intended to replace a flight instructor in learning mountain flying operations.

Information provided in this book is provided "as is" without warranty of any kind, either express or implied, including but not limited to the implied warranties of suitability or fitness for a particular purpose.

The user assumes the entire risk as to the accuracy and the usefulness of this book. Mountain Flying, LLC and the author shall not have liability, nor responsibility to any person or entity for the loss or damage that is caused or alleged to be caused, directly or indirectly, by the information, maneuvers or procedures contained within this book.

If you do not agree with the above, you may return this book to the publisher for a full refund.

PART 1 PREFLIGHT

Table of Contents

TABLE OF CONTENTS

INTRODUCTION
Conventions i-1
Introduction i-1
What exactly is so different about mountain flying? i-3
Complacency i-4
Do's and Don'ts of Mountain Flying i-6
Minimum Knowledge—Mountain Flying i-9
    Basic Premises i-9
    Mountain Meteorology i-9
    #1-Remain in position to turn to lower terrain i-9
    #2-Never fly beyond the point of no return i-9
    Density Altitude i-10
    Runway Length i-10
    Leaning the Mixture .i-10
    Approaching Ridges i-10
    Flying Canyons i-10
    Airspeed Control i-10
    Darkness i-11
    Gross Weight i-11
    Climb out i-11
    Downdrafts i-11
    Course Reversal i-11
    Arrival i-12
    Summary i-12
Introduction—Rules of Thumb i-12

Part 1—PREFLIGHT

CHAPTER 1—BASIC PREMISES
Introduction 1-3
Must Know Information 1-4
Fly Your Experience Level 1-5
Mountain Flying Rules .1-5
    Basic premise #1—Remain in position to turn... . . .1-5
    Basic premise #2—Do not fly beyond the point... . . .1-5
Mountology 1-7

CHAPTER 2—CONSIDERATIONS
Flight Planning Considerations 1-9
Cruise Altitude 1-10
Cruise Performance .1-11
Thin Air 1-11
Optimum Cruise Altitude 1-11
Rule of Thumb—Do not climb more than 10 min... . . .1-12
Fuel Systems 1-12
Fuel Sampling Procedure 1-13
Fuel Management .1-14
Fuel Facilities 1-14
Fuel System Icing 1-15
Prevention Procedures 1-15
Alcohol Blending Technique 1-15
Alcohol Mixture 1-16
Fuel/Air Mixture 1-16
Temperature and Fuel/Air Ratio 1-17
Proper Leaning Altitude 1-17
Carburetor Icing 1-18
Water Vapor 1-18
Humidity 1-18
Vaporization 1-19
    Favorable Carb Icing Conditions 1-19

Categories of Carburetor Icing 1-19
    Fuel Ice 1-19
    Impact Ice (Atmospheric Ice) 1-19
    Throttle Ice (Expansion Ice) 1-20
    Carburetor Heat 1-20
    Indications of Carburetor Icing 1-22
    Prevention Procedures 1-22
Effect of Wind 1-23
Section Lines 1-23
Preflight Safety Tips .1-24
Plan Early Morning Flights 1-24
Oxygen 1-25
Atmosphere Problem Areas 1-25
Oxygen Physiology .1-26
Air Composition 1-27
Respiration Categories 1-28
Respiration 1-29
Hypoxia 1-30
    Causes 1-30
    Symptoms 1-31
    Hypoxia Prevention 1-33
    Pressurized Aircraft 1-34
Hyperventilation 1-35
Pressurization 1-35
Turbocharging 1-36

CHAPTER 3—PREPLANNING
Charts 1-37
Current Charts 1-38
Chart Reading 1-38
Routes 1-38
Flight Planning 1-40
Methods of Navigation 1-40
    Pilotage 1-40
    Dead Reckoning 1-41
    Radio Navigation 1-41
The Double Cross 1-41
Preflight Preparation 1-44
Navigation Log 1-45
VFR Flight Plan 1-45
Flight Log 1-46
Rule of Thumb—Add One Minute per 1,000' Climb . . .1-47
    1. Draw a True Course Line 1-47
    2. Measure the True Course 1-48
    3. Measure the Course Distances 1-49
Mileage Conversions 1-49
    Determine the Ground Speed 1-49
    Compute the Time and Fuel Required 1-50
    Diverting to an Alternate Airport 1-50
    Course Measurement 1-51
    Distance Measurement 1-51
Rule of Thumb—Estimating Time 1-52

CHAPTER 4—WEATHER
Weather Accidents .1-53
Mountain Meteorology 1-54
Go/No-Go Decision .1-55
Mountain Airstrip Weather 1-55
Weather Briefings 1-56
    Outlook Briefing 1-57
    Standard Briefing .1-57

Mountain Flying Bible   **i**

Table of Contents

Part 1 PREFLIGHT

Abbreviated Briefing 1-57
 Background Information 1-57
 Briefing Format (ask for these items) 1-58
Buys Ballot's Law 1-58
Tom's Law 1-59
Marginal Weather 1-59
Visibility 1-60
Fog 1-61
Stability 1-61
Lapse Rates 1-62
 Dry Adiabatic Lapse Rate 1-62
 Moist Adiabatic Lapse Rate 1-63
 Dew-point Lapse Rate and Cloud Heights 1-63
 Standard Lapse Rate 1-64
Stability Determinations 1-64
Absolute Stability 1-65
Absolute Instability 1-65
 Some Effects of Stability and Instability 1-65
Wind 1-65
Mountain and Valley Winds 1-66
Mountain and Valley Winds 1-66
Winds Aloft 1-67
Turbulence 1-68

CHAPTER 5—AIRPLANE

Basic Aerodynamics 1-71
Stalls 1-72
 Engineering Modifications 1-73
 Predicting Stalls 1-73
 Why Know Aerodynamics? 1-76
Spins 1-76
Straight-tail versus Swept-tail airplanes 1-78
 Straight-tail spin Recovery 1-79
 Swept-tail Spin Recovery 1-79
 Airplane Familiarity 1-79
 Standard Atmosphere 1-80
 Aircraft Performance 1-80
Engine Preheat 1-81
Cold-engine Starts 1-82
 Frosted Plugs 1-82
Blowing Snow 1-83
Fire Extinguisher 1-84
Multi-viscosity Oil 1-84
Batteries 1-85
 Lead-acid Battery 1-85
Ground Inspections, Checks and Procedures ...1-87
STOL Kits 1-88
 Robertson STOL 1-88
 Leading-Edge Cuff 1-88
 Stall Fence 1-88
 Wash Out 1-89
 Gap Seals 1-89
 Vortex Generators 1-89
STOL Costs 1-89
 Wren 460 1-89
 260SE/STOL 1-89
 Super-Dooper Cub 1-90

CHAPTER 6—WEIGHT AND BALANCE

Introduction 1-91
Rule of Thumb - Takeoff distance varies with the... 1-92
Aircraft Loading 1-92
Types of Weight to Consider 1-93
Weight Limitations 1-93
Center of Gravity 1-93
Dangerous Conditions 1-94
 Forward CG Loading 1-94
 Aft CG Loading 1-94
Overloaded Aircraft 1-95
 Basic Formula 1-95
 Common Errors 1-96

CHAPTER 7—THE MAGNETIC COMPASS

Magnet 1-97
Magnetic Dip 1-98
Magnetic Compass Construction 1-98
Compass Errors 1-99
 Variation 1-99
Rule of Thumb - East is Least, West is Best 1-100
 Deviation 1-101
 Oscillation Error 1-101
 Magnetic Dip 1-101
 Northerly Turning Error 1-101
 Acceleration Error 1-104
 Summary 1-104

CHAPTER 8—AIRSPEED INDICATOR

High-altitude Operation versus Indicated Airspeed ..1-105
Determining True Airspeed 1-106
Rule of Thumb - to Determine True Airspeed ...1-106
Airspeed Markings (Required) 1-106
Other Airspeed Limitations 1-107
V Speeds (V = Velocity) 1-108
Position Error 1-109

CHAPTER 9—ALTIMETER

Types of Altitude 1-111
Altimeter Operation 1-112
Altimeter Errors 1-112
Non-standard Pressure 1-113
Non-standard Temperature 1-114
Rule of Thumb - Altimeter Indications 1-114

PART 1—RULES OF THUMB

Rules of Thumb 1-115

Part 2 — TAKEOFF

CHAPTER 1 - TAXIING

Throttle Usage 2-3
Carburetor Heat Usage 2-3
Thumbs Up Taxiing 2-4
Downwind Taxiing 2-5
Cold Weather Taxi Operations 2-5

CHAPTER 2 - AIRCRAFT PERFORMANCE

Performance Charts 2-7
Cold Air 2-8
Density Altitude 2-8
Rule of Thumb - Altimeter setting equivalent feet...2-9
 Effect of Altitude 2-9
 Effect of Temperature 2-9
 Effect of High Humidity 2-9
 Combined Effect of Altitude, Temperature and...2-11
Density Altitude Computations 2-11
 Density Altitude Procedure 2-11
Rule of Thumb - Determine Density Altitude 2-12
 Density Altitude Formula 2-12
Density Altitude Takeoff Distance 2-13
Rule of Thumb - Fixed-Pitch Prop Density Alt... 2-13
Rule of Thumb - Constant-Speed Prop Density Alt... 2-15
Rule of Thumb - Density Altitude Rate of Climb... 2-15
Rule of Thumb - Density Altitude Rate of Climb... 2-15
Other Factors 2-15
Gross Weight 2-16
Rule of Thumb - The takeoff distance varies as the... 2-16
Wind 2-17
Rule of Thumb - Headwind Reduces Takeoff Dist... 2-17
Wind Component 2-17
Tailwind Component 2-18
Humidity 2-18

PART 1 PREFLIGHT

Table of Contents

Runway Surface 2-18
Rule of Thumb - Takeoff from various surfaces 2-18
Gradient (Sloped Runway) 2-19
Aircraft and Engine Condition 2-19
Pilot Skill 2-20
Effect of Local Terrain 2-20

CHAPTER 3 - ENGINE OPERATION

Engine Operation 2-21
    Intake Stroke 2-21
    Compression Stroke 2-22
    Power Stroke 2-22
    Exhaust Stroke 2-22
Mixture Control 2-22
Fuel-Air Mixture 2-23
Temperature and Fuel-Air Ratio 2-24
Recommended Leaning Altitude 2-26
Mixture Distribution 2-26
Mixture Definitions 2-27
    Best Economy Mixture 2-27
    Recommended Lean Mixture 2-27
    Best Power Mixture 2-27
Procedure for Leaning - Takeoff 2-27
    Fixed-Pitch Propeller 2-28
    Constant-Speed Propeller 2-28
Procedure for Leaning - Cruise 2-28
    Fixed-Pitch Propeller 2-28
    Constant-Speed Propeller 2-29
Procedure for Leaning - Landing 2-30
Takeoff and Climb Power Settings 2-30
EGT Equipment 2-30
Cruise Power Settings 2-31
Combustion Analyzer 2-31
Pressure Carburetor 2-32
Detonation 2-32
Preignition 2-32
Carburetor Icing 2-33
    Favorable Carb Icing Conditions 2-33
    Indictions of Carburetor Icing 2-34
    Carburetor Heat 2-34
    Fixed-pitch Prop - Carb Ice 2-34

CHAPTER 4 - TAKEOFFS

Takeoff Considerations 2-37
Airspeed 2-37
Takeoff Power 2-38
Runway Length Requirement 2-39
Rule of Thumb - for sufficient runway length for... 2-39
Gusty Wind Takeoff 2-40
Tail Wind Takeoff 2-40
Rule of Thumb for the effect of a tailwind on... .. 2-41
Upslope or Downslope Runway 2-41
Rule of Thumb - Upslope or Downslope Runway... 2-41
Breakeven Headwind 2-41
Determine Runway Gradient 2-43
Flap Settings 2-44
Flap Setting for Takeoff 2-44
Ground Effect 2-46
    Drag 2-46
    Effect 2-47
    Extent 2-47
Rule of Thumb - Ground Effect 2-48
Normal Takeoff 2-48
Normal Takeoff - Tricycle Gear Airplane 2-49
Normal Takeoff - Tail Wheel Airplane 2-50
Short-field Takeoff 2-52
Short-field Takeoff - Tricycle Gear Airplane 2-52
Short-field Takeoff - Conventional Gear Airplane .. 2-53
Advanced Technique Short-field Takeoff - Conven... 2-54
Soft-field Takeoff 2-56
Modified Short/Soft-field Takeoff 2-57
Crosswind Takeoff 2-58

Wind Limits 2-59
Crosswind Takeoff Technique 2-60
    Upsetting Wind Action 2-61
    Skipping During Takeoff 2-62
    Weather Vane Tendency 2-62
    Crosswind Takeoff Procedure 2-62
    Ground Loop 2-62
    Airspeed for Rotation 2-62
    After Takeoff 2-65
    Ground Loop 2-65
    Airspeed for Rotation 2-65
    Use of Flaps 2-65
Cold Weather Takeoffs 2-66

CHAPTER 5 - AFTER TAKEOFF

Cycle Gear 2-67
Climb Out 2-67
False Horizon 2-69
Natural Horizon 2-69
Rate of Climb 2-70
Angle of Climb 2-71
Climb per Nautical Mile 2-72
Part 2 - Takeoff — Rules of Thumb 2-73

PART 3 - EN ROUTE

Introduction 3-1
Rule of Thumb - Increased Takeoff Distance 3-4
Rule of Thumb - Increased landing Distance 3-4
How Reliable are Aviation Weather Forecasts? 3-4

CHAPTER 1 - PRECAUTIONS

Altitude 3-7
Rule of Thumb - Wind and Cruise Altitude 3-7
Horizon Check Line 3-8
Flying Blind 3-9
Collision Avoidance 3-9
Flying the Terrain 3-10
Common Sense 3-10
Climbout 3-11

CHAPTER 2 - NIGHT FLYING

Night Vision 3-14
    Dark Adaptation 3-14
    Preservation of Dark Adaptation 3-15
    Scanning Techniques 3-16
    Visual Effects of Hypoxia 3-16
    Visual Illusion 3-17
Night Takeoff and Departure 3-17
    Runway Alignment 3-17
    Takeoff 3-17
    Climb Out 3-18
    Terrain Clearance 3-18
    Vertigo 3-18
    Weather 3-20
Approach for Landing 3-20
Landing 3-21
Emergency Landing 3-21
Night Flying Tips 3-21

CHAPTER 3 - MOUNTAIN FLYING TECHNIQUES

Approach Ridges 3-24
Rule of Thumb - Stall Speed Increase 3-24
Mountain Flying Designations 3-26
Determine Adequate Altitude 3-28
Crossing Ridges 3-28
Rule of Thumb - Crossing the Ridge 3-29
Mountain Downdrafts 3-30
Speed-to-Fly in a Downdraft 3-32
Flying Canyons 3-33
Rule of Thumb - Canyon Flying 3-33

Mountain Flying Bible

iii

Table of Contents

Part 1 PREFLIGHT

Wires Across Canyons .3-35
    Marginal Weather 3-35
    Snags 3-36
Flying Up Canyons 3-36
Beyond the Point of No Return 3-36
Pass at Head of a Canyon 3-37
Subsidence and Downdrafts 3-39
Crossing the Ridge at the Head of a Canyon 3-39
Flying Up Narrow Canyons 3-40
Course Reversal Procedures 3-42
Rule of Thumb - Canyon Turn Around 3-43
    Hammerhead Turn .3-43
    Wing Over 3-44
    Chandelle 3-44
    Box Canyon Turn .3-45
    Box Canyon Options 3-46
    Natural Horizon 3-48
    Box Canyon Turn Procedure 3-49
    Initiate the Turn 3-51
    Recover 3-51
    Summary 3-51
    Caveat 3-51
    Steep Turn 3-52
Rule of Thumb - Turn Radius versus Airspeed 3-52
Rule of Thumb - Minimum Width for any Canyon... .3-53
Parameters of Canyon Flight 3-54
    Load Factor 3-54
    Increased Stall Speed 3-54
    Power Limits 3-55
    Maneuver Speed .3-55
Rule of Thumb - Box Canyon Turn 3-56
Formulas 3-57
Flight Load Factors 3-58
    Ultimate Loads 3-59
Maneuvering Speed 3-60
Rule of Thumb - Determine Maneuvering Speed 3-60
    Maneuvering Speed and Weight 3-63
Canyon Downdraft 3-63
Loction of Updrafts 3-63

CHAPTER 4 - MOUNTAIN FLYING TURBULENCE

1. Convection Currents (Thermals) 3-68
Rule of Thumb - Base of Convective Activity 3-69
2. Mechanical (Obstruction to Wind Flow) Turb... 3-69
Turbulence Penetration Procedures 3-71
Rule of Thumb - Reduce Turbulence Effects 3-71
Rule of Thumb - Change in Weight/Stall Speed 3-72
Rule of Thumb - Maneuvering Speed Determina... . .3-72
    Aircraft Control 3-73
3. Wind Shear 3-73
Rule of Thumb - Turbulence 3-75
    1. Low-Level Temperature Inversion 3-75
    2. Wind Shear in a Frontal Zone 3-76
    3. Mountain Wave Wind Shear 3-76
    4. Sea Breeze Fronts 3-78
    5. Clear Air Turbulence (CAT) 3-79
    6. Thunderstorms .3-79
Detecting Wind Shear 3-80
Airpane Performance in Wind Shear 3-82
    1. Power Compensation 3-82
    2. Angle of Attack in a Downdraft 3-83
    3. Energy Trade 3-83
    4. Trading Altitude for Speed 3-83
    5. Trading Speed for Altitude 3-83
    6. Adding Speed for Wind Shear 3-83
Procedures for Coping with Wind Shear 3-83
    1. Takeoff 3-84
    2. Approach to Landing 3-85
    Pireps 3-85

CHAPTER 5 - THE MOUNTAIN WAVE

Introduction 3-87
Jet Stream 3-88
Polar Front 3-89
Polar Outbreak 3-89
Mountain Wave Conditions 3-91
    Mountain Wave Formation 3-92
    Mountain Wave Dimensions 3-93
    Wave Length 3-93
    Amplitude 3-94
    Typical Clouds 3-95
Turbulence 3-100
Flight Planning Procedures/Precautions 3-100

CHAPTER 6 - SCUD RUNNING

1. Inadequate Preflight 3-103
2. Landing Accidents 3-104
3. VFR into Adverse Weather 3-105
Scud Running 3-105
    1. Establish Minimum Weather Conditions 3-106
    2. Fly in the Lower Third of the Cloud Quadrant .3-106
    3. Keep Navigation Simple 3-106
    4. Turn on the Lights 3-106
    5. Fly Like you Drive 3-106
Lifesaving Maneuver 3-107
Estimating In-Flight Visibility 3-107
    The Cockpit Cut-off Angle and In-Flight Visibility 3-107
Rule of THumb - Estimating In-Flight Visibility 3-108

CHAPTER 7 - LOST PROCEDURES

Bracketing 3-111
Error Semicircle 3-112
Triangular Pattern 3-114

CHAPTER 8 - AIRCRAFT STRUCTURAL ICING

Beware of Mountain IFR 3-115
Basic Ingredients for Ice 3-117
Types of Ice 3-117
    Clear Ice (Glaze) .3-118
    Rime Ice 3-119
    Mixed Ice 3-119
    Frost 3-119
Cloud Types and Icing .3-119
    Stratus Clouds 3-120
    Cumulus Clouds .3-122
    Cirriform Clouds .3-122
    Frontal-Zone Clouds 3-123
Rates of Accretion and Icing Intensities 3-123
    Accretion 3-123
    Rate of Accumulation 3-123
    Weight of Ice 3-123
    Most Severe Icing 3-123
    Insidious 3-124
    Supercooled Water Droplets 3-124
    Effects of Ice 3-124
    Reporting Airframe Icing 3-124
    Icing Probability 3-125
In-Flight Icing 3-126
    Aircraft Structure .3-126
    Anti-Icing/Deicing Equipment 3-127
    Pitot-Static System 3-127
    Propeller Icing 3-128
    Pneumatic Boots .3-129
    Windshield 3-131
    Fuel System Icing 3-131
Legality of Flight 3-132
Ground Use of Deice Fluids 3-132
    Deice Procedure .3-133
    Anti-Ice Procedure 3-133
    Warning 3-134
GLYPRO System 3-134
Takeoff Performance .3-135

Mountain Flying Bible

PART 1 PREFLIGHT

Table of Contents

Effect of Frost	3-136
Unpredictable	3-137
Icing Forecasts	3-137
Most Severe Icing	3-137
Ice Avoidance Altitude	3-138
Icing Clouds	3-138
Stratiform Clouds	3-138
Cumuliform Clouds	3-138
Conditions Favoring Icing	3-138
Seasons	3-139
Wing Shape and Airspeed	3-139
Freezing Drizzle/Freezing Rain	3-140
Mountain Ice	3-141
Mountain Wave Ice	3-141
Instrument Approach Ice	3-143
Landing with Ice	3-144
IFR in Mountainous Areas	3-145
Case in Point	3-145
Good Operating Practices: IFR Operations in...	3-147
How Reliable are Aviation Weather Forecasts?	3-148
Weather Check	3-150
Concentrate On...	3-151
Weather Depiction Chart	3-152
Constant Pressure Charts	3-153
Summary	3-156
Basic Premise of Ice	3-156
Rule of Thumb - Aircraft Icing	3-156
Temperature Inversions	3-157
Weather Check	3-157
Procedures to Avoid/Minimize Icing Effects	3-157
Go/No-Go Decision	3-158
Ice Encounter Solutions	3-158
Outs	3-159

CHAPTER 9 - SURVIVABLE EMERGENCY LANDING...

Types of Emergency Landings	3-162
Precautionary Landing	3-162
Psychological Hazards	3-163
Basic Concepts of Crash Safety	3-163
Energy Absorption	3-164
Occupant Restraint	3-164
Speed and Stopping Distance	3-164
Attitude and Sink Rate Control	3-165
Simulated Forced Landings	3-165
Low-Altitude Forced Landing	3-166
Terrain Selection	3-167
Field Selection	3-167
Changing Fields	3-167
Field Length	3-167
Aircraft Configuration	3-168
Approach	3-169
Determining Wind Direction	3-169
Planned Approach	3-169
Touchdown	3-170
Confied Areas	3-170
Trees (Forest)	3-171
Mountainous Terrain	3-171
Water (Ditching)	3-172
Snow	3-173
IFR and Night	3-173
Conclusion	3-174

CHAPTER 10 - SURVIVAL AND RESCUE

Survival Equipment	3-176
Winter Woes	3-177

PART 4 - ARRIVAL

INTRODUCTION...4-1

CHAPTER 1 - MEDICAL CONSIDERATIONS

Barotitis Media	4-3
Treatment	4-4
Valsalva Maneuver	4-4
Barosinusitis	4-5

CHAPTER 2 - AIRPLANE CONSIDERATIONS

Thermas Shock	4-7
Constant-Speed Propeller	4-7
Fixed-Pitch Propeller	4-7
Detuning the Engine	4-8
1. Rapid Throttle Operation	4-9
2. Propeller Feathering	4-9
3. High Engine Speed and Low Manifold Pressure	4-10
4. Excessive Speed and Power	4-10
Overspeed/Overboost Maintenance Procedures	4-10

CHAPTER 3 - DESCENT RULE

3-Degree Glide Slope Descent Rule	4-11

CHAPTER 4 - DESTINATION AIRPORTS

Over-Flight Observation	4-13
Ferry Flights	4-14
Sparky's 10 Commandments	4-17

PART 5 - LANDINGS

INTRODUCTION...5-1

Approach Airspeed	5-2
Rule of Thumb - Approach Indicated Airspeed	5-3

CHAPTER 1 - DRAG CURVE

Parasite Drag	5-5
Induced Drag	5-6
Drag Curve	5-6
Front Side of Drag Curve	5-7
Backside of Drag Curve	5-7
Rule of Thumb - Landing Flight Path Adjustments	5-8
Backside of Drag Curve Operation	5-8
Best Glide Speed	5-9
Glide Speed and Weight	5-9
Effect of Altitude	5-10
Effect of Configuration	5-10
Effect of Wind	5-10
Area of Reversed Command Operation	5-10

CHAPTER 2 - FLAPS

Effects of Flaps	5-13
Flaps for Landing	5-14
Rule of Thumb - Centrifugal Force During a Swerve	5-15

CHAPTER 3 - LANDING IRREGULARITIES

Ballooning	5-17
Bouncing	5-18
Corrective Action	5-18
Wheelbarrowing	5-19
Corrective Action	5-20
Porpoising	5-20
Corrective Action	5-20
Ground Loop	5-21
Corrective Action	5-21

CHAPTER 4 - LANDING CONSIDERATIONS

Landing Uphill/Downhill	5-23
Rule of Thumb - Upslope Runway Takeoff Distance	5-23
Rule of Thumb - Downslope Runway Takeoff Dist...	5-23
Landing in Rain	5-25
Stabilized Landing Approach	5-25

Mountain Flying Bible

Table of Contents

Part 1 PREFLIGHT

Landing Practice 5-26
Vision 5-26
Eye Focus 5-27
Ground Effect 5-27
Airspeed Indicator Errors 5-28
Airspeed Calibration Chart .5-28
    Landing Flaps, Maximum Landing Weight 5-28
Gusty Wind Conditions 5-30
Mountain Strip Operations .5-28

CHAPTER 5 - SPOT METHOD LANDING TECHNIQUE

Optimum Approach Speed .5-34
Stabilized Approach 5-34
    3-Degree Glide Slope .5-35
    Best Approach Angle 5-35
Landing Requirements 5-35
    Aiming Point 5-36
    Windshield Mark 5-36
    Touchdown Point 5-37
    Go-Around Point 5-37
Spot Method for Landing Technique 5-37
    Performance 5-37
    Pitch Changes 5-38
    Gusty Wind Conditions 5-38
    Windshear Awareness .5-38
    Spot Landing Uses 5-38
Summary 5-40

CHAPTER 6 - SOFT-FIELD LANDING

Soft-Field Landing Procedure 5-42

CHAPTER 7 - SHORT-FIELD LANDING

Rule of Thumb - Approach Speed/Landing Dist... 5-43
Short-Field Landing 5-44
    Review of Attitude Flying 5-47
Short-Field Landing - Without an Obstacle 5-47
    Short-Field Precautions 5-47
Emergency Forward Slip to Landing 5-48
Turbulent Air 5-48

CHAPTER 8 - CROSSWIND LANDING

Crab/Kick-Out Method 5-49
    Forward Slip 5-50
        Sideslip 5-50
Sideslip to a Landing 5-50
Preferred Crosswind Landing Method 5-51
Curved Path Landing 5-53
Crosswind Landing Errors .5-53

CHAPTER 9 - PARKING

Nose Over 5-55
Tie-Down 5-55
Mosquitoes 5-56

PART 5 - LANDINGS — RULES OF THUMB

Rules of Thumb 5-57

APPENDIX

Aeronautical Information A-1
Formulas A-2
Mountain Flying Lesson A-5

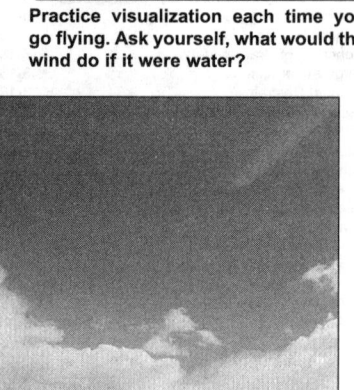

Practice visualization each time you go flying. Ask yourself, what would the wind do if it were water?

IT FEELS MORE COMFORTABLE TO FLY THE CENTER OF A CANYON, AWAY FROM THE SIDES. IT IS MORE PROPER TO FLY THE SIDES OF THE CANYON. THIS AVOIDS THE SHEAR NEAR THE CENTER OF THE CANYON AND PLACES YOU IN A BETTER POSITION TO TURN AROUND IF ESCAPE BECOMES NECESSARY (CACHE CREEK, EAST OF JACKSON, WYO.)

INTRODUCTION

CONVENTIONS

The knowledge and the amount of material presented in this book requires a different approach from the normal presentation of books. In order to assure that certain pieces of information stand out and become more meaningful, icons have been incorporated to assist you in sorting out nice-to-know, need-to-know, advisory, precautionary and warning information.

The "Advanced" icon has been placed to serve as a warning that inexperienced pilots should not attempt the procedure or maneuver without first seeking instruction.

The "Note" icon denotes information that you should know before flying in the mountains and you should, at the least, spend a moment reading the content.

The "Remember" icon marks information that you will use over and over. It should be remembered to enhance the safety of flight.

The "Rule of Thumb" icon points out procedures that save time and trouble. They are roughly correct, but not meant to be scientifically accurate, while promoting safety.

The "Warning" icon represents a situation, event, or area that can get you in trouble (serious trouble) or cost you money (airplane damage), if you do not adhere to the recommendations.

INTRODUCTION

All flying involves risk. Presumably, that's part of the glamour of becoming a pilot. Perhaps some pilots want to imbue this facade to impress their non-flying friends. Knowledge reduces the risk for the pilot, but does not reduce the glamour of flight or of the perceived mystique.

This book is not designed to allow you to disregard established procedures for mountain flying, but in an emergency situation some of the information gained from the book may help you deal with a situation that goes beyond the limits of your experience or capabilities as well as situations that go beyond the capabilities of your airplane.

There are many valid reasons for mountain flying, such as personal enjoyment, aerial photography, training, fire patrol, law enforcement, business travel, search-and-rescue, game and fish surveys, and the like. Regardless of your

INTRODUCTION

motivation for flying the mountains, it is necessary to develop good judgment and proper technique.

 Some of the techniques presented for flying the mountains may tax your skills if you are a novice mountain pilot. Keep in mind that this book has been written for the advanced pilot as well as the novice pilot. If a particular maneuver causes you concern rather than challenging your skills; avoid this maneuver until you have more experience. If you aren't certain about a procedure or maneuver, check with an experienced mountain pilot. If you don't know, avoid the situation until you do know. It is necessary for you to fly your experience level, not the author's. *Experience is a wonderful teacher, but it gives the test first and the lesson afterwards.*

This book contains advice, warnings, data, rules of thumb, and possible courses of action for the pilot to keep in mind when flying in mountainous terrain. It is difficult to remember everything of importance pertaining to mountain flying. This is further complicated by the fact that all pilots are subject to the "if you don't use it, you lose it" syndrome.

You don't actually forget something you've learned, you just fail to recall it without a review of the information. Occasionally some half-forgotten piece of information may be essential to the safe operation of the airplane. For these reasons this book is divided into parts representing the phases of flight: preflight, taxiing, takeoff, en route, arrival and landing. It makes it easy to find what you need when you need it.

Some *learn to fly* manuals describe and then dictate how to perform a particular maneuver in a specific way. Those books may contain a caution against doing it in some other manner. They may not provide an explanation of what is going on, why you should do it that one way only, or what will happen if you do it some other way. Apparently they assume pilots do not have the intelligence to understand the whys and wherefores if they were to clarify it. They don't explain, only admonish. We aren't robots. If we understand why we do something, it makes sense to do it; it makes further sense when we know why we shouldn't do it in some other way.

Perhaps I'm guilty of providing too much material in an attempt to avoid an esoteric style and to help you understand what is happening and why. An understanding is basic to the elimination of the "do it my way because I say so" method used in so much of flight training. My purpose isn't just to arouse your curiosity, but to satisfy it. In doing so I've found I am not writing so much to answer your questions, but rather my own ... providing explanations that satisfy me. You can always sort through and cross out what you don't need.

INTRODUCTION

You may seem overwhelmed by the number of rules of thumb contained in this book; however, it's like learning to fly. Remember all those instruments and dials? You might have thought you'd never be able to look at so many things all at once. You discovered you don't use them all at once. The same is true for rules of thumb. You will find some you use all the time; others you may never need. But, they are available.

NOTE Not every pilot is as sharp as he should be for every flight. Many of the hints in this book are directed to this end. For example, *up-right* is used during the control check before takeoff. It's pretty simple to reason out what the controls should be doing as they are moved. If you are making a right turn, the control wheel is moved to the right; the left aileron moves down to increase the camber (lift) on the left wing. The right aileron moves up to reduce the lift (or provide lift in a downward direction) on the right wing. This all makes sense, but why have pilots, after some maintenance procedure, taken off in an airplane with reversed aileron control? They swear that they have performed the control check. Something just didn't click.

This *up-right* procedure is so simple that if you establish it as a habit pattern for the before takeoff control check and you look to the right expecting to see "up," and the aileron is down, something definitely *clicks,* without consciously thinking about it.

NOTE Operations in the mountains are little different than any place else. It's just that the safety margins are reduced to a greater extent, so a pilot can't get away with many practices that are common at lower elevations (with better aircraft performance) and more hospitable terrain (that allows the pilot to go where he wants to go).

This doesn't mean we can't fly safely in the mountains. It means we have to be aware of the differences to be able to effectively deal with them.

What exactly is so different about mountain flying?

- ✔ The air is thin. Thin air affects the lift of the wings, the thrust of the propeller and the power output of the engine.
- ✔ This thin air is moving creating updrafts, downdrafts and turbulence. Thin, moving air requires specialized flying techniques in the mountains.
- ✔ The airplane is in close proximity to the terrain. For someone inexperienced in mountain flying this can be very intimidating.
- ✔ The terrain creates airflow modifications that may vary from the steady-state wind aloft. This requires visualization to determine the wind direction at any particular point of location.

INTRODUCTION

- ✔ Over flat land when you take off and climb you might expect the upper winds to increase in velocity and switch somewhat clockwise from the surface wind direction. You can't always expect this to occur in the mountains; ridges, mountains and valleys may change the airflow.
- ✔ Density altitude adversely affects the aircraft performance.
- ✔ And, you can't take off from all mountain fields and turn directly on course. Often it is necessary to circle while gaining altitude before turning on course.

COMPLACENCY

Webster's defines complacency as a *calm sense of well-being and security,* or *self-satisfaction accompanied by un-awareness of actual dangers or deficiencies.*

Smug, familiar, bored, overconfident, and *self-contented* are adjectives describing complacency. Lack of judgment and overconfidence can often result from repetition.

You might discover yourself becoming complacent if you scrutinize the manner in which you do your preflight inspection. Do you really examine the airplane or are you paying less attention to detail? The same thing applies to the actual flight. Do you think ahead of the airplane, planning for all contingencies? If not, you might be setting yourself up for an accident. Remember, *complacency kills!*

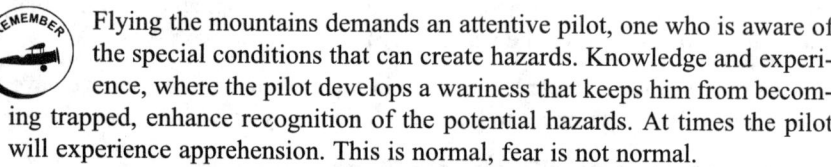

Flying the mountains demands an attentive pilot, one who is aware of the special conditions that can create hazards. Knowledge and experience, where the pilot develops a wariness that keeps him from becoming trapped, enhance recognition of the potential hazards. At times the pilot will experience apprehension. This is normal, fear is not normal.

A wariness of mountain flying is good. A true fear of mountain flying means you should not be flying in the mountains. A concern for where you are and what you are doing is healthy; and, as all veteran mountain pilots will expound, you must maintain a constant vigilance of your surroundings and have an escape route in mind should one be needed. Do not fear flying in the mountains. Learning of the dangers that might exist and knowing how to minimize or avoid them replaces fear with knowledge.

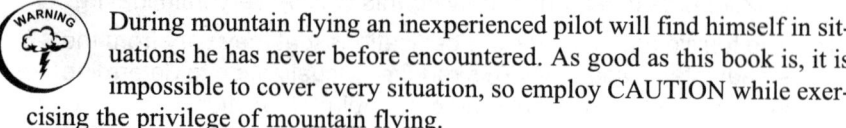

During mountain flying an inexperienced pilot will find himself in situations he has never before encountered. As good as this book is, it is impossible to cover every situation, so employ CAUTION while exercising the privilege of mountain flying.

INTRODUCTION

Some pilots may develop an attitude of fearing the mountains. If this extends beyond a normal protective reaction, do not fly in the mountains without additional dual instruction. Another extreme, having no respect for the mountains at all, is almost as bad, leading the pilot toward an accident.

The novice mountain pilot requires a basic knowledge and appreciation of mountains, airplanes and weather.

NOTE: Your mountain flying techniques will be developed over a period of time. Don't expect to know everything before flying in the mountains.

Let me take some liberty with an old saying and paraphrase it to state: *Mountain flying in itself is not inherently dangerous, but even more so than flatland flying, it is terribly unforgiving of carelessness, neglect and incompetence.* It's mighty easy to ignore your surroundings when gazing at wildlife or unique terrain features; perhaps more so for the experienced pilot than the novice. The new pilot or pilot new to mountain flying will be wary and will be looking around.

This book is an attempt to collect all the information necessary to function safely in the mountains under various conditions. As a result, it is a subjective view, colored by the author's prejudices and requirements. Since my requirements of flying in and with the mountains may differ from your requirement of operating from point-to-point, without any desire to fly close to the mountains, both viewpoints are given. Although flying over the mountains is encouraged and promoted, there is definitely a bias toward flying *amongst and betwixt* those scary old peaks. You might also note the author's preference for mountain airstrip operations.

DO NOT BE TOO PROUD OR TOO VAIN TO ASK A LOCAL PILOT FOR ADVICE.

INTRODUCTION

DO'S AND DON'TS OF MOUNTAIN FLYING

✘ DON'T fly into unimproved mountain strips without a minimum of 150-hours total flight experience. Even then, be proficient at slow flight maneuvering.

✘ DON'T plan a cross-country flight into the mountains when the wind at mountaintop level exceeds 30 knots unless you are experienced in this type operation (strong updrafts, strong downdrafts and moderate or greater turbulence). This does not preclude taking a "look-see." Often with a stable air mass the air will contain very little turbulence during these high-wind conditions. Expect the wind velocity to double or more in mountain passes and over the ridges due to a venturi effect.

✘ DON'T choose a route that would prevent a suitable forced-landing area.

✘ DON'T leave the airplane without a compelling reason if you have executed an emergency or precautionary landing. Temporary evacuation may be necessary if a fire hazard exists.

✘ DON'T become quiescent with weather reports of ceilings of 1,000-2,000 feet. The ceiling is reported above ground level. Often, in the mountains, the weather reporting facility will be surrounded by mountains that extend thousands of feet higher than the facility. Clouds may obscure the mountains and passes in the vicinity.

✘ DON'T go if the weather is doubtful or "bad."

✘ DON'T fly VFR or IFR in the mountains in an unfamiliar airplane make and model. It is required that you learn the flight characteristics, slow flight and stalls in various configurations, beforehand.

✘ DON'T make the landing approach too slow. Some pilots feel they have to make a low approach on the backside of the power curve to get into a mountain strip. This "hanging on the prop" is a dangerous operation. Use a stabilized approach for all landings.

✘ DON'T operate low-performance aircraft into marginal mountain strips. If in doubt about your takeoff, use the "sufficient runway length" rule of thumb.

✘ DON'T rely on cloud shadows for wind direction (unless you are flying at or near the cloud bases). Expect the wind to be constantly changing in direction and velocity because of modification by mountain ridges and canyons.

✘ DON'T fly close to rough terrain or cliffs when the wind approaches 20 knots or more. Dangerous turbulence may be encountered.

INTRODUCTION

✗ DON'T fail to realize that air, although invisible, acts like water and it will "flow" along the contour of the mountains and valleys. Visualize where the wind is from and ask yourself, "What would water do in this same situation?"

✗ DON'T slow down in a downdraft. By maintaining your speed, you will be under the influence of the downdraft for a lesser period of time and lose less altitude overall.

✗ DON'T forget or fail to realize the adverse effect of frost. Less than 1/8 inch of frost may increase the takeoff distance by 50 percent and reduce the cruise speed by 10 percent. Often, if the airplane becomes airborne, the smooth flow of air over the wings is broken up by the frost and the extra drag prevents the airplane from climbing out of ground effect.

✗ DON'T give insufficient attention to the importance of fuel and survival equipment. It is important to keep the airplane light, but don't skimp on these items.

✗ DON'T fly the middle of a canyon. This places you in a poor position to make a turnaround and it subjects you to shear turbulence.

✗ DON'T fail to use the same indicated airspeed at high-altitude airports that you use at low-altitude or sea level airports for the takeoff or for the approach to landing.

✗ DON'T be too proud or too vain to check with experienced mountain pilots concerning operations to and from unfamiliar fields.

✗ DON'T attempt VFR flight in mountainous terrain unless you have the minimum visibility you have established as a personal safety standard.

✗ DON'T become complacent about the horizon when flying with outside visual reference. A gentle upslope terrain may cause an unknown constant climb with the possibility of an inadvertent stall. The horizon is the base of the mountains some six to eight miles away.

☐ DO file a flight plan for each leg of your flight. Also, make regular position reports to allow search and rescue personnel to narrow down the search area if you are overdue on the flight plan.

☐ DO check all aspects of the weather including weather reports and forecasts.

☐ DO familiarize yourself with the high-altitude characteristics and performance of your airplane. This includes the takeoff and landing distance and rate of climb under various density altitude conditions.

☐ DO spend some time studying the charts to determine the lowest terrain along the proposed route of flight. If possible, route the flight along airways.

INTRODUCTION

☐ DO have confidence in the magnetic compass. The compass (unless it has leaked fluid or someone has placed interfering metal near its magnets) is the most reliable instrument. Charts will show the areas of local magnetic disturbance that may affect the accuracy of the compass reading.

☐ DO plan the fuel load to allow flight from the departure to the destination airport with a reserve to counter unexpected winds.

☐ DO fly a downdraft, that is, maintain speed by lowering the nose of the airplane. Unless the airplane is over a tall stand of trees or near a shear cliff, the downdraft will not extend to the ground (exception: microburst).

☐ DO use Sectional Aeronautical Charts instead of World Aeronautical Charts (WAC) because of the greater detail (8 miles per inch).

☐ DO approach ridges at an angle. The recommendation is to use a 45-degree angle approach when in a position of one-half to one-quarter mile away. This allows an escape, with less stress on the pilot and airplane, if unexpected downdrafts or turbulence are encountered. Flying perpendicular to the ridge, rather than at a 45-degree angle, does not mean you cannot escape the downdraft or turbulence by making a 180-degree turn. But, it does mean the airplane will be subjected to the effects of the downdraft and turbulence for a greater period of time. Usually, a steeper bank will be required to make the 180-degree turn. This will increase the g-loading stress on the airplane.

☐ DO count on the *valley breeze* (wind blowing upstream during the morning hours) and the *mountain breeze* (wind blowing downstream during the evening hours). In an otherwise calm wind condition the valley breeze will create an approximate 4-knot tailwind for landing upstream. The mountain breeze will cause an approximate 8-knot to 12-knot tailwind for takeoff downstream.

☐ DO use horse sense (common sense) when performing takeoffs or landings at mountain strips. If you have any doubt about the operation, confirm the aircraft performance using the Pilot's Operating Handbook or Owner's Manual. If the physical conditions are adverse and compromise the operation, delay the operation until conditions are better.

☐ DO make a stabilized approach for landings. Since the late '60s the power-off approach has been discouraged because of thermal shock to the engine.

☐ DO remember your study of aerodynamics. It is possible to stall the airplane at any airspeed and any attitude (providing you are strong enough and the airplane doesn't break first). If a stall is entered in the same manner, for example, with a slow deterioration of the airspeed, it will stall at the same indicated airspeed at all altitudes.

INTRODUCTION

MINIMUM KNOWLEDGE—MOUNTAIN FLYING

The following is a summation of the minimum knowledge needed to fly safely in the mountains. Additional study and flight instruction is required prior to flight in the mountains. This minimum knowledge information is intended to supplement—not replace—such preparation.

BASIC PREMISES

Adhere to the two basic premises of mountain flying to keep out of trouble.

#1–Always remain in a position where you can turn toward lowering terrain.

The novice mountain pilot should plan the flight to remain 2,000 feet above the terrain along the route of flight. When approaching mountain ridges, turn to approach the ridge at a 45-degree angle when about one-half to one-quarter mile away. This permits an easy escape with less stress on the airplane if downdrafts and/or turbulence are encountered.

Never fly in a canyon where there is not room to execute a turnaround maneuver.

#2–Never fly beyond the point of no return.

When flying upslope terrain, the "point of no return" is defined as the point where, if you reduce the throttle to idle, you can lower the nose of the aircraft for a normal glide and perform a 180-degree turn without impacting the ground. At or prior to this "point of no return," circle (away from the mountain) to gain additional altitude before proceeding.

MOUNTAIN METEOROLOGY

A complete check of the weather is necessary to develop a go/no-go decision. Stay out of marginal weather areas. For the novice, winds aloft greater than 30 knots at cruise altitude usually means the flight should be delayed or postponed until more favorable conditions prevail.

DENSITY ALTITUDE

Density altitude is the altitude the airplane thinks it is flying and performs accordingly. High, hot and humid conditions may raise the physical altitude to a performance altitude by many thousands of feet higher.

INTRODUCTION

RUNWAY LENGTH

A handy rule of thumb for operations from a short runway (or high-density altitude) is:

If you obtain 71 percent of the speed necessary for rotation at the halfway point of the runway, you can take off in the remaining distance. If not, abort the takeoff.

LEANING THE MIXTURE

Lean the mixture in accordance with the airplane manufacturer's recommendations. With no recommendation, lean the mixture at 5,000-feet density altitude during a climb at full throttle. Do not lean turbocharged or supercharged engines for takeoff, even at high mountain strips.

APPROACHING RIDGES

Turn to approach ridges at a 45-degree angle to provide the option of turning toward lowering terrain.

The visual aspects of mountain flying can be deceiving, but if you can see more and more of the terrain on the other side of the ridge, you are higher than the ridge and can probably continue.

When approaching a ridge and the airplane is in a position where the power can be reduced to idle and it will glide to the top of the ridge line, a commitment to cross the ridge can be made. At this position, the airplane is close enough to the ridge line not to experience an unexpected downdraft of a nature to cause a problem. If a downdraft is encountered, keep the power on, lower the nose to maintain airspeed and the airplane should clear the ridge.

FLYING CANYONS

Until you have experience, do not fly up canyons. If it is necessary to fly in a canyon, gain altitude, fly to the head of the canyon, then fly downslope terrain.

AIRSPEED CONTROL

Landing at short mountain strips requires exact airspeed control to eliminate float. A 10-percent increase in the proper approach speed results in a 21-percent increase in the landing distance.

Use the same indicated airspeed for approach when landing at a high-elevation mountain strip as you would at a sea-level airport. The thin air at high altitudes affects the airspeed indicator to result in an automatic compensation of the correct amount.

INTRODUCTION

A rule of thumb states that the airplane flies faster than the indicated airspeed at altitudes above sea level. This is approximately two-percent-per-thousand feet faster than indicated airspeed.

DARKNESS

Allow a minimum of an extra half-hour of daylight if your destination is in the mountains. There may be plenty of daylight at cruise altitude, but darkness may exist at your valley destination.

GROSS WEIGHT

The takeoff distance varies with gross weight. A 10-percent increase in takeoff gross weight (while not exceeding the maximum allowable gross) will cause a:

- ☑ 5-percent increase in the speed necessary for takeoff.
- ☑ 9-percent decrease in acceleration to takeoff speed.
- ☑ 21-percent increase in the takeoff distance.

CLIMBOUT

The first consideration for takeoff from a strip surrounded by mountains is one of terrain clearance. A considerable amount of time may be required to circle and circle, climbing to the en route altitude prior to turning on course.

DOWNDRAFTS

Use visualization to determine possible downdraft areas. Air behaves like water. Ask yourself, "What would water do if it were flowing as the winds aloft flow?" You can then picture areas of downdrafts, updrafts and splashes (turbulence). If you encounter unexpected downdrafts, diving to maintain airspeed will generally lessen the total displacement effect of the downdraft (altitude loss). At the higher airspeed you will be under the influence of the sink for a shorter period of time.

COURSE REVERSAL

Everyone flying in the mountains will encounter situations when it becomes necessary to make a 180-degree turn. Forget the hammerhead turn, wingover, chandelle and other fancy maneuvers.

For course reversal, slow down—to decrease the radius of turn—by pulling back on the control wheel to trade airspeed for altitude. In conjunction with this airspeed/altitude trade, make the steepest turn you can safely make.

INTRODUCTION

ARRIVAL

The mountainous terrain surrounding many strips prevents a normal descent from cruise altitude to pattern altitude. It is necessary to make progressive power reductions to prevent thermal stresses from being induced in the engine. This allows the engine to cool slowly, preventing thermal shock of the engine. Do not detune the engine.

SUMMARY

Although the preceding is considered the minimum knowledge for mountain flying, it barely touches the surface of the "mountain" of information available to those contemplating a safe flight over or through the mountains.

The summarized information is presented here—in the introduction section—to provide the background information that will "flag" the text that follows as something that is important and that requires further study.

Be sure to read the following chapters very carefully so you can pass the final exam. Failure of the final exam will result in a "mountain flying prohibited" endorsement on your pilot certificate.

INTRODUCTION – RULES OF THUMB

- If 70.7 percent of the speed necessary for rotation is obtained at the halfway point of a runway, you can take off in the remaining distance. If not, abort the takeoff.
- A 10-percent increase in the proper approach speed results in a 21-percent increase in the landing distance.
- Use the same indicated airspeed for approach to a high-elevation mountain strip that you would use at a sea-level strip.
- The airplane flies faster at altitudes above sea level, by approximately two-percent-per-thousand feet above sea level.
- A 10-percent increase in takeoff gross weight will cause a 5-percent increase in the speed necessary for takeoff, a 9-percent decrease in acceleration to takeoff speed, and a 21-percent increase in takeoff distance.

PART 1 PREFLIGHT — Part 1 - Introduction

INTRODUCTION

Part 1
PREFLIGHT

- Chapter 1—BASIC PREMISES 1-3
- Chapter 2—CONSIDERATIONS 1-9
- Chapter 3—PREPLANNING 1-37
- Chapter 4—WEATHER 1-53
- Chapter 5—AIRPLANE 1-71
- Chapter 6—WEIGHT AND BALANCE 1-89
- Chapter 7—THE MAGNETIC COMPASS......................................1-95
- Chapter 8—THE AIRSPEED INDICATOR..................................1-103
- Chapter 9—THE ALTIMETER..1-109
- Part 1—RULES OF THUMB..1-113

Flying, especially in the mountains, requires a total commitment that becomes the ultimate challenge of exploring yourself, your airplane, the terrain and the elements. You must have some basic knowledge and appreciation of each of these before attempting mountain flight.

Questions of concern when contemplating a mountain flight might be:

✔ How does the service ceiling (or absolute ceiling) of the airplane compare with the terrain along planned routes?

✔ How much time and distance will it take to get to this altitude?

✔ How much safety margin will I have operating at en route altitudes and high altitude airports?

✔ How is the weather different in the mountains?

✔ How and where will winds create updrafts, downdrafts and turbulence?

✔ What are the special techniques used for flying in the mountains?

Part 1 - Introduction   **Part 1 PREFLIGHT**

✔ An examination of aeronautical charts may bring to mind questions about chart reading and interpretation.

This book is designed to provide this information.

Part 1, consisting of nine chapters, covers the preflight portion of the flight. Much of the information might already be familiar to you. In this case, peruse the table of contents and find an area where you want to begin. Although basic, it is not meant to be superfluous; this information deserves your thought prior to a mountain flight. ✈

1-2   *Mountain Flying Bible*

PART 1 PREFLIGHT   Chapter 1 - Basic Premises

CHAPTER 1—BASIC PREMISES

➤ MUST KNOW INFORMATION..1-4
➤ FLY YOUR EXPERIENCE LEVEL..1-5
➤ MOUNTAIN FLYING RULES 1-5
➤ *MOUNTOLOGY* 1-7

INTRODUCTION

Every pilot faces two limitations or restrictions in his quest for safety throughout his flying career. First, he is concerned with his own limitations as a pilot. His aviation background, education, training and experience delineate what he can and can't do. Second, the airplane defines the types of operations that can be safely conducted, such as IFR or high-altitude flight.

Technical advances in the manufacture of airframes and engines combined with improved pilot training techniques have reduced the inherent risk of flight. Follow-up safety programs are important to eliminate the element of risk, but the people who need to go to these programs, the ones who are involved in accidents, never have the time or inclination to attend.

The pilot's liability to err prevents total elimination of aircraft accidents. If you, personally, establish safety standards and adhere to them, you, at least, will be prepared to avoid an accident. You might begin by inculcating a rule to avoid mountain flight when the ceiling is less than 2,000 feet or the visibility is less than 5 miles. Only knowledge and experience will allow you to change these self-imposed limits. But, changing this restriction before having the knowledge and experience to do so may rule out the occasion of changing them in the future.

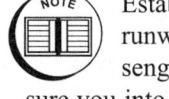 Establish your own personal limitations of weather and night flying, runway length, loading and range and abide by them. Don't let a passenger—especially someone who knows nothing about flying—pressure you into compromising these standards. Learn to accept the inconvenience and expense incurred when you have to cancel a flight due to questionable weather. Don't let an important business engagement become a compelling reason to venture out in bad weather. *Pilot error* leading to an accident may occur

Mountain Flying Bible

when you want to prevent disappointment for your family when a long anticipated flight has to be canceled because of weather.

The same thing applies to equipment. The most qualified pilot in the world can still get into trouble trying to push an aircraft beyond it's limitations. If the equipment available is not suitable for the flight, change the flight or change the airplane.

For example, a Cessna 172 may not be able to operate at a high-elevation mountain airstrip at gross weight on a hot day. Changing to a Cessna 182 may allow the desired operation. With the Cessna 172 it may be necessary to off-load passengers, baggage or fuel. Ferry partial loads of passengers and baggage to a nearby airport that allows the desired operation.

In recognizing the airplane's limitations, you have to bear in mind that even though you may hold an instrument rating or an ATP certificate, the weather is not always such that you can fly your small plane.

There's an old adage—if you have time to spare, travel by air—that, when adhered to, has kept many pilots out of trouble.

MUST KNOW INFORMATION

You do not have to learn everything about mountain flying prior to flying in the mountains. Specialized techniques do not have to be learned all at once. It will take time to become proficient in all areas of mountain flying. Start out slow. Recognize and abide by your limitations until you are able to learn, absorb and practice the advanced techniques.

It makes sense to:

- ✔ Know your limitations
- ✔ Use a checklist
- ✔ Pre-plan your flight
- ✔ Preflight your airplane
- ✔ Know your aircraft systems
- ✔ Know your aircraft performance limits

You must have some basic knowledge and appreciation of mountains, airplanes and weather before attempting mountain flying. Few pilots read a book about aerobatics then go out to practice by themselves. The same is true for many of the procedures in this book. If the techniques impose stress, rather than challenging your skills, you should fly with an instructor.

PART 1 PREFLIGHT   **Chapter 1 - Basic Premises**

By the way, you can never learn everything about mountain flying. If you could, it would become boring. Instead, mountain flying remains a constant challenge, providing year after year of enjoyment.

FLY YOUR EXPERIENCE LEVEL

This book provides you with knowledge of mountains, airplanes, yourself and weather. An appreciation and understanding of advanced operations develops after you fly the mountains with a qualified mountain pilot. The advice given herein for mountain flying—contour, drainage or terrain flying—is not bold, macho or foolhardy. But, it does require background, education, knowledge, training, practice and experience. Don't try to fly my experience level, fly yours!

MOUNTAIN FLYING RULES

There are only two rules that you must know to be able to fly in the mountains with safety. You need to *ingrain these truisms into your mind*. With these axioms firmly adhered to, you will not get into trouble when flying the mountains.

  **Basic premise #1 of all mountain flying— ALWAYS REMAIN IN A POSITION WHERE YOU CAN TURN TO LOWERING TERRAIN.**

This encompasses the idea that you will not fly in an area where there is insufficient room to turn around, for example, a narrow canyon. It also means that you will approach ridges at an angle to allow an escape turn at any time.

  **Basic premise #2 of all mountain flying—DO NOT FLY BEYOND THE POINT OF NO RETURN.**

This rule pertains to flying upslope terrain. It is actually an extension of the first axiom. The *point of no return* is the place defined by reducing the throttle to idle and having sufficient altitude to turn around. (It is not meant to be implied that it is proper technique to reduce the throttle to idle to turn around.)

When you arrive at a position, where if you reduce the throttle to idle and lower the nose for the proper glide attitude, and can complete the 180-degree turn without impacting the terrain, this is the *point of no return*. Do not fly beyond this point. Turn the airplane (away from the mountain) and gain additional altitude before flying beyond this point.

When a pilot flies beyond the *point of no return,* the terrain outclimbs the airplane. The pilot has two options when this occurs and both lead to an accident. The first, and usually less serious, involves landing the airplane straight ahead into whatever terrain exists. The second choice involves the stall-spin accident because there is either insufficient altitude or insufficient maneuvering space to complete the turn. By trying to hurry the turn, excessive bottom rudder is used leading to a tuck-under spin entry.

The majority of accidents classified as flight into a blind canyon result from flying beyond the point of no return or entering an area that does not allow the physical space for a turn around.

FLY A POSITION THAT ALLOWS A TURN TO LOWERING TERRAIN.

Make a placard for the aircraft's panel that lists the two basic premises. Then adhere to them and you will fly safely in the mountains.

> 1. Be able to turn to lower terrain.
> 2. Do not fly beyond the point of no return.

Learning is often enhanced when you are exposed to the same information in different ways. Another way of stating the basic premises is: Always have an escape route in mind and be in a position where you can exercise this option. Or, constantly evaluate where you are and decide if you can lose altitude prior to having to turn the airplane. If not, you are narrowing your options and approaching an area where you may not be able to extricate yourself.

You will often find that instinct does not work in an airplane. For example, look at a pilot who has never experienced a spin. If he finds himself in a situation where the aircraft's nose appears to be pointing straight down while rotating, his "instinct" is to pull back on the control wheel to raise the nose. It doesn't work. He must first break the stall, then recover with back pressure.

PART 1 PREFLIGHT   Chapter 1 - Basic Premises

You will find the basic axioms of mountain flying are not instinct. They must be ingrained as conditioned responses. They will become a part of your innermost being.

MOUNTOLOGY–The PSYCHOLOGY of MOUNTAIN FLYING

In trying to persuade you to train yourself to react to mountain flying situations the same way Pavlov got his dogs to react to stimulus (no, you won't have to drool), it is necessary to provide some basic definitions. The three terms are *conditioned, reflex* and *instinct.*

- *Conditioned* in psychology means *exhibiting or trained to exhibit a conditioned reflex (response).*

- *Reflex* in psychology means an *unlearned or instinctive response to a stimulus.*

- *Instinct* means an innate aspect of behavior that is unlearned, complex and normally adaptive.

An instinctive response to a stimulus does not work all the time in an airplane. For example, when an airplane is in a spin, your instinct is to pull back on the control wheel to raise the nose. It has worked before, but now it is not adaptive. You must be trained to "break" the stall before pulling back on the control wheel. This is a conditioned response. The basic premises of mountain flying must also be ingrained as a conditioned reflex.

True mountain flying (terrain, contour or drainage flying as opposed to flying above the mountains) can be done with total safety only when the pilot becomes conditioned to apply the basic premises during flight without having to think about them.

Let's take a "for instance." Shortly after you began your flight training, the person sitting next to you (your opinion is rapidly transforming him from one of the gods to a sadistic ogre), reached up and pulled back on the throttle and said, *"Your engine just quit, proceed as you would in an actual emergency."* You probably tried, without success, to glide the airplane to a spot where an emergency landing could be made. Your experience level did not allow you to make the proper choice of a field, its suitability for landing, or its location in relation to your glide distance. This training continued until at some point the instructor (maybe he switches the fuel selector to the off position without your noticing) says, *"Egad, the engine quit!"* You, without consciously thinking about it, head for a field that your subconscious picked out in advance.

Chapter 1 - Basic Premises   **Part 1 PREFLIGHT**

And that's the way it will continue—you don't have to think about the engine quitting. This type of training unconsciously caused you to seek an emergency landing area each time you were with the instructor. Eventually the training transfers to encompass all the time you are flying.

At the risk of boring you to the extent that you put this book away, never to look at it again, I'm going to restate the two basic premises of all mountain flying. They are the most important information you can gain from this book.

Basic premise #1: *Always remain in a position where you can turn toward lowering terrain.* Another way of stating this truth is to have an escape route in mind and be in a position to exercise this option.

Basic premise #2: *Do not fly beyond the point of no return.* Constantly evaluate where you are and decide if you can lose altitude prior to having to turn the aircraft. If not, you are narrowing your options substantially.

The two golden rules of mountain flying are not instinctive. They must be conditioned responses. It is not necessary to have Pavlov (an instructor) to condition you for mountain flying. But, you must *constantly* think about the axioms of flight until you become conditioned to remain unconsciously in a position where you can turn toward lowering terrain and never fly beyond the point of no return.

If you know and abide by these two basic premises of mountain flying, you can go flying, with safety. ✈

SOME AREAS REQUIRE MODIFICATION OF THE STANDARD TRAFFIC PATTERN. MANEUVER THE AIRPLANE AFTER TAKEOFF TO STAY IN A POSITION TO TURN TOWARD LOWERING TERRAIN. (Paul Imeson, Horse Creek, Jackson, Wyo.)

PART 1 PREFLIGHT   Chapter 2 - Considerations

CHAPTER 2—CONSIDERATIONS

➤ Flight Planning Considerations 1-9
➤ Cruise Altitude 1-10
➤ Cruise Performance 1-11
➤ Thin Air 1-11
➤ Optimum Cruise Altitude 1-11
➤ Fuel Systems 1-12
➤ Fuel Sampling Procedure 1-13
➤ Fuel Management 1-14
➤ Carburetor Icing 1-18
➤ Effect of Wind 1-23
➤ Section Lines 1-23
➤ Preflight Safety Tips 1-24
➤ Plan Early Morning Flights 1-24
➤ Oxygen 1-25
➤ Hypoxia 1-30

You must prepare for mountain flying. Regulations specify the pilot is responsible for the safety of the flight. He must be physically fit and mentally knowledgeable to exercise judgment while performing the flight. The weather must be suitable for the proposed operation. The flight must be planned and the airplane must be prepared. Regardless of whether these items are regulation or not, it is only after evaluating each of these and being aware of the basic premises of all mountain flying, that you are ready to go flying.

FLIGHT PLANNING CONSIDERATIONS

Before spending a lot of time planning a flight, call the Flight Service personnel (or crank up your computer to DUATS) to determine the trend of the weather along the route of flight.

Chapter 2 - Considerations   **Part 1 PREFLIGHT**

 If the ceilings vary en route, look with suspicion at what is causing the weather fluctuations. It may be rare, but ceilings have lowered as much as 2,000-feet per minute over portions of the intermountain west.

 Trying to sneak through a narrow pass under a low ceiling is asking for trouble. Strong downdrafts and turbulence may not be encountered until the airplane is far enough into the pass to be committed to continue.

 For more than 30 years (that's all the longer I have been flying) a rule of thumb has stated when the temperature and dew point are within 5 degrees, with a trend showing closure, you can expect low clouds and fog (BR or mist on the new weather reports). It remains a valid rule, especially in the mountains. Once the temperature/dew point are within 4 degrees, head for the nearest airport before encountering a dangerous situation that can get you into trouble.

 The sun sets earlier in a canyon because the sun's rays are blocked by the mountains. Flying en route to a valley destination may pose problems. You are flying along in beautiful sunlight, but the airstrip may already be shrouded in darkness. A destination airstrip without runway lighting means you have to divert to your alternate airport.

Have one or two flashlights (with extra Alkaline batteries and bulbs) if the flight extends into darkness. It's easy to distinguish the pilot who has experienced an electrical failure while flying at night ... his flight bag contains a minimum of two flashlights. If your flashlight is stored in the airplane, reverse one battery to break the electrical connection and eliminate any power drain.

Seldom, if ever, will you have to refuel from a barrel or drum, but if you do, have a chamois and funnel to filter the fuel. (See *Refueling*)

The novice pilot may fail to realize the importance of making long trips in the mountains in easy stages. Several hours of low altitude navigation along highways and between mountains can be the stress equivalent of a full day's VOR or GPS navigation over flatland. The unusual environmental conditions encountered in the mountains may place additional stress on you and may impair your flying ability unless you deliberately pace yourself, taking time to adjust, and refusing to hurry on or fly in marginal weather.

CRUISE ALTITUDE

To fly cross-country as quickly and efficiently as possible, advanced planning can save much time and money. Maximum speed and maximum efficiency do not always go hand-in-hand. With a headwind, usually maximum cruise power yields the greatest efficiency. With a tail wind, the minimum cruising power will produce the greatest efficiency.

To obtain the best point-to-point speed requires consideration of the cruise altitude, wind, ground speed and cruise power setting.

CRUISE PERFORMANCE

The cruise performance of an airplane is dependent upon the desired power output and the altitude. Suppose it is desired to operate the engine at 65-percent power. By climbing to the highest altitude where the engine can produce this desired power, it will have the advantage of the least amount of aerodynamic drag. The airplane will perform at its fastest speed (for a given power setting) and will give good range.

THIN AIR

The density of the air decreases with altitude. The airplane in flight experiences two kinds of drag, *induced drag* (greatest at low speeds) that is related to lift being produced and *parasite drag* (greatest at high speeds) that is associated with air flow interference, eddy and form drag. For a particular power setting, the higher the airplane climbs, while still being able to maintain the desired power setting, the faster the airplane will fly. Remember the rule of thumb about indicated airspeed and true airspeed? For each 1,000 feet above sea level, the true airspeed is two percent faster than indicated.

As with most things in life, it's not a free ride. You can't get something for nothing. The *best power mixture* results when the mixture is leaned to obtain a fuel/air ratio of one pound of fuel for each 12½ pounds of air. Regardless of altitude, the airplane engine with a certain volume or capacity (for example, 200-cubic inches) will "pump" that volume of air through the engine with each cycle of the engine. With increasing altitude, although the same amount of air goes through the engine (by volume), its weight is reduced. Therefore, it is required that you reduce the weight of the fuel with the mixture control.

OPTIMUM CRUISE ALTITUDE

To realize the *optimum cruise altitude* for your airplane requires some homework. If you want to fly at 75-percent power, look in the Pilot's Operating Handbook (POH) to determine the maximum altitude where application of full throttle produces 75-percent power.

This highest altitude where the desired power setting can be obtained is the altitude that will provide the best performance. It results in the maximum obtainable cruise speed for the 75-percent-power setting because it is the highest altitude where 75-percent power can be developed. The highest altitude you can fly and obtain your desired power setting will provide the maximum advantage from the decreased drag of the thin air.

The normally aspirated engine (non-turbocharged, non-supercharged) develops 75-percent power at full throttle somewhere around 6,000 feet. Colder than standard temperature raises the altitude and warmer than standard temperature will lower this optimum altitude. The normally aspirated engine develops 65-percent power at full throttle somewhere between 8,000 feet and 12,000 feet depending on temperature, the engine condition, and whether or not it is equipped with a fixed-pitch propeller or a constant-speed propeller.

Suppose, while flying at the optimum cruise altitude, terrain requires a climb. Increasing altitude causes a decrease in the aerodynamic drag, but the loss of air by weight into the engine causes a loss of power. The overall effect is a loss of true airspeed in an airplane with a normally aspirated engine.

Many areas of the intermountain west, Canada and Alaska have terrain that dictates flight at altitudes higher than the optimum cruise altitude. In this case you sacrifice efficiency and economy for safety and fly at the higher altitudes that are required.

The lower the desired power setting used, the higher the optimum altitude will be, assuming full throttle is used for the cruise power setting. The time and power it takes to climb to a favorable operating altitude must be considered when selecting your cruise altitude. Generally, the airplane equipped with a normally aspirated engine having a cruise speed under 130 knots, should not be climbed to a cruise altitude above 9,000- or 10,000-feet above ground level unless the proposed flight is of two hours or greater duration or terrain features require greater altitude. It takes this long to amortize the additional time for the climb. However, the presence of a favorable tail wind could change this recommendation.

 **RULE OF THUMB**—Do not climb more than 10 minutes for each hour of en route flight time.

If the terrain dictates a higher altitude than that specified by this rule, you will have to sacrifice efficiency. Depending upon the performance of your airplane, it is usually inefficient to climb more than 10 minutes per hour of estimated time en route for the entire trip. If the rate of climb in your airplane is 500 feet per minute, you shouldn't climb more than 5,000 feet above ground level for each one hour of flight time.

FUEL SYSTEMS

As responsible pilots we all get a checkout before beginning a flight in an unfamiliar airplane. This checkout must include the fuel system components and operation. Become familiar with the fuel selector. Learn the proper operation of fuel boost pumps and whether they are used for takeoff, landing, switching fuel tanks or purging vapor from the system.

Of course, other than for insurance requirements, there is no regulation requiring a checkout if we want to fly solo. Even to carry passengers we only need to make three takeoffs and landings in the preceding 90 days. The *single-engine land* endorsement on our pilot certificate allows you to fly any single-engine land airplane weighing less than 12,500 pounds (excluding turbojet and warbird airplanes). This legality, however, doesn't lend itself to safety. But, if there is someone out there who is going to do it, for heaven's sake study the airplane flight manual beforehand. The worst time to be studying about an emergency is in the middle of one.

Sometimes it is necessary to park the airplane overnight without *topping* the tanks. There is a possibility of water contamination from condensation even when the airplane is in a heated hangar. Some pilots are unaware of the proper procedure to take a fuel sample to check for contamination.

FUEL SAMPLING PROCEDURE

Fuel contamination in airplanes is always a possibility even though we use modern fuel-pumping facilities and oil companies deliver pure fuel. Because of this, most airplanes are equipped with quick drain valves for each tank sump and fuel filter. During the first preflight of the day and after each refueling, drain sufficient fuel into a transparent container to see that it is free of contaminants.

Drain 4- or 5-small samples into your fuel tester to eliminate the fluid swirl that can cause water and contaminants to move away from the sump drain.

The experienced pilot will place the airplane in a level flight position and allow the fuel to settle for five to 10 minutes, then drain the sumps and filters. The proper technique for obtaining the fuel sample is not to drain the container full of fuel all at once.

FUEL-SAMPLING TECHNIQUE

The **proper fuel sampling technique** is to open and close the sump, taking many small samples. The reason for not opening the drain to obtain one large sample is simple. In the northern hemisphere, a low pressure area results in a counterclockwise rotation of a fluid—whether it be liquid or gas—creating a miniature tornado. When you drain the sump by holding the quick drain valve open, the venturi effect results in a low pressure area that causes water and contaminants to be swirled and slung to the outside of the whirlpool. By opening and closing the drain you allow the water to settle into the drain for collection in the sampler cup.

If you collect more water than usual, grab the wing tip and move it up and down to slosh the fuel and wash down any condensation from the walls of the tanks. Again, it will be necessary to wait another five to 10 minutes before taking another fuel sample. The reason you have to wait is because the water may be in suspension with the fuel and it takes some amount of time for it to separate and settle to a drain.

FUEL MANAGEMENT

The fuel systems of some airplanes requires changing the position of the fuel selector valve to select a different tank(s) as the flight progresses. This provides for proper weight and balance while using the full capacity of the airplane. It is wise, in the winter, to change to the other tank(s) while leaving a 30-minute reserve in the original tank. It is possible to have condensation or contamination in the tank you are switching to, and the engine just won't run. You then have the option of going back to the original tank and having a 30-minute reserve to find a landing place. Should the 30-minute fuel supply in the original tank be required, you will be able to select it without worry since it has already been used and there is less chance that condensation exists that will cause it to freeze.

During cold weather operations, even though a tank has been previously used, it is possible for its supply line to freeze during the time you are burning fuel from another tank. By changing back to this tank while leaving a reserve, you can test it. If there is a problem you have an "out" or "escape route" available ... at least for 30 minutes.

 Use isopropyl alcohol or anti-icing fluid in the fuel, as recommended by the manufacturer, during cold-weather operations.

FUEL FACILITIES

Be cautious when using makeshift fueling facilities. Older fuel drums, even if refinery sealed, may contain rust, water and other contaminants. Avoid using anything other than the proper grade of aviation fuel specified for your airplane. If the proper grade is not available, consult the Pilot's Operating Handbook to determine the proper substitute fuel. Adhere to the following precautions:

- ✔ Always fuel from modern facilities and fill your tanks (if not weight limited) as soon as possible after landing.
- ✔ Drain the sumps ten minutes after refueling if the airplane is to remain outside overnight if there is a possibility of freezing temperature. You will still need to drain them again the next morning. Take several small samples, instead of one large sample.
- ✔ Check that the fuel is of the proper grade by looking at the color. A mixture of 80/87 and 100/130 will create clear fuel. Always

- smell clear fuel to check for jet fuel contamination and feel it to make certain that it is not jet fuel.
- ✔ If using a makeshift facility, be certain to filter the fuel. Attach a static ground and have a fire extinguisher available.
- ✔ Do not wear nylon clothing while refueling. This clothing generates static electricity.
- ✔ Do not use additives unless authorized by the manufacturer and approved by the FAA.
- ✔ A chamois skin does not filter the fuel. It only removes water, providing it is not wet. Once saturated with water, it will not filter water. If water is observed or suspected, wring out the chamois. Do not use an imitation chamois, it will not filter water.
- ✔ When water contamination is likely (temperature and dew point come close together overnight), add isopropyl alcohol or ethylene glycol monomethyl ether (EGME) compound. This provides two distinct benefits:
  1. The alcohol has a freezing-temperature depressant effect.
  2. This fluid should be blended with the fuel, not poured into the fuel after fueling. It is most effective when it is completely dissolved in the fuel.

FUEL SYSTEM ICING

Ice formation in the fuel system results from undissolved free water or dissolved water in suspension with the fuel. Free water can usually be drained through sump drains during preflight; however, if the airplane is parked outside during freezing temperatures, the free water may be frozen. If such a condition is detected (the sumps won't drain), place the airplane in a warm hangar to thaw and drain the sump drains. Water in suspension may freeze and form ice crystals that could block fuel screens, strainers and filters.

PREVENTION PROCEDURES

The use of anti-icing additives has been approved for use in some piston-engine-powered aircraft. The use of hexylene glycol (1% by volume), certain methanol derivations (1% by volume), and EGME (at a maximum 0.15% by volume) substantially inhibits fuel system icing. Check your flight manual for the manufacturer's recommendation.

Alcohol Blending Technique—Add isopropyl alcohol and anti-icing fluid (in a concentration of one percent by volume) to the fuel by pouring or injecting it (from a pressurized canister) directly into the fuel stream coming from the fuel nozzle. An alternative method is to use a clean container with a minimum 2-gallon capacity. Premix the alcohol with fuel and pour this mixture evenly among all tanks before refueling.

Alcohol Mixture—One percent by volume is obtained by mixing one cup of alcohol per six gallons of total fuel or one quart of alcohol per 25 gallons of total fuel.

FUEL/AIR MIXTURE

The complete burning of the fuel introduced into the cylinders of a gasoline engine, requires the proper fuel/air (F/A) ratio to be established. This fuel/air ratio is based on *weight,* not quantity of fuel or air. The chemically correct mixture uses about 15 pounds of air for each pound of fuel.

Airplanes, regardless of the elevation of their home base, have the carburetor adjusted to provide this 1:15 F/A ratio when the mixture is in the full rich position at sea level. This is done because the airplane has the capability of going to a sea level airport and it must be able to obtain sea level performance.

When an airplane departs a sea level airport and begins to climb, it is exposed to less dense or thinner air. The higher you fly, the thinner the air. In fact, about half the atmosphere, by weight, lies below 18,000 feet.

With the decreasing air density during a climb, the fuel/air ratio becomes rich. It is true that the engine is an air pump and that the quantity of air entering and exiting the engine is the same regardless of altitude. But, the fuel/air ratio is based on the ratio of the weight of fuel and the weight of air, not the quantity.

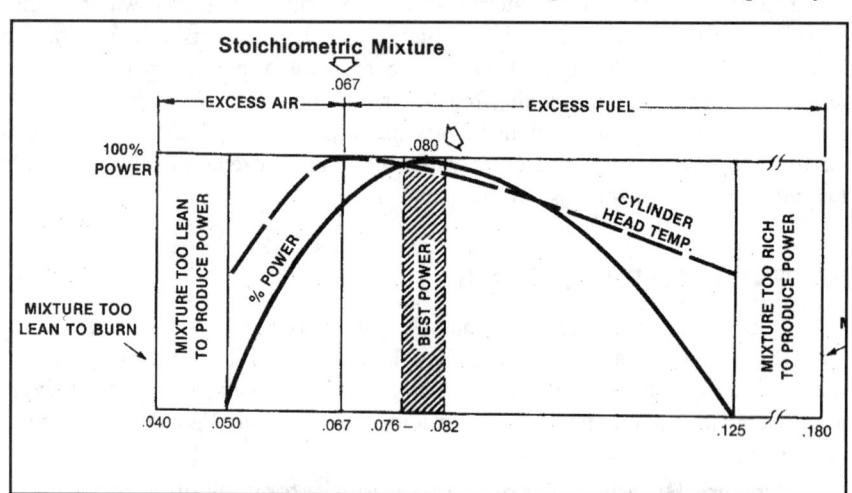

NOTE: THE STOICHIOMETRIC MIXTURE (.067) RESULTS IN THE GREATEST CYLINDER HEAD TEMPERATURE AND A LOSS OF POWER. AT THE BEST POWER MIXTURE (.080) THE CYLINDER HEAD TEMPERATURE IS LESS AND THE POWER GREATER.

As the airplane climbs the mixture must be adjusted to maintain the ratio of fuel and air by weight. This is called *leaning the mixture,* a method of compensating for decreased air density by metering less fuel to the carburetor.

TEMPERATURE AND FUEL/AIR RATIO

The *stoichiometric mixture* is the chemically correct mixture required to use all the air and all the fuel during combustion. This is achieved at a fuel/air ratio of 1 to 15 (0.067). Even though this is considered a *chemically correct mixture* for combustion, it produces the greatest heat, causing the engine to run its hottest. Therefore, the fuel/air ratio of 1 to 12½ (0.080) is used and is known as the *best power mixture.* The best power mixture is the fuel/air ratio required for a specific power output obtained with the lowest manifold pressure or throttle setting for that particular power.

PROPER LEANING ALTITUDE

Back in the "old days," engine manufacturers cautioned us not to lean the mixture below 5,000 feet. The only reason for this recommendation was the manufacturer's feeling that pilots were not knowledgeable enough to properly lean the mixture. They felt that below 5,000 feet there was no noticeable increase in engine efficiency even if it was leaned. Above 5,000 feet it was harder for the pilot to get into trouble by using improper leaning techniques. This is because above 5,000 feet, the normally aspirated engine is not capable of developing more than 75 percent of its rated power.

The advent of the "energy crisis" of the '70s created thinking and ideas of conservation. Depending upon which FAA publication you read, you may find you are still cautioned to lean the mixture only when operating at 75 percent or less power and above 5,000 feet (Accident Prevention Program literature).

Many knowledgeable pilots go along with the recommendations of the *Flight Training Handbook* (AC 61-21A). Its recommendation is to not lean the mixture during climb until passing 5,000 feet; otherwise, lean the mixture when operating above 3,000 feet with power settings of 75 percent or less.

Experience may suggest that you lean the mixture at any altitude above sea level when operating at 75 percent power or less. Remember, though, during a climb excess fuel is needed to help cool the engine. Some carburetors are equipped with a power enrichener valve to add extra fuel during full throttle operation. This helps cool the engine.

Caution: Do not lean turbocharged or supercharged engines for takeoff, even from high altitude mountain strips. These engines can produce sea level power up to their critical altitude and they require sea level mixture settings.

Leaning the mixture is covered in Part 2, Procedure for Leaning.

CARBURETOR ICING

The carburetor of the engine is designed to convert liquid fuel into vapor (minute droplets) because liquid fuel is not combustible in the engine. The fuel/air mixture is a function of the carburetor. After air enters the carburetor, fuel is added and vaporization and expansion occur causing a temperature drop of as much as 60°F. The intake manifold (tunnels or channels that lead to each cylinder) directs the fuel/air mixture to the cylinders. Within the carburetor itself, ice can form under conditions where structural icing can not form on the outside of the airplane.

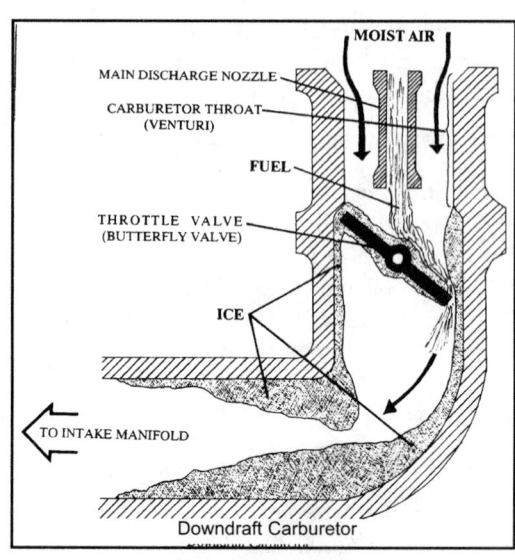

CARBURETOR ICING

WATER VAPOR

Air always contains some water vapor. The amount of water vapor that air can contain at a given temperature is limited. As the temperature of the air is increased, its capacity to hold moisture is increased. When air contains the maximum amount of moisture that it can hold at a given temperature, the pressure caused by the water vapor is also at a maximum and the air is then said to be *"saturated."*

HUMIDITY

Humidity is moisture. The *relative humidity* is the ratio of the amount of moisture the air contains compared to the amount of moisture it could contain at that temperature. Generally, if you double the temperature of the air, it doubles the amount of moisture the air can contain. Conversely, if the temperature is reduced by half, it reduces the air's capacity to hold moisture by half. A relative humidity of 100 percent means the air is saturated. If 100-percent-saturated air is cooled, water vapor will condense. The temperature at which moisture begins to condense is called the *"dew point."*

VAPORIZATION

Vaporization is the conversion of a solid or liquid to vapor. A solid can change to a liquid, and a liquid can change to a gas or vapor.

The carburetor takes liquid fuel and changes it to a gaseous fuel for mixture with the air in a process known as vaporization. Vaporization involves the absorption of heat from the environment. Thus, inside the carburetor, there is a cooling of air when vaporization takes place. As the fuel/air mixture passes from the carburetor to the intake manifold (where it is channeled to each cylinder) expansion takes place. Expansion also cools the air.

Favorable Carb Icing Conditions

During the late fall, through the winter, and extending into the early spring, the outside air temperature may fall in the 40°F range or colder. As a general rule, air 40°F or colder does not have the capacity to hold sufficient moisture to form carburetor icing. Even on summer days, when the temperature is greater than 80°F, vaporization and expansion of the fuel does not cool the mixture sufficiently for ice to form. It is on those perfect flying days with the temperature between 49°F and 60°F when sufficient humidity (greater than 60 percent) poses the threat of carburetor icing. Don't become lax just because the conditions do not meet those most conducive for icing, for carburetor icing has occurred at temperatures from 14°F to 100°F.

CATEGORIES OF CARBURETOR ICING

Three categories of carburetor icing have been established: *fuel ice, impact ice* and *throttle ice*.

FUEL ICE (Fuel Evaporation Ice - Fuel Vaporization Ice)

Fuel ice forms downstream (between the carburetor and intake manifold) from the point where fuel is introduced. The mixture has been cooled to below freezing by fuel vaporization. This condition usually occurs in conjunction with throttle icing. It is most prevalent in airplane engines equipped with conventional float type carburetors. Fuel ice may occur at temperatures from 32°F to as high as 100°F with a relative humidity of 50 percent or greater. In general, when the temperature-dew point spread is 20°F or less and you have a relative humidity of 50 percent or greater, you are in potential icing conditions.

IMPACT ICE (ATMOSPHERIC ICE)

Impact ice is formed by the impact of water (rain, snow, sleet or liquid droplets in clouds) in suspension in the atmosphere, coming in contact with parts of the induction system at temperatures 32°F or below. On an airplane with a carburetor and no alternate air, it is possible for ice to cover the air filter. In this case, carburetor heat must be used. Not to melt the ice, it won't, but to provide an alternate source of air for the engine.

Impact ice may affect an engine with fuel injection by ice build-up on air scoops, intake screens and alternate air valves. It may be necessary to use alternate air before the selector valve is frozen.

The use of partial heat for ice prevention without a carburetor air temperature gauge may be worse than using none at all. Partial heat may raise the mixture temperature to a danger range where throttle ice forms, whereas, full carburetor heat would bring the mixture temperature well above any danger of icing.

THROTTLE ICE (EXPANSION ICE)

Throttle ice is caused by the freezing of the condensed water vapor of the air at or near the throttle valve (butterfly valve) in the carburetor. This occurs when the water vapor in the air is condensed and frozen due to the cooling and lowering of pressure when the air passes through the throttle restriction (venturi of the carburetor). If this icing is allowed to continue, the ice build-up may stop the engine. The effect of throttle icing is a progressive decline in power. With a fixed-pitch propeller this is evidenced by a loss of RPM. With a constant-speed propeller, this is confirmed by a decrease in manifold pressure.

CARBURETOR HEAT

Except for extreme conditions, when your flight is performed at cruise power settings, the engine generates sufficient heat to prevent carburetor icing. It is when the throttle is reduced that the engine becomes susceptible to carb icing. When the throttle is closed (power reduced), the butterfly valve inside the carburetor throat closes to cut down the flow of air. This restriction of the size of the opening in the carburetor permits only a small amount of icing to block the airflow to the engine and cause engine failure.

The carburetor heater is an anti-icing device (not a deicing device) that preheats the air before it reaches the carburetor. The heater is usually adequate to prevent icing, but it will not always clear out ice that has already formed. When using reduced throttle settings, the manufacturers generally suggest you use carburetor heat. Some tachometers incorporate a green arc that indicates the use of carburetor heat when power is reduced below the lower limit of the green arc, around 2,000 rpm.

Use the carburetor heater whenever it is needed, but remember the carb heat shunts the air from the air filter. If you are on the ground, parked over dust and debris, this dirt could enter the engine. The intake air passes around the muffler or exhaust manifold to become heated. When carb beat is applied, this unfiltered air, at temperatures up to 200-degrees Fahrenheit, enters the throat of the carburetor. When in flight with the intention of reducing the throttle below the green arc, apply the carb heat for 10 to 30 seconds before closing the throttle.

The throttle body of a carburetor consists of the venturi with a butterfly valve near the center. The butterfly valve is connected to the throttle, regulating the airflow into the engine. *Float-type* carburetors have a fuel-discharge nozzle in the venturi with fuel flow dependent on the amount of air entering the venturi. *Pressure-type* carburetors use a pump or venturi suction to vaporize the fuel at a point beyond the venturi. The float-type carburetor is more susceptible to icing since vaporization occurs in the venturi. Pressure-type carburetors are less susceptible to icing because the fuel is introduced to the air after passing through the venturi.

Carburetor icing can and does cause an engine to fail. In an emergency (if the engine fails, it is an emergency), it may be possible to dislodge carburetor icing by leaning the mixture until the engine backfires. There are recorded instances of the pilot turning the magnetos off for a few seconds, allowing fuel to build up in the cylinders, and when the mags are turned back on the engine backfires with sufficient force to dislodge the ice. This can also dislodge the cylinder heads, so use this procedure for emergencies only. If all else fails, close the throttle and wait as long as possible (probably for more than a minute) for the heat from the engine to be conducted to the carburetor and clear the ice.

 Often the temperature and moisture conditions that produce carburetor icing are restricted to a few thousand feet of altitude. If you are having trouble with carb icing, use the carb heat at once. When applying carb heat, use full heat, not a partial setting. When the engine is running normally (it may be necessary to lean the mixture to compensate for the heated air), change altitude and reduce the carb heat gradually while attempting to restore full power.

Carburetor icing is dangerous at any time but especially so during the takeoff. Some pilots check the carburetor heat during the before-takeoff check by pulling the heat on and, before a drop in rpm or manifold pressure can occur, turning it off. Pull the heat on, determine there is a drop of rpm or mp, wait a moment to see if there is a rise (indicating ice), then turn it off. If you don't wait to see that the carb heat actually works, don't even bother with the check. If the carb heat control is not functioning, get it fixed before flying. By the way, carb heat is not used for the takeoff except in extremely cold condition where it is required to allow vaporization of the fuel.

Because the air diverted by carb heat is unfiltered, your *before-takeoff* check should be done in an area where loose gravel and dirt particles are at a minimum. When operating at a field where it is impossible to avoid dirt, make the carb heat check while taxiing. This will cause the dirt to be blown back instead of being taken into the engine.

Chapter 2 - Considerations   Part 1 PREFLIGHT

The FAA used to have a "trick" question on the written exam stating "closing the cowl flaps will prevent or cure carburetor icing." Cowl flaps allow the air to flow from the front of the engine to the rear in a continuous efficient movement, helping to cool the engine, especially during the climb. Another of their "tricks" is to talk about fuel-injected engines experiencing carb icing. With fuel injection there is no carburetor, the fuel goes directly to the cylinders, so there can be no carb icing with the fuel-injected engine.

Indications of Carburetor Icing

Carburetor icing is easily detected in airplanes equipped with a fixed-pitch propeller or constant-speed propeller. The first indication of carburetor icing will be:

- ☆ Fixed-pitch propeller - loss of rpm
- ☆ Constant-speed propeller - loss of manifold pressure (rpm remains the same)

If the pilot fails to notice these indications, there is a progressive decrease in engine power until it is necessary to re-trim to maintain altitude. Next, engine roughness will occur. If carburetor heat is not applied now, complete stoppage may occur.

PREVENTION PROCEDURES

Induction system icing characterized as *fuel ice, impact ice,* and *throttle ice* can cause a serious loss of power by restricting the flow of the fuel/air mixture to the engine. The pilot can prevent induction icing.

- ☒ Check the carburetor heat effectiveness by noting a power drop when the heat is applied during run-up.

- ☒ If induction system ice is suspected of causing a power loss, apply full heat or alternate air. Do not move the throttle until an improvement is noted. Expect a further power loss momentarily and then a rise in power as the ice is melted, along with some engine roughness.

 If throttle ice is suspected, transition to the best angle-of-climb speed to heat up the engine. The use of full carburetor heat may require leaning the mixture; however, use caution to prevent killing the engine. A restart with ice may be difficult.

Prior to a prolonged descent with reduced power settings, apply carburetor heat for a short time to warm the induction system. Periodically, apply power (with the carburetor heat still on) to warm the engine.

With the *fixed-pitch prop,* if there is carb ice, upon applying heat there will be a drop in rpm, engine roughness due to water ingestion, and then a rise in rpm when the ice melts (even though you are using heated air, there will be more of it if the carburetor passage is cleared out). When the carb heat is turned off there will be another rise in the rpm to a setting that is higher than before the application of carb heat. If you noticed a loss of rpm and there is no ice present, the loss is probably due to throttle creep. This is confirmed, when upon adding heat, the rpm would drop (due to the less dense heated air being taken into the cylinders and a loss of ram-air effect), remain at that rpm, and then return to the original rpm setting when the carb heat is turned off.

If carb ice is present in an aircraft equipped with a *constant-speed prop,* the addition of carb heat will cause a drop in manifold pressure (MP), then an increase as the ice melts and another increase to a higher setting than the original when the carb heat is turned off. If ice is present, the engine will run rough as it melts. If there was no ice, upon application of carb heat the MP would drop, remain at that setting, and then return to the original MP setting when carb heat is turned off.

> TAKE CARE OF YOUR AIRCRAFT ENGINE
> AND IT WILL TAKE CARE OF YOU!

EFFECT OF WIND

Occasionally the winds aloft are less at high altitudes than near the ground. For this reason it is wise to check the winds aloft at all altitudes where it is possible to fly. Although a headwind may be stronger at a higher altitude, its direction may be more favorable, producing less of a ground speed reduction. Additionally, the increase in true airspeed at higher altitudes may more than compensate for a stronger headwind as well as provide a smoother flight void of convection currents or mechanical turbulence.

After takeoff, while climbing to the en route cruising altitude, it is recommended you climb at the best rate-of-climb airspeed whenever a no-wind condition or tail wind is present. A maximum rate schedule is used to conserve climb fuel for the more efficient operating environment at altitude, unless a lower pitch attitude is required for better forward visibility or engine cooling. When climbing into a headwind, use a faster cruise climb airspeed to minimize the effect of a lower ground speed.

SECTION LINES

Because mountainous terrain is not favorable for farming operations you may fly for hours without seeing section lines. Pilots often, either consciously or sub-

Chapter 2 - Considerations — Part 1 PREFLIGHT

consciously, maintain their course based on section lines. If you feel some uneasiness flying in an area void of section lines, check the compass a little more often and reset your heading indicator to put yourself at ease.

PREFLIGHT SAFETY TIPS

- ✘ Be familiar with the airplane's operating limitations.
- ✘ Check the weather. If the weather is marginal, delay or postpone the flight.
- ✘ File a flight plan and make regular position reports.
- ✘ Route your trip along airways and over valleys choosing a route that allows for a forced landing.
- ✘ Keep the airplane as light as possible, but do not compromise on reserve fuel or survival equipment.
- ✘ Become familiar with the destination field. Talk to someone familiar with operating at the strip or study the state-published airport information.
- ✘ Take advantage of early-morning air, but beware of *flying blind*.
- ✘ Carry survival equipment in the aircraft (not buried in a baggage compartment where you cannot gain access).
- ✘ Have oxygen available for flights above 10,000-12,000 feet MSL.

PLAN EARLY MORNING FLIGHTS

Flight instructors generally recommend that mountain flights should be made early in the morning or late in the afternoon to take advantage of the calm air. Usually, by 10:00 a.m. convection makes the air unstable. The air becomes progressively worse until around 4:00 or 5:00 p.m., when it slowly improves. (See *Flying Blind* caution)

You might be surprised by the number of days the air is calm and it is not hazardous to fly during the middle of the day. Be aware, however, that the density altitude increases, with the possibility of convection currents creating additional turbulence. Beware also of flying blind.

OXYGEN

Federal Aviation Regulations require the pilot (and required crewmembers) to use supplemental oxygen when flying between 12,500 and 14,000 feet MSL (or cabin altitude for pressurized aircraft) for more than one-half hour. The pilot (and required crewmembers) must use supplemental oxygen at any time when flying above 14,000 feet. At 15,000 feet, all occupants of the airplane must be *provided with* supplemental oxygen. *Provided with* suggests that its use is optional. We have heard stories of the guy, flying along with fussy kids, who climbs to altitude (without providing the children with supplemental oxygen) to put them to sleep...stupid!

LACK OF OXYGEN! Can cause the same effect as a couple of Martinis

OVERCONFIDENCE...InCoOrDiNaTiOn

You may not agree with all Federal Aviation Regulations, but this regulation is very realistic and you are well advised to stay within its parameters. Flying contrary to this regulation, whether illegal or not, exposes the pilot to hypoxia, a deficiency of oxygen. Lack of oxygen can cause permanent brain damage.

Medical research has proven that the pilot who lives at a high elevation cannot extend his physiologic altitude by the amount equal to the elevation of his domicile above sea level. For example, the pilot living at 7,000 feet cannot safely fly 7,000 feet above the limits of the FAR (14,000 + 7,000).

The pilot living at 7,000 feet does have a greater number of red blood cells than a pilot who lives at sea level. This requirement is automatically compensated for by the body for more efficient oxygen transportation throughout the body. But other variables enter into the calculation in determining how much higher the acclimated pilot can fly. Physical conditioning, smoking habits, fatigue and business pressure can, individually or combined, affect the body's functions. The pilot who lives at 7,000 feet may (illegally) extend the FAR requirements 1,000-2,000 feet, but definitely he cannot extend his hypoxia tolerance by 7,000 feet.

It's not prudent to do other than what the regulation requires. If there is a possibility of flying above 10,000 feet, carry supplemental oxygen. Remember, while the regulation is based upon physical altitude, the body responds to the density altitude.

ATMOSPHERE PROBLEM AREAS

The composition and distribution of the atmosphere poses special considerations for the pilot. The composition is only about 21 percent oxygen. It is 79.02 percent nitrogen, 20.95 percent oxygen, and 0.03 percent carbon dioxide by vol-

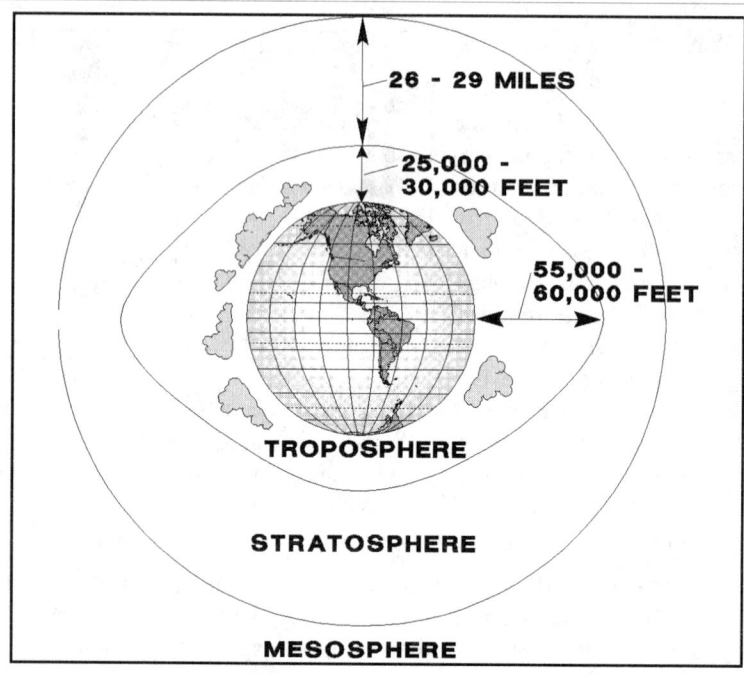

MAJOR REGIONS OF THE ATMOSPHERE
THE BULGE IN THE TROPOSPHERE (OVER THE EQUATOR) IS DUE TO UNEVEN SURFACE HEATING. THE LINE OF DEMARCATION BETWEEN THE TROPOSPHERE AND THE STRATOSPHERE IS CALLED THE TROPOPAUSE. THE TROPOPAUSE OCCURS AT AN ALTITUDE WHERE THE STANDARD LAPSE RATE DECREASES FROM 15°C AT SEA LEVEL TO –54°C.

ume. Included with the nitrogen are small amounts of rare gases (argon, neon, helium, krypton, hydrogen, xenon, and radon) that apparently have no physiological significance on us mere mortals.

Next, half the atmosphere by weight is located below 18,000 feet msl. When climbing to higher altitudes, the atmospheric pressure decreases. Although the percentage of oxygen remains the same at higher altitudes, this decrease in pressure prohibits the body from absorbing and using the oxygen.

OXYGEN PHYSIOLOGY

Without the proper use of oxygen equipment or cabin pressurization, the decreased partial pressure of oxygen encountered at low barometric pressures (increasing altitude) can quickly lead to incapacitation or death. Deaths have occurred at altitudes between 17,000 and 20,000 feet; a fact that emphasizes, that under no conditions, can the lethal effects of acute altitude hypoxia be underestimated.

Hypoxic episodes that lead only to mental confusion or even unconsciousness, but not necessarily death, may result ultimately in the loss of the airplane and occupants because of the mental disorientation during or after the episode.

While not trying to sound like the prophet of doom, to understand and appreciate the nature of altitude hypoxia requires a basic understanding of the physiology of respiration. According to the *Flight Surgeon's Guide, Department of the Air Force, AFP 161-18*, "...deaths occurred at altitudes between 17,000 and 20,000 feet, a fact which emphasizes that, under no conditions can the lethal effects of acute altitude hypoxia be underestimated. ...Even hypoxic episodes that lead only to mental confusion or unconsciousness, but not necessarily death, may result ultimately in the total loss of the aircraft, crew, and passengers, because of the mental disorientation during and following the episode."

The main purpose of the respiratory process is to supply the lungs, blood and body tissues with adequate oxygen, and to eliminate the carbon dioxide that is generated by the metabolism of the body tissues. Thus, a homeostatic state (physiological equilibrium) is maintained in spite of a wide variety of conditions and activities. The respiratory process, along with the renal system (kidneys), also plays a role in maintaining the acid-base balance of the body within narrow limits under normal environmental conditions.

AIR COMPOSITION

Quantities of gas at various altitudes, expressed in percentages of the atmosphere, have little significance, for percentage represents the relative volume of a gas and not its molecular concentration. Since molecular concentration determines the availability of the gas to the body, the actual concentration of any gas is best expressed in terms of *partial pressure*.

The **partial pressure** of a gas, in a mixture of gases not interacting with one another, is equal to that pressure which that particular gas would exert if it alone occupied the space taken up by the mixture (Dalton's Law—Law of Partial Pressure). The **total pressure** of a mixture of gases, therefore, is the sum of the pressures of the individual gases composing the mixture.

The total standard pressure (barometric pressure) of the atmosphere at sea level is 760mm Hg (millimeters of mercury) or 14.7 psi (pounds per square inch). Since oxygen comprises about 21 percent of the air, we would expect the dry air oxygen partial pressure in the lungs to be 159.6mm Hg (760 times 21 percent), but through physiologic processes, the partial pressure of oxygen in the arterial blood is normally about 100mm Hg. The dry atmosphere contains essentially the same concentration or percentage composition of gases throughout up to 80,000 feet. The partial pressure of oxygen in the alveoli determines how much oxygen reaches the blood and tissues.

Chapter 2 - Considerations   Part 1 PREFLIGHT

Ventilation, the mass movement of air in and out of the lungs, causes alveolar air to be mixed with atmospheric air. The alveolus are small air sacs used to exchange or supply oxygen and eliminate carbon dioxide. The partial pressure of oxygen in the alveoli is responsible for combining dissolved oxygen with the hemoglobin molecules in the red blood cells for distribution to the tissues. Standard pressure at sea level is 14.7 psi or 760 mm Hg. According to *Dalton's Law*, the partial pressure of a gas mixture is equal to the pressure that particular gas would exert if it alone occupied the space. The partial pressure of oxygen at sea level is (20.95 percent by volume, divided by 100, times 760 total pressure) 159 mm Hg. This results in a hemoglobin saturation of approximately 97 percent.

The atmospheric pressure decrease with altitude is not linear. Half the atmosphere by weight lies below 18,000 feet. At 10,000-feet msl, the oxygen partial pressure is 109.5 mm Hg (20.95/100 x 522.75 total pressure), resulting in a hemoglobin saturation of about 87 percent. At 15,000-feet msl, the oxygen partial pressure is 98.9 mm Hg (20.95/100 x 429.08 total pressure).

According to the *Flight Surgeon's Guide, Department of the Air Force, AFP 161-18*, "For the unacclimatized man, an alveolar oxygen tension of less than 50 mm Hg is considered as approaching a severe state of hypoxia and an oxygen tension of 30 mm Hg is not adequate for supporting consciousness, and collapse is imminent."

In studying density altitude we learn that the airplane may be located at a certain physical altitude, but the effects of non-standard temperature and pressure can raise that altitude to represent a much higher altitude in the standard atmosphere. It is possible to try to fly over a mountain having a density altitude higher than the service ceiling of the airplane. The density altitude also affects the body's physiological processes. When flying a turbocharged airplane, it is possible to fly above the body's service ceiling for the requirement of oxygen. If you are flying along and feel light-headed, compute the density altitude and apply the regulation for oxygen usage as required.

RESPIRATION CATEGORIES

Respiration is divided into three general categories: the *pulmonary phase*, the *blood transport phase*, and the *tissue phase*.

PULMONARY PHASE

The pulmonary phase involves the exchange of gases between the external or ambient atmosphere and the alveolar air, and between the alveolar air and the blood in the pulmonary capillaries. **Alveolus** is an air sac of the lungs, at the termination of a bronchiole. This is the point where the exchange of oxygen and carbon dioxide occurs.

Mountain Flying Bible

TRANSPORT PHASE

The transport phase depends on an adequate cardiovascular system and blood constituents for transporting the respiratory gases in adequate quantities between the lungs and tissues.

TISSUE PHASE

The tissue phase of respiration involves the exchange of gases between cells of the body and the blood in the tissue capillaries.

RESPIRATION

The major physiologic functions of the lungs are grouped under three main headings: *ventilation, diffusion,* and *perfusion.*

VENTILATION

Ventilation is the mass movement of air in and out of the lungs. This is the process where alveolar air is periodically mixed with atmospheric air.

Adequate ventilation is dependent upon the creation of a pressure gradient or difference between the alveoli and the external atmosphere by the bellows action of the chest and diaphragm acting upon the lung.

DIFFUSION

Diffusion of gases across the alveolar-capillary wall refers to the mechanism whereby the respiratory gasses are transferred from the alveolar air to the blood in the pulmonary capillaries and vice versa.

The following explanation provides some understanding of the process of diffusion, not because it is necessary, or even desirable, that you know about diffusion; but rather, so you can perceive what is going on in the body when we talk about the *partial pressure of oxygen.*

For end-capillary blood in the pulmonary circulation to become adequately saturated with oxygen, the oxygen must diffuse across the alveolar membrane, through the interstitial fluid and the capillary endothelium. Within the capillary, the dissolved oxygen must then diffuse through the plasma, the red blood cell membrane, and the intracellular fluid within the red cell to combine with the hemoglobin. Hemoglobin is the oxygen carrying agent of the blood. Thus, oxygen must diffuse from a gaseous state in the alveoli to a dissolved state within the alveolar membrane and the pulmonary-capillary tissues and fluids. The solubility of a gas, and its partial pressure, greatly influences its diffusion characteristics. Carbon dioxide is about 25 times more soluble than oxygen in pulmonary tissues and fluids and its capacity for diffusion is about 20 times greater than oxygen.

PERFUSION

Perfusion of blood through the lung capillaries results in oxygen reaching the tissues.

HYPOXIA

Hypoxia, mountain sickness or *altitude sickness,* is the lack of oxygen at the tissue level of the body due to a decrease of the oxygen pressure in the inspired air or by conditions that prevent or interfere with the diffusion of oxygen across the alveolar membrane. Hypoxia is serious. If unconsciousness occurs, without remedy, it may cause death.

A syndrome, *anoxia,* meaning literally *without oxygen,* is sometimes erroneously used to denote a deficiency, rather than a lack of oxygen in the tissues. This term should not be used for flight below 55,000 feet, for even in acute cases, the tissues are never entirely without oxygen.

CAUSES

Hypoxia may be caused by:
- Flight at an altitude where there is insufficient oxygen partial pressure to cause oxygen transfer.
- A mechanical malfunction of the oxygen equipment.
- Introduction of drugs (carbon monoxide, nitrites, sulfa, etc.) that reduced the amount of hemoglobin available to form oxyhemoglobin.
- Malfunction of the circulatory system (heart failure, occlusion of a blood vessel, positive g forces).

TYPES OF HYPOXIA

The pilot has no built-in warning system against hypoxia. It is not painful. To the contrary, the greatest danger of hypoxia is that it renders the pilot euphoric.

eu.pho.ria \ yu-"for-e-a\ noun: *a feeling of well-being or elation.*

This is similar to the effects of alcohol and the pilot is unable to sense that anything is wrong. Because it is insidious, the pilot does not perceive the onset of his forthcoming incapacitation.

(1) **Histotoxic Hypoxia**—This type hypoxia follows when alcohol, narcotics, and certain poisons (cyanide) interfere with

the tissue's ability to metabolize the delivered oxygen.

(2) **Hypemic Hypoxia**—The reduction in the ability of the blood to carry oxygen because of a decreased hemoglobin content is caused by chronic anemia, a large blood loss, or the forming of compounds with hemoglobin (carbon monoxide, nitrites, sulfa drugs, etc.) that reduces the amount of hemoglobin available to form oxyhemoglobin.

> SMOKERS BEWARE: The *Flight Surgeon's Guide, Department of the Air Force, AFP 161-18* states, "Oxygen must diffuse from a gaseous state in the alveoli to a dissolved state within the alveolar membrane and the pulmonary capillary tissues and fluids. The solubility of a gas, as well as its partial pressure, greatly influences its diffusion characteristics. Carbon dioxide is about 25 times more soluble than oxygen in pulmonary tissues and fluids and, its capacity for diffusion is about 20 times greater than oxygen."

(3) **Hypoxic Hypoxia**—This is the classic "lack of oxygen," condition that results from a decrease in oxygen partial pressure at high altitudes or by conditions that prevent or interfere with the diffusion of oxygen across the alveolar membrane (asthma, pneumonia, tumors, arterial venous shunts).

(4) **Stagnant Hypoxia**—Stagnant hypoxia is also due to a malfunction of the circulatory system. It differs from hypemic hypoxia because there is plenty of oxyhemoglobin, but inadequate circulation to the tissues. It can be caused by heart problems, arterial spasm, occlusion of a blood vessel, exposure to temperature extremes, high g loads or sudden emotional disturbance.

SYMPTOMS

A particular person's symptoms of hypoxia may be quite different from another person's indicators. Once a person has gone through an altitude chamber and has discovered his symptoms, they generally remain a valid indicator of hypoxia. The onset of hypoxia depends upon the following variables:

- ✔ Absolute altitude
- ✔ Rate of ascent
- ✔ Duration at altitude
- ✔ Ambient temperature
- ✔ Physical activity

Chapter 2 - Considerations   Part 1 PREFLIGHT

Individual factors:
- ✔ Inherent tolerance
- ✔ Physical fitness
- ✔ Emotionality
- ✔ Acclimatization

Because it is possible to ascertain your own signal for the onset of hypoxia, you are urged to pick up an application form at any FAA office to attend an *altitude chamber* training session. The cost is reasonable, the training invaluable.

Hypoxia is divided into stages relating to the approximate pressure, the altitude, and the oxygen saturation of the blood.

INDIFFERENT STAGE

The only adverse effect of the indifferent stage of hypoxia is on dark adaptation.

COMPENSATORY STAGE

Physiological compensations provide some defense against hypoxia so that the effects are reduced unless the exposure is prolonged or unless exercise is undertaken. Respiration may increase in depth or slightly in rate, and the pulse rate, the systolic blood pressure, the rate of circulation and the cardiac output increases.

DISTURBANCE STAGE

In this stage, the physiological compensations do not provide adequate oxygen for the tissues.

Subjective symptoms may include:

Fatigue, lassitude (state of exhaustion), somnolence (drowsiness, sleepiness), dizziness, headache, breathlessness, and euphoria.

Objective symptoms include:

Special Senses—Both the peripheral and central vision are impaired and visual acuity is diminished.

Extraocular muscles are weak and incoordinate—Touch and pain are diminished or lost. Hearing is one of the last senses to be impaired or lost.

Mental Processes—Intellectual impairment is an early sign and makes it improbable for the individual to comprehend his own disability. Thinking is slow. Calculations are unreliable. Memory is faulty. Judgment is poor. Reaction time is delayed.

Personality Traits—There may be a release of basic personality traits and emotions as with alcoholic intoxication (euphoria, elation, pugnaciousness, overconfidence, or moroseness).

Hyperventilation Syndrome—Over-breathing due to excitement or stress.

Cyanosis—Blue discoloration of the skin.

CRITICAL STAGE

This is the stage where consciousness is lost. Death follows shortly.

HYPOXIA PREVENTION

Prevention of hypoxia is the best cure. Using supplemental oxygen in accordance with the FAR and monitoring the cabin altitude of a pressurized airplane, will keep the pilot safe. If you develop hypoxia symptoms at altitudes lower than the suggested use of supplemental oxygen, descend below 10,000 feet to experience almost instantaneous relief.

ALTITUDE WITHOUT OXYGEN	TIME OF USEFUL CONSCIOUSNESS
18,000	20 to 30 minutes
22,000	10 minutes
25,000	3 to 5 minutes
28,000	2½ to 3 minutes
30,000	1 to 2 minutes
35,000	30 to 60 seconds
40,000	15 to 20 seconds
43,000	9 to 12 seconds

TIME OF USEFUL CONSCIOUSNESS AT VARIOUS ALTITUDES WITHOUT THE USE OF SUPPLEMENTARY OXYGEN

EQUIPMENT

An oxygen system in an airplane consists of a container for storing the oxygen supply, tubing to conduct the oxygen from the main supply to a metering device, a metering device to control the flow of oxygen, and a mask or nasal canula to direct the oxygen to the respiratory system.

Portable oxygen bottles may be carried that incorporate the oxygen supply, metering device, and mask, in one unit.

Constant Flow Oxygen System

The constant-flow oxygen equipment has the ability of providing the equivalent of sea level breathing when using 100-percent oxygen at 24,000 feet. Theoretically, 100-percent oxygen breathed at 40,000 feet is the same as breathing the air at 10,000 feet. Because of the possibility of an oxygen mask leak and the physical conditioning of the pilot, it is wise to restrict the use of constant-flow oxygen systems to a maximum of 35,000 feet.

Diluter Demand Oxygen System

The diluter-demand system is hard to use. It requires forced breathing to inhale and forceful muscle contraction of the diaphragm to exhale.

PRESSURIZED AIRCRAFT

Pressurized airplane engines compress air and feed it into the cabin area to maintain a cabin pressure altitude that is less than the physical altitude. Unless the cabin pressure altitude exceeds 12,500 feet for more than one-half hour, or 14,000 feet for any amount of time, the use of supplemental oxygen is not necessary.

Sometimes you may be concerned about the health of one of your passengers. And, knowing that your mountain flight will require a climb to higher altitudes, you may want to determine the cabin pressure altitude, that is, the effective altitude inside the airplane. A physician may caution you not to exceed 5,000 feet (or some other arbitrary altitude).

The cabin altitude can be determined in flight by looking at the cabin altitude gauge. On the ground, it is sometimes desirable to determine what the cabin altitude will be for flight at any particular altitude. The system's pressure differen-

ALTITUDE	PSI
Sea Level	14.70
1,000	14.20
2,000	13.71
3,000	13.21
4,000	12.71
5,000	12.22
6,000	11.77
7,000	11.34
8,000	10.91
9,000	10.51
10,000	10.10
11,000	9.72
12,000	9.34
13,000	8.98
14,000	8.62
15,000	8.29
16,000	7.96
17,000	7.64
18,000	7.33
19,000	7.03
20,000	6.75
21,000	6.47
22,000	6.20
23,000	5.94
24,000	5.69
25,000	5.45
26,000	5.21
27,000	4.99
28,000	4.77
29,000	4.56
30,000	4.36

ALTITUDE PRESSURE CHART

tial (from the POH) is compared to the altitude pressure from the **altitude pressure chart** for the desired cruise altitude.

> Example: Flying at 17,000 feet (7.64 altitude pressure) plus the 4.4 differential, results in a total of 12.04 psi. Comparing this value on the Altitude Pressure Chart shows a cabin altitude between 5,000 and 6,000 feet. Interpolation provides a value of 5,400 feet for the inside cabin altitude.

HYPERVENTILATION

Hyperventilation occurs when rapid breathing (from stressful situations) causes carbon dioxide in the system to be expelled in excess. As a result the blood becomes alkaline. Because of some similar symptoms, it is often difficult to differentiate between hypoxia and hyperventilation.

The symptoms include:
- ✔ **Numbness of fingers and toes.**
- ✔ **Tingling of fingers and mouth.**
- ✔ **Dizziness.**
- ✔ **Unconsciousness.**

Because of the difficulty in distinguishing the differences between hypoxia and hyperventilation, the best remedy is to use supplemental oxygen while regulating your breathing rate at 12 to 16 times per minute (about once every five seconds). After the symptoms go away, discontinue using supplemental oxygen If the density altitude permits). If the symptoms reappear, it is hypoxia; if not, it was hyperventilation.

If you feel rapid breathing is causing the symptoms, regulate your breathing rate to once every five seconds. The symptoms should disappear within a matter of minutes if it is hyperventilation.

PRESSURIZATION

Unless you will regularly fly at altitudes in the high teens or low twenties, the additional cost of a pressurized aircraft is not feasible. Pressurization (and turbocharging) is a great aid for escaping turbulence and ice over the mountains, but using this type airplane for high altitude operations is not true mountain flying. Generally the pressurized airplane will experience more engine problems or expense than non-pressurized airplanes.

Most pilots prefer the pressurized airplane for operation at altitudes that require supplemental oxygen. Oxygen masks are uncomfortable. Yet the expense of a portable or built-in oxygen system is a mere fraction of that of a pressurization system.

TURBOCHARGING

The Cessna TU-206 (turbo utility) is one of the workhorses of backcounty aviation. The turbo allows sea level power at high-density altitude fields, allowing operation at greater gross weights than the non-turbocharged airplane.

The benefits of turbocharging greatly outweigh those of the normally-aspirated airplane. These benefits include *ice avoidance* because of the ability to fly at high altitudes, avoidance of *convective turbulence,* shorter *takeoff* and greater *climb* capability from high density-altitude airstrips, and faster *cruise speeds.*

Generally, the turbocharged airplane will cost half again as much to operate when considering the cost of overhaul.

If your airplane is used as a serious cross-country machine, going when and where you want in all types of weather, consider turbocharging and pressurization.

If your airplane is used as a work tool with occasional escapes from the everyday work world, your fun machine need not be turbocharged or pressurized.

Flight safety in the normally-aspirated-engine airplane in the mountains is every bit as safe as in an airplane with a turbocharger. Just follow the suggestions in this book to make your flight safe and enjoyable. ✈

If you can't laugh at yourself, make fun of other people

CHAPTER 3—PREPLANNING

- CHARTS 1-37
- CURRENT CHARTS 1-38
- CHART READING 1-38
- ROUTES 1-38
- FLIGHT PLANNING 1-40
- METHODS OF NAVIGATION 1-40
- PREFLIGHT PREPARATION 1-44

CHARTS

Because of the expense, some pilots refuse to purchase current navigational charts for all their flights. Their biggest argument is, "Well, the terrain doesn't change." That's certainly true, with the exception of landslides, earthquakes, volcanoes or other natural phenomena.

Charts provide more than terrain information. Airspace classifications, airspace restrictions, man-made obstructions and new communication and navigation frequencies are handy to have.

Some mountain areas are so vast and the terrain so varied that even pilots with adequate charts can get lost by attempting short cuts, or by mistaking logging roads for a main road or river forks for the main river. The conscientious pilot will make notes during the flight. If he takes up a different heading from that listed on his flight log, he notes the heading and time. If the short cut doesn't work out —you're temporarily misplaced—it's easy to plot where you probably are.

The sectional aeronautical chart turns out to be the chart of choice for VFR flight in mountainous areas. With its scale of eight miles to the inch, there is plenty of detailed topographical information. Cultural and geographic landmarks are depicted with the physical characteristics to provide sufficient detail for accurate identification.

The aeronautics division of some western states produce a state aeronautical chart with the same scale as the WAC chart (1:1,000,000 or 16-nautical miles to the inch). Information pertinent to aviating within the state is included on the back panel.

Some states also publish an airport directory showing all airports accessible to the public. You can call or write to obtain information on what is available and the cost.

To obtain the address or phone number, if the telephone operator can't find a listing, phone the state government main information number and ask them for the aeronautics department phone number.

Some popular states with their addresses and phone numbers are listed in the Appendix.

CURRENT CHARTS

Responsible pilots agree that it is important to use current aeronautical charts for all cross-country flights. The use of outdated charts may cause the unknowing and unsuspecting pilot to fly into Class D airspace (airport traffic area, terminal control area), Class C airspace (ARSA), TRSA, Class B airspace (TCA), or restricted areas without proper authorization.

CHART READING

If you are not proficient at chart reading and interpretation, purchase a copy of the *NOAA Aeronautical Chart User's Guide*. It serves as both a learning aid and a reference document providing the following subjects:

Section 1—Explanation of Terms and Symbols (VFR and IFR)
Section 2—Listing of NOAA Aeronautical Products
Section 3—Aeronautical Planning Chart Symbols
Section 4—VFR Aeronautical Chart Symbols
Section 5—IFR Aeronautical Chart Symbols

ROUTES

The shortest distance between two points is a straight line. Pilots like direct flights because they reduce flight time, and time is money. There are circumstances that make direct flights in the mountains undesirable.

For instance, suppose I want to fly from Denver, Colorado, directly to Jackson, Wyoming, in a Cessna 170. Because of the high mountains encountered on a direct flight, the additional time-to-climb to clear the mountains negates any cost-cutting advantage and may take more time than routing the flight north of Denver towards Laramie, Wyoming, then direct. Although the distance flown will be greater, the flight time may be less.

PART 1 PREFLIGHT   **Chapter 3 - Preplanning**

Another consideration in choosing the route will be the anticipated density altitude at cruise altitude. The service ceiling of the airplane will be reached at the density altitude, not the physical altitude.

Remember the body's need for supplemental oxygen will also be reached at the prevailing density altitude, not the physical altitude.

The majority of mountain flights made in the typical single-engine general aviation airplane are routed along highways that roughly parallel the desired course. Even if this route requires additional flight time, following a highway in isolated or unfamiliar terrain is a good idea. Highways are routed along the best terrain (lowest altitude) and they pass through populated areas.

Don't blindly follow a highway or railroad tracks. Flying west from Denver, following Interstate 70, the sectional chart shows the road disappearing into the Eisenhower tunnel at Loveland Pass (the Denver VOR 250-degree radial at 48-nautical miles). Another popular crossing, V8 from Denver to Kremmling avoids most of the high elevations on a westbound flight. Near Corona Pass (Denver VOR 269-degree radial at 37-nautical miles) the railroad tracks disappear into the Moffat RR Tunnel for seven miles.

Diamond-shaped, blue-colored "foot prints" ◆◆◆◆ mark the preferred routes through some mountain areas and passes. The first consideration in establishing these routes is that of terrain clearance, followed by radio reception. Finally, the emergency landing places are taken into account.

 In choosing a route:

✗   Determine the time-to-climb to the required cruise altitude versus the time required for following more favorable terrain.

✗   Determine the density altitude at the planned cruise altitude and compare this to the service ceiling of the airplane (and the pilot).

✗   Determine if supplemental oxygen will be required.

✗   Check for blue-diamond footprints on charts.

✗   Plan your route along highways if feasible. Study the terrain along the route of highways and railroads, checking for tunnels.

Before the advent of GPS, it was possible to select the wrong canyon or valley when flying through widely ranging mountain areas. In Alaska, for example, the fuel supply may be exhausted before conceiving a problem exists.

When selecting a route during a time of suspected or reported mountain wave activity, try to route the flight on the windward side of the mountains if the winds aloft report (or forecast) is 20 knots or greater. The leeward side of the mountains will be predominantly downdrafts with the resulting turbulence.

Check with Flight Service personnel (ask for a pilot), FAA Accident Prevention counselors, local senior airmen, FBO personnel and the like. Most pilots are willing and able to share their knowledge of a particular area, if you ask.

FLIGHT PLANNING

Judgment errors are magnified in the mountains. You must monitor the weather and fuel reserve constantly. Because of this, the value of preflight planning can't be overstated.

The airplane's performance parameters must be taken into account. The service ceiling and rate of climb influence your choice of flight path. Determine the maximum no-reserve range and the power setting you will be using. Plan legs that will put you on the ground with at least one-hour fuel reserve.

Your flight course often depends on the characteristics of the terrain. Plan the route of flight within the parameters of your airplane's altitude and range capability.

METHODS OF NAVIGATION

There are several methods of navigating from one point to another. While you can use any one of them for a flight, it is best to use a combination of them. This redundancy will keep you from becoming temporarily misplaced (lost).

PILOTAGE

Flying cross-country when using only a chart and flying from one visible landmark to another is known as pilotage. This method requires the flight be conducted at comparatively low altitudes so the landmarks ahead may be easily seen and identified. Therefore, it cannot be used effectively in areas that lack prominent landmarks or under conditions of low visibility.

Advantages—It is comparatively easy to perform and it does not require special equipment. If the navigational equipment fails en route, you can keep track of your position.

Disadvantages—A direct course is usually impractical because it is often necessary to follow a zigzag route to prominent geographical landmarks, often resulting in a longer flight.

PART 1 PREFLIGHT — Chapter 3 - Preplanning

DEAD RECKONING

Dead reckoning is the navigation of an airplane solely by means of computations based on airspeed, course, heading, wind direction and speed, ground speed and elapsed time. To oversimplify, it is a system of *determining where the airplane should be on the basis of where it has been.* It is literally, deduced reckoning, and the term has been shortened from *deduced to dead* reckoning.

The most common form of VFR navigation is a combination of dead reckoning and pilotage, where the course flown and the airplane's position are calculated by true dead reckoning and then constantly corrected for error and variables after visually checking nearby landmarks.

RADIO NAVIGATION

Radio navigation includes any method that allows a pilot to follow a predetermined flight path over the earth's surface by utilizing the properties of radio waves. The primary systems are VOR, ADF, LORAN, and GPS.

Often you cannot maintain *line of sight* when using VORs in the mountains, rendering these radio stations unusable.

THE DOUBLE CROSS

With the advent of LORAN and GPS, more and more pilots are becoming reliant on these black boxes for their navigation. Either they haven't learned or they haven't used basic navigation for so long that they have forgotten how to plot courses and compute headings for a flight.

Confusion often exists when dealing with the terms true, magnetic and compass courses and headings. It seems the definitions seldom make sense and if they do, there are so many definitions you never have the capacity for remembering everything. The *double cross* system is designed to be easily remembered. From it, definitions can be derived to answer any test question, but more importantly, you eliminate the possibility of making errors when dealing with courses and headings.

The double cross *should be committed to memory* and used whenever a course or heading is used. To make a double cross, draw a vertical line with two crossing horizontal lines:

Make the cross large enough to allow numerals to be written into the spaces between the lines.

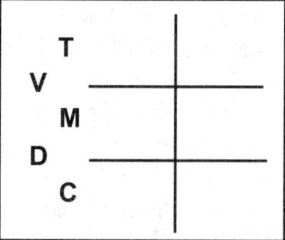

MEMORIZE HOW TO DRAW THE DOUBLE CROSS.

Next, label each alternate space and line using the mnemonic aid, **T**rue **V**irgins **M**ake **D**ull **C**ompany. The space in the upper left corner is the **T**, the line is **V**, the next space is **M**, the line is **D**, and the last space is **C**.

Chapter 3 - Preplanning   Part 1 PREFLIGHT

The vertical line is labeled **WCA**, representing the **w**ind **c**orrection **a**ngle. Whenever a course is corrected for the effect of the wind, a heading results. Courses are on the left side of the double cross. Headings are on the right side.

	WCA	
TC		TH
VAR		
MC		MH
DEV		
CC		MH

The top left space will be used to log the true course. The horizontal line represents variation. The next space is magnetic course, the line is deviation and the last space is the compass course.

This is all the memorization required. Just be able to draw the *double cross* and label it using the memory aid. It will be of immense value to you throughout your flying career.

How does the double cross work? In the upper left of the cross is the *true course,* represented by *TC.* This is the line drawn on the chart from the departure airport to the first checkpoint and between each checkpoint. It is measured in relation to a meridian of longitude (the lines printed on the chart that connect the South Pole and the North Pole.) If you use the VOR compass azimuth to determine your course, it is a *magnetic course* and should be placed in the space labeled *MC.*

A new double cross must be drawn for each route segment.

TRUE COURSE is the intended track (path over the ground) measured clockwise from true north (meridian of longitude) on the aeronautical chart.

Beneath the true course is a line that separates true course from magnetic course. This is the *variation* line. If you cross this line, going from true course to magnetic course, you must correct for variation. *Magnetic course is the true course corrected for variation.*

Variation is the angular difference between the geographic North Pole (True North Pole) and the Magnetic North Pole. It results because the Magnetic North Pole is located some 1,300 miles south of the True North Pole in Canada at 70 degrees north latitude and 100 degrees west longitude (in 1975). It drifts about 0.2 degrees west each year. An *agonic line* (zero variation) passes through the east central United States. To the east and west of the agonic line are *isogonic lines.* These are represented by dashed lines on aeronautical charts and denote the number of degrees of east variation or west variation for any particular area. A compass in an airplane located west of the agonic line (western U.S.) points to the Magnetic North Pole. In doing so, it points east of the True North Pole. This is called *east variation.* If an airplane was pointed at Magnetic North and east variation was subtracted from the compass indicated direction, true north would be determined.

When moving from the magnetic course to the compass course, you have to cross the line labeled deviation. Apply the deviation from the compass correction card that is found in the airplane.

In a no-wind condition a flight from the departure airport using the compass course would end up over the first checkpoint after a certain amount of time. However, the wind is usually blowing. Therefore, when a course is corrected for wind (wind correction angle), a heading results. The right side of the double cross is labeled in the same manner as the left, but instead of *c* for *course,* use *h* for *heading.* The vertical line separating the courses and headings is called the *WCA line* This value is obtained from the wind side of the flight computer.

There are two simple rules to help you remember how to correct for variation and wind correction angle.

- *Variation Rule*—East is least, west is best. Subtract an east variation and add a west variation. This works only when moving vertically downward from either *True Course* to *Magnetic Course* or *True Heading* to *Magnetic Heading.*
- *WCA Rule*—Left is least. The WCA rule doesn't really need to be memorized, since its use involves common sense. If you are flying in any one direction of the 360 degrees of a circle and turn to the left for the wind correction angle, it will result in a smaller heading. So *left is least* just reminds one to subtract a left WCA. This works only when moving horizontally in the double cross from left to right. That is, from any course (true, magnetic, or compass) to any heading.

Whenever you do flight planning involving courses or headings, there is a chronological order to the use of the double cross, down and to the right. The variation rule and WCA rule is based on this premise. You always begin the double cross with the true course, measured from the chart at the mid-point in relation to the meridian of longitude, or the magnetic course, read from the chart using the VOR compass azimuth that is aligned with magnetic north.

If you take a written exam to further your certificates or ratings, you may be given a compass heading and then asked to figure the true course. This will require reversing the variation rule and WCA rule. Instead of subtracting east variation when moving in the double cross from magnetic heading to true heading or magnetic course to true course, it is necessary to add. For example, you may be told the compass heading is 090 degrees, the WCA is 7 degrees left, the deviation is +2 degrees and the variation is 12 degrees east. In determining the true course, write 090 in the bottom right of the double cross. If you were moving from the CC to the CH, you could subtract the 7 degrees left WCA; but instead, you add it, arriving at a CC of 097 degrees. Moving up from CC to MC, the deviation is +2; but it is now subtracted, making the MC 095 degrees. Moving from the MC to the TC would involve adding the 12 degrees east variation (that is normally subtracted), the TC would be 107 degrees.

After working through a test problem in this manner, it is a good idea to go back through the double cross using the proper rules to check your math. Instead of moving down to the magnetic course and compass course and over to the compass heading, try moving to the true heading and then the magnetic heading and finally the compass heading. Apply variation and deviation in the proper manner. If you obtained the CH of 090 degrees, you worked the double cross correctly. This confirms that you performed the reversed rules properly while working your way backward through the double cross.

Whenever working with the double cross your **main objective** is to determine the compass heading. The *Compass Heading* is the value that allows you to fly from point *a* to point *b,* compensating for variation, deviation and wind drift. There is no need to determine the TH and MH if you originally moved vertically downward, then to the right; however, by determining them, it serves as a check of your mathematics.

PREFLIGHT PREPARATION

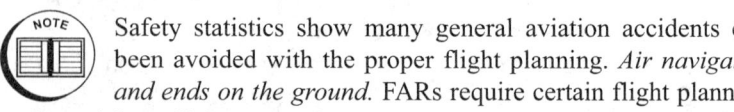
Safety statistics show many general aviation accidents could have been avoided with the proper flight planning. *Air navigation begins and ends on the ground.* FARs require certain flight planning be performed for a flight *not in the vicinity of an airport.* This has been interpreted to mean a flight of more than 25-nautical miles from the departure airport. The regs also require weather and aircraft performance determinations. This includes obtaining pertinent weather information, plotting the course on an aeronautical chart, selecting checkpoints, measuring distances and computing flight time, headings, fuel requirements, weight and balance and takeoff and landing distances under the expected conditions of runway elevation and temperature (density altitude).

Equipment

Assemble all the materials needed for flight planning. In order to facilitate this, as well as to assist during en route navigation, it is a good idea to keep all of your equipment in one place. A flight bag is recommended for your charts, computer, plotter, lap board or knee board, airport diagram book, notebook, pens and pencils, flashlight (with spare bulb and batteries), ear plugs, stop watch, screw driver and pliers.

PART 1 PREFLIGHT   Chapter 3 - Preplanning

You have to use some common sense in preparing a flight bag. I have seen student pilots who carry more on a 50-mile cross-country flight than I take on an international flight.

Checking Weather

Check the weather to see if the flight is feasible and that route would be the best. This is just a preliminary check called an *outlook briefing,* to determine the weather is VFR and to obtain the winds aloft forecast to use in computing ground speeds and wind correction angle. A comprehensive check is made later and is called the *standard weather briefing.*

Plotting the Course

Sectional aeronautical charts are the best for cross-country flight planning because of their scale of 1:500,000 and the abundance of detail, as compared to the WAC Chart (World Aeronautical Chart) with a scale of 1:1,000,000.

Sectional Aeronautical Chart
Scale 1:500,000
8 statute miles per inch (6.95 nautical miles)

World Aeronautical Chart (WAC) and ONC Chart
Scale 1:1,000,000
16 statute miles per inch (13.9 nautical miles)

If your route of flight takes you near the border of the chart be sure to have the charts of the area adjoining the flight route. In this way you are prepared if you need to circumnavigate weather or need to find your position should you become temporarily misplaced.

NAVIGATION LOG

Military flight departments often carry a sign, "Plan your flight and fly your plan." This is sound advice. When preflight planning is completed on the ground there is less chance that mistakes in measuring courses or computer time and distance will occur because there is no pressure from flying duties, adverse weather, or the radio blaring. It might be a good idea for the novice pilot to double the required VFR fuel reserve for the first few flights into the mountains, keeping in mind that fuel may not be available at the destination airstrip.

Planning a mountain flight with a mountain wave present means you must know what to expect. Know how and where to fly to avoid downdrafts and turbulence. (See *MOUNTAIN WAVE*)

VFR FLIGHT PLAN

Except when crossing the border into Mexico or Canada, the Federal Aviation Regulations do not require pilots to file a VFR flight plan. Common sense requires otherwise. When a VFR flight plan is filed, it guarantees the activation of search and rescue if the airplane becomes overdue to missing. It is important to make regular position reports along the route of flight. Then, if the airplane is overdue, it narrows the search area between the last position report and the destination.

FLIGHT LOG

It is necessary and important to have a systematic approach to flight planning. Using a *flight log* will give you the *need to know* information and eliminate the unnecessary information. A flight log will promote accurate and complete preflight planning. With a flight log all the information for the actual flight is *in your lap,* not scattered around the cockpit or stored in a flight bag.

This will eliminate confusion, prevent the omission of important information and make valid use of the time you spend planning. The item that allows this is the flight log.

Another advantage of a flight log is that it becomes an accurate and permanent record of the flight, allowing a review of performance, pilot techniques and flight after-the-fact, in the leisure of your home.

Any flight log that you decide to use should be satisfactory, whether it is purchased from a pilot supply store or picked up free from the Flight Service Station (if they are still available).

Regardless of the type flight log used, it should provide columns for at least the following information that is completed prior to the flight:

- ☐ Navigational aid identification and frequency (if any)
- ☐ Route (Victor airway or direct).
- ☐ Course *to* and *from.*
- ☐ Leg mileage.
- ☐ Mileage remaining, determined after the total mileage has been computed.
- ☐ Point-to-point time, based on the ground speed and distance.
- ☐ Cumulative time.
- ☐ Ground speed.
- ☐ Fuel required.

FIXES or checkpoints—Starting with the point of departure, list all other check points in chronological order.

FREQUENCY COLUMN—The frequency of a radio navigation aid at the fix, if any.

MAGNETIC COURSE—LIST THE MAGNETIC COURSE *TO* and *FROM* the checkpoint on the same line. The departure airport will only have a "from" listing and the destination airport will only have a "to" listing. If you are not using radio navigation aids, you can substitute the compass heading for the magnetic course.

DISTANCE—The miles between fixes are logged here. The total distance is logged either at the bottom of the form or at the top if there is a provision for determining the miles remaining. Try to get into the habit of using nautical miles. There is an advantage because winds aloft are in knots and any reports to air traffic control should be in knots.

TIME—This column or combination of columns should provide an area where the ground speed can be divided into the distance to obtain a time for each leg of the flight or *point-to-point* time. There should be a column to allow you to add up all the point-to-point times for a cumulative time. Another column should provide a space to record the takeoff time. To this time is added the first point-to-point time to obtain an ETA for that fix. While the times are computed and written on the flight log prior to flight using the winds aloft forecast, the takeoff time and ETA (estimated time of arrival) is not completed until after takeoff. After arrival at the checkpoint the ATA (actual time of arrival) is written down and the next point-to-point time is added to this to derive an ETA for the next checkpoint. If there is a large discrepancy between the ETA and ATA, you may be able to determine why and adjust the estimated time en route to the next fix.

RULE OF THUMB—Add one minute for each 1,000 feet of climb altitude

Compute the altitude difference between the departure elevation and the cruise altitude. Use the computed ground speed for time and distance calculations along the entire distance. Add one minute per 1,000 feet of climb to the en route time for the first leg to compensate for the reduced true airspeed during the climb. If your airplane has greater performance than most general aviation planes, you may find one minute too much. If so, try adding one minute for each 2,000 feet of climb. If this doesn't work out, modify it to suit your airplane.

1. Draw A True Course Line

Draw a line representing the course to be flown. This is the course line. If it is measured in relation to true north, it is called the *true course*. This course line should be drawn between the points of intended flight. It is not necessarily a direct line from the departure to the destination airport.

Chapter 3 - Preplanning — Part 1 PREFLIGHT

The course line originates at the center of the departure airport and ends at the center of the destination airport. If a VOR is located near the departure airport or along the route of flight, it is recommended the flight go from the departure airport to the VOR and then on to the next checkpoint or VOR. Many pilots plan and fly their entire route from one VOR to another rather than making direct flights, since this makes navigation easier. Remember though, radio navigation is not always possible in the mountains.

The course line is drawn between the points (checkpoints) of the intended flight. This line should be dark enough to be seen, but not so heavy as to obscure the symbols on the chart. A pencil is better than a felt tip marker. Do not get into the habit of using a red pen or pencil for drawing the true course line. At night the red lights used in many airplanes for cockpit lighting may make the line seem to disappear.

Select appropriate checkpoints along the route and note them on the chart in some way. They should be easily recognizable.

Check along and to either side of your route for airspace designations such as alert areas, warning areas, restricted areas, prohibited areas, intensive student jet training areas, Class B airspace (TCAs - terminal control area), Class C airspace (ARSAs - airport radar service area) and Class D airspace (TRSAs - terminal radar service area). Also, at this time, check for towers and other man-made obstructions.

Study the terrain along your route for the highest and lowest elevations. The highest elevation is needed to determine adequate terrain clearance. The lowest elevation is needed to conform with the VFR hemispherical rule (cruising altitude requirement of FAR 91.159), stating that when flying 3,000 feet or more above ground level (AGL) on a magnetic course of 0 degrees through 179 degrees, fly any odd thousand-foot altitude plus 500 feet. On a *magnetic course* of 180 degrees through 359 degrees, fly any even thousand foot altitude plus 500 feet.

2. Measure The True Course

Measure the course of each route segment. You want to ultimately end up with the *compass heading* to fly from point *a* to point *b*. The compass heading is compensated for variation, deviation and the wind correction angle.

Measure the *true course* of each route segment. This is the angle between the course line and the meridian of longitude midway between the straight-line segments of the route. Because the earth is round, the meridians taper toward the Poles. It is important to make the measurement of the true course on a meridian that is approximately halfway between checkpoints. This provides an accurate reading, averaging the error caused by the tapering meridians.

PART 1 PREFLIGHT   Chapter 3 - Preplanning

Meridians are the vertical lines printed on the chart that converge at the North Pole and South Pole.

Determine the variation from the mid-isogonic line. Apply it using the rule, *east is least, west is best,* to the measured true course to obtain the *magnetic course.*

If there is a VOR station located on the airport, the magnetic course can be determined by reading where the course line intersects the compass rose on the chart. This eliminates the need to measure the true course. Remember though, if your flight is *TO* a VOR, the course determined by reading the VOR compass azimuth is always *FROM* the station. You must determine the reciprocal when flying *TO* the station.

3. Measure The Course Distances

Measure the course distance between each checkpoint and note this on your flight log. Check the scale on the plotter against the distance scale on the bottom of the chart. If there is any discrepancy, use the distance scale on the chart. Sometimes the paper is stretched during printing or folding and it will have an error when compared with the plotter; but since the paper is stretched, its scale is also stretched, making it the more accurate.

MILEAGE CONVERSIONS

    1 nautical mile (6,076.115 feet) = 1.150779 statute miles
    1 statute mile (5,280 feet) = 0.868976 nautical mile
    1 kilometer (3,280.333 feet) = 0.621369 statute mile
    1 kilometer (3,280.333 feet) = 0.539955 nautical mile

Based upon this information, the following mileage conversions can be made on the flight calculator:
    Statute miles = 1.15 x nautical miles
    Nautical miles = .87 x statute miles
    Statute miles = .62 x kilometers
    Nautical miles = .54 x kilometers
    Kilometers = 1.61 x statute miles
    Kilometers = 1.85 x nautical miles

Determine the Ground Speed

Use the winds aloft forecast and the estimated true airspeed (TAS) with your computer to determine the ground speed for each route segment (between checkpoints). Since most pilots fly from VOR to VOR (magnetic courses) or use a flight log incorporating magnetic courses, it is recommended that the wind be converted from true north to magnetic north. This usually results in only one conversion, rather than changing each magnetic course to the true course for each leg of the flight. This simplifies flight planning and eliminates one source of error.

Compute the Time and Fuel Required

From the computed ground speed and measured distance, use the flight computer to compute the time and fuel required for the flight. In preflight planning, accurate estimates of the estimated time en route (ETE) must be made to establish the fuel requirements for the flight. The amount of fuel required and any necessary fueling stops en route can be determined by computing the en route time versus the rate of fuel consumption. The fuel capacity and rate of fuel consumption can be found in the Airplane Flight Manual, Pilot's Operating Handbook (POH), or Owner's Manual.

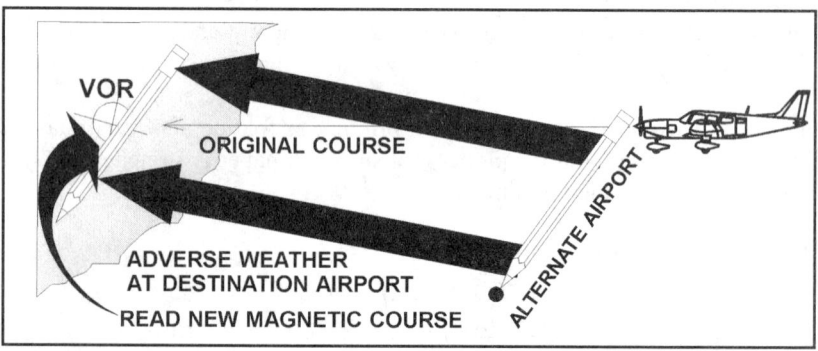

EMERGENCY COURSE MEASUREMENT: ALIGN A STRAIGHT EDGE (PENCIL) ALONG THE DESIRED COURSE FROM YOUR PRESENT POSITION TO THE ALTERNATE. CAREFULLY MOVE THE PENCIL PARALLEL TO THE COURSE TO A COMPASS AZIMUTH TO READ THE COURSE.

Diverting To An Alternate Airport

A mechanical malfunction, adverse weather, medical emergency or some other reason, may necessitate diversion to an alternate airport. There may not be time to dig out your plotter and computer to measure a new course and compute the flight time; yet it is essential to become established on the new course in the least amount of time.

> **NOTE** Among the aeronautical skills all pilots must have is the ability to plot courses in flight to alternate destinations when flight to the original destination becomes impractical. This may be accomplished by means of pilotage, dead reckoning or radio navigation. Advantage must be taken of all possible shortcuts and rule-of-thumb computations.

It is rarely practical while in flight to actually plot a course line on the chart and then mark checkpoints and distances as is usually done during preflight planning. Because the alternate airport selected in an emergency is usually not very far from the original course and known position, such actual plotting is seldom necessary.

Course Measurement

Assume radio navigation is not practical or possible and you are not familiar enough with the area to rely on pilotage. That leaves us with dead reckoning. Courses to alternates can be measured accurately with a protractor or plotter. But they can also be measured with reasonable accuracy using a straight edge and the compass rose shown at VOR stations on the chart. We navigate by reference to the magnetic compass. The VOR radials, compass azimuth and airway courses are already oriented to magnetic north. So we use these aids for course determination.

By knowing your approximate position on the chart, you can align a pencil from this position to the alternate airport. Move the pencil to any VOR compass rose, carefully paralleling the desired course to the alternate airport. Read the magnetic course from the azimuth scale of the VOR compass rose.

To complete all plotting, measuring and computations involved *BEFORE* diverting toward the alternate airport may only aggravate an actual emergency.

Another method to determine the magnetic course is to hold the chart on your lap. Pick it up on each side so the top and bottom edges fold down. Pinch your known position with one hand and the new destination with the other. Pull the chart taut and crease it between the known position and destination. Turn the chart on your lap so the crease is horizontal. Locate a VOR compass azimuth on either side of the crease. Roll the edge containing the VOR and move it to the crease. Another crease can be made through the center of the VOR. This will provide the magnetic direction to the destination. This is quite accurate since rolling the chart keeps the VOR parallel to the creased course.

Distance Measurement

When a plotter is not handy and it is inconvenient to try to fold the aeronautical chart so the mileage scale along the bottom can be used, distances can be very accurately measured by using a straight edge such as a pencil or piece of paper, in conjunction with the minute scale along any meridian of longitude (true north line).

The meridians of longitude that run vertically from the Poles through the equator are divided into degrees. The equator is the starting point or zero degrees. From the equator to either Pole is a quarter of a circle or 90 degrees. The Pole itself represents the 90-degree position. Each degree is divided into 60 minutes and is marked with a ticked line on the aeronautical chart. One minute of longitude is 6,076.115 feet (1,852 meters). A nautical mile, by definition, is an inter-

Chapter 3 - Preplanning   Part 1 PREFLIGHT

national unit of measurement based on the length of a minute of arc of a great circle of the earth.

 The distance around the earth along a parallel of latitude decreases north or south of the Equator. Do not use a minute of arc along a parallel of latitude to determine a nautical mile.

By placing the point of a pencil (any straight edge) at one end of the course for which distance is to be measured, you can pinch the pencil along its length at the other end of the course to be measured. Then, move the pencil to a vertical position. The pinched part is held on any parallel of latitude (parallels of latitude run horizontally across the chart) with the pencil point up or down. Count the ticks vertically up or down (the minutes of longitude) to the point of the pencil. This will be the number of nautical miles of the route segment.

 CAUTION: Do not measure distance horizontally along the parallels of latitude, only vertically along the meridian of longitude.

 RULE OF THUMB — Estimating Time

Use rule of thumb computations. If the airplane flies 120 knots per hour, the speed is two miles per minute. If 20 miles away from the alternate, it will take about 10 minutes.

To find out how much time is required to fly to the alternate airport, at various *groundspeeds,* use the following estimates:

80 knots groundspeed, multiply the distance by 0.75 to get minutes.

100 knots groundspeed, multiply the distance by 0.6 to get minutes.

120 knots groundspeed, divide distance by 2 to get minutes.

150 knots groundspeed, multiply the distance by 0.4 to get minutes.

180 knots groundspeed, divide distance by 3 to get minutes.

Drop the last digit of the groundspeed (airspeed, if the groundspeed is not known); you will fly that many miles in six minutes. ✈

Mountain Flying Bible

PART 1 PREFLIGHT   Chapter 4 - Weather

CHAPTER 4—WEATHER

- ➢ WEATHER ACCIDENTS 1-53
- ➢ MOUNTAIN METEOROLOGY 1-54
- ➢ GO/NO-GO DECISION 1-55
- ➢ MOUNTAIN AIRSTRIP WEATHER 1-55
- ➢ WEATHER BRIEFINGS 1-56
- ➢ TOM'S LAW 1-59
- ➢ MARGINAL WEATHER 1-59
- ➢ VISIBILITY 1-60
- ➢ FOG 1-61
- ➢ STABILITY 1-61
- ➢ LAPSE RATES 1-62
- ➢ WIND 1-66
- ➢ MOUNTAIN AND VALLEY WINDS 1-66
- ➢ WINDS ALOFT 1-67
- ➢ TURBULENCE 1-68

WEATHER ACCIDENTS

Statistically, weather accidents are the most severe in general aviation, where severe means those accidents with the most injuries, fatalities, and aircraft damage. Weather demands your respect.

How do these weather accident occur? There is a pattern and the sad fact is that we are not learning from that pattern. The FAA has done an admirable job since the initiation of their accident prevention program in 1971. Often the pilots who need to attend these meetings find some excuse for not going. Whatever the reason, every year many VFR-only pilots intentionally fly into marginal weather and do not come back. If you and the airplane are not equipped for instrument flying, don't do it. It's a guaranteed way of getting seriously killed.

Mountain Flying Bible   1-53

Chapter 4 - Weather   Part 1 PREFLIGHT

When examining the National Transportation Safety Board (NTSB) accident statistics for any year they have records available, you will find the same things causing the same accidents, year after year, in almost the exact same proportion.

When a non-instrument-rated pilot tries scud running or suddenly and unintentionally becomes trapped by weather and he no longer has outside visual reference, statistics say he is going to be involved in an accident. The FAA has determined that the one likely to be involved in a weather accident is a private pilot having gained between 100-300 hours flight experience. After receiving a reasonably accurate weather briefing he crashes during daylight hours with one additional passenger, after having failed to file a flight plan.

These pilots do not intentionally get into instrument weather. The conclusion is that they did not recognize the instrument weather and flew into it without an escape route. Once into the weather, statistics bear out that a crash is highly probable.

This study strongly points out the need to:

- ✔ Learn what comprises critical weather situations from weather reports and forecasts.
- ✔ Learn to recognize critical weather situations visually from the air, from a distance.
- ✔ Do not scud run in the mountains with less than a 2,000-foot ceiling or less than 5-miles visibility. Be ready to land or turn back before becoming vulnerable to entering an area of obscuration or clouds that reduce visibility.
- ✔ Analyze a weather briefer's caution for the potential of encountering a critical weather situation en route. Always have an out to keep from becoming trapped by the weather.

MOUNTAIN METEOROLOGY

Mountain weather is not so much different than weather occurring elsewhere. It just seems that there's more of it–and sometimes it is very intense. Sure, there are katabatic winds (any wind blowing down an incline) and mechanical lifting that don't normally occur over flatland. But the basic weather is the same. However, flying in the mountains when adverse weather conditions exist, does require more judgment and skill than when flying over the flatland.

In the mountains, when the weather is good, it is really good; when the weather is bad, it is terrible. Typical summer forecasts state, *"Partly cloudy with widely scattered afternoon and early evening rain showers and thunderstorms."* As long as the forecast remains valid, that is, *widely scattered,* there

PART 1 PREFLIGHT   Chapter 4 - Weather

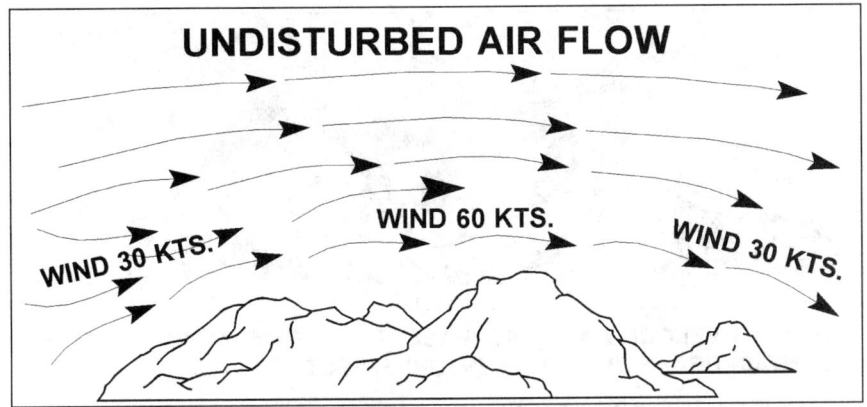

THE WIND VELOCITY MAY DOUBLE OVER A RIDGE DUE TO A VENTURI EFFECT CAUSED BY THE RIDGE AND AN UNDISTURBED AIR FLOW ABOVE. THE LOW PRESSURE ASSOCIATED WITH THE VENTURI CAUSES THE ALTIMETER TO READ HIGHER THAN THE TRUE ALTITUDE (LOOK OUT BELOW).

is no problem circumnavigating the weather over flatland. Thunderstorms, scattered or not, can set up a total roadblock when operating in the mountains.

Probably the biggest trap for the unsuspecting pilot is his choice to make a VFR flight based upon the lowest reported ceiling along his route. With the scarcity of reporting stations, the forecast weather may not occur. Look at the total weather pattern to make a go/no-go flight decision.

GO/NO-GO DECISION

There have been times when the FSS (Flight Service Station) or DUATS (Direct User Access Terminal Service) has been unable to provide the information necessary to make an intelligent go/no-go decision. This isn't their fault; the weather information just isn't available to them. Sometimes a phone call to an FSS or weather bureau near your destination can clear up any question of doubt in your mind.

With the proliferation of computers, many pilots subscribe to a private weather service or use DUATS. Even with the computer, there will be times when the pilot must talk with a Flight Service Station specialist to make an informed decision.

MOUNTAIN AIRSTRIP WEATHER

Most mountain strips (as opposed to mountain airports) do not have weather reporting facilities or personnel. If it is necessary to further check the weather, call the closest town for information. This call may be made to the sheriff's

Chapter 4 - Weather   **Part 1 PREFLIGHT**

THE WIND VELOCITY MAY INCREASE (DOUBLE OR MORE) BETWEEN MOUNTAIN PEAKS DUE TO A VENTURI EFFECT.

NOTE: IF THERE ARE EXTENSIVE CUMULUS BUILDUPS, A MOUNTAIN WAVE WILL NOT EXIST BECAUSE THERE IS NO STABILITY LAYER ALOFT.

department, police department, game and fish department, forest service, state aeronautics department, or radio station. Although this isn't "official" weather, it may be invaluable information.

WEATHER BRIEFINGS

Sometimes the pilot gets what he asks for from the FSS. Don't call and say, *"How's the weather from Jackson to Denver?"* Your request may provide you with very little information; although the briefer will solicit background information from you so he can provide a briefing appropriate to the proposed flight. This is especially true if you know the briefer and he thinks you know something about flying.

There are three basic types of preflight briefings, *Outlook Briefing, Standard Briefing,* and *Abbreviated Briefing.* The *preflight briefing* should be obtained in person or by telephone. Pilots flying at remote mountain strips use the *In-flight Briefing*. It can provide the same information as the outlook, standard or abbreviated briefings.

It is your responsibility to specify to the briefer the type of briefing you want (except for the in-flight briefing) along with background information. The FSS briefer is not authorized to make original forecasts, but he is authorized to translate and interpret available forecasts and reports directly into terms describing the weather conditions that you can expect along your flight route and at your destination. He may not read weather reports and forecasts verbatim unless specifically requested by you.

Outlook Briefing —

The *outlook briefing* is designed to provide forecast information for planning purposes only. Request an outlook briefing whenever your proposed departure is six or more hours in advance.

Standard Briefing —

If you have not received a previous briefing such as TWEB, PATWAS, VRS or DUATS, you should request the *standard briefing*. The briefer will automatically provide the following:

- ☐ *Adverse Conditions* of a meteorological and an aeronautical nature.
- ☐ *VFR Flight Not Recommended* when conditions make the flight doubtful.
- ☐ Synopsis.
- ☐ Current Conditions.
- ☐ En Route Forecast.
- ☐ Destination Forecast.
- ☐ Winds Aloft.
- ☐ NOTAMs.
- ☐ ATC Delays.

Ask for any information you feel the briefer may have missed. Jot down notes for these questions to allow the briefer to make a chronological presentation without interruption. Ask the questions after his briefing. This will provide you a better briefing.

Abbreviated Briefing —

Request an *abbreviated briefing* when you need to update a previous briefing or when you need only one or two specific items.

BACKGROUND INFORMATION (provide to the briefer)

Request specific information using a checklist.

- ☐ Type of Flight, VFR or IFR
- ☐ Aircraft Identification
- ☐ Aircraft Type
- ☐ Departure Airport
- ☐ Route of Flight
- ☐ Destination
- ☐ Flight Altitude(s)
- ☐ Estimated Time of Departure
- ☐ Estimated Time En Route, or
- ☐ Estimated Time of Arrival

Chapter 4 - Weather

Part 1 PREFLIGHT

BRIEFING FORMAT (ask for these items)
- ☐ Adverse Conditions
- ☐ Synopsis
- ☐ Current Weather
- ☐ En Route Forecast
- ☐ Destination Forecast
- ☐ Winds and Temperatures aloft and on the ground
- ☐ Aeronautical Information (NOTAMs)
- ☐ Request PIREPs
- ☐ Miscellaneous (icing level, lapse rate, inversions, alternates)

BUYS BALLOT'S LAW

If an observer in the Northern Hemisphere stands with his back to the wind, low pressure will be to his left. This is known as *Buys Ballot's Law*.

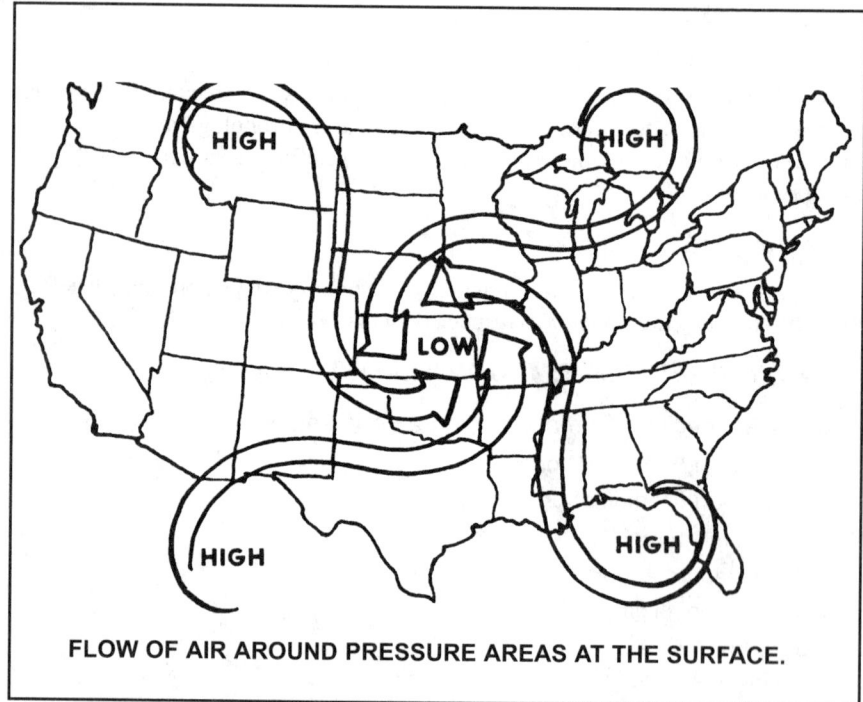

FLOW OF AIR AROUND PRESSURE AREAS AT THE SURFACE.

THE WIND ON THE SURFACE BLOWS 45-DEGREES INWARD TOWARD A LOW PRESSURE AREA AND 45-DEGREES OUTWARD FROM A HIGH PRESSURE AREA.

PART 1 PREFLIGHT   Chapter 4 - Weather

TOM'S LAW

Modifying Buys Ballot's Law is helpful when at a mountain strip without a telephone. The only thing you can do is look outside to see what is happening with the weather. Tom's Law, for Tom Herrod, states that you can face the surface wind and determine general weather trends. Extend your left arm 45° to the left, your right arm 135° to the right. The left hand points to a high-pressure area and good weather. The right hand points to a low-pressure area and bad weather. Obviously you can not tell how *good* or how *bad* the weather is, but this tool is better than nothing. (See figure page 1-58)

MARGINAL WEATHER

Present day weather forecasts are very accurate, but they have limitations. Some pilots have complete faith in forecasts and tend to ignore warning signs en route. Other pilot have no faith at all. It is best to consider forecasts as professional advice instead of the unmitigated truth.

The mountains, like the plains, experience frontal movement and weather phenomena. It's just that in the mountains a weather system moving across uneven terrain receives greater modification than it would over flat land. This is what makes *mini-weather* systems so unpredictable and often violent.

Spend some time thinking about marginal weather situations prior to flying in the mountains and establish some personal safety standards. To begin with, you should consider parking the airplane and waiting for better conditions whenever the ceiling is less than 2,000 feet or the visibility is less than five miles. If you aren't instrument rated, you must learn to recognize instrument weather from a distance and be ready to divert to the nearest airport and land or go back before getting into instrument weather. Even if you have an instrument rating, without the proper equipment (altitude capability, anti-icing and deicing equipment), it may be foolhardy to try IFR.

Stay out of unfamiliar areas–or even familiar areas–when marginal weather prevails along your route of flight. It is difficult to determine your position because everything looks different when clouds obscure a portion of the terrain. From a safety standpoint, you must learn there is no marginal weather that allows safe VFR flight. If it is VFR, fly it VFR. If it is IFR, do not try to fly VFR.

The author was born and raised in Jackson, Wyo. and spent a lot of time in the mountains with his father on foot and on horseback. He has flown there for 29 years. Flying VFR on top one day, we felt that it would be safe to duck down through a hole in the clouds to save time. Knowing the country as well as anyone and knowing my approximate position, once through the hole I had no idea where I was. It's strange–and it can be scary–how things look different when clouds obscure most of the mountains. (See *Scud Running*)

Chapter 4 - Weather Part 1 PREFLIGHT

VISIBILITY

One of your personal limitations to be established for flying the mountains is a minimum visibility. This is a value that is colored by your experience level and knowledge of the weather situation.

The visibility is every bit as important as the ceiling. Without both your established minimum ceiling and visibility, it is time to turn around. If the weather has deteriorated behind you, find a place to land the plane and wait until conditions improve.

Keep in mind:

- Rain or snow can severely restrict forward visibility and provide a visual illusion of being higher than you actually are.
- A thunderstorm with its accompanied rain can cause darkness in a canyon during the middle of the day.
- The transition from daylight to dusk makes it difficult to discern terrain. A mountain may appear to be just another dark area.

Be careful when evaluating a reported ceiling of 2,000 or 3,000 feet and thinking the weather is suitable to fly to your destination. The ceiling is the lowest layer of clouds (or obscuring phenomena) above the ground (or water) at the reporting station that is classified as broken, overcast or obscuration and not classified as thin or partial.

Although a ceiling of 2,000 or 3,000 feet may match your personal limitation for VFR flight in the mountains, a mountain pass may be enough higher than the reporting station's level that it is obscured by clouds, or it results in a ceiling or visibility below your established personal limitation.

STRATUS-TYPE CLOUDS INDICATE A SMOOTH RIDE AND MAY EXTEND OVER AN EXTENSIVE AREA. (GROS VENTRE AREA, JACKSON, WYO.)

ALTO-CUMULUS FORMING PATTERNS INDICATE CBS IN THE AFTERNOON (SUMMER) AND SNOW WITHIN 2 DAYS (WINTER). (BLACKTAIL BUTTE NE OF JACKSON HOLE AIRPORT.)

FOG

We know there is a lack of weather reporting stations in the mountains. The only way a pilot knows about the actual weather is through pilot reports. Some pilots depart a clear area, unaware of the possibility of interior valley fog, and have their plans spoiled. Valley fog occurs most often after rain showers have passed an area during the late fall months. The excess moisture combined with radiational cooling during the night creates the fog.

Do your fellow pilots a favor and make a PIREP concerning the weather, good or bad, in the vicinity of mountain strips.

STABILITY

The pilot is vitally concerned with the stability of his aircraft. A stable aircraft, if disturbed by the movement of the controls or by an external force (turbulence), will tend to return to a balanced steady flight condition. An unstable aircraft, however, will continue to move away from the normal flight attitude.

So it is with the atmosphere. The normal flow of air tends to be horizontal. If this flow is disturbed, a stable atmosphere will resist any upward or downward displacement and will tend to return quickly to normal horizontal flow. An unstable atmosphere, on the other hand, will allow these upward and downward disturbances to grow, resulting in rough air.

Atmospheric resistance to vertical motion, called *stability,* depends upon the vertical distribution of the air's weight at a particular time. The weight varies with air temperature—hot air is lighter than cold air. Therefore, if air is warmer than its surroundings, it is forced to rise. For example, if a balloon is filled with air of the same temperature as the surrounding air, it will not rise—indicating a stable condition. On the other hand, a balloon filled with air that is warmer than the surrounding air will rise, since the atmosphere–that cannot resist this vertical motion–is unstable. The atmosphere can only be at equilibrium when light air is above heavy air; just as oil mixed with water will rise to the top to obtain equilibrium.

In the same manner that the balloon with warm air rises, the air that is heated near the earth's surface on a hot summer day will rise, too. The speed and vertical extent of its travel depends on the temperature distribution of the atmosphere. Vertical air currents resulting from the rise of air can vary from the severe updrafts and compensating downdrafts associated with thunderstorms, to the closely spaced upward and downward *bumps* that are felt on warm days when flying at low levels.

 The type and intensity of the weather are directly related to the atmospheric stability, stability being affected by temperature and moisture. When air is heated or when moisture is added, it tends to become unstable. These two factors are interrelated. When the air temperature is increased, it will hold more moisture and cause a greater rate of evaporation when it comes into contact with large bodies of water. When moisture evaporates, it carries with it a small amount of latent heat. The latent heat does not affect the surrounding air until the water vapor is condensed into a water droplet, at which time it gives up latent heat. One cubic inch of rain over one square mile releases as much heat as the burning of 65,000 tons of coal. When the water droplet is formed, the latent heat affects the surrounding air temperature. The increased air temperature resulting from condensing water vapor will cause the air to rise still further, and finally it reaches a point called the *point of free convection,* that causes thunderstorms. This represents the height of instability.

The degree of stability also affects the type of clouds that will appear. Stratus-type clouds represent stability, whereas cumulus-type clouds represent instability.

LAPSE RATES

The temperature of air is an index of its density. A comparison of the temperature from one level to another can indicate the degree of the atmosphere's stability—that is, how much it will tend to resist vertical motion. Generally temperature decreases with altitude, and that rate at which it decreases is called the *lapse rate.* The lapse rate, commonly expressed in degrees per thousand feet, gives a direct measurement of the atmosphere's resistance to vertical motion. The degree of stability of the atmosphere may vary from layer to layer as indicated by changes of lapse rate with height.

DRY ADIABATIC LAPSE RATE

When unsaturated air rises, its temperature decreases at the rate of 3°C (5°F) per 1,000 feet, whether the air is forced upward as a result of being heated from below, or through forced ascension such as up a mountain slope. This cooling rate of unsaturated air is known as the *dry adiabatic lapse rate.*

Visualize the rising air as a *bundle* or *parcel* that is separate from the general atmosphere. A balloon that rises gets larger and larger with height because a rising parcel of air expands, causing it to cool. Heat, a form of energy, is consumed as air expands, thus removing heat from the air parcel and promoting a cooling of it. This is called an *adiabatic process,* the word *adiabatic* means that the temperature change takes place without adding or taking away heat from outside of the air parcel. Warming by contraction (compression), the reverse of cooling by expansion, is also an adiabatic process.

PART 1 PREFLIGHT   Chapter 4 - Weather

MOIST ADIABATIC LAPSE RATE

When saturated air rises or is forced to ascend, condensation occurs, and the air absorbs the heat released as the result of condensation. This causes the air to cool at a slower rate than that of unsaturated air. The *moist adiabatic lapse rate* varies from approximately 1.1°C to 2.8°C (2°F to 5°F) per 1,000 feet, depending mostly on the temperature and, to a small extent, on the atmospheric pressure. Since air can hold more water vapor at high temperatures than at low temperatures, a small decrease in the temperature of ascending saturated air at a high temperature causes a relatively large amount of moisture to condense. The amount of heat released by the condensation process is thus greater at high temperatures than at low temperatures, explaining why the moist adiabatic lapse rate is not a fixed value.

The warm, dry chinook wind is a dramatic example of the difference between the *moist adiabatic lapse rate* and the *dry adiabatic lapse rate*. In winter, moist air from the Pacific Ocean is occasionally forced over the Rockies by a strong wind flow. Assume that at 5,000 feet on the western slope, the air is saturated and has a temperature of 44°F. Blowing over the mountains, the air is lifted to 12,000 feet. Because it is saturated, the air cools at the moist adiabatic rate, with condensation occurring throughout the 7,000 feet of rise. At 12,000 feet its temperature is 21°F, having cooled at an average rate of 3.3°F per 1,000 feet. Descending the eastern slope of the mountains the air warms at the dry adiabatic lapse rate. As soon as the air starts to descend, its temperature increases due to compression, and it is no longer saturated. Thus the descending air, warming at 5°F per 1,000 feet, arrives at 5,000 feet on the east side with a temperature of 60°F. In crossing the mountains, its temperature has increased by 16°F and its relative humidity has decreased considerably.

DEW POINT LAPSE RATE AND CLOUD HEIGHTS

The difference between the air's temperature and the dew point temperature gives an indication of the air's relative humidity. When they are the same, the relative humidity is 100 percent–the air is saturated–and condensation may be expected. The *dew point lapse rate* is 1°F (0.56°C) per 1,000 feet during the lifting process. The temperature and dew point in rising unsaturated air, therefore, approach each other at a rate of 4°F (5°F minus 1°F) per 1,000 feet. Knowing the surface air temperature and dew point, one can readily estimate the level where condensation will occur when air rises. By dividing the difference between the surface air temperature and the dew point by 4°F, the height of cloud bases can be estimated in thousands of feet. For example, if the surface air temperature is 80°F and the surface dew point is 62°F, the approximate height of the base of the clouds formed by this lifting process is 4,500 feet (18°F divided by 4°F).

This method of estimating the height of cloud bases is reliable only on warm days when the earth's surface is heated a great deal by the sun.

Chapter 4 - Weather

STANDARD LAPSE RATE

The standard lapse rate is the average rate at which the atmosphere cools with increasing altitude. This cooling rate, approximately 2°C (3½°F) per 1,000 feet, is an average determined by evaluating thousands of atmospheric soundings from various parts of the world.

While the standard lapse rate is used in the United States and most of the world as a basis for calibrating aircraft altimeters, it has no connection with determining the stability of air on a day-to-day basis. However, the following may be concluded from the standard lapse rate:

- Unsaturated air, on the average, is stable.
- Saturated air at high temperatures is normally unstable.
- Saturated air at low temperatures, on the average, is stable.

STABILITY DETERMINATIONS

Stability may be defined as the ability of a mass of air to remain in equilibrium—in other words—its ability to resist displacement of any parcel from its initial position in the mass. There are five types of stability that arise, (1) absolute stability, (2) neutral stability, (3) absolute instability, (4) conditional instability, and (5) convective instability.

To get a general idea of what these terms mean, one can look at the following figure where we have a surface with one part level and one part with a ridge and a valley. A marble placed at point D will resist movement if displaced in either direction and will return to its original position at point D. It is absolutely stable.

When placed at point A on the level surface, the marble will remain at rest in any position on the flat surface. It is neutrally stable.

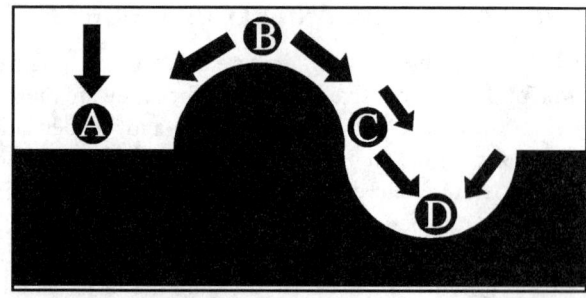

POINT A - *NEUTRAL STABILITY* - A SYSTEM IN EQUILIBRIUM BEING DISPLACED SLIGHTLY REMAINS IN EQUILIBRIUM. POINT B - *CONDITIONAL STABILITY* - IF UNDISTURBED, THE SYSTEM WILL REMAIN IN EQUILIBRIUM. POINT C - *ABSOLUTE INSTABILITY* - THE SYSTEM IS UNSTABLE WITHOUT THE INFLUENCE OF AN OUTSIDE FORCE. POINT D - *ABSOLUTE STABILITY* - IF THIS SYSTEM IS DISPLACED, IT WILL GENERATE A FORCE TO RETURN TO EQUILIBRIUM.

If placed at point C, it will immediately fall down the slope without any outside force being applied to displace it. It is absolutely unstable.

At point B, the marble can be balanced atop the ridge, and so long as it is undisturbed, it will remain at rest. Once displaced, however, it will continue to fall until reaching equilibrium at some other point. It is conditionally unstable, that is, unstable on the condition that it receives an initial displacement.

The term, convective instability, refers to a condition within a layer that becomes unstable after lifting. It does not lend itself readily to illustration here, but it, also, would be best represented by B.

ABSOLUTE STABILITY

When the actual lapse rate in a layer of air is *less than the moist adiabatic lapse rate, the air is absolutely stable,* regardless of the amount of moisture it contains. A parcel of absolutely stable air that is lifted becomes cooler than the surrounding air and sinks back to its original position as soon as the lifting force is removed. Similarly, if forced to descend, it becomes warmer than the surrounding air and, like a hot air balloon, will be forced to rise rapidly back to its original position.

ABSOLUTE INSTABILITY

When the actual lapse rate in a layer of air is *greater than the dry adiabatic lapse rate, that air is absolutely unstable,* regardless of the amount of moisture it contains. A parcel of air lifted even slightly will at once be warmer than its surroundings and, like a hot air balloon, will rise rapidly.

SOME EFFECTS OF STABILITY AND INSTABILITY

The degree of stability of the atmosphere helps to determine the type of clouds, if any, that form. For example, if very stable air is forced to ascend a mountain slope, clouds will be layer-like with little vertical development and little or no turbulence. Unstable air, if forced to ascend the slope, would cause considerable vertical development and turbulence in the clouds.

If air is subsiding (sinking), the heat of compression frequently causes an inversion of temperature, increasing the stability of subsiding air. Sometimes when this occurs, often in wintertime high-pressure systems, a surface inversion formed by radiational cooling is already present. The subsidence-produced inversion, in this case, will intensify the surface inversion, placing a strong *lid* above smoke and haze. Poor visibility in the low levels of the atmosphere results, especially near industrial areas. Such conditions frequently persist for days.

WIND

Although there are exceptions to every rule, normally the inexperienced pilot is advised to avoid mountain flying when the surface wind exceeds 20 knots.

Chapter 4 - Weather — Part 1 PREFLIGHT

This is indicative of stronger winds aloft. The rule does not prevent the pilot from taking a "look-see."

Flying in the flatlands, the pilot discovers the wind will assume a more or less constant speed and direction in a horizontal plane. Under these circumstances it may not be a hazardous operation to fly when moderately strong winds exist. In the mountains, a different situation may occur where mountains, valleys, canyons and obstructions modify the wind flow and create turbulence that may prevent safe flight.

Inexperienced pilots often observe movement of cloud shadows and assume the wind will conform to that shadow movement. This is true only if the pilot is flying at or near the cloud base. At altitudes lower than the cloud base, terrain modification of the wind flow makes the cloud shadow useless, except when used in conjunction with visualization of possible modification.

MOUNTAIN AND VALLEY WINDS

A *katabatic wind* is any wind blowing down an incline. The *mountain breeze* is a type of katabatic wind. To be classified as a katabatic wind, the mountain breeze must be observed to be blowing down an incline, under circumstances such that the incline itself is responsible for the existence of the primary characteristics of the wind. There are many other katabatic winds other than mountain breezes, and some of them have received colorful names of local origin, since they are often quite dramatic in their local effect.

Any katabatic wind originates because a cold, and therefore heavy, air mass spills down over sloping terrain, displacing the warmer and less dense air ahead of it. If the descent persists through a sufficient altitude, the air will become warmed by compression until it is actually warmer than the air ahead of it. But, by that time it has momentum enough to continue displacing the colder air. Under these circumstances, the katabatic wind can usually be observed at the surface for only a relatively short distance, for as soon as the warm air loses its momentum, it will no longer be able to displace the cold air. It will then *ride over* the colder air, leaving the original surface wind unchanged while the katabatic wind may still be observed at some altitude above ground level. Sometimes, however, the cold air receding from the slope, and the warming from the downslope winds may be felt many miles from the steeper slopes. In such cases it is impossible to define a clear-cut line between the katabatic wind and the winds resulting from existing pressure gradient forces.

In areas where the katabatic wind is observed as a cold breeze replacing a warmer air mass, it is sometimes called a *gravity wind* or *fall wind*. Fall winds are found in very cold plateau regions. Because of its heaviness, the cold air flows downhill under the influence of gravity, resulting in a shallow wind that sometimes attains high speeds. These winds usually affect a rather large area and may occur either during the day or night. However, fall winds are usually stronger during the night because radiational cooling of the ground adds to the air's coldness. The ancient Greeks termed this wind *Bora,* meaning cold, from which we have derived our term *boral* to describe a northern or Arctic characteristic. The name Bora is still often used to define the cold blasts that flow down the Alps along the northern Mediterranean upon the coastal populace. In southern Alaska one may hear this same wind called a *Taku,* a term from the Eskimo language meaning cold, that is also applied to the glacier where these winds are observed to originate. A bora is a wind so cold at its source that, even after being heated by compression during the descent, it arrives in the valley at a lower temperature than that of the air it is replacing.

The same wind along the eastern slopes of the Rockies is called *Chinook,* a term applied by the Plains Indians of Montana. The air is heated as its moisture is condensed during the ascent on the windward slopes and then is heated even more by compression as it flows downhill from the high elevations. Following the arrival of a Chinook wind, the temperature at a weather station near the base of the mountain may rise as much as 30 degrees Fahrenheit in a few minutes. On occasions when the cold air slowly settles and moves downslope in the high plains country, the Chinook may bring rising temperatures as far east as the Dakotas, southward to western Oklahoma, and on rare occasions, the downslope warming will be felt as far east as Minnesota, Iowa and Missouri.

The *Santa Ana* winds of Southern California are warm katabatic winds descending from the high Nevada plateau, sometimes at very high speeds. The name was applied by the early Spaniards who observed them along the coast in the region where the Santa Ana River Valley channels them into a narrow band. Thus, there are many local names, but only one cause, as described.

WINDS ALOFT

With the exception of the Uinta mountain range in northern Utah and Colorado, most mountains are oriented more or less perpendicular to the prevailing westerly winds aloft. As a general rule of thumb, the west side (upwind side) of the mountains will contain updrafts; the east side (lee side) produces downdrafts and turbulence.

The venturi effect is a phenomena that may occur when the wind blows across a ridge line. The ridge line itself forms the bottom portion of the venturi. With stable air, a boundary of undisturbed air above forms the top portion of the venturi. Within the constriction, the wind velocity may double or triple over the steady-state wind flow velocity. Often a mountain pass will form a venturi shape where funneled wind may double or triple.

Wind flow characteristics in mountainous areas demand that the pilot spend time studying its causes and effects. (See *Mountain Wave*)

Wind has substance just like water. It obeys the laws of physics in the same manner. Because of this it is possible to study flowing water in various riverbeds to gain some appreciation of lift, sink and turbulence.

When you find an area with obstructions, visualize what you think the water would do, then move up close to check it out. Experience makes it possible to accurately predict areas of updrafts, downdrafts and turbulence.

Previous experience combined with the study of wind allows us to come up with some generally acceptable rules of thumb to apply when contemplating a mountain flight.

- When the surface wind becomes 20 knots or greater, or the ridge-level winds are greater than 20 knots, the flight should be executed with caution. If the Geostrophic wind (wind caused by rotation of the earth) approaches 30 knots or more, consider postponing or delaying the flight. This rule does not preclude a test flight to determine the stability of the air. Sometimes, with winds of 50 knots at the 9,000-foot level, the flight is devoid of turbulence, although the updrafts and downdrafts may be quite strong. It all depends on the air's stability.

- The prevailing winds aloft are westerly throughout the U.S. In the mountains a condition known as a *valley breeze* occurs in the morning and a *mountain breeze* occurs in the evening. The valley breeze begins around mid-morning and lasts until late evening. Heating of the surface causes the air to rise and flow upslope. The mountain breeze occurs due to cooling and the air slides down the slopes.

- Ridges should be approached and crossed at an angle. This allows an escape away from the ridge with the least amount of turn if downdrafts or turbulence are experienced.

TURBULENCE

Whenever moderate turbulence or greater is experienced, it is essential that you immediately slow to the maneuver speed or rough air speed to prevent structural damage. With strong updrafts and downdrafts, fly an attitude rather than trying to hold a hard altitude. It is possible to exceed the structural limits of the airframe or wings when trying to hold the altitude. Allow minor airspeed and altitude deviations. Visualize what is causing the turbulence and fly out of the area. ✈

PART 1 PREFLIGHT   Chapter 4 - Weather

EMERGENCY

An emergency is *a situation or occurrence of a serious nature, developing suddenly and unexpectedly, and demanding immediate action.* While the dictionary definition of an emergency is correct, we, as pilots, have a different definition:

> An emergency is a situation or occurrence involved with the operation of an airplane, where the pilot has the capability of overcoming or dealing with the situation, but does not know how.

Take a minute and think about it. Can you think of an emergency? One fellow at a seminar thought he caught me when he yelled out, *"You're flying along and the wing falls off, that's an emergency."* I replied, *"No, that's not an emergency, that's a certainty."*

Know the operating limitations, performance, normal and emergency procedures and the operational information for your airplane. The worst time to be studying about what to do in an emergency is in the middle of one.

I'm obviously being facetious here, to drive home the point that it is extremely important to know your airplane inside and out ... its systems and performance characteristics.

Flight instructors are often wrong, but never without an opinion.

Mountain Flying Bible   1-69

Chapter 4 - Weather Part 1 PREFLIGHT

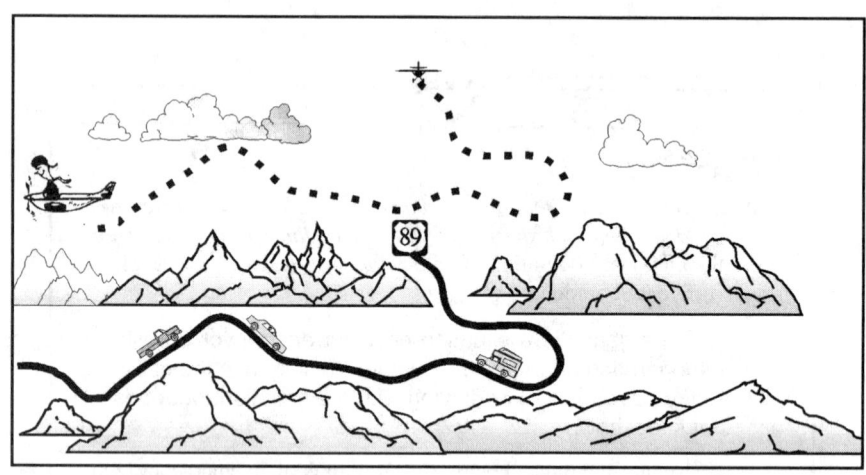

SELECTING THE ROUTE OF FLIGHT

SELECTING THE ROUTE OF FLIGHT FOR A MOUNTAIN FLIGHT INVOLVES CONSIDERATIONS OTHER THAN MAKING A DECISION TO FLY A STRAIGHT-LINE ROUTE. MANY TIMES IT IS BENEFICIAL TO FOLLOW A MAJOR HIGHWAY, ESPECIALLY IN AN AIRPLANE THAT DOES NOT HAVE THE POWER TO FLY HIGH ABOVE THE RIDGES.

FOLLOWING A HIGHWAY PROVIDES AREAS FOR A PRECAUTIONARY LANDING OR A FORCED LANDING (WITHOUT HAVING TO WALK FAR FOR HELP SHOULD YOU HAVE TO PUT IT DOWN). GENERALLY THE HIGHWAY PROVIDES THE LOWEST-TERRAIN ROUTE THROUGH AN AREA OF MOUNTAINS AND PEAKS.

IN UNFAMILIAR AREAS OR A REGION WITH ISOLATED AND RUGGED TERRAIN, FOLLOWING THE HIGHWAY CAN KEEP YOU FROM BECOMING LOST.

THIS DOG-LEG PROCEDURE, USED TO AVOID HIGHER TERRAIN, REALLY DOESN'T ADD TOO MANY MILES TO THE FLIGHT. EVEN ON YOUR LONGER LEGS IT WILL ADD ABOUT 10 MINUTES IN MOST CASES.

CHAPTER 5—AIRPLANE

- ➤ BASIC AERODYNAMICS 1-71
- ➤ STALLS 1-72
- ➤ STRAIGHT-TAIL VERSUS SWEPT-TAIL AIRPLANES 1-78
- ➤ AIRPLANE FAMILIARITY 1-79
- ➤ ENGINE PREHEAT 1-81
- ➤ COLD ENGINE STARTS 1-82
- ➤ BLOWING SNOW 1-83
- ➤ FIRE EXTINGUISHER 1-84
- ➤ MULTI-VISCOSITY OIL 1-84
- ➤ BATTERIES 1-85
- ➤ GROUND INSPECTIONS, CHECKS & PROCEDURES 1-87
- ➤ STOL KITS 1-88

BASIC AERODYNAMICS

Stalls used to bother me a lot. In my student pilot days, solo practice of stalls caused a lot of consternation. The darned airplane would do something different each time it stalled. One day the wing would fall off to the left, the next day to the right, and occasionally the wings would fall through the horizon in a level attitude. Since I didn't know what to expect—the unknown—I was scared of stalls.

By the time I became a flight instructor, I was comfortable with stalls. I came to the conclusion that stalls are not scary if you can predict what the airplane is going to do beforehand. Then I went out with a guy who was afraid of stalls, and after a few, I was too.

We all fear the unknown. You do and I do. We definitely are afraid of something we know nothing about. For example, if a snake slithers across the floor right now, you will find me perched on top of my computer, hollering for help. I don't know much about snakes. The little snake on the floor might be a harmless garden snake. But I still fear it. Stalls used to instill the same dread, until I determined what was going on.

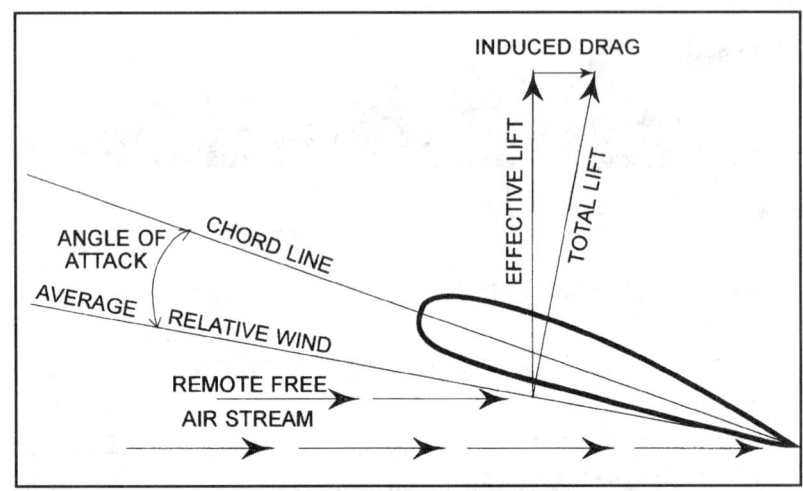

AERODYNAMIC DEFINITIONS

STALLS

Some pilots are not comfortable with slow flight and stalls. In mountain flying, especially during approach for landing, it's important to be comfortable with slow flight and to understand stalls so you can direct your full attention to the task at hand and not have a nagging doubt in the back of your mind. *If you are not at ease with slow flight, mountain flying is like dancing with a porcupine...even if you put your feet in the right places, it's hard to concentrate on the music.*

Another reason to have an understanding of stalls is because of their correlation with mountain flying. Next to weather accidents, the stall/spin accident causes the greatest number of serious injuries and deaths.

As a typical general aviation pilot you were probably taught that lift is created by a pressure differential explained by Bernoulli's Principle. Daniel Bernoulli—a Swiss scientist who lived in the 1700s—is credited with being the first to explain the relationship between fluid flow and pressure.

What you may not have been taught is that lift is also created by *Newton's Third Law of Motion* that states, "every action has an equal and opposite reaction." The wing pushes down on the air and the equal and opposite reaction is for the air to push up on the wing.

Bernoulli's Principle explains how most of the lift is derived, where about 85 percent of the lift is created by the fluid dynamics involved. Old timers in aviation knew about Newton's laws, but an attitude problem caused many important items to be omitted from publications. Some authors felt it wasn't necessary to know aerodynamics in depth, and some even felt it was beyond a pilot's capability to understand.

ENGINEERING MODIFICATIONS

When we recall our basic training about how and why an airplane flies, we remember that it creates a relative wind, relative to the airplane's flight path. During slips or skids the flight path is not parallel to the longitudinal axis. Prove it to yourself. At a ground-reference maneuver altitude (about 600-800 feet agl), try a slip and see the airplane move towards the inside of the turn. Now skid the airplane and watch it move towards the outside of the turn. Look at the ball of the turn-and-bank indicator while doing this and notice the airplane always moves towards the ball.

The airplane designer wants the cockpit area of the airplane level in relation to the horizon during cruise flight. The engineer determines an angle—angle of incidence—for both wings to be attached to the plane in order to create enough lift for this level-flight condition at cruise speed and cruise power settings. This is a fixed angle that the pilot can't change.

This hasn't solved the problem. Due to the torque of the engine that produces a slight left twisting or turning action, the airplane flies sideward through the air. To eliminate this problem of twisting, the left wing is mounted at a slightly greater angle of incidence, called *wash-in*.

Lift and drag are directly proportional, so if the lift is increased on the left wing, the drag is increased. The airplane responds by flying sideward to the left.

To eliminate this undesired effect engineers use various techniques that produces the same effect as stepping on the right rudder (the forward edge of the vertical stabilizer may be offset to the left or the engine may be mounted at an angle).

PREDICTING STALLS

These engineering modifications cause some very predictable results when the airplane is stalled.

During climbs with the power on, you step on the rudder (usually the right rudder) to compensate for torque, p-factor, asymmetrical thrust of the propeller (gyroscopic action) and the corkscrewing effect of the propeller slipstream.

If you didn't compensate for these factors (during a climb with the power on), the ball of the turn and slip instrument would be to the right of center. If you stalled the airplane with the ball to the right, it falls in a direction opposite the ball. (Instructors have to be careful when explaining this to their students. It causes a lot of undue stress when they say, *"Now watch this, the left wing is going to fall off."*)

Chapter 5 - Airplane   Part 1 PREFLIGHT

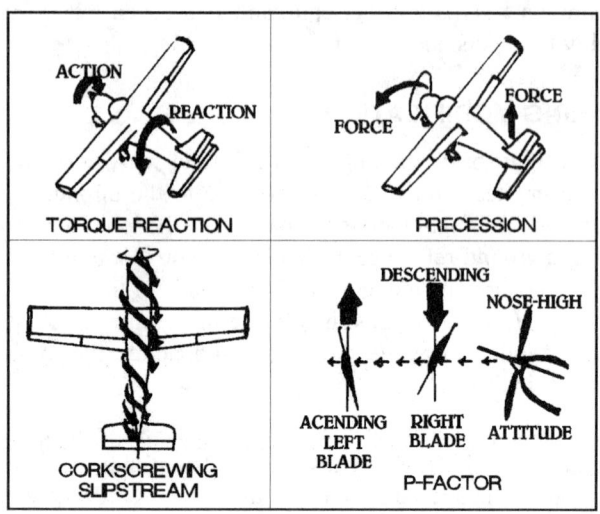

THE FOUR FORCES

Why did the left wing stall first? The airplane is creating a relative wind—relative to the direction the airplane is moving. During slips and skids the flight path is not parallel to the longitudinal axis. You can prove this to yourself. At a ground-reference altitude, 600-800 feet agl, try a slip and see the airplane move toward the inside of the turn. The ball is toward the inside of the turn. The skid causes the airplane to move toward the outside of the turn. Look at the ball of the turn coordinator. In each case the airplane flies toward the ball.

Most American-built airplanes have clockwise rotation of the propeller when viewed from the cockpit. When climbing with the power on, the ball of the turn coordinator is to the right. With the ball to the right, the airplane is moving to the right. The relative wind (parallel to and opposite from the flight path) is from the right. The fuselage blocks some of the airflow to the left wing. Now you can guess which wing stalls first and why.

If the right rudder is pressed too hard during the climb, it moves the ball to the left of its index. Again, the airplane falls away from the ball. In this case the airplane rotates to the right—away from the ball—but it does so at a rate slower than when it rotates to the left. This slower rate occurs because the stall's rotation is fighting against the torque of the engine.

Next, try stalling with the power on and with the ball centered. We might (and probably do) expect the airplane to fall straight down with no tendency to go off to either side. It doesn't. The airplane falls to the right. Why? The left

PART 1 PREFLIGHT   **Chapter 5 - Airplane**

wing is washed-in. It has a slightly greater angle of incidence than the right wing to compensate for torque in cruise flight. Also, the vertical stabilizer is offset to the left; causing the same effect as adding some right rudder to compensate for the extra drag of the left wing.

These design features are balancing forces only during cruise flight, so at the slower airspeed of the climb, they overcompensate. More importantly, the corkscrewing effect of the propeller slipstream moves up on the vertical stabilizer as the angle of attack increases. When the airplane stalls, not as much right rudder is needed and the airplane falls to the right.

If you hold less right rudder pressure so the ball is half-way to the right of the index, the airplane will stall straight ahead with the wings remaining level as the nose passes through the horizon.

With this understanding you can go out and practice stalls, anticipating what the airplane is going to do and why it is doing it. You may not be comfortable with stalls, but they are no longer to be feared as the unknown.

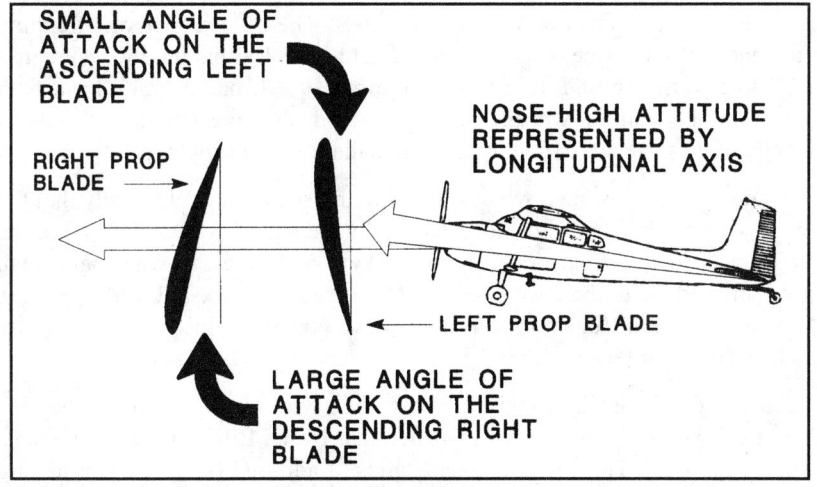

P-FACTOR

IF A GENERAL AVIATION AIRPLANE HAD ENOUGH THRUST TO PERMIT IT TO CLIMB AT AN ANGLE REPRESENTED BY WHERE THE NOSE IS POINTED, THERE WOULD BE NO P-FACTOR. BECAUSE THE AIRPLANE IS CLIMBING AT AN ANGLE THAT IS LESS THAN THE ANGLE WHERE IT IS POINTED, THE DESCENDING BLADE ON THE RIGHT SIDE HAS A LARGER ANGLE OF ATTACK (ASSUMING CLOCKWISE ROTATION OF THE PROPELLER AS VIEWED FROM THE COCKPIT) THAN THE ASCENDING BLADE ON THE LEFT SIDE OF THE AIRPLANE. THIS FORCE, KNOWN AS P-FACTOR, ADDS TO THE LEFT-TURNING TENDENCY DURING A CLIMB.

Chapter 5 - Airplane   Part 1 PREFLIGHT

WHY KNOW AERODYNAMICS?

I didn't really learn about stalls until the late '60s. A fellow came to my flight school in Jackson, Wyo. wanting to learn to fly, with concentration on doing spins. He didn't want to waste time by going through the gradual build-up to the cross-control stall entry procedure, thereby slowly building up so that we would allow the airplane to work itself into a full spin.

I demonstrated about six or eight three-turn spins with him holding onto the controls. He thought he had them down. When he tried his first spin I was surprised after saying, "Okay, let's recover." Glancing to the left I saw stark terror on his face. He had locked up on the controls, full left rudder and full left aileron with the control wheel back into his gut.

We had started the spin around 11,000 feet msl. Ground level was at about 7,000 feet msl over the practice area. Since we were rapidly approaching the ground, I thought it wise to effect a recovery. I stepped on the right rudder. Nothing happened. I looked out the back window of the Cessna 150 and stomped back and forth on the rudder pedals. The little rudder was flopping back and forth just fine, yet, we continued to spin. By this time we were getting close to the ground. In a last-ditch effort of self preservation I put both hands on the control wheel, pushed forward and exclaimed, "Oh, sh--." (Really, it was shucks.) The airplane immediately began flying.

About 30 minutes later, while I was shaking so hard I could barely dial the phone (rotary dial back in those days), I called the FAA GADO (General Aviation District Office) in Cheyenne, Wyo. to figure out what happened. They referred me to the Denver office. Denver referred me to Oklahoma City. Apparently I didn't talk to the proper person there because Oklahoma City said, "Gee, I don't know."

That night I needed a seatbelt in bed. The world kept spinning around. I decided to get to the bottom of my dilemma. I used Bill Kershner's manuals in learning to fly. He was one of the "gods" I admired (still do). Not having any idea of who else to call, I tried him.

Mr. Kershner explained what happened; telling me about the horizontal stabilizer and elevator blocking the airflow to the rudder in swept-tail airplanes. These airplanes require the use of forward-elevator control in conjunction with the rudder control to effect a recovery.

SPINS

General aviation's number two killer continues to be the stall/spin accident. Many modern airplanes have to be forced to spin and require considerable judgment and technique to get started when loaded with the student and an instructor. But, put a passenger or some baggage in the back and these same airplanes may be accidentally put into a spin with surprising ease. With the aft loading, recovery may be difficult or impossible.

Some pilots develop an unconscious aversion to spins because of reports in newspapers and other aviation trade publications. The definition of a spin doesn't help much when it states that, "it is an aggravated stall that results in autorotation with a corkscrew path downward." Talk about stalls being scary; think of the mental anxiety of a pilot intentionally going out the first time to do spins.

Want to start an argument? Try telling a pilot he needs spin training to enhance his and his passenger's safety. Some pilots have the attitude, *my mind's made up, don't confuse me with facts.* Flight schools also have excuses for avoiding spin training. One of these is that spins will ruin the gyro instruments. Horse pucky! The modern trainer is equipped with non-tumbling gyros. Sure, they might tumble and the wear-and-tear on the gimbals might require overhaul a little sooner, but the benefits of spin training outweigh this cost.

There is no need to fear spins—only the lack of knowledge about them. Spin training does not have to be a hair-raising experience. I know whereof I speak. I owned a flight school and trained more than 2,000 students in spins. One thing a successful business owner is not going to do is run off his customers by scaring them. All our student pilots did spins before their first solo flight. Not one student quit his flight training as a result of being terrified.

The technique we incorporated into flight training to make spin training an enjoyable experience involved a detailed explanation of the aerodynamics involved during stalls. Next we practiced cross-control stalls, beginning with the first introduction of stalls. These were gentle stalls, not violent maneuvers.

The airplane was stalled while climbing with partial power and the ball of the turn coordinator off to the right side. The student expected the airplane to fall to the left side and was conditioned to use the rudder and elevator to stop the stall.

The use of the rudder is a *conditioned reflex* as opposed to *instinct.* Instinct in an airplane is sometimes wrong. For example, if the airplane is in a spin, instinct says you should pull back on the control wheel to raise the nose. It won't work. The stall must be broken with neutral or forward elevator control, and then backpressure is applied to fly out of the resulting dive.

The student continues to practice cross-control stalls during each dual lesson before solo. The instructor gradually used more power to create a faster rotation of the airplane and asked the student to delay the recovery allowing the airplane to roll more, and the nose to pitch down further. Notice that during this training the instructor is not flying the airplane. And the instructor did not ever mention the dreaded word "spin."

Chapter 5 - Airplane   Part 1 PREFLIGHT

Eventually the student did a spin and effected the recovery. When asked, *"How did you like your first spin?"* The student would say something like, *"Oh, was that a spin? I thought a spin was something scary."*

If you decide to *rent* an instructor and go for a *spin,* find an instructor who will introduce you to the maneuver gradually, using the cross-control stall technique. You don't want him to demonstrate spins to you; you want to do them yourself. You will find they aren't as bad as you imagined, although spins are the worst of the *inside* aerobatic maneuvers. If you enjoy the spins, try aerobatics. They will increase your proficiency as a pilot and proficiency means safer flying.

STRAIGHT-TAIL VERSUS SWEPT-TAIL AIRPLANES

Somewhere around 1960, some aircraft manufacturers switched from the straight-tail to the swept-tail design. This was an important sales tool. Just look at the airplanes on the ramp and compare the straight-tail models versus the swept-tail models. The swept-tail airplanes look good; in fact, they appear to be going 20 mph just sitting there.

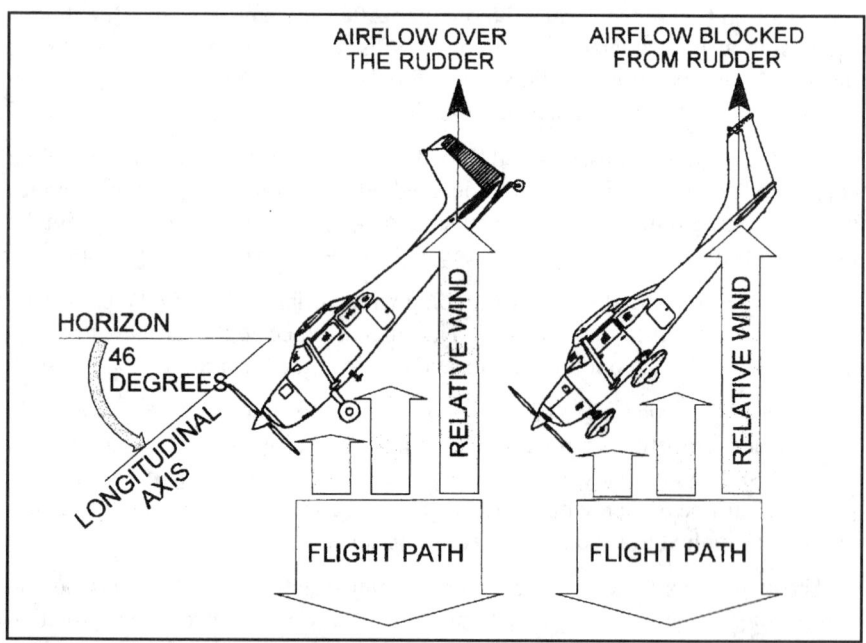

STRAIGHT-TAIL AIRPLANES HAVE RUDDER CONTROL DURING A SPIN BECAUSE A PORTION OF THE AIRFLOW CONTINUES OVER THE RUDDER. SWEPT-TAIL AIRPLANES REQUIRE FORWARD ELEVATOR MOVEMENT TO ALLOW AIRFLOW OVER THE RUDDER, BEFORE THE RUDDER IS EFFECTIVE IN STOPPING THE ROTATION OF A SPIN.

It is important to realize the swept-tail airplane incorporates a different spin-recovery technique from the straight-tail airplane.

STRAIGHT-TAIL SPIN RECOVERY

The straight-tail airplane uses the traditional spin-recovery technique; step on opposite rudder to stop the rotation, then stick forward to break the stall, and stick back to recover from the resulting dive.

SWEPT-TAIL SPIN RECOVERY

Many airplanes assume a nose-down attitude of approximately 45 degrees below the horizon while in a spin. The uninitiated swear the nose is pointing straight down. Despite the attitude of the airplane, the flight path is downward. The resultant relative wind is upward.

During a spin recovery, if opposite rudder is pressed to stop the rotation, nothing happens (of any consequence). The horizontal stabilizer and elevator block the airflow to the rudder because of the swept-tail design. Recovery in swept-tail designs requires the stick (control wheel) to be moved forward to allow airflow over the rudder. Only then will rudder application stop the rotation.

AIRPLANE FAMILIARITY

We have determined the importance of the airplane's service ceiling in flight planning. What is the service ceiling? The service ceiling of a single-engine airplane is the altitude in the standard atmosphere, where operating at maximum allowable gross weight produces a climb rate of 100 fpm. The airplane may be climbed above this altitude. It will not harm the airplane to do so. When the airplane performance deteriorates so that the best angle-of-climb speed produces level flight, the airplane has reached its *absolute ceiling*. It is possible to fly above the absolute ceiling—using mountain wave lift, thermal lift, or mechanical lift—and again, this will not damage the airplane. If the airplane, such as a pressurized model, has a maximum altitude listed as an operating limitation, it is illegal to fly above that altitude.

Notice the service ceiling is based on operation at maximum allowable gross weight. If the weight is less, the service ceiling will be higher. The service ceiling is based on the density altitude. Speaking of density altitude, what is it? When the altimeter is set to 29.92 inches of mercury, we read the pressure altitude, then compensate for non-standard temperature. This gives the textbook value known as density altitude. The author prefers to think of density altitude as *the altitude at which the airplane thinks it is flying*. This is because the airplane will perform at the density altitude the same as it would at the same altitude in the standard atmosphere, even though the physical altitude may be much lower.

Chapter 5 - Airplane　　　　　　　　　　　Part 1 PREFLIGHT

Aircraft performance is based upon density altitude. Leaning the mixture to obtain maximum engine performance is predicated upon the density altitude, not the physical altitude.

STANDARD ATMOSPHERE

It is necessary to adopt a standard atmosphere to be used as a reference for the computation of an airplane's performance. Because conditions in the atmosphere vary each day, this standard provides a yardstick to compare results with other similar computations under varying conditions. The standard atmosphere is defined as the average properties of pressure, temperature and density existing at 40°-north latitude. Standard sea level pressure is 29.92 inches of mercury and 59°F (15°C). The lapse rate is 3½°F (2°C) per 1,000 feet.

AIRCRAFT PERFORMANCE

An airplane's rate of climb assumes more importance in the mountains. Over flat terrain, you take off and climb on course using an attitude and airspeed that is comfortable. In the mountains you fly precise airspeeds; best angle-of-climb airspeed for terrain clearance or best rate-of-climb airspeed for the greatest altitude gain per unit of time. The terrain surrounding many mountain airports will not allow you to climb on course, even if you use the proper airspeed for maximum performance. Also, when approaching mountain ridges or passes, the rate of climb may not be great enough to cross. You will learn to maneuver away from the higher terrain in these circumstances. While circling for additional altitude, visualization will help you find mechanical lift (air being forced up terrain) or anabatic lift (convection currents).

In the mid-1970s, aircraft manufacturers got together and standardized the information in their manuals (Pilot Operating Handbook - POH). They are now divided into usable sections:

1 - **General**
2 - **Limitations**
3 - **Emergency Procedures**
4 - **Normal Procedures**
5 - **Performance**
6 - **Weight and Balance/Equipment List**
7 - **Airplane & Systems Descriptions**
8 - **Airplane Handling, Service & Maintenance; and,**
9 - **Supplements.**

Manufacturers go to a lot of trouble to test and verify the documented information. Spend some time looking over the POH and be able to find the performance information appropriate to flight operation.

You can expect to do as well as the performance chart data only if your airplane is kept in the peak of condition. It isn't necessary to consult performance charts for every takeoff and landing. Your pilot skill, proficiency, familiarity with equipment, along with density altitude, gross weight, wind and runway type, length and condition, will dictate whether or not you will use the charts. Use performance charts anytime there is doubt in your mind.

If you are preflight planning one of your first trips to the mountains, look at the performance charts to determine the takeoff and landing distance required for the density altitudes you could conceivably encounter. This allows you to determine beforehand the possibility of restrictions on your flight.

ENGINE PREHEAT

It is possible to start an airplane engine without preheating, even in temperatures as low as –25°F, because of the advent of multi-viscosity oils. This will decrease the life of the engine. Generally, 20°F or lower is considered *preheat* temperature. Below the pour point, oil quickly turns to a molasses-type liquid and any colder temperature results in the oil rapidly approaching a solid.

Besides the change in oil viscosity, batteries lose a high percentage of their effectiveness and instruments stick or freeze.

When you have determined to preheat the engine, adhere to the following:

- ☐ Do not use a heater if it is not in good condition. Do not refuel the heater or the airplane while the heater is operating.
- ☐ Do not leave the airplane unattended during heating.
- ☐ Keep a fire extinguisher nearby.
- ☐ Do not direct the heat directly on combustible parts or engine accessories.
- ☐ In a sheltered area, the engine may be kept ready to go with the use of a mechanic's drop cord with a 60- to 100-watt bulb installed. Place this light near the bottom of the engine, inside the cowling. Use an insulated engine blanket (old quilt) when parking the airplane outside.

It is possible to direct the hot air blast from an engine heater at the cylinders and when the engine appears heated and ready to go, the oil is still in a near-frozen state. It is best to direct the hot air blast at the bottom of the oil pan. When the engine is shut down after a flight, moisture condenses on the inside and outside of the case. Preheating causes the tiny, frozen droplets to melt and disappear. If the preheating continues until the moisture disappears entirely on the outside of the engine and the propeller turns easily, the preheating process is complete.

Chapter 5 - Airplane   Part 1 PREFLIGHT

COLD ENGINE STARTS

 Above 20°F the engine may be started without preheat, but the oil may be partially congealed. It is recommended the propeller be turned over by hand at least four to six times to relieve some of the stress on the starter and battery. Never operate a starter motor for more than 90 seconds continuously. If the engine does not start, allow a full minute before attempting another start. This allows the starter motor to cool down. After the initial attempt, do not operate the starter for more than 30 seconds continuously.

Primer—Some pilots have a tendency to overprime during cold starts. This washes oil from the cylinder walls, since raw fuel is directed into the cylinders without passing through the carburetor and intake manifold. When starting, lack of lubrication causes scoring of the cylinder walls. This in turn causes lack of compression and causes hard starting.

Over priming can also cause induction fires. If this occurs, continue operating the starter in an attempt to suck the fire back into the engine where it belongs.

 **Frosted Plugs**—Another problem that plagues the airplane engine that has not been preheated is that of *frosted* spark plug electrodes. The engine fires a couple of times and then quits. Any further attempt at starting is futile since there has been sufficient combustion to cause some water (a by-product of combustion) in the cylinders, but insufficient combustion to heat up the spark plugs. As a consequence, the water condenses on the spark plug electrodes, freezes to ice and shorts them out. The only remedy is heat. If a heater is not available, remove the plugs and heat them until all moisture disappears.

For prolonged cold weather operations, switching to fine-wire spark plugs helps eliminate the frosted-plug problem and improves cold starts.

When the temperature is extremely cold, fuel vaporization becomes a problem. Immediately after starting, apply carburetor heat to help vaporize the fuel. Turn the carb heat off. If there is engine roughness turn it back on immediately. As soon as the engine runs smoothly without carburetor heat, turn the carb heat off.

During cold-weather operations aircraft engines have a habit of quitting during prolonged idling because insufficient heat is produced to keep the plugs from fouling. Avoid prolonged idling and you'll avoid iced-over or fouled spark plugs.

Oil Pressure Indication—You should look for an oil pressure indication within 30 seconds after starting in warm temperatures. There should be an indication within 60 seconds during cold temperatures. If there is no indication, investigate. Turn off the mags, rather than pulling the mixture control, to stop the engine faster. Sometimes, even with engine preheating, the oil pressure line to the gauge may contain frozen oil that requires preheating too.

Immediately after the engine starts, **DO NOT OPERATE THE ENGINE ABOVE 800-1,200 RPM** until several minutes of running loosens (warms) the oil to provide lubrication. Revving the engine to as little as 1,500 rpm immediately after starting (even in warm weather) destroys the engine. The pilot who does rev the engine could easily reduce the TBO (time between overhaul) of his engine by half.

Turbine engines can accumulate internal ice overnight and resist rotation when trying to start them. With any indication of locked rotor, unusual noise, or low RPM, discontinue the start. Be aware that rotors can freeze on any cold-weather start and be alert enough to stop the start before damaging the engine. If weather forecasts suggest snow, ice or sleet, install engine cowl plugs. This should be done anyway, if the airplane is parked outside, summer or winter.

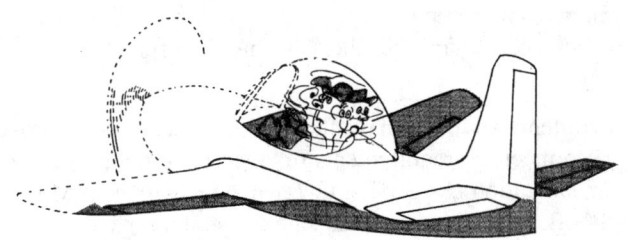

White out...

BLOWING SNOW

When the airplane is exposed to blowing snow, direct special attention to all aircraft openings where snow can enter and freeze solid. Even if the controls are free, an ice accumulation could affect weight and balance.

These openings must be free of snow and ice before flight:
- Pitot tubes
- Wheel wells
- Heater intakes
- Carburetor intakes
- Tail section—Check for snow that could result in an aft cg
- Tail wheel area—Check the elevator, rudder-steering and spring-steering controls
- Fuel tank vents

Chapter 5 - Airplane	Part 1 PREFLIGHT

- ☐ Fuel cap vents
- ☐ Control surface openings—If snow accumulates in these openings and temperature fluctuations cause it to melt and refreeze as ice, a serious balance problem occurs. During flight the control surface may begin to flutter. The resonance of the flutter may cause structural failure.

FIRE EXTINGUISHER

Check your fire extinguisher. Liquid extinguishers may freeze and break. CO_2 bottles must have a full charge. Even with a full charge, their effectiveness diminishes in cold weather. As the temperature outside lowers, the pressure inside the bottle decreases. At –60°F, a fully charged bottle may contain as little as 5 psi, where 750 psi is normal. The extinguisher may be useless.

MULTI-VISCOSITY OIL

Oil is the engine's lifeblood. It is required to lubricate, cool, seal, and clean the engine. You can't blindly pour any motor oil into the engine. Using automotive oils in an airplane engine can lead to problems, expensive problems. The flight manual, or perhaps the filler opening, will specify oils of a particular type and grade.

Phillips Petroleum and Shell have their multi-viscosity oil approved by the FAA. They also meet the requirements of Avco Lycoming (now TEXTRON Lycoming) Specification No. 301F and Teledyne Continental Motors specification MHS-24B, meaning you can safely use Phillips or Shell in your Lycoming or Continental engine.

The petroleum industry devised a classification system for engine lubricants to identify oils. This system is based on grades. Viscosity, or thickness, determines the grade. Viscosities have been assigned identifying SAE (Society of Automotive Engineers) numbers.

The viscosity of the oil is very important for cold weather operations. If the oil is too thick, it will not lubricate the engine when cold. If too thin, it will

COMMERCIAL AVIATION NUMBER	COMMERICAL SAE NUMBER	AN SPECIFICATION NUMBER
65	30	1065
80	40	1080
100	50	1100
120	60	1120
140	70	

OIL CLASSIFICATION

break down at high temperatures. In the past it was necessary for pilots to switch back and forth between *summer* and *winter* grades. (See: *Pour-point of oil* next page) And, some pilots changed oil whenever they operated in different parts of the country. Even if you aren't bothered by seasonal oil changes, multi-viscosity oil is for your engine.

Multi-viscosity oils may be synthetic, semi-synthetic, or non-synthetic. They will prolong the engine life as the airplane climbs or descends through temperature extremes. They add to engine life because they are thin enough to flow when cold and thick enough to be effective when hot. The wear and tear is not only reduced on the engine itself, but also on accessories such as the battery, starter, oil pump, oil cooler, and propeller governor. The multi-viscosity oils are compounded with a complete package of anti-scuff, anti-wear, anti-oxidation, anti-acid, anti-corrosion, and other additives. Some of the anti-wear additives will make scored and galled surfaces inside the engine heal themselves. That's something the best straight-grade oil could never do.

COMMERCIAL AVIATION NUMBER	POUR POINT
100	+10°F
65	0°F
20w-50 Phillips X-C	–25°F
15w-50 Shell	–30°F

POUR-POINT OF OIL

Claims that multi-viscosity oils will permit longer intervals between oil changes should be disregarded. Most people think that as long as the dipstick is not a black molasses consistency, the oil is still doing its job. But, since there are many by-products an oil must clean, such as rust, corrosives, acids, and varnishes, stick to your regular oil change schedule.

BATTERIES

The airplane battery requires special consideration during cold weather for acceptable performance. If an airplane is kept outside during freezing temperatures, the wet-cell storage battery (like your car battery) must be kept fully charged to prevent loss of power and freezing.

Neglecting to maintain the correct fluid level is the most common reason for the battery to freeze. Inactivity may cause the battery to become drained of its electrical charge, allowing it to freeze. If a battery is frozen, it may crack and leak sulfuric acid. If it doesn't break from the freezing, when subjected to a high-charge rate, it may explode.

During cold weather (below zero Fahrenheit), if the battery is not fully charged and no provision exists for charging it, remove it, and store it in temperatures of 60° to 75°F.

Lead-Acid Battery—A lead-acid battery consists of lead plates (positive lead peroxide and negative spongy lead) surrounded by an electrolyte consisting of a mixture of sulfuric acid and water. The sulfuric acid breaks up into positive and negative ions by chemical action when the battery delivers current.

This chemical action will continue until the lead plates are coated with lead sulfate; then no further chemical action can occur and the battery is *discharged*.

Charging the battery results when current passes in a reverse direction causing the ions to move back into solution, where they combine, reforming sulfuric acid.

The wet-cell storage battery is able to deliver a large amount of power for a short time. After starting, the engine generator or alternator system provides the electrical power for operation of the electrical system and re-charging the battery for the next start.

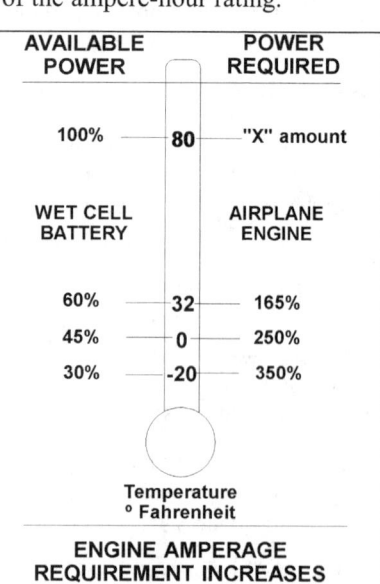

STORAGE BATTERY
STATES OF CHARGE/ FREEZING POINTS

SPECIFIC GRAVITY*...FREEZING POINT, °F

1.000........No Charge........	+32
1.050.................................	+27
1.100...Fully Discharged...	+19
1.125.................................	+13
1.150.................................	+5
1.175.................................	–4
1.200.................................	–16
1.225.................................	–35
1.250......Older Battery......	–62
1.275.....Fully Charged.....	–80
1.300......New Battery.......	–95

*Specific gravity is an expression used when batteries are tested with a hydrometer which determines the ratio of the weight of the electrolyte to the weight of pure water at +40°F (+4°C).

The capacity of the lead-acid battery is measured in *ampere-hours*. A one ampere-hour battery can produce a current flow of one amp for one hour before becoming exhausted. The battery will produce any combination of current flow and time that equals the product of the ampere-hour rating.

For example, a 20 ampere-hour battery can deliver 20 amps for one hour, or 40 amps for one-half hour, and so on. If your particular airplane requires 400 amps for starting, the battery could turn the starter for three minutes (20 divided by 400 times 60). With cold weather, sluggish oil could easily double this draw. Also, at 32°F the chemical action takes place at a much slower rate, reducing the battery to near one-half its normal capacity.

The battery's total capacity (ampere-hour measurement) depends on the amount of lead plate material it contains. Each time the battery discharges, even a small amount, recharging causes deterioration of the plates. That is, some of the material falls off. This is a normal process, and when insufficient plate material remains, the battery is worn out.

If a battery is not kept fully charged, sulfation occurs—hard lead-sulfate crystals—that cannot be easily changed back to the active material.

GROUND INSPECTIONS, CHECKS AND PROCEDURES

In the mountains, even more than in the flatlands, a good preflight is necessary because there are fewer forced-landing areas available should you have to make one because of carelessness on the ground.

STOL KITS

Are STOL kits and other enhancements such as droop wingtips and winglets worth the time, effort and money to have your airplane modified? The answer ... it depends ... depends on how much money you are willing to spend and what you are doing or what you want to do with your air machine.

Droop tips make a 'mean-lookin' machine.' The claim is that the droop tips change the airflow (prevents some of the low pressure air from the bottom of the wing curling around to fill in the high pressure area on the top of the wing) and as a consequence reduce the induced drag associated with low-speed flight. Unless the manufacturers have changed something drastically in the last few years, I didn't notice a large difference in performance in the before and after modification.

What about other devices such as the stall fences, leading edge cuffs, drooped ailerons and similar modifications?

ROBERTSON STOL

The Robertson STOL kits by Sierra Industries have been very popular with performance-minded pilots for years and years. This kit has often been promoted more as a safety device, rather than a performance booster. It can reduce the takeoff and landing distance significantly without adding unacceptable weight to the aircraft structure. Some dual instruction is required to get used to the difference in attitude between the 'normal' attitude and the 'flat' takeoff, climbout and approach to landing of the Robertson STOL.

LEADING-EDGE CUFF

My preference for a STOL conversion is the leading edge cuff, mainly because the cost of this modification is affordable for many aircraft owners. The shape of the cuff allows slower flight maneuvering, a lower stall speed and greater lifting ability without a large penalty in the normal cruise speed.

The leading edge cuff, called by Cessna the camber-lift wing, is often sold as a kit combined with stall fences.

STALL FENCE

Stall fences run from the front of the wing toward the back (chord-wise) on the top surface of the wing. These are small 'walls;' that keep air directed over the inboard portion of the wing. They reduce the spillage of air over the outboard portion of the wing that can cause a burble, thus keeping the outer part of the wing flying when the inboard part of the wing may be stalled.

WASH OUT

Some aircraft manufacturers perform a similar enhancement through manufacturing in what is called wing 'washout.' The wingtips are twisted down at the forward edge to produce a smaller angle of incidence than that at the wing root (where the wing joins the fuselage). When approaching a stall at a high angle of attack, the wing tips and a portion of the outer wing do not reach the critical angle of attach at the same time as the inner portion of the wing. This provides aileron control during a stall.

GAP SEALS

Gap seals provide a cover between the hinged areas of the wing (ailerons and/or flaps). This reduces the turbulent airflow associated with such areas thus reducing the interferrence or eddy drag. When drag is reduced, lift is enhanced.

VORTEX GENERATORS

Vortex generators are small tabs installed (generally with epoxy) on the top surface of the wings. They redirect the airflow over the wing to reduce airflow separation. They work.

STOL COSTS

If money is not an object, the ultimate STOL aircraft for providing safety and short-field operations is the 260SE/STOL built by Todd Peterson since 1986.

Back in the late 1950s, Jim Robertson of Robertson STOL fame, designed an airplane called the *Skyshark*. It would 'eat-up' any airplane in sight, but not many people could afford it. Many of its enhancements were applied to the Cessna 182 to produce the Wren 460.

WREN 460

The Wren incorporates a high-lift canard (back in the days before most pilots could spell canard), full span, double-slotted flaps and 'wren's teeth,' a system of spoilers to produce roll control.

260SE/STOL

Todd Peterson (Performance Plus Inc., El Dorado, Kansas) came up with a new design, the 260SE/STOL, to replace his Wren 460 design. This airplane has a faster cruise speed, a greater useful load, a higher service ceiling and no compromise in safety and performance. Like the Robertson STOL, the 260SE/STOL maintains a flat attitude at slow speeds and exhibits stall resistant performance.

A word of caution for helicopter pilots. The 260SE/STOL flies so slow that you may be fooled into believing you are in a helicopter. Forget about grabbing the collective control ... it doesn't have one.

Chapter 5 - Airplane
Part 1 PREFLIGHT

SUPER-DOOPER CUB

Hal Goddard and his son Mike (Airborne Research, Ryan Field, near Tucson), developed the Goddard Lift Kit for the Super Cub (and Pawnee). John A. Lindholm flew the modified Cub and was impressed.

He reports the kit adds about 28 pounds total weight with the leading edge slats (that extend nearly the full length of each wing) and the aileron gap seals. Lindholm reports the Cub will fly at an airspeed under 20 mph. ✈

HINT: SMOOTH LANDING

Many passengers are still of the opinion that they have had a wonderful flight if the landing is exceptionally smooth. The pilot may have been lost for half the flight and he may not have been able to maintain the altitude within 500 feet of that desired. But, if the landing is good, it was a good flight.

In order to make a "squeeker" landing, the following advise may be handy. Often one lands with the power reduced to idle, especially in the mountains. If it is your intention to land with the power off, the point of power reduction or the technique of power reduction becomes important.

If the power is reduced before the beginning of the flare, there is no problem. The landing may be performed with a two-stage flare. There is an initial flare to level flight attitude, then as the speed bleeds off and the aircraft starts to settle, the nose is transitioned to the landing attitude.

If the power is reduced during the flare, it must be done slowly and smoothly because of a disturbance to the airflow over the tail when the power is reduced. The airflow over the tail is reduced in some models and blocked in other models. Regardless, this change in airflow usually causes the nose to sag or drop. Catching this dip is more often a matter of luck than skill. It's really hard to time the back pressure on the elevator with a too rapid power reduction. Make the reduction slow and smooth. Then, perform the two-stage flare.

CHAPTER 6—WEIGHT AND BALANCE

- ➤ AIRCRAFT LOADING 1-92
- ➤ TYPES OF WEIGHT TO CONSIDER 1-93
- ➤ WEIGHT LIMITATIONS 1-93
- ➤ CENTER OF GRAVITY 1-93
- ➤ DANGEROUS CONDITIONS 1-94
- ➤ OVERLOADED AIRCRAFT 1-95
- ➤ WEIGHT AND BALANCE CALCULATIONS 1-95

INTRODUCTION

Overloading has frequently been cited as a cause of accidents involving aircraft operating in the mountains. There are two basic types of accidents. One occurs because the airplane is overweight and lacks the performance to takeoff or to climb in order to avoid the terrain once airborne. The other occurs because of lack of control from an out-of-balance airplane. An airplane loaded outside the center of gravity limits sets up a porpoising tendency. The pilot trying to catch and stop this oscillation often makes it worse.

For mountain flying you should carry only the essentials, but do not be frugal by reducing the fuel reserve or by off-loading survival equipment to stay within weight limitations. It is wiser to off-load passengers or baggage and make several ferry flights, than to run out of fuel or wish you had some survival equipment.

The maximum allowable gross weight is established for an aircraft as an operating limitation both for safety (aircraft structural strength) and performance considerations. It is interesting to note the effect of an increase in gross weight on the performance of the airplane. These values are not limited to an increase in gross weight above the maximum allowable gross weight. They are valid for any increase of 10 percent over a particular operating condition. For example, suppose an airplane with a maximum allowable gross weight of 2,300 pounds is being flown at a reduced weight of 1,900 pounds. Add a 190-pound passenger (10 percent) and this increases the gross weight to 2,090 pounds. The airplane is well below the maximum allowable gross weight, but its performance will be affected.

Chapter 6 - Weight and Balance　　　　　　　　Part 1 PREFLIGHT

 **RULE OF THUMB**—The takeoff distance varies with the square of the gross weight.

Whenever the gross weight of an airplane is increased, the performance is decreased. *The takeoff distance varies with the square of the gross weight.* This makes sense. If the gross weight of the airplane is increased, it is logical that the takeoff speed must be increased to compensate for the additional weight.

It will also take more runway for the airplane to accelerate to this increased speed. For an airplane with a 10 percent increase in the gross weight, with the total weight remaining at or less than the maximum allowable gross weight, the effects are:

GROSS WEIGHT INCREASED 10% MEANS:
- 5% increase in rotation speed
- 9% decrease in acceleration
- 21% increase in takeoff distance

The majority of our general aviation airplanes have relatively low thrust-to-weight ratios, causing these figures to be slightly higher.

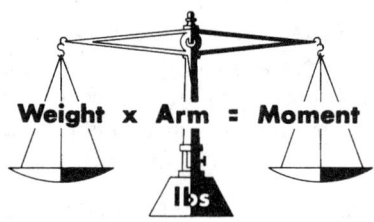

AIRCRAFT LOADING

Airplane engineers design each make and model of airplane to accommodate a certain maximum allowable weight. This weight, and the limit load factor, defines the structural strength of the airplane. How the weight is arranged within the airplane affects the cg range and the airplane's stability.

An airplane loaded outside of its cg range, either forward or aft, is very dangerous. Once airborne the airplane may be completely uncontrollable because of pitch oscillations. The more the pilot does to control these oscillations, the worse the situation becomes. You have a problem. If you have a parachute, you might consider it's use in a timely manner.

An airplane loaded outside the CG range is inviting disaster. Unless you practice solipsism, it is not always proper or possible to fill all the seats, to fill the fuel tanks, and to fill the baggage compartment and then try to fly the airplane.

Pilots displaying knowledge and respect for the aircraft's limitations usually have a system worked out whereby they figure that if they have full fuel, they can carry two passengers and limited baggage. With half fuel, the airplane will carry four occupants and their baggage. This system usually works, but as the title, "weight and balance," suggests, we are concerned also with the distribution of the weight. That is, how it affects the balance of the airplane because balance affects the stability, control and performance.

TYPES OF WEIGHT TO CONSIDER

In the determination of weight and balance computations, there are three weights the pilot considers: *empty weight, useful load* and *gross weight.*

Empty Weight—The empty weight consists of the airframe, engine(s), and all items of operating equipment that are permanently installed. It includes optional equipment, fixed ballast, hydraulic fluid, *unusable fuel*, and undrainable oil.

Useful Load—The useful load or payload, is the weight of the pilot, passengers, baggage, *usable fuel* and drainable oil. It is the empty weight subtracted from the maximum allowable gross weight.

Gross Weight—The gross weight is the total weight of the empty weight and the useful load. Each airplane is certificated for a maximum allowable gross weight. If the maximum load exceeds the maximum allowable gross weight, passengers, baggage or fuel must be off-loaded.

WEIGHT LIMITATIONS

Density altitude (high pressure altitude, high temperature and high humidity) may not allow an airplane to be operated at its legal maximum allowable gross weight at high-elevation mountain strips or even some shorter strips at lower elevations.

Usually there is a larger airport or airstrip within 20- to 30-minutes flying time from the mountain strip you have chosen as your destination. If you are concerned about the runway length being adequate, it might be a good idea to land at the longer runway, off-load some of the passengers or baggage and then fly several trips into the destination, ferrying a portion of the load on each trip. This procedure may not be required for the original arrival, but becomes necessary for departure.

CENTER OF GRAVITY

The center of gravity, abbreviated cg, is the one point on the airplane where the airplane would balance if suspended. The allowable cg range has been established to allow some flexibility in loading. As long as the airplane is loaded within the allowable range, it will not exhibit stability or control problems.

Chapter 6 - Weight and Balance — Part 1 PREFLIGHT

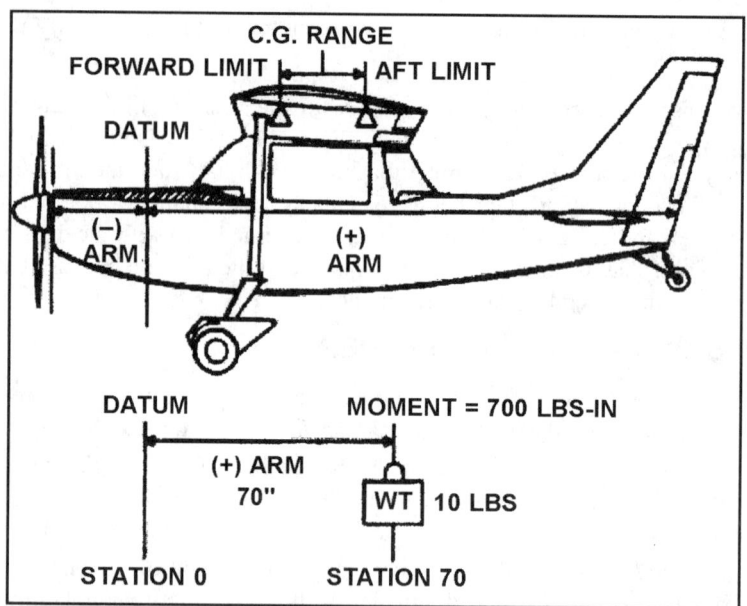

WHEN LOADED OUTSIDE THE CG RANGE THE AIRPLANE WILL EXHIBIT SOME DANGEROUS CHARACTERISTICS.

DANGEROUS CONDITIONS

Again the point must be made, and it cannot be over-stressed, that loading an airplane outside the allowable range is an invitation to disaster. The undesirable and dangerous flight characteristics of a forward and aft cg loading will be examined.

FORWARD CG LOADING

- ✔ Excessive loads on the nose wheel. In a tail wheel airplane there is a tendency to nose-over.
- ✔ Decreased performance because a higher angle of attack is needed to maintain level flight.
- ✔ Higher stalling speeds. The airplane already has a higher angle of attack than normal, placing it closer to the critical angle of attack.
- ✔ Greater takeoff distance required.
- ✔ Hazardous landings. You run the risk of running out of elevator control at normal approach speeds, thus requiring an increased landing speed.

AFT CG LOADING

- ✔ Decreased static and dynamic longitudinal stability. Under some conditions the airplane may be impossible to control.

- ✔ Violent stall characteristics. It is possible to run out of forward elevator control. The tail could then drop resulting in a flat spin.
- ✔ Light control wheel forces. Very good leverage is obtained from the control surfaces.
- ✔ Increased landing distance.
- ✔ Increased landing speed is required.

OVERLOADED AIRCRAFT

The effects of overloading an airplane are undesirable and dangerous.

- ✔ The insurance policy is likely to be null and void.
- ✔ Slower cruise speed.
- ✔ Shorter range.
- ✔ Reduced rate of climb.
- ✔ Less g-force tolerance. The airplane will not tolerate the limit load factor for which it was designed. This can be a problem, maybe not at the time but the airplane's structure becomes weakened over a period of time. Then, someday during normal flight it may fail.

WEIGHT AND BALANCE CALCULATIONS

BASIC FORMULA—Weight times Arm equals Moment

Before the advent of the loading graph and center of gravity moment envelope, pilots used this formula to calculate the weight and balance. Weight is expressed in pounds, the arm in inches from a datum line, and moment as inch/pounds.

The datum line is nothing more than an arbitrary reference point for calculations that is selected by the manufacturer. When multiplying the weight times the arm, the product sometimes results in a large number. For this reason it is common for the moment to be expressed with a reduction factor. This may be 1,000 or 10,000 or more, depending upon the size and weight of the airplane.

Once you multiply the weight times the arm and get the moment for each item of useful load, you can add all the moments, including the empty weight, and divide by the total weight. This gives the center of gravity in inches from the datum line.

Most weight and balance calculations involve a pictorial representation of multiplication rather than the old formula of weight times arm equals moment. By choosing weight along one axis (left side) of the chart and moving to the item of the useful load (arm), a line can be projected down to obtain a number, the moment. Each item of the useful load is determined in this manner. By totaling the weight and the moment, the values can be compared to the center of gravity moment envelope. Any combination of weight and balance falling within the envelope is allowable for flight.

COMMON ERRORS

Pilots just beginning to work weight and balance problems should learn to avoid the most common error. Oil is listed in the owner's manual and Pilot's Operating Handbook (POH) in quarts. We learn that oil weights 7.5 pounds per gallon. It is necessary to convert the POH value to gallons before multiplying.

The other error involves the fuel. The fuel weights 6 pounds per gallon. The *unusable* fuel weight is already included in the empty weight of the airplane. When multiplying to determine the weight of the fuel, use the *usable* fuel quantity. ✈

FAIR-WEATHER CUMULUS AND HIGH-ALTITUDE LENTICULARS OVER GUATEMALA CITY, GUATEMALA. SOME OF THE MOUNTAINS IN THE BACKGROUND ARE ACTIVE VOLCANOS. YOU WILL FIND MOUNTAIN FLYING IS THE SAME ALL OVER THE WORLD.

PART 1 PREFLIGHT   Chapter 7 - The Magnetic Compass

Chapter 7—THE MAGNETIC COMPASS

- ➤ MAGNET 1-97
- ➤ MAGNETIC DIP 1-98
- ➤ MAGNETIC COMPASS CONSTRUCTION 1-98
- ➤ COMPASS ERRORS 1-99

The magnetic compass is essential for flying from one point to another. The reliability of the compass is compromised when the pilot does not understand the four compass errors known as *variation, deviation, oscillation* and *magnetic dip*.

MAGNET

Any metal having the ability to attract another metal is a magnet. Magnets produce a force field. The force field lines are closed loops radiating from the north pole to the south pole on the outside of the magnet. The earth itself is a

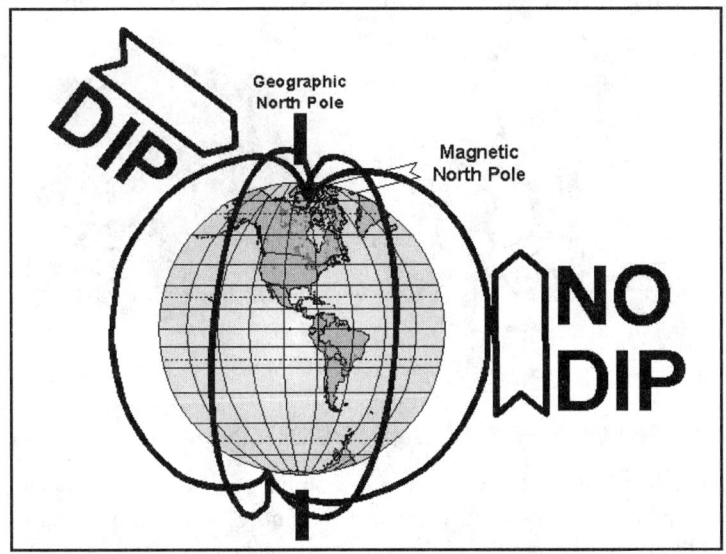

MAGNETIC DIP IS THE RESULT OF THE COMPASS NEEDLES TRYING TO POINT DOWN AS WELL AS TOWARD THE MAGNETIC NORTH POLE.

Mountain Flying Bible

Chapter 7 - The Magnetic Compass   Part 1 PREFLIGHT

magnet and has this force field. The earth's north magnetic pole—called the North Magnetic Dip Pole—is the location where the north-seeking end of a compass needle will point straight into the ground.

MAGNETIC DIP

The compass is the only direction-seeking instrument in the cockpit; it is important to understand the errors that can affect accurate navigation. Northerly turning error and acceleration error are caused when the magnetic needles of the compass align themselves parallel to the earth's magnetic lines of force.

A basic understanding of magnetism is required to appreciate compass errors. Evidence shows the earth is surrounded by a magnetic field with lines of force flowing from the north pole in all directions, bending to return to the south pole. The needles in the magnetic compass parallel the earth's surface at the magnetic equator, where the earth's lines of force have a vertical component of zero. As the compass is moved closer to the magnetic pole (either north or south), the vertical component or pull of the lines of force increase (to 100 percent at the pole itself). This causes the magnetic compass needles to assume the same direction and position as the line of force. The needles point downward as well as toward the magnetic pole.

The property of the compass needles pointing toward and down to the magnetic pole (paralleling the lines of force) is known as magnetic dip.

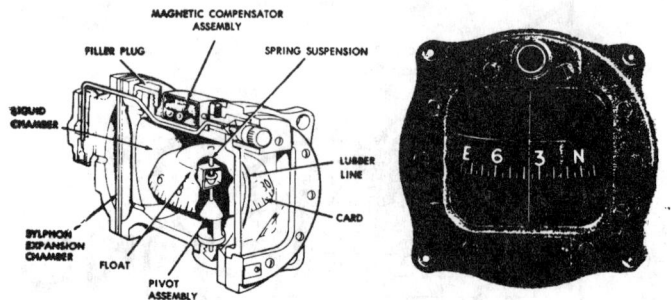

MAGNETIC COMPASS

MAGNETIC COMPASS CONSTRUCTION

The magnetic compass consists of a chamber enclosing two magnetic needles that have been attached to a float assembly. The compass card wraps around the float. This card has letters for cardinal headings and each 30-degree interval is represented by a number with the zero omitted. Between the numbers, vertical lines graduate the card into 5-degree increments.

1-98   *Mountain Flying Bible*

PART 1 PREFLIGHT   Chapter 7 - The Magnetic Compass

The chamber, with an expansion diaphragm, is filled with an acid-free white kerosene to provide lubrication of the jewel bearings used to mount the float assembly on the pedestal. The kerosene also dampens excessive oscillations and provides buoyancy to the card, reducing its weight on the bearings.

The front of the compass has a glass face with a lubber line to read the compass direction.

The compass is adjustable with small screws attached to compensating magnets. A process known as *swinging the compass* is used to adjust the compass if new equipment is installed or if hard landings make it unreliable.

Remember that because the airplane rotates around the magnetic compass, its indication—the compass card—reads opposite of the heading indicator. If the magnetic reading is 10 degrees to the right of E, the compass reading is 80 degrees. This is contrary to the way we normally read and interpret numbers.

COMPASS ERRORS

Courses are drawn on aeronautical charts and measured in relation to meridians of longitude. This course is the true course. The aircraft is flown from point-to-point using the magnetic compass as a reference. The pilot must make an allowance for the difference in location of the geographic and magnetic poles. This difference is known as variation.

VARIATION

Lines of equal magnetic declination called *variation* are plotted on the chart as isogonic lines. These lines are labeled in degrees east and west to represent whether the magnetic compass points to the east of true north (geographic north pole) or west of true north.

The line connecting points of zero-degree variation is called the *agonic line*. These lines are re-plotted periodically on aeronautical charts to correct any changes that may have occurred as a result of the shifting of the magnetic pole or any changes caused by local magnetic disturbances.

Variation results from the angle between the true geographical north pole and the magnetic north pole. This occurs when flying anywhere other than along the agonic line. The compass needle always points toward the magnetic north pole. The magnetic north pole is about 700 miles south of the geographical north pole. The magnetic north pole is located in Canada at 78.3-degrees north latitude and 104.0-degrees west longitude in 1994.

The earth's magnetic field changes with time. The rate of change averages 11.6 km (6.3 nautical miles) per year. From 1831 to 1981 the North Magnetic Pole moved 800 km.

Mountain Flying Bible

Chapter 7 - The Magnetic Compass Part 1 PREFLIGHT

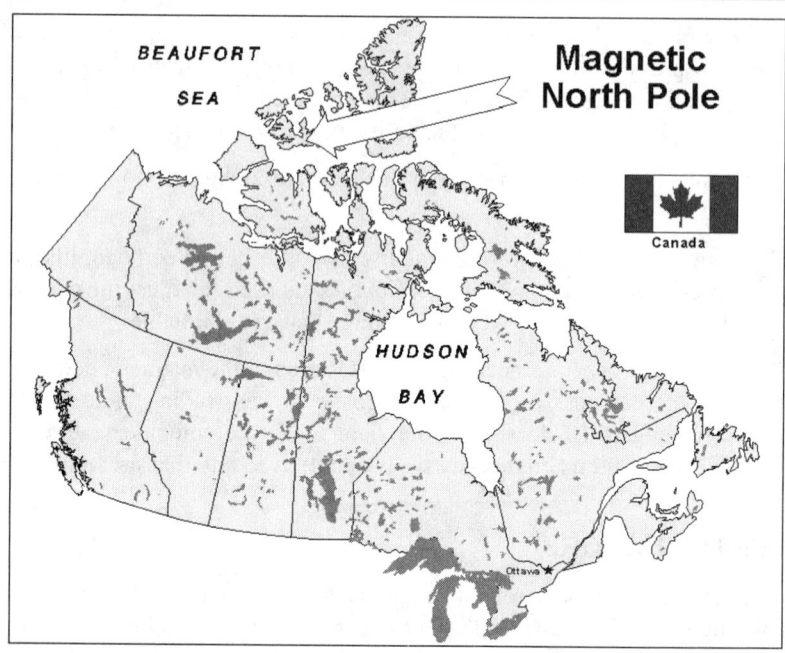

THE MAGNETIC NORTH POLE, IN EARLY 1994, WAS LOCATED ON ELLEF RINGNES ISLAND, CANADA, AT 78.3°N LATITUDE, 104.0°W LONGITUDE. THE LOCATION WAS FIRST PLOTTED IN 1831 BY J.C. ROSS. THE POLE HAS MOVED TO THE NORTHWEST AN AVERAGE OF 9.4 KM (5.84 STATUTE MILES, 5.08 NAUTICAL MILES) PER YEAR SINCE 1904.

The offset between the geographic and magnetic poles causes an angular difference between true and magnetic north at any point east or west of the agonic line. For example, an airplane flying true north over Denver, where there is about 12-degrees east variation, would result in the magnetic compass pointing 12-degrees to the right (east) of true north.

To plot courses on charts with the true north reference and fly the courses with a magnetic compass we add west variation and subtract east variation from the true course or the true heading in order to find the magnetic course or the magnetic heading. The memory aid, *east is least, west is best,* is helpful in remembering when to add or subtract variation.

RULE OF THUMB – East is least, west is best.

Using the true course, subtract east variation or add west variation to obtain the magnetic course.

Mountain Flying Bible

PART 1 PREFLIGHT   Chapter 7 - The Magnetic Compass

DEVIATION—

Magnetic disturbances arising from magnetic fields generated by airplane radios and other electrical equipment can cause deviation, a condition where the magnetic compass needles are diverted from their normal alignment with the lines of force. sometimes, if the compass receives a jolt from a hard landing, it will change the magnetism of the needles.

To compensate for deviation (or changed magnetism of the needles), "swinging the compass" is performed, adjusting out most of the error. That deviation that remains after swinging the compass is written on a compass correction card that is attached on or near the compass.

OSCILLATION ERROR —

When flying in turbulence, the compass card swings back and forth. This is called oscillation. Oscillation can also be caused by rough pilot technique or jerky movements on the airplane controls.

MAGNETIC DIP —

Magnetic dip results when the needles of the magnetic compass try to parallel the earth's lines of force as well as align themselves toward the magnetic pole. The force is zero at the equator and increases to 100 percent at the poles.

When the needles dip they are limited in their movement about 18 degrees due to the construction of the float assembly and pedestal. Beyond 18 degrees the card rubs and retards its movement any further.

The design of the magnetic compass allows it to work properly when the airplane is horizontal to the plane of the earth. When the airplane banks, it allows magnetic dip to influence the compass reading. Magnetic dip causes two errors known as *northerly turning error* and *acceleration error*.

NORTHERLY TURNING ERROR

The center of gravity of the card in the magnetic compass is below the pivot point where the float assembly is balanced on the pedestal. When banking the airplane this allows the card to also bank due to centrifugal force. When the card is banked, it allows its alignment with the magnetic lines of force, creating an erroneous indication of a turn.

The compass gives an indication of a turn in the opposite direction when turning *from* north. It lags behind the actual turn rate when turning *to* north. When making a turn *to* or *from* south, it gives an indication of a turn in the correct direction, but at a much faster rate than is actually occurring.

Northerly turning error does not occur on headings of east or west. If the card dips, it still reads east or west because there is no turning associated with the dip.

Mountain Flying Bible

Chapter 7 - The Magnetic Compass						Part 1 PREFLIGHT

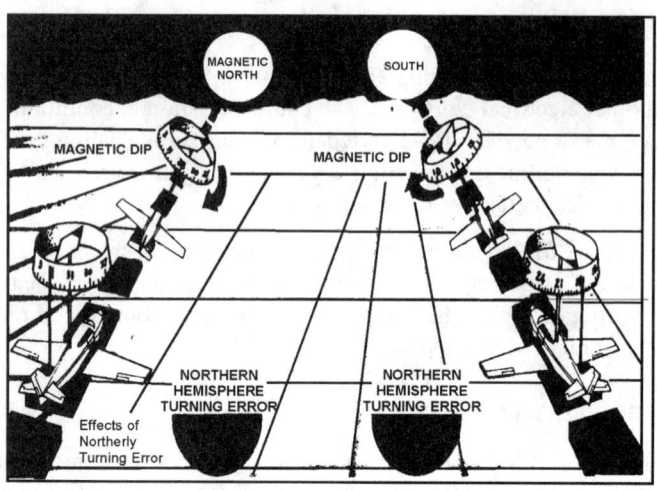

NORTHERLY TURNING ERROR IS DUE TO MAGNETIC DIP.

The dip error (northerly turning error) is greatest when headed north or south and the bank allows the dip to turn to the compass card.

Northerly Turning Error—LAG

While making a turn to or from the north, there is an erroneous reading on the compass. To visualize what follows, it is necessary to understand the construction and operation of the compass card. N on the compass card is on the south end of the compass needles. If the airplane is flying N, east is physically to the right. On the compass card east is to the left. If you turn to the right, towards east, the compass keeps pointing toward north because of lag, or the tendency of the compass needles to point downward (paralleling the lines of force) as well as toward the magnetic north pole. The aircraft rotates about the compass. When on a heading of east, the E of the compass shows under the lubber line (assuming the bank angle has not exceeded 15-18 degrees).

The aircraft on the left side of this figure is flying toward the magnetic north pole. The compass card is constructed so that when the airplane is headed north, west is on the right side. If the airplane pivots around the compass to the left, it indicates west on the compass card. When the airplane banks, it allows the compass needles to align themselves with the earth's lines of force. In this case the airplane is turning to the right, but the compass card rotates to indicate a turn in the opposite direction, toward the west.

Do not exceed a 15-degree to 18-degree bank when using the magnetic compass for turns. This prevents the compass card from rubbing and minimizes the magnetic dip error.

PART 1 PREFLIGHT   Chapter 7 - The Magnetic Compass

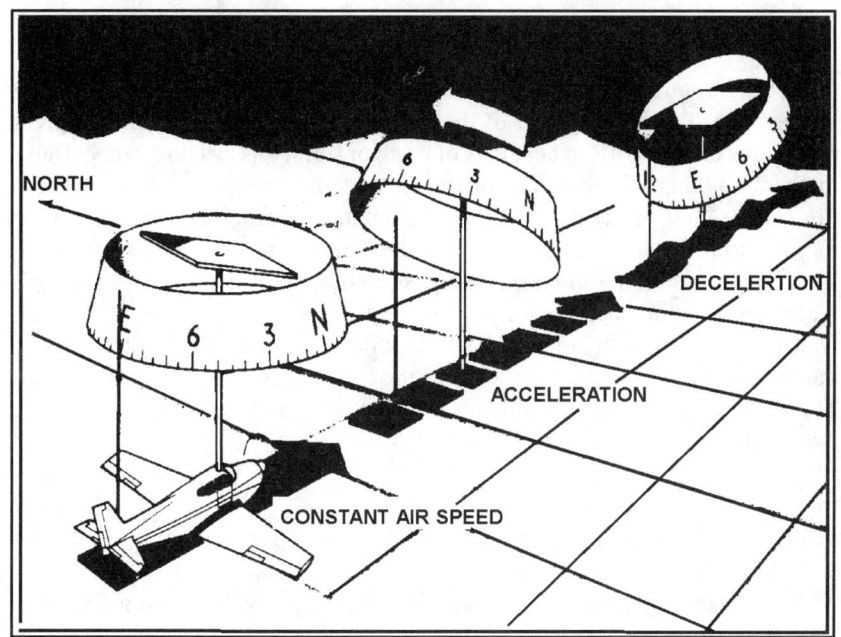

Part 1

ACCELERATION ERROR IS DUE TO MAGNETIC DIP

PREFLIGHT

- Chapter 1—BASIC PREMISES 1-3
- Chapter 2—CONSIDERATIONS 1-9
- Chapter 3—PREPLANNING 1-37
- Chapter 4—WEATHER 1-53
- Chapter 5—AIRPLANE 1-71
- Chapter 6—WEIGHT AND BALANCE 1-89
- Chapter 7—THE MAGNETIC COMPASS 1-95
- Chapter 8—THE AIRSPEED INDICATOR 1-103
- Chapter 9—THE ALTIMETER 1-109
- Part 1—RULES OF THUMB 1-113

Flying, especially in the mountains, requires a total commitment that becomes the ultimate challenge of exploring yourself, your airplane, the terrain and the elements. You must have some basic knowledge and appreciation of each of these before attempting mountain flight.

Chapter 7 - The Magnetic Compass   Part 1 PREFLIGHT

ACCELERATION ERROR

Acceleration error acts just the opposite of northerly turning error. With acceleration, the forward part of the compass card, located below the pivot point, dips downward. On headings of north or south this has no effect because the card aligning with the lines of force maintains the same direction indication. On headings of east or west, an acceleration causing the forward part of the card to point downward, will allow the compass needles to align with the lines of force changing the compass indication as the card rotates. Acceleration will cause an erroneous indication of a turn to the north. Deceleration, where the rear of the card points downward gives an erroneous indication of a turn toward the south as the card aligns with the lines of force. There's an easy way to remember this, ANDS, means Accelerate, North error; Decelerate, South error.

SUMMARY

Follow these recommendations to minimize compass errors.

- ☐ Using the magnetic compass on headings near north or south, it is important to maintain the wings level until all oscillation disappears.
- ☐ Using the magnetic compass while heading east or west requires a constant airspeed (level flight, climb or descent).
- ☐ On intermediate headings, to use the compass, maintain wings level and unaccelerated flight.
- ☐ Avoid placing flashlights or other metal objects that may induce deviation near the compass . ✈

Good judgement comes from experience, experience comes from bad judgement

Mountain Flying Bible

PART 1 PREFLIGHT   Chapter 8 - The Airspeed Indicator

CHAPTER 8—AIRSPEED INDICATOR

- ➢ HIGH ALTITUDE VERSUS INDICATED AIRSPEED 1-105
- ➢ DETERMINING TRUE AIRSPEED 1-106
- ➢ AIRSPEED MARKINGS (REQUIRED) 1-106
- ➢ OTHER AIRSPEED LIMITATIONS 1-107
- ➢ V SPEEDS (V=VELOCITY) 1-108

I have never felt that it is necessary to memorize stalling speeds; but it is wise to know the ballpark figure of the indicated airspeed for stalling in various configurations (with flaps retracted or extended, and if applicable, with the gear retracted or extended) in level flight and during banked turns.

The airplane stalls at the same indicated airspeed at all altitudes in a given flight condition. For example, if the airplane stalls at 50 knots *indicated* airspeed at sea level during a slow deceleration, power-off and level flight, then it will stall at the same indicated airspeed at high altitudes under the same flight conditions, even though the true airspeed is greater.

HIGH-ALTITUDE OPERATION VERSUS INDICATED AIRSPEED

The indicated airspeed and true airspeed are the same at sea level under standard conditions of pressure and temperature, assuming the airspeed indicator is properly calibrated. As the airplane climbs above sea level, the indicated airspeed will be of a lesser value than the true airspeed.

The airspeed indictor works on the principle of a pitot tube directing air to a Bourdon tube inside the airspeed indicator case. This tube—similar to a party whistle—expands (unrolls) and contracts, depending on the airflow, to show increasing or decreasing airspeed.

An airplane flying at 70 knots indicated airspeed at sea level has a true airspeed of 70 knots (again, assuming the airspeed indicator is properly calibrated). At 10,000 feet the same airplane flying at 70 knots *true* airspeed will have an indicated airspeed of approximately 58 knots. The air is less dense and its impact on the Bourdon tube is less, resulting in the reduced indicated airspeed reading.

Mountain Flying Bible

Chapter 8 - The Airspeed Indicator   Part 1 PREFLIGHT

For the takeoff, or for the approach to landing, at an airport with a high density altitude, use the same takeoff indicated airspeed or approach indicated airspeed that you use at a sea level strip. There is a *built-in* compensating factor that automatically adjusts for the reduced air density of higher altitudes.

We know it is necessary to have a higher true airspeed for operating at high elevation airports to compensate for the thinner air. The thin air affects the lift of the wings, the power output of the engine and the thrust of the propeller. The high-altitude thin air causes the airplane to stall at a higher *true* airspeed. But, with the built-in safety factor there is no complicated mathematical formula to remember. The airplane is flying approximately two percent per thousand feet above sea level faster than the indicated airspeed.

 Assume an airplane at sea level accelerates for takeoff. If the airspeed indicator is calibrated properly, when the airplane reaches 60 knots, the airspeed indicator reads 60 knots. Next, take the same airplane to 5,000-feet msl. Begin the takeoff roll. As the airplane accelerates the airspeed indicator is influenced by the thinner, less dense air at altitude. The airplane must go faster to get the thin air to register 60 knots. When the airspeed registers 60 knots the airplane is actually going about 2 percent per 1,000 feet above sea level faster than indicated. In this case the true airspeed is about 72 knots when the airspeed indicator registers 60 knots. This is the built-in compensating factor that allows you to use the same indicated airspeed to rotate for takeoff or for approach to landing regardless of the density altitude of the airport.

DETERMINING TRUE AIRSPEED

 RULE OF THUMB to determine true airspeed

The true airspeed will be approximately 2 percent higher than the indicated airspeed for each 1,000 feet above sea level (add to the indicated airspeed 2 percent of the indicated airspeed for each 1,000 feet of altitude).

AIRSPEED MARKINGS (REQUIRED)

Airspeed indicators for all airplanes weighing 12,500 pounds or less and manufactured after 1945 are required by regulation to use a standard color-coded marking system for some of the operating limitations of the airplane. These markings are:

PART 1 PREFLIGHT   Chapter 8 - The Airspeed Indicator

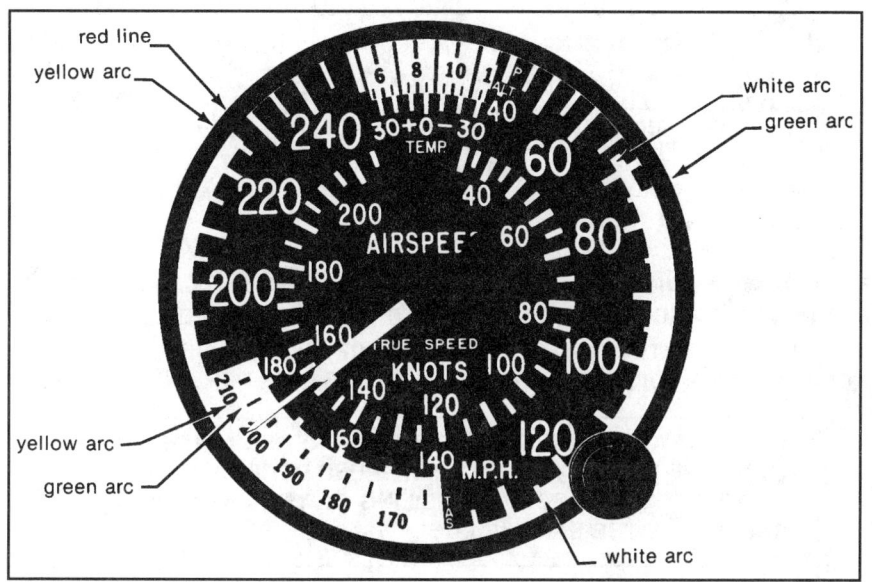

THE AIRSPEED INDICATOR

WHITE ARC—The white arc is the flap operating range. The lower limit of the white arc is the power-off stalling speed with the wing flaps and landing gear in the landing position. This is abbreviated V_{SO}. The upper limit of the white arc is the maximum flap extension speed or V_{FE}. Some airplanes allow partial extension of the flaps, 10 or 15 degrees, above this mark.

GREEN ARC—The green arc is the normal operating range. The lower limit of the green arc is the power-off stalling speed with the wing flaps and landing gear retracted, abbreviated as V_{S1}.

YELLOW ARC—The yellow arc is the caution range. The pilot should avoid this area unless in smooth air.

RED LINE—The red line, abbreviated V_{NE}, is the never exceed speed.. This is the maximum speed at which the airplane can be operated in smooth air. This speed should never be exceeded intentionally. The reason for avoiding speeds faster than the red line is due to flutter. Once flutter begins it propogates itself and tears the airplane apart.

OTHER AIRSPEED LIMITATIONS

There are other important airspeed limitations not marked on the face of the airspeed indicator. These speeds are generally found on placards in view of the pilot and in the Airplane Flight Manual, Owner's Handbook, or Pilot's Operating Handbook.

Chapter 8 - The Airspeed Indicator — Part 1 PREFLIGHT

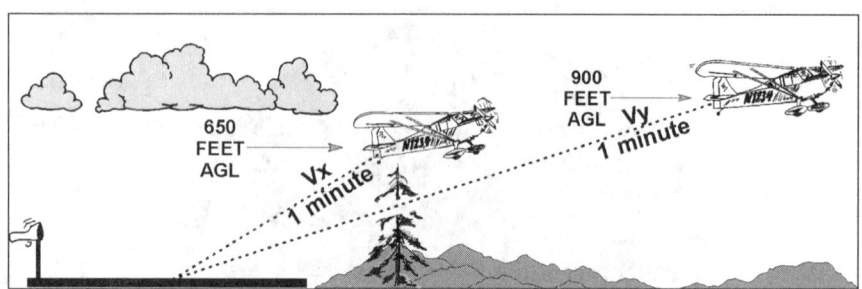

COMPARISON OF THE BEST ANGLE-OF-CLIMB SPEED, V_X, (THE GREATEST ALTITUDE GAIN PER DISTANCE) TO THE BEST RATE-OF-CLIMB SPEED, V_Y, (THE GREATEST ALTITUDE GAIN PER UNIT OF TIME).

> THE BEST ANGLE-OF-CLIMB SPEED INCREASES WITH ALTITUDE. THE BEST RATE-OF-CLIMB SPEED DECREASES WITH ALTITUDE. AT THE SERVICE CEILING OF THE AIRPLANE V_X AND V_Y ARE THE SAME VALUE.

MANEUVERING SPEED (V_A) is the maximum speed for operation during moderate or greater turbulence or for performing full-control movement maneuvers. (See V_A)

LANDING GEAR OPERATING SPEED (V_{LO}) is the maximum speed for operating the gear mechanism.

LANDING GEAR EXTENDED SPEED (V_{LE}) is the maximum speed for operating the airplane after the gear is down and locked.

BEST ANGLE OF CLIMB AIRSPEED (V_X) is the airspeed that will give the greatest amount of climb in a given distance.

BEST RATE OF CLIMB AIRSPEED (V_Y) is the speed that will give the most altitude gain per unit of time.

V SPEEDS (V = VELOCITY)

V_A means design maneuvering speed. This is the *rough air speed* and is the maximum speed for abrupt maneuvers or full-control deflection. If, during flight, rough air or moderate or severe turbulence is encountered, the airspeed should be reduced to maneuvering speed or less to minimize the stress on the airplane structure. Maneuvering speed is the speed that allows the airplane to relieve stress with an aerodynamic stall at around 3.8 gs. If you fly an older airplane without documentation of the maneuvering speed, use the value of 1.7 V_{SO}.

PART 1 PREFLIGHT — Chapter 8 - The Airspeed Indicator

V_C means design cruising speed.

V_D means design diving speed.

V_F means design flap speed.

V_{FE} means maximum flap extended speed. This is the upper limit of the white arc on the airspeed indicator.

V_{LE} means maximum landing gear extended speed. Once the gear is down and locked, this is the maximum speed for flight in this configuration.

V_{LO} means maximum landing gear operating speed.

V_{LOF} means lift-off speed.

V_{MC} means minimum control speed with the critical engine inoperative on multi-engine aircraft. This is determined at sea level with maximum allowable power, rear-most allowable CG, flaps in takeoff position, gear up and the inoperative engine windmilling. V_{MC} depends on and varies with power and CG. (See *Cold Weather Takeoffs*)

V_{NE} means never-exceed speed, this is the red line on the airspeed indicator.

V_R means rotation speed.

V_S means the stalling speed or the minimum steady flight speed at which the airplane is controllable.

V_{SO} means the stalling speed or the minimum steady flight speed in the landing configuration. Sometimes it is called the *stall speed dirty*, that is, with the gear down and locked and the flaps fully extended. It is the lower limit of the white arc on the airspeed indicator.

V_{S1} means the stalling speed or the minimum steady flight speed obtained in a specified configuration. *Stalling speed clean* is with the gear up and the flaps retracted. It is the lower limit of the green arc on the airspeed indicator.

V_X means the speed for the best angle of climb. Use this speed to clear obstructions. This speed, to the exclusion of all others, results in the greatest altitude gain in a given distance. This particular airspeed generally increases in value with an increase of altitude.

V_Y means the speed for the best rate of climb. Use it for normal operations. This speed, to the exclusion of any other, results in the greatest altitude gain in a given amount of time. The particular airspeed necessary to obtain V_Y generally decreases from the specified value with an increase of altitude.

POSITION ERROR

When the value of airspeed is read from the dial of the airspeed instrument it is called *indicated airspeed*. Indicated airspeed is the same as true airspeed at sea level under standard conditions, assuming no pitot position error.

Chapter 8 - The Airspeed Indicator   Part 1 PREFLIGHT

Airplanes manufactured before the mid-1970s have performance charts based on the *calibrated airspeed* (CAS) or *true indicated airspeed* (TIAS). There may be a large difference between the indicated airspeed (read from the dial) and the calibrated airspeed (providing performance), especially at low airspeed with a high angle of attack. This is because of installation error, often called position error.

Position error occurs because of the angle of the pitot tube to the air. At cruise airspeeds the pitot tube looks like the letter "O." At high angles of attack the pitot tube approaches the air looking like an oval. At a high angle of attack the ram air striking the pitot tube is restricted resulting in a pitot-static differential that causes the airspeed to read low. ✈

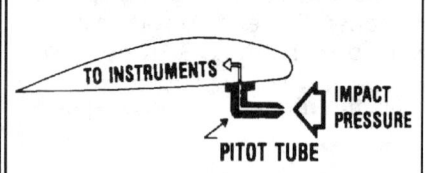
When the wing is flown at the cruise angle of attack, it allows the impact pressure to enter the pitot tube straight on.

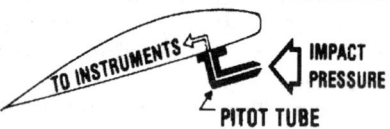
When the wing is flown at the slow flight angle of attack, it allows the impact pressure to enter the pitot tube at an angle.

CROSS-SECTION OF A WING

PITOT TUBE POSITION ERROR.

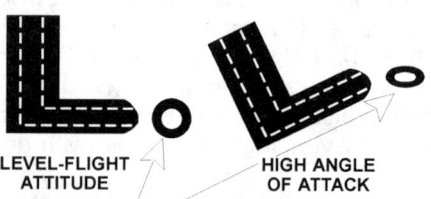

LEVEL-FLIGHT ATTITUDE   HIGH ANGLE OF ATTACK

FRONTAL VIEW OF THE COLLECTION END OF THE PITOT TUBE. IN LEVEL FLIGHT THE PITOT TUBE COLLECTS AIR IN ITS CIRCULAR OPENING. WHEN CLIMBING, THE PITOT TUBE FORMS AN ANGLE TO THE AIR THAT CUTS DOWN THE AMOUNT OF AIR ENTERING THE PITOT TUBE.

PART 1 PREFLIGHT — Chapter 9 - The Altimeter

CHAPTER 9—ALTIMETER

> ➤ TYPES OF ALTITUDE 1-111
> ➤ ALTIMETER OPERATION 1-112
> ➤ ALTIMETER ERRORS..1-112
> ➤ NON-STANDARD PRESSURE...1-113
> ➤ NON-STANDARD TEMPERATURE 1-114

TYPES OF ALTITUDE

Absolute altitude is the vertical distance of an aircraft above the terrain.

Calibrated altitude is the altitude read directly from the altimeter after being corrected for instrument errors.

Density altitude is the pressure altitude corrected for non-standard temperature variation. When conditions are standard, pressure altitude and density altitude are the same. If the temperature is above standard, the density altitude will be higher than pressure altitude. If the temperature is below standard, the density altitude will be lower than pressure altitude. This is an important altitude because it is directly related to the aircraft's takeoff and climb performance. My definition may lead to less confusion, "density altitude is the altitude the airplane thinks it is at and performs in accordance with."

Indicated altitude is that altitude read directly from the uncorrected altimeter after it is set to the current altimeter setting.

Pressure altitude is the altitude indicated when the altimeter setting window is adjusted to 29.92. This is the standard datum plane, a theoretical plane where air pressure corrected to 15-degrees Celsius is equal to 29.92 inches of mercury. Pressure altitude is used for computer solutions to determine density altitude, true altitude and true airspeed.

True altitude is the true vertical distance of the aircraft above sea level, the actual altitude. Airport, terrain, and obstacle elevations found on aeronautical charts are listed as a true altitude.

ALTIMETER OPERATION

Mechanical Discrepancy. Unless you examine the operation of the altimeter and think about its function as an altimeter in comparison to its setting mechanism, confusion might exist. The altitude indication functions in an inverse order with the pressure. At sea level, the pressure is at its greatest and the altimeter indicates zero. At higher altitudes, where the pressure is less, the altimeter indicates a higher reading. That's easy to understand. The confusion enters when setting the altimeter's Kollsman Window.

When the Kollsman value is turned down, the indicted altitude goes down. When the number is increased, the altitude increases. This is the opposite of the altimeter's function. What's going on? Suppose you park the airplane in the afternoon during a low pressure area with the altimeter set to 29.80 inches of mercury. The altimeter indicates the field elevation. Overnight a high pressure area moves in with the pressure now at 30.20 inches of mercury. When you check the altimeter, it reads 400 feet below the field elevation.

Remember that pressure works inversely to the altimeter indication, where higher pressure gives a lower altimeter indication. Subtract 29.80 from 30.20 and arrive at 0.40 difference. One inch of mercury approximates 1,000 feet, so 0.1 inch equals 100 feet. The 0.40 difference is the 400-foot difference in the altimeter reading. When the altimeter is changed from 29.80 to 30.20, moving up, the indicated altitude moves up.

When dealing with weather maps, you might find it useful to know that one inch of mercury is equal to 34 millibars.

ALTIMETER ERRORS

Not all altimeters are created equal. This is readily apparent when flying airplanes with duplicated instrument panels, one for the pilot and one for the copilot. It is easy to determine a large discrepancy between altimeters in this situation, and they may be within legal tolerance. You know one of the altimeters is in error, but which one. When flying with only one altimeter there is no way to know that it is functioning properly. Periodic checking and calibration is the only way.

Hysteresis or after effect is an error affecting the altimeter due to its lag in adjusting to various altitudes. An airplane sitting on the ramp for several hours or longer becomes "used-to" its surroundings. That is, the altimeter assumes a state of equilibrium. When taken to altitude, the pressure is less, and the altimeter requires time, maybe an hour or two, to reach another state of balance. As the altimeter adjusts, *drift* or a small increase in altitude occurs. The same thing happens on descent, with the indicated altitude remaining higher

PART 1 PREFLIGHT   Chapter 9 - The Altimeter

than the actual altitude until the period of adjustment transpires. The error, although real, is small enough not to cause concern.

The standard atmosphere is a hypothetical condition derived from averaging values of temperature and pressure. Theoretically the standard atmosphere exists when, at sea level, the temperature is 59-degrees Fahrenheit (15-degrees Celsius) and the pressure is 29.92 inches of mercury (1,013.2 millibars).

The altimeter was designed to operate in a standard atmosphere. Large errors can occur when it encounters nonstandard temperature or pressure.

NON-STANDARD PRESSURE

It is unusual to make a flight of any length and have the barometric pressure (altimeter setting) the same at the departure airport and at the destination airport. The pressure at the destination will be higher or lower than the departure station. If an airplane departs an airport having a high pressure area and proceeds to a destination with a low pressure area, without adjusting the altimeter to the current reported altimeter setting, the airplane will follow the *isobar* or line of equal

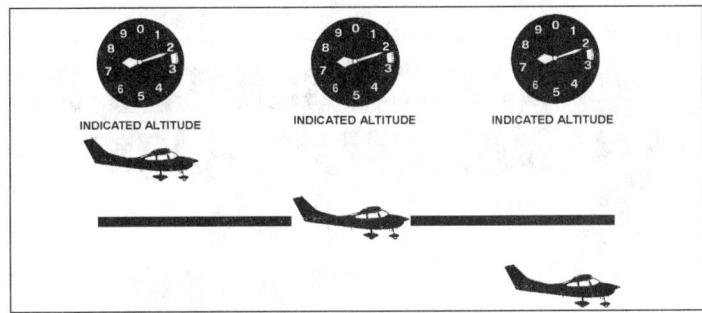

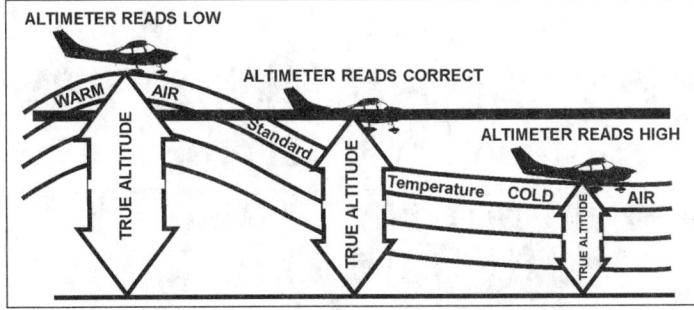

ALTIMETER ERROR DUE TO NON-STANDARD ATMOSPHERIC TEMPERATURE. WHEN THE TEMPERATURES LOWER EN ROUTE, THE AIRPLANE IS LOWER THAN THE ALTIMETER INDICATES. "WHEN FLYING FROM A HOT TO A COLD, LOOK OUT BELOW."

Mountain Flying Bible   1-113

Chapter 9 - The Altimeter   Part 1 PREFLIGHT

pressure. In this instance the airplane will be lower than the altimeter indicates. *When flying from a high to a low, look out below.*

NON-STANDARD TEMPERATURE

Temperature has a direct effect on the air density. Look at a hot air balloon. The hot air is less dense than the surrounding air as it lifts into the atmosphere. Under standard conditions the altimeter operates correctly with indicated altitude and true altitude being the same. When the air is warmer than standard, the altimeter can't compensate and it reads too low, that is, the airplane is at an altitude that is higher than the indicated altitude. The opposite is true for cold air. When the altimeter indicates too high, the airplane is physically lower than the indicated altitude. *When flying from a hot to a cold, look out below.*

 **RULE OF THUMB—Altimeter Indications.**

WHEN FLYING FROM A HIGH TO A LOW OR HOT TO COLD—LOOK OUT BELOW!

1-114   *Mountain Flying Bible*

PART 1 - PREFLIGHT— RULES OF THUMB

 BASIC PREMISE #1—ALWAYS REMAIN IN A POSITION WHERE YOU CAN TURN TO LOWERING TERRAIN. (See Page 1-5, 1-8)

 BASIC PREMISE #2—DO NOT FLY BEYOND THE POINT OF NO RETURN. (See Page 1-5, 1-8)

 RULE OF THUMB—Do not climb more than 10 minutes for each hour of en route flight time. (See Page 1-12)

 RULE OF THUMB—Add one minute for each 1,000 feet of climb altitude.

Use computed ground speed to calculate flight time. Add one minute per 1,000 feet of climb to the en route time for the first leg. (See Page 1-47)

 RULE OF THUMB-Estimating Time (See Page 1-52)

 RULE OF THUMB—The takeoff distance varies with the square of the gross weight. (See Page 1-92)

 RULE OF THUMB—East is least, west is best.

Use the true course and subtract east variation or add west variation to obtain the magnetic course. (See Page 1-100)

 RULE OF THUMB to determine true airspeed.

Add two percent for each 1,000 feet above sea level to the indicated airspeed to determine true airspeed. (See Page 1-106)

Chapter 9 - The Altimeter   Part 1 PREFLIGHT

 **RULE OF THUMB—Altimeter Indications.**

When flying from a high to a low or a hot to a cold—look out below. The airplane is lower than the altimeter indicates. (See Page 1-114)

RULE OF THUMB - CONVERTING CELSIUS TO FAHRENHEIT

Double the Celsius temperature and add 30°. This rule is only an approximation.

CELSIUS	FAHRENHEIT	CONVERTED
-40°C	-40°F	-50°F
-30°C	-22°F	-30°F
-20°C	-04°F	-10°F
-10°C	+14°F	+10°F
+00°C	+32°F	+30°F
+10°C	+50°F	+50°F
+15°C	+59°F	+60°F
+20°C	+68°F	+70°F
+30°C	+86°F	+90°F
+40°C	+104°F	+110°F

ALTHOUGH THIS TEMPERATURE CONVERSION RULE OF THUMB IS NOT EXACT, IN THE NORMAL TEMPERATURE RANGE THAT IS USED (FROM +10°F TO +90°F) ON A DAILY BASIS, THIS CONVERSION RESULTS IN A DERIVED TEMPERATURE SUITABLE FOR US TO GAIN AN IDEA OF THE ACTUAL TEMPERATURE AS WE RELATE TO IT ON THE FAHRENHEIT SCALE.

For an exact conversion, double the temperature in Celsius, subtract 10% and add 32. Example: 15°C = ?°F.

15 + 15 = 30 − 10% = 27 + 32 = 59°F

PART 2 TAKEOFF — Introduction

INTRODUCTION

Part 2
TAKEOFF

- CHAPTER 1 – TAXIING 2-3
- CHAPTER 2 – AIRCRAFT PERFORMANCE 2-7
- CHAPTER 3 – ENGINE OPERATION 2-21
- CHAPTER 4 – TAKEOFFS 2-37
- CHAPTER 5 – AFTER TAKEOFF 2-67
- PART 2 - RULES OF THUMB 2-73

INTRODUCTION

The takeoff associated with mountain flying varies little from the takeoff at lower elevations with more hospitable terrain. You might be exposed so some new and more efficient techniques as you peruse the following information.

The techniques described are not new and revealing. They have been deduced over many years by pilots trying to gain the greatest safety and efficiency from the planes in an unforgiving environment devoid of mercy when the wrong technique is used.

Some mountain airstrips have been designated "one-way" strips. For example, if the strip is oriented north-to-south with high terrain adjacent to the north end, then all landing approaches will be to the north.

TAKEOFF FROM RUNWAY 35, JOHNSON CREEK AIRPORT, IDAHO. ELEVATION 4,933. NOTE: ELEVATION RISES TO SOUTH, RECOMMEND TAKEOFF RUNWAY 35.

Mountain Flying Bible

Introduction — PART 2 TAKEOFF

All takeoffs will be to the south. Airspeed control and the use of the spot method are critical to landing the airplane where you want or need to land on a short runway. Do not try to make a go-around once you are committed to land on a one-way strip.

For example, if the approach has resulted in the airplane being too high to land near the end of the runway, it may be proper to go ahead and land even though you know the airplane will overrun the runway and experience damage. Get the airplane on the ground and begin decelerating. The damage encountered while decelerating is nothing in comparison to the damage when you try to go-around from a one-way strip and crash at flying speed.

Mountain airstrip operations demand expertise for each takeoff. Before cranking the engine consider the control manipulation and coordination that will be required to compensate for updrafts, downdrafts, turbulence and crosswind conditions. ✈

IMPROPER GROUND OPERATIONS CAN BE COSTLY. USE CAUTION WHEN TAXIING BEHIND OTHER AIRPLANES. USE DIFFERENTIAL BRAKING TO TURN IN TIGHT AREAS. USE A TAXI SPEED CONSISTENT WITH SAFETY. POSITION THE FLIGHT CONTROLS FOR THE EXISTING WIND CONDITION. DO NOT MAKE LOCKED-WHEEL TURNS.

PART 2 TAKEOFF — Chapter 1 - Taxiing

CHAPTER 1 - TAXIING

- THROTTLE 2-3
- CARBURETOR HEAT 2-3
- THUMBS UP TAXIING 2-4
- DOWNWIND TAXIING 2-5
- COLD WEATHER TAXI OPERATIONS 2-5

THROTTLE USAGE

Treat the throttle with respect whether the airplane is on the ground or in the air. Occasionally after parking the airplane, the airplane will settle and the wheels may create small dimples in the ground. When you try to taxi, the airplane may refuse to budge. Full throttle should never be used to break the resistance. Use partial power while moving all the control surfaces. The elevator and rudder are the most effective.

If it has been raining and the airplane is parked with the propeller over a puddle of water, push the airplane to an area void of puddles. If not, once the engine starts the spinning propeller creates a low-pressure area. Water droplets can be pulled to the lower arc of the propeller in a funnel that resembles a miniature tornado. When the prop strikes the water droplets they can be fully as destructive as rocks causing the leading edge of the prop to resemble a chain saw blade.

CARBURETOR HEAT USAGE

Application of carburetor heat shunts the air filter allowing unfiltered air to enter the carburetor. Do not use carb heat in an area of dust or sand. Occasionally it is necessary to taxi through an area of dust, sand or gravel to reach the takeoff position. Try to avoid slow-speed taxi through these areas. If there is an extensive area of dust or sand, perform the before takeoff engine runup during the taxi to blow the dirt back away from the engine air intake.

If caught in a dust storm or sandstorm while airborne, do not use the carburetor heat. There are times when the dust or sand is so thick that it plugs the air filter and the engine will not run without air. In this case it will be necessary to use carb heat (or alternate air if fuel injected). Shut down as soon as possible after landing and change the oil, oil filter and air filter.

Chapter 1 - Taxiing PART 2 TAKEOFF

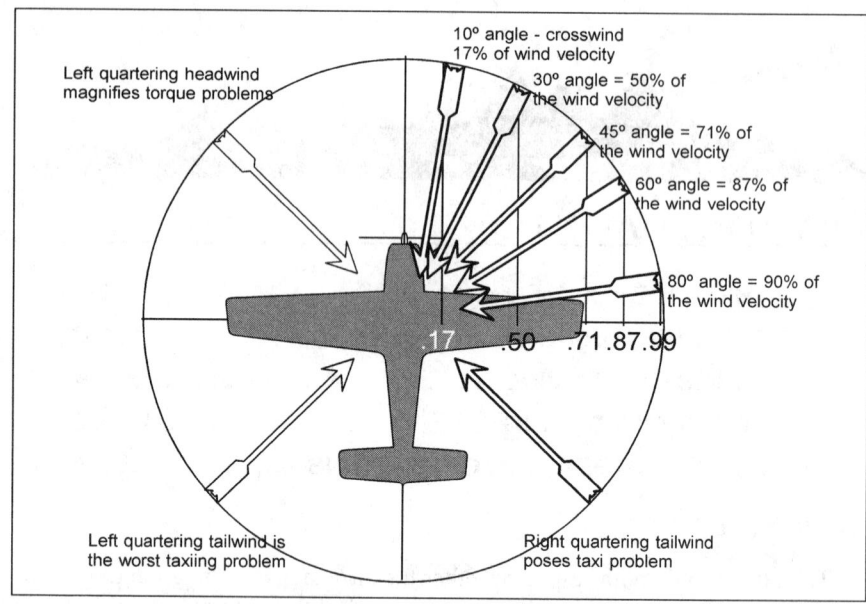

WIND CIRCLE - THE CROSSWIND EFFECT CAN BE DETERMINED BY APPLYING THE VALUES IN THE UPPER RIGHT QUADRANT TO ANY OTHER QUADRANT. IN THE LOWER QUADRANTS THE 10° ANGLE BEGINS TO THE LEFT OR RIGHT OF THE TAIL. FOR EXAMPLE, A 30° CROSSWIND TO THE LEFT OF THE TAIL WOULD BE EQUAL TO 50% OF THE WIND VELOCITY.

THUMBS UP TAXIING

Improper ground handling of the airplane under the influence of a surface wind can result in weather cocking, ground looping, nosing over or tipping over. When taxiing in a crosswind, the wind flows under the windward wing and tries to flip the plane over. (The wind doesn't really try to tip the airplane over, but that's the effect.) For this reason the ailerons should be positioned to increase the lift of the downwind wing when taxiing into a quartering headwind or to block the wind from flowing under the wing when taxiing with a quartering tailwind.

Instead of trying to memorize this information or even taking the time to reason it out while taxiing, it is easier and faster to use the *thumbs up technique*. Stick your thumb up vertically while holding the control wheel (stick) in the neutral position, and then parallel the wind with your thumb.

For example, with a left-quartering tailwind or a right-quartering headwind, paralleling the wind with the thumb results in the control wheel being turned to the right. This places the left aileron down, blocking the left-quartering tailwind or increasing lift to oppose the right-quartering headwind. The right aileron moves up when the control wheel is turned to the right.

PART 2 TAKEOFF   **Chapter 1 - Taxiing**

THUMBS-UP METHOD - PARALLEL THE WIND WITH YOUR THUMB TO PROPERLY POSITION THE AILERONS DURING CROSSWIND TAXIING.

The memory aid "up-right" works well when performing the "Before Takeoff" control movement check. This check is especially appropriate after maintenance. It means that if the control wheel is turned to the right, the right aileron is positioned up, therefore, the "up-right."

The left-quartering tailwind provides more airflow under the right wing to oppose the tipping tendency when the control wheel is turned right. The down aileron of the left wing blocks some of the airflow to the left wing. Paralleling the wind with your thumb does all this thinking automatically. Similarly, paralleling the wind with the thumb in a left quartering headwind or a right quartering tailwind causes you to turn the control wheel left, automatically positioning the ailerons. This thumbs-up method works especially well when making a clearing turn on the ground before takeoff; just keep the thumb paralleling the wind.

DOWNWIND TAXIING

A strong quartering tailwind requires extra caution when taxiing. It is easy to acquire excess taxi speed that can result in tipping over when making the turn to the runway. Fuel in partially filled tanks will slosh to the outside of the turn to add to this tipping tendency. Eliminate the risk of tipping over by avoiding sudden bursts of the throttle, sharp braking and excess speed when taxiing downwind.

COLD WEATHER TAXI OPERATIONS

Clean the windshield of snow and ice before attempting taxi operations. This might not be as simple as it sounds during cold weather. Aircraft windows made of plastic will not withstand the scraping and pounding that automobile glass

Chapter 1 - Taxiing   PART 2 TAKEOFF

windows allow, without the possibility of serious damage. Putting the airplane in a heated hangar or applying isopropyl alcohol onto the windows may be your only solution.

Airplanes and surface vehicles have a habit of not being parked in their proper positions when snow and ice obscure ground markings. Use extra caution when taxiing near other airplanes. Lead all turns to allow for slipping.

Operations on wheels are difficult in deep snow and on packed snow or ice. Braking action is generally poor to nil, unless the temperature is well below zero.

During cold weather operations, special attention should be given to avoidance of snow banks along the sides of runways; they may be frozen solid. Pilots feel they can taxi through the small snow piles or wind rows caused by plowing operations. When snow is plowed, it compacts. Trying to taxi through these small piles may cause an abrupt halt. Even if the airplane passes through the pile, snow may pack into the wheels and brakes or the propeller may pick up a small piece of ice that causes damage.

Use the brakes as little as possible while taxiing. The heat of friction can warm the brake assembly sufficiently to allow prop blasted snow to melt and freeze the brakes after takeoff.

- Taxi on bare ground or snow-covered ground as opposed to ice. If the taxiway is ice covered, stay on the upwind side.
- Check the heater operation before takeoff. Gasoline cabin heaters should be run at reduced output so they do not overheat and pop an inaccessible circuit breaker.
- Run the engine several minutes from each fuel tank to assure yourself that ice does not obstruct a line.
- Be mentally alert for carbon monoxide (CO) contamination. Although CO is a tasteless, odorless, colorless gas, it is the product of combustion. If exhaust fumes are detected, determine their source and correct the problem before flight.
- With very cold surface-level temperatures, spend as little time as practical on the ground. Climbing after takeoff may place the airplane in a warmer temperature environment because of an inversion.
- Under certain ice conditions it may be impossible to perform a run-up while parked because of slippery conditions. Under these circumstances, plan to do the run-up while taxiing, if the wind and taxiway conditions allow. ✈

Mountain Flying Bible

CHAPTER 2 – AIRCRAFT PERFORMANCE

- PERFORMANCE CHARTS 2-7
- COLD AIR 2-8
- DENSITY ALTITUDE 2-8
- OTHER FACTORS. 2-15

Operating during a period of high outside temperature and low atmospheric pressure creates a high density altitude. An airplane performs in accordance with the altitude where it thinks it is flying, or the density altitude.

Airplanes aren't smart. They are easily fooled because they can't think. You have to think for the airplane. When you are exposed to high density altitude situations it is up to you to determine if the airplane has the required performance to make the takeoff and to outclimb the terrain once airborne. Remember density altitude is an expression of the thickness of the air. A high density altitude means the air is thin and this affects the engine performance, thrust of the propeller and lift of the wings. Let's look at Jackson, Wyo. with an elevation of 6,445 feet. Assume it is a beautiful day with the barometric pressure at 29.80 and temperature 92-degrees Fahrenheit. Under these conditions the density altitude is 9,752 feet. So, physically the airplane is at 6,445 feet, but performance-wise, it is a 9,752 feet in the standard atmosphere.

PERFORMANCE CHARTS

The performance charts provided with your airplane have changed from a sales tool of the early days of aviation to a usable and valuable set of figures. It used to be that a manufacturer could claim that their 85-horsepower "SkyCraft" would takeoff after a 146-foot ground run over a 50-foot obstacle from a 5,000-foot elevation airstrip on a 95°F day, with a 10-knot tailwind and loaded at the maximum allowable ground weight.

The manufacturer did not fib. The airplane actually did what was claimed. It did it with a professional pilot in an airplane with a new engine (no old gray mares) and under ideal conditions. The figure quoted was usually the best of several tries.

These numbers may have given the SkyCraft salesman an advantage over another airplane manufacturer whose test pilots were not as good. But, pity the poor (and foolishly optimistic) pilot in a 10-year-old SkyCraft that relies on these performance numbers for takeoff from a backcountry strip.

During the 1970-1980 period, the author participated in measuring aircraft takeoff distance and takeoff distance over a 50-foot obstacle for many makes and models of general aviation planes. The charts of all manufacturers provided surprisingly (to the author) accurate information, even for those airplanes with engines approaching overhaul.

You may want to leave a little room for error, but you will find the performance charts and graphs of these airplanes will provide you with reliable information. Use caution in placing total trust in the charts. They don't always provide the information you need to make accurate determinations (for example, there is no upslope information). If the charts cover the various parameters encountered for the computation, the information is likely to be valid.

COLD AIR

Cold air is heavy and dense providing the perfect medium for flying. Compared with warmer air, cold air gives the wings more lift, the engine more air (by weight) to provide power and the propeller more air (thicker) to produce thrust.

DENSITY ALTITUDE

The novice pilot who does not heed density altitude warnings, or even knowledgeable pilots who become complacent, often have a rude awakening when experiencing the effect of density altitude. Four variables, *altitude, pressure, temperature* and *humidity*, comprise density altitude. *Altitude* and pressure are used to determine the *pressure altitude*. The value of pressure altitude can be read directly from the altimeter when it is adjusted to 29.92 inches of mercury. Using a flight computer or calculator, non-standard temperature is applied to the pressure altitude to determine the value of density altitude.

Occasionally a pilot will confuse the term "high density altitude," thinking this means the airplane will perform well. The term means the air is experiencing a low density that is associated with a high altitude in the standard atmosphere.

When the altimeter setting is lower than 29.92 and the altimeter is adjusted (Kollsman window turned up) to obtain the pressure altitude, the pressure altitude will be higher than standard.

The pressure altitude can be determined without adjusting the altimeter. This is accomplished with the rule of thumb that 1-inch of mercury equals 1,000 feet.

 **RULE OF THUMB**—The altimeter setting's equivalent-feet values

1 inch of mercury equals 1,000 feet; 0.1 inch equals 100 feet; 0.01 inch equals 10 feet.

When the reported altimeter setting is lower than 29.92, subtract the setting from 29.92 and convert to equivalent feet of altitude. Add this value to the field elevation to obtain pressure altitude. EXAMPLE: The altimeter setting at Jackson, Wyo. is 29.66. What is the pressure altitude? Jackson's elevation is 6,445. Subtract 29.66 from 29.92 (0.26) and convert to 260 feet. Add 260 feet to the elevation and the pressure altitude is 6,675.

Conversely if the reported altimeter setting is higher than 29.92, subtract 29.92 from the altimeter setting. Subtract this value from the field elevation to obtain pressure altitude. EXAMPLE: The altimeter setting at Centennial airport, Denver, is 30.21. What is the pressure altitude? Subtract 29.92 from 30.21 to obtain 0.29. Convert this to 290 feet and subtract from Centennial's elevation of 5,883 to obtain the pressure altitude of 5,593.

There is an easy way to remember whether to add or subtract the equivalent feet of altitude value to or from the field elevation. If the altimeter is turned up, it results in a higher indicated altitude; add the equivalent feet. If the altimeter is turned down, it results in a lower indicated altitude; subtract the equivalent feet. (See page 1-112, ALTIMETER OPERATION)

If one considers only the effect of pressure altitude on the performance of the airplane, the takeoff distance, rate of climb and landing distance will change very little. This may lull one into ignoring density altitude when the combined effects of altitude, pressure, temperature and humidity may present a completely different picture requiring serious consideration.

EFFECT OF ALTITUDE

The operating altitude can be increased by flying to a field with a higher elevation or by operating at a field with nonstandard higher temperature. In either case the air density is decreased resulting in increased takeoff and landing distances and a decrease in the rate of climb.

EFFECT OF TEMPERATURE

Heated air expands reducing its density. A decrease in density will have a pronounced effect of flight.

EFFECT OF HIGH HUMIDITY

A pilot determines to fly an hour or two over the weekend to maintain currency. He goes out on a beautiful Saturday and stays in the pattern. On Sunday,

Chapter 2 - Aircraft Performance   PART 2 TAKEOFF

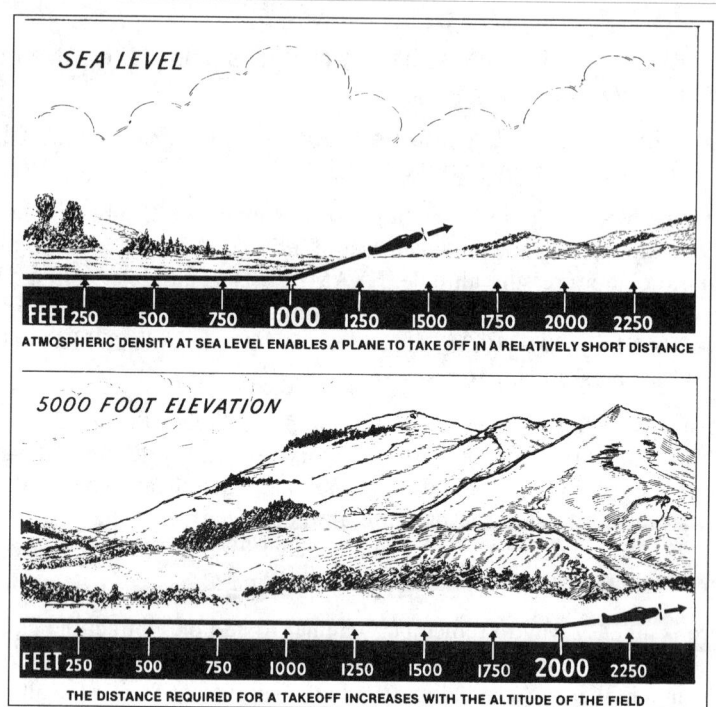

LOSS OF AIRCRAFT PERFORMANCE DURING HOT WEATHER

the weather has changed to a light mist with occasional rain. The pilot perceives a noticeable change in the airplane's performance—for the better—while it is raining. He reasons that the moisture in the air has provided the extra performance. What he failed to consider was the temperature difference between Saturday and Sunday.

To dispel this common misconception that moist air is "thicker" than dry air, consider that air containing water vapor weighs approximately five-eighths as much as an equal volume of dry air.

The air is composed of about 21 percent oxygen. The molecular structure of oxygen is represented as O_2, meaning two atoms combined. The atomic weight unit (atu) of the "O" element is 16; therefore, O_2 weighs 32 atu.

Moisture in the atmosphere takes the form of H_2O. Two hydrogen (1 atu each) atoms combined with one oxygen atom. The molecular weight of water (H_2O) is 18 atu, compared to the molecular weight of oxygen (O_2) at 32 atu.

An equal amount of dry air will have greater density than moist air because only 21 percent of the air contains oxygen. If water is present, it must combine with some of the oxygen that is present.

When the temperature and pressure are the same, the air density varies inversely with the humidity. This means that as the humidity increases, the air density decreases; and, as the humidity decreases, the air density increases.

As air is heated its moisture-carrying ability increases. For each 20°F increase in temperature, the air's capacity for holding moisture is doubled. If the relative humidity is 80 percent on a hot day and again on a cool day, the air will contain more moisture on the hot day.

The aerodynamic effects of humidity have been mostly ignored because humidity affects the power output of the engine more than the aerodynamic efficiency of the wings. There is no rule of thumb for determining the effect of humidity on aircraft performance. If high humidity exists, add 10 percent to the computed takeoff distance. Anticipate a reduced rate of climb.

COMBINED EFFECT OF ALTITUDE, TEMPERATURE AND HUMIDITY ON FLIGHT

Even at near sea-level airports, density altitude affects an airplane. At mountain airports--with higher elevations--the effects of density altitude are more dramatic. When altitude, temperature and humidity are combined their adverse conditions are aggravated. BEWARE OF HIGH, HOT, HUMID CONDITIONS. The only way to guarantee that the aircraft performance is sufficient to deal with the condition is to check the Airplane Flight Manual, Owner's Manual, or Pilot's Operating Handbook to delve into the performance charts.

DENSITY ALTITUDE COMPUTATIONS

By now you should agree that high density altitudes not only can, but do affect the airplane's performance capabilities. What is needed now is some way to determine the density altitude and estimate its effects on the airplane's performance.

Density altitude is the pressure altitude corrected for non-standard temperature variation.

DENSITY ALTITUDE PROCEDURE

- Step 1 - To accurately determine the density altitude, an electronic calculator, flight calculator or flight computer is required. Obtain the pressure altitude. Pressure altitude is the value indicated on the altimeter when 29.92 is dialed into the Kollsman Window.
- Determine the outside air temperature.
- Compute the density altitude by imputing the pressure altitude and temperature.

Although not as accurate, a rule of thumb can be used for determining the density altitude that rarely results in errors of more than 200 or 300 feet.

 **RULE OF THUMB – Determine Density Altitude**

For each 10°F above or below standard temperature for the airport's elevation, add or subtract 600 feet to (from) the field's elevation.

For example, assume the pressure is 30.18 at the Centennial Airport (elevation 5,883), Denver, Colo. and the temperature is 87 degrees. To determine the standard temperature (in degrees Fahrenheit), multiply the altitude in thousands (5.883) by 3.5 (lapse rate) and subtract from 59 (standard sea level temperature).

Standard temperature at Centennial would be 59 minus 20.6 or 38.4°F. Subtract the standard temperature, 38.4, from that given (87), and the actual temperature is 48.6°F above standard. The rule states to add 600 feet for each 10 degrees above standard temperature (or subtract 600 for each 10 degrees below standard temperature). Multiply 4.86 (48.6 divided by 10 to determine the number of 10-degree intervals) by 600 feet to arrive at 2,916 feet. Add this to the field elevation, 5,883 plus 2,916, to equal 8,799 feet density altitude.

Using an electronic calculator the value is 8,613 feet density altitude. The rule of thumb is off 186 feet. Usually it is more accurate and rarely will it be off by 300 feet. The rule of thumb accuracy is sufficient to provide valid takeoff and rate of climb information.

The DENALT performance computer is helpful in determining the expected performance of the airplane under various density altitude conditions. The surprising thing is, it does not compute density altitude. This device provides an area to write down the sea-level takeoff distance and rate of climb for the airplane. By setting the temperature and moving to the pressure altitude, a factor can be obtained for the takeoff and rate of climb. Merely multiply the sea-level numbers by the factors to determine the takeoff distance and the rate of climb under the existing conditions of nonstandard temperature and pressure.

The DENALT performance computer can be purchased from aviation supply stores and mail order. It provides scales for both the fixed-pitch propeller airplane and the constant-speed propeller airplane.

DENSITY ALTITUDE FORMULA

For those pilots who like to play with computers, the density altitude formula is:

```
10 C=288.16
20 INPUT "Enter pressure altitude in feet" ,PA
30 INPUT "Do you want to use degrees C or degrees F? (D/F)" ,CF$
40 IF CF$="C" THEN 100 ELSE GOTO 200
```

| PART 2 TAKEOFF | Chapter 2 - Aircraft Performance |

```
50 IF CF$="F" THEN 200 ELSE 100
100 INPUT "Enter temperature in degrees Celsius",DC
150 GOTO 300
200 INPUT "Enter temperature in degrees Fahrenheit",DF
210 DC=(DF-32)/1.8
300 DA=(145426*(1-(((C-PA*.001981)/C)^5.2563/   ((273.16+DC)/c))
    ^.235))
310 DA=INT(DA)
320 PRINT "The density altitude is DA;" FEET
330 END
```

DENSITY ALTITUDE TAKEOFF DISTANCE

Having determined the density altitude from the computer or the rule of thumb, it does little for you unless you use the performance charts in the POH. There is a rule of thumb that is useful to determine the takeoff distance.

> Remember that these rules of thumb provide estimations of expected performance. Before relying on the rule of thumb, compare POH computations to the rule of thumb value to ascertain the applicability to your particular make and model airplane.

RULE OF THUMB—Fixed-Pitch Propeller Density Altitude Takeoff Distance

To the standard, sea level takeoff distance, add 12 percent for each 1,000 feet of density altitude up to 8,000 feet. Add an additional 20 percent for each additional 1,000 feet density altitude above 8,000 feet.

For example, a Cessna 172M operating at 2,300 pounds (maximum) gross weight requires 865 feet of ground roll for takeoff at sea level under standard conditions. This is obtained by looking in the Pilot's Operating Handbook in the Performance section at the "Takeoff Distance, Maximum Weight 2,300 Pounds" chart, and interpolating between the 10°C and 20°C listing. Using the same chart to determine the takeoff ground roll distance for a density altitude of 7,500 feet, we interpolate between 7,000 and 8,000 feet pressure altitude and between 0°C and 10°C. (1,505 feet ground roll at 0°C and 7,000 feet pressure altitude and 1,665 feet ground roll distance at 0°C and 8,000 feet pressure altitude. The mean is 1,585 feet.) The standard temperature at 7,500 feet is 32.25°F or 0.141°C. This manipulation of numbers gives us 1,586.8 feet ground roll for takeoff. This is a lot of mechanical work, which is subject to math errors.

Rule of thumb computation:
  Ground roll for takeoff at sea level under standard conditions = 865 feet
  Density altitude = 7,500 feet
  Percent increase = 7.5 times 12 = 90% (represented as .90)
  New takeoff distance = 865 + (865 x .90) = 1,643.5 feet

Chapter 2 - Aircraft Performance — PART 2 TAKEOFF

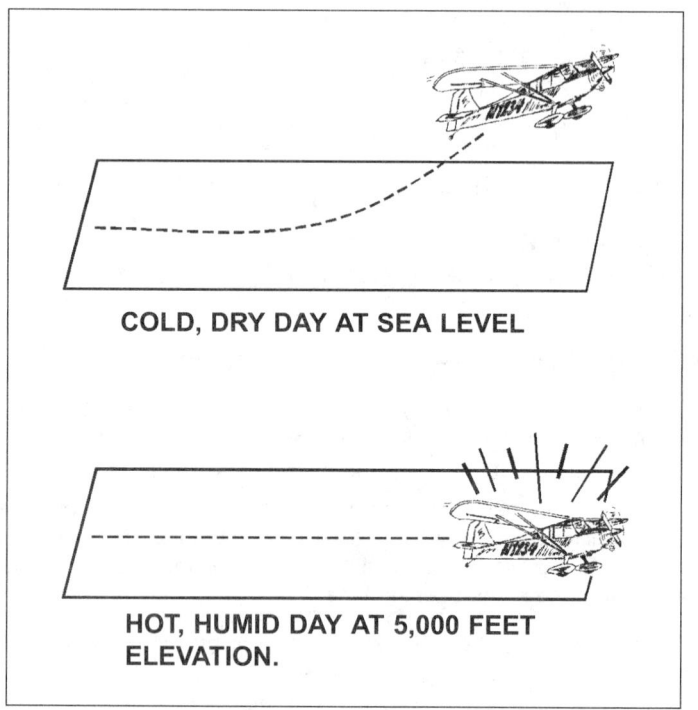

COMBINED EFFECT OF ALTITUDE, TEMPERATURE, AND MOISTURE ON THE TAKEOFF AND RATE OF CLIMB

THIN AIR REDUCES LIFT. HOT AIR AT HIGH ALTITUDE IS THIN. DO YOU REALIZE THAT KANSAS CITY AIRPORT, WITH AN ELEVATION OF 758 FEET ABOVE SEA LEVEL CAN HAVE AN EFFECTIVE ELEVATION IDENTICAL TO DENVER INTERNATIONAL AT 5,431 FEET ABOVE SEA LEVEL, UNDER CONDITIONS OF EXTREME HEAT AND LOW PRESSURE?

LARAMIE, WYOMING, AT 7,273 FEET CAN BE ABOVE THE SAFE OPERATIONAL ALTITUDE OF SOME AIRCRAFT DURING HOT WEATHER. THE EFFECTIVE ELEVATION AT 86°F IS 10,250 FEET.

THE RARIFIED AIR AT HIGHER ALTITUDE LOWERS THE EFFICIENCY OF THE ENGINE AND THE PROPELLER AND LESSENS A PLANE'S RATE OF CLIMB.

REMEMBER: ANY INCREASE IN OPERATING ALTITUDE, DUE TO ELEVATION, HIGH TEMPERATURE OR LOW PRESSURE WILL GREATLY INCREASE THE TAKEOFF AND THE LANDING ROLL.

DENSITY ALTITUDE IS THE ALTITUDE THE AIRPLANE THINKS IT IS AT AND PERFORMS IN ACCORDANCE WITH.

PART 2 TAKEOFF   **Chapter 2 - Aircraft Performance**

 **RULE OF THUMB—Constant-Speed (Variable Pitch) Propeller Density Altitude Takeoff Distance**

To the standard, sea level takeoff distance, add 10 percent for each 1,000 feet density altitude up to 8,000 feet. Add 15 percent for each additional 1,000 feet density altitude above 8,000 feet.

For example, a Cessna 180H, operating at maximum allowable gross weight, 2,800 pounds, under standard conditions at sea level requires 625 feet ground roll for takeoff. At 7,500 feet it requires 1,100 feet ground roll for takeoff.

Rule of thumb computation:

Ground roll for takeoff at sea level under standard conditions = 625 feet
Density altitude = 7,500 feet
Percent increase = 7.5 times 10 = 75% (represented as .75)
New takeoff distance = 625 + (625 x .75) = 1093.75 feet

Since this rule does not provide exact performance information, now is a good time to grab your owner's manual and determine if the rule if applicable to your airplane by working a few examples.

 **RULE OF THUMB—Density Altitude Rate of Climb—Fixed-Pitch Propeller Airplane**

Rule of thumb - fixed pitch props - Reduce sea level rate of climb 7% for each thousand feet density altitude up to 8,500 feet and 8% for each thousand feet above 8,500 feet.

 **RULE OF THUMB—Density Altitude Rate of Climb—Variable-Pitch Propeller Airplane**

Rule of thumb - variable pitch props - Reduce sea level rate of climb 6% for each thousand feet density altitude up to 8,500 feet and 8% for each thousand feet above 8,500 feet.

OTHER FACTORS

While density altitude is a good gauge of the performance you may expect, some other factors that require consideration for takeoff would be: gross weight, wind, humidity, runway surface, gradient, aircraft and engine condition, pilot skill and effect of local terrain.

Chapter 2 - Aircraft Performance   PART 2 TAKEOFF

GROSS WEIGHT

Because the takeoff distance varies with the square of the gross weight, there may be conditions of elevation, temperature, and tailwind operations that require an "off-load" of part of the useful load in order to obtain a margin of safety during takeoff from short mountain airstrips.

 Remember the takeoff distance varies with the square of the gross weight. A 10 percent increase in takeoff gross weight will cause:

- a 5 percent increase in the speed necessary for takeoff;
- at least a 9 percent decrease in acceleration; and,
- at least a 21 percent increase in takeoff distance.

Conversely, a 10 percent decrease in takeoff gross weight will cause:

- a 5 percent decrease in the speed necessary for takeoff;
- at least a 9 percent increase in acceleration; and,
- at least a 21 percent decrease in takeoff distance.

 **RULE OF THUMB**—The takeoff distance varies as the square of the gross weight.

Suppose you are operating a Cessna 172 at 2,000 pounds gross weight. The maximum allowable gross weight is 2,300 pounds. To obtain the percent of gross weight, divide the actual weight by the maximum allowable gross weight. You are operating at 2,000 pounds; divide this by the maximum, 2,300 and obtain 0.8695, or 0.87. Square this number, 0.87 x 0.87 equals 0.76. The takeoff distance is equal to 0.76 multiplied by the normal takeoff distance for the density altitude at which you are operating.

Another example that the change in takeoff distance varies as the square of the change in gross weight would be:

A Cessna 180 flies into a backcountry strip to pick up some passengers and equipment. The airplane lands and the pilot finds a note explaining the passengers are delayed for one day. The pilot takes off at 2,300 pounds gross weight and uses 1,000 feet of runway. The next day he returns to pick up the people. The weight of the passengers and equipment is 500 pounds. How much additional runway will be required with the addition of 500 pounds? Assume the temperature and pressure still requires 1,000 feet for takeoff at 2,300 pounds.

The change in takeoff distance varies as the square of the change of the gross weight. The weight change is the new weight, 2,800 pounds, divided by the original weight, 2,300 pounds, or 1.217, rounded off to 1.22. The square of the change is 1.22 multiplied by 1.22 for a total of 1.49, rounded to 1.5. The new

PART 2 TAKEOFF **Chapter 2 - Aircraft Performance**

takeoff distance is this factor, 1.5, multiplied by the original takeoff distance, 1,000 feet, for a total of 1,500 feet.

WIND

The presence of a headwind will assist in the takeoff and landing in terms of shortening the distance required to takeoff or land. For an approximation of the effect of the wind use the following rule of thumb.

 **RULE OF THUMB—Headwind Reduces Takeoff Distance**

A headwind will reduce the normal takeoff distance for any particular density altitude equal to 90 percent of the takeoff distance minus the value of the ratio of the headwind component divided by the rotation speed.

If you don't want to do any mathematical computations, use the following for a rough estimate of the effect of the headwind.

Headwind—Reduce Takeoff Distance
- 10 knots = 27%
- 15 knots = 39%
- 20 knots = 52.5%
- 25 knots = 65%

Whenever operating with a crosswind present, the wind is divided into two vector forces. One component is a crosswind, the other component a headwind (this does not apply to a direct headwind or a 90-degree crosswind). The headwind (or tailwind) component is equal to the Cosine of the wind angle multiplied by the wind velocity. The direct crosswind component (90-degree angle crosswind) is equal to the Sine of the wind angle multiplied by the wind velocity.

WIND COMPONENT

Example: Runway 18 with wind 2215 (220° at 15 knots). The wind angle is 220° wind

WIND ANGLE-DEGREES	CROSS-WIND-SINE	HEAD-WIND-COSINE
0	0.0	1.0000
10	.1736	.9848
20	.3420	.9397
30	.5000	.8660
40	.6428	.7660
50	.7660	.6428
60	.8660	.5000
70	.9397	.3420
80	.9848	.1736
90	1.0000	0.0

WIND COMPONENT TABLE

Mountain Flying Bible **2-17**

direction less 180° runway alignment, or 40°. The crosswind is the Sine of the 40° wind angle or .6428 multiplied by the wind velocity; .65 x 15 = 9.64 knots crosswind component. The headwind is the Cosine of the 40° wind angle or .7660 multiplied by the wind velocity; .7660 x 15 = 11.49 knots headwind component.

TAILWIND COMPONENT

Occasionally, especially at a one-way strip, it is necessary to depart with a tailwind if the flight is going to be made. In an airplane with a rotation speed of 60 knots, a tailwind of 6 knots (10 percent of the takeoff speed) will increase the takeoff distance by 21 percent. This may create one of the situations where you think to yourself, "Gee, I don't know if I can make it." Whenever doubt creeps into flight, it's time to dig out the Airplane Flight Manual or Pilot's Operating Handbook to determine the takeoff distance. Until you gain experience and can judge that the airplane does what the book states it will do, it would be wise to add a safety factor to the 21 percent you add to the takeoff distance, probably an additional 10 percent.

HUMIDITY

If the temperature and pressure are constant, air density varies inversely with humidity. If the humidity increases, the air density decreases.

RUNWAY SURFACE

The performance data provided by manufacturers in airplane manuals for takeoff assumes the surface will be a paved runway. Whenever the airplane's wheels are exposed to a surface that increases the drag due to friction, the takeoff distance will be increased. Those surfaces increasing the takeoff distance include long grass, dirt, mud, sand, slush, snow, or gravel. The following rule of thumb lists takeoff and landing data that may be helpful.

RULE OF THUMB—Takeoff from various surfaces

Increase the takeoff distance based on the runway surface:
- Firm turf - add 7%
- Rough, rocky, or short grass (up to 4") - add 10%
- Long grass (4" or more) - add 20 to 30%
- Soft field - add 23 to 75%
- Mud or snow - add 50% or more

For combinations of various surfaces, add the percentage of each variable. For example, if the surface is soft (recent rain) and grass covered, to the normal takeoff distance add 10 percent for the grass, plus 23 percent for the soft surface.

These computations provide "ball park" figures. Because they are only an approximation of the performance you may expect, inexperienced pilots should add a 25- to 50-percent safety factor until they have developed the ability and experience to determine a "soft" field.

Snow and Water—maximum depth for takeoff:
- ½ inch slush or water
- 1 inch of wet snow
- 4 inches of dry snow

GRADIENT (SLOPED RUNWAY)

Few airports are "flat." Whenever a slope exists, even if it is a slight incline of only a few degrees, it can affect the takeoff. *Normal operation* calls for landing upslope and takeoff downslope.

"Normal," in this case, assumes that the existing wind and any obstructions that may exist do not create a factor that you need to consider.

A one-percent downslope is generally equivalent to a 10-percent reduction in takeoff distance. But, if the wind is more than 15 knots, an upslope takeoff is recommended into the headwind, providing the aircraft has enough performance available to clear intervening obstructions and will outclimb any rising terrain. The additional drag and rolling friction caused by a one-percent upslope can result in a two percent to four percent increase in the takeoff distance.

To the normal takeoff distance for any particular density altitude, add 10% more runway for each one-degree of upward slope in the runway.

To the normal takeoff distance for any particular density altitude, subtract five percent of the takeoff distance for each one-degree of downward slope in the runway.

The following list is more accurate than the general rule of thumb:
- 2% downslope reduces takeoff distance 11%.
- 4% downslope reduces takeoff distance 19.5%.
- 6% downslope reduces takeoff distance 28.5%.

- 1% upslope increases takeoff distance 7.5%.
- 2% upslope increases takeoff distance 14%.
- 4% upslope increases takeoff distance 25.5%.
- 6% upslope increases takeoff distance 39.5%.

AIRCRAFT AND ENGINE CONDITION

When computing takeoff distance and rate of climb consider that an older airplane with a worn engine cannot be expected to perform in accordance with the performance charts.

Chapter 2 - Aircraft Performance — PART 2 TAKEOFF

Through experimentation and comparison to the airplane performance charts, it is possible to develop a "fudge" factor to be applied for your particular airplane.

For example, make several takeoffs and landings soliciting a friend to help you measure the distances. Compare these distances to the performance charts. Likewise, time your climb for five minutes and get an average rate of climb. Compare this rate of climb to the midpoint rate of climb in the performance charts. If there is a significant difference, note it in the performance charts and apply whatever correction is needed to subsequent values.

PILOT SKILL

The more experience you have, the greater the performance you can obtain from your airplane. Often gaining experience will place the pilot in a precarious position. If you are delving into unknown aircraft performance areas, it is wise to enlist the aid of an experienced flight instructor.

EFFECT OF LOCAL TERRAIN

Local terrain around a mountain airstrip can modify the wind circulation patterns from that of the general wind flow. Strong downdrafts or wind shear may exist shortly after takeoff that will prevent the airplane from climbing above the terrain if the flight path is maintained. It is wise to have a plan of action in mind to allow maneuvering away from the higher terrain whenever climbing. Before proceeding on course, be certain that you have gained sufficient altitude so you can execute a turn toward lowering terrain if an unexpected downdraft occurs. ✈

DENSITY ALTITUDE AFFECTS THE AIRPLANE DURING EN ROUTE OPERATIONS TOO.

PART 2 TAKEOFF   Chapter 3 - Engine Operation

CHAPTER 3 – ENGINE OPERATION

- ➤ ENGINE OPERATION 2-21
- ➤ MIXTURE CONTROL. 2-22
- ➤ FUEL-AIR MIXTURE 2-23
- ➤ TEMPERATURE AND FUEL-AIR RATIO 2-24
- ➤ RECOMMENDED LEANING ALTITUDE 2-26
- ➤ MIXTURE DISTRIBUTION 2-26
- ➤ MIXTURE DEFINITIONS 2-26
- ➤ PROCEDURE FOR LEANING - TAKEOFF 2-27
- ➤ PROCEDURE FOR LEANING- CRUISE 2-28
- ➤ PROCEDURE FOR LEANING - LANDING. 2-30
- ➤ DETONATION 2-32
- ➤ PREIGNITION 2-32
- ➤ CARBURETOR ICING 2-33

ENGINE OPERATION

If you are experienced in "hangar flying," (the art of talking about flying when the weather is bad, mechanical delays occur, or finances keep you grounded) you have probably heard a pilot refer to his airplane engine as a motor. It isn't. A motor is an electrical device. An internal combustion engine, on the other hand, uses chemical reaction from burning fuel to create heat inside the cylinders. The heat expands to push the piston down. One end of the connecting rod is attached to the piston that moves up and down within the cylinder; the other end is connected to a crankshaft to convert straight-line motion into rotary motion to turn the propeller.

There are four strokes of the piston required to complete one cycle of the engine: the *intake, compression, power* and *exhaust* strokes.

INTAKE STROKE

During the intake stroke, the fuel-air mixture is sucked into the cylinder as the piston moves down in the cylinder. The exhaust valve is closed and the intake valve is opened.

Chapter 3 - Engine Operation — PART 2 TAKEOFF

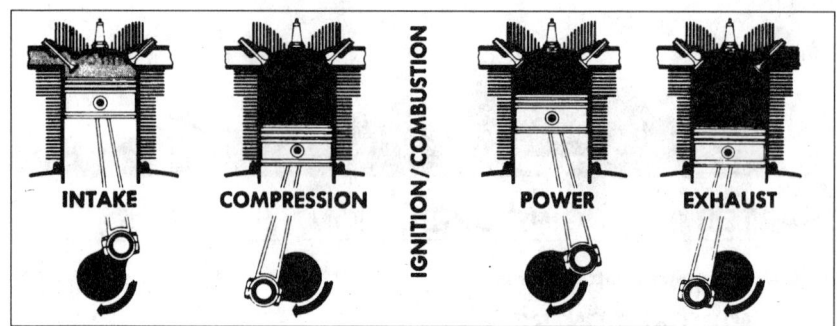

THE FOUR STROKES OF THE INTERNAL COMBUSTION ENGINE.

COMPRESSION STROKE

When the piston reaches the bottom of its travel, the intake and exhaust valves close. The piston moves up compressing the fuel-air mixture. Using the wrong grade fuel may allow the heat of compression to ignite the fuel-air mixture before the piston reaches top dead center (TDC), leading to engine damage.

POWER STROKE

Shortly before the piston reaches TDC during its upswing on the compression stroke, the spark plugs ignite the fuel/air mixture to allow it to begin burning. As the piston passes TDC the remaining fuel/air mixture burns at about 34 mph. The burning gases expand, forcing the piston downward during the power stroke. As the piston passes bottom dead center (BDC), the exhaust valve begins to open.

EXHAUST STROKE

During the exhaust stroke the rising piston scavenges the burned gases into the exhaust manifold. The valve closes and the intake valve opens to begin the cycle again.

An exhaust gas temperature (EGT) gauge can measure the exhaust gas temperature for use in adjusting the mixture. It is more accurate than other methods. The "mixture" is adjusted with a throttle that controls air flow and the mixture control lever that adjusts flow fuel.

MIXTURE CONTROL

The mixture control is a knob located near the throttle or propeller control. It's red color serves as a warning against improper adjustment. When an airplane climbs above sea level, the air becomes thinner. An engine of a certain cubic-inch displacement continues "breathing" the same quantity of air regardless of altitude, but that air weighs less above sea level. The mixture control is used to reduce the eight of the fuel for more efficient engine operation and greater fuel economy.

 An FAA publication states, "Leaning more than the manufacturer's recommendation presents the risk of rough engine operation, sudden 'cutting out,' backfiring, detonation, overheating, loss of power, and eventual engine failure."

Leaning the mixture when operating at high-altitude airports is critical in order to achieve maximum power for takeoff. It is important, too, to lean the mixture for the landing approach in case a go-around becomes necessary.

 WARNING: Never lean a turbocharged or super-charged engine for takeoff. These engines provide full sea-level power up to their critical altitude. Whenever takeoff power is used, adjust the mixture for sea level fuel flow (full rich).

FUEL-AIR MIXTURE

The balance between the weight of the fuel and the weight of the air that enters the cylinders of the engine is known as the *fuel-air ratio*. The proportion of approximately 15 pounds of air is required to completely burn one pound of fuel in a gasoline engine.

This mixture of the fuel and air is a function of the carburetor. Air enters the carburetor and fuel is added before this mixture enters the cylinders. Liquid gasoline cannot ignite, so another function of the carburetor is to break up the liquid into minute droplets, known as atomization or vaporization.

If the airplane remained at sea level there would be no need for a mixture control. At altitudes above sea level, air density decreases. While the volume of air entering the carburetor is the same at all altitudes, the weight of the air decreases with altitude. The fuel-air ratio is based upon the weight of fuel and the weight

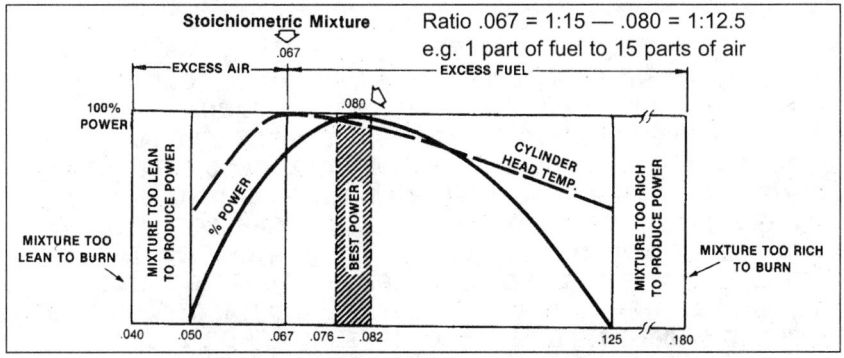

FUEL-AIR RATIO VS. POWER AND TEMPERATURE

of air. For this reason the mixture control is used to reduce the weight of fuel to correspond with the weight of air at altitudes above sea level.

TEMPERATURE AND FUEL-AIR RATIO

The fuel/air mixture is adjusted to obtain maximum performance of the engine. When the fuel/air ratio is adjusted to a ratio of 1 pound of fuel to 15 pounds of air (1:15), it is the chemically correct mixture referred to as the stoichiometric mixture. It is considered the optimum mixture to burn the greatest amount of fuel possible. While considered chemically correct, the engine produces more power when adjusted to a ratio of 1:12.5.

With the mixture control in the full-rich position, there is excess fuel delivered to the engine. By adjusting the mixture control outward, the excess fuel is reduced and the exhaust temperature increases. This can be viewed on airplanes equipped with an exhaust gas temperature (EGT) gauge. Leaning the mixture reduces the excess fuel and increases engine power. Further leaning until there is excess air causes the EGT gauge to show a drop in temperature. At the first sign

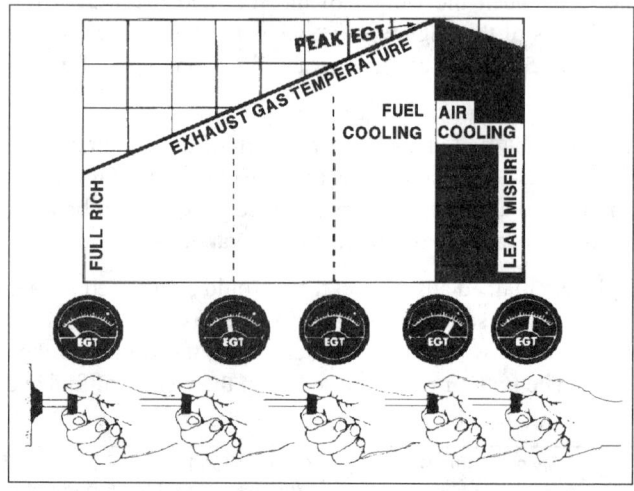

AS THE MIXTURE IS LEANED FROM THE FULL RICH POSITION, THE EGT INCREASES AS SHOWN BECAUSE THE AMOUNT OF EXCESS FUEL IS BEING DECREASED. THE LESSER THE EXCESS FUEL, THE GREATER THE EGT READING. AS LONG AS EXCESS FUEL IS PRESENT, THE EGT INCREASES WITH MIXTURE LEANING UNTIL NO EXCESS FUEL EXISTS, AT WHICH POINT "PEAK EGT" OCCURS. FURTHER LEANING DECREASES THE EGT AS SHOWN BECAUSE OF THE COOLING FROM THE EXCESS AIR. "PEAK EGT" IS THE KEY TO THE EGT METHOD OF MIXTURE CONTROL AND IT IS THE MIXTURE SETTING WHERE THERE IS NO EXCESS FUEL, NOR EXCESS AIR, BOTH OF WHICH CAUSE COOLING OF THE EXHAUST.

PART 2 TAKEOFF — Chapter 3 - Engine Operation

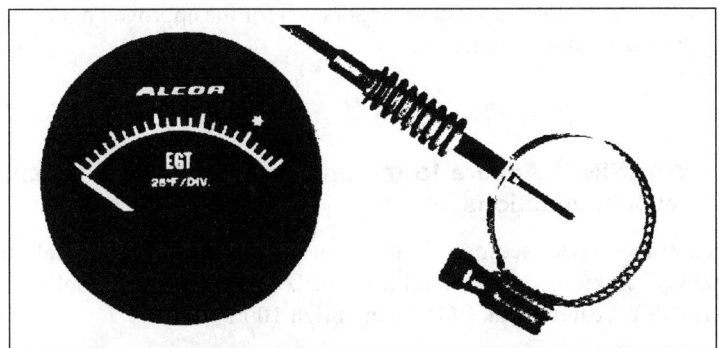

THE EGT GAUGE AND WIRING HARNESS. THE TEMPERATURE-SENSITIVE EXHAUST PROBE IS INSTALLED INSIDE THE EXHAUST.

of an EGT drop or engine roughness, move the mixture control in until the temperature is at the hottest again. This is called leaning to "peak EGT" temperature.

Operation at peak EGT may be the chemically correct mixture for combustion, where every reactant is used up completely, but it causes the engine to operate at its hottest temperature.

ALCOR Aviation, Inc is a manufacturer of EGT and Engine Analyzers. ALCOR recommends leaning to peak EGT at 65-percent power or less.

If the engine is operated above 65-percent power, lean to peak EGT, then enrich 50 degrees. If you are using an EGT rather than an engine analyzer (that allows selection of the leanest cylinder), run the engine a little rich, enriching 50 degrees for normally aspirated engines and 75 degrees for turbocharged engines. You will find that burning a little extra fuel is cheaper than buying engine parts.

ALCOR has found no evidence to suggest that operating at the peak EGT at power settings of 65 percent or less, will shorten the life of the engine. This assumes use of an analyzer where the leanest cylinder is chosen for mixture adjustment.

Teledyne Continental has not approved operating at peak EGT at cruise power settings above 55-percent power (except 65-percent power may be used with some engines, provided there is adherence to certain RPM limitations).

Lycoming has approved operating at peak EGT for cruise up to 75% power (except for geared-supercharged engines where they set the limit at 65% power).

Chapter 3 - Engine Operation   PART 2 TAKEOFF

Check your POH (Pilot's Operating Handbook) for the approved operations concerning your particular engine.

 **WARNING! Adhere to the engine manufacturer's leaning recommendations.**

When cruise power settings greater than 65-percent power are selected, the "best power" mixture setting should be used. This occurs at a fuel/air ratio of 1:12½ (0.080). Lean to peak EGT, then enrich 100°F.

RECOMMENDED LEANING ALTITUDE

The U.S. economy suffered an initial oil shock with the Arab-Israeli war of 1973, followed by a second shock after the Iranian revolution in 1979. The energy "crisis" had arrived. U.S. aircraft manufacturers traditionally recommended that the aircraft engine should not be leaned below 5,000 feet. With the advent of the crisis they responded rationally to allow the mixture to be leaned at 3,000 feet or above.

The original rationale for the 5,000-foot level is that below this altitude there is no noticeable increase in engine efficiency. At 5,000 to 7,000 feet the normally-aspirated (non-supercharged) engine is capable of developing about 75% of its rated power. At this setting it is easier to stay out of trouble when using improper leaning techniques.

There is a trend toward better education for pilots on the procedures and hazards of the mixture control. But some confusion still remains. Some FAA documents admonish us to never lean the mixture below 3,000 feet. Other documents state that the mixture should be leaned whenever the cruise power setting is 75 percent or less, at any altitude. You will be safe adhering to the aircraft manufacturer's recommendations.

MIXTURE DISTRIBUTION

The majority of airplane engines use a carburetor located at the back of the engine. This keeps it out of the slipstream and prevents wind chill. Intake air passes through the venturi of the carburetor to create a fuel/air mixture. Distribution of this mixture is through an intake manifold that leads to each cylinder. The mixture distribution of an engine equipped with a carburetor is inefficient and wasteful because the cylinders farthest away from the carburetor are the leanest, while those cylinders close to the carburetor are too rich. Fuel injection was invented to provide the same mixture distribution to each cylinder.

PART 2 TAKEOFF   Chapter 3 - Engine Operation

MIXTURE DEFINITIONS

BEST ECONOMY MIXTURE

The *best economy mixture* is defined as operation at "peak EGT." Compared to the best power mixture setting, the best economy mixture setting results in a small loss of true airspeed, but there is a range increase of about 10 to 15 percent. Never adjust to peak EGT when the power is set above 65 percent.

 NOTE: Follow the engine manufacturer's specific recommendations for leaning.

RECOMMENDED LEAN MIXTURE

 Lean the mixture to peak EGT, then enrich 50°F. This is referred to as "peak minus 50." Compared to the best power mixture setting, the *recommended lean mixture* setting produces a slight loss of true airspeed and a range increase of about 5 to 7 percent.

BEST POWER MIXTURE

Lean the mixture to peak EGT, then enrich 100°F (peak minus 100). Maximum speed for any desired cruise power setting is obtained at the *best power mixture* setting.

PROCEDURE FOR LEANING—TAKEOFF

The mixture must be leaned in accordance with the manufacturer's recommendation. In the absence of any recommendation, the following techniques may be incorporated to properly lean the mixture.

Maximum performance at high altitude airports is obtained only after the mixture is adjusted to obtain maximum engine efficiency. It is equally important to lean the mixture for landing as well as for takeoff in the event a go-around maneuver must be performed. Leaning the mixture at high altitude airports to obtain maximum power available for takeoff is based on the DENSITY ALTITUDE, not the physical altitude.

You may be operating from a mountain strip during the winter when no leaning of the mixture is required. In fact, if the mixture is leaned under these conditions, it may result in damage to the engine.

Do not lean a turbocharged or super-charged engine for takeoff. These engines are capable of producing sea level or greater manifold pressures and they need full-rich mixture.

Many pilots cringe when the see another pilot performing a full-power run-up to adjust the mixture. This practice is hard on the brakes, airframe, engine and

Chapter 3 - Engine Operation   PART 2 TAKEOFF

propeller. If you can't be convinced to do otherwise and prefer to lean to the maximum RPM at full throttle prior to takeoff, limit the engine operation at full throttle on the ground to a minimum.

After starting the engine at a high-altitude mountain strip (or airport), adjust the mixture for engine smoothness and taxi to the departure end of the runway. Perform the normal "before takeoff checklist." Smoothly add full power during the takeoff roll. Adjust the mixture according to the equipment as follows:

Keep in mind that it is not critical to adjust the mixture with a greater amount of accuracy than that provided by the following methods; however, it is important that the engine is not run too lean. The engine requires extra fuel for cooling during the takeoff and climb out.

Fixed-pitch propeller

No EGT, no fuel-flow gauge: Begin the takeoff roll and lean the mixture until there is some engine roughness. Enrich until the engine runs smoothly.

Fuel-flow gauge equipped: Begin the takeoff roll and at maximum power, lean the mixture until obtaining the proper fuel flow for the existing density altitude.

EGT gauge equipped: Begin the takeoff roll and at the full-power setting, lean the mixture until there is a slight engine roughness. Enrich the mixture until the engine runs smoothly.

Constant-speed propeller

No EGT, no fuel-flow gauge: Begin the takeoff roll and with full power lean the mixture until it begins to run rough. Enrich the mixture until the engine runs smoothly.

Fuel-flow gauge equipped: Begin the takeoff roll. After obtaining full power, lean the mixture until engine roughness, then enrich until the engine runs smoothly.

EGT gauge equipped: Begin the takeoff roll and at the full-power setting, lean the mixture until there is a slight engine roughness. Enrich the mixture until the engine runs smoothly.

PROCEDURE FOR LEANING—CRUISE

Fixed-Pitch Propeller

Tachometer method—No EGT, no fuel-flow gauge: When the cruise power setting has been selected and the friction-control lock activated on the throttle, begin leaning the mixture. Watch the tachometer. The rpm will increase slightly until there is some engine roughness at which time the rpm indication will begin decreasing. Enrich the mixture slowly (push the mixture control forward) until obtaining maximum rpm (peak RPM) and the engine runs smoothly. This is the "best economy mixture" setting. The author prefers to move the mixture control in ⅛ to ¼ inch to obtain the "recommended lean mixture" setting.

Fuel-flow gauge equipped: Lean the mixture to obtain the proper fuel flow for the existing density altitude.

EGT gauge equipped: Lean the mixture while watching the EGT gauge. At or near the peak EGT there is a slight engine roughness. Enrich the mixture slowly watching the EGT needle indication. For normally aspirated engines, enrich 50°F. For turbocharged or supercharged engines, enrich 75° to 100°F.

Constant-Speed Propeller

For the pilot, even engines in good mechanical condition pose a problem concerning the best manner to adjust the mixture. The cylinders located near the carburetor may receive as much as 50 percent more fuel than the cylinders located farthest from the carburetor.

Changing the flight altitude or power setting changes the mixture distribution throughout the engine. Perhaps cylinder #4 is the leanest cylinder (determined with an engine analyzer) during cruise at 8,500 feet. Reversing course and climbing to 9,500 feet may show that cylinder #3 is operating the leanest.

If the manufacturer has recommended specific procedures for adjusting the mixture, use their recommendation; otherwise, the following may be helpful.

Engine Rough Method—No EGT, no fuel-flow gauge: Begin leaning the mixture. Since the propeller governor will maintain a constant rpm there is no need to watch the tachometer. Slowly lean the engine until there is some engine roughness. Enrich until obtaining engine smoothness. This is the "best economy mixture" setting. The author prefers to move the mixture control in ⅛ to ¼ inch to obtain the "recommended lean mixture" setting.

Fuel-flow gauge equipped: Lean the mixture to obtain the proper fuel flow for the existing density altitude.

EGT gauge equipped: Lean the mixture while watching the EGT gauge. At or near the peak EGT there is a slight engine roughness. Enrich the mixture slowly watching the EGT needle indication. For normally aspirated engines, enrich 50°F. For turbocharged or supercharged engines, enrich 75° to 100°F.

The engine manufacturer specifies which cylinder to use for the installation of a single-channel EGT. This is supposed to allow the pilot to lean the mixture based on the leanest cylinder. Since the mixture distribution can change with altitude and power settings, the pilot doesn't really know that the single-probe EGT is giving him information about the leanest cylinder. If you want to be absolutely certain that the mixture is never too lean, and maybe fuel is cheaper than parts, the following recommendation is offered.

- For power settings of 65 percent or less, adjust the mixture to peak, then enrich 50°F. This is the *recommended lean* mixture setting and the terminology is "peak minus 50."
- For power settings above 65 percent (cruise flight, not climb), adjust the mixture to peak, then enrich 100°F. This is the best power mixture setting and the terminology is "peak minus 100."

PROCEDURE FOR LEANING—LANDING

After descending to pattern altitude, follow the *procedure for leaning—cruise* to obtain the go-around mixture setting.

TAKEOFF AND CLIMB POWER SETTINGS

When operating an airplane with a normally aspirated engine, use full power for all takeoffs. When the takeoff is from airports below 3,000-feet density altitude (not physical altitude), the manufacturer generally recommends using a full-rich mixture setting. Above 3,000 feet the mixture is leaned to obtain maximum performance, not economy, from the engine. Many of our general aviation airplanes incorporate a power enrichment valve in the carburetor. This provides extra fuel to assist in cooling the engine at climb attitudes and airspeeds that restrict the flow of air over the engine.

Unless you can't chew gum and pat your belly at the same time, the technique preferred over leaning at full throttle prior to takeoff is to begin the takeoff roll, advance full throttle, and ease the mixture control back until you get engine roughness. Then adjust the mixture control inward to obtain smooth operation.

Airplanes equipped with turbocharged engines enjoy the ability of having sea-level power available for all takeoffs, regardless of elevation (up to the critical altitude of the engine). Because the engine is compressing the air to provide sea-level capacity, it must have sea-level fuel flow. Always use full-rich mixture for takeoff. Often it is necessary to lean the mixture while taxiing, but during the take-off roll, do not fail to go to full-rich mixture.

EGT EQUIPMENT

The exhaust gas temperature (EGT) system is to an aircraft engine what a thermostat is to a home furnace. The EGT system allows the pilot to efficiently adjust the fuel/air mixture of the engine for the minimum fuel consumption consistent with the safe, non-damaging operation of the engine. This will provide the maximum time between overhaul (TBO) for the engine.

PART 2 TAKEOFF   **Chapter 3 - Engine Operation**

The author has used the ALCOR Aviation, Inc. EGTs and Combustion Analyzers (Engine Analyzer) with reliability and satisfaction over many years. All airplanes should have at least an EGT, but the Combustion Analyzer is preferred. Generally the EGT will pay for itself—in fuel savings and prevention of engine damage—in fewer than 100 hours. It may only take one flight if you consider your safety, peace of mind, engine power, and reduced maintenance costs.

Also, I'm adamant in my conviction of installing at least an EGT (Combustion Analyzer preferred) in all my airplanes. They will pay for themselves in one flight if you consider your safety, power and maintenance. They will pay for themselves in less than 100 hours if you consider fuel savings for an engine burning over 10 gallons per hour. It takes a few more hours to pay off with a small airplane, but it certainly does.

When you go to a facility for the installation of a single-channel EGT, the mechanic will check the engine manufacturer's recommendation for installation of the temperature probe in the leanest cylinder's exhaust. This probe is very sensitive to temperature changes. It is connected to a millivolt meter that reflects the reading on the EGT meter in the cockpit. The needle indicator of the EGT meter begins to move at about 1,200-degrees Fahrenheit. Full-scale deflection occurs at around 1,700-degrees F.

A multi-channel EGT is better than a single-channel EGT since it provides information about each cylinder. And, obviously, the multi-needle EGT gauge is better than the switchable EGT gauge in making comparisons. The multi-needle EGT shows all cylinders and their relationship to each other on one dial. The switchable EGT gauge allows you to select only one cylinder at a time. This makes it harder to see the relationship with other cylinders.

CRUISE POWER SETTINGS

Prior to the mid-1970s, it was recommended that the mixture be full rich for operations below 5,000-feet msl. The FAA now recommends the mixture be properly leaned when operating at cruise power settings of 75-percent or less at any operating altitude.

COMBUSTION ANALYZER

The single-channel EGT is much better than no EGT indication, but the combustion analyzer (multi-channel EGT) is the ultimate for optimum mixture control. Because the multi-channel EGT has a temperature probe installed in the exhaust of each cylinder, the cylinder providing the leanest mixture can always be determined and selected for adjustment of the mixture.

The equipment involved for the EGT Combustion Analyzer is the same as for the EGT mixture control indicator with added exhaust probes (one for each cylinder) and a cylinder selector switch or multi-needle gauge.

Another advantage is provided by having a multi-channel EGT. It can detect, locate and identify engine operating abnormalities such as a faulty ignition system, detonation, sticking valves, or poor fuel injection. The manufacturer provides troubleshooting data to be used by the pilot to monitor the engine and determine when a mechanical problem is beginning to occur. Corrective action can be initiated before the problem becomes mechanically threatening or more expensive.

PRESSURE CARBURETOR

Some aircraft engines are equipped with a pressure carburetor, so called because changes in the pressure when climbing or descending allows the carburetor to automatically control the fuel/air mixture. If the engine you fly has an automatic mixture control, do not try to adjust the mixture.

DETONATION

Detonation occurs when unburned gases—remaining in the cylinders after normal ignition—incur a spontaneous and destructive explosion. This sudden and violent explosion, with pressures in excess of 4,000 psi, takes place at about 1,500 mph, compared with the smooth burning of normal combustion that occurs at around 34 mph. Noticeable unusual sounds or engine roughness are generally not recognizable from the cockpit, unless the detonation is particularly heavy. Light to moderate detonation may not be determined until engine teardown (or failure). The detonation is then indicated by extensive engine damage, including dished piston heads, collapsed valve heads, damaged valve seats, broken ring lands, or eroded portions of the valves, pistons, or cylinder heads. Detonation may also cause sudden and complete engine failure. It is best to protect against detonation.

 The major cause of fuel detonation in the cylinders is leaning the fuel-air mixture excessively. Other causes include using fuel with an octane rating less than specified by the manufacturer, developing excessive cylinder head temperatures, operating with excessive manifold pressure, and an abrupt opening of the throttle that causes an excess of air (similar to over-leaning).

PREIGNITION

Detonation may lead to preignition, but preignition is normally caused by a fouled spark plug, lead deposit, particle of carbon in the combustion chamber that glows red hot, or excessively hot exhaust valves. Where it is difficult to detect detonation, preignition is generally recognizable by the pilot because of engine roughness, backfiring and the sudden increase in cylinder head temperature.

Preignition occurs when ignition of the fuel/air mixture occurs prior to normal ignition, or the ignition happens before the electrical arcing of the spark plugs. It is possible to have both detonation (usually in all the cylinders) and preignition (may occur in only one or two cylinders) occurring at the same time. Of the two, preignition is the most harmful in a time sequence. The effects of preignition are so harmful that the engine may operate normally for only a short period of time.

A form of preignition can occur after the flight when the engine has been shut down. If the pilot jumps out and tries to center the propeller (because it looks good while parked), there may be a small amount of fuel in the cylinder(s), or the prop movement may draw some fuel. With a glowing hot spot inside the combustion chamber, the engine may fire (kick over) for a revolution or two, certainly sufficient to cause a serious or fatal accident.

Thanks to ALCOR Aviation, Inc. for permission to use information from *EGT and Combustion Analysis In a Nutshell.*

CARBURETOR ICING

Vaporization of fuel and expansion of the air while passing through the carburetor causes a sudden cooling of the fuel-air mixture. The air temperature through the carburetor may drop as much as 60 degrees Fahrenheit. Ice will form when there is water vapor in the air and the temperature is below freezing inside the carburetor.

The purpose of the carburetor is to convert liquid fuel into a gaseous fuel for mixture with the air. This process is known as *vaporization*. Vaporization, or the conversion of a liquid to a gas, involves the absorption of heat from the environment. Inside the carburetor, there is a sudden cooling of the air when vaporization takes place. As the fuel/air mixture passes from the carburetor to the intake manifold—where it is channeled to each cylinder—expansion takes place. Expansion also cools the air.

Favorable Carb Icing Conditions

We might expect carburetor icing during the winter, but with temperatures of 40°F or lower, the air is usually too cold to contain enough moisture for carburetor ice to form.

On hot summer days when the temperature is 85°F or above, there is too much heat for ice to form in the engine.

Look out during the early summer or early fall when the temperature ranges from 45°F to 85°F. These days can provide a high relative humidity or visible moisture (clouds or rain). With low-power operations, all the conditions that cause carburetor icing exist.

Chapter 3 - Engine Operation   PART 2 TAKEOFF

Indications of Carburetor Icing

Fixed-pitch Propeller

In an airplane with a fixed-pitch propeller, the first indication of carb ice will be a loss of rpm.

Constant-speed Propeller

In an airplane with a constant-speed propeller, the first indication of carb ice will be a loss of manifold pressure.

Carburetor Heat

Carburetor heat is a device that directs unfiltered air over the exhaust for heating. The heated air is diverted directly into the carburetor.

An indication of carburetor ice (loss of rpm with fixed-pitch prop, loss of manifold pressure with constant-speed prop) would alert you to apply carb heat. When used, the pilot pulls back on the carburetor heat knob all the way. Remember, if needed, apply carb heat fully.

Fixed-pitch prop—carb ice

With the fixed-pitch prop, if there is carb ice, upon applying heat there will be a drop in rpm, then a rise in rpm when the ice melts (along with rough engine operation) and when the carb heat is turned off there will be another rise in the rpm to a setting that is higher than before the application of carb heat. If there was no ice present, upon adding heat, the rpm would drop (due to the less dense heated air being taken into the cylinders), remain at that rpm, and then return to the original rpm setting when the carb heat is turned off.

If carb ice is present in an aircraft equipped with a constant-speed prop, the addition of carb heat will cause a drop in manifold pressure (MP), then an increase as the ice melts (even though you are using heated air there will be more of it if the carburetor passage is cleared out), and another increase to a higher setting than the original when the carb heat is turned off. If ice is present, the engine will run rough as it melts. If there was no ice, upon application of carb heat the MP would drop, remain at that setting, and then return to the original MP setting when carb heat is turned off.

If the ice in the carburetor has built up to the point of causing the engine to quit, move the mixture control to full rich and turn off the mags. Count slowly to five and turn on the mags. This may "load up" the cylinders with fuel so the resulting explosion when the mags are turned on will cause a backfire. If the engine has not quit, but there is a serious loss of power, it is sometimes possible, in an emergency, to free the carburetor passageway by leaning out the mixture (be careful not to kill the engine) until the engine backfires and dislodges some ice.

As soon as there is some response to the preheating being done with the carburetor heater, it is advisable to restore full power to the engine by diminishing the carb heat gradually, while seeking a more favorable altitude for your flight. If you find it necessary to operate with the carb heat on, lean the mixture. The hot air from the carb heat will make the engine run too rich.

The most dangerous time for carburetor icing to occur is during takeoff. The use of carb heat during your "before takeoff checklist" should be mandatory to preclude the risk of a power failure or loss at a critical moment.

On the other hand, consistent use of carburetor heat when unnecessary is wasteful of fuel and may harm the engine. Because the air diverted by carb heat is unfiltered, your check during the "before takeoff checklist" should be done in an area where loose gravel and dirt particles are at a minimum.

Carburetor heat reduces power. Generally carb heat is not used during the takeoff.

Closing the cowl flaps, incidentally, does not prevent or cure carburetor icing, and, of course, fuel-injected engines (having no carburetor) do not experience carb icing. ✈

THE TAKEOFF TRAFFIC PATTERN MAY INVOLVE A NON-STANDARD CLIMBOUT.

(GARDEN CITY, IDAHO)

Chapter 3 - Engine Operation   PART 2 TAKEOFF

REMEMBER TO TAKE CARE OF YOUR AIRCRAFT ENGINE AND IT WILL TAKE CARE OF YOU. ✈

LEFT-TURNING TENDENCY OF AN AIRPLANE

STEP ON THE RIGHT RUDDER TO COMPENSATE FOR:

1. **TORQUE**

   "Every action has an equal and opposite reaction." Most general aviation airplanes have a clockwise rotation of the propeller when viewed from the cockpit. The torque reaction is counter-clockwise or a yawing force to the left.

2. **P-FACTOR**

   Propeller factor, or asymmetric thrust of the propeller, results when the right side of the propeller's plane of rotation develops more thrust than the left side causing the airplane to yaw left.

3. **CORKSCREWING EFFECT OF THE PROPELLER SLIPSTREAM**

   The slipstream from the propeller strikes the vertical stabilizer and rudder on the left side of the airplane, yawing the airplane to the left.

4. **GYROSCOPIC PRECESSION OF THE PROPELLER**

   Any spinning object having mass will exhibit the properties of a gryoscope. One property is that it reacts to an outside force, but the reaction is 90 degrees in the plane of rotation. With clockwise rotation of the propeller, the force acts 90 degrees in the plane of rotation, yawing the airplane to the left.

PART 2 TAKEOFF   Chapter 4 - Takeoffs

CHAPTER 4 – TAKEOFFS

- TAKEOFF CONSIDERATIONS 2-37
- AIRSPEED................................... 2-37
- TAKEOFF POWER 2-38
- RUNWAY LENGTH REQUIREMENT 2-39
- GUSTY WIND TAKEOFF....................... 2-40
- TAILWIND TAKEOFF......................... 2-40
- UPSLOPE OR DOWNSLOPE TAKEOFF.......... 2-41
- DETERMINE RUNWAY GRADIENT.............. 2-43
- FLAP SETTINGS............................. 2-44
- GROUND EFFECT 2-46
- NORMAL TAKEOFF 2-48
- NORMAL TAKEOFF - TAILDRAGGER 2-50
- SHORT-FIELD TAKEOFF 2-52
- SHORT-FIELD TAKEOFF - TAILDRAGGER 2-53
- SHORT-FIELD TAKEOFF - ADVANCED 2-54
- SOFT-FIELD TAKEOFF........................ 2-56
- MODIFIED SHORT/SOFT-FIELD TAKEOFF 2-57
- CROSSWIND TAKEOFF 2-58
- COLD WEATHER TAKEOFF 2-66

TAKEOFF CONSIDERATIONS

The worst time to be studying about an emergency is during the middle of one. Before beginning a takeoff, consider the following topics. Familiarization makes it easy to cope with adverse conditions or an emergency, should one arise.

AIRSPEED

Airspeed control is important during the takeoff and climb from a mountain strip. With exact airspeed control you are able to extract the maximum performance from the airplane.

Mountain Flying Bible   2-37

Chapter 4 - Takeoffs — PART 2 TAKEOFF

Very few operations can associate a rule with the "always" or the "never" monicker without exception...because there are always exceptions to the rule. But, for normal operations, as opposed to special exceptions like adding half the wind-gust factor to the takeoff speed or approach speed, we will, at any airport elevation regardless of density altitude, always use the same indicated airspeed for takeoff as that used at sea level. We will always use the same indicated airspeed for approach to landing that we use for approach to landing at a sea-level airport. Let's see why this is true.

An airplane accelerating for takeoff from a sea-level airport under standard conditions (assuming no instrument error) will register the true airspeed of the airplane on the airspeed indicator. That is, the indicated airspeed and true airspeed are the same. When the airplane operates at a high altitude airport (any airport above sea level) the indicated airspeed is less than the true airspeed.

Assume an airplane is departing from Leadville, Colorado, elevation 9,927 feet msl. At sea level this airplane uses 65 knots true airspeed to rotate. You know the true airspeed must be faster at high altitudes to compensate for the increased true airspeed stalling speed. The thin air affects the power output of the engine, the thrust of the propeller, and the lift of the wings.

As the airplane accelerates and reaches a true airspeed of 65 knots, the airspeed indicator will only indicate about 56 knots (with standard conditions) because the thin air cannot expand the diaphragm inside the airspeed indicator as much as the thicker air does at sea level. By the time the airspeed indicator shows 65 knots (the speed used to rotate), the airplane is actually going about 75.5 knots true airspeed, automatically compensating for the thin air.

TAKEOFF POWER

Many years ago, the FAA conducted tests to determine the benefits of setting full power before brake release for takeoff. They determined that, aerodynamically, the prop must move forward through the air before becoming efficient; therefore, this static run-up does not increase the takeoff performance by shortening the take-off roll. On a rough field this technique of setting full power before brake release may damage the propeller and horizontal stabilizer.

Although I know, theoretically, that it does no good to make a full-power application before brake release, I prefer to hold the brakes on a short-field takeoff, assuming it can be done without damaging the propeller or horizontal stabilizer. This is especially true if the engine is turbocharged or supercharged. A progressive power application without surging or over-boosting is the reason. This technique reduces the urgency to shove the throttle through the panel as the end of the runway approaches.

On a landing strip where it is unwise to make the full-power application before brake release, with practice, the pilot can begin adding the power during

PART 2 TAKEOFF
Chapter 4 - Takeoffs

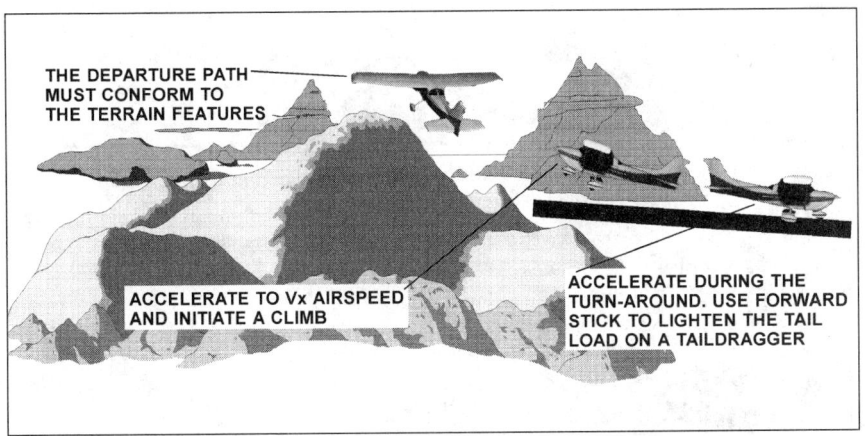

RULE OF THUMB: WHEN THE RUNWAY LENGTH IS DOUBTFUL, MARK THE MIDPOINT OF THE RUNWAY. IF 71% OF THE TAKEOFF SPEED IS OBTAINED AT THE 50% POINT ON THE RUNWAY, SUFFICIENT RUNWAY IS AVAILABLE FOR THE TAKEOFF. IF NOT, ABORT THE TAKEOFF AND WAIT FOR BETTER CONDITIONS. (COOLER TEMPERATURE, MORE HEADWIND, OR OFF-LOAD SOME PASSENGERS AND BAGGAGE, FERRYING THEM OUT IN SEVERAL TRIPS.

the turn to align with the runway. During the last 30-degrees of turn full power can be set without incurring any damage because of the forward movement of the airplane.

RUNWAY LENGTH REQUIREMENT

There is a simple rule to determine if a particular runway length is sufficient for takeoff.

RULE OF THUMB for sufficient runway length for takeoff

Multiply 10 times the square root of the percentage of liftoff distance required. This equals the percentage of liftoff speed that should be attained in that distance.

A fellow experiencing mechanical difficulties (lack of fuel) landed in a small hay field and was hesitant to try to fly the airplane from this short field. He contacted me to see if it could be flown from the field.

The performance charts for this airplane turned out to be worthless under the existing condition of density altitude and the 12-inch high hay.

When you fly from a short runway and you have doubts that the performance of the airplane is adequate to takeoff in the distance available under existing con-

Mountain Flying Bible 2-39

Chapter 4 - Takeoffs

PART 2 TAKEOFF

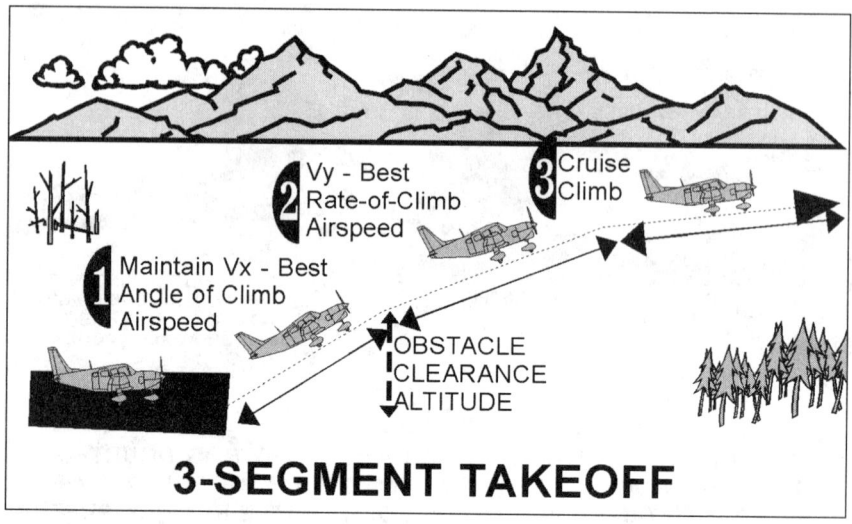

ditions of density altitude and aircraft loading, use the "runway length sufficient" rule of thumb.

Mark the mid-point of the runway. The reason for this is because the airplane stops better than it accelerates. If you accelerate to the halfway point and determine you have insufficient speed for takeoff, you can easily stop in the remaining distance.

Take the square root of 50 (percentage of liftoff distance required equals half or 50 percent of the runway). This value is 7.07. Multiply this by 10 (10 times the square root), for a total of 70.7. If 71 percent of the liftoff speed is attained by the halfway point of the runway, the airplane will take off in the space remaining.

This does not guarantee the rate of climb will be sufficient to clear any obstacles that may be present after takeoff, but it does guarantee that you can takeoff in the space available.

GUSTY WIND TAKEOFF

For takeoff operations during gusty wind conditions, keep the airplane on the ground until obtaining a speed of V_R plus one half the gust factor.

TAILWIND TAKEOFF

Due to terrain considerations, backcountry airstrips are generally located beside creeks and rivers where more or less flat terrain exists. It is desirable to land upstream and takeoff downstream at backcountry strips to let the sloping terrain work with you. But, you must be mindful of the wind.

When wind is created by solar effect, the air rises and begins moving upslope. The sun heats the canyon creating convection currents and these morning winds—called a *Valley Breeze*—blow up the canyons. The valley breeze is generally 4-6 knots. This means, when landing upslope (upstream), the airplane will experience a tailwind.

In the evening, as the air cools and becomes heavier, it slides down the mountains creating evening winds—called a *Mountain Breeze*. The mountain breeze is stronger than the valley breeze, usually around 10-12 knots. This means a flight departing during the late afternoon or evening, flying downslope, will be exposed to a tailwind.

RULE OF THUMB for the effect of a tailwind on takeoff distance

The tailwind takeoff distance is equal to 110 percent of the computed takeoff distance for the existing density altitude plus the value of the tailwind component divided by the rotation speed.

How does a tailwind affect the takeoff distance? For an airplane with a takeoff distance of 1,000 feet, a rotation speed of 50 knots and a 10-knot tailwind, the takeoff distance would be:

1,000 x 1.10 = 1,100 feet (takeoff distance x 110 percent) plus

1,000 x 10/50 = 200 feet (tailwind/rotation speed)

Total 1,100 feet plus 200 feet = 1,300 feet

UPSLOPE OR DOWNSLOPE RUNWAY

RULE OF THUMB Upslope or Downslope Runway Takeoff Distance

For takeoff on an upslope runway, from one degree up to two degrees, add 10 percent per degree.

For downslope runways, decrease the takeoff distance five percent per degree.

BREAKEVEN HEADWIND

Often when I am speaking before a group of pilots someone asks, "How can I determine whether to takeoff upslope into the wind or down slope with a tailwind?"

Chapter 4 - Takeoffs   PART 2 TAKEOFF

> **ONE WAY STRIP**
>
> OFTEN THE PRESENCE OF OBSTACLES NEAR THE RUNWAY OR ALONG THE DEPARTURE PATH WILL DETERMINE THE TAKEOFF AND LANDING DIRECTION. DO NOT FLY INTO OR FROM A "ONE-WAY" STRIP THE WRONG DIRECTION REGARDLESS OF THE WIND DIRECTION.

TAILWIND TAKEOFF DOWNHILL

AS A GENERAL RULE, WHEN THE WIND IS FEWER THAN 15 KNOTS, TAKE OFF DOWNHILL UNLESS OBSTACLES OR TERRAIN DICTATE OTHERWISE. THE TAILWIND INCREASES THE GROUNDSPEED RESULTING IS A MORE SHALLOW CLIMB GRADIENT. GENERALLY A 1% DOWNSLOPE IS EQUIVALENT TO 10% MORE RUNWAY.

HEADWIND TAKEOFF UPSLOPE

WHEN THE WIND IS MORE THAN 15 KNOTS, IT MAY BE NECESSARY TO TAKE OFF UPHILL, PROVIDING THAT THE AIRPLANE HAS SUFFICIENT PERFORMANCE TO OUTCLIMB THE TERRAIN. IT WILL TAKE LONGER TO BECOME AIRBORNE, BUT THE TOTAL DISTANCE WILL BE SHORTER. USE THE "RUNWAY LENGTH SUFFICIENT" RULE OF THUMB.

John Lowry, Ph.D., Flight Physics, Billings, Mont. handed me a note during one of these question-and-answer periods. He states the following formula will tell you when to takeoff—without considering terrain—uphill into the wind or downhill with a tailwind. The breakeven wind speed is:

$$V_{BE} = \frac{\theta° d_{LO}(0,0)}{5 V_{LO}}$$

V_{BE} = velocity break-even wind speed in knots

$\theta°$ = runway slope up in degrees

$d_{LO}(0,0)$ = POH distance to liftoff with 0 slope and 0 wind (in feet) under the existing density altitude condition

5 = a constant

V_{LO} = velocity of liftoff speed in knots true airspeed

The breakeven headwind is that wind resulting in the same amount of distance for takeoff whether you take off uphill or downhill. If the wind velocity is less than the computed breakeven headwind, take off downslope. If the wind is greater than the breakeven headwind, takeoff upslope.

This formula is fine for determining if the airplane will take off, but don't rely on it totally. Consider the terrain surrounding the airport. If the breakeven headwind indicates you should take off upslope, but you have doubts about out climbing the terrain, it may be necessary to delay the flight until the takeoff can be made downslope where the terrain is less of a consideration.

My personal method to deal with this problem is to use the rule-of-thumb numbers for an upslope (Page 2-19 – 2% upslope = 14% more runway) to determine the takeoff distance. If there is sufficient runway for takeoff, monitor the takeoff using the *Runway Length Requirement* (Page 2-39 – if 71% of the speed necessary for takeoff is obtained at the halfway point, continue the takeoff).

DETERMINE RUNWAY GRADIENT

Subtract the low-end elevation of the runway from the high-end elevation. Divide this by the runway length and multiply by 100. This equals the gradient or slope of the runway.

For example, at Aspen, Colo. the elevation at the approach end of runway 15 is 7,674 feet. The elevation at the approach end of runway 33 is 7,815 feet. The runway length is 7,004 feet. The gradient equals 7,815 minus 7,674 = 141/7,004 = 0.00201313 times 100 = 2.0 percent upslope on runway 15.

For general aviation VFR airports the FAA has established a maximum gradient of 2 percent. They state the takeoff length must be increased 20 percent for each 1 percent of effective gradient up to the maximum 2 percent gradient.

Chapter 4 - Takeoffs   PART 2 TAKEOFF

FLAP SETTINGS

Some people express their opinion that flaps were invented to allow airplanes to land slower and to reduce the stalling speed. This doesn't bother me, but when they start telling other pilots, "Never use flaps for takeoff and never use more than half-flaps for landing," this causes some concern.

Flaps were designed to allow the pilot to make a steeper approach angle to a runway without an increase in airspeed. By increasing the camber or curvature of the wing, lift is increased. Lift and drag are directly proportional. The increased lift increases drag. A side benefit of flaps is that flaps do lower the stall speed and allow for a slower touchdown speed.

We will discuss the use of flaps for takeoff now and defer the use of flaps for landing until Part 4 - Arrival.

FLAP SETTING FOR TAKEOFF

Experienced pilots using backcountry strips use flaps for all takeoffs (including crosswind takeoffs). It's not that these strips are particularly rough or short (many of them are), it's just that this technique reduces the overall wear-and-tear on the airplane and provides practice for when flaps are required.

How much flap should be used for takeoff? It's a good idea to follow the manufacturer's recommendation. If the manufacturer doesn't specify a flap setting, move the control wheel or stick to the side for full aileron deflection. Look at the down aileron. The angle formed produces a camber that is optimum for the airfoil, producing the maximum lift and minimum drag. Next, match the flap deflection to the aileron deflection. This will give you the maximum lift available for the particular airfoil design. (Photo page 5-16)

Some airplanes may have excess power available, which would allow the use of a greater amount of flaps. The extra drag from, say one-half flap application, is not detrimental to the takeoff and does not limit the rate of climb. Using a runway of sufficient length to allow experimentation (be able to take off and land again in the same length), see how your airplane performs with and without flaps on the takeoff roll and climb out.

One technique used for a flap takeoff from a short field is to wait until takeoff speed before "popping" the flaps to the desired deflection. While I occasionally do this to reduce drag and decrease the possibility of a rock striking the flaps, it is not necessary. The amount of drag caused by setting the flaps before the takeoff roll, at these slow speeds, would be infinitesimal (or at least negligible on the ground roll for takeoff, unless operating at short strips where 10 or 20 feet can make a difference). Do what works best for you.

PART 2 TAKEOFF   **Chapter 4 - Takeoffs**

Once airborne, what technique should be used to raise the flaps? Well, usually two terms are used for flap retraction, "dumping" and "milking." *Dumping* means exactly that, retracting the flaps all at once. You have to have excess airspeed, excess power, or excess altitude to use this technique. *Milking* means the incremental retraction of the flaps a few degrees at a time while catching any sink tendency with back pressure on the control wheel. This is the best method for flap retraction.

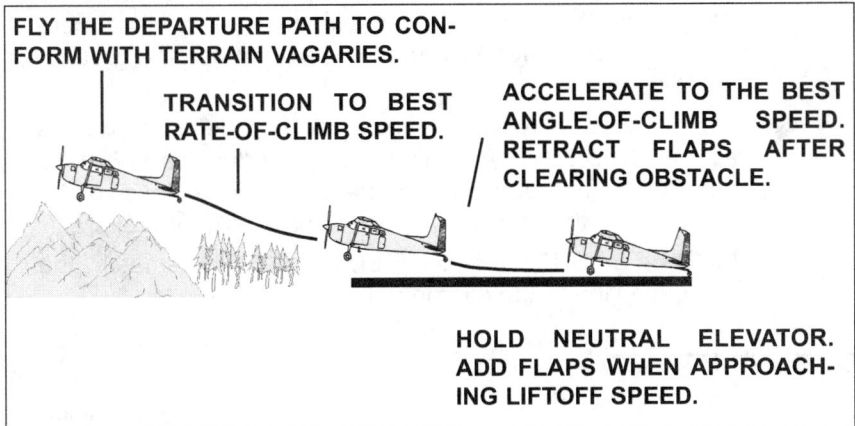

FLY THE DEPARTURE PATH TO CONFORM WITH TERRAIN VAGARIES.

TRANSITION TO BEST RATE-OF-CLIMB SPEED.

ACCELERATE TO THE BEST ANGLE-OF-CLIMB SPEED. RETRACT FLAPS AFTER CLEARING OBSTACLE.

HOLD NEUTRAL ELEVATOR. ADD FLAPS WHEN APPROACHING LIFTOFF SPEED.

SHORT-FIELD TAKEOFF

The aircraft manufacturer, in the Owner's Manual, Airplane Operating Handbook or Pilot's Operating Handbook, may provide recommendations for flap settings for the normal, short-field and soft-field takeoff. If recommendations are given, follow the recommendations. In the absence of such recommendations, use the following guidelines:

The general aviation, two-passenger or four-passenger airplane equipped with a fixed-pitch propeller and fewer than 180 horsepower (excluding high-performance aircraft like the SuperCub) generally provide best performance by using the flaps as indicated:

NOTE: To obtain maximum lift from a particular airfoil section (design), make full aileron deflection and match the flap deflection to the aileron deflection. For example, on the Cessna 172 this will result in the application of approximately 12 degrees of flaps.

- NORMAL TAKEOFF—zero flaps (flaps retracted).
- SHORT-FIELD TAKEOFF—match flap deflection to aileron deflection; zero flaps with rising terrain or obstacles in the takeoff path.
- SOFT-FIELD TAKEOFF—match flap deflection to aileron deflection.

Chapter 4 - Takeoffs PART 2 TAKEOFF

The general aviation airplane with more than 180 horsepower has the advantage of greater performance capabilities and incorporates a different recommendation for flap settings:

- NORMAL TAKEOFF—zero flaps or match the flap deflection to the aileron deflection, as desired.
- SHORT-FIELD TAKEOFF—match the flap deflection to the aileron deflection. If the aircraft is powerful and you have determined from previous experience (testing) that more flaps can be safely used, their use will reduce the ground-run distance.
- SOFT-FIELD TAKEOFF—match the flap deflection to the aileron deflection. If the aircraft is powerful and you have determined from previous experience that more flaps can be safely used, their use will reduce the abuse on the aircraft.
- MODIFIED SHORT/SOFT-FIELD TAKEOFF—match the flap deflection to the aileron deflection.

GROUND EFFECT

The term "ground effect" is discussed in ground school, flight school and in hangar sessions. When its importance is not stressed, the actual mechanism of how it works and its consequences is often forgotten. In hangar sessions I have heard it described as a cushion of air between the wing and the ground. That's not correct, but it's okay if the pilot understands how to deal with ground effect.

Accident reports describing ground effect mishaps display the same appearance. An airplane, sometimes heavily loaded or experiencing the adverse effects of density altitude, begins the takeoff roll from a short runway (sometimes the runway is not short). The pilot, after accelerating to the speed he feels is sufficient for takeoff, rotates and struggles to miss the upcoming fence. The airplane begins to climb and then sinks back to the ground. What went wrong?

DRAG

To see that this type of accident is not an isolated incident, let us examine drag and the aerodynamics of the wing to determine what course of action caused the accident. An airplane in flight is exposed to both induced drag and parasite drag.

Induced drag results from lift being produced. Induced drag is greatest at slow speeds where the angle of attack is higher. There are a couple of ways to explain induced drag. First, when a wing pushes down on the air through which it is flying, the air pushes back creating a downwash and drag. The harder the wing works (by increasing the angle of attack), the more downwash is created. Second, lift always acts perpendicular to the wing. If the wing is at a high angle of attack with the lift acting perpendicular, there is a vertical component of lift. The rearward component that acts opposite weight (between the lift component and the total lift component) is a retarding force known as induced drag.

Parasite drag is caused by the stickiness of the air and is greatest when the airplane goes fast. Stick your hand out of a car window (cautiously, if the speed is fast) and you can feel parasite drag.

EFFECT

During the study of aerodynamics it is convenient to explain the relative wind as being parallel to the longitudinal axis of the airplane. In actuality, there is an upwash ahead of the wing and a downwash behind the wing. During operation close to the ground, the free-flight upwash and downwash cannot evolve. Close to the runway the rearward component (induced drag) between the lift component and the total lift component will be reduced allowing the airplane to produce the same amount of lift at a smaller angle of attack than it could out of ground effect without a larger angle of attack. When the airplane initially lifts off the ground and the wing is at a height equal to 10 percent of its span, there is a 48-percent reduction in induced drag. Induced drag increases rapidly with height above the takeoff surface. At a height equal to half the wing span, about 18 feet above the ground, there is only an 8-percent reduction in induced drag.

EXTENT

Ground effect no longer reduces the induced drag once the airplane is 20 to 30 feet above the ground. The typical accident occurs when an airplane is "horsed" into the air, a high angle of attack is maintained, and the airplane climbs out of ground effect to encounter the full effect of induced drag. At this point the wings stall, and the plane drops suddenly to the ground.

A combination of short runways, rough ground, grass and snow, high airport altitude, high air temperature, a weak engine and a heavy load, in any of many combinations, is the danger signal.

When you find yourself in a marginal takeoff situation, know your plane's takeoff speed for the operating weight, the distance required to accelerate to that speed, and then allow a margin of safety after takeoff by accelerating just off the ground in ground effect before trying to climb. If the plane is still dragging its wheels when it should be airborne, abort the takeoff while you can, for you're heading into a stall a dozen or fifty feet up.

Using the *runway length sufficient* rule of thumb, mark the halfway point of the runway. During the takeoff roll, if 71 percent of the takeoff speed is attained at or before the halfway point of the runway, the airplane will take off in the runway remaining.

Rather than accelerating the airplane to a certain speed and then pulling back on the control wheel to force the airplane to fly, a safer technique is to accelerate until approaching the rotation speed. Then ease the control wheel back to the takeoff attitude and wait for the airplane to fly off by itself.

 **RULE OF THUMB – GROUND EFFECT**

When trying to accelerate after a soft-field or short-field takeoff, maintain the wing as close to the ground as possible. During the acceleration to V_X or V_Y, fly no higher than one-half the wing span above the ground.

NORMAL TAKEOFF

During a normal takeoff, the airplane becomes airborne smoothly and with positive control. This is done by "rotating" the airplane about its lateral axis to establish a flying attitude. Do not pull back on the control wheel to cause the airplane to start flying.

The normal takeoff from a paved or smooth grass strip assumes plenty of runway length. After power application the airplane will begin to accelerate. Before it reaches a speed where it will fly, pull back on the control wheel (rotate) to assume a pitch attitude of about 7.5 degrees. That's it. Don't do anything else. When the airplane is ready it will fly off the runway. Hold the same pitch attitude for the climb out.

General aviation airplanes, depending on excess power available, should be rotated to a nose up attitude of between three and seven and one-half degrees. This technique has its advantages. If there is frost (polished smooth, of course) on the wings or a very high density altitude, the airplane will not fly until it can fly. The technique also compensates for ground effect. It is possible to fly an airplane using ground effect, lifting off with too great a load or with insufficient power to allow the airplane to climb out of ground effect. By rotating to and maintaining the best rate of climb airspeed attitude (the position of the nose in relation to the natural horizon), the airplane will continue to fly once it is clear of the runway.

The normal takeoff technique is just that, for normal takeoffs. If the wind is gusty, if there are obstacles immediately after takeoff, or if there is a crosswind, this technique is not used. The gusty-wind takeoff and crosswind takeoff are used to prevent skipping or stalling under those wind conditions. A short-field takeoff is used to depart from a short field with or without obstacles. If a maximum rate of climb is desired, fly the best rate-of-climb speed. The normal takeoff will result in a speed faster than the best rate-of-climb speed. The airplane climbs more steeply at V_Y than at a higher speed.

PART 2 TAKEOFF
Chapter 4 - Takeoffs

NORMAL TAKEOFF

☆ MAKE A SMOOTH APPLICATION OF POWER.

☆ RAISE THE NOSE TO LIFTOFF ATTITUDE WHEN APPROACHING V_X. AT HIGH-ALTITUDE AIRPORTS ROTATE AT THE SAME INDICATED AIRSPEED AS THAT USED AT SEA-LEVEL AIRPORTS.

☆ ROTATE TO THE TAKEOFF ATTITUDE AND ALLOW THE AIRPLANE TO FLY OFF THE GROUND BY ITSELF INSTEAD OF PULLING THE AIRPLANE OFF THE GROUND.

☆ WHEN A POSITIVE RATE OF CLIMB IS ESTABLISHED, RETRACT THE LANDING GEAR AND MAINTAIN THE BEST ANGLE-OF-CLIMB AIRSPEED.

☆ REDUCE POWER AT 400-FEET AGL. LIMIT ANY TURNS TO A MAXIMUM OF 30 DEGREES OF BANK.

☆ THE DEPARTURE PATTERN MUST BE MODIFIED TO AVOID OBSTACLES REMEMBERING TO ALWAYS REMAIN IN A POSITION TO TURN TOWARD LOWERING TERRAIN.

A normal takeoff is defined in the following manner:

**NORMAL TAKEOFF
"TRAINING WHEELS" (TRICYCLE GEAR AIRPLANE)**

- Use partial power until runway alignment is achieved, then smoothly apply full power while maintaining directional control. Use full power for takeoff (use full takeoff power with turbocharged or supercharged engines). Many small airplanes incorporate a "power enrichment valve" in the carburetor for additional engine cooling during the climb. If you do not use full throttle, you will not activate this feature. Do not over-boost

Mountain Flying Bible

(operate beyond the redline manifold pressure) the supercharged/turbocharged engine. As the elevator control becomes effective, apply back pressure to lighten the weight on the nose wheel, maintaining the thrust line of the propeller parallel to the ground. If this is done, the thrust will be more effective and aerodynamic drag will be at a minimum.

- As the airspeed approaches the best angle-of-climb speed, rotate to the liftoff attitude. If you rotate to the takeoff attitude too soon, or if you rotate beyond the proper attitude, increased drag (induced drag) will delay the takeoff and increase the takeoff distance.

- The airplane will fly off by itself, hold the takeoff attitude and the airplane will accelerate to V_X (best angle of climb speed). Climb at V_X until obstructions are passed. Accelerate to V_Y (best rate-of-climb speed). Maintain full power until at least 400 feet agl. Full power in conjunction with the best rate of climb speed will result in the greatest altitude gain in a minimum of time. Using this procedure, if you experience an engine failure you are in a better position to cope.

- Maintain runway alignment with coordinated use of the controls. It is not proper to fly the airplane in a slip to maintain runway alignment. Fine tune the trim of the airplane and maintain V_Y, unless a higher speed is necessary to improve visibility.

- High-elevation (or high density altitude) mountain airstrips often result in takeoff distances that double or require even more runway surface than at sea level (5,000-feet elevation requires more than double the sea-level takeoff distance). To avoid ground effect problems that can send you crashing back to the ground, make all takeoffs using an attitude for rotation and climb out.

NORMAL TAKEOFF
TAIL WHEEL (CONVENTIONAL GEAR AIRPLANES)

The "tail dragger" will have a tendency to yaw to the left during the takeoff run because:

(1) TORQUE – Every action has an equal and opposite reaction. Have you noticed other people in a restaurant trying to get ketchup out of a bottle? They hold the bottle inverted and pound on the base ... and pound on the base ... and pound on the base. The equal and opposite reaction is not for the ketchup to be squirted out, but for it to retract back into the bottle. (Proper technique is to hold the bottle inverted and using the palm of your

other hand, strike your hand on the side of the bottle in an UP direction). Most general aviation airplanes have a clockwise rotation of the propeller when viewed from the cockpit. The torque reaction to this rotation is counterclockwise. This causes the left main wheel to be pressed on the ground harder than the right main wheel. The extra drag from friction causes the airplane to yaw to the left.

(2) P-FACTOR – Propeller factor (asymmetric thrust of the propeller) results in the right side of the propeller's plane of rotation developing more thrust than the left side causing the airplane to yaw to the left.

- The conventional gear airplane's longitudinal axis is pointed up into the air during the takeoff run. The angle of attack is still the angle between the chord line of the propeller blades and a line perpendicular to the ground; however the propeller blades are tilted away from the perpendicular line. This tilt causes the large angle of attack on the right plane of rotation and the small angle of attack on the left plane of rotation.

- The tricycle gear airplane is not subject to P-factor during takeoff because the propeller blades are both at the same angle of attack.

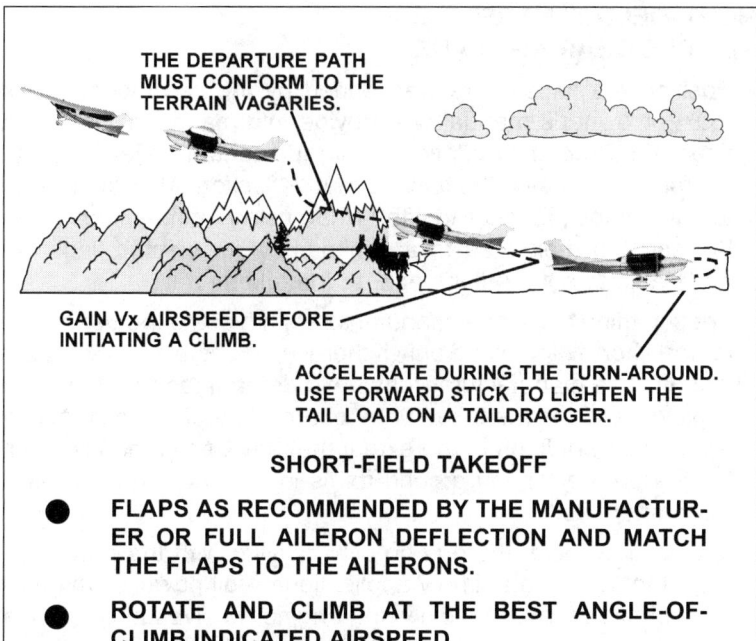

THE DEPARTURE PATH MUST CONFORM TO THE TERRAIN VAGARIES.

GAIN Vx AIRSPEED BEFORE INITIATING A CLIMB.

ACCELERATE DURING THE TURN-AROUND. USE FORWARD STICK TO LIGHTEN THE TAIL LOAD ON A TAILDRAGGER.

SHORT-FIELD TAKEOFF

- FLAPS AS RECOMMENDED BY THE MANUFACTURER OR FULL AILERON DEFLECTION AND MATCH THE FLAPS TO THE AILERONS.

- ROTATE AND CLIMB AT THE BEST ANGLE-OF-CLIMB INDICATED AIRSPEED.

(3) **CORKSCREWING EFFECT OF THE PROPELLER SLIP-STREAM** – The slipstream from the propeller strikes the vertical stabilizer and rudder on the left side of the airplane, which yaws the airplane to the left.

(4) **GYROSCOPIC PRECESSION OF THE PROPELLER** – Any spinning object having mass will exhibit the properties of a gyroscope. One property of a gyro is that it reacts to an outside force, but the reaction is 90 degrees in the plane of rotation. When the tail is raised with the elevator control, the effect is the same as if a force in front of the airplane is pushing down on the bottom of the propeller's plane of rotation to force the tail up. With clockwise rotation (viewed from the cockpit) of the propeller, 90 degrees in the plane of rotation is where the force acts, which will tend to yaw the airplane to the left.

SHORT-FIELD TAKEOFF

The short-field takeoff is used whenever the field length is limited or there are obstacles near the windward end of the runway or along the departure flight path. Determine the takeoff distance for the existing density altitude, and then apply the OTHER FACTORS information provided in Chapter 2.

We will define the short-field technique as follows:

SHORT-FIELD TAKEOFF
TRICYCLE GEAR AIRPLANE

- ✔ Position the flaps as recommended by the manufacturer. The POH or owner's manual will provide information on the use of flaps. If no recommendation, make full control deflection of the ailerons, and match the flaps to that deflection. My preference is to lower flaps just prior to liftoff when using manual flaps, thereby reducing their drag to a minimum. With electric flaps, it is preferable to set the flaps prior to the takeoff roll.

- ✔ Keep in mind that some manufacturers advocate the use of flaps for the short-field takeoff only if there in no obstacle present after takeoff. The manufacturer may have determined that the use of flaps will shorten the takeoff run, but the rate of climb is reduced with the use of flaps to the extent that any benefit of using flaps to shorten the takeoff ground roll is lost in the reduced rate of climb after liftoff.

- ✔ With a short field, there is no dilly-dallying with the power. It is important to make a timely application of full power. If the throttle is shoved forward rapidly, the engine receives a "gulp" of air that will cause hesitation and detonation. The power application must be smooth. For an airplane equipped with a supercharged or turbocharged engine, you may want to hold the brakes while you make a smooth application of power to prevent over-boosting.

✔ Don't lock the brakes and add full power (unless necessary to prevent over-boosting). The propeller must be moving forward through the air before it becomes efficient. Also, locking the brakes and adding full power can cause damage to the propeller and horizontal stabilizer as small rocks and debris are picked up and accelerated rearward. Hold the elevator control at neutral to minimize aerodynamic drag during the ground run. Use the ailerons as appropriate to the wind condition. Rotate at the best angle-of-climb speed and maintain this attitude until clear of obstacles, then accelerate to the best rate-of-climb speed after clearing obstacles.

✔ If the runway is short enough to cause you concern and you've checked the manual and determined you can take off under the existing conditions, you might feel more comfortable by having some extra takeoff speed. As you approach the end of the runway (there probably will not be a taxiway), move to one side. If there is any wind, make the turnaround into the wind. During the turnaround, begin applying power and when the airplane is within 30 degrees of runway alignment, apply full power. With a taildragger, push forward on the stick to relieve the weight on the tail wheel. This maneuver should be practiced with an instructor to determine the speed of the turnaround. Remember the centrifugal force during the turn will sling the fuel to the outside and increase the tendency to tip over. While with the instructor, look at the ball of the turn and bank instrument. It shouldn't exceed one and one-half ball widths during the turn.

SHORT-FIELD TAKEOFF
CONVENTIONAL GEAR AIRPLANE

✔ Flaps as recommended by the manufacturer. If no recommendation, make full control deflection of the ailerons, and match the flaps to that deflection.

✔ Prompt, smooth application of full power. Do not lock the brakes. Add full power (unless necessary to prevent over-boosting on a turbocharged or supercharged engine); the takeoff distance will not be shortened; the propeller must move forward before it becomes efficient. Also, using full power with the brakes locked can pick up small rocks and debris, which may damage the propeller or be accelerated rearward to damage the horizontal stabilizer.

✔ As soon as the elevator control becomes effective, use forward control pressure to assume an attitude similar to normal cruise attitude, which will minimize aerodynamic drag.

✔ Accelerate to the best angle-of-climb speed and rotate to an attitude that will maintain this speed until obstacles are cleared. Then transition to the best rate-of-climb airspeed.

ADVANCED TECHNIQUE – SHORT-FIELD TAKEOFF CONVENTIONAL GEAR AIRPLANE

When operating at short mountain airstrips that tax the ability of the airplane and the pilot, a different technique is incorporated to assure takeoff in the space available.

Because most general aviation taildraggers require more runway for takeoff than they do for landing, keep in mind the go/no-go point on the runway before applying takeoff power. If you do not mentally calculate a position along the runway where you must be airborne or you will abort the takeoff, use the *runway length adequate* rule of thumb. If 71 percent of the takeoff speed is attained by the half-way point of the runway, there is sufficient runway remaining for the liftoff. If the airplane does not have the required speed at the half-way point, shut it down.

There are two choices available to the pilot at the half-way point of the runway. The first is to abort the takeoff and stop, changing the aircraft loading or waiting for better conditions (cooler temperature, stronger headwind). The second choice is to continue the takeoff. Unfortunately, although there may be two choices available at the half-way point, only the first is viable.

The skilled pilot is one who is the master of flying techniques, being adept in various airplane operations. This "skilled pilot" is not measured by the number of hours in his logbook. His skill is demonstrated in the advanced-technique for the short-field takeoff. The takeoff is described as:

✔ Smoothly apply takeoff power.

This is important to improve engine-life and prevent propeller damage. I've seen some propellers flown by "bush pilots," that look like chainsaw blades. Other bush pilots (the masters) go into short gravel strips with no damage to the prop. The difference is the power application. I don't mean that you use up most of the runway before reaching full power. Just allow the airplane to move forward so rocks are not drawn into the blades.

Do not lock the brakes. Small rocks can damage the propeller and the horizontal stabilizer/elevator. The propeller must move through the air before it becomes efficient. There may be a small advantage, maybe 5 or 10 feet, in going to full power before brake release. If you can't make yourself go psychologically without the locked-brake takeoff, do what's best for you.

✔ When the elevator becomes effective, raise the tail to reduce aerodynamic drag.

Because the taildragger is operating at a high angle of attack during ground operations, it is important to reduce the drag as quickly as possible during the takeoff. Lifting the tail to assume an attitude close to normal cruise attitude reduces the aerodynamic drag.

It becomes a matter of experience as to when to raise the tail. If it is done too soon, it adds to the aerodynamic drag. If done too late, it is ineffective in reducing the takeoff distance. When you reach the position in the takeoff roll where the elevator is effective enough to raise the tail using only one-third of the elevator forward travel, this is the time to raise the tail.

✔ Flaps are used differently on the really short strips. When the airplane is ready to fly, apply half of the flaps. Accelerate in ground effect before the climb out.

Most of the taildraggers used for operation to short fields have hand-operated mechanical flaps. The flap lever is called the *Johnson Bar*. If you have trouble reaching the flap lever while keeping your eyes on the runway, pull them up to 10 degrees before starting the takeoff roll.

When the airplane will be flying in ground effect, smoothly apply one-half the flaps. Jerking the flaps will balloon the airplane into the air, which adds drag and could cause the airplane to touch down again. If the strip is really short, do not use the flaps to lift off even though you can. Use the full length to avoid lifting off too soon.

When the airplane is established in the air, fly close to the ground, within one or two feet. Accelerate in ground effect until obtaining the best angle-of-climb speed. Slowly bleed off (sometimes called "milking") the flaps.

After clearing any obstacles, accelerate to the best rate-of-climb speed.

Chapter 4 - Takeoffs   PART 2 TAKEOFF

This technique provides better performance than the conventional short-field takeoff; however, the novice can get into trouble if he does not understand flight in the region of reversed command (back side of the power curve).

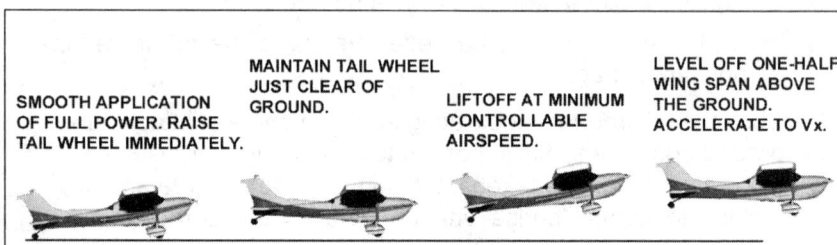

SMOOTH APPLICATION OF FULL POWER. RAISE TAIL WHEEL IMMEDIATELY.

MAINTAIN TAIL WHEEL JUST CLEAR OF GROUND.

LIFTOFF AT MINIMUM CONTROLLABLE AIRSPEED.

LEVEL OFF ONE-HALF WING SPAN ABOVE THE GROUND. ACCELERATE TO V_x.

THE SOFT-FIELD/ROUGH-FIELD TAKEOFF TECHNIQUE IS USED FOR OPERATING FROM FIELDS THAT ARE ROUGH OR THAT HAVE STANDING WATER, SLUSH, SNOW, MUD, HIGH GRASS, WET GRASS OR LOOSE ROCKS. RAISE THE NOSEWHEEL/TAIL WHEEL AS SOON AS POSSIBLE AND MAINTAIN A HIGH ANGLE OF ATTACK. LIFTOFF IS FORCED AT THE MINIMUM AIRSPEED. DO NOT CLIMB AT THIS AIRSPEED BECAUSE OF THE POSSIBILITY OF A STALL. WITHIN ONE-HALF WING SPAN ABOVE THE GROUND, REDUCE THE ANGLE OF ATTACK AND ACCELERATE TO V_X OR V_Y.

SOFT-FIELD TAKEOFF

SOFT-FIELD TAKEOFF

The soft-field or rough-field takeoff is used when the surface is soft, rough, rock, grass, mud, sand, gravel, snow or slush covered. The object is to transfer the weight of the aircraft from the wheels to the wings as soon as possible; assuming the drag of the wheels on the surface is greater than the induced drag resulting from a high angle of attack. The nose wheel or tail wheel is lifted off the surface when the elevator is effective.

Normally flaps will be used for the soft-field takeoff; however, a high density altitude may preclude a low-powered airplane from climbing once it is off the ground. If the manufacturer advises otherwise, such as when an obstacle is present, perform the takeoff in the manner prescribed in the flight manual.

✔ Use sufficient back pressure (tricycle-gear airplanes) to obtain a high angle of attack, exercising caution. It is desirable to raise the nose wheel off the ground as soon as possible, but it is poor technique to experience a tail strike. For conventional gear airplanes, use enough forward pressure to lift the tail wheel as soon as possible, but keep the tail close to the ground. With a tricycle gear airplane, don't over-rotate and strike the tail!

- ✔ As the speed increases, the angle of attack, if maintained at the original attitude, will cause a tail strike. It is important to decrease the angle of attack, as required, to maintain the nose wheel or tail wheel off of the surface.

Maintaining the attitude to keep the nose wheel or tail wheel clear of the ground will result in liftoff at an airspeed that is slower than a safe climb speed. If it is maintained the airplane will stall or settle back to the ground as soon as it climbs out of ground effect.

- ✔ Level off at a height of one-half wing span and accelerate to V_X or V_Y.

- ✔ Immediately after liftoff, lower the nose to accelerate to the best angle-of-climb speed if there are obstacles to consider, or the best rate-of-climb speed for a normal climb out. At a safe altitude, maybe 100-feet agl, begin retracting the flaps. The flaps are not dumped, a procedure called "milking the flaps" is used, where partial flap retraction is made and any sink is arrested with back pressure on the control wheel. This continues until the flaps are totally retracted.

- ✔ The purpose of the soft-field procedure is to allow the airplane to take off in the space available from a high-drag surface. This assumes that the drag on the wheels will be greater than the induced drag on the wings. In actuality, the technique also diminishes the wear and tear on the landing gear and aircraft components.

- ✔ Low-powered airplanes have to exercise caution in making a soft-field takeoff from a short field. The induced drag from the high angle of attack in combination with the drag on the wheels may make it impossible to take off in the space available. In this case, a modified short-field/soft-field takeoff must be used.

MODIFIED SHORT/SOFT-FIELD TAKEOFF

Those pilots who have never flown under-powered airplanes in the mountains don't realize the thrills they are missing. To reduce the adrenaline level—but not all of the excitement—it is necessary to use the modified short-field/soft-field takeoff technique for the soft-field takeoff.

Airplanes with marginal performance may not be able to accelerate and obtain the speed necessary for takeoff from a short/soft field. The induced drag of a high angle of attack is combined with the drag of the surface.

Chapter 4 - Takeoffs — PART 2 TAKEOFF

Using the *runway length sufficient* rule of thumb, if 71 percent of the required takeoff speed is not obtained by the halfway point of the runway, abort the takeoff and taxi back. Then try the modified short/soft-field takeoff. During the takeoff roll, raise the nosewheel slightly, if at all. This produces some "abuse" for the aircraft. The mistreating of the airplane is necessary to be able to takeoff and is less harmful than crashing off the end of the runway if the takeoff is continued, or running through the fence if the takeoff is aborted. It's probably a good idea to walk along the length of the strip to determine if one side is firmer than the other. Make the takeoff along the best path.

Once the airplane is clear of the ground—operating in ground effect—maintain an attitude that will keep the airplane clear of the ground, yet will allow acceleration to the best angle-of-climb or rate-of-climb airspeed before climbing.

CROSSWIND TAKEOFF

Approximately one-half of all aircraft involved in ground incidents or accidents during crosswind operations are equipped with tricycle landing gear. Maybe there is some complacency on the part of pilots who assume that tricycle-gear airplanes are easier to operate in a crosswind. Regardless, the statistics point out the need for crosswind operation proficiency.

In the early days of aviation, when an aerodrome consisted of a large square area that was suitable for operations in any direction, it was possible to direct the airplane's nose into the wind for all landings. Today, with limited runways and given the fickle nature of the wind, crosswind proficiency is required.

Crosswind takeoffs involve different techniques from the normal takeoff because the wind coming from the side tries to veer the airplane in the direction of the wind (weathercocking tendency), while lifting the upwind wing. This produces a tendency to tip the airplane over.

The weathercocking tendency is due to the airplane having more surface area (fuselage, vertical stabilizer and rudder) exposed to a crosswind aft of the main wheels than ahead of them. The "tail dragger" airplane (center of gravity located aft of the main wheels) encounters a stronger weathercocking tendency than a tricycle-gear airplane (center of gravity located forward of the main wheels).

A normal takeoff into the wind requires very little control input by the pilot as the airplane tends to maintain a straight heading; however, the crosswind takeoff requires special control input. Performed within the experience level of the pilot and the operating limitations of the airplane, the crosswind takeoff is relatively simple. The biggest problem and the most common cause of crosswind takeoff accidents is lifting off without sufficient airspeed to remain airborne.

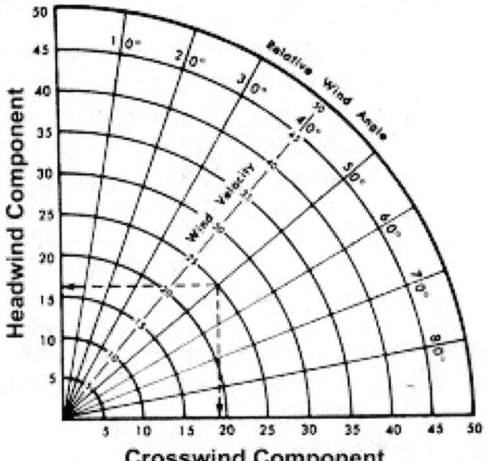

CROSSWIND COMPONENT CHART
GO/NO-GO DECISION

Instructions:

- Determine the maximum 90° crosswind for your plane. If this is not listed in your owner's manual, use 20% times the stall speed. Place a dot on the "Crosswind Component" line of the chart at this value.

- Determine the maximum 45° crosswind for your plane. Suggest 30% times the stall speed. Place a dot on the "Headwind Component" line of the chart at this value.

- Connect these dots with a red line.

    ✔ Any values determined to be left of the red line are **GO**.

    ✔ Any values determined to be right of the red line are **NO-GO** wind directions and velocities.

WIND LIMITS

As a general rule, never attempt to taxi when the crosswind exceeds 50 percent V_{SO}. Taxi slowly and with caution when the crosswind is 30 percent of V_{SO}.

Federal Aviation Regulations governing airplane design require than an airplane is controllable in a 90-degree crosswind with a wind velocity of 0.2 V_{SO} (stall speed in the landing configuration).

Chapter 4 - Takeoffs   PART 2 TAKEOFF

Experienced pilots operate in 90-degree crosswinds of greater than 20 percent V_{SO} and would find the regulation to be quite restrictive if it were a limiting factor. An airplane may be controllable in a 90-degree crosswind greater than 0.2 V_{SO}. Only you know your capability as a pilot. As with all flight operations, you should allow some margin for safety.

Some manufacturers list a maximum demonstrated crosswind velocity that is greater than 1.2 V_{SO}. They may state the maximum demonstrated crosswind velocity is not a limiting factor (perhaps there wasn't a stronger wind available for their demonstration to the FAA), and this implies that it is okay to takeoff or land in crosswinds stronger than that listed. You might want to check with your insurance carrier and ask what their policy is concerning crosswind operations at a crosswind speed greater than 0.2 V_{SO}.

CROSSWIND TAKEOFF TECHNIQUE

The crosswind takeoff is relatively simple for the pilot who understands the principles involved. It may, at times, be quite exciting, yet it is still simple. A

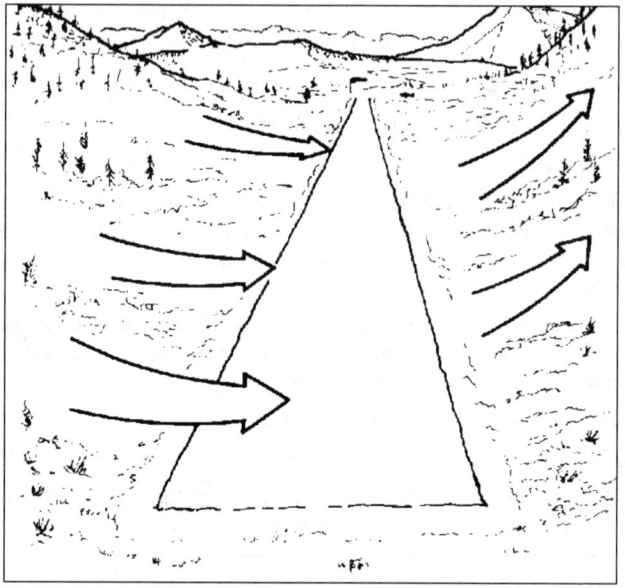

CROSSWIND TAKEOFF

CROSSWIND CONDITIONS ARE PREVALENT AT AIRSTRIPS LOCATED NEAR THE CONFLUENCE OF CREEKS. DETERMINE THAT THE EXISTING CONDITIONS ARE WITHIN THE CAPABILITIES OF THE AIRPLANE. STUDY TERRAIN FEATURES TO VISUALIZE THE POSSIBILITY OF DOWNDRAFTS IN THE CRITICAL AFTER-TAKEOFF AREA OF THE DEPARTURE.

PART 2 TAKEOFF Chapter 4 - Takeoffs

crosswind, affecting the wings and other control surfaces, does not move in the same direction that the wheels roll along the ground. Therefore the takeoff technique results in part taxiing, part flying and the transition between the two.

While taxiing into the takeoff position, check the wind indicator for the trend of the crosswind. The action of the wind from the side does two things to the airplane. First, the wind tries to get under the upwind wing with a tendency to tip the airplane over. Second, the airplane has a tendency to weathervane (streamline itself into the wind).

Upsetting Wind Action

The upsetting action of the side wind is originally counteracted by holding the wings level or banking slightly into the wind by application of *full* aileron into the wind. If the wind is from the right, full right aileron deflection is held. The right-wing aileron is up and the left-wing aileron is down. A left crosswind requires left aileron pressure.

As the speed increases during the takeoff roll, the upwind wing will develop more lift, causing it to "fly" or begin rising before the downwind wing. The use of aileron pressure is merely to keep the wings level.

It's a good idea to understand the order of control effectiveness when flying an airplane in a crosswind. While accelerating for takeoff the order is A-E-R. That is, the ailerons are the first control surface to provide a response, elevators are next, followed by the rudder. With increasing speed during the takeoff roll, the ailerons become sufficiently effective to be able to maneuver the airplane

SKIPPING DURING THE CROSSWIND TAKEOFF IS DUE TO INSUFFICIENT AILERON CONTROL USAGE TO KEEP THE UPWIND WING DOWN AND/OR INSUFFICIENT FORWARD ELEVATOR PRESSURE TO KEEP THE AIRPLANE ON THE GROUND.

Chapter 4 - Takeoffs PART 2 TAKEOFF

about its longitudinal (roll) axis. While decelerating they become ineffective in the R-E-A order.

With the increasing speed and greater aileron effectiveness, less aileron pressure is required. Until you develop a "feel" for the airplane, try relaxing one-half the aileron pressure when one-half the takeoff speed has been obtained. With experience, there is a gradual reduction of aileron pressure throughout the takeoff roll, rather than making mechanical movements.

Skipping During Takeoff

If not enough aileron pressure is maintained during the takeoff roll and the upwind wing rises, a "skipping" may result. This is a series of very small bounces caused by the airplane attempting to fly and then settling back onto the runway while drifting some distance downwind. These bounces impose sideward stress on the landing gear and may cause the gear structure to fail.

Weather Vane Tendency

In addition to the use of aileron during the takeoff roll, it is necessary to use rudder opposite the wind direction to counteract the weathercock tendency.

A weather vane is a thin plate of wood or metal that has often been shaped to resemble a rooster or arrow. Pilots are more familiar with the tetrahedron or wind tee. The weather vane pivots to indicate the direction of the wind.

The airplane's vertical stabilizer and rudder make an excellent, but undesired, weather vane. The airplane tries to turn into the wind to become streamlined.

During takeoff in a conventional gear airplane with a light crosswind from the right, the normal torque and p-factor may be sufficient to counteract the weathercock tendency. Conversely, with a left crosswind, it will add to the weathercock tendency, aggravating the situation. Regardless of the wind direction, use sufficient rudder to maintain directional control.

During the takeoff ground roll the pilot must maintain a ground track parallel to the runway while compensating for the side force that tries to tip the airplane over by lifting the upwind wing and the side force that tries to weathercock the plane.

The difference between a normal takeoff and a crosswind takeoff involves maintaining directional control while on the ground and maintaining directional control while in the air, with a transition between a ground vehicle and an air vehicle occurring at the moment of liftoff. It is important that once the airplane is lifted into the air it is not allowed to contact the ground again.

Crosswind Takeoff Procedure

✗ To perform the crosswind takeoff, begin the takeoff roll with full aileron deflection into the wind. It may be necessary to use differential braking until the rudder becomes effective. If the crosswind is from the right, the airplane will try to turn right, into the wind. The left brake is used, but only until the rudder becomes effective enough to counteract the weathercocking tendency. The use of the brake will lengthen the takeoff distance.

For the conventional gear airplane (or tricycle gear airplane) when the wind is too strong to takeoff otherwise, you might consider using the following technique. Assume the wind is from the right. For this example, assume we are operating from runway 18 and the wind is from 230 degrees at 25 knots.

✘ Taxi to the downwind edge of the runway. Instead of aligning the longitudinal axis parallel to the runway length, point the nose about 10 to 20 degrees into the wind, toward the upwind edge of the runway.

This angle is variable and depends on the pilot's experience, the takeoff performance of the airplane and the runway surface. For a hard surfaced runway, it is determined by pointing the nose at an imaginary spot along the upwind edge of the runway. This imaginary spot is located down the runway at a distance equal to two-thirds the takeoff distance required for the density altitude at which you are operating. If you point the nose farther down the runway, much of the advantage of using this technique is lost. If you point the nose less than this distance down the runway, you may be unable to complete the required turn to parallel the runway.

For a soft field, such as grass or gravel, the angle cannot be as large as with a paved runway or the airplane will chatter (skid) off the runway while turning to parallel it.

✘ Perform the crosswind takeoff. As the airplane approaches the upwind side of the runway, make a left turn so the longitudinal axis parallels the length of the runway.

There is a reduction of the velocity of the crosswind component realized by turning into the wind and reducing the wind angle. But, more important, the centrifugal force created by the left turn, which fights against the weathercocking tendency of the wind, keeps the upwind (right) wing down.

How much reduction in the velocity of the direct crosswind component is realized by angling into the wind?

Let's examine two different airplanes, one with a total ground roll takeoff distance of 400 feet and the other with a total ground roll takeoff distance of 1,200 feet. We will use the same data as before; runway 18 and wind 2325.

For the airplane that requires 400 feet for the takeoff ground roll, the angle formed by pointing down the runway for two-thirds the takeoff distance (266.4

Chapter 4 - Takeoffs — PART 2 TAKEOFF

feet in this case) will vary with the width of the runway. For a runway 50 feet wide, the airplane would be turned 10.63 degrees into the wind (direct crosswind component of 15.86 knots); for a runway 75 feet wide, the heading would be 15.73 degrees to the right (direct crosswind component of 14.08 knots); and for a runway 100 feet wide, the angle would be 20.56 degrees (direct crosswind component of 12.29 knots). If the airplane made the takeoff, paralleling the runway, using a heading of 180 degrees, the direct crosswind component would be (50 degree angle, 25 knot wind) 19.15 knots.

For the airplane requiring 1,200 feet for takeoff, the angle formed by pointing down the runway for two-thirds the takeoff distance, 799.2 feet, also varies with the width of the runway. For a 50 foot wide runway the airplane is turned 3.58 degrees into the wind (direct crosswind component of 18.11 knots); for the 75 foot wide runway the airplane is turned 5.36 degrees into the wind (direct crosswind component of 17.57 knots); and for the 100 foot wide runway the airplane is turned 7.13 degrees into the wind (direct crosswind component of 17.01 knots).

Angling into the wind reduces the amount of crosswind affecting the takeoff. But, again, it is the centrifugal force from the turn to parallel the runway, that really helps in fighting the weathercocking tendency and in keeping the upwind wing down.

> ✘ The elevator control is maintained in a forward position (conventional gear pilots pull back on the control wheel/stick) to keep the wheels solidly on the runway while a straight heading is maintained. The pressure of the wind on the fuselage and empennage (complete tail assembly) imposes a side strain on the landing gear. As long as a straight heading is maintained, this side strain is acceptable. If the aircraft is not held down firmly, it could skip sideways on the runway putting an unacceptable strain on the landing gear and its components.

If the wind is from the right side, the right wing will develop more lift than the left wing and will tend to lift the upwind wheel off the ground. This occurs because the dihedral effect increases the angle of attack of the right wing and the fuselage blankets some of the left wing airflow. To counteract this lifting action, move the control wheel/stick to the right. The left aileron deflects down, increasing the lift on the downwind wing; the right aileron deflects up, decreasing the lift on the upwind wing. As the speed increases and the ailerons become more and more effective, it is necessary to roll out some of the deflection. Use only enough aileron control to keep the wind from lifting the upwind wing, maintaining the wings level. In a strong crosswind which requires full aileron deflection, especially with a conventional gear airplane, the downwind wheel will lift off first. The airplane is flown (on the ground) with the upwind wheel on the ground and the downwind wheel in the air, maintaining a straight ground track, until the proper airspeed for takeoff is obtained. The airplane is difficult to handle and you must force the airplane to remain on the runway. You must avoid the temptation to haul the airplane off the ground before it will continue to fly without settling back to the runway. This procedure of maintaining only one wheel on the ground will prevent damaging side loads on the gear assembly.

AFTER TAKEOFF

After takeoff, with sufficient airspeed to prevent the possibility of settling back to the runway, make a coordinated turn into the wind in an amount that will compensate for drift. It is poor technique to climb with one wing low (slip) after liftoff instead of crabbing. A slip will adversely affect the airplane's climb performance.

GROUND LOOP

Howard Ballew always told me, "Fly the thing until it's tied down." While this applies to the conventional gear airplane, it's sage advice for the airplane with training wheels (tricycle gear) too.

Most pilots associate the ground loop with the after-landing roll in a conventional gear airplane, in which the airplane makes an uncontrolled turn. It may occur during the takeoff and it can happen to tricycle gear airplanes.

Essentially, something causes the airplane to swerve. This may be improper use of the rudder, uneven ground, a crosswind, or a soft spot that retards one wheel. When the swerve occurs, centrifugal force causes the airplane to veer even more. Centrifugal force increases as the square of the speed at which it starts, so the faster the airplane is going, the worse the centrifugal force. If the swerve cannot be controlled with power, brake and coordinated use of the rudder, the airplane will tip and may strike the wing on the ground.

AIRSPEED FOR ROTATION

For a steady crosswind it's a good idea to have about 10 percent more airspeed than normal so that the airplane will not settle back to the runway in a crab. If the wind is gusting, use 10 percent more airspeed than normal or one-half the gust factor, whichever is greater.

USE OF FLAPS

The use of flaps during a crosswind takeoff is a controversial subject. To do what is right for you requires some experimentation on your part. See the discussion about flaps under Part 4 - Landings.

I can hear some of you saying, "That's a cop-out. What do you do?" Well, when flying an airplane with mechanical flaps (the old Johnson Bar), I use flaps, but not during the start of the takeoff roll. The flaps are applied smoothly at the time of liftoff.

Mountain Flying Bible

With electric flaps the same technique can be used, but most pilots usually do not use them unless there is some compelling reason, like a short runway. Electric flaps do not provide a feel for application and unless there is a detent that allows you to preselect the desired amount, it is best to direct your attention outside the airplane, not to look at a small dial while trying to set the flaps.

If flaps are used during the takeoff it is not a good idea to retract them immediately after takeoff. Level off to remain in ground effect. When the airspeed increases and is approaching the best angle-of-climb speed or the best rate-of-climb speed, slowly retract the flaps. Increase the back pressure while "milking" the flaps to prevent settling.

COLD WEATHER TAKEOFFS

Cold weather operations are ideal for flying; the denser air allows the engine to produce more power, the propeller develops more thrust and the wings create more lift. There are three disadvantages to operating in cold air that require consideration:

- ★ The *normally aspirated engine* (normally aspirated means the engine has no supercharger or turbocharger to maintain sea level atmospheric pressure at altitudes above sea level) has the ability of increasing its power output about one percent for each 10-degrees Fahrenheit below standard temperature at any particular altitude. At 40 degrees below the standard temperature, the engine will develop about 10 percent more power even though the manifold pressure and rpm are maintained within indicated limits.

- ★ V_{MC} is the single-engine minimum control speed for multiengine airplanes. It's value is established at sea level, under standard conditions, with the rearmost allowable cg. V_{MC} depends on and varies with power and cg location. Consult performance charts during cold weather to establish the proper power setting; otherwise, the engine may develop greater than rated power. If this is the case, V_{MC} will be a value greater than listed. ✈

CHAPTER 5 – AFTER TAKEOFF

- CYCLE GEAR 2-67
- CLIMB OUT 2-67
- FALSE HORIZON 2-69
- NATURAL HORIZON 2-69
- RATE OF CLIMB 2-70
- ANGLE OF CLIMB 2-71

CYCLE GEAR

During the late fall or early spring (and sometimes during the winter), mountain flying may involve a takeoff from a surface that has water or slush, with the outside temperature at or near freezing. Operating an airplane with a retractable landing gear requires the proper technique to prevent the wheels from freezing or the gear from freezing in the wheel wells.

The usual procedure after takeoff is to ease on the brakes and retract the gear. Using the brakes eliminates centrifugal force that can expand the wheels so they don't fit into the wheel wells properly. With a wet surface, allow the wheels to spin down by themselves before the initial gear retraction. This will allow the tires to rid themselves of excess water. When a safe altitude and airspeed have been reached, extend the gear at least once to allow the extension jolt to sling water from the gear.

CLIMB OUT

Terrain clearance at a mountain strip is the first and foremost consideration during the approach for landing and especially for the takeoff and climb out. Some airstrips are obviously one-way strips, having an obstacle at one end that prohibits approach or takeoff in that direction. Other strips are more subtle. The obstruction isn't adjacent to the strip, but if the takeoff is made in the direction of the impediment, it may be impossible to outclimb or maneuver the airplane into a course reversal to avoid a collision. When approaching an unfamiliar airport for the first time, survey the surrounding terrain for the best approach for landing and for departure.

Chapter 5 - After Takeoff

PART 2 TAKEOFF

FORGET THE STANDARD PATTERN DEPARTURE AT MANY MOUNTAIN STRIPS. THE DEPARTURE PATTERN MUST CONFORM TO THE TERRAIN FEATURES. THE DEPARTURE ROUTE MAY REQUIRE FLIGHT THROUGH NARROW CANYONS OR AN IMMEDIATE COURSE REVERSAL WITH CIRCLING OVER THE AIRSTRIP TO GAIN ALTITUDE.

We become conditioned to operating the airplane in a certain manner and do it mostly without conscious thought. At some airports, we have to consciously abandon the normal traffic pattern and make the flight path conform to the terrain vagaries, often devoting considerable time to circling during the climb to obtain altitude before turning to the en route course.

At short strips, the departure might require takeoff toward formidable terrain where it is necessary to make a turn immediately after takeoff. Perform the appropriate takeoff technique (short-field or soft-field), then accelerate to a speed equal to 1.4 V_{so}. The load factor in a 60-degree bank is 2 gs. The stall speed increases at the square root of the wing load factor. The square root of 2 is 1.41, or a 41 percent increase in stall speed. When this speed is achieved make the turn, limiting the bank to 45-50 degrees. Remember, if flaps are used during the turn the speed will be less, resulting in a smaller radius of turn.

If it is a hot day, monitor the engine cylinder head temperature and oil temperature. It may be necessary to level off at an intermediate altitude and circle momentarily to allow the engine to cool.

Turbulence concerns all prudent pilots. If the mountain strip provides an opportunity for a weather briefing you will have some idea of reported or forecast turbulence; if not, use your eyeballs to check for a mountain wave, cumulus clouds with the edges moving, snow or dirt blowing off mountain peaks and ridges, gusty wind, ripples or white caps on bodies of water and the like. These indicators do not prohibit flight, but they give you an indication that turbulence may exist. You can depart for a "look-see" to determine the stability during the climb out. If the turbulence is uncomfortable, return to the airstrip and delay the flight for an hour or two. It might even be necessary to postpone the flight until the next day. If the turbulence doesn't limit the flight, but is uncomfortable, try climbing to a higher altitude in an attempt to escape the bumpiness.

The takeoff and climb out requires the use of precise airspeed control to eliminate the possibility of the false horizon effect. Maintaining a constant attitude (where the nose is located in relation to the horizon) and constant power setting, will result in a constant airspeed. Once V_X has been used to clear obstacles and V_Y has been used to gain altitude, it is wise to transition to a cruise climb. The difference in aircraft performance, that is, the rate of climb, between the best rate-of-climb speed and a cruise-climb speed is small enough that the cruise-climb speed is preferred for better engine cooling and better visibility.

FALSE HORIZON

For the pilot who learned to fly in the flatlands, it is easy to use the attitude of the airplane to maintain straight-and-level flight. You look at the nose position in relation to the horizon and look at the wing spacing in relation to the horizon. This allows straight-and-level flight without constantly monitoring the heading indicator and altimeter.

When operating in an area where mountains replace the natural horizon, it is often difficult to discern a slight upslope to the terrain when it appears to be level. If clouds obscure the mountaintops or if the cloud layers are angled, there is an illusion of straight-and-level flight when the airplane is banked. An unwary or uninformed pilot maintaining level flight by visual reference with the terrain may unsuspectingly climb the airplane. The continuous climb leads to airspeed degradation. When the steadily rising terrain and steadily decreasing airspeed come together, the pilot is likely to come face-to-face with a stall entry.

 The solution to visual illusions? Monitor the attitude indicator, airspeed and outside visual reference and learn how to visualize the natural horizon (the base of the mountains about six to eight miles away).

NATURAL HORIZON

During attitude flying the position of the nose in relation to the natural horizon is used to maintain level flight. The nose is positioned so the horizon is below the nose a certain amount. If the airplane, due to turbulence or inattention,

Chapter 5 - After Takeoff
PART 2 TAKEOFF

FALSE HORIZON

USE THE BASE OF THE MOUNTAINS SOME 6-8 MILES FROM THE AIRPLANE AND INSTRUMENT REFERENCE TO ESTABLISH THE HORIZON FOR VISUAL ATTITUDE FLYING. GENTLY UPSLOPE TERRAIN CREATES AN ILLUSION OF LEVEL FLIGHT WHILE UNINTENTIONALLY CLIMBING AND REDUCING AIRSPEED.

(APPROACHING RUNWAY 15, ASPEN, COLORADO)

transitions to a climb or a descent, the pilot can easily adjust the nose back to the level-flight attitude and be very precise in this determination. The problem arises when flying upslope terrain and the nose is placed below what appears to be the horizon. In reality, the nose is above the level flight attitude. To eliminate this false horizon effect requires visualization of the natural horizon. Use the base of the mountains at least six or eight miles away (or farther is better). Adjust the nose position in relation to this visualized horizon.

RATE OF CLIMB

Some pilots use an *IFR en route low altitude chart* in combination with their sectional chart to monitor the required altitude along the route. The instrument chart provides the minimum en route altitude (MEA) and minimum obstruction clearance altitude (MOCA). The *Terminal Instrument Procedures* manual (TERPS), written by the FAA defines the minimum rate of climb to transition from one MEA to another MEA along an airway.

If the MEA does not have a crossing restriction (where you have to climb to the restricted altitude before proceeding along the airway), then a rate of climb of 152 feet-per-nautical mile guarantees both terrain and obstruction clearance. This doesn't require excessive aircraft performance. An airplane maintaining 120 knots needs only 250 feet-per-minute rate of climb to maintain the 152 feet-per-nautical mile criteria.

To determine the rate of climb per nautical mile, divide the ground speed by 60. This gives the nautical miles per minute travelled. Example, at 80 knots, how many nautical miles per minute are travelled? 80/60 = 1.33. Next, the miles per minute multiplied by 152 (rate of climb established by TERPS) yields the rate of climb necessary to transition between MEAs (1.33 x 152 = 202.7 fpm).

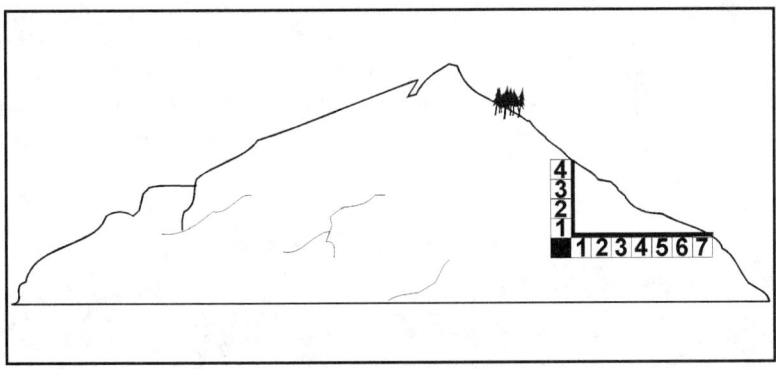

CALCULATING THE SLOPE OF A MOUNTAIN USING VISUALIZATION. THIS MAY OR MAY NOT BE ACCURATE DEPENDING UPON YOUR VISUALIZATION SKILL.

ANGLE OF CLIMB

I've never found much use for determining the aircraft's angle of climb except for aircraft accident litigation. The information doesn't do much good unless you know or can determine the topographical angle of the terrain.

Most light aircraft have an angle of climb of about two and one-half degrees, so if there is a visible change in the terrain, watch out. The terrain will probably climb faster than the airplane.

The slope of a mountain can be estimated through visualization, if your visualizing skills are good. In this example we have a slope of 4 over 7. Divide 4 by 7 and come up with .57. Multiply the .57 by 90 degrees to find the slope is 51.3 degrees. The small general aviation airplane, climbing at an angle of about 2½ degrees has no chance of outclimbing this terrain. An airplane flying below the

Chapter 5 - After Takeoff   **PART 2 TAKEOFF**

altitude of discernable changes in terrain may require maneuvering for additional altitude prior to continuing on course.

CLIMB PER NAUTICAL MILE

To determine the rate of climb per nautical mile, use the flight computer, placing the ground speed in knots over the "60" speed index. Look above "10" (actually 1) to determine the distance traveled per minute. Divide the rate of climb by the distance traveled per minute to obtain the rate of climb per nautical mile.

> **EXAMPLE**: With a ground speed of 120 knots and a rate of climb of 500 feet per minute, what is the rate of climb per nautical mile?
>
> **SOLUTION**: Place the ground speed, 120 knots, over the "60" speed index. Look above "10" to find 2 miles per minute. Divide 500 feet per minute rate of climb by the 2 miles per minute ground speed (place 500 on the outside scale, 2 on the middle scale, and read above 1 on the middle scale 250 feet), and obtain 250 feet per nautical mile. ✈

FRONT OFFICE OF THE CITATION X. NOT TOO GOOD FOR MOUNTAIN FLYING, BUT IT WILL CRUISE AT MACH 0.92.

Mountain Flying Bible

PART 2 TAKEOFF — Rules of Thumb

PART 2 - TAKEOFF – RULES OF THUMB

ALTIMETER SETTING EQUIVALENT-FEET VALUES
One inch of mercury equals 1,000 feet; 0.1 inch equals 100 feet; 0.01 inch equals 10 feet. (See page 2-9)

DETERMINE DENSITY ALTITUDE
For each 10°F above or below standard temperature at an airport's elevation, add or subtract 600 feet to (from) the field's elevation. (See page 2-12)

FIXED-PITCH PROPELLER DENSITY ALTITUDE TAKEOFF DISTANCE
To the standard, sea level takeoff distance, add 12 % for each 1,000 feet of density altitude up to 8,000 feet. Add an additional 20 % for each additional 1,000 feet density altitude above 8,000 feet. (See page 2-13)

CONSTANT-SPEED (VARIABLE-PITCH) PROPELLER DENSITY ALTITUDE TAKEOFF DISTANCE
To the standard, sea level takeoff distance, add 10 percent for each 1,000 feet density altitude up to 8,000 feet. Add 15 percent for each additional 1,000 feet density altitude above 8,000 feet. (See page 2-15)

DENSITY ALTITUDE RATE OF CLIMB — FIXED-PITCH PROPELLER
Reduce sea level rate of climb 7% for each thousand feet density altitude up to 8,500 feet and 8% for each thousand feet above 8,500 feet. (See page 2-15)

DENSITY ALTITUDE RATE OF CLIMB — VARIABLE-PITCH PROPELLER
Reduce sea level rate of climb 6% for each thousand feet density altitude up to 8,500 feet and 8% for each thousand feet above 8,500 feet. (See page 2-15)

Mountain Flying Bible

Rules of Thumb — PART 2 TAKEOFF

TAKEOFF DISTANCE VARIES AS THE SQUARE OF THE GROSS WEIGHT
New weight divided by original weight squared equals takeoff distance factor to be multiplied by the original takeoff distance at original weight. (See page 2-12)

HEADWIND REDUCES TAKEOFF DISTANCE
Determine takeoff distance for the density altitude. Multiply by 0.90 and subtract the value of the ratio of the headwind divided by rotation speed. (See page 2-17)

TAKEOFF FROM VARIOUS SURFACES
Increase the takeoff distance: Firm turf – add 7%; Rough, rocky or short grass – add 10%; long grass – add 20 to 30%; soft field – add 23 to 75%; mud or snow – add 50% or more. (See page 2-18)

RUNWAY LENGTH SUFFICIENT FOR TAKEOFF
Take 10 times the square root of the percentage of liftoff distance required. This equals the percentage of liftoff speed that should be attained in that distance. (See page 2-39)

TAILWIND INCREASES TAKEOFF DISTANCE
The tailwind takeoff distance equals 110% of normal takeoff distance plus the percentage of tailwind speed divided by rotation speed. (See page 2-41)

UPSLOPE TAKEOFF DISTANCE
For takeoff on an upslope runway, from one degree up to two degrees, add 10% per degree to the density altitude takeoff distance. (See page 2-41)

DOWNSLOPE TAKEOFF DISTANCE
For downslope runways, decrease the density altitude takeoff distance 5% per degree. (See page 2-41)

GROUND EFFECT
Fly no higher than one-half the wing span above the ground after takeoff until obtaining V_X. (See page 2-48) ✈

Mountain Flying Bible

PART 3 EN ROUTE Introduction

INTRODUCTION

Part 3
EN ROUTE

- CHAPTER 1—PRECAUTIONS 3-7
- CHAPTER 2—NIGHT FLYING 3-13
- CHAPTER 3—MOUNTAIN FLYING TECHNIQUES . . 3-23
- CHAPTER 4—MOUNTAIN FLYING TURBULENCE . . 3-67
- CHAPTER 5—THE MOUNTAIN WAVE 3-87
- CHAPTER 6—SCUD RUNNING 3-103
- CHAPTER 7—LOST PROCEDURES 3-111
- CHAPTER 8—AIRCRAFT ICING 3-115
- CHAPTER 9—EMERGENCY LAND TECHNIQUES . 3-161
- CHAPTER 10—SURVIVAL AND RESCUE 3-175

INTRODUCTION

Operating safely in a mountain environment requires you to establish some personal safety standards relating to mountain flying such as weather, night flying, minimum runway lengths and aircraft loading.

Depending on your experience, these weather minimums might be a 2,000- or 3,000-foot ceiling and five miles visibility. If the ceiling or the visibility drops below your established minimum, divert to an alternate and wait on the ground until conditions improve.

C150 APPROACHING THE TETON MOUNTAINS

Introduction

PART 3 EN ROUTE

Once you have established your personal safety standards, only experience will allow you to expand them. Don't let a passenger—especially someone who knows nothing about flying—pressure you into compromising these standards. A passenger impatient to get home might say, "The weather looks okay, let's go."

The same thing applies to equipment. The most qualified pilot in the world can still get into trouble trying to push an aircraft beyond it's limitations. If the equipment available is not suitable for the flight, change the flight or change the airplane.

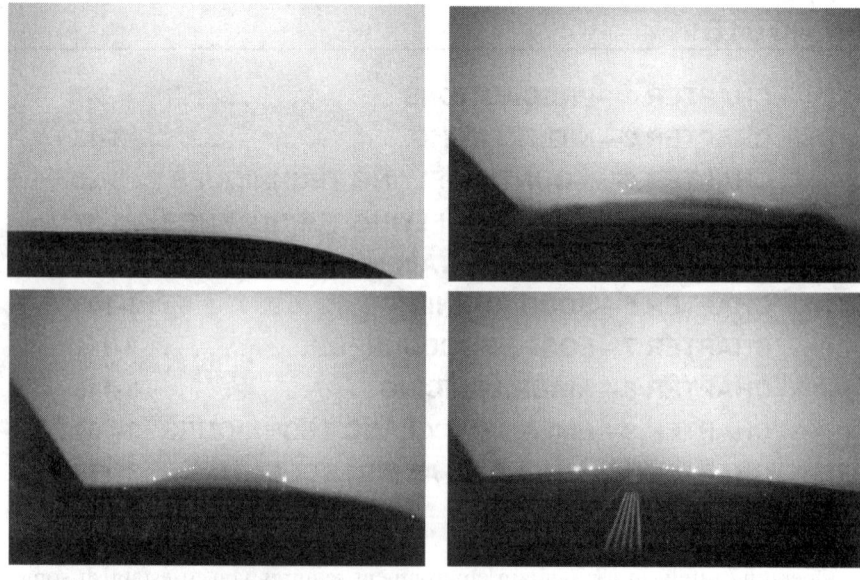

THIS ILS APPROACH TO JACKSON, WYO. DEMONSTRATES THE UNPREDICTIBILITY OF MOUNTAIN WEATHER. THE MOST CRITICAL ASPECT OF MOUNTAIN FLYING IS THE WEATHER; CHECK IT CAREFULLY. FEW MOUNTAIN STRIPS HAVE AN ILS APPROACH PROCEDURE.

Weather is the most dangerous aspect—and the primary cause—of general aviation accidents. This includes flatland and mountain operations. Weather is the final determining factor in making any mountain flight. The pilot may be physically and mentally prepared and the airplane may have the performance capability to deal with the en route terrain. But, unless you are foolishly optimistic, obtain a weather briefing before spending a lot of time on flight planning. The weather briefer may discourage you from making the flight. Or, he may suggest an alternate route that would skirt the weather.

Statistics show weather-involved accidents cause more general aviation injuries and deaths than any other operating factor. Weather is the most important consideration in determining the suitability or probability of making a particular flight. Do not push the weather. When operating in an familiar area and the weather is marginal, you may experience confusion over your location. Easily recognizable landmarks, that appear during good VFR weather, seem to disappear when you need them.

THIS IS VFR?

It is best to listen to the advice of experienced pilots, but you may wish to make your own mistakes. One thing you will learn—whether it is from the advice of others or through your own experience—what affects the safety of flight is that the weather in the mountains is either good VFR or it is IFR and it should be flown as such. Do not fly during marginal VFR conditions in the mountains.

The basic truisms of mountain flying should always be kept in the front of your mind. Always remain in a position where you can turn to lowering terrain if you encounter downdrafts, if you have inadequate terrain clearance, or if you experience a power loss or a power failure. Do not fly beyond the point of no return when flying upslope terrain. Before reaching the point of no return, circle to gain additional altitude before proceeding.

For the pilot new to mountain flying the visual aspects are often deceptive. It is recommended that you start out flying the mountains with 2,000-feet terrain clearance. As your experience, skills and techniques improve; you may be able to lower this personal limitation.

During your preliminary flight planning you may decide to use an 8,000 or 9,000-foot mountain as a landmark. While these figures may infer that this is a prominent landmark, you may miss it during the flight because the large mountain may be little more than a knoll encompassed within other mountains.

Rely on the magnetic compass in the airplane. If the compass appears to be in error, compare its reading to section lines when flying over farming areas. Fly along any section line. The compass should then read N, E, S or W when the magnetic course is corrected for variation (add east variation and subtract west variation).

Maintain an awareness of the wind direction and velocity. Visualize the wind as water and ask yourself what water would do as it flows up and down the

Introduction   **PART 3 EN ROUTE**

mountain ridges and slopes. In areas where there is an abrupt change in terrain, turbulence may occur.

Keep in mind the false horizon effect. The natural horizon will be represented by the base of the mountains about six to eight miles from the airplane.

Some pilots have been tempted to fly up a blind canyon while climbing out from a valley airport. It is usually best to circle and gain altitude before turning on course. If you do fly into a blind canyon—sometimes called a box canyon or dead end canyon—stay to the side. If the canyon narrows, perform a 180-degree turn before getting trapped. If the terrain out climbs the airplane, turn around before passing the point of no return.

Bush Pilot

RULE OF THUMB – Increased Takeoff Distance

For each 1,000 feet above sea level, the takeoff run will increase approximately 12 percent.

RULE OF THUMB – Increased Landing Speed

The landing speed (true airspeed) will increase about 2 percent for each 1,000 feet above sea level when using the same indicated airspeed for approach as at a sea level airport.

Do not fly close to terrain that has abrupt changes—such as cliffs or other rugged areas—when there are strong winds aloft. Dangerous turbulence may be generated in these areas.

Watch for wires and cables strung across canyons and rivers. Unmarked power lines are nearly impossible to see.

HOW RELIABLE ARE AVIATION WEATHER FORECASTS?

The reliability of weather reports and forecasts depend to a large extent on the pilot's understanding of the limitations and capabilities imposed by the state of the art of present day meteorology. The meteorologist understands some atmospheric behaviors and has watched them long enough to know that his knowledge of the atmosphere is not complete.

PART 3 EN ROUTE   **Introduction**

Pilots who understand the limitations of observations and forecasts usually are the ones who make the most effective use of the weather forecast service. The safe pilot continually views aviation forecasts with an open mind. He knows that weather always is changing and, consequently, that the older the forecast, the greater the chance that some part of it will be wrong. The weather-wise pilot looks upon a forecast as professional advice rather than an absolute surety. To have complete faith in weather forecasts is almost as bad as having no faith at all.

Recent studies of the aviation forecasts indicate the following:

1. Up to 12 hours—and even beyond—a forecast of good weather (ceiling 3,000 feet or more and visibility three miles or greater) is much more likely to be correct than a forecast of conditions below 1,000 feet or below one mile visibility.

2. If poor weather is forecast to occur within three to four hours, the probability of occurrence is better than 80 percent.

3. Forecasts of poor flying conditions during the first few hours of the forecast period are most reliable when there is a distinct weather system, such as a front, a trough, precipitation, etc. There is a general tendency to forecast too little bad weather in such circumstances.

4. The weather associated with fast-moving cold fronts and squall lines is the most difficult to forecast accurately.

5. Errors occur when attempts are made to forecast a specific time that bad weather will occur. Errors are made less frequently, of course, when forecasting that bad weather will occur during some period of time.

6. Surface visibility is more difficult to forecast than ceiling height. Visibility in snow is the most difficult of all visibility forecasts. Skill in these forecasts leaves much to be desired.

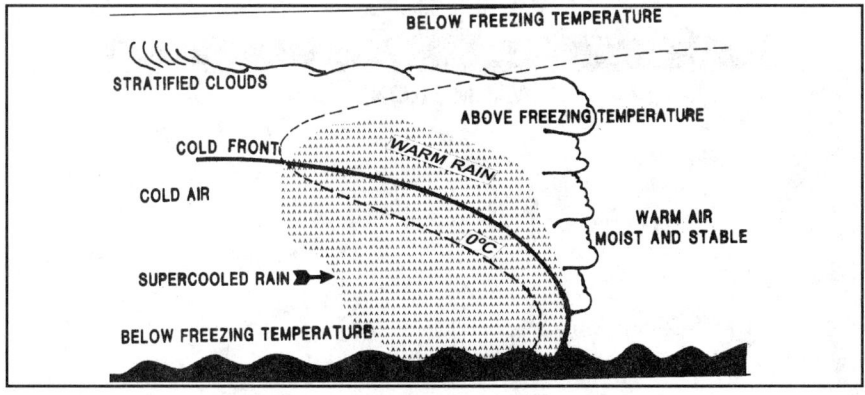

COLD FRONT

Introduction   PART 3 EN ROUTE

Available evidence shows that forecasters can predict the following at least 75 percent of the time:

- ✔ The passage of fast-moving cold fronts or squall lines within plus or minus two hours, as much as 10 hours in advance.
- ✔ The passage of warm fronts or slow-moving cold fronts within plus or minus five hours, up to 12 hours in advance.
- ✔ The rapid lowering of ceiling below 1,000 feet in pre-warm front conditions within plus or minus 200 feet and within plus or minus four hours.
- ✔ The onset of a thunderstorm one to two hours in advance, if radar is available.
- ✔ The time rain or snow will begin, within plus or minus five hours.
- ✔ You can see that while weather forecasting is not yet an exact science, it does provide the tools necessary to make an intelligent decision concerning your proposed flight. ✈

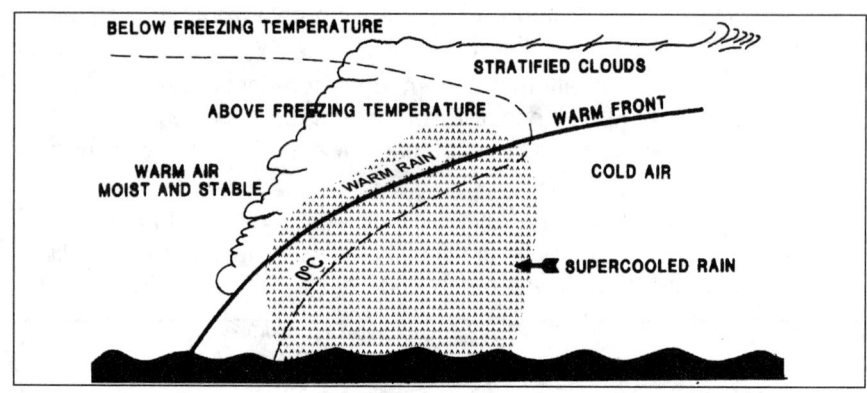

WARM FRONT

Mountain Flying Bible

PART 3 EN ROUTE   Chapter 1 - Precautions

CHAPTER 1—PRECAUTIONS

- ALTITUDE 3-7
- HORIZON CHECK LINE 3-8
- FLYING BLIND 3-9
- COLLISION AVOIDANCE 3-9
- FLYING THE TERRAIN 3-10
- COMMON SENSE 3-11
- CLIMB OUT 3-11

ALTITUDE

The novice pilot generally tries to fly over mountains at the highest altitude his airplane will climb. This provides a feeling of comfort when he is the farthest he can be away from those mountains. If you have supplemental oxygen or a pressurized airplane this is an acceptable method of crossing the mountains. If you are restricted to lower altitudes by aircraft performance, oxygen limitations, or extremely strong winds aloft, follow the mountain pilots' advice of flying 2,000 feet above the terrain. This is the recommended altitude for crossing higher ridges and mountains during the en route phase of flight.

The recommended crossing altitude varies with the upper airflow. A strong-wind condition will require more clearance. A no-wind condition will allow flight at a lesser clearance altitude. When flying in strong winds with the possibility of downdrafts or turbulence, flying half again as high as the mountains will avoid destructive turbulence.

 **RULE OF THUMB – Wind and Cruise Altitude**

When the wind exceeds 20 knots at mountaintop level, fly half again as high as the terrain.

This does not mean that when you are flying over a 14,000-foot mountain that you should fly at 21,000 feet (half the altitude, 7,000 feet, plus the mountain height). It means that you should subtract the prevailing terrain elevation from the mountain elevation and use half of this value. For example, the terrain surrounding the 14,000-foot mountain might approximate 10,000 feet. The moun-

Mountain Flying Bible   3-7

Chapter 1 - Precautions PART 3 EN ROUTE

tain is 4,000 feet above the terrain. Half of this value means you would fly 2,000 feet above the mountain.

HORIZON CHECK LINE

The altitude of the airplane in relation to the mountains can be deceptive for the inexperienced mountain pilot. It is desirable to determine whether the airplane is at an altitude that will provide clearance to cross the mountain ridge before arriving at the ridge. While this is desirable, it is not always possible. There are several techniques that assist in making this determination.

By checking the sectional aeronautical chart and identifying the mountain by its location on the chart, it is simple to fly 2,000 feet above the known elevation. With the possibility of human error in chart reading, it is a good idea to establish a habit of checking the terrain clearance altitude by using the *spot method* (sometimes called the *flight-path horizon* or *visual check line*).

ho•ri•zon \hó-"rí-zön\ *noun* - 1 the apparent junction of earth and sky

Pilots use the horizon line for visual attitude flying. Mountains destroy the perception of where the Earth and sky meet, making it difficult for the inexperienced pilot to know where the actual horizon exists. If you use the base of the mountains at least six to eight miles (or more) ahead of the airplane, the natural horizon can be approximated. If the terrain requires that you use a side window to determine the base of the mountains six to eight miles away, with minimal practice, it is easy to circumscribe a line to the front of the airplane.

Sometimes—in some canyons—you will be flying in an area where you cannot determine or see the base of the mountains. Visualization has to be used. There is no easy rule for this interpretation; it comes with experience.

The spot method, as you will learn in *Part 5—Landings*, consists of a *windshield mark* and an *aiming point* on the ground. The windshield mark is what you use in determining terrain clearance for crossing ridges. The windshield mark is established during cruise flight with cruise power. It is where the natural horizon appears about two to four inches up from the base of the windshield. This depends on the airplane and your parallax as you sit in the airplane.

For your first few mountain flights it is desirable to make a China pencil mark (easy erased with a Kleenex) or use a sticky corner of a 3M Post-it paper to make the windshield mark. When you approach a ridge in level flight, the airplane will pass easily over any mountain or ridge that is seen clearly below this spot method mark.

If the ridge juts up above the windshield mark, the mountain is higher than your airplane and it will be necessary to maneuver for additional altitude before trying to cross the ridge.

 Remember, this spot method to determine ridge crossing capability only works when the airplane is in level flight.

FLYING BLIND

 Flight instructors recommend that mountain flights be made during the early morning or late afternoon when the air is calmer and there is less concern about density altitude and turbulence. When your flight direction is toward the sun and the sun is at a low angle to the horizon, you may not be able to see the mountains ahead of you. This becomes a serious problem when you are flying at an altitude below the highest terrain.

The following might seem like a contrived situation, but "Smokey" Bear (Norman Ray Bear) and myself were employed by the Teton County Sheriff's Department, Jackson, Wyo. in 1968. We received a call that some "bad guys" had broken into the J-Y Ranch. Because of unproductive roadblocks we figured the perpetrators were trying to escape up Death Canyon.

We jumped into my Cessna 172 and headed into Death Canyon at low altitude. At the mouth of the canyon, it is fairly narrow and the canyons are nearly vertical. We spotted the suspects shortly after entering the canyon and turned around to face the rising sun. Everything in front of the airplane disappeared. We quickly moved over to the side of the canyon—the visibility is good in all directions except into the sun—did a tight 180-degree turn and climbed for all we were worth. As we reached the point of no return, we did another 180 and flew the side of the canyon, maneuvering back and forth until we were above the terrain.

If you get caught in this predicament, transition to the shadow side of the canyon. Normally the shaded side is avoided because of the probability of downdrafts, but here it is required to avoid the blind spot. The best solution to this problem—and remember, it can occur with the setting sun also—is to climb 2,000 feet above the terrain before going on course.

COLLISION AVOIDANCE

Whenever you become concerned about another airplane's flight path that might be approaching you on a collision course, look at the airplane through any window. If the other airplane remains in a constant spot on the window and the flight path is converging, you are on a collision course. If the airplane moves from the spot in any direction—up or down, forward or rearward—you are not on a collision course. If the airplane is climbing or descending, you will have to continue to watch it. If it maneuvers to a position where it becomes stationary on the window, look out. This technique works regardless of the window (windshield or side windows) where you view the other airplane.

Chapter 1 - Precautions **PART 3 EN ROUTE**

"FLY THE TERRAIN" ALONG THE SIDE OF THE MOUNTAIN. TURN AWAY FROM THE MOUNTAIN, THEN MOVE BACK INTO THE AREA OF LIFT.

FLYING THE TERRAIN

"Flying the terrain" is a technique used to fly close to a ridge, mountain side or canyon wall for the purpose of gaining orographic lift (wind blowing up the mountain) or anabatic lift (convection currents). Flying the terrain is used by sailplane pilots to gain lift. When lift is located in a particular area, the sailplane "works" the lift by flying back and forth through the area.

Disregard the sailplane pilot advice to make the turn toward whatever wing raises. If you want to fly back and forth in an area of lift, always turn away from the mountain.

 Fly along the side of the mountain. When lift is discovered, continue until the lift dies out, then make a 180-degree turn away from the mountain. If everything looks right, maneuver back to the area of lift, paralleling the mountain. Continue back and forth until obtaining the desired altitude gain.

Flying the terrain is used mainly to take advantage of orographic lift. The airplane must be flown close to the terrain, within 100 yards or closer. This, in itself, is not dangerous. Ravines may create danger.

When the pilot attempts to fly the terrain in an area with gullies, small draws and ravines, if the airplane is turned into this area, there may not be enough room to complete a turn out of the small area. When flying the terrain, cut across gullies and ravines.

COMMON SENSE

Common sense is defined as sound and prudent but often-unsophisticated judgment, horse sense, native good judgment, or wisdom.

Flight instructors get into arguments about whether or not a student can be taught good judgment. Perhaps good judgment can be taught, mainly by example if the instructor establishes parameters of flight (personal safety standards) that are carefully explained. For example, crosswind limitations should be addressed as well as the minimum ceiling and the minimum visibility for scud running.

"Use common sense and sound judgment." That sounds easy enough, but people do not always exercise common sense. Ask a pilot what he would do if the fuel supply were running low on a cross-country flight? Most will explain that they would make an unscheduled fuel stop. Or, what if the landing approach turns sour? You would be surprised how often these people—safely on the ground—will make the right decision, but in the airplane they might try to save some time by stretching the fuel, or continue on the landing approach when he knows he should make a go around.

Why do people gamble on life threatening decisions? When a few minutes inconvenience are weighed against the possible loss of life, Las Vegas odds makers will not play those odds.

Many of us have a subconscious feeling where we regard certain actions unworthy of a pilot. Don't let your "professional pride," prevent you from making that necessary go-around just because someone is watching you.

Use good old common "horse sense" in all your flying. Many of us have been in situations where we have doubt. I know I have. Usually it's late at night, and not in an airplane. I tell myself, "Gee, I don't know if I should be doing this." And sure enough, I shouldn't have been doing that. This is when you have the opportunity to exercise common sense.

CLIMB OUT

Terrain clearance is the most important consideration during climb out from a mountain airstrip. It may be necessary to maintain the best rate-of-climb airspeed or the best angle-of-climb airspeed until above the terrain. At some backcounty strips this requires a considerable amount of time for the climb.

Learn to fly by attitude. It is possible to cover the airspeed indicator and fly an exact airspeed by using outside visual reference; that is, checking where the nose is in relation to the horizon. Often there will not be a natural horizon. It is necessary to use the base of the mountains some six to eight miles (farther is preferable) from the airplane. With experience, a natural horizon can be imagined when flying in canyons that do not allow the reference of mountains six to eight miles away.

Ignore all you have learned about using a standard pattern departure. Fly the terrain. Survey the area before takeoff and decide if a left or right turn would place you in an area with the greatest probability of lift, either orographic or anabatic.

It is during the climb out that you can test the air for turbulence. If the conditions are not favorable, return to the airport and wait it out. Remember to maintain the maneuvering speed when encountering turbulence classified as moderate or greater.

Remember that the visual cues relating to your altitude above the terrain can be confusing when approaching ridges. Use the *spot method* to determine terrain clearance. Or, if you can see more and more of the terrain on the other side of the ridge, the airplane is higher than the ridge.

When flying toward upslope terrain, your left arm seems to become shorter. The result of this phenomena is that the airspeed is lower than anticipated. The tendency to pull back on the control wheel when approaching rising terrain is a normal self-protection reaction. Be aware that it may occur. ✈

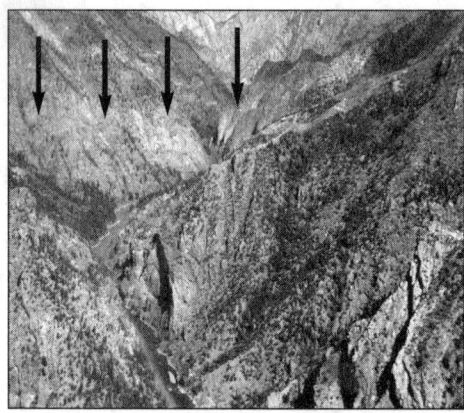

POWER LINES CROSS THE BLACK CANYON OF THE GUNNISION (COLORADO). UNDER CERTAIN LIGHT CONDITIONS THEY ARE IMPOSSIBLE TO SEE (LOOKING TOWARD THE WEST-NORTHWEST). WATCH FOR SUPPORTING STRUCTURES SUCH AS TOWERS OR POLES. REMEMBER, NOT ALL THE WIRES ARE MARKED WITH HIGH VISIBILITY BALLS.

THESE ARE THE SAME POWER LINES VIEWED FROM SOUTH TO NORTH. BECAUSE OF THE CHANGE IN LIGHTING, THEY ARE EASIER TO SEE.

PART 3 EN ROUTE — Chapter 2 - Night Flying

CHAPTER 2—NIGHT FLYING

- NIGHT VISION. 3-14
- DARK ADAPTATION 3-14
- PRESERVATION OF DARK ADAPTATION 3-15
- SCANNING TECHNIQUES 3-16
- VISUAL EFFECTS OF HYPOXIA. 3-16
- VISUAL ILLUSION 3-17
- NIGHT TAKEOFF AND DEPARTURE 3-17
- RUNWAY ALIGNMENT 3-17
- TAKEOFF 3-17
- CLIMB OUT. 3-18
- TERRAIN CLEARANCE 3-18
- VERTIGO. 3-18
- WEATHER. 3-20
- APPROACH FOR LANDING 3-20
- LANDING 3-21
- EMERGENCY LANDING 3-21
- NIGHT FLYING TIPS 3-21

The Aeronautical Information Manual states *"Mountain flying at night in a single-engine light aircraft is asking for trouble."* This statement elicits a negative response from many responsible pilots. Night flying under the proper conditions may be one of the most pleasant experiences connected with aviation. But with improper equipment, ineptitude on the part of the pilot, or bad weather, it is one of the most dangerous.

About one-tenth of all general aviation accidents takes place at night. Statistics seem to indicate that less than 10 percent of the general aviation flying is done after dark. So maybe the AIM is correct in its statement. But presuming that night flying is more dangerous than day flying on the basis of statistics is a fallacy. The airplane does not discriminate between light and dark. Conditions of of knowledge, combined with the absence of visual cues that presents an extra challenge.

During the course of flying about the country, a pilot is subjected to times when the destination airport lies an hour or so beyond the rays of the setting sun; or an important business engagement becomes a compelling reason to venture out into the black of night.

The question that comes to mind is, "Should I fly a single-engine airplane at night in the mountains?" The ground, horizon and sky blend into one on dark nights and emergency landing sites are obscure. On moonlit nights, especially with snow-covered ground, many of the physical aids that are used for day flying are distinct, usable and offer little difference from day flight. This argument, pro and con, can continue on and on. It's not an easy question to resolve.

I'm not going to try to convince you one way or the other about night flying in the mountains or elsewhere. In fact, it's ridiculous for anyone to extol the beauty and safety of night flying in an attempt to convince someone else to fly at night. The fact remains that it is a personal choice. If your choice is to do it, learn to do it safely.

NIGHT VISION

Even if you are competent at attitude instrument flying, you will still use vision during a night flight, if only in the transition for takeoff and landing. Night vision is a skill that needs understanding and practice before proficiency is achieved.

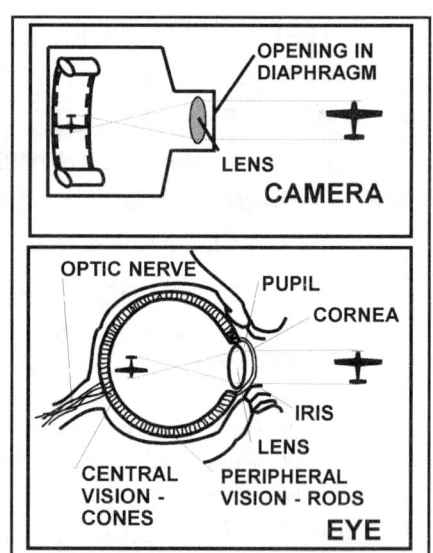

DARK ADAPTATION

What you see or don't see in the dark is dependent on the state of dark adaptation of your eyes. When you enter a dark area from a light area, your vision improves slowly. After six to seven minutes, the eyes are 100 times more sensitive than when you entered the dark. Full dark adaptation takes at least 30 minutes, at which time the rods are 100,000 times more sensitive that when first exposed to the dark. This is due to the buildup of a photosensitive chemical called *visual purple*. Visual purple is the key to night vision and is dependent on vitamin A (carrots, eggs, milk, cheese, and most vegetables). The

VIEW AS SEEN WITHOUT BEING DARK ADAPTED.

SAME VIEW WITH DARK ADAPTATION, LOOKING ABOVE THE OBJECT

DARK ADAPTATION

body cannot store Vitamin A. Because of this; it is necessary to eat a well-balanced meal before going on a night flight.

PRESERVATION OF DARK ADAPTATION

Adaptation can occur in bright lights if you wear red goggles; otherwise you have to spend about 30 minutes in a darkened environment. Although it takes 30 minutes for dark adaptation to occur, it can be lost in a second or two of exposure to bright lights. Avoid bright lights. If you use white light in the airplane, keep it as dim as possible and use it for the shortest time possible.

Dark adaptation is an independent process in each eye. If you are exposed to bright light in the cockpit or to an airplane's landing light (or just have to light a cigarette), close one eye until the bright light is gone to preserve half your dark adaptation.

CENTRAL BLIND SPOT IN DIM LIGHT PREVENTS SEEING OBJECTS LOOKED AT DIRECTLY.

OBJECTS CAN BE SEEN BY LOOKING ABOVE, BELOW OR TO ONE SIDE.

ECCENTRIC FIXATION

SCANNING TECHNIQUES

The cones of the eye (day vision) provide central vision. The cones do not work in the dark and this causes a blind spot in the center of the eye at night. If you detect something with peripheral vision, the natural tendency is to turn and look directly at it. This will not work.

Night vision is impossible at the center of the eye, so a technique called off-center scanning must be practiced and used. By looking six to 12 degrees away from the object you wish to see, you can take advantage of the rods that provide night vision.

Seeing at night is not a natural function, but rather, a technique to be learned and practiced until it becomes automatic. Practice moving the eyes frequently in dim light. The rods tire quickly and lose efficiency when static. Remember that you can't see anything while your eyes are in motion, although they are sensitive just after moving. Short movements, scanning 15 to 30 degree arcs, seems to provide the best vision.

VISUAL EFFECTS OF HYPOXIA

Hypoxia influences your ability to see. The area from sea level to 10,000 feet is known as the *indifferent zone,* since daytime vision is virtually unaffected. There is a slight impairment of night vision due to changes in the blood vessels of the eye, but unless you are a fighter pilot searching for enemy aircraft, it is not significant.

The range from 10,000 to 16,000 feet is called the *zone of adaptation,* because even though visual functions are impaired, the pilot can continue to function, unless these higher altitudes are maintained for a long period of time.

At about 16,000 feet there is a loss of 40 percent in night-vision ability when supplemental oxygen is not used. Changes occur in the eye:

- ✔ Retinal vessels become dark and cyanotic.
- ✔ Retinal arterioles increase in diameter 10 to 20 percent.
- ✔ Retinal blood volume increases 400 percent.
- ✔ Retinal arteriolar pressure increases.
- ✔ The pupil constricts.

These changes are returned to normal with the administration of supplemental oxygen or descent below 10,000 feet.

The region between 16,000 and 25,000 feet is called the *zone of inadequate compensation* in which night vision is seriously impaired without supplemental oxygen.

Above 25,000 feet is the *zone of decompensation* which may cause permanent damage to the retina and brain due to the death of neurons (nerve cells and their processes) and lack of circulation.

VISUAL ILLUSION

A visual illusion may occur at night if you stare at one light for a long period of time. Involuntary muscle twitches cause the light to be displayed on a different portion of the eye, creating false motion, and the light appears to move. This is called *autokinesis*. Avoid autokinesis by scanning.

NIGHT TAKEOFF AND DEPARTURE

When you have determined that you are going to depart from a mountain airport at night you should fix firmly in your mind the nature of the terrain adjacent to the airport and the location of obstructions which are nearby. This is of major importance at unfamiliar airports so that you can formulate a safe departure procedure.

While you have no intention of making an emergency landing shortly after takeoff, it doesn't hurt to survey the terrain during daylight conditions to form a plan of action.

RUNWAY ALIGNMENT

At uncontrolled airports, execute a 360-degree turn in the direction of traffic flow, searching for other aircraft. Line up on the centerline of the runway. There probably won't be runway markings or runway-edge lights, so parallel the runway edge at the midpoint.

TAKEOFF

With the interior lights adjusted to the minimum brightness that affords instrument readability, initiate a normal takeoff. By way of definition, a normal takeoff does not mean acceleration to a certain speed where the airplane is forced off the ground. Rather, as the airspeed approaches normal takeoff speed, hold a pitch attitude that allows the airplane to fly off when it is ready.

Now is the time some pilots experience trouble. Even in low powered airplanes, there is some acceleration error in the attitude indicator (artificial horizon). This causes an indication of a higher nose attitude than during a regular climb. As a consequence, some pilots have lowered the airplane's nose to the normal attitude indicator mark and have flown back into the ground.

The moment the airplane leaves the ground on a dark night, it is enveloped in black. Even with the landing lights turned on, outside visual reference becomes impossible. The airspeed indicator becomes all-important.

A positive rate of climb based on airspeed indication (best rate of climb or best angle of climb) must be maintained, regardless of the attitude indicator display. Initially you will be unable to tell if the airplane is getting closer to or farther from the surface. More dependence must be placed on the instruments and they should be used to a greater degree in controlling the airplane.

When flying in sparsely settled areas, turn the landing lights off after establishing the climb. They are ineffective and may be deceptive when reflected by haze, smoke or fog. At high-traffic airports, leave the landing lights on to help with the "see and be seen" concept.

CLIMB OUT

If you become disoriented during the climb out to the extent that you are concerned about terrain clearance, fly toward the rotating beacon. If you have flown away from the airport, or if you are operating at a mountain airstrip that has no lighting, fly toward any light on the ground.

One technique that works well is to make a smooth 90-degree turn to the left or right (depending on terrain), and a 270-degree turn back to the runway. Once over the runway, do a shuttle climb in holding until the en route altitude is reached.

TERRAIN CLEARANCE

Even with the proper preflight planning, studying charts, and developing a plan and altitude for terrain clearance, at some time during night flying you are going to experience a moment of fear (or even stark terror) arising from your concern about terrain avoidance.

If there are any lights around, use them. Fly directly toward the light. When you get near it, select another light. If the light flickers or disappears, there is an obstacle between you and the light. Remember any flickering means there is some obstacle between you and the light.

If there is only one usable light in the area, try a shuttle climb while holding. Since you know there are no obstructions between your position and the light (it is not flickering), fly toward the light. Before passing beyond the light perform a 180-degree turn and fly one minute, then turn back toward the light. Continue this maneuvering while climbing to a safe altitude before proceeding on course. Be sure to check the chart for obstructions in your immediate vicinity to determine if you will make left or right turns in the holding pattern.

VERTIGO

On dark nights, with an absence of visual references available, it becomes natural to stare at whatever illumination exists. Lights on the ground or stars on the horizon may appear to move due to autokinesis. This leads to the possibility of

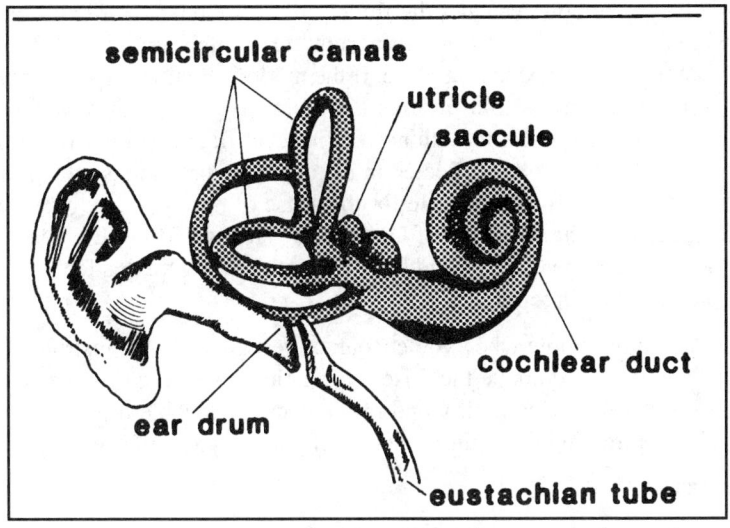

INNER EAR

confusing stars for horizon lights, accompanied by an airplane attitude correction causing vertigo.

Instrument flight proficiency is a necessity when flying over sparsely populated sections of the country, particularly when there is an overcast hiding the stars.

Pilots know vertigo is a condition in which you are unable to tell which way is up. Inexperienced pilots accept this definition, but trying to convince them that everyone is susceptible to vertigo becomes another matter.

The vestibular system (semicircular canals, utricle, and saccule) is located in the inner ear. It is a tiny, but powerful body computer controlling balance, spatial orientation, detection of motion, and some types of eye movement.

As a ground animal, the utricle and saccule tell us the direction of forces causing acceleration and deceleration. The three semicircular canals tell us whether we are turning or rotating when the enclosed fluid moves past receptor hairs imbedded in the tubes.

Mother Nature did not plan on centrifugal force, during turns, creating the same motion as produced by gravity. Also, tilting the head while picking up a chart or pencil on the floor of the airplane causes the alignment of the semicircular canals to be in a different position with respect to gravity and the movement of the plane. When the head is straightened, with no visual confirmation of the actual attitude, all heck may break loose.

Chapter 2 - Night Flying

PART 3 EN ROUTE

Initially, any rotation causing the fluid to deflect the receptor hairs transmits a signal to the brain telling it a left turn, right turn, climb, or dive, or some other form of angular motion is taking place. If the motion remains constant for roughly 20 seconds, another signal informs the brain that rotation has stopped. In a medium left turn the brain may think it is in level flight. Rolling back to level flight causes the hairs to be deflected in the opposite direction, so the pilot feels he is in a right turn. To compensate for the sense of turning, he adjusts the controls to the left for the "feeling" of level flight. This is vertigo. Even very gradual turns that aren't detected, if suddenly corrected, will give this feeling of turning in the opposite direction.

The remedy is simple when you encounter vertigo ... fly the instruments, and believe them over and above the false information transmitted by the vestibular system. Instrument flying ability and proficiency is valuable training. You may never need the training for night flying, but if you do, you will need it all at once.

WEATHER

It is difficult to see weather at night and your first indication may be a glow emanating from the navigation lights or a brilliant flash of the strobes being diffused throughout a cloud. VFR pilots should do an immediate 180-degree turn. Restricted visibility conditions become apparent with the gradual disappearance of lights on the ground or when they become fuzzy and glow. Remember, the horizontal visibility through a restriction such as fog, haze or smoke will be vastly less than when looking down through it from above. Pilots have gotten into trouble trying to land at an airport with fog because they can fly over and see the runway, but when on final they can't see anything.

APPROACH FOR LANDING

Distances at night are deceptive, due to the lack of illumination and the inability of the pilot to judge them by the usual method of comparing the size of different objects.

If the airport area is unfamiliar, sighting the runway may be difficult until close in. And many airports throughout the country are located near hills, buttes, bluffs, and ridges, rising ground or otherwise precipitous terrain. The pilot should fly towards an airport light (rotating beacon if one exists), then make a standard pattern, rather than attempting a direct approach. Since the perception of distance may be difficult, fly along the downwind leg until the point where you want to land is halfway between the wing tip and tail. Your parallax may make a small change in this point of reference, but the technique works well.

Some pilots are prone to make their approach and landing with excessive airspeed. This creates the hazard of floating during the day, but at night, with limited visibility, it is dangerous.

Approach unfamiliar airports higher than normal because of the possibility of unknown obstructions.

LANDING

In addition to the common training practice of takeoffs and landings, other aspects of night flying should include training with and without landing lights, runway lights, interior cockpit lights and right hand traffic patterns.

The only way to approach a runway in the mountains at night is by using the spot method for landing technique.

The flare and landing is accomplished in the same manner as during the day; although there is a tendency to look too far down the runway, which may cause you to flare too high. Practice develops judgment of height, speed and sink rate.

If the runway and airplane lights are inoperative, but enough ambient light exists so the runway is discernible, it may be helpful to make a power landing; one in which the power is left on until the plane makes contact with the ground. Seaplane pilots use this technique for glassy water landings when there is a lack of visual cues to provide depth perception. This landing should be practiced (maybe with an instructor) before being put to use.

EMERGENCY LANDING

An engine failure at night compels the pilot to maintain positive control of the airplane to avoid a stall. It is natural to pull back on the control wheel to keep away from the ground causing the airplane to slow down too much. Force yourself to trim for the best glide speed and fly toward an area that affords the best chance for landing. If attempts to restart fail, and weather conditions will prevent seeing the ground, fly into the wind at the slowest possible airspeed which will afford aircraft control and pray until the ground is contacted.

NIGHT FLYING TIPS

Before flight, check all equipment including the aircraft and interior/exterior lights.

- ✔ Always carry a workable flashlight.
- ✔ Close one eye when exposed to bright light to avoid the blinding effect from loss of night adaptation.
- ✔ Force the eyes to view off-center.
- ✔ Blink the eyes if they become blurred.
- ✔ Do not wear sunglasses after sunset.
- ✔ Contact ATC radar facilities en route and ask for radar flight following.

Chapter 2 - Night Flying   PART 3 EN ROUTE

- ✔ On final approach, use any available descent aids, such as VASI, ILS glide slope, or the spot method.
- ✔ Monitor the ammeter gauge to detect an electrical failure.
- ✔ Don't attempt violent or abrupt maneuvers at night.
- ✔ Watch for disappearance of ground lights or an area of glow around the navigation lights. You may be entering instrument weather conditions.
- ✔ Remember the deceptiveness of altitude and speed at night. A normal approach looks steeper at night, creating an illusion of overshooting, which may result in undershooting.
- ✔ Distance judgment at night is often less accurate than by day; simple visual assessment can lead to a premature descent. ✈

PART 3 EN ROUTE   Chapter 3 - Mountain Flying Techniques

CHAPTER 3—MOUNTAIN FLYING TECHNIQUES

- APPROACHING RIDGES 3-24
- DETERMINE ALTITUDE IS ADEQUATE 3-28
- CROSSING RIDGES 3-28
- MOUNTAIN DOWNDRAFTS 3-30
- FLYING CANYONS 3-33
- WIRES ACROSS CANYONS................... 3-35
- MARGINAL WEATHER 3-36
- FLYING UP CANYONS 3-36
- PASS AT HEAD OF CANYON 3-38
- CROSSING RIDGE - HEAD OF CANYON 3-40
- COURSE REVERSAL PROCEDURES 3-43
- PARAMETERS OF CANYON FLIGHT............ 3-54
- FLIGHT LOAD FACTORS 3-58
- MANEUVERING SPEED 3-60
- CANYON DOWNDRAFT 3-63
- LOCATION OF UPDRAFTS................... 3-63

   Although I taught a ground school for 11 years for private and commercial students, I have never taught a private ground school or a commercial ground school. It was always a combined private-commercial school. My reasoning was that the private pilot applicant would be a safer pilot having been exposed to the additional information of a commercial pilot. And the commercial pilot benefited from the review of the private pilot curriculum.

   This combination ground school reflects the same philosophy in which some pilots prefer to fly over the mountains; while other pilots prefer to fly with the mountains.

   This chapter is directed at each distinct and separate pilot group. The first group wants and needs to know how to fly safely from a departure airport, such as Denver, to a destination airport, such as Aspen. The other group wants and needs to know how to operate safely within the canyons and drainage areas of the mountains. The information presented will answer both groups. It is not necessary for the first group to fly close to the mountains to benefit for the additional

Mountain Flying Bible

Chapter 3 - Mountain Flying Techniques   PART 3 EN ROUTE

knowledge, but they will be more knowledgeable having been exposed to the techniques and procedures.

APPROACHING RIDGES

When approaching a mountain ridge from the upwind side the pilot will encounter an updraft (there are exceptions) that will normally help in crossing the ridge.

When approaching the mountain ridge on the lee side or downwind side, and the wind velocity is 20 knots or more at mountaintop level, the airflow will come over the ridge and flow downward producing turbulence and downdrafts. Twenty knots of wind velocity seems to be the magic number for turbulence under most atmospheric stability conditions. With fewer than 20 knots of wind, there isn't much turbulence. More than 20 knots and the wind will create eddy currents that translates into turbulence.

FLYING THE "BACK SIDE" OF THE GRAND TETON, JACKSON, WYO. (THE WEST SIDE.) NOTE THE ORIENTATION OF THE CIRRIFORM CLOUDS FROM LEFT TO RIGHT (WEST TO EAST) INDICATING THE WINDS ALOFT (AT THE ALTITUDE OF THE CLOUDS) IS FROM THE WEST. AS A GENERAL RULE, AT LOWER ALTITUDES THE WIND WILL SHIFT COUNTERCLOCKWISE.

The possibility of encountering eddy currents and downdrafts from which there is no escape is the basis for establishing the rule that all mountains and ridges (or any higher terrain) are approached at a 45-degree angle.

 **RULE OF THUMB—Approach all mountains and ridges at a 45-degree angle.**

It is not necessary or beneficial to approach the mountains at a 45-degree angle when you are four or five miles away from the ridge. If you are not comfortable using the one-quarter mile from the ridge recommendation, try one-half mile.

You may determine that the existing weather conditions do not produce downdrafts and feel that it is not necessary to approach the ridges at the 45-degree angle. This is not true. What the lack of downdrafts means is that instead of transitioning to the 45-degree angle for approach when one-half mile or one-quarter mile from the ridge, it is acceptable to wait until you are several hundred yards from the ridge to move to the approach angle.

| PART 3 EN ROUTE | Chapter 3 - Mountain Flying Techniques |

 The lack of downdrafts and turbulence doesn't change the rule, it just changes the distance from the ridge where the transition to the 45-degree angle approach is made.

If you approach the mountains straight-on (perpendicular), the airplane must be turned beyond 90 degrees if an escape becomes necessary. Once a strong downdraft is encountered, the natural tendency is to pull back on the control wheel with the resultant decrease in airspeed. Safety is behind the airplane and to avoid the mountain and reach the safety of lowering terrain, a steep turn is required. The stall speed increases with bank angle to further complicate matters (the stall speed increases as the square of the wing load factor).

APPROACH ALL RIDGES AT A 45-DEGREE ANGLE WHEN WITHIN 1/2 TO 1/4 MILE. TERRAIN CLEARANCE OF 2,000 FEET IS SAFE UNDER MOST CONDITIONS. FEWER THAN 500 FEET OF CLEARANCE MAY BE ADEQUATE WITH LIGHT WINDS AND STABLE AIR.

Approaching the mountain at the perpendicular isn't necessarily bad, but when you combine the g loading of the turn with the stress of the turbulence, the decrease in airspeed, and the increase in stall speed, it is safer and more comfortable for the airplane (and occupants) to have approached at a 45-degree angle. With the 45-degree approach, any turn greater than 45 degrees will place the airplane in a position to advance toward lowering terrain.

Once the ridge is crossed, the course can be resumed in any direction (either a diagonal or perpendicular direction) providing the airplane maintains a position that allows turning toward lowering terrain.

If there are a series of closely spaced ridges along the flight path and the wind is creating downdrafts on the lee side of each ridge, it is easy to zigzag, making a series of course alterations back and forth to stay more or less on the planned course. The first ridge is crossed at the 45-degree angle, then the heading is

Mountain Flying Bible

Chapter 3 - Mountain Flying Techniques PART 3 EN ROUTE

changed approximately 45 degrees to the opposite direction, and so on, for any more ridges.

RULE OF THUMB—Stall Speed Increase

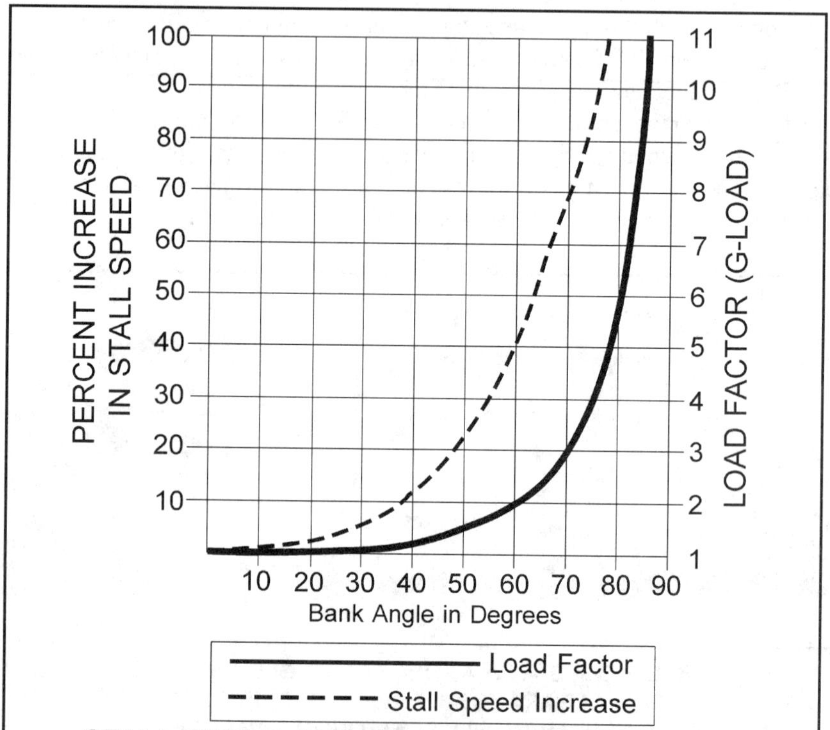

STALL SPEED CHART – LOAD FACTOR CHART

The stall speed increases as the square root of the wing load factor. For example, in a 60-degree bank the load factor is 2 Gs. The square root of two is 1.41, resulting in a 41 percent increase in stall speed.

MOUNTAIN FLYING DESIGNATIONS

Mountain flying can be broken down into four designations or types.

- ☐ Flatland to flatland over the mountains
- ☐ Flatland to a mountain destination.
- ☐ Mountain departure to a flatland destination.
- ☐ Contour/Drainage/Terrain flying, simply called mountain flying.

| PART 3 EN ROUTE | Chapter 3 - Mountain Flying Techniques |

When departing a flatland airport and flying to a flatland destination with mountains in between, the novice pilot could climb to an altitude 2,000 feet above the highest terrain along his route and proceed to the destination without much concern for the mountains unless there is bad weather.

The same logic applies for departure from a flatland airport and going to a mountain destination. The flight may be made at 2,000 feet above the terrain and then circle down for landing at the mountain airport destination.

Departure from the mountain airport would involve circling while climbing to 2,000 feet above the terrain and flight to the flatland destination.

For most conditions the inexperienced mountain pilot will find that 2,000 feet terrain clearance will be comfortable and adequate. With experience, and the confidence experience instills, the minimum altitude will decrease.

Classic mountain flying—sometimes called *contour, drainage* or *terrain flying*—is practiced mainly by the purist or the pilot having a need to operate close to the terrain (search and rescue, game and fish surveys, fire patrol, law enforcement, aerial photography, training, or personal enjoyment). This mountain pilot adheres strictly, not only to the tradition, but also to the rules of mountain flying.

THE GRAND TETON (NORTH OF THE TOWN OF JACKSON, WYO.) CHOOSE THE UPDRAFT SIDE WHEN FLYING THROUGH A CANYON. IF YOU DESIRE TO FLY AT LOW ALTITUDE TO OBSERVE SOMETHING ON THE GROUND AND THE TERRAIN SLOPES, GAIN SUFFICIENT ALTITUDE TO ALLOW YOU TO FLY FROM THE HIGH END TO THE LOW END.

Chapter 3 - Mountain Flying Techniques   **PART 3 EN ROUTE**

This is not to suggest that it is inappropriate to fly 2,000 feet above the terrain. Under certain conditions, such as a mountain wave, even the purist will maintain a terrain-clearance altitude that provides safety, rather than hugging the ridges. This qualified mountain pilot will fly an altitude (maybe even more than 2,000 feet above the terrain) that avoids strong downdrafts and escapes the associated turbulence.

An altitude that generally provides adequate terrain clearance and escape from destructive turbulence is determined by subtracting the elevation of the base of the mountain from the top. Use one-half of this value as the altitude to cross the mountain.

 Remember the rule for crossing mountains: approach the mountain at a 45-degree angle, even in a no-wind condition. The lack of wind (and hopefully downdrafts) does not invalidate the rule, it only changes the distance from the ridge that the approach is commenced.

DETERMINE ADEQUATE ALTITUDE

There are several methods that can be used to determine if you have sufficient altitude to cross a ridge.

- **Fly 2,000 feet above the known elevation of the ridge.**
- **If you see more and more of the terrain on the other side of the ridge, you can probably continue.**
- **A variation of this is to choose two spots. If the distance between the two is increasing, you are higher than the ridge.**
- **Use the spot method to determine the horizon check line.**

CROSSING RIDGES

If you elect to make your mountain flight without maintaining a 2,000-foot clearance altitude above the ridges, there are several techniques you can use to eliminate the deceptive visual aspect of crossing ridges.

Using the technique of choosing two spots, one spot would be the terrain seen at the ridge line and the other spot would be an arbitrary point above this first point. If the airplane is higher than the ridge, when it approaches closer and closer, the first spot will be visible at a lower point. The distance between the two points is increasing. This confirms that the airplane is higher than the ridge.

Many instructors have discontinued using this explanation to provide a method to determine adequate altitude to cross a ridge. The reason for this is because the pilot can develop "tunnel vision," where his whole world is encompassed in paying attention to the spacing between the chosen points. Nothing else matters and nothing else is recognized. This pilot could fly into trouble and have no awareness of what is going on around the airplane.

It is better to use the spot method or merely look at the ridge line to see if more and more of the terrain is coming into view.

As you approach the ridge at a 45-degree angle, it is a simple matter to turn toward lowering terrain if you determine you do not have sufficient altitude to cross the ridge.

What is this elusive "sufficient altitude?" It depends on the winds aloft that influence updrafts, downdrafts and turbulence. The clearance may be as little as 100 feet, or less, terrain clearance under a stable atmosphere with little or no wind.

A ridge may be defined as a mountain where the terrain on the approach side of the ridge slopes down toward the approaching airplane and the other side slopes down away from the top of the mountain.

RULE OF THUMB – Crossing a Ridge

When approaching a ridge and arriving at a position where you can dive, with the power reduced to idle, and hit the top of the ridge, you can commit to crossing the ridge.

It is not proper technique when approaching a ridge to reduce the power to idle and dive at the ridge. This is merely used as a "yardstick" for you to judge when you are in a position to continue.

If you don't have the altitude required to reduce the power and glide to the top of the ridge, you don't have sufficient altitude to continue flying toward the ridge.

Assume you are approaching the ridge at an angle with the ridge off to your left. You haven't entered a downdraft, but you don't have quite enough altitude to conform to the rule of thumb that allows you to continue. Make a turn away from the ridge, in this case to the right. If you want to cross the ridge at this point, make the right turn more than 225 degrees and move in close to the ridge. A 180-degree turn would put you in a position of flying away from the ridge at the 45-degree angle at which you approached it. A 225-degree turn would parallel the ridge. More than 225 degrees of turn allows you to move in close to the terrain where you can search for lift. When you think you have a little more than half the additional altitude you need to cross the ridge, turn around, always making the turn away from the ridge. In this case it will be a left turn of more than 225 degrees. You should gain the remaining required altitude as you fly back to the point at which you want to cross the ridge.

When you approach a ridge with less than 2,000-feet clearance altitude, look at the terrain on the other side of the ridge. If you can see more and more of the

Chapter 3 - Mountain Flying Techniques — PART 3 EN ROUTE

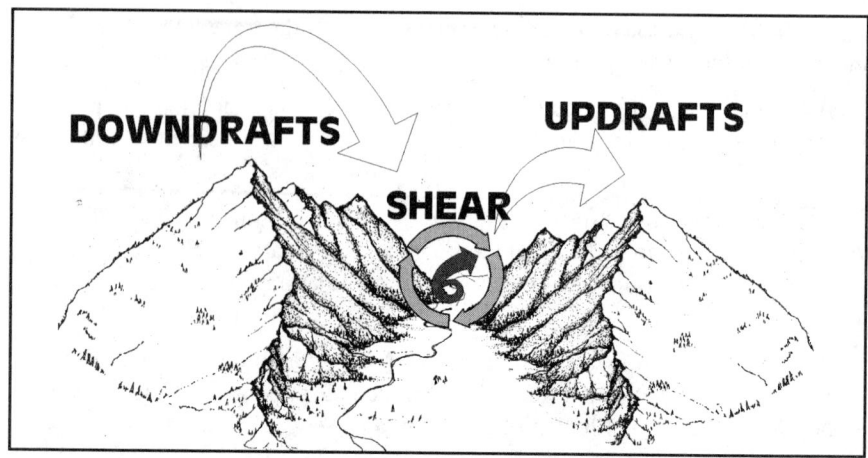

THE INTERMIXING OF THE AIR IN THE CENTER OF A CANYON SETS UP EDDY CURRENTS THAT PRODUCE AN AREA OF SHEAR TURBULENCE. AVOID THE SHEAR BY FLYING THE SIDE OF THE CANYON. FLYING THE CENTER, BESIDES EXPOSING YOU TO TURBULENCE, WILL PLACE YOU IN A POOR POSITION TO MAKE A COURSE-REVERSAL TURN-AROUND.

other side as you approach closer and closer, there will probably be sufficient altitude to cross the ridge; however, if the terrain starts to disappear, climb to a higher altitude before continuing.

If this technique of crossing ridges causes you worry or concern, rather than challenging your flying ability, do not do it. You should elect instead to maintain 2,000 feet clearance altitude above the terrain along the route of flight.

If you are flying during strong wind conditions or if a mountain wave exists, generally you can subtract the ground elevation from the mountaintop elevation and use one-half of this value as the terrain-clearance altitude. This helps avoid the stronger downdrafts and aids in escaping destructive turbulence.

Not many of us read a book about aerobatics and then go out and learn the maneuvers by ourselves. So it is with mountain flying. Mountain flying should include some dual instruction from a qualified instructor.

MOUNTAIN DOWNDRAFTS

If you fly the mountains long enough, in all types of weather conditions, eventually you may take a short cut to cross a ridge. You haven't found any downdrafts and have now come to ignore the 45-degree angle approach. When the airplane encounters an unexpected downdraft while in a position to cross the ridge, it may make turning dangerous or impossible.

PART 3 EN ROUTE   **Chapter 3 - Mountain Flying Techniques**

The only technique that can be used for an emergency escape during daylight is a dive. Diving into the face of danger is hard to do and requires strict discipline to keep the nose down while maneuvering to get into the cushion of air next to the ridge. Even if there isn't an updraft, the downdraft cannot extend into the ground unless tall trees cover the top of the ridge. Then the wind flow could pass through the trees and the airplane could experience the downdraft to an area below treetop.

It is difficult, but not impossible, to dive at a mountain ridge. Self-preservation keeps rearing its ugly head and tries to get you to pull back on the control wheel to avoid the ridge. While you should never have gotten into this predicament in the first place, you must surmount any reluctance at diving in order to escape from this emergency.

A normal reaction to a downdraft is to transition from the normal climb speed to the best angle-of-climb speed or slower. This subjects the airplane to the effects of the downdraft for a longer period of time than if the airplane was placed in a dive with a faster speed. The slow-speed climb results in a greater loss of altitude than will be incurred in a dive.

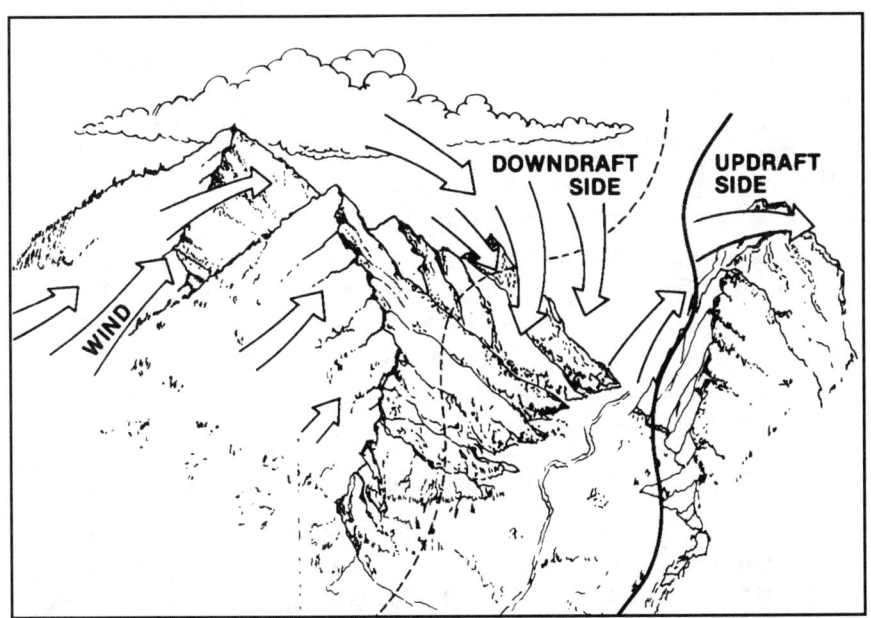

FLY THE UPDRAFT SIDE OF A CANYON. AVOID THE DOWNDRAFT SIDE (OFTEN THE SHADOW SIDE). STAY AS CLOSE TO THE SIDE AS CONDITIONS ALLOW TO AFFORD PLENTY OF ROOM FOR A TURN AROUND. TO FLY AT LOW ALTITUDE FOR GROUND OBSERVATION, FLY FROM THE HIGH END TO THE LOW END.

Chapter 3 - Mountain Flying Techniques   PART 3 EN ROUTE

Steven H. Philipson, Mountain View, CA, in his paper, *Mountain Wave and Speed-to-Fly for Light Airplanes, American Institute of Aeronautics and Astronautics, August 1995*, explains how to maximize the airplane's performance while flying through a descending air mass. He uses the performance data from 26 different general aviation planes from light trainers to medium twins to determine the speed-to-fly in a downdraft. His complex mathematical data has been reduced to his important rules of thumb.

> *Conway's* Joy of Soaring *defines* speed-to-fly *as "The indicated airspeed that produces the flatest glide in any situation of convection without considering the effect of the wind."*
>
> *Typical aircraft climb performance in mountainous areas is in the range of 300 to 500 fpm, making the airplane incapable of climbing or maintaining altitude in a strong mountain wave downdraft.*
>
> *Most pilots react to a downdraft by attempting to climb. If the airplane is able to maintain altitude, continue; however, once the intensity of the downdraft exceeds the airplane's climb ability, the airplane will begin to descend. As the intensity of the downdraft increases, attempts to climb become counterproductive and actually cause a steeper descent angle than flying at cruise airspeed.*
>
> *The situation can be complicated by encountering the downdraft while operating IFR. The controller may say, "Try to maintain altitude," and vector the aircraft along the shortest route toward lower terrain. Pilot compliance may make a ground impact unavoidable. If you can't speed up on the vector course without losing altitude critical to terrain clearance, turn around and fly downslope terrain.*
>
> *The most critical case in dealing with a mountain wave downdraft is when flying directly into the wind. Ground speed is greatly reduced increasing the length of time the aircraft is exposed to the downdraft, increasing the altitude loss, and increasing the angle of descent.*
>
> *Accounting for wind direction and velocity versus direction of flight yields* three rules of thumb:

STEVE'S RULES OF THUMB for Speed-to-Fly in a Downdraft

At Vy, if the airplane is descending faster than you should be going up (aircraft's rate of climb for the density altitude), speed up to cruise speed. This requires lowering the nose.

At Vy, with a tailwind, and you are going down three times as fast as you should be going up, speed up to cruise speed.

PART 3 EN ROUTE   Chapter 3 - Mountain Flying Techniques

 The greater the headwind, the sooner you should increase to cruise speed. All else being equal, it is better to fly downwind and fast.

Used with permission. ©1993-95 Steven H. Philipson

FLYING CANYONS

Mention the word "canyon" and some pilots conjure a vision of a narrow canyon with steep rocky walls. It's true, flying up a narrow canyon requires an experienced mountain pilot's skill, knowledge and judgment. The majority of canyon flying is done in canyons that afford plenty of room to turn around if the terrain outclimbs the airplane or if downdrafts are encountered.

 When using the "flying the terrain" technique to follow the contour of the terrain, remember the caution to cut across small gullies and ravines. Turning into a narrow area may not afford the opportunity to get out.

Flying in canyons or through canyons could involve a path through a mountain drainage where the terrain is fairly level. Or, it may embody a path through a drainage with sloped terrain, either flying up the canyon or flying down the canyon.

 Occasionally it is desirable to fly at low altitude in a canyon for search and rescue, law enforcement or some other valid reason. The recognized technique for flying in a canyon with upslope is to gain altitude, fly to the head of the canyon, then fly down the canyon.

There is nothing wrong with flying up canyons ... when it is done properly.

 **RULE OF THUMB – Canyon Flying**

- Never enter a canyon in which there is not room to turn around (remain in a position to turn toward lowering terrain).
- Never fly beyond the point of no return.
- Fly the side of the canyon

The novice pilot flying through a canyon for the first time will invariably fly in the center of the canyon. This places him the farthest away from the scary old mountains. It also places him in a poor position to make a turnaround if he encounters strong downdrafts or determines that the terrain is climbing faster than the airplane. He has only half the canyon width to effect the turn.

When air flows over one side of the canyon it swoops down and goes up the other side. In the center, there is an intermixing of the airflow that causes shear turbulence. Flying the side of the canyon avoids this type of turbulence.

Mountain Flying Bible

Chapter 3 - Mountain Flying Techniques   PART 3 EN ROUTE

There are several factors that must be considered in determining how close the airplane is positioned to the canyon wall. The winds aloft, turbulence, downdrafts, updrafts, terrain features, and width of the canyon must all be considered.

When flying the updraft side of a canyon the airplane must be positioned within 100-300 yards of the canyon side to obtain the maximum amount of orographic lift. Flying farther from the side may result in little or no lift. Some wind and turbulence conditions will prohibit flying this close to the canyon side. In that case, don't.

The sides of a canyon are not straight. They weave in and out forming rounded knolls, areas of steepness and gentle curving terrain. Once you have determined the spacing interval from the side that produces lift, maintain the spacing while traversing the canyon side. As the terrain moves in, the airplane moves in. As the terrain moves out, the airplane moves out. But, be careful of narrow ravines.

 **WARNING: Many pilots will fly the contour of the canyon maintaining the spacing interval of about 100 yards from the canyon wall. There is nothing wrong with this, but if there is a side canyon, gully or narrow ravine that the pilot flies into while maintaining the same spacing interval, when the pilot gets to the position where a turn is necessary, he will be flying perpendicular to the terrain. The turn to maintain the spacing will be 90 degrees or more and when approaching the wall it will be quite exciting. It is necessary to lead the turn quite a bit. A better technique is to cut across any narrow areas.**

When there is not sufficient wind to produce updrafts and downdrafts, fly either side of the canyon. Divide the canyon into thirds and maintain the aircraft's flight path within one third of the area on one side or the other. Avoid the center third. If one side of the canyon is shadowed, fly the sunny side. There may not be enough solar activity to produce convection that will help the airplane climb, but there may be enough convection to produce a neutral area. If there is any convection—whether it helps you climb or not—downdrafts will occur on the shadow side.

When the wind is blowing at a sufficient speed that you suspect updrafts and downdrafts (20 knots or more), yet you are unable to find updrafts on what you suspect is the updraft side of the canyon, try the other side. Occasionally Mother Nature can fool us. The wind may be modified by the terrain or by a high-pressure area that may produce a subsidence downflow that is stronger than the effect of the wind.

If you have sufficient altitude and performance to fly in the canyon without regard to lift, fly where you want; however, it is still a good technique and habit pattern to fly an area next to the canyon side within one-third the canyon width.

For the majority of canyon flying, choose a path on the updraft side. An exception occurs when flying up a narrow canyon (discussed shortly). If the canyon is visibly sloped, indicating the airplane cannot outclimb the terrain, the best technique is to obtain altitude and maneuver to the high end of the canyon and fly downslope terrain.

If you have ever flown over water beyond the power-off gliding distance from the shore you have probably encountered a situation or illusion where the engine goes to *automatic rough*. Whether imaginary or real, the engine will occasionally shudder, begin vibrating, or make a strange noise. When you check the engine gauges, you discover the oil pressure gauge quivers on an irregular basis. That doesn't seem to happen over land.

A similar phenomena occurs when flying in an upslope canyon. Your left arm becomes shorter than normal. This is a common reaction to rising terrain. You subconsciously try to keep as far away from the ground as possible and keep nudging the airplane up. Because of this "short-arm" effect, fly a speed faster than the best angle-of-climb speed. If there is not sufficient performance to outclimb the terrain, reverse course and gain additional altitude before trying it again. The best rate-of-climb speed or even a higher speed is recommended. If you experience turbulence, increase the speed. Monitor the airspeed and never fly below your selected speed except in an emergency. Your chosen speed provides you with a margin for error.

WIRES ACROSS CANYONS

Power lines are strung across canyons and rivers in populated and unpopulated areas. You have to be ever alert, looking more for the structures that support these lines rather than the lines themselves. Under many light conditions the wires will be impossible to see. (see Page 3-12.) This is why you want to look for metal towers or wooden poles.

When pilots have complained—usually by filling out a hazard to safety report, or by notifying the local FAA—the lines are marked with balls. There are more wires that are not marked than there are marked wires and worse, the majority of wires are not indicated as a hazardous marking on sectional or WAC charts. Remember, unless sunlight reflects off the wires, they may be impossible to see.

MARGINAL WEATHER

Do not attempt to fly through a canyon in marginal weather such as low stratus and fog, rain showers, or snow showers that restrict visibility. This is especially true if you are unfamiliar with the area. If you are unacquainted with the terrain of a canyon, you may discover too late, because of reduced visibility, that it narrows down or becomes a dead end, making it difficult or impossible to make a turnaround.

SNAGS

Snags are dead trees that have turned a silver-gray color with age. They obviously do not have leaves or vegetation associated with them and they are often devoid of branches.

More pilots than you might suspect experience mountain flying at low altitude. They determine that the mountains don't "bite," and then get into the habit of flying as closely as possible to the terrain because of the rush or exhilaration. When they come close to a snag, they are stimulated and roused. Snags, like power lines are very difficult to see.

DEAD TREES (LOCATED IN A PASS AT 8,700 FEET, AT THE HEAD OF CACHE CREEK, JACKSON, WYO.) ARE SOMETIMES IMPOSSIBLE TO SEE UNDER CERTAIN LIGHT CONDITIONS. BE VERY CAREFUL FLYING CLOSE TO THE TERRAIN.

FLYING UP CANYONS

Flying up a canyon is sometimes advantageous or even necessary. It can be accomplished safely with a few rules in mind, but remember the general recommendation is to fly, at altitude, to the head of the canyon and then fly down the canyon.

 As you begin mountain flying, never, never enter a canyon at an altitude below the elevation of the head of the canyon if there is not lateral room to make a comfortable turn around. As you gain experience, by flying with an instructor or an experienced mountain pilot, you may enter some canyons without sufficient altitude to cross the head of the canyon providing there is room to turn around and you do not fly beyond the point of no return.

Flying in canyons often involves maneuvering to find lift while in the canyon area. If you can't climb to obtain sufficient altitude to cross the head, get out. By the way, dead-end canyons do not pose a problem if you stay in a position to turn around and do not cross the point of no return.

BEYOND THE POINT OF NO RETURN

So what happens if a pilot flies beyond the point of no return? The terrain out climbs the airplane. The pilot has two options and they both lead to an accident.

While not good, the first choice is the best. This involves landing the airplane straight ahead into whatever terrain exists.

Because of the upslope it will be hard to go against the self-preservation instinct of pulling the nose up to avoid the terrain. Rather than landing the plane under control—albeit inhospitable terrain—the pilot in a frenzy tries to keep the airplane flying until it stalls. Treat the treetops like a runway at an international airport.

It is required that the nose be lowered to obtain a speed faster than the normal approach speed. The excess speed is used in the transition to parallel the terrain before a normal flare is continued to the landing.

The second option involves the stall-spin accident. There is insufficient altitude or maneuvering space to complete the turn toward lowering terrain. Once the bank reaches a certain steepness, the only thing remaining is the rudder. When the turn is hurried with the use of rudder, a tuck-under spin entry occurs. It doesn't seem to matter how good you are as a pilot (or how good you think you are); you've just lost 400 feet of altitude. This is true even if the recovery is begun just as the spin starts. Usually there are fewer than 400 feet separating the airplane and the ground.

"Never fly beyond the point of no return" is pretty sound advice, but quite useless without the experience to determine this point. One useful explanation would be to never fly beyond a point, where if you reduce the throttle to idle, you would still have sufficient altitude to complete a 180-degree turn. I am not suggesting that it would be proper technique to reduce the power during the turn-around, the power reduction analogy is merely a gauge for you to determine the point of no return.

BEHIND THE GRAND TETON
NOTE THAT THE AIRPLANE (AERONCA CHAMP) IS POSITIONED TO ALLOW A LEFT TURN-AROUND USING THE FULL CANYON WIDTH.

PASS AT HEAD OF A CANYON

Year after year pilots get into trouble flying up a canyon without sufficient altitude to cross the pass at the head of the canyon. The problem isn't flying up

Chapter 3 - Mountain Flying Techniques   PART 3 EN ROUTE

the canyon. The dilemma occurs when the pilot enters a narrow area where he cannot turn around, or when he flies beyond the point of no return.

A prime example is flying from Aspen, Colo. up the Roaring Fork River to Independence Pass (to the east of Aspen). Prevailing westerly winds aloft generally provide strong orographic lifting along the west side of slopes in this area.

The pilot starts out fully alert, flying the side of the canyon and remaining in a position to turn toward lowering terrain. So what goes wrong?

After passing Lincoln Creek and Green Mountain the canyon narrows. Most pilots stay to the right (south side) because a right turn has to be made into the basin on the west side of Independence Pass. When this last turn has been made, the basin opens up and the pass can be seen. Instead of continuing to follow the terrain—that would allow a left turn back down the canyon—the pilot cuts straight across toward the pass anticipating an updraft to provide the additional altitude that is needed. Now he is no longer in a position to be able to turn around and he may be rapidly approaching the point of no return. Expecting an updraft, but finding a downdraft (caused by subsidence) the airplane becomes parked on the side of the mountain.

There are several things to watch out for when flying up a canyon.

- ✔ The orographic lift may provide extra aircraft performance that lulls the pilot into a state of complacency.
- ✔ The pilot may continue flight into an area "beyond the point of no return" while anticipating further updrafts that do not materialize.
- ✔ The pass may not be a well-defined ridge that allows an escape route to lowering terrain. It may be necessary to circle, gaining additional altitude, before trying to cross the head of the canyon.
- ✔ The air flows like water. If you have a tailwind when flying up the canyon, it will likely provide an updraft at the head of the canyon to assist in crossing the area. CAUTION: See Subsidence and Downdrafts, next section.
- ✔ A headwind encountered while flying up a canyon will most likely cause a downdraft at the head of the canyon.

While flying up a canyon it's not unusual to be able to climb over 1,000 fpm in a Cessna 172-type airplane when operating at density altitudes in excess of 12,000 feet. This increased aircraft performance is due to updrafts created by wind blowing upslope. This is known as orographic lift or mechanical lift.

Remember you should approach a ridge at a 45-degree angle. When you are in a position where you could reduce the power to idle and then dive so the airplane can glide to the top of the ridge, you are in a position to continue. This yardstick assumes further flight toward lowering terrain on the other side of the ridge.

The majority of canyons—at least the ones wide enough to fly in—are formed at the head of the canyon in a curved or circular area. When flying the side of the canyon toward the head and by following the curved slope of the terrain (See: *Flying the Terrain*) as you reach the head of a canyon, it places the airplane in a position where it is easy to escape toward lowering terrain.

Do not continue flying at any point in the canyon or at the head of the canyon unless you can adhere to the basic premises of mountain flying:
- Remain in a position where you can turn to lowering terrain.
- Do not fly beyond the point of no return.

SUBSIDENCE AND DOWNDRAFTS

Occasionally you will encounter a situation that goes completely against everything you have learned about updrafts and downdrafts. This may occur when a high-pressure area dominates a high plateau region and you approach the plateau from a lower altitude.

Independence Pass again provides a good example. With a high-pressure area centered over the upper Arkansas River valley near Leadville, the entire area falls under the influence of the high. When this happens it is possible to have downdrafts on the west side of Independence Pass in an area where you usually find a predominance of updrafts. This extends to passes north (especially Hagerman Pass that leads from Leadville to Aspen) and south of Independence Pass.

The high-pressure area can be thought of as a mountain of air that creates an instability in the atmosphere. High-pressure areas subside or flow downward and outward, filling in low-pressure areas, in an attempt to re-establish stability.

The sinking air can slide under the updrafts on the west side of the pass and provide quite a surprise for the unsuspecting pilot. If you've worked at staying in a position to turn to lower terrain, this is more of an annoyance than a problem. Just circle around, gain additional altitude and continue on your way. It's likely that the additional altitude will put you above the downdraft area and back into an area of updrafts.

CROSSING THE RIDGE AT THE HEAD OF A CANYON

Assume that you are following the terrain to obtain lift in a canyon area and arrive at the head of a canyon with less than 2,000-feet terrain clearance. How do you know when you can continue?

If you are following the terrain, the natural curve of the terrain will place you at a 45-degree angle when you arrive at the head of the canyon. This is true unless the canyon is a box canyon with perpendicular walls joining the end (the author has never seen a true box canyon). Following the terrain allows an easy escape if a substantial downdraft is encountered.

 As you approach the head of the canyon, if you can see more and more of the terrain on the other side, you can probably continue. You can commit to crossing the ridge when you are in a position where with the throttle reduced to idle you can glide to the middle of the ridge line. If you have flown this close to the ridge without encountering a downdraft, any downdraft can be overcome with a slight nose-low attitude.

> **SAFE TO CROSS A RIDGE**
> - Position allows a power-off dive where the airplane would hit the center of the ridgetop.
> - Any downdraft encountered from this position will not pose a problem.

FLYING UP NARROW CANYONS

Flying in narrow canyons can be extremely hazardous or it can be pleasant. Even when it is an agreeable experience, you will have to remain constantly alert. One thing can be said with certainty about flying in a narrow canyon...if it is not performed correctly, it will not be habit forming.

What is a narrow canyon? By definition, a narrow canyon is one where, if you have to turn around, the turn radius will exceed one-half the canyon width.

 Pay attention to the wind. Flying with a tailwind indicates the possibility of an updraft at the head of the canyon. Flying with a headwind is almost a certain indication of a downdraft at the head of the canyon.

There are occasions when it becomes necessary to fly in a canyon at low altitude such as for law enforcement, search and rescue, or the airdrop of medication or supplies. A narrow canyon may be physically configured so the pilot cannot, at altitude, go to the head of the canyon and fly down to reach the desired point. In this case, it may be necessary to fly up the narrow canyon.

 My best advise is that it is wise to stay out of narrow canyons in an airplane. With flight experience and age comes caution. Unless there really is some compelling reason to venture into a narrow canyon, it's best to remain clear.

 Flying up a narrow canyon requires a different technique from flying up a normal canyon. First, you are going to anticipate making a 180-degree turn. And second, you fly up the downdraft side of the canyon. The rea-

PART 3 EN ROUTE — Chapter 3 - Mountain Flying Techniques

LEVEL STALL SPEED	STALL SPEED at DEGREE OF BANK / MINIMUM MANEUVER SPEED at DEGREE OF BANK							
	30	35	40	45	50	55	60	65
30	32.2	33.1	34.3	35.7	37.4	39.6	42.4	46.1
	34.6	36.6	39.2	42.4	46.7	52.3	60.0	71.0
35	37.6	38.7	40.0	41.6	43.7	46.2	49.5	53.8
	40.4	42.7	45.7	49.5	54.5	61.0	70.0	82.8
40	43.0	44.2	45.7	47.6	49.9	52.8	56.6	61.5
	46.2	48.8	52.2	56.6	62.2	69.7	80.0	94.6
45	48.4	49.7	51.4	53.5	56.1	59.4	63.6	69.2
	52.0	54.9	58.7	63.6	70.0	78.5	90.0	106.5
50	53.7	55.2	57.1	59.5	62.4	66.0	70.7	76.9
	57.7	61.0	65.3	70.7	77.8	87.2	100.0	118.3
55	59.1	60.8	62.8	65.4	68.6	72.6	77.8	84.6
	63.5	67.1	71.8	77.8	85.6	95.9	110.0	130.1
60	64.5	66.3	68.6	71.4	74.8	79.2	84.9	92.3
	69.3	73.2	78.3	84.9	93.3	104.6	120.0	142.0
65	69.8	71.8	74.3	77.3	81.1	85.8	91.9	100.0
	75.1	79.4	84.9	91.9	101.1	113.3	130.0	153.8
70	75.2	77.3	80.0	83.2	87.3	92.4	99.0	107.7
	80.8	85.5	91.4	99.0	108.9	122.0	140.0	165.6
75	80.6	82.9	85.7	89.2	93.5	99.0	106.1	115.4
	86.6	91.6	97.9	106.1	116.7	130.8	150.0	177.5
80	86.0	88.4	91.4	95.1	99.8	105.6	113.1	123.1
	92.4	97.7	104.4	113.1	124.5	139.5	160.0	189.3
85	91.3	93.9	97.1	101.1	106.0	112.2	120.2	130.8
	98.1	103.8	111.0	120.2	132.2	148.2	170.0	201.1

LOCATE THE LEVEL-FLIGHT STALL SPEED IN THE LEFT COLUMN. MOVE HORIZONTALLY TO THE RIGHT TO THE DEGREE OF BANK COLUMN. THE TOP FIGURE IS THE BANKED-FLIGHT STALL SPEED AT THE PARTICULAR BANK ANGLE. THE BOTTOM FIGURE IS THE MINIMUM *MANEUVER SPEED* AT THAT PARTICULAR BANK ANGLE.

THE PUBLISHED MANEUVERING SPEED (V_A) IS FOR WINGS-LEVEL FLIGHT. MANEUVER SPEED (V_P) IS A STRUCTURAL LIMITATION FOR BANKED FLIGHT. MANEUVER SPEED DEPENDS ON THE STALL SPEED, G-FORCE TOLERANCE AND POWER AVAILABLE. MANEUVER SPEED IS THE *MINIMUM SPEED* TO FLY IN A CANYON WHEN A TURNAROUND MANEUVER IS TO BE EXECUTED.

son for flying the downdraft side is when you make the turnaround, you will be turning into an area of lift (updrafts) instead of complicating the turn by encountering sink along the downdraft side.

Be aware that when you do turn around that the turn will be subject to a tail wind. This will increase the radius of turn. Actually the radius to turn remains the

Chapter 3 - Mountain Flying Techniques   PART 3 EN ROUTE

TRUE AIRSPEED KNOTS	RADIUS OF TURN BANK ANGLE IN DEGREES							
	25°	30°	35°	40°	45°	50°	55°	60°
30	171.4	138.4	114.2	95.3	79.9	67.1	56.0	46.1
35	233.3	188.4	155.4	129.7	108.8	91.3	76.2	62.8
40	304.7	246.1	202.9	169.3	142.1	119.2	99.5	82.0
45	385.7	311.5	256.8	214.3	179.8	150.9	125.9	103.8
50	476.1	384.6	317.1	264.6	222.0	186.3	155.5	128.2
55	576.1	465.3	383.7	320.2	268.7	225.4	188.1	155.1
60	685.6	553.8	456.6	381.0	319.7	268.3	223.9	184.6
65	804.7	649.9	535.9	447.2	375.2	314.8	262.7	216.6
70	933.2	753.7	621.5	518.6	435.2	365.1	304.7	251.2
75	1071.3	865.3	713.4	595.3	499.6	419.2	349.8	288.4
80	1218.9	984.5	811.7	677.4	568.4	476.9	398.0	328.2
85	1376.0	1111.4	916.4	764.7	641.7	538.4	449.3	370.5
90	1542.7	1246.0	1027.4	857.3	719.4	603.6	503.7	415.3
95	1718.8	1388.3	1144.7	955.2	801.5	672.5	561.2	462.8
100	1904.5	1538.2	1268.3	1058.4	888.1	745.2	621.9	512.7
105	2099.8	1695.9	1398.3	1166.9	979.1	821.6	685.6	565.3

LOCATE THE *TRUE* AIRSPEED IN KNOTS IN THE LEFT COLUMN. (ABOVE SEA LEVEL USE THE INDICATED AIRSPEED PLUS 2% PER 1,000 FEET ABOVE SEA LEVEL). MOVE HORIZONTALLY RIGHT TO THE COLUMN DENOTING THE MAXIMUM ANGLE OF BANK YOU DESIRE TO MAKE IN A CANYON. THE FIGURE GIVEN IS THE RADIUS OF TURN IN FEET.
NOTE: THE RADIUS OF TURN VARIES AS THE SQUARE OF THE TRUE AIRSPEED. EXAMPLE: LOCATE 40 KNOTS TAS AT 40° OF BANK. THE RADIUS OF TURN IS 169.3 FEET. DOUBLE THE SPEED TO 80 KNOTS AT THE SAME 40° BANK AND THE RADIUS OF TURN QUADRUPLES.

same. It is the drift from the wind that can cause the airplane to have insufficient space to complete the turn.

Depending on the strength of the wind, there may not be room for a turn-around maneuver and the flight into the canyon will have to be delayed until more favorable conditions exist.

COURSE REVERSAL PROCEDURES

One of my first mountain flying students had learned to fly while in the military. John had been exposed to some aerobatic maneuvers. He advocated the hammerhead turn for escaping from a canyon if the terrain out climbed the airplane. I didn't ever let him demonstrate it to me.

At this point in my career (1968), my aerobatic experience included being able to perform one, two and three turn spins with entries and recoveries to within 10 degrees of a preselected heading. That was it. Harold Price, Billings, Mont. had demonstrated some rolls, loops and hammerheads, but I didn't know how to perform them.

I did, however, keep this thought about using the hammerhead turn in the back of my mind to evaluate after learning to perform aerobatics. I learned aerobatics and quickly came to the conclusion that the hammerhead turn, in a canyon, equates to gross stupidity.

Other maneuvers, such as the wing over and chandelle have also be mentioned at the ultimate means of extricating yourself from a "tight." None of them work because they require maneuvering speed or greater to perform.

When you get into trouble in a canyon or in any situation comprising rising terrain, your airspeed will probably be at a minimum. It will not allow a hammerhead turn, wing over or chandelle. The safest and the best way to turn around (the author considers it the *only* way) is to make a slow turn.

RULE OF THUMB - Canyon Turnaround

When you approach a "tight," maintain your composure and slow down because the radius of turn decreases as the airspeed decreases. Do not reduce power to slow down. Trade airspeed in excess of the best angle of climb for altitude by climbing as you make a 180-degree turn at the steepest bank you can comfortably make.

HAMMERHEAD TURN

The hammerhead turn is an aerobatic maneuver executed by obtaining maneuvering speed (or the aircraft manufacturer's recommended entry speed). The airplane is pulled to the vertical. Before the stall, rudder is applied in the desired turn direction (usually to the left because the torque of the engine aids the turn). As the airplane starts to turn, the top wing circumscribes a larger arc, thus producing more lift than the bottom wing. Because of this, full aileron opposite the turn is used. The airplane pivots to the vertical down position and is recovered at the same or even a higher altitude than when it started.

Sound like something you want to do in a canyon? Probably not. Even with proficiency the hammerhead turn or hammerhead stall is not a maneuver to be performed in a canyon. Even if turbulence were not restrictive, by the time you recognize the need for the turn-around, the decreased airspeed of normal flight in the canyon would not allow this maneuver.

WING OVER

For playing in the mountains, the wing over is a great maneuver to use for a course reversal. When it is performed during play, regulations require that a parachute be provided for the student and instructor since the wing over meets the definition of aerobatic flight.

The wing over is a maximum performance steep climb turn. At the apex of the climb the bank angle reaches 90 degrees and the airspeed falls below the stall speed. Without adding back pressure until the airspeed increases, the airplane is allowed to fall through by itself. When the airspeed begins increasing, back pressure is applied on the elevator control, slowly increasing until the recovery is made at the same or higher altitude than started.

Again, the problem with preselecting this maneuver in one's mind for an emergency escape in situations requiring a turnaround, is that the pilot is generally close to the terrain before he considers the 180-degree turn and has unconsciously reduced his airspeed to a minimum by constantly adding back pressure in an effort to make the plane climb.

If you want to impress (and probably scare) a passenger, the wing over is a great maneuver providing it is properly planned in advance. For real-life situations, forget it.

CHANDELLE

The chandelle is a 180-degree maximum performance climbing turn. It is usually entered at maneuvering speed. For this reason it is impractical for a canyon turn-around. By the time you realize you need to reverse course the airspeed will probably be too slow.

As mentioned previously (page 3-35), when flying over extended bodies of water, the airplane's engine goes to "automatic rough." You start hearing weird sounds and feeling strange vibrations that you have never noticed before. It doesn't seem to matter whether it is a single-engine, twin-engine, turboprop or turbojet airplane.

The same type of thing happens when flying in a canyon—your left arm gets shorter. By the time you notice this phenomena, the airspeed has decreased substantially from what it was or what you expect it to be.

The "short-arm" effect is a normal reaction, especially for an inexperienced pilot flying upslope terrain. It is merely a matter of self preservation. You unconsciously try to avoid the terrain by pulling back on the control wheel.

PART 3 EN ROUTE   Chapter 3 - Mountain Flying Techniques

BOX CANYON TURN

Mountain flying, like Mother Nature, can be harsh and unforgiving for the novice who fails to adhere to the two basic premises for mountain flying. It's really a simple matter to flirt with the mountains if you always remain in a position to be able to turn toward lowering terrain and never fly beyond the point of no return.

The first law, being able to turn while having some extra altitude to descend, encompasses the idea that you never enter into a canyon if there is not sufficient room to turn around.

APPROACHING TWIN MOUNTAIN, GREAT BEAR WILDERNESS, MONTANA

The second law requires the pilot to establish a turn-around point whenever flying upslope terrain. The point of no return is defined as a point on the ground of rising terrain where the terrain out climbs the aircraft. The turn-around point is determined as the position where, if the throttle is reduced to idle, the aircraft could be turned around during a glide without impacting the terrain. Obviously, if you exercise this option, the power is not reduced to idle. This merely is a gauge to judge and establish the point over the ground where an escape turn must be made.

THE "NATURAL HORIZON" IS THE BASE OF THE MOUNTAINS ABOUT SIX TO EIGHT MILES AWAY

Conditioned Response

Even the unconcerned aviator flitting through the mountains at cruise power and cruise airspeed must cultivate a conditioned reflex to maintain a position

Chapter 3 - Mountain Flying Techniques   PART 3 EN ROUTE

allowing a turn to lowering terrain and guarding against flight beyond the point-of-no-return.

These axioms must be a conditioned reflex rather than instinct, because instinct may be wrong in an airplane. Entering a spin for the first time gives you the impression that the airplane is pointing straight towards the ground while rotating. In the Cessna 172, for example, the nose is 45 degrees blow the horizon, only about halfway from the horizon to the vertical. Your instinct will be to raise the nose with backpressure. It's always worked before. But now you must use the conditioned reflex of relaxing the controls (or pushing the control wheel forward) to break the stall and then fly out of the resulting dive without exceeding the critical angle of attack.

Box Canyon Options

Released from the confines of the traffic pattern, you find yourself heading for the mountains to swoop over ridges and soar beside majestic peaks. Caught up in the thrill, you lose track of your position and suddenly find yourself in a box canyon requiring course reversal maneuvering to escape what might become a precarious position.

The hammerhead turn, wing over or steep turn may appear to be viable options to extricate yourself from the predicament. Pilot have, in all seriousness, asked my advice about performing the hammerhead turn as an emergency procedure for getting out of a tight spot. The hammerhead turn is an aerobatic maneuver. Definitely it is best to avoid this maneuver in a "tight."

The wing over (another aerobatic maneuver) is more often performed while playing in the mountains rather than being used as an emergency escape maneuver. The pilot must preplan the wing over, allowing sufficient airspeed to transition from level flight to a climbing pitch attitude of about 40 degrees.

Until you have practiced the box canyon turn and understand the mechanics of and the ramifications of an unintentional stall close to the terrain, the safest and most commonly used method of course reversal for escaping from a "tight," that is, the rapidly rising terrain or the narrowing confines of a canyon, is to make a steep turn at a slow speed, using flaps if prudent.

APPROACHING THE SOUTH SIDE OF TWIN MOUNTAIN WESTBOUND

The stall speed of an airplane increases as the square root of the wing load factor. In a level, coordinated 60-degree bank, regardless of airspeed, the airplane experiences a 2-g load factor. The square root of 2 is 1.41, so there is a 41-percent increase in stall speed.

The radius of turn is equal to the velocity in true airspeed (knots) squared, divided by a constant of 11.26 times the tangent of the bank angle in degrees. Most pilots could care less about a formula for determining the radius of turn. This isn't Math 101 and we aren't concerned with computations, only the fact that radius of turn can be shorted by either reducing the true airspeed, or by increasing the angle of bank. The greatest benefit is from a combination of both slowing and banking.

THE CANYON IS WIDE ENOUGH FOR THE PILOT TO MAKE AN ESCAPE TURN TO THE LEFT, BUT HE CONTINUES, FOLLOWING THE TERRAIN WITH A TURN TO THE SOUTH

What about using flaps during this steep turn? Use them as appropriate to the flight conditions. Flaps were invented to allow an airplane to increase its approach angle without an increase in airspeed. They work because lift and drag are directly proportional. If the lift is increased (by applying flaps to increase the camber of the wing), the drag is increased (and hence, no increase in airspeed during a steep approach).

For most airplanes the addition of flaps, up to half the total available, provides more lift benefits than drag because the drag can be "subdued" with excess power.

At a high-density altitude it may not be possible to use full flaps without intentionally losing altitude to maintain a safe airspeed. If a trade-off between altitude and airspeed cannot be made because of rapidly ris-

THE BOX CANYON TURN IS REQUIRED WHEN THE CANYON ABRUPTLY NARROWS OR THE TERRAIN BEGINS TO OUT CLIMB THE AIRPLANE

ing terrain, limit the use of the flaps to the extent that the airplane will maintain a constant altitude during the turn.

Remember too that flaps reduce the structural strength of the airplane. The POH (pilots operating handbook) may say the airplane is certified for 3.8 Gs, and with the flaps extended 2.2 Gs (a 42-percent reduction). Many of the normal category airplanes are stressed for 3.8 Gs (g = gravity unit). This is the limit-load factor that should not be exceeded during maneuvering flight. Okay, some say, what about the ultimate load factor, you know, that 50-percent safety factor built into the airplane? Shouldn't the airplane be capable of flying at 5.7 Gs?

THE TURN AROUND RESULTS IN THE AIRCRAFT GETTING CLOSE TO THE TERRAIN (NOTE: FULL FLAPS ARE EXTENDED - SMOKE IS FROM FOREST FIRES)

Unless, like Peter Pan, you can fly without your airplane's wings, do not exceed the limit load factor. For certification the airplane must be able to withstand the ultimate load factor for a period of fewer than 2 seconds without permanent deformation of the structure. Otherwise the airplane may experience structural failure.

AS AIRSPEED AND ALTITUDE PERMIT (A POSITIVE RATE OF CLIMB IS ESTABLISHED), THE FLAPS ARE RETRACTED

Natural Horizon

It is imperative that the pilot knows his attitude in order to safely perform a box canyon turn. Attitude is the relationship of the airplane to the horizon. The natural horizon is "hidden" by mountains.

The natural horizon is used to teach flying by outside visual reference. An instructor demonstrates a climb attitude at the best rate-of-climb airspeed. The student mimics this attitude. The airspeed indicator can be covered and the student, by learning the pitch attitude in relation to the horizon (where the horizon intersects the side of the nose cowling), is able to fly at the best rate-of-climb airspeed within plus or minus one knot.

The instructor also demonstrates the nose position in relation to the horizon for level flight, the wing position in relation to the horizon in level flight, and the nose position in relation to the horizon during steep turns left and right.

This natural horizon is easy to use in the flatlands as a reference for basic attitude flying. In the mountains, the natural horizon may disappear. By visualizing a horizon, basic attitude flying can still be maintained. The base of the mountains, at least six to 8 miles away, represents the natural horizon. What if the airplane is closer than the six to eight miles? Visualization is still used. Perhaps the mountains at least six to eight miles in the distance are visible out the side window. Project the same horizon visually to the front of the airplane.

Box Canyon Turn Procedure

The box canyon turn is often initiated from minimum controllable airspeed. This minimum controllable airspeed is probably not an intentional flight condition and it definitely is not desired. It is caused by a condition similar to flying over water beyond the power-off gliding distance from the shore. You know the feeling: the oil pressure gauge beings ticking. And it hasn't done that before. The engine gives a little shudder of roughness. This continues until you approach the safety of the shoreline.

A similar phenomenon occurs when flying upslope terrain in the mountains. Your left arm becomes shorter. This is a normal self-preservation aspect of flight. You unconsciously pull away from the rising terrain and often the deterioration of airspeed goes unnoticed.

The box canyon turn varies from a steep tern in that it is either performed from level flight at such a slow airspeed than in unintentional stall is imminent, or some excess airspeed at the beginning of the maneuver allows the nose to be raised above the horizon prior to initiating the bank and the airspeed, during the turn, will be too slow to sustain level flight.

We have learned the airplane always stalls at the same critical angle of attack. When banking the airplane, the stall speed increases (remember, it increases as the square of the wing load factor). Whenever the airplane is banked in a coordinated turn, it is balancing the centripetal force (horizontal lift component that causes the turn) and the centrifugal force (the opposing force of the turn). The turn takes place because the centripetal force pulls the airplane towards the inside of the turn.

Chapter 3 - Mountain Flying Techniques   PART 3 EN ROUTE

BOX CANYON TURN COURSE REVERSAL – SIMULTANEOUSLY BEGIN THE BANK, ADD POWER AND EXTEND FULL FLAPS

Without a compensating increase in the amount of total lift during a turn, the airplane will lose altitude. The total lift is divided between a vector force that sustains the weight of the airplane and the portion of lift that is directed sideward to cause the turn.

To maintain level flight while turning it is necessary to increase backpressure (more lift equals an increase in the angle of attack). This increases the load factor and stall speed. Some pilots get into trouble with the box canyon turn without realizing it because they have been "conditioned" to maintain level flight when performing steep turns.

The first time a pilot has to perform a box canyon turn in a true-life situation, he may feel like the lady who climbs on a stool to avoid a mouse scampering across the floor ... it's kind of scary. A little scream to get the adrenaline flowing wouldn't hurt here either.

The box canyon turn could be described as a combination of the steep turn and the wing over maneuver. With excess airspeed (above V_X or V_Y) the nose is raised above the horizon, but nowhere near the 40-degree pitch attitude of the wing over maneuver. An attitude of about five to 20 degrees above the horizon is about right, depending on the airspeed. Use less pitch when beginning with a slow airspeed.

This does two things for you. First, it trades excess airspeed for altitude, and second, it slows the airspeed for a smaller radius of turn. This might be a critical situation instead if the airspeed is slower than V_Y or V_X due to the "short arm" effect.

At the same time, full power is added and full flaps (providing the airspeed is within the flap operating range) are applied while beginning the bank. The bank will be a minimum of 60 degrees and may approach 90 degrees.

To insure that the g-load factor is not exceeded during the steep bank it is necessary to relax the backpressure once the bank passes about 45 degrees. The backpressure is not increased again until the bank passes through about 45 degrees toward zero degrees during the rollout.

Initiate the turn

The procedure requires coordination to accomplish all the items at the same time:
- Increase pitch attitude (if beginning at a slow speed - maintain the same pitch attitude initially).
- Increase the power.
- Begin a bank.
- Apply full flaps.

At approximately 45 degrees of bank (if beginning from a slow speed - 30 degrees of bank) increasing toward 60-90 degrees:
- Relax backpressure from the control wheel.
- At slow speed, the pitch attitude will fall below the horizon.

Recover

At approximately 45 degrees of bank, decreasing from 60-90 degrees:
- Increase backpressure on the control wheel to arrest any further loss of altitude.
- When the airplane is in a position that allows, reduce the flaps to one half.
- As airspeed and altitude permit, retract the flaps. This will be when the airplane exhibits a positive rate of climb.

Summary

The box canyon turn is an emergency procedure that without practice can lead to an accelerated stall that exacerbates the original critical situation. It is best to practice it with an experienced instructor prior to the time when it becomes necessary as a life-saving maneuver.

Caveat

You must exercise caution in using full flaps during the practice of the box canyon turn because of the possibility of the flaps failing in the extended position. You might consider practicing in an area where the drainage leads toward lowering terrain that would allow for an emergency landing.

STEEP TURN

In a "tight"—defined as a situation that requires immediate action to prevent an accident—the steep turn becomes paramount for safety during the course reversal.

Due to the fact that the radius of turn increases with an increase in speed, it is mandatory that the airplane be flown at the slowest speed possible. Although the desired speed is slow, it must be fast enough to provide a safety margin for the increased stall speed of maneuvering while banked and it must be fast enough so that it prevents an accidental stall if turbulence is encountered.

The importance of speed and its effect on the radius of turn is easily demonstrated. Use a string about three-feet long. Attach an object, maybe a pocketknife, pen or other available doodad. While holding the end of the string, slowly move your hand in a circular pattern. The weight at the end of the string will create a circular pattern similar to the movement of the hand. Increase the speed of your hand movement and the radius of turn for the suspended weight increases.

There is an easy way to measure the effects of the ratio-of-turn radius to an increase in airspeed.

RULE OF THUMB—Turn Radius versus Airspeed

The radius of turn varies as the square of the true airspeed.

The radius of turn varies as the square of the true airspeed means that if the speed is doubled, the radius of turn is quadrupled.

As an example, an airplane in a turn with a constant 30-degree bank that doubles its speed, would increase the distance traveled in completing a 360-degree turn four times over the distance of the original turn. So, even though the airplane is going twice as fast, it would take twice as long to complete this turn.

The canyon turnaround rule of thumb advocates slowing down and making the steepest bank possible. The novice pilot may not be comfortable making a bank greater than about 30 degrees, especially if there is turbulence. In this case the 30-degree bank is the steepest bank possible. Having decided ahead of time on the maximum bank angle that you will use, the following charts can resolve the distance required (radius of turn) to turn around at the desired airspeed and bank angle.

The airspeed to be used at any particular bank angle is determined from the *Minimum Maneuver Speed* chart on page 3-41. The distance to turn around is calculated from the *Radius of Turn* chart on page 3-42.

After coming up with the value for the radius of turn, it is easy to determine the minimum width for any canyon operation.

RULE OF THUMB – Minimum Width for any Canyon Operation

Double the turn radius and add 200 feet. Do not enter a canyon that is narrower than this computed width.

Whenever you operate in a canyon, be sure that you have maneuvering space to make a 180° turn. Decide that maximum angle of bank that you will perform before entering the canyon area. Don't be overly optimistic by choosing a 60° bank to start with. You may enter the canyon and be intimidated by the terrain. It is best to be somewhat conservative, choosing maybe a 35-degree bank angle as the maximum bank for a turnaround. Then, while flying in a canyon, try different degrees of bank and see what you are comfortable with.

It is helpful to establish certain parameters of flight beforehand when you plan to fly through canyons. Having information (such as the maximum bank you desire to make), prior to flight allows you to decide if a canyon is wide enough to be flown in safely. For example, using the *Radius of Turn* chart on page 3-42, with a true airspeed of 80 knots and using a 35-degree bank, the radius of turn is 916 feet. Double this value and add 200 feet. This would equate to an approximate 2,000-foot width canyon (2,032 feet) as the minimum width before flying in the canyon.

To determine the minimum canyon width for operations, double the radius of turn and add an arbitrary 200 feet. By allowing a little extra margin (the arbitrary 200 feet) to the width, if you have to turn around during a winds aloft condition that produces updrafts and downdrafts, the airplane will not extend beyond the halfway point of the canyon into the area of downdrafts.

To approximate the width of the canyon, convert the groundspeed (true airspeed if unknown) into feet per second. Fly perpendicular to the canyon and determine the time to fly from one side to the other. Multiply the fps by the seconds and get an approximation of the canyon width.

Chapter 3 - Mountain Flying Techniques   PART 3 EN ROUTE

To determine the distance flown in feet per second, multiply the groundspeed (true airspeed) by 6,076.114 (feet in a nautical mile). Divide by 3,600 (number of seconds in an hour). At 80 knots, the airplane travels aproximately 135 fpm.

PARAMETERS OF CANYON FLIGHT

When the width of a canyon narrows to become critical and it is necessary to turn around in the smallest distance possible, slowing the airplane to its slowest speed (maneuver speed) and making the steepest bank possible will result in the smallest radius of turn and the greatest rate of turn. Let's examine the factors that place a limitation on the airplane's ability to fly at slow speed with a steep bank.

Load Factor

Whenever an airplane deviates from straight flight, the circular path causes the structure to be subjected to centrifugal force. In a 60°-banked turn, the airplane experiences a 2-g load factor. This means the wings are supporting double the airplane's weight.

Aircraft certification is based in part upon the structural strength that is built into the plane. Some of the categories are *normal, utility, aerobatic, restricted* and *transport*. The single-engine general aviation airplane is, in most cases, certified as a normal category airplane. It usually is stressed for 3.8 gs and is designated as a limit load factor because it is limiting. Exceeding the limit load factor may cause permanent deformation of some part of the aircraft structure and structural failure is possible.

Increased Stall Speed

An airplane in level flight may be flown at 90 knots. For this speed a certain angle of attack is required. For the sake of example let's assume the angle of attack is 8 degrees. If the same airplane is flown in a 40-degree banked turn at 90 knots, the angle of attack is greater, let's assume it is 12 degrees. Using this logic you can see that the airplane will reach the critical angle of attack at a greater speed when it is in banked flight as opposed to level flight. Remember that the airplane always stalls at the same angle of attack, regardless of airspeed. This is called the critical angle of attack.

When an airplane is banked, the stall speed increases. It increases as the square root of the wing load factor. For example, in a 60-degree bank, the load factor is 2 gs. The square root of 2 is 1.41, or a 41 percent increase in stall speed. Why is this so?

In straight-and-level unaccelerated flight the airplane is acted upon by four forces; lift opposes weight and thrust balances drag. When the airplane is banked, a portion of the lift is directed toward the side to create a horizontal lift component (centripetal force toward the inside of the turn) that causes the turn. Centrifugal force, towards the outside of the turn, opposes centripetal force. Because some of the lift has been diverted for the turn, the total lift must be increased to maintain a constant altitude. The additional lift results in an increase in the angle of attack.

An airplane always stalls at the same angle of attack, regardless of airspeed or attitude. This is called the critical angle of attack. Let's examine an airplane (that stalls at a critical angle of attack of 18 degrees) that is in cruise flight at 90 knots true airspeed. For this level flight condition a specific angle of attack is required to maintain level flight. In this example, we will assume that it is an 8-degree angle of attack. If this airplane is banked 40 degrees (and the power is increased to maintain 90 knots), the angle of attack must increase to maybe 12 degrees. If the bank is increased further, or the airspeed reduced below 90 knots, the angle of attack must be increased again to maintain level flight. Using this logic it is easy to see that the airplane will reach its critical angle of attack at a greater speed when it is in banked flight than it would in level flight.

Power Limits

Check the **AIRCRAFT LOAD FACTOR/STALL SPEED CHART** for your airplane (Pilot's Operating Handbook or Owner's Manual). It demonstrates the increase in load factor for banked flight and the increase in stall speed at any particular bank. To sustain flight at a constant altitude while banked, the total lift must be increased. Lift and drag are directly proportional; meaning that when lift is increased, drag is increased by the same amount. To maintain the same airspeed in banked flight as in level flight requires additional thrust. General aviation airplanes are limited in the amount of excess power available. During high density altitude operations, a light airplane with minimal power may be unable to maintain level flight during a steep-banked turn.

Using the Pilot's Operation Handbook, determine the maximum bank, at various density altitudes, where you can maintain level flight. The aircraft performance, or lack thereof, may place a restriction on some flight operations. If the maximum bank for sustained level flight is 30 degrees, the flight will be restricted to canyons of a width that matches the performance capabilities of the airplane.

Maneuver Speed (V_P)

The minimum speed that an airplane can be operated at a specific bank angle in level flight is dependent on the stall speed at that bank angle, the structural strength or g-force tolerance of the airplane and the power available.

The g-force limit is designed into the airplane. For a normal category airplane, the level flight bank should not exceed 74.7 degrees, the amount of bank that pro-

Chapter 3 - Mountain Flying Techniques — PART 3 EN ROUTE

duces 3.8 gs. Remember, the 50-percent safety factor (3.8 + 1.9 = 5.7 g *ultimate load factor*) is added for certification to compensate for vagaries in materials and workmanship, not to allow flight beyond the 3.8 g limit-load factor.

The maneuver speed (V_P) is the minimum speed required to develop aerodynamically the limit load factor that will produce the minimum turn radius within the aerodynamic limit and structural limit of the airplane. When the stall speed and limit load factor are known (for a particular configuration such as gear and flaps retracted), the maneuver speed is determined by the formula:

Where

$$Vp = Vs \cdot \sqrt{n\ limit}$$

Vp = maneuver speed, knots
Vs = stall speed, knots
N limit = limit load factor

What is the difference between the minimum *maneuver speed (V_P)* and *maneuvering speed. (V_A)*? There is no difference, they are both the same. The difference in designation has traditionally been used to distinguish between wings-level maneuvering speed (V_A) and banked-maneuvering speed, or maneuver speed (V_P).

Maneuvering speed is the maximum speed that full control deflection can be made without deforming the aircraft structure. When the airplane is flown at maneuvering speed it will stall near the 4 gs load factor mark, relieving stress. Maneuvering speed should be flown whenever the aircraft is in moderate or greater turbulence.

RULE OF THUMB - Box Canyon Turnaround

✔ Slow to the minimum maneuver speed. Trade excess airspeed for altitude using back pressure on the elevator control.

✔ Make the steepest bank possible.

✔ Use flaps.

Although the rule of thumb suggests the use of flaps for the box canyon turn, some *caution* must exist. The main purpose of flaps is to allow an airplane to increase its approach angle to a runway without an increase in airspeed (lift and drag are directly proportional and flaps, with reduced power, add drag), they do reduce the stall speed.

The reduction in stall speed allows the airplane to be flown slower, decreasing the radius of turn. For most light airplanes, the addition of flaps up to about one half will create additional lift and drag along with a nose-up pitch change.

When the flaps are increased beyond half, there will be little pitch change, but there is a substantial increase in induced drag. For airplanes with the available power, such as a Cessna Turbo 206, more than half flaps may be used to reduce the radius of turn without the penalty of losing altitude during the turn.

For airplanes with less power available, the use of flaps beyond half might be detrimental to the turn around, causing the plane to lose valuable altitude.

Another important consideration is the fact that flaps reduce the structural strength of an airplane. The limit load factor, with full flaps selected, is decreased anywhere from about eight percent to a whopping 58 percent, depending on the year, make and model of airplane.

Check the operating limitations section of the owner's manual or the POH for your airplane. A 1971 Cessna 182 lists the flight load factor (at design gross weight of 2,950 pounds) as:

Flaps Up . . . . +3.8
Flaps Down . . . . +3.5

This is a 7.9 percent reduction in the structural strength of the airplane.

Checking the POH for the 1977 Cessna Turbo Stationair (TU206G) and 1977 Cessna Turbo Centurion (T210M) give flight load factor limits:

Flaps Up . . . . +3.8
Flaps Down . . . . +2.0

These airplanes have a 47.4 percent reduction in their structural strength with the application of full flaps.

As a general rule of thumb, when moderate or greater turbulence exists in a canyon, do not use flaps during the box canyon turn (although if they are required, don't hesitate to do what you have to do to extricate yourself from a precarious position). If the turbulence is less than moderate, use flaps to reduce the stall speed and allow flight at a slower speed to reduce the radius of turn.

FORMULAS

Most pilot have little regard or use for mathematical formulas, but a few want to see how the information in various charts and graphs come into being. These formulas are included in the Appendix.

Chapter 3 - Mountain Flying Techniques   PART 3 EN ROUTE

FLIGHT LOAD FACTORS

You should remember from your pilot certification days that a coordinated turn at a particular bank angle always produces the same wing load factor. It doesn't matter if the same airplane is flown at different speeds. For example a turn at 60 knots indicated airspeed and a coordinated 60-degree bank will produce a 2-g load factor. If the same airplane is flown at 120 knots in the same coordinated 60-degree banked turn, it still produces a 2-g load factor. A Boeing 757 or a jet fighter, regardless of their speed, produces a 2-g load factor in a coordinated 60-degree banked turn.

Remember the application of flaps reduces the structural strength or g-load tolerance of the airplane. If the airplane is being flown at a 74.7-degree bank (3.8-g load factor) and it experiences a wind gust, or the pilot makes an abrupt elevator change while trying to maintain altitude, the wing load factor may be exceeded, challenging the structural integrity of the airplane.

Federal Aviation Regulations governing the certification of aircraft establish minimum strength limitations for a particular category (normal, utility, aerobatic, limited, provisional, etc.). One way the strength is measured is to calculate or measure the total load the wings are capable of supporting without distortion or permanent damage.

Positive load factors occur when the aerodynamic force acts upward with respect to the airplane. Negative load factors happen when the force acts downward. The action of the force is assumed to be with respect to the airplane regardless of the airplane's attitude in relation to the horizon.

The pilot's indication of an increasing load factor is a feeling of becoming heavier or being pushed down in the seat. An increasing flight load factor increases the perceived weight of the pilot. If the pilot were to sit on a bathroom scale during straight and level flight, the scale would indicate the weight of the pilot. In a 60-degree bank, the scale would indicate twice the weight, since the flight load factor is 2 gs in a 60-degree bank.

If you aren't acclimated to aerobatics, you experience a "pucker factor" some-

BANK ANGLE	AIRCRAFT LOAD FACTOR	INCREASE IN STALL SPEED
20°	1.06	1.03
25°	1.10	1.05
30°	1.16	1.08
35°	1.22	1.11
40°	1.31	1.14
45°	1.41	1.19
50°	1.56	1.25
55°	1.74	1.32
60°	2.00	1.41
65°	2.37	1.54
70°	2.92	1.71
75°	3.86	1.97
80°	5.76	2.40
85°	11.47	3.39

AIRCRAFT LOAD FACTOR
STALL SPEED CHART
THE STALL SPEED INCREASES AS THE SQUARE ROOT OF THE LIMIT LOAD FACTOR.

where around 3 gs, where you notice your cheeks sagging along with a feeling that the blood is draining from your head.

In addition to banked flight, severe vertical gusts can cause a large load factor. Strong gusts have the ability to momentarily replace the relative wind, causing a change in the angle of attack. When a gust input causes a vector force that replaces the relative wind, the angle of attack is increased, increasing the load factor. These wing loads are resisted by the inertia of the airplane and this is what causes the stress to occur on the structure.

For a particular category airplane, such as the normal category, the regulations require the aircraft structure to be capable of supporting the limit loads specified in the regulation before it can become certified for production. Normal category airplanes must be stressed for +3.8 and –1.52 limit loads without detrimental or permanent deformation. (FAR 23.337 provides that the positive limit maneuvering load factor may not be less than 2.1 + (24,000/W + 10,000) for normal category airplanes, except that it need not be more than 3.8. The negative limit maneuvering load factor may not be less than 0.4 times the positive load factor) Deformation may occur at loads up to the limit load as long as it is not permanent and it does not interfere with the safe operation of the airplane. Flexing of the wings is an example of this deformation.

ULTIMATE LOADS

For certification, the airplane must be proven to be capable of supporting the limit loads specified by regulation. Additionally, the airplane must be able to support the ultimate load factor for at least three seconds without failure.

Federal Aviation Regulations—Part 23 - Airworthiness Standards: Normal, Utility, Acrobatic, and Commuter Category Airplanes and Part 25 - Airworthiness Standards: Transport Category Airplanes—require the ultimate load factor to be 50 percent greater than the limit load factor.

CATEGORY	POSITIVE LIMIT LOAD	POSITIVE LIMIT LOAD + 50% SAFETY FACTOR = ULTIMATE LOAD	NEGATIVE LIMIT LOAD
Normal	+3.8	+5.7	–1.52
Utility	+4.4	+6.6	–1.76
Aerobatic	+6.0	+9.0	–3.00

THE AIRPLANE MUST NEVER EXCEED THE POSITIVE *LIMIT LOAD FACTOR* ESTABLISHED BY THE MANUFACTURER EVEN THOUGH AN *ULTIMATE LOAD FACTOR* IS PROVIDED. THE ULTIMATE LOAD FACTOR PROVISION IS TO COMPENSATE FOR VAGARIES IN MATERIALS AND WORKMANSHIP DURING CONSTRUCTION.

This ultimate load factor sometimes causes confusion when pilots think it is okay to fly the airplane and experience the ultimate load factor in flight. The purpose of the ultimate load factor is to compensate for differences in materials and construction irregularities. Do not subject the airplane to stresses greater than the limit load factor.

MANEUVERING SPEED

Maneuvering speed is defined as the maximum speed at which the airplane can be safely stalled, or the controls deflected fully, without exceeding the airplane's limit load factor. This is the "rough air speed," and the maximum speed for abrupt maneuvers. Gust loads increase with increasing airspeed, so rough air of moderate or greater turbulence demands the airspeed be reduced to maneuvering speed or less to minimize the stress on the airplane structure. The airplane has been designed to withstand turbulence loads of considerable intensity providing it is flown at or below the maneuver speed.

Maneuvering speed allows the airplane to experience a brief aerodynamic stall to relieve loads that could result in structural damage at a a faster speed. Even if full control travel is used in maintaining the attitude of the airplane, there is a sufficient margin of safety above the stalling speed and protection against airplane structural damage.

Examination of the aircraft manual reveals that the maneuvering speed changes with a change in gross weight. With a weight decrease, the value of maneuvering speed decreases. This might be the opposite of what you would expect. A 2-percent change in weight causes a 1-percent change in stall speed. If an airplane's weight is reduced from 2,300 pounds to 1,900 pounds, this is a 17.39 percent reduction in gross weight that equates to an 8.7 percent reduction in the stall speed.

If the airplane being operated at the reduced weight is flown at the original (gross weight) maneuvering speed, the reduction in stall speed would allow the airplane to exceed 3.8 gs before stalling to relieve the stress imposed by the turbulence.

RULE OF THUMB to Determine Maneuvering Speed.
$V_A = 1.7\ V_{SO}$

Many older airplanes do not have owner's manuals or any other printed information concerning their operating limitations. If you cannot determine maneuvering speed, multiply the normal stall speed by 1.7. The maneuvering speed may be as much as twice the stall speed in some airplanes, but by using this value you won't break the airplane.

Federal Aviation Regulations provide for a factor of 1.9 to be multiplied by the normal stall speed; however, if the airplane is old enough that there is not an owner's manual, it is old enough to use 1.7 as the value for determining maneuvering speed. It is best to be cautious with older airplanes.

If you have flown very much, you might be cognizant of the fact that an airplane loaded to its gross weight gives a smoother ride in turbulent air than a lightly loaded airplane. Because of this, you might come to the mistaken conclusion that it is best to load the airplane to its maximum if you anticipate turbulence on your flight.

The total stress imposed on an airplane during operation in turbulence is more important than the g-load factor encountered. We can measure the forces involved when an airplane encounters gust loads. An airplane operated at gross weight will resist vertical displacement more than a lightly loaded airplane and will incur less g force than the light airplane.

During flight the pilot perceives the load factor, but the airplane structure (and its operating strength limitation) is influenced by the total load encountered.

Regulations for certification prior to 1987 required general aviation airplanes to be capable of withstanding a +30 feet-per-second (fps) gust during level flight at maximum speed with normal rated power. The FARs were changed on January 15, 1987, to consider more fully the gust effect on the airframe and now specify a +50 fps gust at the design cruise speed.

In straight-and-level unaccelerated flight an airplane experiences a 1-g load factor. Suppose a Cessna Turbo 210 (T-210) operated at gross weight encounters a +30-fps gust. This gust results in a 2-g load factor. The airplane structure is exposed to a total load of 3 gs. Multiply the weight (3,800) by the load factor (3) and the wings supported a total of 11,400 pounds. The pilot doesn't recognize the load on the wings, but he can feel the 3 gs.

The airplane lands and cargo is off-loaded to bring the weight of the T-210 down to 1,900 pounds for the return flight. During this flight the airplane encounters an exact gust, but at the lighter weight, the gust acceleration is greater. With only half the weight (inertia), the gust acceleration will be double, producing a 4-g load factor. Here again we multiply the weight (1,900) by the load factor (5) and determine the wings in this case supported a total of 9,500 pounds. The pilot is aware that 5 gs was much greater than the 3 gs previously experienced, but he may not realize the stress on the airplane was much less (11,400 minus 9,500). The lightly loaded T-210 was exposed to 1,900 pounds less stress on the structure.

The heavily loaded airplane realizes less load factor, but it incurs more strain on the airframe. The lightly loaded airplane "feels" like it is affected more by the

Chapter 3 - Mountain Flying Techniques   PART 3 EN ROUTE

turbulence because the high accelerations and inertial forces tend to intensify the pilot's impression of the turbulence.

When the pilot operates the airplane properly by slowing to maneuvering speed in moderate or greater turbulence, he need not fear exceeding the structural capabilities or limitations of the airplane. At maneuvering speed or below the aircraft cannot be over-stressed. It will stall before the limit load factor is reached.

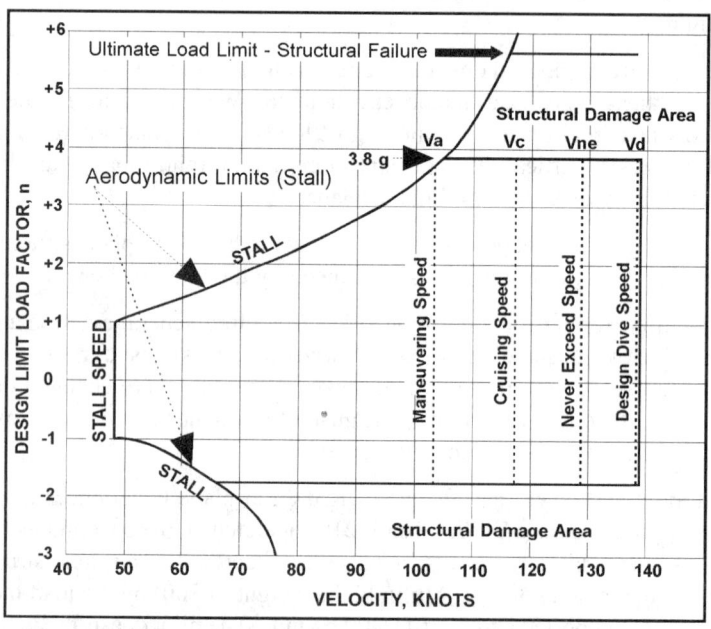

V-n DIAGRAM (V-g DIAGRAM) FOR NORMAL CATEGORY, LOW-PERFORMANCE AIRPLANE. (V-g DIAGRAM TERMINOLOGY NOT USED BECAUSE OF CONFUSION WITH GRAVITATION "g.")

THE MAXIMUM POSITIVE LIMIT LOAD FACTOR FOR A NORMAL CATEGORY AIRPLANE IS +3.8 g EXTENDING FROM THE STALLING SPEED AT POINT "V_A" AND EXTENDING TO POINT "V_D." THE MAXIMUM NEGATIVE LIMIT LOAD FACTOR IS −1.52 gs EXTENDING FROM 67 KNOTS TO "V_D."

THE LIMIT LOAD FACTORS ARE FOR MAXIMUM ALLOWABLE GROSS WEIGHT. THE SPEED FOR VA CHANGES WITH A REDUCTION IN GROSS WEIGHT. THERE CAN BE NO CORROSION, FATIGUE OR OTHER DAMAGE TO THE AIRPLANE FOR THE DATA TO BE VALID.

CAUTION: SAMPLE ONLY, DATA NOT VALID FOR ANY SPECIFIC AIRPLANE

Maneuvering Speed and Weight

Do not forget that if the gross weight is reduced, the value of maneuvering speed is reduced. Maneuvering load factors vary with the square of the speed ratio. Design maneuvering speed, V_A, equals (V_S * sqrt(n)), where V_S is. the computed stalling speed with flaps retracted at the design weight and n is the limit maneuvering load factor used in design. When the aircraft weight is reduced, the stall speed is reduced, causing V_A to be a lesser value.

CANYON DOWNDRAFT

For most flights, when you use visualization to fly through a canyon you can stay in an updraft area or at least a neutral area. Occasionally the visualization doesn't work and you are not able to find lift. In fact downdrafts may make it impossible to maintain your original altitude. If this happens—maintain a position where you can turn toward lowering terrain—and try maneuvering to the other side of the canyon. It may be that subsidence (sinking air from a high pressure area that may be stronger than orographic lift from the winds aloft) is producing a downdraft in a visualized updraft area and it may produce an updraft in an area you visualize as a downdraft area. Mother Nature tries to maintain a balance in the atmosphere, so if there is a downdraft, there has to be a compensating updraft. Updrafts tend to be smaller in size than downdrafts. It may take some searching and experimentation on your part to find the updrafts.

It is important to maintain airspeed when you encounter a downdraft. Even if you are approaching a "tight," fight against the self-preservation instinct of pulling back on the control wheel. Lower the nose to maintain flying speed and maneuver toward lowering terrain. There will be a cushion of air next to the ground–with exceptions.

Exceptions to the ground cushion of air exist when the airplane is very close to a steep mountain or any precipitous terrain, when it is over tall stands of timber (the tree height prevents descending into the ground cushion) and in downburst situations where the downdraft covers an extensive area.

LOCATION OF UPDRAFTS

When the winds aloft blow nearly perpendicular to a mountain range, updrafts occur on the windward side and downdrafts and turbulence occur on the lee side. The amount of turbulence is dependent upon air stability and wind flow velocity. The updraft expands, changing its position when the wind velocity increases. The following figure, page 3-56, demonstrates this phenomenon.

Updrafts become stronger and stronger as the airplane is maneuvered closer to the slope. The best updrafts are encountered, not directly over the ridge, but to the windward side. Even the lee side produces appreciable lift in an area above mountaintop level.

Chapter 3 - Mountain Flying Techniques   PART 3 EN ROUTE

Most mountain ranges in the United States are orientated in a more or less north-south line (the exception being the Uinta Mountains of Utah and Colorado). The prevailing winds aloft are westerly. With these facts in mind, generally there will be oragraphic lift on the west side of mountains and downdrafts with its associated turbulence on the east side of the mountains. There are always exceptions to this generality, so use visualization to determine areas of lift, sink and turbulence. Ask yourself what water would do if it was flowing the same as the wind. ✈

**EISENHOWER TUNNEL ALONG I-70
(APPROACHING A RIDGE FROM THE WINDWARD SIDE)**

NOTE THAT THE CLOUDS ARE PARALLEL WITH THE MOUNTAINTOP RIDGES. THE AIRPLANE IS FLYING EAST-NORTHEAST. THE CLOUDS INDICATE THE WIND IS FROM THE WEST OR THE EAST. PREVAILING WESTERLY WINDS WOULD MAKE THE WIND DIRECTION MOST LIKELY FROM THE WEST; HOWEVER, BY WATCHING THE CLOUD SHADOWS THE ACTUAL WIND DIRECTION CAN BE ASCERTAINED.

APPROACH THE RIDGE AT AN ANGLE. WHEN IN A POSITION WHERE DIVING WILL "REACH" THE TOP OF THE RIDGE YOU CAN MAKE A COMMITMENT TO CROSS THE RIDGE.

PART 3 EN ROUTE Chapter 3 - Mountain Flying Techniques

UPDRAFTS RESULTING FROM MOUNTAIN WIND FLOW DEPEND UPON THE WIND VELOCITY, AIR STABILITY, AND SHAPE OF THE MOUNTAINS.

WINDS LESS THAN 20 KNOTS PRODUCE SLIGHT UPDRAFTS VERY CLOSE TO THE RIDGE. DEPENDING ON THE AIR STABILITY, TURBULENCE ON THE DOWNWIND (LEE SIDE) SIDE SHOULD BE MINIMAL. RARELY WILL IT CAUSE WHITECAPS IN YOUR COFFEE CUP.

WINDS OF 20 KNOTS OR GREATER PRODUCE STRONGER UPDRAFTS AND DOWNDRAFTS WITH ASSOCIATED TURBULENCE. THESE MAY BE SUSTAINED, STRONG UPDRAFTS AND DOWNDRAFTS. TURBULENCE MAY BE EXTENSIVE ON THE LEE SIDE. SOME UPDRAFT MAY EXTEND TO THE LEE SIDE OF THE MOUNTAIN ABOVE MOUNTAINTOP LEVEL. THE CLOSER TO THE SLOPE THE AIRPLANE IS MANEUVERED TOWARD THE SLOPE, THE STRONGER WILL BE THE UPDRAFTS.

Chapter 3 - Mountain Flying Techniques   PART 3 EN ROUTE

UPDRAFTS AND DOWNDRAFTS CAN ALSO BE CAUSED BY WIND FLOW THROUGH UNSTABLE AIR. USE VISUALIZATION TO TRY TO PICTURE THE AREAS OF LIFT AND SINK.

CASTLE-TOP CLOUDS (LOWER CLOUDS) SHOW INSTABILITY. THESE CLOUDS INDICATE THE PROBABILITY OF THUNDERSTORMS DURING THE AFTERNOON DURING THE SUMMER.

PART 3 EN ROUTE   Chapter 4 - Mountain Flying Turbulence

CHAPTER 4—MOUNTAIN FLYING TURBULENCE

- CONVECTION CURRENTS (THERMALS)......... 3-68
- MECHANICAL TURBULENCE 3-69
- WIND SHEAR 3-73
- DETECTING WIND SHEAR................... 3-80
- AIRPLANE PERFORMANCE IN WIND SHEAR..... 3-82
- PROCEDURES FOR COPING WITH WIND SHEAR . 3-83
- PIREPS 3-85

    Computer models and other technical equipment advances provide the guidelines for forecasting mountain turbulence, but the location, extent and severity remain mostly unknown.

    On the opposite side, aeronautical engineers know exactly how much stress will break the airplane. Lacking accurate forecasts, pilots should learn all they can about mountain turbulence, maneuvering speed and the actions to take when turbulence is encountered.

    Weather personnel predict the location and amount of turbulence by following general forecasting guidelines using the winds aloft forecast near the 10,000-foot level. These general guidelines can't take into account the various terrain modifications, funneling effect and venturi effect of the wind as it moves across the mountains. It behooves all pilots to practice visualization—asking yourself, "What water would do if it were flowing the same as the wind?"—in order to picture areas of updrafts, downdrafts and turbulence.

    The study of wind provides some general guidelines for flight based on the wind's velocity, but as with other generalizations, there are always exceptions. Surface winds of greater than 20 knots mean the flight should proceed with caution. Mountaintop winds of greater than 20 knots convey the need for extra caution and greater than 30 knots usually denotes the flight should be delayed or postponed until the wind velocity dies down.

    There may be times when the winds aloft forecast at 12,000 feet suggests winds of 40 or 50 knots. With a stable atmosphere it may be possible to fly in the mountains and avoid any turbulence and downdrafts by using visualization. With

Mountain Flying Bible

Chapter 4 - Mountain Flying Turbulence   PART 3 EN ROUTE

an unstable air mass, you will know before reaching the mountains that the best course of action is the 180-degree turn.

When flying during a period of winds aloft at 20 knots or more, avoid sharp ridges that are perpendicular to the wind flow. These are very dangerous. The air strikes the full face of the mountain from the top to the bottom. The air flow continues moving into the face. The air at the base doesn't have a chance to escape up and over the top before more onrushing air traps it. The replacement air rides over the trapped air, setting up an eddy current with strong downdrafts and possible severe turbulence.

The forecast wind direction and velocity may differ from the condition experienced due to funneling and the venturi effect.

Mountain winds—because of greater modification and the problems inherent with traversing varying terrain features—create a more hazardous flight scenario than flatland winds.

There are three major classifications of turbulence: *convection currents, mechanical turbulence* and *wind shear*. An examination of each classification provides insight into what to expect and shows the necessity of slowing to the maneuvering speed whenever the intensity of the turbulence approaches moderate or greater.

1. CONVECTION CURRENTS (THERMALS)

The sun's heating can cause air at the earth's surface to become heated until it acts like a hot air balloon, moving upward through a colder atmosphere. Whenever an updraft occurs, it leaves a void of air and instability. Downdrafts occur—usually over a larger area than updrafts—when colder air rushes into the evacuated area to alleviate the instability.

Convection currents that cause the annoying turbulence at low altitudes are sometimes welcomed as anabatic lift at other times. The updrafts continue rising until reaching an altitude where its temperature, through expansion cooling, matches that of the surrounding air. If the air contains moisture, cumulus clouds may form. Generally the tops of thermal activity are around 10,000 to 12,000 feet, but can extend beyond 15,000 feet in the mountains.

Mountain pilots advocate that early morning flights are desirable because this will minimize the convective turbulence that occurs once the ground heats up. It also allows operating with reduced density altitudes. If the flight must be conducted during the heat of the day, convective turbulence can be minimized by flying above convective clouds, or if there are no clouds, at a computed altitude. A rough rule of thumb is used to determine the approximate altitude to fly in order to avoid convective turbulence. It's accuracy is dependent upon the stability of the air and is only a rough guide using average values.

 **RULE OF THUMB– Base of Convective Activity**

Subtract the dew point temperature from the surface temperature. Multiply this value by two. This is the altitude in hundreds of feet (add two zeros), of the base of convective activity.

2. MECHANICAL (OBSTRUCTION TO WIND FLOW) TURBULENCE

Obstructions such as mountains, trees and rough terrain (including buildings) disrupt the smooth wind flow into a complicated mishmash of random motion eddies. Winds of fewer than 20 knots create irregular whirls on the upwind and downwind side of the obstruction that results in annoying turbulence. If the air is stable the eddies dissipate slowly.

Mechanical turbulence depends on the wind velocity and degree of roughness of the terrain/obstructions. Winds of more than 20 knots can generate the turbulence to altitudes higher than the mountains and carry the eddies downwind. If the air is unstable, larger eddies form but they tend to break up quickly. As the wind velocity increases, there is less change in the wind direction, but a greater variability in the speed of the eddies. When the speed changes it may set up "lulls" of brief, sudden, irregular periods of low speed wind and "gusts" of high-speed wind (a gust must have at least a 9-knot variation between the peak and lull).

For the most part, gusts and other types of mechanical turbulence provide advanced warning as you approach a ridge. This warning occurs before you cross over, allowing you the opportunity to change your mind.

Turbulence that is encountered when approaching the mountains from a flatland area is almost certain to get worse as you get closer to the mountains. You can judge the air stability to make a decision as to whether to continue or not. If you go on, approach the ridges at an angle to allow an escape to lower terrain with a minimum of aircraft maneuvering. Reducing the maneuvering reduces the stress on the airplane structure.

When you meet with turbulence a long distance prior to reaching the mountains it may cause undue apprehension. You don't know whether to continue or not. This consternation is usually resolved based upon your flight experience, the intensity of the turbulence and your comfort level in turbulence. If you don't know whether you should go on or not, you might consider landing and talking with an experienced pilot or FAA Accident Prevention Counselor. When in doubt...don't.

Chapter 4 - Mountain Flying Turbulence   PART 3 EN ROUTE

As an obstruction to wind flow, mountains are the granddaddy of them all. Destructive turbulence—the kind that has the potential of causing structural failure—may be avoided by flying half again as high as the mountain is above the surrounding terrain. Fly an altitude equal to one-half the distance from ground level (not MSL) to mountaintop level. Flying at this altitude does not and can not guarantee the absence of turbulence, but it does provide a guarantee that you would avoid all destructive rotor turbulence.

IT IS MOSTLY THE WIND FLOW NEAR 10,000 FEET MSL THAT DETERMINES THE EXTENT OF UPDRAFTS, DOWNDRAFTS AND TURBULENCE IN MOUNTAINOUS AREAS.

Downdrafts are similar to stalls as far as the pilot action required. The nose of the airplane should be lowered whenever a downdraft is encountered. This is the opposite of instinct and is more of a conditioned response. But, it is the correct response. For example, when the airplane is in a spin the nose is down about 45 degrees below the horizon. While you might swear it is straight down, it isn't. Instinct causes one to pull back, trying to raise the nose. It's worked before, but not now. It is required that the control wheel be moved forward to break the stall (with rudder opposite the rotation) and then back pressure increased to fly out of the resulting dive.

PART 3 EN ROUTE   **Chapter 4 - Mountain Flying Turbulence**

"SIGNPOST IN THE SKY"
Left – WIND BLOWING SNOW FROM THE MOUNTAINTOPS OF THE TETON MOUNTAIN RANGE.
Right – SNOW BLOWING FROM THE GRAND TETON (elevation 13,766').

The reason for lowering the nose when a downdraft is encountered is to increase the airspeed and get out of the downdraft faster than if the best rate-of-climb or best angle-of-climb speed is used. It is true that by lowering the nose the vertical speed will increase. But when a slower speed is used, the plane is exposed to the downdraft for a greater period of time and loses more altitude overall.

Turbulence Penetration Procedures

At times it is impossible to avoid turbulence in the mountains. Whenever encountering moderate or greater turbulence, slow to maneuvering speed. The danger from turbulence occurs when operating at speeds above normal cruise airspeed, such as during a descent.

The majority of small airplanes do not have a yaw damper, yet the pilot has the ability to effect the same type of function, dampening the effect of turbulence and keeping passengers from getting airsick.

 **RULE OF THUMB – Reduce Turbulence Effects**

When turbulence causes fishtailing, step on the right rudder (one quarter of its travel) and apply left aileron to maintain wings level flight.

You might have to experiment with the rudder pressure. It may require less than one quarter of its travel movement, or it may require as much as one third of its movement, depending upon the make and model of airplane. This technique is very effective in dampening the yaw oscillations caused by turbulence. With experience you will probably apply down aileron to maintain the wings level and step on the opposite rudder without thinking about it. It does not have to be the right rudder and left aileron.

Mountain Flying Bible

Chapter 4 - Mountain Flying Turbulence   PART 3 EN ROUTE

Maneuvering speed, abbreviated V_A, is often called the "rough air speed." This is the highest (fastest) speed that can be used to prevent an accidental stall due to gust loads and it is the lowest speed that allows the limit load factor to be developed aerodynamically to cause a momentary stall to reduce stress before the turbulence can break the airplane.

When a stall is performed intentionally, it may last a few seconds or more. The aerodynamic stall occurs when a gust is of sufficient strength to replace the relative wind and change the angle of attack. It is usually of a short duration and with airplanes that have a stall warning horn, you hear nothing more than a momentary "uumph," that may last for a fraction of a second before the airplane begins flying again.

Pilots get into trouble because of encountering turbulence with excess airspeed, usually during a descent where excess speed is easily obtained. They are lulled into a false sense of security by descent in smooth air. Suddenly and unexpectedly all heck breaks loose (pun). Structural damage or failure is a real possibility.

On the other hand, flight at an airspeed well below maneuvering speed is not recommended or required. The airplane has been built to withstand rough air, providing it is flown at the maneuvering speed in moderate or greater turbulence. Some pilots, fearing structural damage, slow down too much. They have a difficult time controlling the airplane at the reduced speed because the controls are not as effective.

RULE OF THUMB — Change in Weight/Stall Speed

A two-percent change in weight causes a one-percent change in stall speed.

Before making a high-speed descent, check for pilot reports concerning the ride during descent. If not available, study the winds aloft forecast for a change in wind direction occurring throughout the altitudes of the operation. Check also for wind velocity changes. Usually a change of six knots per 1,000 feet of altitude change is sufficient to produce turbulence.

Because of the importance of the value of maneuvering speed in protecting the structural integrity of the airplane, the stall speed and maneuvering speed rules of thumb are repeated.

RULE OF THUMB — Maneuvering Speed Determination

Divide the reduced weight by the gross weight. Multiply the square root of this value by V_A to determine the reduced weight V_A.

DETERMINE MANEUVERING SPEED

$$\frac{\text{REDUCED WEIGHT}}{\text{GROSS WEIGHT}} = X \qquad \sqrt{X} \times V_A = \text{new } V_A$$

Divide the percentage change in weight by two (the reduced weight divided by the gross weight). This is the percentage change in stall speed.

Aircraft Control

Flight control usage and manipulation in severe or extreme turbulence should be with hesitation. The best technique is to try not to move the controls. If control movement is required, do it very gently. Fly attitude, not altitude, and let the airplane go where it will. Concerns about terrain clearance must be addressed with whatever control movement is necessary. Once maneuvering speed (or a slower speed is obtained, maneuvering speed is preferred), full-control deflection may be used in controlling the airplane. Use coordinated rudder and aileron to control the flight path and the elevator to control pitch attitude. If the turbulence is moderate or greater, try using more rudder instead of coordinated aileron/rudder.

Continuous light turbulence often causes an uncomfortable ride where the airplane seems to wallow through the air and the empennage fish tails. A built-in yaw damper (the one sitting in the left-front seat) will eliminate this with a little practice with cross-control technique. Trying to catch the oscillations of the nose or tail moving back or forth may aggravate the situation; cross-control will dampen the oscillations. When the nose moves to the right, apply some right rudder pressure (about one-quarter of that available) to hold the nose to the right. Use enough left aileron to hold the airplane steady. Continue this control application until out of the turbulence.

3. WIND SHEAR

Wind shear occurs when there is a difference of wind direction (wind shift) or wind speed (gradient) or both occurring in a short distance in the atmosphere. Wind shear generates eddies (shear zones) between the two wind currents of differing velocities. The shear zone consists of irregular motion in either the vertical or the horizontal dimensions, or both.

Horizontal shear occurs when the flight path passes through a wind shift plane such as when crossing a cold front (frontal activity) or when flying in thunderstorm areas.

Chapter 4 - Mountain Flying Turbulence — PART 3 EN ROUTE

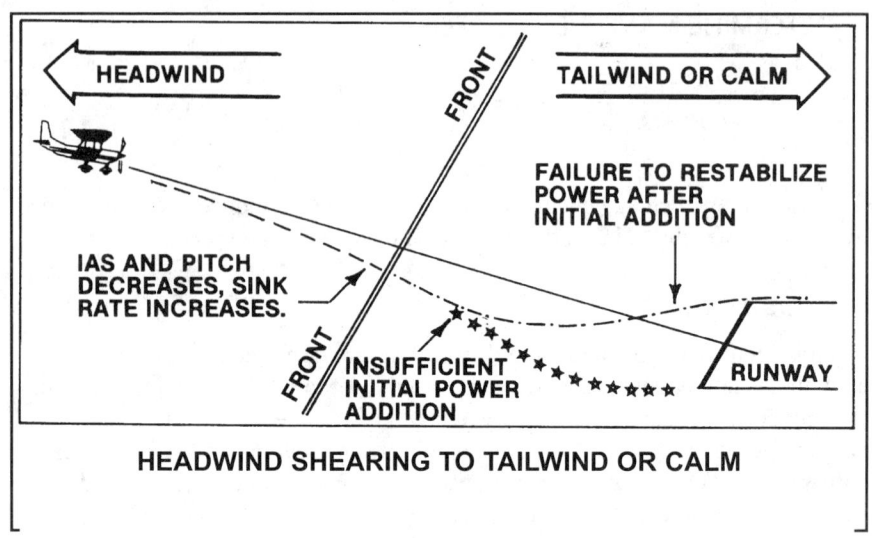

HEADWIND SHEARING TO TAILWIND OR CALM

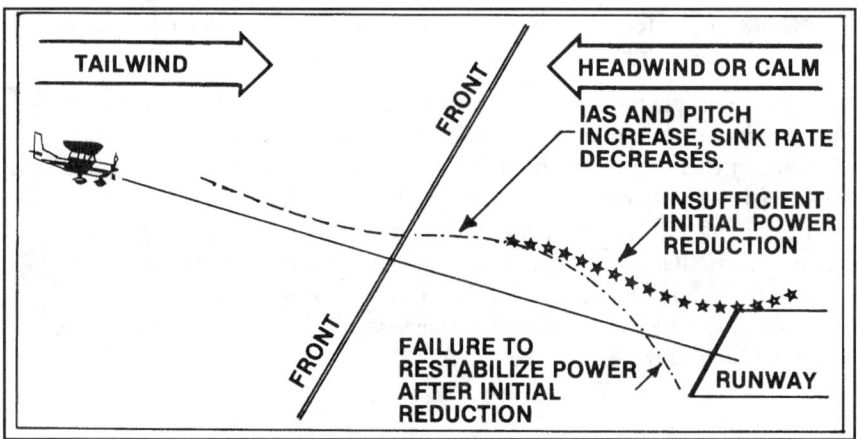

TAILWIND SHEARING TO HEADWIND OR CALM

WIND SHEAR IN A FRONTAL ZONE

Vertical shear caused by temperature inversions or surface obstructions (buildings or mountains) is most often associated with the takeoff and climb out or approach and landing.

Suppose the winds aloft forecast reports the wind at 9,000 feet as 2715 (270° at 15 knots) and at 12,000 feet as 2936 (290° at 36 knots). The shear is 7-knots per 1,000 feet. This is sufficient to produce wind shear turbulence.

| PART 3 EN ROUTE | Chapter 4 - Mountain Flying Turbulence |

 RULE OF THUMB– Turbulence

A wind velocity change of 6 knots per 1,000 feet is sufficient to produce wind shear and turbulence.

Vertical shear of 6-knots per 1,000-feet altitude change causes turbulence. With increasing shear values or differences in wind direction comes greater turbulence. The shear of greatest importance to pilots is that shear of vertical dimensions that cause changes in the aircraft's angle of attack and may result in a stall.

Conditions associated with shear can occur at any level in the atmosphere, but three are of special interest to the pilot.

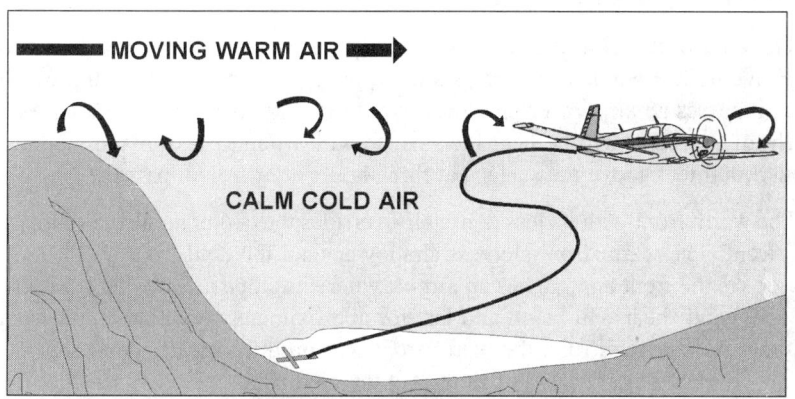

WIND SHEAR TURBULENCE

1. Low-Level Temperature Inversion

A temperature inversion forms near the surface on a clear, cool night with calm or light surface wind. This allows the layer of air next to the ground to cool at a rate faster than the air above. The inversion or reversal of the normal lapse rate causes the temperature to increase with altitude rather than decrease. A wind shear zone of eddy turbulence develops between the calm air of the inversion and the wind flow above. This is particularly hazardous when the low-level jet stream provides the wind.

Some pilots have been taught that a taxiing airplane is subject to, not only the prevailing wind direction and velocity, but also to the relative wind due to the motion of the aircraft. We may have been told that once the airplane leaves the ground that the wind would have no effect on its flight other than creating drift and modifying the groundspeed.

Mountain Flying Bible

Chapter 4 - Mountain Flying Turbulence PART 3 EN ROUTE

This is not true if the wind changes faster than the aircraft's mass can be accelerated or decelerated. It is helpful to discuss some other conditions, then talk about the causes, effects and procedures to deal with wind shear.

2. Wind Shear in a Frontal Zone

When two air masses meet a frontal zone is developed with abruptly changing wind along the zone. The degree of turbulence depends on the magnitude of the wind shear. The clouds associated with the frontal zone give an indication of turbulence, but when two dry air masses meet the area may be devoid of all indicator clouds.

Wind shear height above an airport cannot be accurately measured, but weather forecasters, using a model of frontal characteristics, can make an estimation of the height of the wind shear.

The cold front, with its heavy, dense air, forms a wedge that pushes warmer air above it. The wind shear occurs along the line between cold air and warmer air as it passes an airport. Frontal movement of 30 knots or greater indicates the height of the shear will be near the surface with frontal passage and sloping to about 5,000 feet above the surface at three hours after frontal passage.

The warm front with its less dense air overrides the cooler air ahead of the surface front. The warm front slope is shallower than the cold front and it moves slower. As the front approaches an airport where its slope is 5,000 feet above the surface, wind shear will begin and last for approximately six hours until frontal passage. As a general rule, the warm front will produce greater wind shear turbulence over a longer period of time than the cold front.

If the front is moving to the east at about 20 knots, it will produce light turbulence. If its movement is 30 knots, expect moderate or greater turbulence.

Check the winds aloft before departing or arriving at an airport where you suspect wind shear. Horizontal shear with the wind direction changing 15 degrees per one-thousand feet or vertical shear exceeding 6 knots per one-thousand feet will produce turbulence. Shear values greater than these numbers will create greater turbulence.

3. Mountain Wave Wind Shear

When stable air flows across a mountain range, a condition known as a mountain wave or standing wave may occur. It is so named because lenticular clouds associated with the wave remain essentially stationary in position with the mountain. Associated with the mountain wave, on the lee side, is rotor turbulence that can create hazardous shear values. It is best to avoid destructive turbulence by flying half again as high as the mountain (half the value of the base elevation subtracted from the top elevation).

PART 3 EN ROUTE   Chapter 4 - Mountain Flying Turbulence

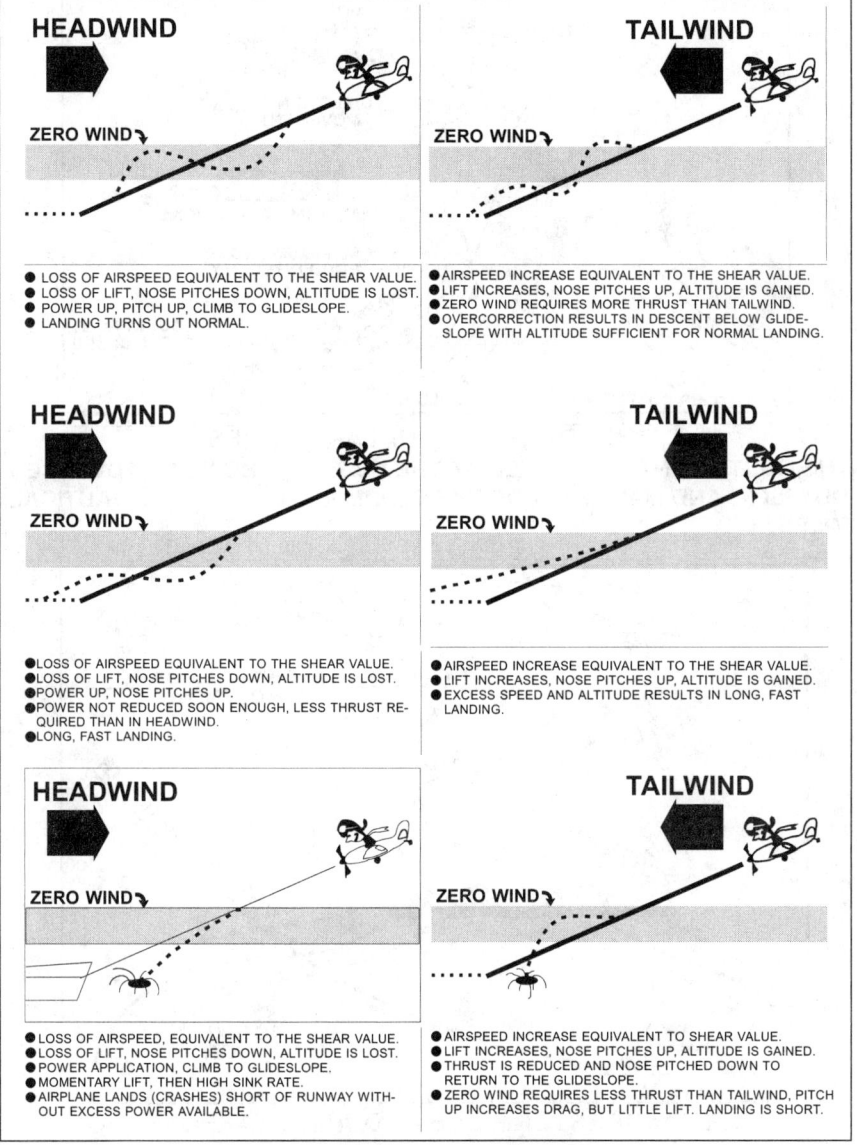

LOW-LEVEL WIND SHEAR

LEFT – SHEAR FROM A HEADWIND TO ZERO WIND ZONE.
RIGHT – SHEAR FROM A TAILWIND TO ZERO WIND ZONE.

Unstable air crossing a mountain may rush down on the leeward side, spilling and creating eddies that are carried downwind. Airports located on the downwind side of mountains, especially those with a gradual slope from the mountain to the airport, are susceptible to the accelerated wind and eddies.

Chapter 4 - Mountain Flying Turbulence   PART 3 EN ROUTE

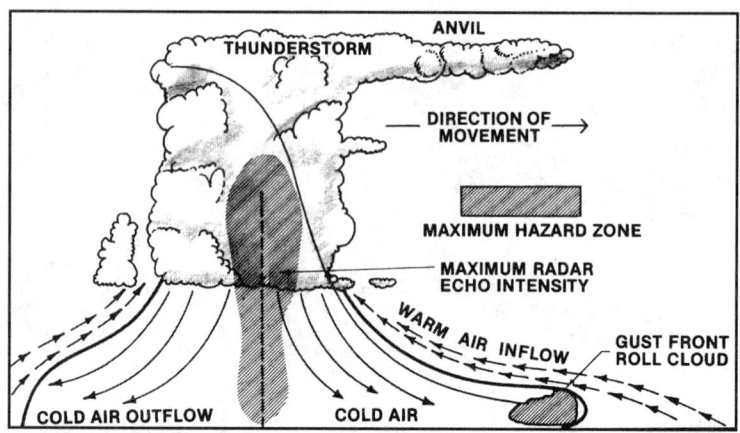

THUNDERSTORM HAZARD ZONES
THE GUST FRONT IS LOCATED AT THE EDGE OF THE MOST ADVANCED OUTFLOW AND MAY PRECEDE THE STORM IN EXCESS OF 15 NAUTICAL MILES.

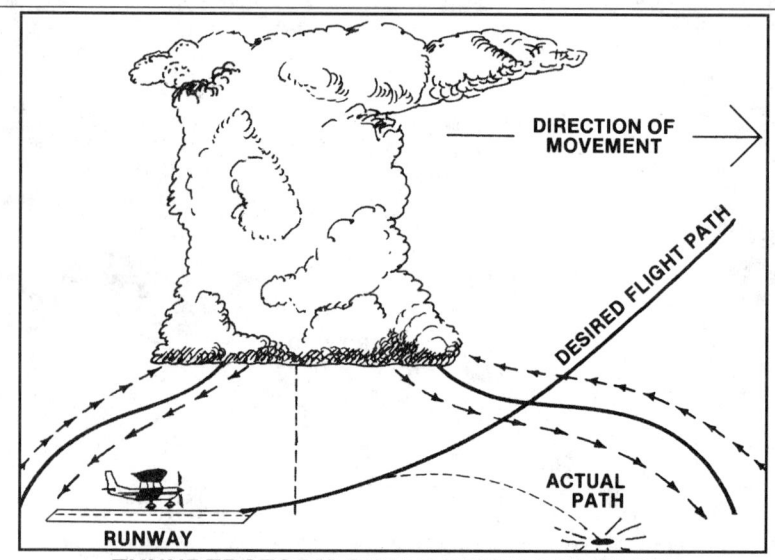

THUNDERSTORM SHEAR DURING TAKEOFF

4. Sea Breeze Fronts

A localized airflow condition may be created when there is uneven surface heating occurring between a land mass and a water mass such as the ocean, bays or lakes. Convection currents are set up over the land. As the air rises, it creates an instability in the atmosphere that is filled by cooler air from the water. This causes the wind to flow on-shore during the daytime. At night there is a reversal of the airflow. Wind shear is set up because of changes in the wind velocity and direction over a short distance.

5. Clear Air Turbulence (CAT)

Clear air turbulence (CAT) is a phenomenon associated with turbulence in areas lacking clouds, usually at high altitudes. Two conditions are responsible for CAT, the jet stream and the mountain wave. When related to the jet stream, its occurrence is mostly on the polar side of the jet or to the north or northeast of a rapidly deepening surface low pressure area. CAT caused by the mountain wave can extend into all altitudes usable by general aviation aircraft (including jets) and can range 100 to 300 miles downstream from the mountains that caused the wave.

6. Thunderstorms

Three conditions are required for a thunderstorm to occur: moist, unstable air, and lifting action. Rising and descending air is modified by atmospheric pressure. Air that is lifted expands. Air that descends is compressed. These pressure changes cause the air to change temperature, cooling as it expands and heating as it is compressed. The mode of temperature change does not affect the surrounding air temperature, only the parcel of air that is lifting or sinking. This process is called an *adiabatic* change.

When unstable air is caused to rise by frontal action, convection or wind flow forcing its ascension up a mountain (or any combination of these), it cools, but the rate of cooling may be less than that of the surrounding air. When the lifting action is removed, the parcel of air is warmer than the sur-

IT IS IMPOSSIBLE TO DISCERN THE INTENSITY OF A THUNDERSTORM BASED UPON A VISUAL EXAMINATION OF ITS EXTERNAL CHARACTERISTICS. COMPARING THE VISUAL ASPECTS OF THE CB WITH RADAR OR STORMSCOPE-TYPE EQUIPMENT OFTEN PROVIDES SURPRISES. SOMETIMES THE WORST-LOOKING STORMS ARE THE MOST BENIGN OR THE MOST INNOCENT APPEARING STORM WILL HOLD SURPRISES.

AVOID FLYING UNDER THUNDERSTORMS REGARDLESS OF THEIR APPEARANCE.

NOTE THE LIGHTNING FROM THIS SEEMINGLY BENIGN STORM.

Chapter 4 - Mountain Flying Turbulence   PART 3 EN ROUTE

HUGE CBS OVER THE FRONT RANGE BETWEEN FORT COLLINS AND DENVER.

THUNDERSTORM MOVING OVER THE JACKSON HOLE AIRPORT, JACKSON, WYO.

rounding air and will continue to rise by itself. If the air is moist and unstable, the conditions may render a thunderstorm.

DETECTING WIND SHEAR

A pilot—no matter how good he is or no matter how good he thinks he is—and his general aviation airplane does not have the ability to fly through all intensities of low-level wind shear. It is better to devise a method of detecting, predicting and avoiding wind shear than it is to deal with it. Wind shear provides warnings the pilot can use to avoid its consequences.

Check the weather during preflight for thunderstorms observed or forecast near the airport. They can cause wind shear in the departure or arrival areas. Check surface weather charts for frontal activity. Determine the surface temperature difference immediately across the front and the speed the front is moving. A 10-degree Fahrenheit or greater temperature differential, and/or movement of the front at 30 knots or more is indicative of significant low-level wind shear.

Thunderstorms in the vicinity of the airport and frontal activity showing movement at greater than 25 knots or more than a 10-degree Fahrenheit temperature difference are indicators of low-level wind shear.

THUNDERSTORM ROTOR CLOUDS

PART 3 EN ROUTE — Chapter 4 - Mountain Flying Turbulence

RAIN SHAFTS CREATE STRONG DOWNDRAFTS. NOTE THE ROTOR CLOUDS ON THE LEFT. MAMMATIFORM CLOUDS (RIGHT) FORM AT THE BOUNDARY BETWEEN CLOUDY (UNSTABLE) AND CLOUD-FREE (STABLE) AIR.

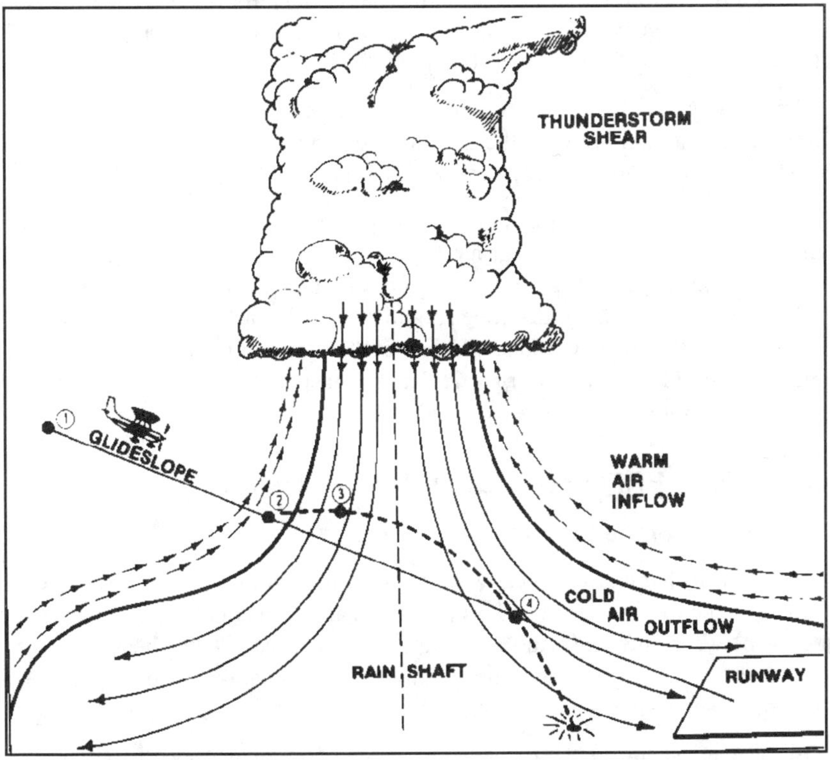

THUNDERSTORM "DOWNBURST CELL" CAUSING DOWNDRAFT SHEAR.

Check PIREPS and avoid areas that report airspeed loss of 15 knots or more on final approach for landing.

Chapter 4 - Mountain Flying Turbulence PART 3 EN ROUTE

For practical purposes *wind shear will be present* when there is a combination of two or more of the following conditions:

- Extreme variation in wind velocity and wind direction in a relatively short time.
- Any evidence of an approaching gust front.
- The surface temperature in excess of 80°F.
- A temperature/dew point spread of 40°F or more.
- Virga in the vicinity of the airport (precipitation aloft falling from the bases of high-altitude cumulus clouds that evaporates before reaching the ground).

To determine whether or not a front has passed an airport, compare the reported METAR surface wind to the current reported wind. With frontal passage there will be a wind shift from 90 to 180 degrees.

Any navigational aid that provides groundspeed (DME, GPS or LORAN) allows a comparison between the groundspeed and the true airspeed throughout the approach, indicating a headwind or tail wind.

Lacking a groundspeed readout, use the ILS (even if you don't have an instrument rating) as an indicator of groundspeed. Although it varies, the glide path is normally adjusted at 3 degrees to the horizon. This means the rate of descent while established on the glide slope should be (based on ground speed) 375 fpm at 70 knots, 430 fpm at 80 knots, 485 fpm at 90 knots, and 540 fpm at 100 knots. If your rate of descent (for your particular groundspeed) is less, you have a headwind; if it is more, you have a tail wind.

AIRPLANE PERFORMANCE IN WIND SHEAR

1. Power Compensation

Wind shear that causes a headwind to shear to a calm wind or tailwind causes the airplane to experience an abrupt drop in airspeed equal to the velocity difference between the headwind and calm/tailwind speed. This shear causes the nose to drop. Pulling the nose up aggravates the situation. Add full power to accelerate back to normal airspeed.

A tailwind shearing to a headwind or calm wind causes the airspeed to increase. Although a power reduction is initially required to compensate for the ballooning effect, power must be added to counter the headwind.

T. Theodore Fujita, *The Downburst – Microburst and Macroburst*, explains the downburst cell contains a strong downdraft in the center of the thunderstorm cell that flows downward. Near the surface it spreads to form strong horizontal winds. Refer to figure, page 3-81. The airplane (1) is on the glide slope at normal approach airspeed. At (2) the airplane encounters an increasing headwind that causes a ballooning effect along with an airspeed increase. The pilot lowers the nose and reduces power to recapture the glide slope beginning at (3). Between (3) and (4) the headwind transitions to a tailwind with a loss of airspeed. The airplane sets up a high sink rate from which there may not be sufficient altitude or thrust to recover before ground contact. Groundspeed is the best indication of entering a downburst cell. When the airspeed increases and the groundspeed decreases, the airplane may be entering position (2).

2. Angle of Attack in a Downdraft

A downdraft increasing as a headwind may be stronger than the relative wind causing an increase in the angle of attack, the ballooning at (2). If the pilot fails to compensate, the airplane may experience a stall. After lowering the nose, then encountering a tailwind, between (3) and (4), the angle of attack is reduced through vectorial addition, setting up a high sink rate.

3. Energy Trade

The only two means of correcting for wind shear are an energy trade or a thrust change. During flight the kinetic energy can be converted to potential energy where there is a trade of airspeed for altitude or a trade of altitude for airspeed.

4. Trading Altitude for Speed

A pilot experiencing low-level wind shear will apply full power, but the airspeed may still be slow. He will be tempted to lower the nose to trade altitude for speed, but this isn't the safest course of action. There will be a large loss of altitude and only a small gain of airspeed. The pilot is better off maintain the airspeed with the application of full power.

5. Trading Speed for Altitude

If the pilot experiences and notices the low-level wind shear before an airspeed loss, he may be tempted to trade his airspeed for altitude. The speed will dissipate rapidly and if the airplane is carried to the ground there will be no airspeed to flare.

6. Adding Speed for Wind Shear

It is tempting to carry extra airspeed when there are reports of wind shear in the vicinity of an airport. The problem is, if the extra airspeed is not used in the shear, the airplane may be too fast to land in the runway space available.

PROCEDURES FOR COPING WITH WIND SHEAR

An awareness of an imminent wind shear confrontation prepares the pilot to take immediate action at the first sign of the shear.

Chapter 4 - Mountain Flying Turbulence — PART 3 EN ROUTE

TURBULENCE REPORTING CRITERIA

VARIATION IN AIRSPEED AIR-SPEED	INTENSITY	AIRCRAFT REACTION	REACTION INSIDE AIRCRAFT	REPORTING TERM DEFINITION	DERIVED GUST VELOCITY CRITERIA
5-15 KNOTS	LIGHT	Turbulence that momentarily causes slight, erratic changes in altitude and/or attitude (pitch, yaw, roll). Report as "**Light Turbulence.**" -or-	Occupants may feel a slight strain against seat belts or shoulder straps. Unsecured objects may be displaced slightly. Food service may be conducted and little or no difficulty is encountered in walking in transport aircraft.	Occasional - Less than 1/3 of the time.	
NONE	LIGHT CHOP	Turbulence that causes slight, rapid and somewhat rhythmic bumpiness without appreciable changes in altitude or attitude. Report as "**Light Chop.**"		Intermittent - 1/3 to 2/3. Continuous - More than 2/3.	5-20 fps
15-20 KNOTS	MODERATE	Turbulence that is similar to Light Turbulence but of greater intensity. Changes in altitude and/or attitude occur but the aircraft remains in positive control at all times. It usually causes variations in indicated airspeed. Report as "**Moderate Turbulence;**" -or-	Occupants feel definite strains against seat belts or shoulder straps. Unsecured objects are dislodged. Food service and walking are difficult in transport aircraft.	Occasional - Less than 1/3 of the time. Intermittent - 1/3 to 2/3.	
SLIGHT FLUCTUATION	MODERATE CHOP	Turbulence that is similar to Light Chop but of greater intensity. It causes rapid bumps or jolts without appreciable changes in aircraft altitude or attitude. Report as "**Moderate Chop.**"		Continuous - More than 2/3.	20-35 fps
EXCESS OF 20 KNOTS	SEVERE	Turbulence that causes large, abrupt changes in altitude and/or attitude. It usually causes large variations in indicated airspeed. Aircraft may be momentarily out of control. Report as "**Severe Turbulence.**"	Occupants are forced violently against seat belts or shoulder straps. Unsecured objects are tossed about.	Occasional - Less than 1/3 of the time. Intermittent - 1/3 to 2/3.	35-50 fps
RAPID, EXCESS OF 25 KNOTS	EXTREME	Turbulence in which the aircraft is violently tossed about and is practically impossible to control. It may cause structural damage. Report as "**Extreme Turbulence.**"			Over 50 fps

*HIGH LEVEL TURBULENCE—NORMALLY ABOVE 15,000 FEET MSL—THAT IS NOT ASSOCIATED WITH CUMULIFORM CLOUDINESS, INCLUDING THUNDERSTORMS, SHOULD BE REPORTED AS CLEAR AIR TURBULENCE (CAT) PRECEDED BY THE APPROPRIATE INTENSITY, OR LIGHT CHOP OR MODERATE CHOP.

1. Takeoff

Wind shear alerts and PIREPS notify the pilot of the possibility of the wind shear phenomenon. If it is reported as severe, avoid the area.

Increased airspeed results from an increasing headwind or decreasing tailwind, causing a balloon. This doesn't pose a problem in most cases.

Decreased airspeed results from a rapidly increasing tailwind, a decreasing headwind, or a downdraft. This is a critical situation for takeoff or approach

PART 3 EN ROUTE — Chapter 4 - Mountain Flying Turbulence

causing the airplane to pitch downward with a loss of lift.

Reports of severe wind shear for departure means the flight should be delayed, period, no discussion.

A pilot caught in severe wind shear during takeoff should apply full power and fly an attitude to maintain the best rate-of-climb airspeed. If it appears that ground contact is imminent, slowly increase the pitch attitude, but not to the point of a stall.

2. Approach to Landing

If wind shear is reported near the approach and landing path to an airport and you determine it is not severe, make a normal approach. Be ready to apply power if needed. If the approach becomes unstable at 500-feet agl or below, execute an immediate go-around procedure.

PIREPS

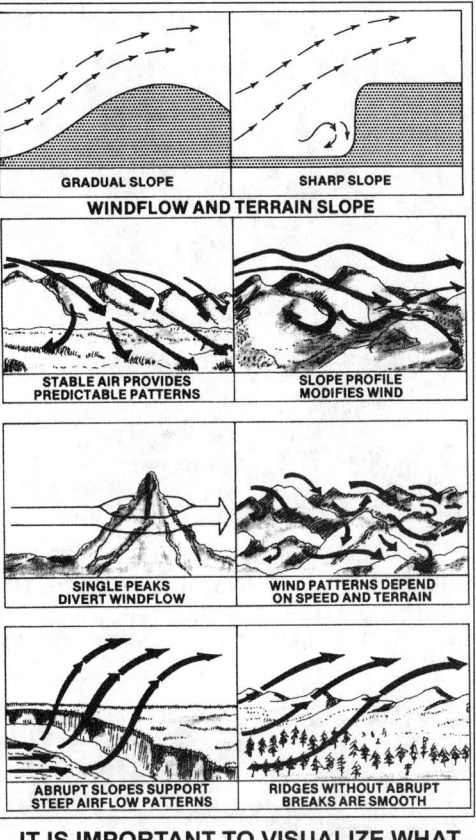

IT IS IMPORTANT TO VISUALIZE WHAT THE WIND IS DOING. WHAT WOULD WATER DO IN THE SAME SITUATION?

For airports without wind shear alert systems, the PIREP is the most valuable source of information. If wind shear is encountered, your PIREP should include the following information:

1. Location of shear encounter.
2. Altitude of shear encounter.
3. Airspeed changes experienced, including the number of knots gained or lost.
4. Type of aircraft. ✈

Mountain Flying Bible

Chapter 4 - Mountain Flying Turbulence   PART 3 EN ROUTE

PROBABLE TURBULENCE PRODUCERS

KELVIN-HELMHOLTZ BILLOW CLOUDS
THE BILLOW CLOUDS ARE SIMILAR TO WHITE CAPS IN A LAKE AND INDICATE TURBULENCE. THE CLOUDS GENERALLY HAVE A VERY SHORT LIFE SPAN AND DISAPPEAR RAPIDLY.

LENTICULAR CLOUDS WITH ROTOR TURBULENCE NORTHWEST OF NORTHWAY, ALASKA

3-86   *Mountain Flying Bible*

PART 3 EN ROUTE   Chapter 5 - The Mountain Wave

CHAPTER 5—THE MOUNTAIN WAVE

- INTRODUCTION 3-87
- JET STREAM 3-88
- POLAR FRONT 3-89
- POLAR OUTBREAK 3-89
- MOUNTAIN WAVE CONDITIONS 3-91
- TURBULENCE 3-100
- FLIGHT PLANNING PROCEDURES 3-100

INTRODUCTION

"Your first experience of flying over mountainous terrain (particularly if most of your flight time has been over the flatland of the Midwest) could be a never-to-be-forgotten nightmare if you are not aware of the potential hazards awaiting ... Many pilots go all their lives without understanding what a mountain wave is. Quite a few have lost their lives because of this lack of understanding. One need not be a licensed meteorologist to understand the mountain wave phenomenon," from the *Aeronautical Information Manual.*

This is good information, if it hasn't scared you off from flying in the mountains—by knowing the hazards associated with the wave, and by knowing where to fly to avoid the hazards, you are able to conduct flights with greater pleasure and safety.

Aviation, more so than any other aspect of our lives, has a profusion of terms used to describe the same thing. When the wind blows over the mountains, with certain parameters present, a mountain wave may occur. Somebody—and it isn't pilots—has come up with a superfluous list for the *mountain wave* that includes *standing wave* (more properly applied to the cloud over the mountain), *lee wave* (more properly applied to the clouds extending down range from the mountain), *standing lenticular*, *ACSL* (altocumulus standing lenticular, or *wave*. (Pilots have a few names of their own, but we can't mention them here.)

After hearing that a log or rock in a stream can create a water flow with the troughs and crests, I wandered along many a stream and river trying to find the

Mountain Flying Bible

Chapter 5 - The Mountain Wave   PART 3 EN ROUTE

textbook description of an analogy between water flow and air flow. It's not impossible to find, I've discovered a couple of them over the years.

Because of the lack of a suitable area where I could sit down and study the water flow, I created my own situation by placing a two-by-four in a frame perpendicular to the water flow. Here I changed the elevation of the two-by-four and altered the angle the stream struck the obstruction.

It is fun to see the water flow over the obstruction, pouring down into a trough area, then rising up again to form a crest. Depending on the velocity of the stream, this pattern is continued downstream for some distance. The crest forms a series of bars that are parallel to the two-by-four and with only slight fluctuations, remain in a stationary position.

Air, although invisible, can create the same flow pattern. Substitute a wind flow for the water and a mountain for the two-by-four and you can visualize the form of lee waves in the atmosphere.

There is a misconception that the wave is found only in high mountain areas. The wave can form on a ridge whose top is only several hundred feet in the air. Waves form over the ocean when a mass of dense air affects the upper winds similar to a mountain.

Because the mountain wave is associated with upwards of 60 miles or more visibility, it is deceiving. The pilot may misconstrue the weather, with unlimited visibility, believing the air is smooth.

Questions about the wave need to be addressed by all pilots flying the mountains. *What is a mountain wave? What forms it" Why is it of concern to pilots? What are its distinguishing characteristics? How do we deal with it?*

The intermountain west experiences, on the average, two mountain waves each week, during the summer. The frequency may be greater during the spring and fall. There may be five or six occurrences a week during the winter months. Increased winter activity is due to more stable air. Also the jet stream shifts south in the winter and becomes stronger. During the night the air becomes more stable (no convection).

JET STREAM

The atmosphere is divided into layers with the lowest layer extending from the earth upward to the troposphere. Next is the stratosphere. An abrupt change in the temperature lapse rate is the line of demarcation (tropopause) between the two layers. The tropopause over the Equator rises to about 65,000 feet, due to the heating of the air. Over the poles it dips to 20,000 feet or lower.

The tropopause descends stepwise from the equator to the poles and is not continuous. The "break" between the polar tropopause and the tropical

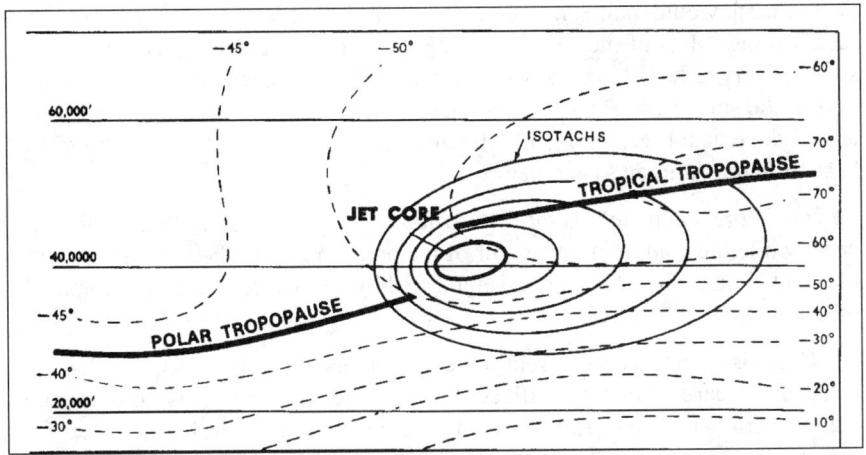

A CROSS SECTION OF THE UPPER TROPOSPHERE AND LOWER STRATOSPHERE SHOWING THE TROPOPAUSE AND ASSOCIATED FEATURES. NOTE THE "BREAK" BETWEEN THE HIGH TROPICAL AND THE LOWER POLAR TROPOPAUSE. MAXIMUM WINDS OCCUR IN THE VICINITY OF THIS BREAK.

COURTESY "AVIATION WEATHER"

tropopause is the favored location of the jet stream, a narrow band of strong winds meandering through the atmosphere at a level near the tropopause. Because the jet stream is associated with the tropopause, jet pilots are the most concerned. But, during the winter a "polar outbreak" may allow the jet stream to dip down as low as 15,000 feet and at times down to 10,000 feet.

POLAR FRONT

We learned in grade school that the earth's orbit forms an ellipse on its path around the sun. The Earth's geographic poles lean at a 23½-degree angle as the earth orbits around the sun. This angular difference places the north pole in darkness for about half of the year. During the winter, the polar air mass is modified over a larger area than during the summer months. It then spreads out and creeps southward. The leading edge of this cold air mass is called a *polar front*. It is a semipermanent, semicontinuous front that separates the air masses of tropical and polar regions. The polar tropopause corresponds to the polar air mass; causing the "break" to be located farther south during the winter months.

POLAR OUTBREAK

Like the oceans maintaining a constant level, the atmosphere desires to maintain an equal pressure over the entire earth. It does so by transporting air from high pressure areas to low pressure areas. The movement of air is known as circulation.

Chapter 5 - The Mountain Wave — PART 3 EN ROUTE

The earth would maintain a constant equilibrium if it were not for uneven surface heating. Most of the sun's direct heat is concentrated at the equator, where some of it is reflected back toward space. The polar regions receive only a portion of the sun's rays. Because the poles do not continue to get colder and colder and the equator does not get hotter and hotter, there must be some transfer of heat from one latitude to another.

The theoretical pattern is for the warming air of the equatorial region to move north while the cold, more dense air of the poles moves to the south setting up a constant circulation. This pattern is modified by many forces, the most important of which is Coriolis force.

"Coriolis force" is an apparent force—but to us, on earth, it is real—that, as a result of the earth's rotation, deflects moving objects (air currents) to the right in the northern hemisphere and to the left in the southern hemisphere.

Coriolis force modifies the earth's circulation pattern. The heated air over the equator, like a hot air balloon, rises and beings moving northward. It is deflected to the right of its normal path, toward the east. By the time it has traveled about a third of the distance to the pole, it is no longer moving northward, but eastward. This causes a high-pressure area at about 30-degrees north latitude (the horse latitudes). Some of the air continues northward and some returns to the equator area.

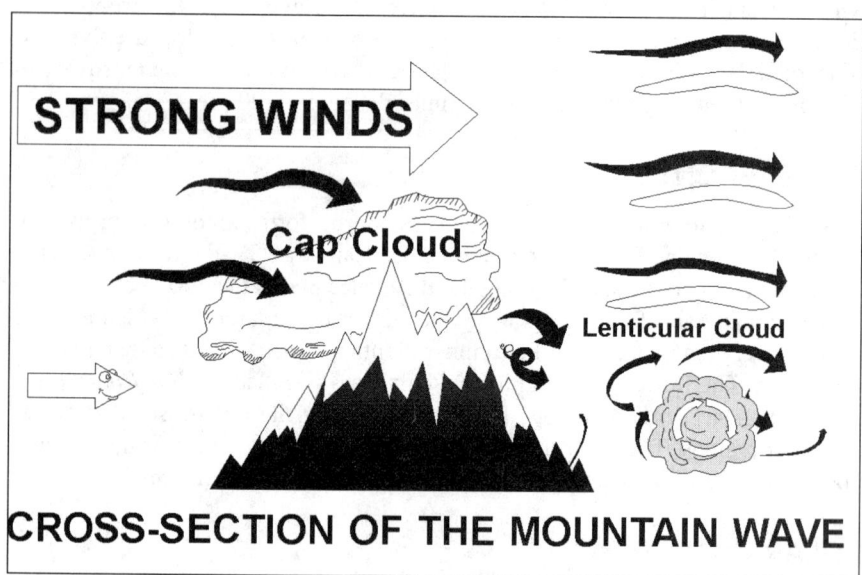

CROSS-SECTION OF THE MOUNTAIN WAVE

THE MOUNTAIN WAVE OR STANDING WAVE MAY CONTAIN SEVERE TO EXTREME TURBULENCE IN THE ROLL CLOUD AREA WITH STRONG UPDRAFTS AND DOWNDRAFTS.

A similar process is going on in the polar region where southward moving polar air is deflected to the right of its normal path becoming an east wind. This air comes into conflict with the warmer air from 30-degrees north latitude.

A high pressure area is an accumulation or pile of air that causes disruption of the earth's pressure systems. The atmosphere has an instability and in trying to regain the stability, air masses begin to move.

The accumulated air mass at the horse latitudes is forced northward. Again Coriolis causes it to veer to its right where it becomes a west wind. The winds of the middle latitudes are the so-called "prevailing westerlies."

The air over the polar regions takes on the characteristics of the region, namely cold and dry. It continues to stack up until additional incoming air forces it to erupt or escape as a wedge of cold polar air. This intermittent break away occurs in series of waves that swell toward the equator. This is called a polar outbreak or cold wave. The area or boundary zone where the two different polar and tropical air masses meet is called the *polar front*.

The polar front forms an irregular line around the Earth, surging toward the equator in one area and pulling back in another area. The weather of the U.S. occurs along this line where the unequal air masses meet to do battle, usually as a cold front. Following the passage of a cold front, conditions are ripe for generating a mountain wave condition.

MOUNTAIN WAVE CONDITIONS

Three elements are required for the formation of the mountain wave phenomenon. If one element is missing, the mountain wave cannot be generated.

1. The wind direction must be within 30 degrees of perpendicular to the mountains.
2. There must be an increasing wind velocity with altitude on the windward side of the mountains with mountaintop winds 20 knots or more.
3. There must be a stable air mass layer aloft or an isothermal layer of inversion below 15,000 feet (near mountaintop elevations).

The stability of the air mass itself is important to the formation of the wave. All three conditions may exist, yet if the air mass is too stable, it tends to dampen the propagation of the wave. If the air mass is too unstable, vertical currents can destroy any undulating pattern of the wave.

Mountain waves can form when the wind flow is within 60-degrees of perpendicular to the mountain range. Generally when a wave forms because of airflow at this acute angle there is not much development

Chapter 5 - The Mountain Wave   PART 3 EN ROUTE

MOUNTAIN WAVE FORMATION

With the three conditions described above (wind within 30 degrees of perpendicular, mountaintop wind 20 knots or more, and a stable air mass layer), the air is lifted on the windward side and shoots up and over the mountain. On the leeward side it falls to its original altitude, but due to acceleration, it overshoots the original position. This creates the wave-like oscillations of the mountain wave. Looking at lapse rates may help explain this unique event.

"Unsaturated" air has a lapse rate of about 5°F per 1,000 feet. When this air is forced up a mountain slope, it cools at the "dry adiabatic lapse rate." If the air began to rise from sea level with a temperature of 59°F, it would cool to 4°F by the time it gets to 10,000 feet.

The standard "free-air" lapse rate is 3½°F per 1,000 feet. With the standard lapse rate the ambient air temperature at 10,000 feet is 24°F.

Once the lifting action is removed from the unsaturated air, the temperature difference between the air being forced to ascend and the surrounding air will cause the unsaturated cold parcel of air to sink back down to its original altitude, descending on the lee side (where the lifting action is removed).

An analogy might explain why an unstable airflow encountering a ridge line does not set up a mountain wave. Compared to a weak spring, the air flow would offer little opposition to vertical motion, where the spring moves up and over the mountain. The jolt from the mountain range is not sent very far upward into the spring.

Neither can a completely stable airflow set up a mountain wave. A heavy spring forced over a mountain is too strong for the required oscillations to be set into motion.

AN UNSTABLE AIR MASS CAN BE LIKENED TO A WEAK SPRING. THE LOWER AIR FLOW MOVES OVER THE MOUNTAIN WITHOUT TRANSMITTING A SHOCK TO THE REST OF THE AIR FLOW.

A stable air mass layer near mountaintop elevation that is caused by an inversion uses the analogy of a sandwich of two weak springs surrounding a strong spring. Once this arrangement is lifted over the mountain, its descent to it original position will cause it to bounce up and down, up and down, up and down (isothermal layer means equality of temperature, there can be changes of volume or pressure under conditions of constant temperature).

PART 3 EN ROUTE   Chapter 5 - The Mountain Wave

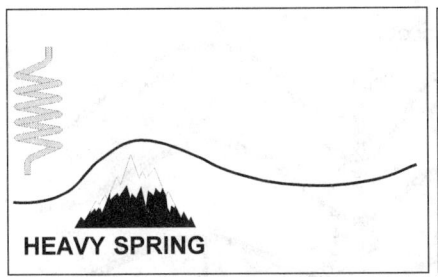

HEAVY SPRING

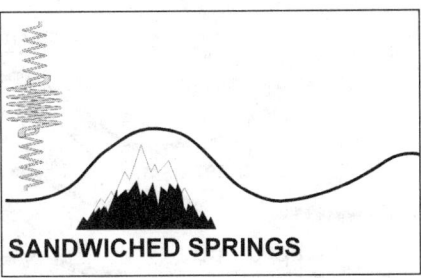

SANDWICHED SPRINGS

THE STABLE ATMOSPHERE CAN BE LIKENED TO A HEAVY SPRING THAT IS TOO TOUGH TO SET UP OSCILLATIONS.

A STABLE AIR MASS LAYER OR INVERSION ALOFT WILL ALLOW THE AIRFLOW TO BOUNCE UP AND DOWN

THE MOUNTAIN WAVE IS FORMED WHEN THE WIND FLOW IS PERPENDICULAR TO THE MOUNTAIN RANGE, WITH INCREASING WIND FLOW AT MOUNTAINTOP LEVEL, AND A STABLE AIR MASS LAYER OR INVERSION ALOFT.

MOUNTAIN WAVE DIMENSIONS

The wavelength and amplitude are used to describe the mountain wave flow and intensity. Without an understanding of these dimensions it is impossible to visualize the wave.

WAVE LENGTH

The wavelength is the distance from crest to crest or trough to trough. This value is important for visualizing lift, sink and turbulence. According to *Aviation Weather,* AC 00-6A, "The wavelength is directly proportional to wind speed and inversely proportional to stability. Lenticular clouds form in a series of successive bands downstream from the mountain that forms them."

With sufficient moisture in the air, lenticular clouds will form and mark the crest of each wave. The distance between the lenticular clouds marks the wavelength. Throughout the Rocky Mountain area the wavelength averages eight nautical miles, but has been observed to vary between two miles and 25 miles depending upon the shape of the mountain, the wind velocity and the air's stability. The average distance this wave action extends down range is 150 nautical miles. With the advent of satellites, the wave has been photographed spreading 700-nautical miles downwind from the mountains. The author has observed small lenticulars over Chicago (about 700-nautical miles from the Front Range at Denver). This area contained very slight updrafts and downdrafts.

Compared to the mountain wave that forms over the Rocky Mountains, the mountain wave that is generated by the Appalachian Mountains is much weaker,

Chapter 5 - The Mountain Wave — PART 3 EN ROUTE

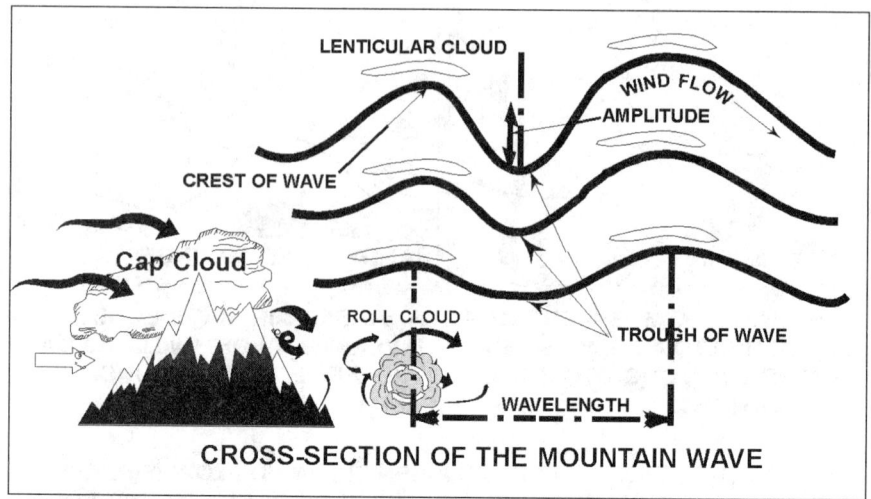

NOTE THE MOUNTAIN WAVE DIMENSIONS: WAVELENGTH AND AMPLITUDE WITH THE TYPICAL CLOUDS.

but occur with great frequency. The smaller amplitude occurs because of the height of the mountains. Associated with the reduction in amplitude is an increase in wavelength, averaging 10 nautical miles.

AMPLITUDE

The lee wave amplitude is defined as half the vertical distance from wave trough to crest. The only reason for knowing this bit of trivia is that the amplitude is related to the strength of the wave.

In a typical wave, amplitude varies with height above the ground. The smallest amplitude is near the surface and near the tropopause. The greatest amplitude generally occurs between 3,000 and 6,000 feet above the ridge top.

The size and shape of the mountain ridge and the wind velocity and atmospheric stability controls the amplitude. A shallow layer of great stability and moderate wind produces greater wave amplitude than does a deep layer of moderate stability and strong winds.

The greater the amplitude, the shorter is the wavelength. Waves offering the strongest, most consistent lift are those with great amplitude and short wave length.

Amplitude information courtesy Aviation Weather, AC 00-6A

In 1961, Paul Bikle set the world altitude sailplane record at 46,267 feet. This was in the Tehachapi Wave or Sierra Wave near Bishop, California.

PART 3 EN ROUTE   **Chapter 5 - The Mountain Wave**

TYPICAL CLOUDS

The formation of a mountain wave does not mean that the distinctive clouds associated with the wave will be present. There must be sufficient moisture for the various clouds to form.

The presence of lenticular clouds does not mean there is a certainty for strong updrafts and downdrafts. The appearance of clouds at any particular level in the atmosphere is not an absolutely sure sign that this is the area of strongest updrafts and downdrafts. The clouds are merely an indication of the level in the atmosphere containing sufficient moisture for the clouds to form.

Four cloud types are associated with the mountain wave, but it requires sufficient moisture for any of them to form. There is the *cap* cloud, *lenticular* cloud, *rotor* cloud and *mother-of-pearl* cloud.

Cap Cloud or Foehnwall

The cap cloud or foehnwall is so named because it forms a "cap" over the mountain. As the airflow is forced up the mountain on the windward side, the air expands in the lesser atmospheric pressure, cools to its dew point, and condenses out moisture. The largest mass of the cap cloud is found on the windward side. As the air descends on the lee side, it compresses. The heat of compression causes the cloud to dissipate in this area where large amounts of moisture can be absorbed.

LENTICULARS IN THE JET STREAM MADE THICKER BY LIFT FROM THE GRAND TETON MOUNTAINS (WYOMING)

Chapter 5 - The Mountain Wave — PART 3 EN ROUTE

CAP CLOUD FORMING OVER MT. McKINLEY AT 11:00 PM. THIS CLOUD LOOKS LIKE A PILIUS. AIRCRAFT AT APPROXIMATELY 19,000 FEET.

Lenticular

The familiar "signpost of the sky" indicating a wave condition is the lenticular cloud. A mountain wave can exist without the physical presence of the lenny cloud. The name "lenticular" means lens-shaped (when viewed from the side) or almond-shaped clouds.

Lenticulars are composed of water vapor, super-cooled water droplets or ice crystals.

"Lennys" are usually found from 20,000 to 40,000 feet. The development of lenticular clouds is entirely dependent on the humidity of the air aloft. When the mountain wave exists without any indication of clouds, it is called a "dry wave."

Once the atmosphere sets up the wave flow, air moves continuously through an undulating pattern. As the air is forced to rise, it cools

INDIVIDUAL ROTOR CLOUD LOCATED NORTHWEST OF BIG DELTA, ALASKA.

Mountain Flying Bible

by expansion and condenses out moisture to form the leading edge of the lenticular. As it moves through the crest area it continues to produce cloud. When it moves over the crest of the wave and down the other side, the heat of compression evaporates and reabsorbs the moisture.

This process continues downwind at succeeding crests forming the lenticular clouds that may occur as a series of waves downstream from the mountains.

Looking at the lenticular gives one the impression that it is a stationary cloud, just hanging in one place. The lenticular is constantly being formed on the upwind edge and dissipated on the downwind edge, with the wind moving through the area at 30 knots or more.

Separate lenticular cloud layers can stack up, one on top of the other. Each lenticular may be separate and distinct or it may be melded in with others above and below. The cooling air ascending and saturating the crest forms the cloud, then the warming of air as it descends causes the cloud to evaporate.

In the photo on page 3-87, the high-level moisture gives an indication of high-level lenticulars. There is an absence of low-level moisture and the wave activity is not marked by lenticulars in the lower levels. The strongest wave condition of up-drafts and downdrafts may exist at the lower level. The appearance of lenticular clouds simply points out wave activity—not wave intensity—at any particular level.

Some pilots have indicated their scorn for the mountain wave by stating that they will fly over any wave that gets in their way. The winds associated with a mountain wave extend to the tropopause (the line of demarcation between the troposphere and the stratosphere). Often the lift and sink will also extend to the troposphere, more than 10 miles above sea level, depending on latitude.

Lenticular clouds are the "signpost of the sky" indicating a mountain wave exists, but not all mountain wave conditions require the general aviation pilot to park his airplane. The majority of mountain waves allow flight with total safety. The pilot must check the weather reports and PIREPS to determine if the wave is causing problems for other pilots.

Roll, Rotor or Arcus

The *roll* cloud, sometimes referred to as a *rotor* or *arcus*, forms on the leeward side of the mountains. There are standing rotors that may be as stationary as the lenticular, or they may be transitory eddies producing various degrees of turbulence. When you look at a rotor cloud, you will be able to distinguish movement along its edges. When such a cloud is spotted, avoid it. The rotor is a "signpost of the sky" that mandates avoidance.

As the air flows over the mountain crest it cascades downward similar to a cataract creating strong downdrafts. It reverses course and flows upward. The

Chapter 5 - The Mountain Wave

interaction of descending and rising air between the crest-to-trough and trough-to-crest area of the wave is what causes the rotor.

When two objects are mixed or rubbed together without an emulsifier, the result is friction. When two air currents having different properties of composition (temperature and moisture) and varying wind flow velocities, they set up friction that results in a mixing zone where eddies occur. These eddies cause the rotor cloud.

The rotor is similar to the lenticular in that it is continuously formed on the upwind side and dissipated on the downwind side of the cloud. When formed close to the ground, the rotor may pick up dust and debris. If moisture is present this cloud takes on a very dark and threatening appearance. But not all rotors appear menacing. They often look like a fair-weather cumulus, but with the characteristic rotating edges. Avoid these clouds.

On some tremendously strong mountain waves, the downdraft air becomes so violent that it will bend back at ground level rather than flowing away from the mountain. Although extremely rare, when this violent overturning occurs, a series of rotors are formed. As the surface wind flows back toward the mountain it is forced upward by the rising terrain or by intermixing with the portion of wave flow that is ascending. Once again the flow is away from the mountain. The formation of the rotor cloud requires sufficient low-level moisture for condensation to appear.

Rotor clouds may appear as a long band of stratocumulus in an area of overturning air. The rotor might appear to remain stationary and forms parallel to the

**LINE OF ROTOR CLOUDS
(CALGARY, ALBERTA)**

mountain range at a distance equal to the wavelength on the leeward side of the mountains.

Once you have observed the rotor a time or two, it is easy to pick it out without watching intently for the rotational movement. You will observe fragments of the clouds being torn from the trailing edge while the top of the cloud moves faster than the bottom. Instead of a solid cloud with compact edges, look for a wispy cloud. Often it looks like a cotton ball with the edges pulled out away from the main body of cotton.

Whenever you detect rotational movement, detour the area. If weather or terrain constraints require flight in the area, the first choice is to fly over the cloud. Next choice is to fly around the cloud. Try to avoid flying beneath the cloud. The rotor diameter may vary between 600 feet and two miles, with typical vertical velocities of 2,000 to 5,000 feet per minute. This can and does produce severe turbulence.

General aviation airplanes are usually classified in the normal category with 3.8 gs limit load factor tolerance. Sailplanes are generally stressed for 6.0 gs limit load factor. The rotor has torn sailplanes apart, so imagine what it could do to us.

The turbulence is of greater duration and greater severity in the standing rotors just beneath the wave crests ranging from ground level to mountaintop level. Flying from Denver to Calgary once a week for 10 years, the author has observed the rotor between 25,000 and 35,000 feet above Denver's Front Range.

If the airplane is flown at an altitude half again as high as the mountain (measured from ground level to mountaintop, not sea level to mountaintop), the destructive-type turbulence can be avoided.

Usually during a period of mountain wave activity, the rotor cloud is downwind from the mountain range, centered beneath the lenticulars (crests). And while most of the rotors are fairly stationary, rotors have been known to be transitory in nature. The rotor can move back and forth between the updraft air on the upwind side of the crest and the downdraft air on the downwind side of the crest. Rotors can also break away from their stationary position and "float" downwind with the wind flow.

Mother-of-Pearl

The fourth cloud type is called the *mother-of-pearl (nacreous)*. It is seen most often above 50-degrees north latitude in the northern part of Canada and in Alaska (and Antarctica) as a huge pancake-shaped cloud at 80,000 to 100,000 feet above sea level. Being extremely thin, it is generally visible shortly after sunset or before sunrise when the sun is below the horizon. It's presence us evidence of tremendous vertical development.

Chapter 5 - The Mountain Wave — PART 3 EN ROUTE

TURBULENCE

All mountain waves have turbulence in the area between the ground and about 20,000 feet. The degree of turbulence depends on wind velocity, shape of the mountain, and air stability. Visible rotors indicate turbulence that should be flown around. The lenticular area, unless it has ragged and irregular edges, is smooth with the area demonstrating updrafts and downdrafts. The upwind side of the lenticular can hold tremendous amounts of supercooled water droplets. The majority of mountain waves can be flown without concern of destructive turbulence. The problem and main concern with most mountain waves is not turbulence, but rather the magnitude of the sustained updrafts and downdrafts.

Next to the thunderstorm, rotor turbulence from a mountain wave condition is about the worst that occurs throughout the altitudes general aviation planes operate.

FLIGHT PLANNING PROCEDURES/PRECAUTIONS

If, during your pre-flight weather briefing you learn of the possibility of mountain wave development or occurrence, consider the following:

- ✔ Check the PIREPS to determine the severity of the wave, along with METARs to see if "ACSL" is mentioned.
- ✔ If you are unfamiliar with the area, ask an accident prevention counselor or a local senior pilot about the best course of action.
- ✔ Because the mountain wave often occurs with the approach of a cold front, check the reports and forecasts to see if there is a cold front in the vicinity of the proposed flight.
- ✔ When approaching a mountain range from the upwind side, generally the west, there will usually be a smooth updraft.
- ✔ When approaching the mountain ridge from the downwind side it is always a good idea to approach at a 45-degree angle to the horizontal direction of the ridge to allow a quick turn from the ridge to an area of lower terrain and add an extra thousand feet or so of altitude to the normal 2,000-foot clearance because downdrafts can exceed the climb capability of the aircraft.
- ✔ One of the more important skills you can develop as a mountain pilot is the ability to visualize what is going on and what is causing it. Use visualization to determine the wavelength and then fly in the updraft area when the course parallels the mountain range.
- ✔ When your route of flight penetrates a front at an angle, and the front has to be crossed, often it is best to turn perpendicular to the front and get through the weather in the shortest distance. This is true of the mountain wave also; however, you must pick an area to penetrate the wave that is over suitable terrain.

PART 3 EN ROUTE   **Chapter 5 - The Mountain Wave**

- ✔ When a wave exists, it is best to choose an altitude that is half again as high as the mountain before trying to cross. This means half the distance between the ground elevation and mountaintop level. Rarely will this exceed 3,000 to 4,000 feet above the ridge line. Again, as you get close to the mountains it is a good idea to turn to a 45-degree angle approach to allow an escape if any downdrafts encountered exceed the rate of climb of the airplane.
- ✔ Other than the rotor, the most dangerous characteristic of the standing wave for the uninformed pilot beginning his first mountain flight is the magnitude of the sustained updrafts and downdrafts. If caught in a downdraft, speed up to get out of the area faster. This results in less altitude loss than flying at the best rate-of-climb or angle-of-climb speed. Those slower speeds prolong your exposure to the wave's effects.
- ✔ Avoid ragged and irregular-shaped lenticular clouds. They have the potential of creating turbulence can be as bad as the rotor cloud area.
- ✔ The level that lenticulars occur does not have any significance about the strength of the wave. This is merely the elevation where there is sufficient moisture for the cloud to appear. High altitude lenticulars may have weak updrafts and downdrafts accompanied with an area below them that is devoid of lenticulars, but with strong updrafts and downdrafts; or, the opposite may occur.
- ✔ Avoid the rotor area. The rotor may appear as a single cumulus-type cloud, or it may appear in a line. Generally it will be located near the elevation of the ridge line and extends up to the base of the lenticular cloud (it may extend downward to the ground and upward to over 30,000 feet). You will be able to see rotation with the top moving away from the mountains and the bottom curling toward the mountains.
- ✔ If there are strong downdrafts that prevent you from crossing the mountains, consider a turn around and climb to a higher altitude before making another attempt. If you need to fly (unpressurized airplane) at 12,000 feet for more than 30 minutes, or if you need to climb above 14,000 feet, have supplemental oxygen available.
- ✔ Trying to sneak through mountain passes and valleys during a period of wave development with strong winds aloft is not wise and is not a safe procedure for the most part. If the wind at ridge level is strong, fly over the mountain at high altitude or fly around them. ✈

Chapter 5 - The Mountain Wave — PART 3 EN ROUTE

ACCIDENT SITE

The *Tribesman II* DC-3, owned by the New Tribes Mission, Chico, Calif. was en route to Billings, Mont. on Nov. 21, 1950.

The 21 members were to attend a rally on their first leg of their missionary trip to South America.

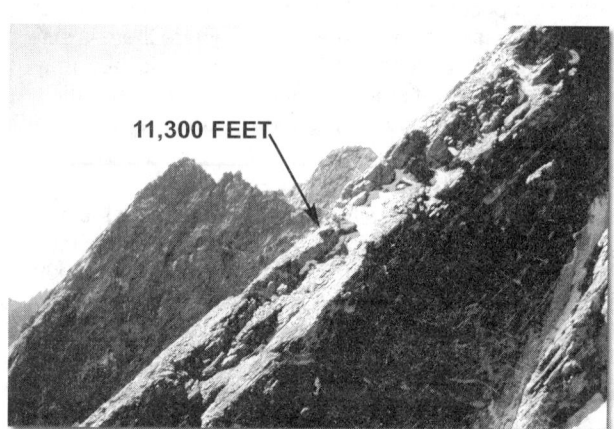

11,300 FEET

The pilots became disoriented in the clouds.

The DC-3 crashed on Mt. Moran, in the Teton Mountain Range, Jackson, Wyo. on Thanksgiving Day.

TAIL

The empennage section is all that remains today.

Use caution flying IFR in the mountains. Have the proper equipment for the prevailing conditions.

Mountain Flying Bible

PART 3 EN ROUTE   Chapter 6 - Scud Running

CHAPTER 6—SCUD RUNNING

> SCUD RUNNING 3-105
> LIFESAVING MANEUVER 3-107
> ESTIMATING IN-FLIGHT VISIBILITY 3-107

It takes very little research into the files of the National Transportation Safety Board (NTSB) to determine the general aviation accident statistics for any particular year during the past decades. These statistics provide information about the most frequent causal factors for these general aviation accidents. The quantitative data also point out the startling conclusion that this list of causes remains relatively stable year after year. That is, the same items are causing the same accidents. Looks like we should learn from our mistakes.

The FAA began their accident prevention program in 1971 and the program has been instrumental in helping to improve statistics. But, while the accident rate has been reduced, it is still the same errors committed by the pilot that continue to cause the accidents. This points out the need for continued refresher training to establish a higher level of flight proficiency for all pilots. In the case of mountain flying, the novice pilot should receive a mountain check-out from a competent mountain flight instructor.

The three top "got yas" are inadequate preflight preparation, landing accidents, and continued VFR flight into adverse weather conditions.

1. INADEQUATE PREFLIGHT

Examining a list of the individual elements responsible for the general aviation accidents provides the insight to see they are silly and preventable. The first on the list is *"inadequate preflight preparation and/or planning."*

What does this tell us? We need to spend some time thinking about the flight before jumping into the airplane and departing.

We have all seen the student pilot that takes more equipment and supplies on his cross-country flight than an airline pilot takes on an overseas flight. This is okay, but if that equipment is not used or not used properly, it is worthless. Ask yourself some questions that are appropriate to the planned flight.

We all get lazy when it comes to actual flight planning. With the use of a computer the flight plan (that provides surprising accuracy for the estimated flight

Mountain Flying Bible   **3-103**

Chapter 6 - Scud Running   PART 3 EN ROUTE

time en route) can be printed out in fewer than five minutes. We can even obtain the departure, en route and destination weather, along with forecasts and notams. But if you don't spend some time reading, deciphering and digesting this information, you can run into trouble.

What other information should you consider for a mountain flight?

- ✓ Is the weather suitable for a VFR flight over or through the mountains? Does the winds aloft forecast indicate any problems? Is turbulence expected? What is the trend of the weather?
- ✓ Are my charts current? (Yeah, I know, they don't change the terrain.) But what if the weather sours and you need to communicate with someone on the ground. Are the frequencies on an out-of-date chart valid?
- ✓ Should the route of flight be direct or dog-leg?
- ✓ Am I familiar with the airplane's operating limitations, performance, normal and emergency procedures and other operational information?
- ✓ How is the aircraft loading going to affect the flight (range, performance, endurance)?
- ✓ Will the flight extend into the night? Do I need a flashlight? Is the destination airport lighted? During the late afternoon a mountain airstrip may be dark in shadows, preventing a safe approach and landing. Allow an extra half-hour when the destination is in the mountains.
- ✓ Does my destination airstrip have fuel or services?
- ✓ Do I have a survival kit that is carried in the cockpit so that it is accessible if needed?
- ✓ What if I run into the venturi effect over the mountains causing the forecast winds aloft to double? Will I have sufficient fuel to continue to the destination?
- ✓ Suppose un-forecast weather crops up, where will I go?

You can see by these brief examples that preflight planning isn't just digging out the plotter and computer, or plugging in the computer.

2. LANDING ACCIDENTS

The next item on the NTSB causal-factor list is *"landing accidents—excessive speed on the landing roll or failure to correct for crosswind conditions."* Crosswind operations (using full flaps) are a common part of landing at backcountry strips. Get some practice with an instructor.

One problem that I have encountered is that the student performs the crosswind landing with mechanical precision. He knows that he has to slip the airplane to counteract drift. He has been taught that if the wind is from the left, the left aileron is used to compensate for the drift and right rudder is used to maintain longitudinal runway alignment. This causes problems in gusty wind conditions.

Rather than making mechanical corrections where the landing is thought of in terms of a slip, try flying the airplane back and forth with the ailerons to maintain *lateral* runway centerline alignment. Use the rudder back and forth to maintain *longitudinal* runway centerline alignment.

3. VFR INTO ADVERSE WEATHER

We all agree that pushing the weather on a VFR flight is not wise. If anyone asked us, we would vehemently reject any suggestion that we could get into a situation of continued flight when the ceiling or visibility begins to deteriorate so that it will disallow forward visibility.

But, look at the statistics. Each year some 200 accidents are listed as *"continued VFR flight into adverse weather conditions."* The sad thing about these accidents is that about 65 percent are fatal accidents.

The first two items on the NTSB list are easy to fix because they involve pilot education, practice and experience. The third causal factor is harder to control, because, not only does it require education, but it also demands pilot judgment. Not all of these accidents occur because the pilot cannot recognize "adverse weather conditions" from a distance. Some of the 200 accidents caused by unintentional weather encounters may be unplanned, but most of the time *scud running* is the culprit.

In open country you can easily detour around scattered clouds, but in a narrow canyon these clouds may pose a big problem. It's not generally the scattered clouds that will "get ya." It is a complete weather system that the pilot has been warned about, and maybe even given the warning, "VFR not recommended." The pilot has "gethomeitis" and scud running is his only way home. Not all "scud runners" are low time pilots who don't know better. Some are high-time pilots and may even hold an instrument rating.

SCUD RUNNING

There are some valid reasons for scud running. IFR flight at minimum en route altitudes may not be practical because of icing, winds, or turbulence aloft. Or, the pilot may have navigational or communication equipment failure. Also, a flight to a destination without an instrument approach facility is a good reason for not flying IFR if there is not another air-

SCUD-RUNNING WEATHER

port within the vicinity that would allow an instrument approach with continued VFR flight to the destination.

Whatever the reason, pilots scud run. Some pilots scud run successfully. They do so by learning how to scud run safely.

 To an experienced mountain pilot, VFR during changeable weather with a 2,000-foot ceiling and five-miles visibility is marginal. Weather conditions less than these, in the mountains, can make the flight turn into a terrifying adventure. What can a pilot do to make scud running a safe operation?

1. ESTABLISH MINIMUM WEATHER CONDITIONS

The smart—and usually experienced—pilot develops rules, and he will not, under any circumstances, breach these rules. If you select 2,000 feet and 5 miles as your minimums, adhere to them. Reverse course and land if it gets worse. If this is impossible, make a precautionary landing.

2. FLY IN THE LOWER THIRD OF THE CLOUD QUADRANT

The experienced pilot listens to his mom, "Fly low and slow, sonny." So throttle back to a comfortable slow-speed cruise and keep the terrain features clearly in sight.

Mentally divide the area from ground level to the cloud base into thirds. Fly in the lower third. The reason for this is simple. A pilot, flying near the cloud base, can fly into trouble before knowing it. At the cloud base the forward visibility is restricted. It is possible to enter a cloud without ever having seen it. And it is possible to fly into a mountainside without seeing it in time to perform an evasive maneuver.

3. KEEP NAVIGATION SIMPLE

Keep navigation simple by following a highway or railroad. Pay attention to your chart to make sure there isn't a tunnel. Be cautious about following a river when the temperature and dew point are close together. That's usually where the poorest visibility is encountered because of low clouds and fog.

4. TURN ON THE LIGHTS

Turn on all the aircraft's lights. It's not likely that anyone else will be out there with you, but if they are, you want them to see and avoid you.

5. FLY LIKE YOU DRIVE

When flying through the Gorge—between Portland and The Dalles, Ore.—or any narrow canyon, it is customary to remain to the right side, just as on a highway, to avoid pilots going the other way. If you are not concerned about other traffic in a remote area, fly the updraft side.

PART 3 EN ROUTE   Chapter 6 - Scud Running

LIFESAVING MANEUVER

Presentation of the following information is with a certain amount of reluctance and is not meant as encouragement for pilots to scud run. It is mearly a means of avoiding the terrain if you get caught in bad weather.

Because some pilot is going to use this as a crutch to go scud running when he shouldn't, I hesitate to mention this lifesaving maneuver. It is not difficult to perform, but some scud runners haven't thought about it or about what they are going to do when they get into trouble. It is an emergency life-saving procedure only. It is not to be used or performed as a routine part of flying.

When the ceiling is less than 2,000 feet or the visibility is fewer than five miles, park the airplane on an airport, not the side of a mountain. This is the original emergency lifesaving maneuver.

If you have checked the weather and find the parameters along the route and extending beyond your destination meet your idea of a safe flight, you are set to go. The takeoff and en route portion of the flight may show weather conditions better than forecast. This could lead to complacency, lulling one into a situation where if the visibility is reduced, there are no immediate warning bells or whistles going off in the pilot's mind.

When you become trapped, slow down and descend to a ground reference maneuver altitude, about 600 to 800 feet agl. Find a *prominent* landmark such as a tree, large rock, small pond or whatever. Don't spend time fussing about the landmark. Determine that you can circle this landmark without worrying about the lateral terrain clearance. Then fly. Fly around and around and around and around and around this landmark until the visibility improves. You might be stuck there for a half-hour or more. But it's better to be stuck there than against the side of a mountain. Don't concern yourself with flying the perfect "turn about a point" or "on-pylon eight." The object is to remain flying without running into something during the period of reduced visibility. Please reserve this maneuver for a real emergency and don't use it as a standard practice.

ESTIMATING IN-FLIGHT VISIBILITY

There is a rule of thumb that can be used to determine your approximate in-flight visibility. Depending on the make and model of airplane and your parallax when seated, this rule may be more accurate for some airplanes than others. It should take less than 10 minutes of your time to do the simple measurements and math to be able to use this method.

The Cockpit Cut-off Angle and In-flight Visibility

A pilot might rely on reports of the surface visibility that indicate a value greater than his established personal minimum for conducting a VFR flight. Even with reduced visibility at his cruise altitude he may continue simply because the

Mountain Flying Bible   3-107

reported visibility is above his comfort level. But, this can be downright foolish when the visibility at his location is much less than reported. The pilot should have some method of determining the in-flight visibility with reasonable accuracy to provide his own assessment of the restriction to vision.

RULE OF THUMB Estimating In-flight Visibility

The approximate visibility in miles will equal the number of thousands of feet above the surface when the surface is just visible over the nose of the airplane.

The rule of thumb is not equally accurate for all airplanes, but it is better than guessing. By using the following procedure, the cockpit cut-off angle can be determined for your particular make and model of airplane.

In other words, when the cockpit cut-off angle is used, if you are flying 2,000 feet above the surface and the ground surface is visible over the nose of the airplane, your slant-range visibility will be approximately two miles.

The cockpit cut-off angle for any airplane can be determined rather easily, to make the rule more accurate. Once it is determined for a given airplane, it will remain constant as long as the eye level (parallax) of the pilot is not changed.

The steps in determining this cut-off angle on the ground are as follows:

1. Adjust the aircraft attitude as close as possible to the normal cruise-pitch attitude.
2. Sit in the airplane and adjust the pilot's seat to the same position you would use in flight. Wiggle around a bit to get comfortable and use your normal posture.
3. Solicit the help of a friend to measure the distance between the ground and your eye level (example–six feet).
4. Look over the nose of the aircraft (cockpit cut-off angle) at the point where the ground surface is just visible. Measure this distance from your eye position along the surface (example—30 feet). Again, you will probable need the help of a friend.
5. In this example we have a six-foot eye height and thirty-foot cockpit cut-off distance. The tangent value is determined through division.

$$\frac{6}{30} = .20$$

6. Look at the following list for the nearest tangent value you computed and you will find the corresponding angle, which will be the cockpit cut-off angle of your aircraft. ✈

PART 3 EN ROUTE — Chapter 6 - Scud Running

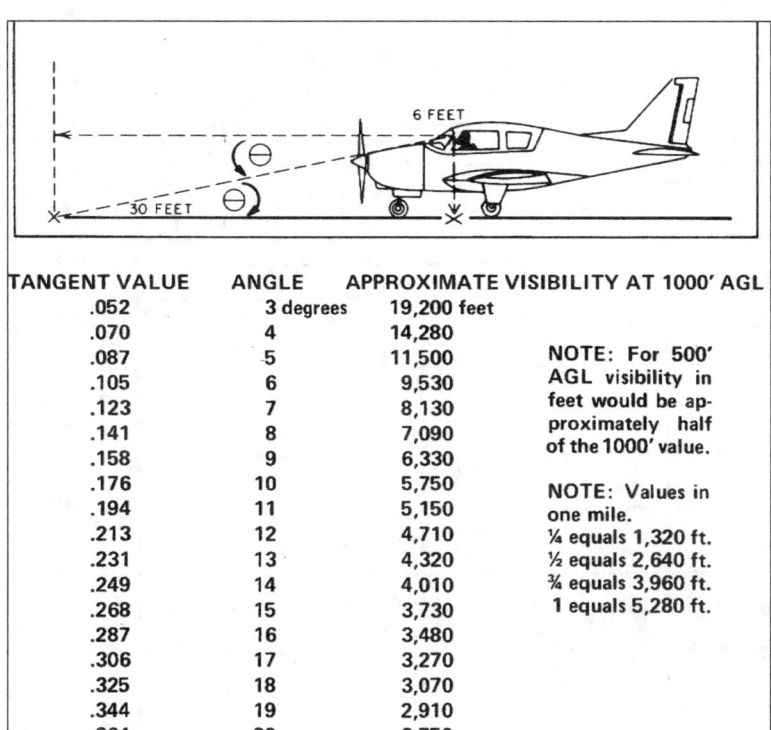

TANGENT VALUE	ANGLE	APPROXIMATE VISIBILITY AT 1000' AGL	
.052	3 degrees	19,200 feet	
.070	4	14,280	
.087	5	11,500	NOTE: For 500' AGL visibility in feet would be approximately half of the 1000' value.
.105	6	9,530	
.123	7	8,130	
.141	8	7,090	
.158	9	6,330	
.176	10	5,750	NOTE: Values in one mile.
.194	11	5,150	
.213	12	4,710	¼ equals 1,320 ft.
.231	13	4,320	½ equals 2,640 ft.
.249	14	4,010	¾ equals 3,960 ft.
.268	15	3,730	1 equals 5,280 ft.
.287	16	3,480	
.306	17	3,270	
.325	18	3,070	
.344	19	2,910	
.364	20	2,750	

THE APPROXIMATE VISIBILITY IN MILES WILL EQUAL THE NUMBER OF THOUSANDS OF FEET ABOVE THE SURFACE WHEN THE SURFACE IS JUST VISIBLE OVER THE NOSE OF THE AIRPLANE.

MARGINAL WEATHER CAN CLOSE IN FAST. BE PREPARED TO GET ON THE GROUND. (NOTE POWER LINE POLES)

Chapter 6 - Scud Running — PART 3 EN ROUTE

RADIUS OF TURN

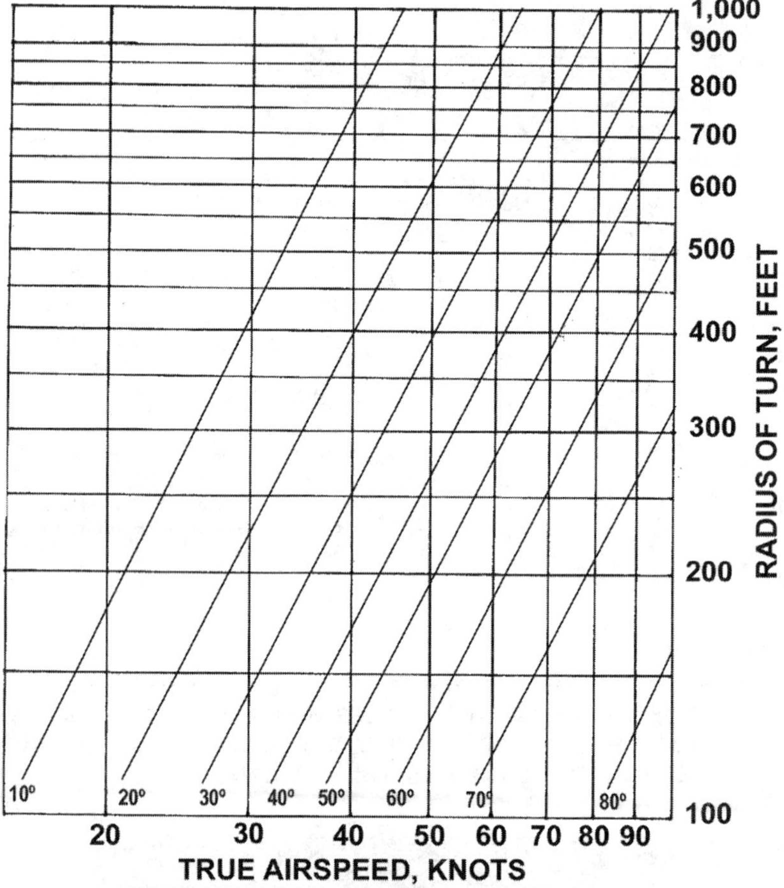

(chart: TRUE AIRSPEED, KNOTS on x-axis from 20 to 90; RADIUS OF TURN, FEET on y-axis from 100 to 1,000; diagonal lines for bank angles 10°, 20°, 30°, 40°, 50°, 60°, 70°, 80°)

TRUE AIRSPEED, KNOTS
(AT HIGH ALTITUDE, USE INDICATED AIRSPEED PLUS 2% PER 1,000 FEET ABOVE SEA LEVEL)

TO DETERMINE THE RADIUS OF TURN, MOVE FROM THE TRUE AIRSPEED (IN KNOTS) ALONG THE BOTTOM VERTICALLY UPWARD TO INTERCEPT THE DIAGONAL ANGLE OF BANK LINE. MOVE HORIZONTALLY TO THE RIGHT TO DETERMINE THE RADIUS OF TURN IN FEET.

A MORE EXACT COMPUTATION CAN BE FOUND IN THE RADIUS OF TURN CHART ON PAGE 3-42.

Mountain Flying Bible

PART 3 EN ROUTE　　　　　　　　　Chapter 7 - Lost Procedures

CHAPTER 7—LOST PROCEDURES

- ➢ BRACKETING 3-111
- ➢ ERROR SEMICIRCLE 3-112
- ➢ TRIANGULAR PATTERN 3-114

Pilots are never lost, just temporarily misplaced. Misplacement can occur during periods of restricted visibility, such as when experiencing heavy rain, smoke, dust storms, or the low clouds and reduced visibility of scud running operations. Occasionally inadequate preflight planning is the culprit.

Recalling my first flight from Jackson, Wyo. along the coast route to Vancouver, B.C., Juneau, and Anchorage, Alaska, brings to mind the technique used to prevent getting lost. The weather was crappy along most of the route. Keeping a sectional chart in my lap the entire time and using my trusty Jimmy Mattern plotter, I kept track of where I was within a tenth of a mile at all times during the entire 17-hour flight.

Flight with marginal weather in unfamiliar territory causes one to pay very close attention. Favorable weather with unrestricted visibility seems to soothe the pilot causing a temporary calm, causing complacency. This temporary calm before the storm may result in becoming lost.

BRACKETING

To avoid becoming lost, select easily identifiable landmarks or "brackets" as a means of keeping oriented. There is no set rule for choosing brackets, but rivers, highways, or the intersecting lines of railroads, highways and power lines, all make good reference brakets. Rather than trying to identify a particular highway or road, look for a pattern of road, mountains, rivers and other specific landmark features that can confirm a locality.

As a general rule don't choose a small lake or city as a bracket. They are too small and you may never see them as you fly past the area. Avoid wandering around, backtracking or zigzagging.

If you get misplaced, fly to the nearest bracket, reorientate yourself using the general pattern of several features to establish an accurate position. To rapidly establish the new course and determine the distance to go, we can use a trick.

Meridians of longitude (the north/south lines on the aeronautical chart) are divided into degrees-minutes-seconds. From the equator to the north pole is 90 degrees. Each degree is divided into 60 minutes. One minute of longitude is 6,076.113 feet, the definition of a nautical mile.

We can measure the distance from the present position to the destination using the length of a pencil, piece of paper or any straight edge. Place the straight edge vertically on the chart (it won't work horizontally on a parallel of latitude) and count the tick lines (nautical miles). The direction is determined by paralleling the course to be flown and moving the pencil to a compass rose (VOR azimuth) to read the magnetic course. (See Page 1-50.)

ERROR SEMICIRCLE

"Plan your flight, fly your plan." This advice comes from the military. When a pilot completes his preflight planning on the ground, instead of in the air, he has no problem finding himself should he become "temporarily misplaced." (lost). If you are using dead reckoning and can't find a particular checkpoint when the arrival time at the checkpoint has expired, maintain your heading (unless a large course change is to be made at that checkpoint) and try to determine if you might have more of a headwind, tailwind or crosswind than computed. This will give you an area on the chart to look for a recognizable feature.

If you use cities, towns, lakes and the like as checkpoints, be sure to use at least three distinguishing characteristics to identify each checkpoint. For example, if you have chosen a town for a checkpoint, ascertain that highways and roads enter and exit the town in the position shown on the chart with the same north-south or east-west orientation. Check for racetracks, cloverleaves, small lakes or other features that can be associated with the town.

When you are lost, use the error semicircle to find a landmark that can establish your position. It might be better to fly a steady course for several minutes while working out the problem. Establishing a new flight path based on a hunch is generally a poor idea. You can end up not knowing where you are.

From your last known position, extend a line between 30-degrees and 45-degrees left and right of the proposed course. Use your computed groundspeed to make a mark on the left line, the planned course, and the right line. Connect these points with a curved line (connect the dots). The airplane should be near the curved line. Use pilotage (recognizable land marks) to establish your position. If unable to find yourself, follow a highway or river to a city or town, maintaining orientation in relation to the chart, to find yourself.

PART 3 EN ROUTE   **Chapter 7 - Lost Procedures**

Lost in Brazil

Flying in Brazil is generally a pleasant experience, but one particularly dark and stormy night quickly became one of those days I wished I had stayed in bed. I was demonstrating a Piper Cheyenne 400LS for a U.S. company.

As a general rule, I will not fly an airplane after an annual inspection without making a daytime, VFR flight test. In this case, the airplane was needed in Cascavel that night and I was threatened that if it was not delivered, the sale of the airplane would be cancelled.

Rationalizing, I thought, "Heck, I have about 3,800 hours in the 400LS and I have flown this particular airplane for 100 hours in Brazil. I feel comfortable with the airplane's systems and flight characteristics. I'll go ahead and go." Mistake.

Bill Clinton won his presidential bid by a landslide on this day, but I felt far from first place. I applied power (this airplane accelerates rapidly) for the flight from Porta Alegre (SBPA) to Cascavel (SBCA). Liftoff, with a rate of climb in excess of 6,000 fpm, placed me inside the low clouds within seconds. The radios quit. All of them.

Was I lost? Not yet, but everything was leaning in that direction. All radios were inoperative because the connector (lacking its safety clamp) in the spar area had vibrated out. There was no VOR, no ADF, and no KNS-660. Lost yet? No, but the flux gates had been swapped to test a heading indication problem. I discovered, in comparison to the magnetic compass, the #1 HSI was +49 degrees and the #2 HSI was –33 degrees.

It was necessary to periodically turn off the electric windshield to check the magnetic heading. A preflight weather briefing showed the wind forecast as 330 degrees at 10 knots at 28,000 feet, requiring very little wind correction angle. The course was 350 degrees for 324 nautical miles. I figured I should be over Cascavel by holding a one-degree left wind correction angle and flying for 58 minutes.

It seems when a problem develops it is often complicated by other problems. This flight was no exception. Climbing through 28,000 feet, the baggage door pressure seal blew out (two holes were poked into the rubber while doing some filleting work on the door frame). This required cycling the environmental control unit to Hi (until a bleed air overtemp annunciation required it be turned to Lo. This caused the cabin pressure to fluctuate at over 6,000 fpm between a 7,000- to 10,500-foot cabin. But, I finally got it down to a science. I would turn one bleed air on until the overtemp indication, then turn the other on and the hot bleed off.

There's a reason why I didn't just go on oxygen and quit fiddling with the bleed airs. (If you've every tried to repack and stow the passenger oxygen masks

Mountain Flying Bible

Chapter 7 - Lost Procedures   PART 3 EN ROUTE

you know why.) Next the #1 inverter failed. By the way, the autopilot was inoperative during all this.

I would like to think it was my exceptional piloting skills that saved the day, but it was probably dumb luck that allowed me to descend through the clouds prior to my eta and end up with a city slightly to my left with an airport beacon to the south. After landing I was tempted not to ask what city, but what country I was in (it was Cascavel).

The point is, if you're lost or might become lost, a little perseverance will prevail.

TRIANGULAR PATTERN

The triangular pattern advocated in the Airman's Information Manual of old, recommended that a lost pilot maintain a straight heading for two minutes, turn 120-degrees right and fly two minutes, followed by another 120-degree right turn (left turns were used to indicated communications failure). Maintain the last heading for 15 minutes and repeat the pattern. Theoretically, a radar controller would see the pattern and send someone (usually military) to help. Forget it. The controller is unlikely to notice your pattern and winds aloft will distort the ground path so it doesn't look like a triangle. ✈

NOTE THE HIGH-ALTITUDE LENTICULAR CLOUDS. WHAT APPEARS AS LOW-LEVEL CLOUDS IS ACTUALLY SMOKE FROM FOREST FIRES THAT ALLOWS VISUALIZATION OF THE WAVE LENGTH.

PART 3 EN ROUTE   Chapter 8 - Aircraft Icing

CHAPTER 8—AIRCRAFT STRUCTURAL ICING

- ➤ BEWARE OF MOUNTAIN IFR 3-115
- ➤ BASIC INGREDIENTS FOR ICE 3-117
- ➤ TYPES OF ICE 3-117
- ➤ CLOUD TYPES AND ICING 3-119
- ➤ RATES OF ACCRETION AND ICING INTENSITIES 3-123
- ➤ ICING PROBABILITY 3-125
- ➤ IN-FLIGHT ICING 3-126
- ➤ LEGALITY OF FLIGHT 3-132
- ➤ GROUND USE OF DEICE FLUIDS 3-132
- ➤ TAKEOFF PERFORMANCE 3-135
- ➤ ICING FORECASTS 3-137
- ➤ ICING CLOUDS 3-138
- ➤ CONDITIONS FAVORING ICING 3-138
- ➤ MOUNTAIN ICE 3-141
- ➤ MOUNTAIN WAVE ICE 3-141
- ➤ GOOD OPERATING PRACTICES 3-147
- ➤ IFR OPERATIONS IN THE MOUNTAINS 3-147
- ➤ HOW RELIABLE ARE WEATHER FORECASTS 3-148
- ➤ CHECK WEATHER 3-150
- ➤ SUMMARY 3-156

BEWARE OF MOUNTAIN IFR

Pilots encountering clouds while flying IFR in the mountains will encounter icing conditions unlike anything that exists over the flatlands. Part of this is due to the high en route altitudes that are a combination of the minimum en route altitude (MEA) and the minimum reception altitude (MRA).

The MEA in mountain terrain is established to provide 2,000-foot clearance from the highest terrain located within four-nautical miles on both sides of the airway. When the mid-point of the airway exceeds 51 nautical miles, it is wider, established by measuring a 4½° angle from the VOR. The MRA guarantees minimum signal strength for reception of VOR signals. Combined, the MEA and MRA are at altitudes that are conducive to structural icing year-round. Although

Mountain Flying Bible

Chapter 8 - Aircraft Icing   PART 3 EN ROUTE

winter icing can be bad, summer icing can sneak up on the pilot. Flying through cumulus buildups, at the statistically worst icing temperature of 0°C to –10°C, can lead to tremendous ice accretion rates.

You can improve your comfort level and your chances of survival when exposed to an aircraft structural icing encounter through knowledge of the classification of ice, knowledge of the in-flight aspects, and knowledge of the required weather briefing. You have a responsibility to yourself and your passengers to know what aircraft structural icing is, how to properly cope with it, and when and where to expect it.

Flying IFR exposes the pilot to the possibility of aircraft structural icing. When icing occurs, the pilot thinks, "Something needs to be done here, and immediately." The following classification of icing will give you the background information required to make an intelligent decision about the proper solution to an icing encounter.

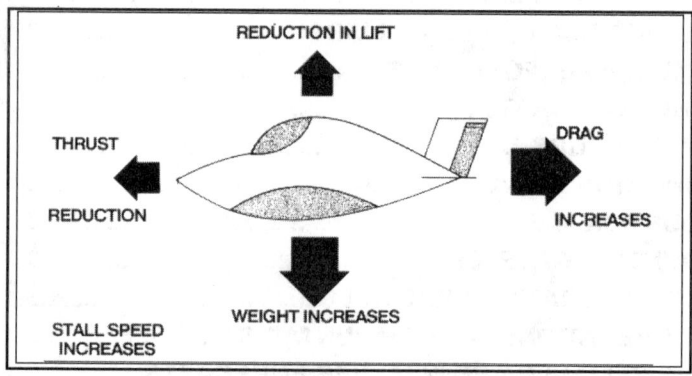

EFFECTS OF STRUCTURAL ICING

The in-flight aspects of icing will detail the anti-icing and deicing equipment, the area of icing to watch out for, and the good operating practices that will keep you out of trouble.

Weather personnel know the atmospheric conditions that cause icing. They know icing is going to occur, but they are unable to forecast exactly where and how much ice there will be. From experience, the icing and its intensity can vary considerable with the passage of only a few minutes. The weather briefing is the most important aspect of dealing with icing. You can predict areas of icing with a high degree of accuracy. Knowing this allows you to avoid those areas.

With a thorough knowledge of the elementary weather conditions that cause in-flight structural icing, the proper in-flight procedures, and a big picture of the actual weather conditions, you are ready to embark upon the flight.

PART 3 EN ROUTE — Chapter 8 - Aircraft Icing

BASIC INGREDIENTS FOR ICE

For structural icing to occur during flight, two basic elements are required.

1. The airplane must be exposed to rain, wet snow or clouds during flight, and,
2. The outside air temperature (or the temperature of the airplane if it has become cold-soaked from flight at a higher altitude) must be at or below freezing. It is possible for the outside air temperature to be slightly above freezing, and aerodynamic cooling can lower the temperature to the freezing point.
3. The amount of icing encountered and the form of ice encountered depends on the size of the water droplets, how fast they freeze, and how long the airplane remains in these conditions. When water droplets form and exist in as water droplets in temperatures below freezing, they are called "supercooled" water droplets. To supercool water means to cool it below the freezing point without solidification or crystallization. This water exists in an unstable state where anything (like an airplane) that disturbs its delicate balance will quickly turn it to ice (on the wings and structure).

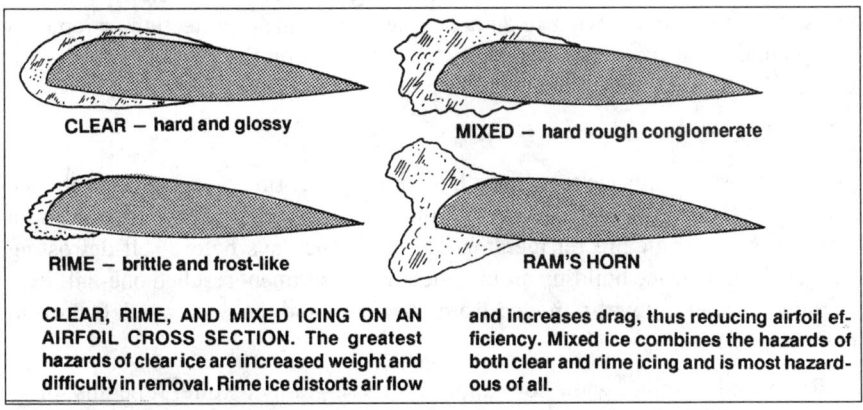

CLEAR – hard and glossy

MIXED – hard rough conglomerate

RIME – brittle and frost-like

RAM'S HORN

CLEAR, RIME, AND MIXED ICING ON AN AIRFOIL CROSS SECTION. The greatest hazards of clear ice are increased weight and difficulty in removal. Rime ice distorts air flow and increases drag, thus reducing airfoil efficiency. Mixed ice combines the hazards of both clear and rime icing and is most hazardous of all.

CLEAR, RIME AND MIXED ICING ON AN AIRFOIL CROSS SECTION

TYPES OF ICE

The type of icing that forms on the airplane depends primarily upon the water droplet size and its temperature. Structural icing types include *clear*, *rime*, a *mix-*

Chapter 8 - Aircraft Icing   PART 3 EN ROUTE

ture of clear and rime, and *frost*. Because of individual characteristics, each type of icing can be easily identified.

CLEAR ICE (GLAZE)

Clear ice is easy to identify. It looks like an ice cube, although it can appear smooth or rippled. It is transparent or translucent and has a glassy appearance. Clear ice is usually found in cumulus clouds and freezing drizzle or freezing rain at temperatures between 0°C and –10°C, but it can be encountered in cumulonimbus clouds as cold as –25°C.

Clear ice obtains its smooth and clear appearance due to large water droplets and slow freezing. The water droplet flows once it strikes the aircraft structure, freezing slowly. The main problem with clear ice is that it can run back (14 inches or more) on the wing. Even with boots it will be difficult, if not impossible, to cope with.

When clear ice begins to form on the wing leading edge at cruise flight (low angle of attack) it conforms to the shape of the airfoil initially, then it begins to build forward at a 45-degree angle upward and a 45-degree angle downward in the *ram's horn* shape (a cross-sectional view resembles a ram's horn). This is also referred to as a *doublehorn*.

Clear ice is the most serious form of icing because it adheres firmly to the aircraft. It's removal with boots or a heated wing is difficult, especially if the ice has spread back on the wing in an area where there is no protection or removal equipment. Clear ice is heavy. One inch of clear ice on the frontal surfaces of a Cessna 182 weighs approximately 800 pounds.

RIME ICE

In contrast to clear ice that looks like an ice cube, rime ice resembles the ice that forms around the outside edges of the freezer compartment. (When I was a kid, we had a Frigidaire refrigerator. This is in the days before self-defrosting fridges. When the ice build-up around the ice compartment reached one-half inch or more, everything was removed from the fridge and the door was left open to melt the ice.)

Rime ice is a milky while formation that has a grainy texture. It begins forming on the curved portions of windshields, landing gear, wind and empennage leading edges, struts, antennas, and other parts exposed to the airflow. Rime ice is usually found in stratiform clouds. Its formation on the leading edge of the wing conforms with the center of the leading edge, but the rest of the ice can develop weird shapes.

Stratiform clouds contain much smaller water droplets than cumuliform clouds. When rime ice begins forming, the small droplets freeze, almost instantaneously, before it can spread. The next drop freezes between the other drops. Air is trapped between these drops to cause the white, rather than clear, coloring.

While rime ice is lighter than clear ice, its effects are often worse because the rough surface is effective in destroying the smooth aerodynamic flow of air over the airfoil surfaces. De-icing boots are more capable in removing rime ice because of the brittle nature of the ice.

MIXED ICE

Mixed icing, as the name implies, is a mixture of clear ice and rime ice. When clear ice is mixed with snow or sleet, it may resemble rime ice with a whitish color and rough shape, but it is mixed icing. In addition to mixing with snow, sleet or small hail, the cause is usually uneven water droplet sizes. It is most common at temperatures from –10ºC to –15ºC. It can form accumulations on the airplane rapidly. At low angles of attack this ice can form a mushroom shape or inverted mushroom (ram's horn or doublehorn) on the leading edges.

FROST

Frost generally occurs on the aircraft while parked on the ramp. In rare instances a cold-soaked aircraft descending from altitude into warm, moist air (or climbing through an inversion), can experience in-flight frost. The danger here is not the decreased aerodynamic lift, but rather a lack of visibility until the frost sublimates.

The formation of ice crystal deposits is caused by sublimation when the temperature and dew point are below freezing. It is really dangerous and stupid to attempt to takeoff with any accumulation of frost on the airplane. Frost can cause up to a 10-percent increase in the stall speed. Because frost forms such a thin layer that conforms to the shape of the airfoil, some pilots are not alarmed when they arrive at the airport and find frost all over the plane. Frost is like sandpaper to the air. It is rough and it destroys the smooth flow of air over the airfoils. If there is no hangar available to dispatch the frost and you can't remove it, polish it smooth before attempting flight.

CLOUD TYPES AND ICING

Clouds are visible evidence of what the atmosphere is doing; its movement, water content and stability. Atmospheric stability is the air's resistance to vertical motion when both temperature and pressure decrease at normal rates with altitude.

From the flier's point of view, there are two basic types of clouds: *cumulus* and *stratus*. True, these come in several varieties and there are many subspecies.

Chapter 8 - Aircraft Icing — PART 3 EN ROUTE

The weather-book description of clouds accompanying fronts is often deceptive. The actual cloud forms may be quite variable from the projected model used in textbooks.

 If you are flying IFR and the outside air temperature approaches freezing temperature, climb or descent, as appropriate, to fly above or below the clouds. Some of the worst icing occurs in the tops of cumulus clouds at or below freezing. Often a climb of as little as 1,000 feet can put the airplane on top of these clouds and out of the icing.

STRATUS CLOUDS

In stable air, stratus clouds form in layers with little or no vertical development. Stratus is shapeless. Within 50 feet of the ground it is fog. It may occur over a large area, or may be patchy. Thickness may range from a few hundred feet to several thousand feet. On the average, stratus clouds contain only about half the liquid water content found in cumulus-type clouds. Precipitation is drizzle, continuous light rain or snow. Stratus clouds may form behind slow-moving cold fronts, well ahead of warm fronts and with temperature inversions (especially in industrial areas where there is an abundance of condensation nuclei). Icing is confined, on the average, to a layer between 3,000 and 4,000 feet thick.

There is little or no turbulence associated with stratus formations, but the danger of structural icing is great if the free air temperature is 0°C or colder. Carburetor ice is likely if the temperature is 25°C or lower. In short, the presence of middle and low stratus usually means poor flying weather.

An isotherm is a line of equal temperature. It may be at a constant elevation or it can undulate up and down like a wave, only over a much larger scale. When you fly in an area with widespread precipitation from stratiform clouds, avoid the 0°C isotherm. Below this area (if the MEA will allow flight), the temperature is above freezing. Above the 0°C isotherm the moisture is changed mostly to ice crystals. Near the 0°C isotherm, above and below in a shallow layer, you may find an area with concentrated liquid water droplets that can produce icing. If the precipitation is intermittent, supercooled water droplets can exit up to the –20°C isotherm and can pose a serious icing problem.

When flying on top of a cloud layer with sunshine at your back, look at the airplane shadow. If you spot the shadow, the cloud is composed of ice crystals; however, if you see a *glory* instead, the cloud is composed of liquid water. The colored rings (circular rainbow) replacing the shadow are caused by a diffraction phenomenon. If the temperature at cloud level is freezing or below when you see the glory, expect icing.

When an airplane flies above a cloud layer composed of small water droplets, a set of colored rings, called the "glory" may appear around the shadow of the airplane. Sunlight entering the small water droplet along its edge is refracted downward, then reflected off the bottom center (backside) of the droplet. The light then exits at the other side of the droplet, being refracted once more. This returning light is what causes the glory.

Cumulus clouds are formed by instability with icing concentrated mainly in the updraft areas. Stratiform clouds occur over a large, horizontal area in comparison to the cumulus clouds. The stratiform icing conditions occur in a relatively narrow band, usually near the tops of the clouds. If you experience ice, try changing the flight level 2,000 feet (sometimes 1,000 feet will eliminate icing) to get out of the heavy water concentrations. If the airplane's performance is capable of a 4,000-foot climb, it just about guarantees that you will be out of the icing, remembering there are no guarantees in aviation.

The ice encountered in these stratiform clouds can usually be dealt with effectively and safely in small airplanes over the flatlands since a minimal altitude change will eliminate the icing. Over mountains, it may be a different story. The main hazard lies in the great horizontal extent of some of these cloud decks, along with mechanical lifting along the mountains.

Use visualization to determine areas of freezing drizzle or freezing rain. These areas present hazards most general aviation airplanes (even those certified for *flight in known icing conditions*) cannot cope with. A warm front, with its less dense air, will override colder air in its path. The warm front precipitation (warm water droplets) falls into the cold air, so any freezing precipitation will occur ahead of the surface front position. The cold front, forming a wedge of air, will shove warm air in its path up along its slope. The warm air cools and condenses moisture. The moisture falls through the cold air changing to freezing precipitation immediately behind the surface position of the cold front.

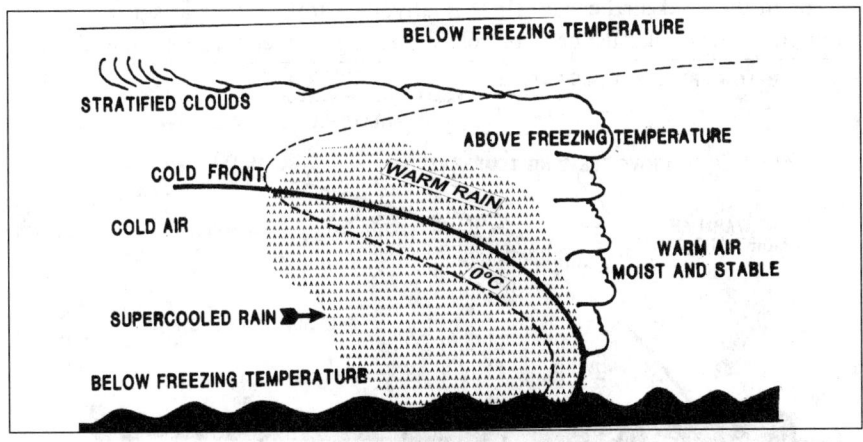

COLD FRONT ICING ZONE

Chapter 8 - Aircraft Icing   PART 3 EN ROUTE

CUMULUS CLOUDS

Although the individual cumulus cloud occupies a much smaller area than stratus-type clouds, combined, the cumulus can prevail over a large area. Cumulus has the ability to transport water droplets vertically to a great extent. As the drops move upward they increase in size combining with other drops. When they become supercooled, severe icing conditions exist. Icing can exist at any altitude above the freezing level, but it is most intense in the upper half of the cloud, especially within the top 1,000 to 2,000 feet.

Building cumulus contains liquid water at temperatures well below the –10°C level, that is considered the lower limit of severe icing potential. Sharp, well-defined cumulus edges indicate the cloud contains liquid moisture; whereas, if the edges are soft and fuzzy, the cloud is most likely composed of ice crystals. Cumulus clouds represent convective or mechanical lifting. Although the icing potential in cumuliform clouds is smaller horizontally than in stratiform clouds, it has greater vertical dimensions. Small airplanes usually cannot deal with the ice encountered in this type of cloud when the temperature-dewpoint spread is zero and the temperature is between 0°C and –10°C. Icing is typically of the clear type, but will be mixed with rime in the upper levels of the cloud.

CIRRIFORM CLOUDS

Ice formation in cirrus clouds is extremely rare, although some cirriform do contain small amounts of water droplets that could cause trace or light accumulations of ice.

FRONTAL-ZONE CLOUDS

Nearly 85 percent of all aircraft icing conditions occur in the vicinity of frontal zones. This icing may be in the relatively warm air above the frontal surface or in the cold air beneath (it is relatively warm in comparison to the air below it; however, it must be at or below freezing temperature for ice to form).

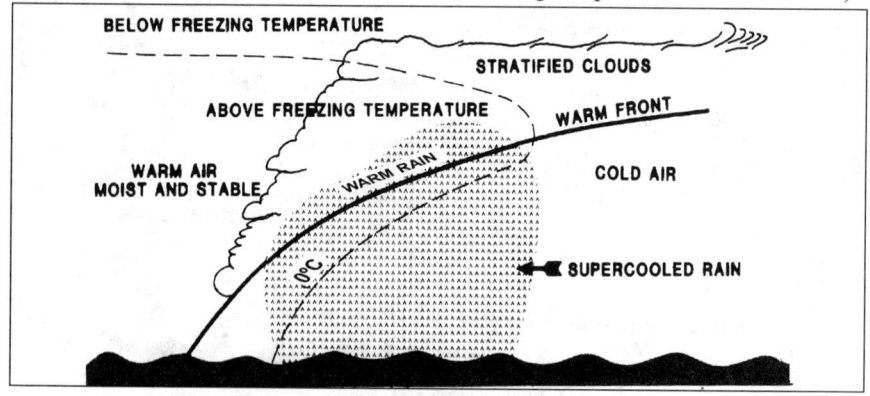

WARM FRONT ICING ZONE

PART 3 EN ROUTE   **Chapter 8 - Aircraft Icing**

For significant icing to occur above the frontal surface, the warm air must be lifted and cooled to its condensation level at temperatures below freezing. This causes it to contain supercooled water droplets. If the warm air is unstable, icing may be spotty; if it is stable, icing may be continuous over an extended area. Icing may form in this manner over either a warm frontal surface or a shallow cold frontal surface.

Icing below a frontal surface outside of the clouds occurs in freezing drizzle or freezing rain. Precipitation forms in the relatively warm air above the frontal surface at temperatures above freezing. It falls into the subfreezing cold air below the front, becomes supercooled, and subsequently freezes on impact with the aircraft. Freezing drizzle and freezing rain occur with both warm fronts and shallow cold fronts. The icing in any freezing precipitation is especially hazardous since it often extends horizontally over such a large area, and can extend downward to the surface, eliminating any escape route. The only escape is an immediate 180-degree turn or flight above the freezing precipitation.

RATES OF ACCRETION AND ICING INTENSITIES

ACCRETION

Accretion is defined as *any growth or increase in size by gradual external addition, fusion, or inclusion.* We will define ice accretion as ice adhesion to exposed aircraft surfaces. Temperatures between 0°C and –20°C cause the most problems, but the worst icing statistically, occurs between 0°C and –10°C.

Generally the warmer the temperature, up to 0°C, the higher the liquid water content of the cloud. The larger the size of the water droplets, and the smaller the size of the wings and components of the airplane, the faster the ice accretion rate.

RATE OF ACCUMULATION

Ice accumulation is variable and dependent on many factors such as the size of the water droplets, whether or not they are supercooled, outside air temperature, airplane wing shape, exposure time and the like. Ice is reported to accumulate as only a trace, where it is barely discernable, to as much as one inch per minute. During an ILS approach into the Idaho Falls, Idaho, airport (with unreported freezing drizzle), I picked up over four inches of clear ice from the outer marker to the runway in less than three minutes.

WEIGHT OF ICE

After formation, ice weighs about 50-pounds per cubic foot.

MOST SEVERE ICING

Statistically the most severe in-flight structural icing occurs with temperatures between 0°C and –10°C. Icing is not uncommon at –25°C and

Mountain Flying Bible

Chapter 8 - Aircraft Icing   PART 3 EN ROUTE

has been noted at temperatures as low as –60°C in thunderstorms and in extreme mountain waves.

INSIDIOUS

Icing is insidious. The dictionary defines insidious as *working or spreading harmfully in a subtle or stealthy manner; intended to entrap; lying in wait for.*

Ice collects first on small objects, having a small radius. Rivets, outside air temperature probes, windshield wipers, steps, fuel vents, the edges of air scoops, antennas and curved portions of the windshield will show the first traces of ice.

Ice formation on the airplane will disrupt the smooth flow of air over the airfoils that will decrease lift, increase weight, increase drag, and increase stalling speed. It will affect the control of the aircraft. When ice forms on the blades of the propeller, its efficiency is decreased and additional power is required to maintain flight. The most significant hazard of ice accumulation on the propeller is a disastrous vibration caused by the uneven distribution of ice on the blades. This usually occurs when one blade slings a portion of ice. This will place stress on the engine mounts and the propeller itself. Other icing effects include engine air intake icing that robs the engine of air to support combustion, loss of proper operating of control surfaces, reduction of outside vision, false flight instrument indications and loss of radio communication and navigation capabilities.

SUPERCOOLED WATER DROPLETS

> su•per•cool \ 'sü-p r-kûl \ verb transitive
> :to cool below the freezing point without solidification or crystallization
> ©1996 Zane Publishing, Inc. and Merriam-Webster, Incorporated. All rights reserved.

A pail of water, ponds and lakes cannot exist at temperatures colder than 0°C. But, water droplets are often influenced by a complex process of freezing. Instead of freezing at 0°C, their freezing temperature varies from –10°C to –40°C. The smaller the droplets, the lower the freezing point. Water droplets colder than 0°C are supercooled.

When water droplets are lifted to great heights by a thunderstorm or a mountain wave condition, the supercooled water can exist at temperatures colder than –40°C; although, they are generally found in the 0°C to –15°C layers.

EFFECT OF ICE

Structural icing alters the flight characteristics of the airplane. Experimenting during controlled conditions will provide additional insight about icing.

Experiments conducted by various independent agencies, confirmed by my own experience, show that one-half inch of ice can reduce the lift by as much as 50 percent. Remember, lift and drag are directly proportional, so this reduction in lift can increase the stall speed tremendously. The FAA reports that as little as 1/8 inch of rough ice can cause a 50-percent loss in rate of climb and a 10-percent loss in cruise speed.

REPORTING AIRFRAME ICING

The "Airframe Icing Report" table on the next page contains the only recognized standard for reporting airframe icing. The problem is that the definitions make no distinction of aircraft size or type. It is important that PIREPS contain this information about the aircraft type.

Pilot Report

To make a pilot report regarding aircraft structural icing, follow this format:
- Aircraft Identification
- Location
- Time (UTC)
- Intensity of Type* (See Page 3-118)
- Altitude/FL (flight level)
- Aircraft Type
- IAS

Rime Ice: Rough, milky, opaque ice formed by the instantaneous freezing of small supercooled water droplets.

Clear Ice: A glossy, clear, or translucent ice formed by the slow freezing of large supercooled water droplets.

ICING PROBABILITY

Examine four areas to determine the potential for aircraft in-flight structural icing: temperature, moisture, stability and lifting action.

Temperature – Most of the icing will occur between 0°C and –20°C, but the worst icing will occur between 0°C and –10°C.°

Moisture – If the temperature-dew point spread (dew point depression) is fewer than 4° and temperatures are between 0°C and -20°C, suspect an icing problem.

Stability – If air is conditionally stable, it resists lifting action. If it is conditionally unstable, it adds to any lifting action.

Lifting Action – There are two types of lifting action: meteorological

Chapter 8 - Aircraft Icing

and orographic. Meteorological lifting is brought about by weather systems. Orographic lifting results because of topographical features where the wind moves the air up slope. When air is lifted, it cools and condenses out the moisture.

IN-FLIGHT ICING

> **(1) TRACE** - Ice becomes perceptible. Rate of accumulation slightly greater than rate of sublimation. It is not hazardous even though deicing/anti-icing equipment is not utilized, unless encountered for an extended period of time (over 1 hour).
>
> **(2) LIGHT** - The rate of accumulation may create a problem if flight is prolonged in this environment (over 1 hour). Occasional use of deicing/anti-icing equipment removes/prevents accumulation. It does not present a problem if the deicing/anti-icing equipment is used.
>
> **(3) MODERATE** - The rate of accumulation is such that even short encounters become potentially hazardous and use of icing equipment or diversion is necessary.
>
> **(4) SEVERE** - The rate of accumulation is such that deicing/anti-icing equipment fails to reduce or control the hazard. Immediate diversion is necessary.

AIRFRAME ICING REPORT

AIRCRAFT STRUCTURE

Ice can and does rapidly destroy the beneficial aerodynamic and stall characteristics of the airplane. It also changes weight and balance, the power output of the engine(s) and the total aircraft performance. It can also form on control surfaces and cause vibrations that actually shake the airplane apart.

The parts of the airplane exposed to the airflow are subject to structural icing. We mostly think of icing as occurring on the wings, but keep in mind that it accumulates on both the wing and tail surfaces, windshield, the propeller spinner and blades, the engine appliances exposed to the air such as alternator or generator wiring, the air intakes and pitot tube (static ports if incorporated with the pitot tube), and radio antennas. The mounting bracket of a sense antenna on a Cessna 182 broke with only about 1/4 inch of ice. As it tore the skin it made a soft slapping noise. As the ice accumulated and the mount tore further, it began making a loud, rhythmic racket.

The danger of aircraft icing is seldom the weight of the ice. Rather, the disruption of the smooth flow of air is the major culprit.

A ground hazard may occur when, during takeoff or landing, splashing water causes ice to form. It may keep control surfaces from operating properly. Or it may cause damage to brakes, hydraulic lines, or even the landing gear.

After landing, use caution in retracting the flaps all the way, unless you are certain they are clear of ice. Low wing aircraft, especially, are susceptible to structural damage if ice is compressed between the flaps and the wing structure.

ANTI-ICING/DEICING EQUIPMENT

Anti-icing/deicing equipment is designed for different parts of the airplane. Manufacturers and owners install various combinations of the *mechanical, thermal* and *chemical* equipment.

Mechanical - Pneumatic deicer boots are installed on the leading edge of wings, horizontal, and vertical stabilizers.

Thermal - Electrical-heating elements are embedded as anti-icing devices in or attached to windshields. Propellers, pitot/static systems, fuel vents and stall-warning systems also incorporate electric heat elements. Turbine engine aircraft may use engine bleed air instead of electric heat.

Chemical - Alcohol is sometimes used on propellers and windshields as an anti-ice/deice fluid. The *weeping wing* is on the wings of some aircraft.

Not all anti-icing/deicing equipment has been designed or intended to allow prolonged flight in icing conditions. Rather, it allows time to find a way out of the ice.

PITOT-STATIC SYSTEM

Pitot heat and static vent heat should be used before entering precipitation or clouds at or below freezing temperatures. It is a good idea to use them whenever encountering clouds or precipitation, regardless of the temperature.

If the pitot tube becomes plugged with ice, the airspeed indicator fails to function as designed. With air trapped in the pitot system, the airspeed indicator acts similar to the altimeter. When climbing, the airspeed shows an increase in speed. A descent will cause an indication of a decrease in airspeed.

If ice clogs the static vents, the altimeter and vertical speed indicator will not function normally. Turn on static heat if available. If it is not available and icing were to occur, an alternate static source may be used. This alternate static source uses air from inside the cabin (non-pressurized airplanes) or outside air (pressurized airplane). Without an alternate static system, the pilot may break the glass on the vertical speed indicator. Damaging this instrument, while breaking the glass, will have less impact than damaging the altimeter or airspeed indicator.

PROPELLER ICING

Propeller icing causes two dangers: the loss of thrust and the creation of vibration.

Vibration occurs when a portion of the ice accumulation is slung off one propeller blade, but not the other(s). The out-of-balance condition can cause failure of the engine mountains or engine failure. Cycle the propeller (or change the throttle on fixed-pitch propeller airplanes) in an attempt to change the centrifugal force and sling ice from the other blade(s). It is important to get the prop back in balance. If there is a warmer area at a lower altitude above the MEA, descend with reduced power.

It is not difficult to recognize propeller icing. There is a loss of power accompanied by vibration as the ice begins building at the prop hub and gradually builds outward covering about one third of its length.

The propeller's performance is degraded by 20 percent or more with ice accretion. Due to the aerodynamics of pressure change and evaporation with a spinning propeller, the temperature may be cooled as much as +4°C. It is possible to taxi in fog and obtain an ice buildup on the prop when there is no other indication of icing. With engine roughness, it would be wise to shutdown and check the prop before attempting takeoff.

Don't back the engine if you are picking up ice. Make all climbs at maximum continuous power (with the highest rpm setting allowed). The high rpms help keep ice off the propeller and the maximum rate of climb will help you get through the icing layer faster.

In a contest involving electric heating elements and alcohol slinger systems, the electric prop wins hands down. The electric prop is generally classified as an anti-ice system. But, because of the high demand for power, it usually cycles continuously as a deice device. There's nothing wrong with alcohol on the props. Centrifugal force distributes the alcohol along the leading edge of each blade, which is an efficient means of removing the ice ... until the fluid capacity is exhausted.

In twin-engine airplanes with reciprocating engines, as ice is thrown off the props it slams against the fuselage with a terrible noise. As long as the noise continues you know the system is working. Turboprop aircraft are not as susceptible to this, because the propeller rpm is much slower.

PART 3 EN ROUTE Chapter 8 - Aircraft Icing

PNEUMATIC BOOTS

Ice avoidance or the use of anti-icing and deicing equipment as you pass through an area of ice is the only acceptable manner for flying IFR. One item of deicing equipment is the pneumatic boots installed on the leading edges of the airfoils. You might read that boots don't do much except provide a psychological advantage for flying in areas with ice. But, psychological or not, when the boot cycle is activated and the ice disappears, you feel a lot better.

If used improperly, boots provide no help in an icing encounter. Boots only work up to a limit, and then only if the pilot follows the manufacturer's recommendations. Most aircraft flight manuals recommend that the pilot allow 1/4 to 3/8 inch of ice to accumulate before inflating the boots; otherwise, *bridging* may occur. Bridging occurs when there is insufficient air pressure (caused by flying too slow or actuating the boots when the ice is too thin) against the cracked ice to remove it. Additional icing fills the cracks, and the boots merely flex beneath the ice from then on.

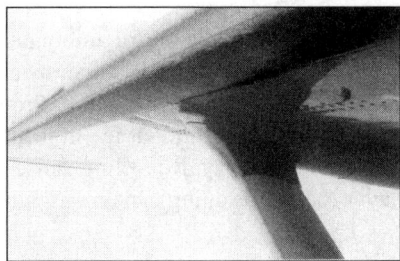

WING ICING

Boot Preparation

Boots are highly technical devices that are glued to the leading edge of the airfoils. They are composed of individual pressure ribs that run horizontally along the surface.1 During flight vacuum is applied to the boots to hold them smoothly against the wing. When the deice cycle is actuated, pressure replaces the vacuum and causes each pressure ridge to expand and crack the ice. The relative wind flowing between the cracks peels the ice and dispenses of it into the slipstream. If the boots are not clean and waxed, the adhesion may be greater than the relative wind's ability to remove the ice.

Wash the boots with a mild detergent and apply wax evenly over their surface. The wax makes the ice come off easier by destroying surface tension.

Manufacturers promote their commercially prepared surface treatments for boots. Most are quite expensive. B.F. Goodrich recommends *Age-Master No. 1* to prevent premature aging of the boots. Their *Icex* is a silicone compound used to reduce ice adhesion. These are good products

For over 17 years I have been using Lemon Pledge (any Pledge wax will work, the lemon just smells good). It works great. Furthermore, it can be applied when the boots are wet and it is raining. Normally the wax is sprayed along the boot and rubbed in. When it is raining, spray the Pledge on the rag or paper towel

Chapter 8 - Aircraft Icing   PART 3 EN ROUTE

and rub it over the boots. I also use the Pledge for cleaning/polishing the Plexiglas windows.

How often should you use the Pledge wax? Preferably after each flight, spend three or four minutes to apply it. Absolutely before each flight into icing conditions, apply it.

Boot Usage

If the boots are not kept clean and waxed, timing in activating the boots can be critical to their effective use. If used too soon, *bridging* occurs. If used too late, they will not crack the ice.

Some older airplane deicing systems have a timer that can be set for automatic operation to actuate the boots at the desired interval. Don't use it. Manual operation after an ice accumulation of 3/8 to and 3/4 inch is the proper method. Premature cycling of the boots may crack the ice enough for additional ice to form in the cracks when there isn't enough bulk to be blown away. Recycling causes expansion and contraction beneath the ice layer (called bridging), making them useless.

With clear ice, experience is a must before using the boots. If the ice has spread out and back beyond the limits of the boots, their use could form a ragged *wall* that effectively destroys lift and creates drag. It may be prudent to save the use of the boots until nothing else works.

Resurfacing

If the boot surface becomes rough or scuffed, apply a coat of conductive neoprene resurfacing cement. This coating will also help to dissipate static electricity. Static electricity can puncture the boots by causing arcing with metal.

Experimenting

One of the best ways of learning the effects of ice is to experiment in carefully controlled conditions. If you are certain you will not encounter any more ice (you are beneath the base of the clouds and expect to remain there, you can see your destination airport, etc.), now is the time to experiment and play with the boots. Actuate the system on different days with varying amounts of ice and a diversity of ice (*rime, clear,* or *mixed*).

If boots are new to you and you are not sure whether you will encounter more ice, select an ice-free cruise altitude. With more than 1/4 inch of ice, ask ATC for a block altitude 1,000 to 2,000 feet above your cruise altitude. After climbing and stabilizing the airspeed at cruise, dive back down to the cruise altitude. When the airspeed reaches the maximum (but not exceeding V_{MO}/M_{MO}), actuate the boots.

If you have waxed the boots before the icing encounter, they should be effective in removing even small accretions (1/8 inch to 3/16 inch of ice).

WINDSHIELD

The most hazardous time for the formation of ice or frost on the windshield is during takeoff or landing. Failure to clean small frost particles from the windshield before takeoff may allow them to act as sublimation nuclei which may reduce visibility to zero during the ground run.

Happiness is an electric windshield—if you turn it on before an anticipated ice encounter. Some pilots advocate you turn on the electric windshield after takeoff to warm the plastic/glass and make it more flexible to prevent breaking if a bird strike is encountered. Others turn it on at 18,000 feet during a climb, regardless of clouds or precipitation.

Some aircraft incorporate an externally mounted bracket to which is attached a removable, small, electrically heated windowpane. This pane lies up against the windshield and is quite effective as an anti-ice system.

Another windshield deicing system uses isopropyl alcohol. The alcohol is squirted on the windshield. It usually requires a reduced airspeed to operate efficiently and can eat holes in thick ice.

When icing extends to ground level, the alcohol system is inadequate. The alcohol must be turned off roughly 30 seconds before DH or MDA to allow the alcohol film to evaporate. If this isn't done soon enough, you can't see through the film. If it is done too soon, additional ice blocks the view.

FUEL SYSTEM ICING

Ice formation in the fuel system results from undissolved free water or dissolved water in suspension with the fuel. Free water can usually be drained through sump drains during pre-flight; however, if the airplane is parked outside during freezing temperatures, the free water may be frozen. If such a condition is suspected, place the airplane in a warm hangar to thaw and drain the sump drains. Water in suspension may freeze and form ice crystals that could block fuel screens, strainers, and filters.

Prevention Procedures

The use of anti-icing additives is approved for use in some piston-engine-powered aircraft. The use of hexylene glycol, certain methanol derivations, and ethylene glycol monomethyl ether (EGME) at a maximum 0.15 percent by volume substantially inhibits fuel system icing. Check your flight manual for the manufacturer's recommendation.

Chapter 8 - Aircraft Icing   PART 3 EN ROUTE

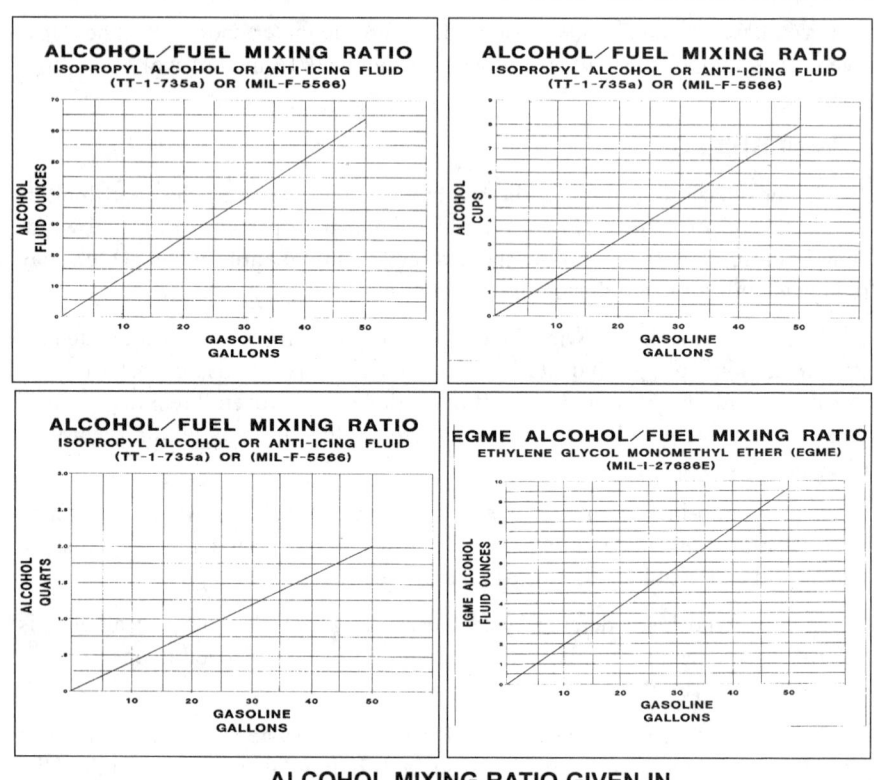

**ALCOHOL MIXING RATIO GIVEN IN
OUNCES, CUPS AND QUARTS.**

LEGALITY OF FLIGHT

General aviation operators (FAR Part 91) will find there is no specific prohibition against flight into icing conditions; however, the FARs state the airplane must be flown in accordance with the operating limitations. Check the *limitations section* of the airplane flight manual for prohibitions on flight in icing conditions. If you get into trouble, an FAA operations inspector will be looking at *careless and reckless* operation. For FAR 135 (air taxi) operators, the FAA demands a higher degree of safety for the paying passenger. Unless the airplane is certified for flight into *known icing* conditions, it is a violation of the FARs to fly into *forecast icing* or *known icing* conditions. *Known icing* may be defined *as a geographical area with vertical dimensions described by pilots in PIREPS (within the past hour), in which they have encountered structural icing.* Another instance of *known icing* occurs if you encounter ice and make no attempt to get out of it.

GROUND USE OF DEICE FLUIDS

Before taxi for takeoff during weather conditions that may allow wet snow to accumulate on the airplane, use an alcohol mixture to prevent ice buildup from the aircraft surfaces. If the ice continues to build-up during taxi or while holding for takeoff, the only solution is to taxi back and have the airplane sprayed down again or wait out the weather.

DEICE PROCEDURE

For small airplanes, removal of structural icing on the ground is best done by placing the airplane in a heated hangar until the snow and ice is melted. Use caution in taking the airplane outside immediately since pooled water can freeze in control surfaces or in the propeller spinner and hub. This can create an unbalanced condition wherein vibration will tear the airplane apart. This is no joke. Vibration can set up a harmonic vibration or oscillation that gets worse and worse until structural failure occurs. If this occurs, slow the airplane and reduce power, then land as soon as possible (not as soon as practical, as soon as possible). This problem can also occur if a warm airplane is taken outside while snow is falling.

When the airplane is covered by an accumulation of dry snow, it is easily removed with a push broom. Snow accumulation in the aileron, elevator, and rudder areas should be removed by blowing out with bottled nitrogen or dry, unheated air.

Sometimes the only deice method available is a heater. Proper procedure is to wipe away the melting ice and snow so the water does not re-freeze on some other, perhaps more critical, part of the aircraft. Use care to prevent overheating and damaging painted surfaces, fiberglass, or hydraulic lines.

If the airplane is covered by ice and snow and a heated hangar is not available:

(1) Use a push broom to remove all snow and ice that is not solidly adhering to the surface. For areas of solid ice, an effective method is to pull a hemp rope back and forth. DO NOT pound or chip the ice because of the likelihood of causing structural damage.

(2) Use an ethylene glycol solution to remove any remaining ice and snow. Application should be done in strict conformance with the recommendations of the aircraft manufacturer and the deicer fluid manufacturer. Some agents, applied full strength, may be injurious to windshields.

Anti-Ice Procedure

The same ethylene glycol solution used for deicing is also used for ground anti-icing, except it is applied full strength. The solution is sprayed or brushed over the aircraft surfaces to retard ice formation and prevent ice accumulation prior to takeoff.

The degree of protection afforded by ground anti-icing varies according to shape of the aircraft and the weather conditions. On streamlined aircraft structures, much of the anti-icing agent runs off onto the ground. Any air traffic delays before takeoff may result in additional snow/ice accumulations that necessitate a return for another deicing session.

How Long will Deicing Last?

This varies with and depends on the type and amount of precipitation (frost, snow, ice), amount of wind, type of deicing fluid, concentration of deicing fluid, thickness of fluid layer, spraying technique, and the aircraft skin temperature versus the outside air temperature. Because of these variables, it is impossible to set a recommended elapsed time limit between deicing and takeoff. Airline procedures state *deicing fluid* does not protect against re-icing resulting from additional precipitation following deicing. For this reason, procedures require another visual inspection if snow or freezing precipitation is in progress and the time elapse from the last visual inspection or deicing exceeds 20 minutes. If the aircraft has left the blocks and is awaiting takeoff clearance, the First Officer will make a visual inspection of the wing surface from the cabin windows. If ice or snow appears to have accumulated (other than a thin coating of loose snow), they return to the gate for deicing. As long as there is no evidence of slush or snow build-up on the wings, the aircraft is acceptable for takeoff.

The fact that a deicing or anti-icing treatment has been applied to an aircraft is never any guarantee that it is ready to fly when you are.

Warning

 Although ethylene glycol is chemically similar to automotive anti-freeze, it is NOT interchangeable. Automotive anti-freeze contains additives which can injure the airframe, the environment, and animals (less than one teaspoon will kill a dog).

GLYPRO System

Some general aviation operators have access to airline deice/anti-ice systems. The Glycol Proportioning System is designed to do most of the deicing with very hot water. It permits varying amounts of glycol to be applied to the aircraft from zero to 65-percent concentration.

Water is pre-heated in a tank to 140°F. When dispensed for deicing, the water passes through a heater that raises the temperature to 180°F as it leaves the nozzle.

Regardless of the outside temperature, hot water can be used to deice the aircraft, then a 30/70 percent glycol/water mixture is applied to prevent the water from freezing. The equipment provides a quick deice while using less glycol than vintage deicers.

The wind chill temperature is the governing factor on how much glycol is necessary.

- ✔ Anti-icing uses 65 percent glycol.
- ✔ Below 10°F, 50 percent glycol is applied.
- ✔ Between 10°F and 20°F, 40 percent glycol is applied.
- ✔ Between 20°F and 27°F, 30 percent glycol is applied.
- ✔ 28°F or higher, normally, the use of glycol in not required.

TAKEOFF PERFORMANCE

The takeoff performance of an airplane can be jeopardized by either an ice or frost accumulation. I've had the unfortunate experience of watching an airplane covered with frost attempt a takeoff, with fatal results. The weight of frost is not a consideration since it doesn't weight enough to affect performance. Frost does destroy the smooth flow of air over the wing significantly affecting takeoff performance.

Most pilots are aware of the hazards of ice on the wings of an airplane, but the effects of hard frost are much subtler. The weight of frost is not a consideration since it doesn't weigh much. But it does destroy the smooth flow of air over the wing.

Viscosity - The air that flows over the airplane is viscous. This means it has resistance to flow. The *viscosity* of the air expresses the degree to which it resists flow.

Friction Effects - Because the air has viscosity, it will encounter resistance to flow over a surface. This is known as *skin friction drag*. Immediately adjacent to the surface, the air particles are retarded to a relative velocity of near zero. Above this area other air particles experience successively smaller and smaller retardation until finally, at some distance above the surface, the velocity of the airflow matches that of the airstream. The layer of air between the surface and the area where the airflow matches the velocity of the airstream is expressed as the *boundary layer*.

At the leading edge of the wing there is a very thin boundary layer with the flow of air occurring in smooth laminations, that is, layers of air flowing smoothly over one another. This is called *laminar flow*.

As the flow continues back from the leading edge, friction dissipates some of the energy of the airstream and the laminar boundary layer increases in thickness and sets up waviness. Beyond this transition region the laminar boundary layer decays into a turbulent boundary layer.

Keep in mind, this is a small scale turbulent flow within the boundary layer; do not confuse it with the large scale turbulence associated with airflow separation known as *burble* that leads to a stall.

Chapter 8 - Aircraft Icing — PART 3 EN ROUTE

Effect of Frost

Frost formation will alter the shape of the airfoil. It also will affect the nature of the boundary layer where the roughness of the frost causes high surface friction and thus, a considerable reduction of boundary layer energy.

The increase in drag and the reduction in maximum lift coefficient requires additional power and will increase stall speed.

The reduction of boundary layer energy (kinetic) will cause incipient wing stalling, meaning that the air flow separation (burble) will occur at lower angles of attack. The frost may require additional speed to produce the lift necessary to become airborne and stay airborne. Typically, frost will cause a 5 to 10 percent increase in stall speed. Even if the airplane becomes airborne, it may have an insufficient margin of airspeed above the stall so that turbulence, gusts, or the increased wing loading in turning flight could produce incipient or complete stalling of the airplane.

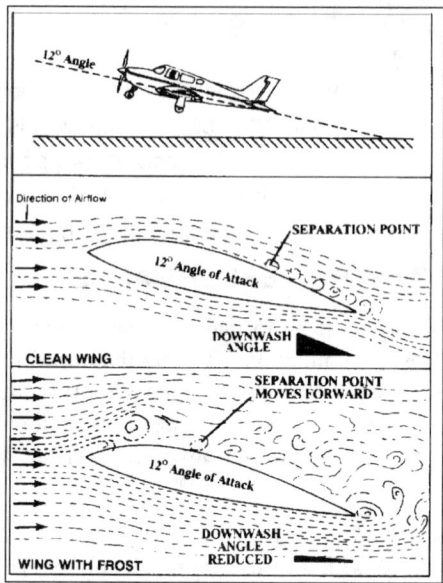

FROST CAUSING THE STALL OF AN AIRFOIL

A 12° angle of attack may result in the best angle of climb speed for a typical general aviation airplane. The critical angle of attack (stall) occurs somewhere around 16 to 18 degrees. When the angle of attack is increased to the critical angle of attack, the airstream can no longer follow the upper curvature of the wing because of the excessive change in direction. The airstream begins separating from the rear of the upper wing surface. The airstream is forced to flow straight back, away from the top surface, causing a swirling or burbling of air. This causes an increase in pressure on the top of the wing and loss of lift or stall.

The clean wing has sufficient lift to cause the airplane to climb. However, the wing with frost causes airstream separation without exceeding the critical angle of attack. Yet the result is the same ... a stall.

The problem with frost occurs because of ground effect. When the airplane is close to the ground, the ground surface will furnish a restriction to the air flow pattern and alter the wing upwash, downwash, and wing tip vortices.

Lift and drag are directly proportional. If lift is increased, drag is increased. In ground effect, with the wing at a height equal to one-tenth the span (the distance from wing tip to wing tip), induced drag is reduced 47.6 percent. At a height of one-fourth the span, induced drag is reduced 23.5 percent. At a height equal to the span, the reduction in induced drag is only 1.4 percent. After rotation the airplane may appear to be flying normally; however, when climbed out of the ground effect, the wing may stall.

Unpredictable

Frost is also very unpredictable. Barbara, a primary student, was reluctant to believe the detrimental effects of frost. She couldn't believe something that thin, that appears innocuous, would keep an airplane from flying.

We climbed into a frost-covered Cessna 150 for a training flight at Jackson, Wyo. We had plenty of runway available to take off, and if things didn't work out right, to land again. Wouldn't you know it, the darned airplane took off and performed perfectly.

However, the next day with the same student, same fuel load and apparently the same frost accumulation, the airplane would not climb out of ground effect. Rather than land right away, we continued to coax the airplane to fly until passing the point where we could safely land. We had to fly the traffic pattern, never getting more than ten feet above the ground.

 Operating in the mountains means a heated hangar is not always available. If not, it is essential that all ice be removed. The frost must be polished smooth, insuring the first third of the wing is very smooth.

You may be able to take off with some amount of frost, but it is difficult to tell how much you can fly with, safely. Operating an aircraft with frost on it is like playing Russian roulette ... you don't know when your time is up.

ICING FORECASTS

Forecast ice conditions are carried in:

- FA's (area forecasts)
- FL's (in-flight advisories) AIRMETS and SIGMETS
- UA's (PIREPS)

The winds aloft forecast provides an indication of temperatures aloft. The worst icing will occur between those altitudes having temperatures of 0°C and –10°C. Check the lapse rate for the degree of stability or instability.

MOST SEVERE ICING

Although rare, in-flight structural icing occurs in thunderstorms and mountain wave conditions at temperatures as cold as –40°C to –60°C. With conditions favoring formation of supercooled water droplets, icing is common at –25°C. But the most severe icing, statistically, occurs between 0°C and –10°C.

Chapter 8 - Aircraft Icing   PART 3 EN ROUTE

ICE AVOIDANCE ALTITUDE

Flying a small, general aviation airplane IFR demands that you have an immediate action response when you begin to get ice. The first option is to change altitude; usually a climb is the best choice. Query ATC about an ice-free altitude. If they don't have any reports, request a different routing that will avoid updrafts near the mountains. Perhaps crossing the mountains to the windward side would be an option. Whatever your choice is, don't just sit in ice.

Choose an altitude 5,000 feet or more above the forecast freezing level, and climb directly to that altitude without an intermediate level off. This should place you in an area where the temperature is colder than –15°C. If there is an inversion or convective activity present, this may not work.

 Avoid the altitude from 0°C to –10°C. Statistically this is the area where the greatest concentration of ice will occur. At colder temperatures the moisture turns to ice crystals.

ICING CLOUDS

Stratiform Clouds

In the layer-like clouds known as stratus or stratiform, the icing is not concentrated in a small area like cumulus clouds. It extends over a large area with the possibility of continuous icing. Experience shows this icing, in an individual cloud layer, is generally confined to about a 3,000-foot layer. Unless there are multiple layers that are nearly merging, an altitude change of 3,000 to 4,000 feet generally places the airplane in an ice-free operation. With merging cloud layers the icing could extend to 6,000 feet in thickness.

Cumuliform Clouds

Cumulus clouds cannot produce the icing over as great a horizontal distance as stratus clouds, but they have the ability of carrying larger water droplets in the supercooled form. The icing can occur throughout a much thicker altitude range because of the vigorous updrafts and downdrafts. When numerous cumulus clouds exist in close proximity to each other, the icing can extend as a more or less continuous icing condition. The rate of accretion is generally greater in cumulus clouds. Remember, although of shorter duration, cumulus clouds can produce severe icing conditions, especially in thunderstorms and the mountain wave at temperatures colder than –30°C and above 25,000 feet.

CONDITIONS FAVORING ICING

Keep in mind the following generalizations.

➢ Icing will occur when flying in liquid water clouds, rain or wet snow with an outside air temperature of 0°C or lower.

PART 3 EN ROUTE   **Chapter 8 - Aircraft Icing**

- The most severe icing when flying over the mountains will occur when within 5,000 feet of the mountaintops.
- The top 1,000 feet of cumulus clouds can produce heavy icing when the temperature is 0°C or lower (down to –25°C).
- Penetration of a mountain wave producing alto cumulus at temperatures of 0°C or lower has the potential of producing heavy icing.

SEASONS

Icing may occur during any season of the year, but in most of the United States, it is most frequent in winter. The freezing level is nearer the ground leaving a smaller low-level layer of airspace free of icing conditions. Frontal activity also is more frequent in winter, and the resulting cloud systems are more extensive.

Geographic regions at higher latitudes, such as Canada and Alaska, generally have the most severe icing conditions in spring and fall. During winter the air is normally too cold in these polar regions to contain heavy concentrations of moisture, and most cloud systems are stratiform and composed of ice crystals.

WING SHAPE AND AIRSPEED

Wing shape and airspeed determine to a great extent the amount of ice accretion on the wings and tail surfaces of the airplane.

When the airplane flies through air it creates its relative wind, relative to the flight path of the plane. There is an upwash ahead of the wing and a downwash behind (the cause of ground effect). At the forward edge of the wing exists a stagnation point and the forward point of the stagnation point is called a *pressure wave*. The pressure wave is the area and the cause of an airflow separation with a portion of the airflow going over the upper wing surface and the remainder along the bottom.

When air containing moisture—rain, drizzle or cloud—strikes the pressure wave, it too, must separate. Depending on the water content and temperature, some of it may collect on the wing.

The pressure wave pattern depends on the leading-edge radius of the airfoil (radius of curvature given the leading edge shape). A leading edge radius of zero (knife-edge) would create a small pressure wave and would collect a great deal of ice. A thicker wing with a larger leading-edge radius would cause a more gentle separation point and less ice forms.

Airspeed affects ice accretion where increasing airspeed decreases the pressure wave pattern and this allows the airflow less time to separate. An airspeed increase allows greater ice accumulation up to about 250 knots. Above 250 knots, aerodynamic heating from the compression of the air usually eliminates icing.

The relatively thick wings of general aviation aircraft have a smaller collection potential than turbojet aircraft that use thinner wings. The actual icing hazard for the general aviation airplane tends to be greater because of less aerodynamic heating. Also, the general aviation aircraft will be exposed to icing conditions over longer periods of time and will be confined to altitudes more conducive to icing.

FREEZING DRIZZLE/FREEZING RAIN

If freezing drizzle or freezing rain is forecast or reported, postponing the flight should be strongly considered. Freezing rain can vary from a layer of several hundred feet thick to near 4,000 feet in depth. This may, at times, require a climb of as much as 6,000 feet in order to reach the warm air above the freezing rain level.

With freezing rain reported at the departure or destination airports, the flight should be cancelled unless the pilot is experienced and has an aircraft equipped for such weather. Experienced in this case means a pilot who has flown in freezing rain previously and knows the effects. He then knows that he will not depart in freezing rain. If the freezing rain is still occurring at his destination, he will arrive there with sufficient fuel to divert to an alternate. If the condition still exists on arrival, he will then divert to that alternate without ever *poking his nose* in the freezing rain. This stuff is bad.

Consider, as an example of how bad it is, an ILS approach to the Idaho Falls, Idaho, airport during a period of light freezing drizzle, where the pilot has not been informed of the freezing drizzle or the fact that a Boeing 737 had previously missed the approach and could barely climb out of the icing. Consider also that freezing rain is much worse.

The airport elevation is 4,741 feet MSL, with an initial approach altitude of 6,700 feet (1,959 feet above the airport elevation).

While descending during the procedure turn inbound in a Cessna 414, just leaving 7,300 feet, I encountered freezing drizzle. The ice accretion rate was so fast that the approach could not be missed. Initially it took METO (maximum except takeoff) power with the gear down just to stay on the glide slope. Halfway through the approach it took full power.

The ice accumulated on the electric windshield faster than it could be shed. I anticipated sticking my arm out the side window using the control lock to scrape some of the ice off in order to see to land. I took off my watch and set it between the seats on the floor, not wanting to lose it in the slipstream.

After arrival (or maybe just a solid landing), the passenger, who was a pilot, said, *"Nice landing. Uh, the approach didn't bother me at all until you took off your watch so you wouldn't hurt it in the wreck."*

Breaking off chunks of clear ice from areas not protected by boots, we took them to the Flight Service Station to measure. They averaged four inches thick. The tail usually has two or three times the ice accumulation of the wing, since it is a thinner airfoil.

If freezing drizzle or freezing rain is forecast en route, ask yourself, "Does the airplane have the performance during single-engine operations to remain in the warm air above the rain?" If not, consider postponing or re-routing the flight. Making the flight in a single engine airplane, even if certified for flight in known icing, is foolish. There is no *out*.

MOUNTAIN ICE

Due to orographic lifting, mountain ranges cause upward air motions on the windward side. As the lifting occurs, moisture is condensed from the air making the windward side slopes and the crest above the mountain into an area of high moisture concentration. The vertical currents are capable of supporting large water droplets.

The most severe icing occurs above the crests and to the windward side of the ridges. This zone usually extends to about 5,000 feet above the tops of the mountains, but can extend much higher when cumuliform clouds have developed.

Route flights over the valleys, if possible, if a mountain wave does not exist.

MOUNTAIN WAVE ICE

Mountain wave icing occurs when the following ingredients assemble:

- ✔ Winds at ridge-level exceed 20 knots.
- ✔ The wind direction is within 30 degrees of perpendicular to the ridges.
- ✔ The air contains moisture.

During preflight planning for an instrument flight, it is wise to use sectional charts in conjunction with the en route low altitude charts to determine if your chosen airway parallels the leeward side of any mountain ranges. Flight in close proximity (within three wave crests, about 24-nautical miles) to the downwind side of the mountain could result in prolonged exposure to wave icing. The late fall through early spring is the worst time period because the wave frequency increases due to the colder, more stable air of winter in conjunction with the jet stream migrating south during the winter, providing the westerly winds aloft.

Using visualization, you can imagine the wind flowing over a mountain and when the lifting action is removed it tries to seek its original level. The mechanics of the mountain wave will cause the air to set up an undulating pattern moving from the lower area, the trough, upward until it reaches its crest and back down again. It is in the area from the trough to the crest where lifting causes cooling and condensing of the air. Supercooled water droplets collect in this area just waiting for some unsuspecting airplane to produce a disturbance that causes the water droplets to form ice on its exposed structure. The general aviation airplane, even with a turbocharger, is not immune to wave icing because of its altitude capability. The wave regularly extends beyond 20,000 feet.

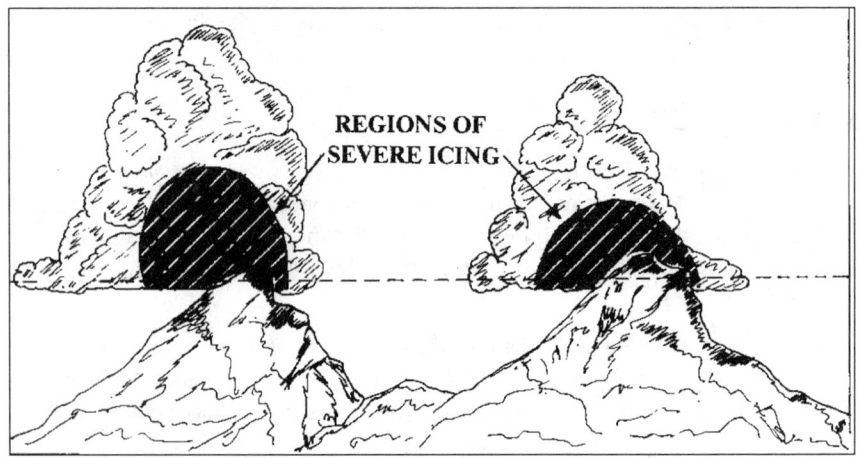

ICING OVER THE MOUNTAINS

The wavelength of a mountain wave is an indiction of its amplitude. Generally, when the wave length shortens, the amplitude becomes greater, meaning the air will be lifted to a greater altitude with the probability of creating more and larger supercooled water droplets.

As an example, assume a flight departing over flat land towards the west will approach mountains in the area of the destination during a period of mountain wave activity. The first awareness, in the form of a downdraft, of the mountain wave may not be too strong, but it will be persistent. Approaching the crest of the wave, traces of ice may appear; however, the updraft portion of the wave produces noticeably greater accretion rates.

Following this, the neutral area between two crests is encountered. As this process repeats itself, it is possible to time the interval between crests and compute the wavelength (if the ground speed is known from DME, Loran, GPS, or ask Center for a ground speed check). The shorter the wavelength, the greater the amplitude and the worse will be the ice. Obviously, if you experience a tremendous amount of ice some 50 miles downrange from the primary wave, the ice at your destination (near the base of the mountains) would approach the unbelievable.

 Remember the wavelength in the inter-mountain west averages 7 to 8 nautical miles. The wavelength in the Appalachian Mountains averages 10 nautical miles. When the wavelength is less than this, flight in icing conditions in an aircraft not equipped with anti-icing/deicing equipment is foolish.

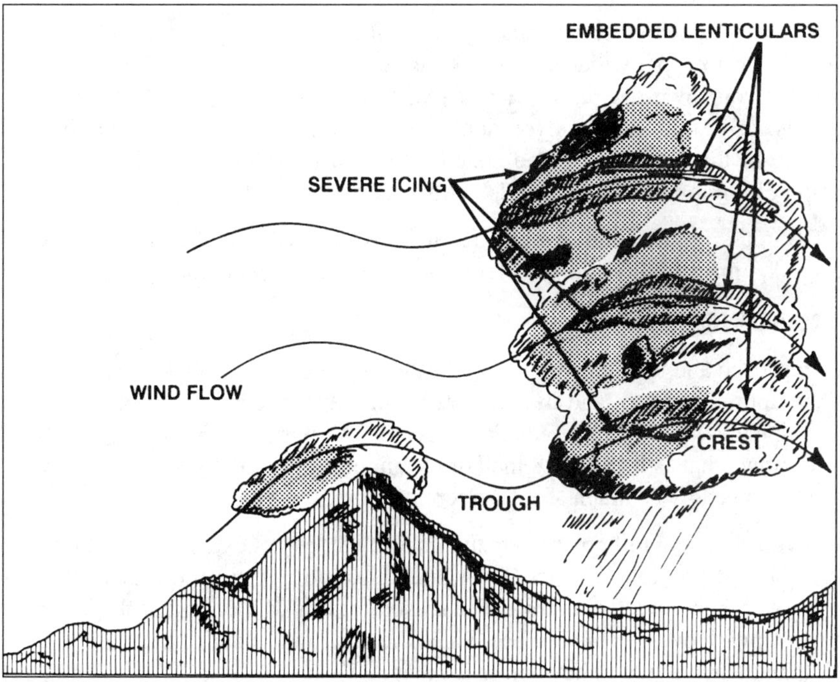

MOUNTAIN WAVE ICING

INSTRUMENT APPROACH ICE

When an airplane is cleared for an instrument approach procedure, it is clearance to descend to the minimum en route altitude until established on a segment of the approach. In low-traffic areas you may receive this clearance 30 miles or more from the initial approach fix. Thirty miles at two miles per minute equates to 15 minutes of flight. If you are operating at an ice-free altitude, it may be a wise decision, depending on the weather, to remain there until you need to descend for the approach.

Chapter 8 - Aircraft Icing   PART 3 EN ROUTE

I have descended upon receiving the original clearance into an area of icing. But, I wasn't worried because I would be descending out of the ice shortly (this is true). The accretion rate was such that it caused me quite a bit of concern before reaching the point where I could descend further. This was stupid and violated the basic premise of icing. If you get ice, get out of it. This is done by changing altitude. I knew there was an ice-free altitude above me, I was there.

You might ask ATC for a climb to a different altitude, mentioning that you are picking up ice. It alerts them to your problem so you can receive more expeditious handling.

One technique to reserve your ice-free altitude is not to alert ATC that you are descending to a particular altitude. When cleared for the approach, descent is made at your own discretion. If you say, "I'm out of 16,000 for 12,000," you must go to 12,000. Suppose you don't start picking up ice until passing through 13,000. In this case if you had stated, "I'm out of 16,000," it allows you the option of climbing without an ATC clearance (up to 15,999).

Do not accept holding pattern instructions that will place you in an area of icing. Again, tell ATC your problem. They are sure to cooperate.

LANDING WITH ICE

An approach and landing with ice on the aircraft demands special considerations. When approaching to land in an aircraft with ANY accumulation of ice on the leading edges of the wings, add 20 percent to the normal approach speed. Tests have shown that as little as 1/8 inch of ice on the wing leading edge will increase the stall speed by as much as 13 percent or more.

If you are using full power to maintain altitude, do not extend the landing gear until the last possible minute. If you use flaps, do not use more than the first *notch,* and then, *milk* them down. The reason for this caution is that flaps change the downwash over the tail surface. Since the horizontal stabilizer is a thinner airfoil than the wing, it will have more ice that may cause it to stall. A small amount of ice on the tail surface will likely change the pitch control and pitch stability. Normally there is a download on the tail. If the tail stalls, the download is removed pitching the plane forward on its nose. Do not reduce the power until you are one foot above the runway.

During the approach with ice on the airplane, the airspeed should be flown faster than normal and more power will be required to maintain the airspeed. Make a gradual flare, trying to attain level flight near the runway surface. Then, if you stall, it won't hurt you. Stall warning systems are designed for a particular airfoil section. With ice on the wing, the airfoil section has changed, but the stall warning system does not know this. The airplane may stall without any warning.

IFR IN MOUNTAINOUS AREAS

Flying IFR in mountainous areas requires extra caution because of the higher en route altitudes. The MEA (minimum en route altitude) is established on two criteria factors: MOCA and MRA.

The MOCA (minimum obstruction clearance altitude) in designated mountainous areas is 2,000 feet above the highest terrain four nautical miles to each side of the airway.

The MRA (minimum reception altitude) is that altitude which guarantees 5 milliwatts of power to the VOR receiver, which is adequate to provide reliable radio navigational signal coverage.

 The combination of MOCA and MRA establishes the MEA at high altitudes in the mountains. These high altitudes are conducive to structural icing, not only in winter, but also during the summer months.

CASE IN POINT

To prevent embellishment or total exaggeration—I have this tendency to remember exciting flights as being worse (or better) than they actually were—it was necessary to refer back to my logbook of Jan. 17, 1973, to determine the facts of an instrument flight with a student.

The Cessna 172 was eased from the hangar where the falling snow did not melt and adhere to its surface. The official weather reported indefinite ceiling, 1,500, sky obscured, visibility three miles, light snow, temperature 5°F (–15°C).

The cold temperature and falling snow held the promise that the obscuration would continue, rather than changing to a cloud condition. Very seldom does one pick up ice in this type obscuration.

My friends, Dave Low and Vince Kirol, departed ahead of us in a Cessna 180. They said they would pass on a PIREP of the actual conditions existing along V-465 from Jackson to Dunoir (a VOR 22 nautical miles northeast of JAC). Their report that they were *in and out of clouds, negative icing to 15,000,* reinforced my decision to make the flight and provide Bob with some actual instrument experience.

In those days it was necessary to call Idaho Falls Radio and we received our clearance by listening to the VOR. The takeoff was customary but the climb in the cold air was better than usual. Through 8,500 feet we went on instruments (Jackson's elevation is 6,444 feet), where a trace of rime ice began immediately. By the time we reached Dunoir it had increased to about 3/16 inch. We reversed course for Jackson.

Eight miles south of DNW, Salt Lake Center told Frontier Airlines to hold at DNW and expect approach clearance in 40 minutes, because of an inbound Cess-

Chapter 8 - Aircraft Icing   PART 3 EN ROUTE

na 172. Feeling a little guilty about holding up a plane load of anxious skiers, we called Salt Lake and told them we would accept holding at DNW to allow Frontier to make the approach first. Center and Frontier thanked us and we felt better. Besides, Bob needed the practice holding.

Arriving over DNW, we noticed over a quarter inch of rime ice. When the ice approached 1/2 inch, we decided to get clearance back to JAC. We called Center three or four times with no response. Apparently the icing on the antennas had impaired or destroyed our communications ability (and navigation signals).

We turned to JAC and informed Jackson Radio (Idaho Falls FSS) of our action (their remote communications site was close enough for communications). We hadn't gone far before hearing the most sickening noise there is in a small airplane that does not have anti-icing or deicing equipment ... wet snow slapping against the little plane. Luckily this turned out to be a small cell and we passed through it after five or ten seconds. But now the ice had accumulated to near the one-inch level.

We weren't in trouble yet, but I told the Bob, *"Maintain 14,000 until the airspeed hits 80, then maintain 80."* My confidence was plummeting with each additional cell we passed through.

Experience is a great and wonderful thing, but it gives the test first and the lesson afterwards. We were accumulating more than experience. We were sinking through the MEA when Salt Lake cleared us for the VOR approach with approach minimums of: Minimum Descent Altitude of 8,000 feet (1,556 feet AGL) and two miles visibility.

We broke out before completing the approach to minimums and landed without incident, except the plane stalled at 78-mph indicated airspeed during the flare with power off in ground effect.

The hangar was warm and cozy. We took our time looking over the airplane and measured over 1 ½ inches of rime ice on the leading edge of the wings, with over 3 inches on the antennas, vertical and horizontal stabilizer.

What is the importance of this one, seemingly isolated, icing encounter? The mountains caused the ice. We were in the clouds for a total of one hour and during that time the weather changed from an obscuration condition to one where pockets of moisture were moving through the area.

Many airways in the western states parallel the downwind side of mountain ranges where this causes prolonged exposure to icing. These icing conditions are most prevalent from October to May, but because of the high minimum en route altitudes in the mountains, icing may exist during the summer. This encounter also pointed out the increased stalling speed with ice. And, it points out the danger of relying totally on PIREPS.

PART 3 EN ROUTE Chapter 8 - Aircraft Icing

Ice is where you find it. You can pick up a load of ice flying directly in the trail of another airplane that didn't pick up ice.

GOOD OPERATING PRACTICES: IFR OPERATIONS IN THE MOUNTAINS

- ✔ Determine the cloud bases and tops from hourly sequence reports, area forecasts and PIREPS.

- ✔ Check the terrain you will be flying over and the minimum en route altitudes required along your route of flight. Compare these with your aircraft's performance capabilities. Carry supplemental oxygen if the possibility exists that you will need to climb above 12,000 feet MSL.

- ✔ For the light plane with a normally aspirated engine (non-turbo), without anti-icing or deicing protection equipment, the best advice is to avoid icing areas by finding low-altitude routes that detour areas with icing potential.

- ✔ If a mountain wave is forecast, plan your flight to avoid icing areas by flying the windward side of mountains or flying a farther distance on the downwind side of mountains.

- ✔ Cycle Gear — When a takeoff is made through water or slush, at or near freezing temperatures, in an airplane with retractable landing gear, it is possible for the gear to freeze in the up position. Precautions should be taken to prevent this by lowering and raising the gear several times after the initial retraction and after reaching a safe altitude and airspeed.

- ✔ After departure, make notes on the temperature each 1,000 feet, cloud bases, the altitudes between layers, cloud tops and the altitude the freezing level was encountered. Use the temperature record to compute the approximate lapse rate. The smaller the number, the greater is the instability because the air being lifted will be warmer than the surrounding air when the lifting action is removed. This creates a greater probability of icing.

- ✔ Use common sense after departure. Many times there are holes or cloud free areas away from the established departure route. Ask ATC for a VFR climb or deviation to avoid weather. Too few pilots take advantage of this technique.

- ✔ Frontal-weather conditions under the influence of mountains can become more intense. If you cannot avoid a front, don't fly in it for longer than necessary. Normal flight procedures call for penetration of the front at a perpendicular, taking the shortest route to cross the weather area.

- ✔ Depending on the airspeed, the temperature probe may give an erroneous reading of the outside air temperature because of aerodynamic heating. The temperature rise will probably be in the range of 2- to

Chapter 8 - Aircraft Icing   PART 3 EN ROUTE

4-degrees Celsius (this can be computed on your calculator), so when the OAT reads +4°C, it is possible to be operating in freezing air.

✔ Once the temperature probe of the OAT (outside air temperature) gauge is covered with ice it will read 0°C regardless of the outside air temperature.

✔ When exposure to aircraft icing demands that the airplane climb for avoidance, don't baby the engine. Use all available power. You may recall reports of airliner accident where the epr (exhaust pressure ratio) power was set, the airplane was approaching the runway end with insufficient airspeed to takeoff, and the plane crashed. Investigation showed icing on the probes provided an erroneous epr indication. Although more than half the throttles (power levers) were available for the addition of more power, they weren't used because the indicated epr limit was reached. When I find myself in a predicament that requires all the available power, the power levers are moved forward ... really forward, maybe creating an indent in the panel as they are moved beyond their normal range of movement.

✔ Climbing in icing conditions will expose more of the under-surface of the wings to icing. Keep the angle of attack low by climbing at a higher speed through ice. I was once told to climb with partial flaps to reduce icing under the wings; however, my small airplane's engine did not have enough power to climb with the additional drag of the flaps being partially extended. Although the addition of flaps increases the lift and changes the nose attitude to a lower angle, lift and drag are directly proportional. Increasing the lift with the use of flaps increases the drag and additional power will be needed to compensate for this.

✔ When ice is encountered, the additional drag will slow the airspeed and require additional power to maintain this reduced airspeed. The result is a greater fuel consumption and reduced range that may require diversion to an alternate airport.

✔ If you receive a clearance that contains an altitude restriction or a stepped climb or a stepped descent to your desired altitude, don't accept it if there is the probability that this will place the airplane in an area of icing. Tell ATC why you don't want to accept their clearance, and more times than not they will accommodate your needs.

✔ Whenever the airplane has more than a trace of ice, operate the controls smoothly. Because of the increase in stall speed, avoid medium or greater banded turns or pullouts that increase the wing loading significantly.

HOW RELIABLE ARE AVIATION WEATHER FORECASTS?

Have you ever wondered about the accuracy of our present-day aviation weather forecasts and services? Many pilots do so and develop an understanding of the limitations as well as the capabilities of our present day meteorology technology. The meteorologist understands some atmospheric behaviors and has watched them long enough to know that his knowledge of the atmosphere certainly is not complete. It is difficult for weather professionals to come up with rules of thumb when Mother Nature creates so many exceptions to what should be an exact science.

Pilots need to understand the limitations of observations and forecasts in order to make effective use of the weather forecast services. A major requirement for safety is to continually view aviation forecasts with an open mind, knowing the weather is constantly changing. If the forecast is old, there is a greater chance that some part of it will be in error. A weather-wise pilot looks at forecasts as professional advice rather than the absolute truth. The pilot who has complete faith in the weather forecasts is almost as bad as the pilot who has no faith at all.

Studies of the aviation forecasts indicate the following:

- Up to 12 hours—and even beyond—a forecast of good weather (ceiling 3,000 feet or more and visibility 3 miles or greater) is much more likely to be correct than a forecast of conditions below 1,000 feet or below 1 mile visibility.
- If poor weather is forecast to occur within 3 to 4 hours, the probability of occurrence is better than 80 percent.
- Forecasts of poor flying conditions during the first few hours of the forecast period are most reliable when there is a distinct weather system, such as a front, a trough, or precipitation. There is a general tendency to forecast too little bad weather in such circumstances.
- The weather associated with fast-moving cold fronts and squall lines is the most difficult to forecast accurately.
- Errors occur when attempts are made to forecast a specific time that bad weather will occur. Errors are made less frequently, of course, when forecasting that bad weather will occur during some *period* of time.
- Surface visibility is more difficult to forecast than ceiling height. Visibility in snow is the most difficult of all visibility forecasts.

Available evidence shows forecasters can predict the following at least 75 percent of the time:

- The passage of fast-moving cold fronts or squall lines within plus or minus 2 hours, as much as 10 hours in advance.
- The passage of warm fronts or slow-moving cold fronts within plus or minus 5 hours, up to 12 hours in advance.
- The rapid lowering of ceilings below 1,000 feet in pre-warm front conditions within plus or minus 200 feet and within plus or minus 4 hours.
- The onset of a thunderstorm 1 to 2 hours in advance, if radar is available.
- The time rain or snow will begin, within plus or minus 5 hours.

Chapter 8 - Aircraft Icing   PART 3 EN ROUTE

WEATHER CHECK

For most flights it is convenient and adequate to check the weather by telephone; however, when adverse weather conditions exist, it becomes difficult to make an intelligent evaluation of a go/no-go nature based upon a description of a surface weather map, a few sequence reports and terminal forecasts.

 When icing is indicated, it is suggested that the weather be checked in person (or by computer) to allow you direct access to weather charts.

Weather forecasters can identify regions or large geographic areas where icing is possible, but they cannot define the exact localities or altitudes. So what the forecasters tell you is not that there will be icing, but rather, that conditions are conducive to airframe icing. The problem with this is that, if there are any clouds and the temperature is near or below freezing, icing will be forecast. Although the conditions may be conducive to icing, the pilot ventures out and encounters not even a trace. This may occur so frequently that pilots begin to disbelieve or ignore icing forecasts. Then, when they do get into icing, many times they find their *escape* route planning has been inadequate because of the complacency instilled by the forecasters.

Your weather briefing should progress as a step-by-step process. It is important to document this information for in-flight analysis, comparisons and conclusions. A written record will also help in making post-flight reviews when you compare what happened with what you thought would happen.

To determine if a flight is feasible in your particular airplane, it is necessary to compare the icing potential to the aircraft performance and anti-icing or deicing equipment capability. Icing forecasts are helpful, but the pilot is responsible for the final decision. Forecasts (and pilot reports) are subjective. Because of the shortcomings of forecasts, the forecasts and reports concerning icing show a tendency toward the conservative side. Also, reported icing is ambiguous. Moderate ice to one type airplane may be a trace to another or heavy icing to another yet.

The only true evidence that icing conditions exist comes from PIREPS. Pilot reports are not always valid since the weather condition can change so rapidly. Use PIREPs in your evaluation of the weather situation, but don't bet your life on them.

 The evaluation of the potential for ice gained from this weather briefing should *concentrate on finding the altitudes containing moisture, the temperature at those altitudes, and the stability of the air.* This is referenced to the fact that **ice accretion is caused by** and **depends on liquid water content in the cloud, water droplet size, temperature, airfoil shape** and **aircraft speed.**

CONCENTRATE ON...

Your weather briefing to determine the icing potential should concentrate on the following:

(1) Check the SURFACE WEATHER ANALYSIS and the WEATHER DEPICTION CHART to form a *big picture* of what is happening, where it is occurring and what is causing it. Check the location of low-pressure areas, fronts and troughs. Fast-moving cold fronts usually offer quick violence, quick clearing and bumpy air. Slow-moving cold fronts may have much the same result as warm fronts with wide frontal zones of poor visibility, precipitation, turbulence, and icing above the freezing level. Frontal danger areas are ahead of a warm front or behind a cold front.

Not all fronts are severe or cause weather, the amount of moisture present is the primary factor in determining what, if any, weather occurs.

(2) Check the CONSTANT PRESSURE CHARTS. These charts depict significant information that pinpoints the location of the moisture and the temperature. Check the moisture content and stability of the air mass where you intend to fly. Temperature-dewpoint spreads and cloud types are indicators.

The constant pressure charts are prepared for five pressure levels beginning at 5,000 feet. The section on constant pressure charts will concentrate on the evaluation of these charts. The information they present is very important in forming your go/no-go decision.

(3) Read the *synopsis, turbulence* and *icing* sections of the AREA FORECAST, relating this information to the previous charts.

(4) Check The WINDS ALOFT FORECAST and compare the wind direction, velocity and temperatures with the CONSTANT PRESSURE CHARTS. The constant pressure chart is not a forecast, but rather, observed data. The winds aloft forecast should generally agree with the observed data. If there is a large discrepancy, view the other forecasts with suspicion.

(5) Look next at lifting and stability. Check the lapse rate for the stability of the air on the PSEUDO-ADIABATIC GRAPH. If not available, consult the CONSTANT PRESSURE CHARTS. The smaller the lapse rate, the greater the instability and the greater the possibility of icing. If the air is unstable, check the surface map to see if there is any type of lifting action (orographic, convective, or frontal) that could add to the instability.

(6) Check the METARs, Aviation Routine Weather Reports (hourly sequence reports) for the departure airport, destination, stations along the route, alternate, and stations in the direction of any incoming weather.

Chapter 8 - Aircraft Icing   PART 3 EN ROUTE

(7) Obtain TAFs, Aerodrome Forecasts (terminal forecasts) for en route, destination and alternate airports. Plan other alternates en route, *other than the legally required alternate,* in case the weather really turns sour.

(8) Check the *tops* from the AREA FORECASTS and PIREPS.

(9) Check for AIRMETS and SIGMETS.

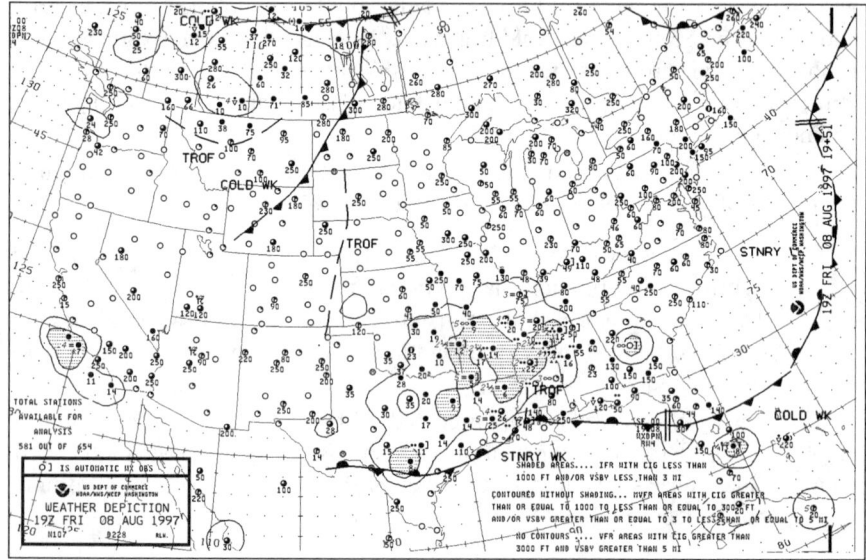

WEATHER DEPICTION CHART

WEATHER DEPICTION CHART

The weather depiction chart is one of the first charts used to begin your weather briefing and flight planning. It is possible to determine the general weather conditions more readily from this chart than any other source, pinpointing areas of favorable weather, adverse weather, and frontal systems. It is transmitted each 3 hours, beginning at 01Z each day. This chart is a computer-prepared overview (derived with information from the aviation routine weather reports) categorizing flying conditions throughout the United States.

Plotted Data

The plotted data shown for each station includes sky cover, cloud height or ceiling, weather and obstructions to vision, and visibility.

Total Sky Cover - is shown by the station circle. This circle is shaded to indicate the amount of sky cover.

| PART 3 EN ROUTE | Chapter 8 - Aircraft Icing |

Cloud Height or Ceiling - The ceiling is the height above the earth's surface (or water) of the lowest layer of clouds or obscuring phenomena that is reported as *broken, overcast,* or *obscuration,* and not classified as *thin* or *partial.* Cloud height, AGL (above ground level), is entered below the station circle in hundreds of feet. It is necessary to add two zeros to the number given. If the sky cover is few or scattered, the cloud height given is the base of the lowest layer of clouds. If the sky cover is broken or greater, the cloud height given is the ceiling. If there is no ceiling, that is, thin broken or thin overcast, the height entry is omitted. An obscured sky has a height indicating the vertical visibility into the obscuration, whereas, a height listed with a partially obscured sky indicates the base of the lowest layer of clouds.

Weather and Obstructions to Vision - are entered left of the station circle.

Visibility - Three categories on the chart (shown on the lower right of the chart for quick reference) show observed ceiling and visibility as follows:
1. IFR - Ceiling less than 1,000 feet and/or visibility less than 3 miles; hatched area outlined by a smooth line.
2. MVFR (Marginal VFR) - Ceiling 1,000 feet to 3,000 feet inclusive and/or visibility 3 to 5 miles inclusive; non-hatched area outlined by a smooth line.
3. VFR - Ceiling greater than 3,000 feet or unlimited and visibility greater than 5 miles; area not outlined.

CONSTANT PRESSURE CHARTS

A constant pressure analysis chart would probably be more properly referred to as a *constant pressure height chart.* While the surface weather chart shows pressure changes at a constant altitude, indicated conditions from the surface upward to about 5,000 feet; the constant pressure charts are prepared twice daily (12Z and 00Z) for five specific pressure levels beginning at 5,000 feet.

The charts show the contoured flow along a specific pressure height depicting highs, lows, troughs and ridges aloft. Additionally, a simplified station model presents information on temperature, temperature-dew point spread and winds aloft.

- ✘ 850-Millibar (5000-foot) Constant Pressure Chart — The 850-mb level is at 1,457 meters (4,780 feet) in the standard atmosphere.
- ✘ 700-Millibar (10,000-foot) Constant Pressure Chart — The 700-mb level is at 3,012 meters (9,882 feet) in the standard atmosphere.
- ✘ 500-Millibar (18,000-foot) Constant Pressure Chart — The 500-mb level is at 5,574 meters (18,289 feet) in the standard atmosphere.
- ✘ 300-Millibar (30,000-foot) Constant Pressure Chart — The 300-mb level is at 9,164 meters (30,065 feet) in the standard atmosphere.
- ✘ 200-Millibar (39,000-foot) Constant Pressure Chart — The 200-mb level is at 11,794 meters (38,697 feet) in the standard atmosphere.

Chapter 8 - Aircraft Icing — PART 3 EN ROUTE

Height Contours

The constant pressure chart consists of solid lines or contours drawn for a particular pressure level, for example, the 700 mb chart plots an approximate 10,000-foot level. Since the pressure changes with temperature at altitude, cold air results in a pressure altitude level lower than that found in the standard atmosphere and warm air causes the pressure level to be higher than in the standard atmosphere. The pattern formed, height contours, is analogous to the isobar pattern on a surface weather map.

These charts are above the surface friction level; therefore, the winds blow parallel to the contours. The spacing of the contours indicates the pressure gradient and gives an indication of wind speed. The closer the contours, and the steeper the gradient, the greater is the wind speed increase.

Isotherms

Isotherms, lines of equal temperature, are drawn as short dashed lines at 5°C intervals. By checking the isotherms it is possible to determine if the flight is towards warmer or colder air. Freezing temperatures and a temperature-dew point spread of 5 degrees or fewer suggest possible icing.

Isotachs

Isotachs, lines of equal wind speed, appear only on the 300-mb and 200-mb charts. These are depicted as dotted lines. Cross-hatching an area indicates wind speeds of 70 to 110 knots. A clear area within the cross-hatching indicates wind speeds of 110 to 150 knots.

Station Model

TT - temperature to the nearest whole degree C; minus sign used if negative. It is left blank if TT is missing. On the 850 mb chart, (mountain regions) where stations may be located above 850 mb of pressure a bracketed temperature (and HGT) is a computed value.

T-D - temperature-dew point spread (or depression) to the nearest whole degree C. It is left blank if T-D is missing. If T-D is less than or equal to 5°C, the station circle is completely blackened. If T-D is greater than 29°C an X is plotted. If TT is colder than –41°C, T-D is left blank because the air is too dry at those temperatures to measure dew point.

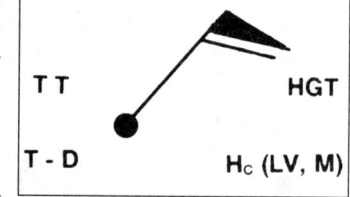

HGT - height of constant pressure surface in meters.

Hc - Height change in meters (add zero to the number) for the previous 12 hours. Not plotted when wind is *LV* (light and variable) or *M* (missing).

WIND - Wind direction and speed is plotted to the nearest 10 degrees and the nearest 5 knots using the station model arrow for direction. An arrow with a barb is 10 knots and each half barb is 5 knots. A pennant represents 50 knots.

Using the Charts

Analyzing and associating weather with upper air features is easier than it might seem. Since there are five different levels to choose from, you must determine which are appropriate for your flight. You will most likely be the most concerned with the 850 mb (5,000-foot level), the 700 mb (10,000-foot level), and the 500 mb (18,000-foot level).

First, look for areas with a temperature-dewpoint spread of less than 4°C. Suspect these areas of containing sufficient moisture to produce icing. If these areas also show temperatures between 0°C and –10°C, there is a good possibility of encountering structural icing. Look at the *station model* to determine the location of the temperature and temperature-dewpoint spread (also called the *dewpoint depression*).

After you have found an area with a dewpoint depression of fewer than 4 degrees and temperatures between 0°C and –10°C along your route of flight, check the depth of this area by referring to the other levels of the constant pressure charts.

Check the slope and wind flow. Highs and lows generally slope westward or northwestward into the upper atmosphere. Due to this slope the winds aloft of the upper system blow perpendicular across the associated surface system, and if strong, will cause the front to move rapidly. However, if the upper winds parallel a front, it moves slowly.

Check the spacing of contours on several of the charts. Closely spaced contours mean strong winds. This gives some idea of the upper air support to a surface system.

Check the temperature-dew point spread from the plotted station model. For flight altitudes between two charts, interpolate. A small spread indicates cloudiness, precipitation and, depending on temperature, icing. To readily delineate areas of high moisture content, station model circles are shaded when the temperature-dew point spread is 5°C or fewer.

There are limitations to these charts. Since they are computer prepared and transmitted every 12 hours, they are history. Even when first available, they are several hours old. But, by comparing the previous chart for the same level, you can determine the trend, whether an area is becoming wetter or dryer, have the moisture areas become larger or smaller, and are the winds aloft moving into the area becoming warmer or colder (source region). This tells you if an area has the probability of becoming better or worse.

Chapter 8 - Aircraft Icing   PART 3 EN ROUTE

As an example, an intense, cold low leans less than does a warm or weaker system. The low becomes almost vertical and is clearly evident on both surface and upper air maps. Upper winds encircle the surface low rather than blow across it. Thus, the storm moves very slowly and usually causes extensive and persistent cloudiness with heavy cumulus and cumulonimbus, precipitation, strong winds, icing, turbulence, and generally adverse flying weather. The term *cold low* describes such a system.

To illustrate why you need to develop an overall picture of what is occurring, consider on the Surface Analysis Chart. The surface weather chart (Surface Analysis Chart) is computer prepared and transmitted every three hours. Isobars depict the sea level pressure pattern. The letters *L* and *H* denote a low-pressure center and a high-pressure center. Frontal positions and types of fronts are depicted as well as a trough of low pressure with significant weather. A station model shows total sky cover, surface wind speed and direction, present weather, pressure, and pressure trend, and cloud types. But, even with all this information, upper cold lows will not show up on the surface chart. This information is acquired from the constant pressure charts.

SUMMARY

BASIC PREMISE OF ICE

If you start picking up ice, don't sit in it. Do something to get out of it ... WHEN YOU START PICKING UP ICE, GET OUT OF IT. Climb, descend, or divert away from it.

RULE OF THUMB - AIRCRAFT ICING

When you start picking up ice, get out of it. Ice is consistently dangerous.

If the water droplets are large—you can tell this if they flow back on the wing before freezing—you won't have much time before the aircraft collects so much ice you will be forced to descend to maintain airspeed. I hesitate to say *the airplane will fall from the sky*. It won't, unless you try to maintain altitude at the expense of airspeed. But, this could cause a stall where the airplane does fall from the sky. The problem here isn't just a stall, but a stall with unpredictable effects.

The atmospheric conditions that produce icing are well known by the weather forecasters. Still, some allowance must be made for the unexpected. The potential for icing and icing intensity can vary a tremendous amount within only a few minutes' time.

TEMPERATURE INVERSIONS

Temperature inversions make the planning process more difficult since there may be two or more freezing levels. Some pilots have become trapped when they climbed to a warm level and found the inversion quit en route.

A safer procedure is to climb into the cold air above the inversion—air at $-15°C$ to $-20°C$ usually contains insufficient moisture for icing—to lessen the probability of encountering ice. Exercise caution about making a flight (departure or approach) when the inversion is within a couple of thousand feet above the airport elevation and the surface temperature ranges from $-3°C$ to $+3°C$. There is frequently severe icing between the surface and the colder air above.

WEATHER CHECK

To accomplish a thorough weather check, the following weather reports, forecasts, and charts should be examined in detail:
1. Surface Weather Analysis
2. Weather Depiction Chart
3. Constant Pressure Charts
4. Radar Summary Chart
5. Area Forecasts (FA)
6. Winds Aloft Forecast
7. Lifted Index Chart
8. Aviation Routine Weather Reports (METARs)
9. Aerodrome Forecasts (TAFs)
10. PIREPS (UA - Pilot Reports)
11. In-flight Advisories (AIRMETS & SIGMETS)

PROCEDURES TO AVOID/MINIMIZE ICING EFFECTS

Be prepared to avoid or to escape the icing hazard. The following procedures will help in reducing the effects of aircraft structural icing:

- Remove all snow and ice from the aircraft before takeoff.
- Use all necessary anti-ice/deice equipment in a timely manner.
- Avoid flying in clouds when the outside air temperature is between 0°C and -20°C.
- If ice is encountered, climb or descend to an altitude where the temperature is warmer than 0°C or colder than -20°C.

Make pilot reports if icing is encountered, or if it is forecast and none is encountered.

Chapter 8 - Aircraft Icing   PART 3 EN ROUTE

GO/NO-GO DECISION

Once the icing potential has been intelligently measured, the decision to go or postpone the flight is made. In an aircraft without anti-icing or deicing equipment, the decision is more difficult. Even an experienced pilot will encounter situations to make him wonder, *"What am I doing here?"*

- ✔ Do not fly into areas of known moderate or greater icing as given in PIREPS.
- ✔ If sleet (ice pellets) occur at the surface, do not takeoff. It is a guarantee that you will run into freezing rain aloft.
- ✔ Do not depart into areas of forecast light-to-moderate icing unless VFR conditions exist under the clouds along the entire route of flight and the freezing level is at least 2,000 feet above the surface along the entire route.

If the answers to the following questions are *yes, the flight can probably be made,* in a light aircraft without ice protection, with no great problems, *IF* there are *outs* available.

- ✘ Can the flight be made avoiding the 0°C to -10°C altitudes?
- ✘ Can the flight be made avoiding the top 1,000 feet of cumulus clouds?
- ✘ Is the ceiling such that it would allow a descent into VFR conditions if too much ice were encountered en route, taking mountains and obstructions into consideration? If the aircraft performance is not adequate to climb through the icing and the freezing level extends down to the MEA, you will have some place to go for safety.
- ✘ Is the aircraft performance adequate to climb a minimum of 3,000 feet above suspected icing altitudes? The rate-of-climb is one of the best weapons available for contending with ice.
- ✘ Is the freezing level above the MEA? It is preferred that the forecast freezing level be at least 3,000 feet above the MEA. The reason for this is that:

Forecasters, through no fault of their own, can not be accurate enough for you to hang all your hopes of survival on their guess of the freezing level. A good technique is to file a couple of thousand feet above the MEA, with the freezing level forecast to be above you. Then, if you encounter ice you have some maneuvering room below you. With the freezing level forecast to be above the airplane, this cushion provides a good chance that you will descend into warmer air. If you fly the MEA and pick up ice, you have run out of options.

ICE ENCOUNTER SOLUTIONS

You only have three choices or courses of action for an ice encounter. With proper preflight investigation, you won't have to waste time trying to figure out what to do.

3-158   *Mountain Flying Bible*

180-Degree Turn

An icing encounter calls for immediate action. Often the first and best course of action for a small general aviation airplane without anti-icing or deicing equipment is the 180-degree turn. The decision to turn around cannot be delayed indefinitely. The amount of ice accumulated considering a course of action will probably be doubled after course reversal and flight to where the ice began.

Climb

If the ice accretion rate is minimal and you want to continue en route, it might be a good idea to climb to an ice-free altitude because even light icing will build up over time to the point of causing concern. If the icing is moderate, climb immediately. Icing, at least moderate icing, is generally confined to a 3,000-foot thick layer of cloud. While it can extend as much as 6,000 feet, it is unusual. Try to avoid flight between the 0°C and –10°C isotherm.

Unless there is a temperature inversion the temperature will decrease as the airplane climbs. Once the outside air temperature is sufficiently cold, any moisture should be in the form of ice crystals that do not collect on the airplane.

Inversions do occur where a climb will put the airplane into warmer air that halts ice accretion, but generally the air will not be this warm.

So why climb? You can always go down.

Descent

The descent is generally reserved as a last resort maneuver. You can always go down, but that doesn't guarantee that you will be out of the icing. When continued icing is experienced after descending to the MEA, you have run out of choices.

The ice accumulation will probably prohibit the airplane from climbing again and additional accumulations of ice will make it impossible to maintain level flight. Do not make a descent during icing unless you are sure you can get out of the icing. Most of the time it's a better choice to climb.

OUTS

Because of the unpredictability of ice, that is, how much will there will be, where it is located, what type of ice it is, and how long will you be exposed to it; it is necessary to have some *plan of action*. This plan of action consists of several *outs,* or options available if icing becomes more than you bargained for.

Outs means being able to make a 180-degree turn to better conditions; being able to climb above the ice; or being able to descend into known above-freezing temperatures at or above the MEA.

Chapter 8 - Aircraft Icing — PART 3 EN ROUTE

It is necessary to plan ahead so that you have some place to go in which to get rid of the ice, if more ice is encountered than anticipated.

To plan ahead means that you must have a proper weather briefing. You must know where the freezing level is located, know the temperature on the ground and know the temperatures aloft. Know also, the locations of cloud layers, the tops of all clouds, and the sky and weather conditions at ground level along the entire route of flight.

If, through all of your careful planning, you get a load of ice and just can't get rid of it, you had better have some place to land. Again, this is part of the preflight planning. ✈

IRREGULAR-SHAPED LENTICULAR CLOUDS (THE LEADING AND TRAILING EDGES) ARE SUGGESTIVE OF TURBULENCE NEAR THE AREA OF THE LENTICULAR.

PART 3 EN ROUTE   Chapter 9 - Emergency Landing Techniques

CHAPTER 9—SURVIVABLE EMERGENCY LANDING TECHNIQUES

TYPES OF EMERGENCY LANDINGS	3-162
PRECAUTIONARY LANDING	3-162
PSYCHOLOGICAL HAZARDS	3-163
BASIC CONCEPTS OF CRASH SAFETY	3-163
SIMULATED FORCED LANDINGS	3-165
LOW-ALTITUDE FORCED LANDING	3-166
TERRAIN SELECTION	3-167
FIELD SELECTION	3-167
DETERMINING WIND DIRECTION	3-169
PLANNED APPROACH	3-169
TOUCHDOWN	3-170
IFR AND NIGHT	3-173
CONCLUSION	3-174

When faced with an emergency landing in the mountains you will be exposed to adverse terrain conditions that have prevented previous training. The lack of exposure to this type of forced landing requires that you rely on the recommendations of others that have been in the same situation.

The probability of an engine failure causing a forced landing in the mountains is much less than running out of fuel, poor pilot technique (forgetting to use carburetor heat, poor preflight, poor flight planning), getting lost or encountering marginal weather.

Chapter 9 - Emergency Landing Techniques   PART 3 EN ROUTE

Except for a biennial flight review, once a private pilot obtains his license he is mostly on his own unless he elects further training. Most of the emergency landing training for the private pilot certificate underscores the need to find a "suitable landing area." Airplanes can be replaced, people can't. Don't make a desperate attempt to continue flying "VFR in IFR conditions," if you need to make a precautionary landing and the terrain doesn't match your mental picture of the "suitable landing area."

 By studying how to use the aircraft structure to protect yourself and your passengers, you can perform a survivable crash landing in almost any terrain.

TYPES OF EMERGENCY LANDINGS

Emergency landings are defined as:

- ✔ **FORCED LANDING**—The forced landing is an unintentional, but required landing on or off an airport, that occurs because the engine has failed or the airplane has experienced structural failure.
- ✔ **PRECAUTIONARY LANDING**—The precautionary landing is a deliberate, on- or off-airport landing caused by forethought and planning due to deteriorating weather, imminent fuel exhaustion, partial power loss or the approach of dusk in rugged terrain.
- ✔ **DITCHING**—Ditching is a planned (precautionary) or imminent (forced) landing on water.

PRECAUTIONARY LANDING

A pilot can elect to set it down (precautionary landing) before he runs out of options when he flies into adverse weather. A controlled precautionary landing into a bad field may produce better results than continuing the flight until you are forced to land.

Generally the precautionary landing is less hazardous than a forced landing because there is more time to select the landing area and the engine is available to adjust the glide path. If the approach hasn't turned out as planned, you have the option of making a go-around.

For the pilot trapped by deteriorating weather, who has ignored the fact that this situation requires a precautionary landing, he has abandoned the beneficial advantages of making a controlled landing. The alternative may be inadvertent flight into the side of a mountain.

PART 3 EN ROUTE   Chapter 9 - Emergency Landing Techniques

PSYCHOLOGICAL HAZARDS

Components of a pilot's mental makeup may interfere with his capacity to act timely and in a appropriate manner when faced with an emergency:

RELUCTANCE TO ACCEPT THE EMERGENCY SITUATION

Some pilots have an unconscious desire to keep the airplane in the air. This may go against all reason because the circumstances may put the airplane on the ground despite everything the pilot does or hopes. The unconscious longing to maintain flight may result in failure to lower the nose to maintain flying speed, procrastination in the selection of a touchdown area, and indecision in general.

DESIRE TO SAVE THE AIRCRAFT

Pre-certificate training that conditions one to expect a safe landing area can influence a pilot to avoid landing where the terrain is likely to cause aircraft damage. This has a tendency to cause pilots to try to stretch the glide to reach a better-looking field. The ensuing stall negates the decision to reach a smoother field. It can also influence the pilot into trying to make a 180-degree turn back to a runway before he has sufficient altitude to complete the maneuver.

Discounting the risks involved in the desire to save the airplane, some pilot's having a financial stake in the airplane believe that if the airplane is not damaged, the people within it will not be damaged. To hell with the airplane. If it can be sacrificed so the people can survive, so be it.

UNDUE CONCERN ABOUT GETTING HURT

Fear is fundamental and vital part of our self-preservation makeup. If fear leads to panic, it can cause improper decisions. Studying beforehand the techniques that result in successful emergency landings in adverse terrain can prevent fear where mind over matter seems to be more important than skill.

BASIC CONCEPTS OF CRASH SAFETY

A pilot who is faced with an emergency landing in terrain that makes extensive aircraft damage inevitable should keep in mind that the avoidance of crash injuries is largely a matter of:

- ✔ Keeping the vital structure (cockpit and cabin area) relatively intact by using dispensable structure (wings, landing gear, fuselage bottom) to absorb the violence of the stopping process before it affects the occupants.

- ✔ Avoiding forceful bodily contact with the interior structure.

Chapter 9 - Emergency Landing Techniques   PART 3 EN ROUTE

ENERGY ABSORPTION

The study of accidents demonstrates that it is important to have crushable structure between the impact point and the occupants. Because there is more structure in front of the occupants, it is better to strike the impact point straight ahead instead of from the side.

Energy-absorbing material has a direct bearing on the severity of the transmitted crash forces. In addition to the aircraft structure, the pilot can use vegetation, trees, fences or other man-made structures. Dense crops such as corn and grain are very effective in stopping the airplane.

OCCUPANT RESTRAINT

The second basic concept involves the requirement that the occupants avoid forcible contact with the interior structure. When seat belts and shoulder harnesses are used, it helps the occupant to decelerate at the same rate as the airplane. Without a shoulder harness, the occupant may experience a violent stop as the result of being forced forward until encountering some part of the airplane in a second collision.

Older airplanes, although not equipped with shoulder harnesses, may contain structural fittings for their installation. A shoulder harness installation is cheap insurance.

SPEED AND STOPPING DISTANCE

Deceleration during an emergency landing is controlled by ground speed and stopping distance. Speed is the most decisive in determining whether grievous harm will occur.

The severity of deceleration is governed by the square of the ratio of the actual speed divided by the desired speed. If the ground speed is doubled, the destructive energy is quadrupled.

The physics of deceleration are such that a small change in the touchdown groundspeed can have an enormous effect in the outcome of the emergency landing. For example, an impact at 80 mph is twice as hazardous as one at 56.6 mph. The occupants are three times safer crashing at 50 mph than at 86.6 mph.

Whenever faced with an emergency landing situation, decelerate, using flaps, to the slowest controllable airspeed possible. Don't worry about finding a large, flat field for your emergency landing. Very little stopping distance is required during a forced landing.

The typical general aviation airplane has been designed to provide occupant protection up to 9 gs. To give you some insight of the required forced landing area, we will examine the minimum stopping distances at various speeds, assuming a uniform 9g crash deceleration.

PART 3 EN ROUTE   Chapter 9 - Emergency Landing Techniques

At 44 knots the required distance is 9.4 feet. At 87 knots the required distance is 37.6 feet. Although the speed is not quite doubled, the distance required is four times as long.

Knowing you should have a uniform deceleration in adverse terrain allows the pilot to choose a landing area that will dissipate or breakup the dispensable structure over a short area. It is not desired that the airplane stop all at once, but rather that it decelerates evenly.

ATTITUDE AND SINK RATE CONTROL

The pilot needs to guard and protect himself from making a critical error during the execution of a forced landing. That error is the loss of aircraft attitude and sink rate at the moment of touchdown. For example, a nose low attitude may cause the nose wheel to stick in the ground and flip the airplane over. Performing last minute steep banks to adjust the flight path may result in catching a wing tip on the ground.

Although an airplane has been designed to provide protection up to 9 gs in a forward direction, there is very little protection against touchdown with a high sink rate. Vertical forces are to be avoided because the lack of cushioning can cause serious compression forces for the occupants. Try to touchdown at 500 fpm or less rate of descent.

SIMULATED FORCED LANDINGS

When a pilot simulates a forced landing, the practice helps ensure he will act promptly and appropriately during an actual emergency situation. This practice, while assisting in the development of accuracy, judgment, planning and confidence, creates two false concepts to be ingrained. The first is that the pilot will always be able to find a suitable landing field. The second false impression is that the only reason for making an emergency landing is when engine failure occurs. The collection of data reveals that flight in marginal weather and fuel exhaustion are the leading causes of forced landings.

An emergency landing demands the pilot to develop an immediate action checklist:

- Maintain aircraft control. Establish a glide at the proper speed. At low altitudes, get that nose down in a hurry to prevent a stall.
- Select a field and plan an approach.
- Perform a cockpit check.

The "cockpit check" includes using the carburetor heat, adjusting the mixture control, changing the fuel selector and adjusting the throttle. The troubleshooting must take a back seat to flying the airplane. Check for problems on a time-available basis.

Chapter 9 - Emergency Landing Techniques   PART 3 EN ROUTE

LOW-ALTITUDE FORCED LANDING

The loss of engine power, at altitudes of less than 500 feet agl, results in the low-altitude forced landing. If the engine failure occurs immediately after take-off, the airspeed will be near the best rate-of-climb. The speed deteriorates rapidly, requiring immediate action to lower the nose and obtain the best glide speed. The procedure of lowering of the nose must be an immediate action. It is wise to practice this maneuver because it is so critical to prevent stalling or to prevent an excessive sink rate.

If you think you might be tempted to turn back to the runway if you experience a power failure immediately after takeoff, it is essential that you determine the minimum altitude that will allow you to make such a turn. A decision to turn back or land straight ahead (allowing slight turns to avoid obstructions) must be punctual and precise. If you are at or above the minimum altitude (your decision height) you have determined by experimentation, you can turn back to the airport. At a safe altitude above the ground, simulate a takeoff by climbing at the best rate-of-climb speed. Reduce power to idle with the nose high attitude and transition to the best glide speed while making a descending 180-degree turn at idle power. It is necessary to add about 25 percent to the altitude you previously determined to compensate for the drag created by a windmilling propeller.

If an engine is going to fail during takeoff, it will probably do so at the time of the first power reduction. If the engine is running, it will probably continue to run until there is a change in the dynamic balance of forces. It is recommended that you maintain full takeoff power until climbing to your "decision height." Then reduce to climb power. Even though you have reached an altitude that will probably allow you to turn back to the runway, it is a hazardous maneuver involving a steep turn close to the ground. If the terrain allows landing straight ahead, or with only slight turns, land straight ahead.

LOW-ALTITUDE FORCED LANDING

GENERALLY, FOR THE LOW-ALTITUDE FORCED LANDING, LAND STRAIGHT AHEAD. IT IS DESIRED THAT YOU MAKE A SLIGHT TURN TO AVOID OBSTACLES, BUT LIMIT TURNS TO FEWER THAN 90° IN EITHER DIRECTION.

PART 3 EN ROUTE   Chapter 9 - Emergency Landing Techniques

TERRAIN SELECTION

A pilot's choice of emergency landing sites en route depends on:
- The preflight planning route that was selected.
- The aircraft's height above the ground when an emergency occurs.
- The aircraft's airspeed. If an emergency landing occurs shortly after takeoff, excess airspeed can be converted into altitude, but this is much less efficient that if you already have the altitude. Always climb at the best rate-of-climb or best angle-of-climb speed until reaching a safe altitude. Some pilots, especially with retractable gear airplanes, stay low over the runway until there is not enough runway left to land on. Altitude is more important to safety.

FIELD SELECTION

Conditioned pilots are constantly, although it may be subconsciously, looking for emergency landing sites. Obviously, you would want your emergency to allow landing at an established airport or road. In reality, the choice involves other hostile environment. Select the best of what is available. If there are cultivated fields, they will work. Even plowed fields can be acceptable if nothing else presents itself. Try to avoid areas with large rocks or boulders or any uneven field that may contain ditches. You are not searching for the largest area in which to land, but rather a suitable area.

Keep in mind that you might be able to change the aircraft heading only a few degrees to take advantage of energy-absorbing terrain that can insure a survivable forced landing.

CHANGING FIELDS

It is difficult to select the perfect forced landing spot from altitude. Pick the area that provides the best prospect for a landing. Even though you may lose a great deal of altitude before you make your final decision, do not hesitate to change one field for another that is obviously better. You just can't change your mind too often or at too low of an altitude. If you are tempted to change your mind more than once, be careful. It is better to perform a well-executed approach and landing into a bad field, than it is to make an uncontrolled landing at an established field.

FIELD LENGTH

Wind velocity and terrain slope influences the distance required to land during a forced landing. Landing on a dirt or grass-covered field may require much less distance than landing on a hard-surfaced runway. Landing on an upslope

Chapter 9 - Emergency Landing Techniques   PART 3 EN ROUTE

demands prior thought as to the technique. Remember, the airplane must transition from its descent attitude to an attitude that parallels the slope, then have enough airspeed to effect a normal landing. Approaching at the normal approach speed may not afford enough speed to complete the flare.

Do not avoid landing at a large, smooth field because of a tailwind landing approach. It may be better than a smaller field aligned with the wind.

AIRCRAFT CONFIGURATION

The purpose of flaps is to allow a steeper approach angle without an increase in airspeed. They do this by increasing lift and drag. Drag is directly proportional to lift. A direct benefit to us is that with flaps the airplane can be maneuvered at slower speeds and the stall speed is reduced. Exercise caution. The premature application of flaps may cause more altitude to be lost than you can afford.

A trick I have used to avoid a last minute disaster during a forced landing uses the flaps. Approaching the emergency landing site you determine the airplane will not make it over the ditch at the approach end. If full flaps have not been used at this point, merely fly along in ground effect until you approach the ditch. Apply the remaining flaps, lower the nose to stay in ground effect, and enjoy the balloon effect that carries you over and beyond the hazard. If you have already used the flaps, at the first moment you discover the ditch, lower the nose and move to about 3-5 feet above the terrain. As you approach the ditch, begin your flare and continue the flare, staying in ground effect, until beyond the obstacle. In either case it is important to move close to the ground. The airplane glides farther in ground effect because it causes a decrease in induced drag.

It is recommended that you practice this technique to hone your piloting skills. It's really quite simple and you will be surprised at how far you can get the airplane to float.

Should a retractable landing gear be extended or retracted during a forced landing? There are too many variables to establish a hard-and-fast rule, but the military recommends that their pilots extend the gear. Landing on a plowed field might have better results with the gear up. This is something you will have to consider and decide at the time, based on the terrain.

If your airplane is equipped with a constant-speed propeller (controllable pitch), engine failure allows the propeller to windmill. Windmilling affects the drag and consequently the glide distance. Pushing the propeller control forward results in high rpm (low pitch blade angle) that will decrease the glide distance and the extra drag steepens the glide angle. By pulling back on the propeller control, the blade assumes low rpm (high pitch blade angle) that increases the glide distance.

Forced landing checklists often recommend the master switch be turned off before touchdown to reduce the chance of a fire. It's good advice, but don't turn off vital electrical systems until they are no longer needed. Don't do it until electric flaps are extended to the desired position (or radio calls have been made).

Checklists are great and useful and needed. But, fly the airplane. Flying the airplane has priority over other considerations, including the cockpit checklist.

APPROACH

Plan your approach considering:

✔ The wind direction and velocity.
✔ The field dimensions and slope.
✔ Final approach path obstacles.

If these three factors do not seem to be compatible under the circumstances, a compromise would be to consider first the wind, then obstacles and finally the terrain. Keep in mind that it is less hazardous to strike an obstacle at the completion of the ground roll than it is while the airplane is close to approach speed. Landing on a bad landing field may be better than not being able to reach a good field.

DETERMINING WIND DIRECTION

Pilots generally maintain an awareness of the wind direction. In the mountains the wind may be modified from the steady-state wind flow. Other than a wind sock, the best wind indicator is smoke. It's obvious that smoke that rises slowly is indicative of a mild wind. If the smoke rises little before paralleling the ground, the surface wind is fairly high. The next best wind indicator is water. Examine lakes and ponds for the edge that is calm. This is the direction the wind is blowing from. I'm not great at looking at grain fields that ripple to determine the wind direction, but if it forms waves, the wind flow is perpendicular to the wave. Another obvious indicator is dust. Less obvious is the fact that cattle usually face downwind. If all else fails, assume the wind is the same as your departure airport.

PLANNED APPROACH

Good judgment in selecting an emergency landing site can be supplemented with pilot technique such as turning from base to final early or late to compensate for altitude, the use of a forward slip to dissipate altitude (preferred over S-turns) and maintain a constant glide speed.

It is difficult to establish a hard-and-fast rule for the pattern to approach a forced landing field. If there is sufficient altitude for a normal pattern, make one. This is familiar and usually results in an accurate arrival. At low altitude there isn't time to use a pattern.

Chapter 9 - Emergency Landing Techniques   PART 3 EN ROUTE

If you have the choice between using a forward slip to dissipate altitude or to use flaps, choose the forward slip because:

1. The airplane will descend rapidly, but you can discontinue the slip if you are losing too much altitude. Flaps, on the other hand also allow a rapid descent, but if too much altitude is lost and you decide to retract the flaps, you will encounter a further sink.

2. Keeping the flaps in reserve until the last moment allows slowing to your minimum approach speed. A hidden obstruction like a ditch or fence can be avoided with the addition of flaps. Merely descend to ground effect and apply the flaps.

Single-engine Cessna aircraft have a placard to "avoid slips with flaps extended." It is wise to follow the manufacturer's recommendation. The reason for the warning is due to the flap and tail configuration. When full flaps are selected, the airflow is directed downward away from the horizontal stabilizers and elevator. If the airplane is slipped, the airflow is blocked (blanketed) by the fuselage on the side opposite the slip. There is still control; however, if the slip is abruptly ended, the airflow is blocked to the other horizontal stabilizer. Now the tail is stalled and the airplane pitches nose down rapidly. My experiments involved about a 50-degree nose down angle.

TOUCHDOWN

Maintain the aircraft attitude (where the nose is in relation to the horizon) at the normal glide attitude and the sink rate will be normal. The sink rate can be reduced during the flare. Let's look at some of the unusual situations that may occur in the mountains.

CONFINED AREAS

Landing in a confined area reminds me of the cartoon where the pilot performed a forced landing between two trees. It wasn't a bad landing, it's just that the trees were the only ones for 500 miles. Sometimes it is necessary to land between two trees. If at all possible, get the airplane on the ground before impact with the trees; otherwise, it's not the impact that will get you, but the fall to the ground.

If you have selected a forced landing area where open space is at a premium, it might be wise to force the airplane down to the ground to begin deceleration before encountering obstacles. Sometimes the airplane can be ground looped to avoid hitting solid objects.

Rivers or creeks devoid of large boulders provide an alternative to rugged mountainous terrain. The area must be wide enough to reach the water without snagging the wings.

PART 3 EN ROUTE   Chapter 9 - Emergency Landing Techniques

A word of caution if you plan to land on a road. Telephone lines and power lines generally parallel the road. It is difficult, if not impossible, to see these lines under certain lighting conditions. Rather, you should search for their support structures (towers or poles).

TREES (FOREST)

Survivable tree landings, although not something to look forward to, can be accomplished by:

- Pretending you are landing at an international airport.
- Using full flaps with the landing gear extended.
- Reducing the groundspeed with flight into the wind.
- Making the touchdown at the minimum airspeed.

Make a normal landing onto the "runway" at your pretend international airport. It is important to avoid a stall where the airplane is dropped down through the trees.

✔ Even after the airplane has made contact with the trees, the rudder can be used to avoid direct contact with heavy tree trunks (even if the wings have been peeled off).

✔ Avoid areas with tall trees and thin tops. These can allow the airplane to drop to the ground. A free-fall from 75 feet beginning at zero speed will result in an impact at 40 knots, generating about 4,000 feet per minute rate of descent. Instead, find trees with lots of branches, especially those that are low.

✔ The ideal landing means wing contact should be symmetrical to prevent the loss of one wing that leads to a spinning descent.

✔ If the airplane is on the ground and contact with trees is unavoidable, try to make contact with both wings at the same time.

MOUNTAINOUS TERRAIN

Mountainous terrain with its irregularity prohibits rules for a forced landing that are cast in stone. Altitude provides more time and options when choosing an emergency landing area. The pilot at a needlessly low altitude over rugged terrain has few options available during an emergency.

The emergency landing when flying in a "v-shaped" canyon means you must land on a slope. Slope landings are always made upslope. Sufficient speed must be obtained to allow the transition from the glide attitude to the landing attitude, and then a normal landing. The importance of airspeed can be seen by examining the performance of a gliding airplane at 50 knots with a 500 feet per minute rate of descent. Such condition results in a 6-degree glide path. If the upslope landing area is 19 degrees, the aircraft's attitude must be changed 25 degrees just

Chapter 9 - Emergency Landing Techniques   PART 3 EN ROUTE

to parallel the slope. This will require a glide speed of 20 knots or more above normal. Remember, another 5-degrees to 10-degrees of pitch is required to complete the flare.

Once the airplane is on the ground, and before its momentum runs out, use full rudder to turn the airplane parallel to the mountain side to prevent sliding backwards.

WATER (DITCHING)

Water landings can be inviting when compared to a poor tree landing or landing in extremely rough terrain. Some pilots may be reluctant to make a water landing because the airplane will be lost and there is the possibility of becoming trapped inside. The only valid reason to pick a very poor landing area over water is when the water temperature is near freezing (or you see schools of sharks).

FIRE PATROL IN THE WIND RIVER MOUNTAINS, WYOMING. THE ONLY SUITABLE TERRAIN FOR A FORCED LANDING MAY BE THE LAKE IN THE CENTER OF THE PHOTO.

Factor in the following considerations before making the decision to ditch the airplane:

- ✔ The water temperature and the estimated time to be spent in the water. The survival time in water with a temperature of 33°F is less than one hour for the average person.
- ✔ The proximity to land.
- ✔ The physical condition of the occupants and their ability to swim.
- ✔ The availability of life vests and other water-survival equipment.
- ✔ The number of occupants and the number of usable exits.

PART 3 EN ROUTE   Chapter 9 - Emergency Landing Techniques

Float-plane pilots learn a method for glassy water landings. As the term implies, a large area of water is smooth and provides no visual reference for depth perception. It usually leads to one of two problems for the uninitiated, either the plane is flown into the water, hitting in a nose-low attitude, or the airplane is stalled from a high altitude. To avoid the consequences of lack of depth perception, establish a constant rate of descent and maintain that minimum descent until water impact. Approach with the landing gear retracted and use no more than half the flaps on a low-wing airplane to preclude sluing from flap failure in the water.

Most of the backcountry airstrips are located adjacent to rivers and streams. If the engine fails immediately after takeoff from one of these strips, a river landing is often the only option. The majority of these landings result in the airplane flipping onto its back. Do not panic and release your seat belt/shoulder harness before bracing your body for a fall. It is possible for this fall to cause more injury than the forced landing.

SNOW

The snow landing technique is performed the same as ditching. During a whiteout condition there is the same problem with loss of depth perception. Any "humps" hidden in the snow should be avoided. Snow is effective in hiding large obstructions with small humps.

IFR AND NIGHT

The most important thing to do during an engine failure at night flight or during IFR flight is to fly the airplane. Transition to the best glide speed. If you have time to be concerned about other IFR traffic (there's really not much in the mountains), go ahead and turn 90-degrees away from the airway.

Your previous experience flying in the area or careful study during preflight planning provides you with some idea of the terrain features you are flying over. It should also give you an indication of the ceiling and visibility to expect during the descent. ATC may be able to provide vectors to the most suitable terrain. If Center hasn't been able to help, fly into the wind. Transition from the best glide speed to the speed for minimum descent and pray.

If time permits during a VFR night flight, use the radio to notify someone of your position and situation.

The Jackson Hole night landing technique involves establishing the proper glide, then turning on the landing light. When the ground comes into view, if you like what you see, go ahead and make the forced landing. If you don't like what you see, quickly turn off the landing light. The reason the landing light is turned on at altitude is because you may be too startled to turn it off if you wait until you descend to a lower altitude.

Mountain Flying Bible

CONCLUSION

A morbid preoccupation with the prospect of a forced landing in the mountains, is grounds for avoiding mountain flight without a twin-engine turboprop or turbojet. However, it is not improper to be concerned about the possibility of a forced landing. The pilot who knows his airplane's performance and studies the proper techniques for mountain flying, need have no fear. ✈

FLYING AT LOW ALTITUDE IN THIS TYPE OF TERRAIN NARROWS YOUR OPTION FOR SELECTING A SUITABLE LANDING AREA.

PART 3 EN ROUTE   Chapter 10 - Survival and Rescue

CHAPTER 10—SURVIVAL AND RESCUE

SURVIVAL EQUIPMENT. 3-176
WINTER WOES 3-177

    The cheapest insurance you can get when flying (for no charge) is the guarantee that search and rescue will be activated if you become overdue on a flight plan. The way to obtain this insurance is to file a flight plan and then make regular position reports en route. The position report narrows down the area if a search becomes necessary.

    If you fail to close your flight plan or fail to forward an updated ETA (estimated time of arrival), a communications search will begin 30 minutes after the ETA. Flight Service personnel begin calling airports along your route of flight to see if your airplane is on the ramp. One and one-half hours after the ETA, if the plane is not found, the combined efforts of the FAA, Air Force, Coast Guard, and Civil Air Patrol, in cooperation with other state agencies and law enforcement agencies are activated for a full air and ground search.

CASCADE CANYON
GRAND TETON MOUNTAINS, WYOMING

Mountain Flying Bible

Chapter 10 - Survival and Rescue   PART 3 EN ROUTE

The expense and inconvenience of a search demands that a flight plan be closed when you arrive on the ground, whether it be your original destination or an alternate airport.

In the event (that means it has happened before and it is going to happen again) that you do make a forced or precautionary landing, remember the search team will be looking for an airplane, not people. Do everything you can to make it conspicuous . The more it looks like a sore thumb, the more likely it will be seen from the air.

Generally, it is better to stay with the airplane once you are down, unless there are compelling reasons to leave, such as the airframe being totally burned out.

Don't wander around at night in the mountains. The mountains contain steep, rugged rocks and cliffs, unguarded holes and other dangers that can be seen and avoided during the daylight.

Not all flights in the mountains are along a straight line. Even though equipped with the latest GPS or LORAN navigational equipment, it is often wise to route the flight to avoid topography that prohibits a safe forced landing.

A small, light weight tool kit should be carried. The wheel covers or propeller spinner can be removed. Some type of flammable material such as brush, moss, green pine boughs, can be added to the spinner along with some fuel to produce smoke. Smoke is internationally used to gain attention.

Occasionally the airplane will be destroyed shortly after the forced landing. In this case you have to work with whatever you have in your pockets. It's a good idea to carry waterproof matches and some type of survival pocketknife when flying remote terrain.

A first aid kit is essential to maintain basic life support after an accident. Extreme temperatures, hot or cold, require suitable protection to maintain normal body temperature. Another life support item is water.

Instead of gathering these items helter-skelter, it is best to devise a survival kit that is accessible from the cockpit.

SURVIVAL EQUIPMENT

Canadian and Alaskan law mandate that emergency rations be carried on cross-country flights (more than 25-nautical miles from the departure airport). Personal preference shapes the contents of most kits, but include the minimum that Alaska requires. In the summer you need:

- Food for each occupant sufficient to sustain life for two weeks.
- One axe or hatchet.
- One first-aid kit.

PART 3 EN ROUTE **Chapter 10 - Survival and Rescue**

- One pistol, revolver, shotgun or rifle and ammunition.
- One small gill net and an assortment of tackle such as hooks, flies, lines, sinkers, etc.
- One knife.
- Two small boxes of matches.
- One mosquito headnet for each occupant.
- Two small signaling devices such as colored smoke bombs, railroad fuses, or Very pistol and shells, in a sealed metal container.

The following additional minimum items are required from October 15 to April 1:

- One pair of snowshoes.
- One sleeping bag.
- One wool blanket for each occupant over four.

I add nylon cord, large garbage bags, warm clothing, fire-starting materials, bottled water and a flashlight to my personal kit.

If you spend your hard-earned money on a commercially prepared kit, check the contents before making the purchase. You may be able to do better with a do-it-yourself kit.

WINTER WOES

Mountain flying in the winter, compared to the summer, has obvious advantages for the light plane pilot. For example, the engine power output is greater, density altitude is lower, and snow-covered frozen terrain results in clear, stable air. There are disadvantages too. Aircraft icing can exist at lower altitudes and  may extend down to the surface. Winter cold fronts move faster than during the summer, as a general rule. Snow may cause an obscuration that obliterates landmarks as well as the horizon, and creates obscured terrain that makes it difficult to find emergency landing sites.

The argument can continue, but the affirmative side tends to equalize the negative side. One factor of primary regard to the pilot (and his passengers) concerns

Chapter 10 - Survival and Rescue   PART 3 EN ROUTE

consideration of what will happen if the airplane goes down in the winter. Will search-and-rescue prevail?

Winter aircraft accidents have a statistically high fatality rate. For the three-midwinter months of December 1979 through February 1980, for example, there were 18 en route accidents in the upper elevations of the predominantly mountainous states in the west. Fourteen of these accidents were fatal—an accident rate about three times as high as that for all general aviation. These 14 fatal accidents accounted for 36 fatalities.

Since the disappearance of Senator Hale Boggs in Alaska, emergency locator transmitters have been required in general aviation aircraft. This may reduce delays in locating a downed airplane, but it does not eliminate all delays. If the airplane crashes in a canyon or ravine, the ELT signal can bounce around and make it impossible to locate the airplane. Sometimes, too, the crash itself renders the ELT unfunctional. Remember, extremely cold weather is debilitating, causing one to succumb quickly to injuries or exposure.

Pilots flying the mountains in the winter must consider the possibility of a forced landing in uninhabited, barren terrain that is devoid of warmth, comfort or hope. Survival gear, including warm clothing, is required. It must be carried where it is accessible, inside the airplane, if the pilot or occupants are injured.

In December 1979, a family of five departed Longmont, Colorado, for a Christmas vacation trip to Southern California in a light twin Piper Apache. The pilot attempted to outclimb a 13,000-foot peak, got caught in a downdraft and crashed near Grand Lake, Colorado, located in Rocky Mountain National Park. The pilot and his three teen-aged daughters survived the impact, and their ELT activated. Because of the high, rugged wilderness terrain, rescue parties could not reach them until two days later, following 48 hours of below-freezing temperatures. After the rescue, the pilot had both legs amputated because of frostbite.

Another December accident occurred at White Pass, Washington, 35 miles west of Yakima. A Piper Comanche, loaded with a family of four, iced up and went down in the Goat Rocks Wilderness Area. After a week of extensive air and ground searching, rescue efforts were discontinued because of severe snowstorms. The wreckage was not found until nine months later when some hikers accidentally came upon it.

The NTSB investigation determined the ELT had not been properly armed and did not operate. Even if the occupants survived the impact, their continued survival would have been in doubt. There were no extra blankets, no winter clothing, no survival gear, and no food onboard the aircraft.

In 1979, a 32-year-old-missionary minister and his family was returning to Eugene, Oregon, from a Christmas holiday trip to Greenville, South Carolina, in a Piper Cherokee 180. The aircraft had been acquired for missionary work in the Philippines, and the pilot had logged 372 hours. He had also received an A & E certificate so he could perform the aircraft maintenance. He held a private pilot certificate and a recently awarded instrument rating. His family consisted of two

PART 3 EN ROUTE	Chapter 10 - Survival and Rescue

daughters, aged 11 and 2, and his 32-year old wife, also a missionary, who was expecting their third child in April.

The return cross-country flight enjoyed good weather as far as Rock Springs, Wyoming. Everyone was eager to return to school and to church commitments in Oregon. At 9 a.m. on January 12, the pilot telephoned the FSS at Rock Springs—Sweetwater County Airport for a weather briefing. He gave his route of flight as Rock Springs to Fort Bridger, Wyoming, Victor 64S to Malad City, Idaho, Victor 4S; then a northerly heading to Pocatello, Idaho. The flight would cover about 220 nautical miles, over sparsely populated, rugged, high terrain. The high, flat plateau between Rock Springs and Fort Bridger later gave way to the 10,000-foot eastern ridges of the Wasatch Range at the Wyoming-Utah border.

Rock Springs Flight Service personnel informed the pilot that airports along his proposed route were reporting low ceilings, mostly between 1,000 and 3,000-feet with visibility three to five miles. Malad City (at an elevation 4,500 feet msl, but surrounded by mountains) was reporting 600-feet obscured, visibility one mile in light snow and fog for the 0900 MST observation. The pilot also received information that the icing level along his route was forecast to be at or near the surface. Winds aloft at 9,000 feet were forecast to be predominantly out of the west-southwest at 15 up to 60 knots, increasing with altitude.

At 10 a.m. the pilot went in person to the Rock Springs FSS to get an updated weather briefing. VFR flight was not recommended because of the icing, possible obscurement in the mountains, and severe turbulence and wind shear that were forecast along his route. At the time of the second weather briefing, PIREPS reported moderate or less icing conditions, but the current area forecast called for possible severe icing in Wyoming, Utah, and Idaho. Cloud tops in the mountains were reported to be at 20,000 feet or more with bases as low as 3,000-feet agl. The pilot said that since Rock Springs was reporting VFR to Fort Bridger, he would see how it looked along the way. If it looked all right he would continue. He would open an IFR flight plan en route if necessary.

The minister-pilot's departure was preceded by another pilot (flying the same route) in a Cessna Skylane, who reported encountering a light snow shower which lasted about 10 minutes. At 8,500 feet he was clear of clouds with good visibility and good ground reference. A preflight agreement between the minister and the Cessna pilot caused them to establish communications en route so the Cessna pilot could report his situation.

After departing the Fort Bridger VOR, some 63 miles west of Rock Springs, the Skylane pilot radioed the minister that the ceiling appeared to be coming down. At this point the two aircraft were about 30-40 miles apart. About 20 miles beyond Fort Bridger, the Skylane pilot radioed the Cherokee pilot again and advised him he was going IFR. This was the last communication between the two pilots. Soon afterwards the Skylane encountered "moderate to severe" turbulence and light rime icing. The turbulence worsened as the pilot neared the area north of Logan, Utah, culminating in prolonged up and downdrafts. He was relieved to arrive safely at Pocatello.

Chapter 10 - Survival and Rescue PART 3 EN ROUTE

The missionary family in the Cherokee reached Fort Bridger at 12:16 p.m. after battling strong headwinds and turbulence. The pilot contacted Salt Lake Center and was given an IFR clearance for 12,000 feet, the minimum en route altitude between Fort Bridger and Malad City. (Normally the Cherokee, with a service ceiling of 13,750 feet, would not be able to go much higher than 12,000 feet while being operated near its maximum gross weight. The cold weather would help the Cherokee to perform better than during standard conditions. Also, there was no supplemental oxygen on board.)

At 1:34 p.m. the pilot desperately called Salt Lake Center saying that he was icing up badly in the clouds and that he was unable to maintain his altitude. He requested a terrain advisory. Center radar showed the Cherokee at 11,000 feet, approximately 1,500 to 2,000 feet above the terrain. Logan Airport, Utah, was 15 miles away at his 10 o'clock position. The pilot requested and was given vectors to Logan. (At this point the Cherokee pilot was traversing the northern end of the Wasatch Mountain Range that runs the length of Utah and bisects the state. Its high spiny ridges—lowest 9,000 feet, highest nearly 12,000 feet—are called Utah's Backbone.)

At 1:43 p.m. radar contact with the Cherokee was lost and a Frontier Airlines flight crew reported hearing an ELT signal near Logan. The Cache County (Utah) Sheriff's office in Logan dispatched deputies on foot and in snowmobiles to the approximate location of the last radar return—Logan Canyon near Tony Grove Lake, at an elevation of about 9,000 feet. They were coordinating with an Air Force C–130 that had taken off from nearby Hill AFB. They were attempting to home in on the ELT signal. Searchers, under the direction of Cache County Sheriff Doug Bodrero—a veteran of many mountain rescues—established a base camp in Logan Canyon at the turnoff for Tony Grove Lake. More than 50 searchers checked into the camp.

Daylight faded rapidly as a heavy snowfall spread over the area. There was already 10 feet of snow on the ground, and temperatures were expected to drop down to zero overnight. Finding the aircraft and its occupants quickly was essential, and the search continued into darkness.

Suddenly at 10 p.m., the ELT signal transmission ceased, forcing a halt to the search.

The next day brought zero visibility in fog and blowing snow—bogging down snowmobiles and grounding aircraft. For nine days, teams on snowshoes continued to search, but eventually the avalanche danger and the depth of the snow cover brought everything to a halt.

The rest of that winter and throughout the spring, the sheriff and his volunteers looked around Logan Canyon every chance they had, but found no sign of the lost aircraft. The spring thaw came late in 1980—not occurring until mid-June. On July 5, two mounted deputies came across the downed Cherokee on a patch of still unmelted snow in a high, narrow canyon about 100 yards from where one search team had spent the night. The four occupants had perished from exposure. The pilot, dazed or in shock, had extricated himself from the wreckage, perhaps with the intention of seeking help. His body was found slumped over the horizontal stabilizer (stabilator). Investigators theorized that the aircraft crash had precipitated a small avalanche which buried the plane below the reach of probing poles. The ELT battery's replacement date had expired nearly a year before the crash, explaining the early signal failure.

Mountainous terrain is inhospitable to downed flyers, but the winter exacerbates all problems. The pilot must be aware of the terrain and have some contingency plan established beforehand of what would happen if a forced landing occurred. When the weather turns bad en route, having the ability to fly IFR is not always an out. Aircraft icing requires not only the instrument ticket, but also an airplane equipped to handle the weather.

The possibility of a forced landing, especially a survivable forced landing, during the winter requires the pilot to plan the flight more conservatively than during another time of the year. Factors influencing the survivability include:

- **Clearing Mountains.** Because of the unique beauty and innocent look of snow-draped mountains, some pilots tend to fly too close to the terrain. Until the stability of the air is determined, fly half again as high at the mountains (subtract the base of the mountain elevation from the mountaintop elevation). Adhere to the recommendation for using supplemental oxygen.
- **Icing.** If weather reports and forecasts indicate that clouds extend to the service ceiling or higher and PIREPS indicate icing, stay on the ground unless equipped with anti-icing and deicing equipment.
- **Turbulence.** Turbulence causes enough apprehension during clear weather. PIREPS of moderate or greater turbulence may suggest the trip should be postponed or delayed.
- **ELT.** Whether or not the law requires an ELT to be equipped with a fresh battery, you are betting your life that it is. Check the ELT for functionality and that the switch is armed before your flight.
- **Sectional Charts.** The WAC chart, with its scale of about 16 miles to the inch is not as suitable for flying in the mountains as the sectional aeronautical chart with a scale of approximately 8 miles per inch. Because we rely on landmarks in the mountains, it is best to be able to see them on the chart.
- **Survival Gear.** The importance of a survival kit (summer too) cannot be over-stressed. It must be located where it is accessible. It is better to off-load fuel, baggage or passengers than it is to leave the survival kit at home.

An examination of an accident near Yosemite, California, stresses the importance of the survival kit. Newspaper reports outline an IFR flight on January 4, 1982, where a pilot, his wife and her 11-year-old son departed Mammoth Lakes

Chapter 10 - Survival and Rescue   PART 3 EN ROUTE

airport in the High Sierra Mountains of northern California. Yosemite National Park is surrounded by 13,000-foot peaks.

The single-engine Grumman Tiger departed for the flight to Concord, California. Over Tioga Pass (87 miles west of Stockton), the pilot reported severe downdrafts of 1,500 feet per minute and that he was unable to maintain his 12,000-foot altitude. The Tiger crashed at the 9,941-foot level.

Search efforts were initiated by a severe winter storm prevented an immediate rescue. Both adults died on impact. The young boy crawled inside sleeping bags and survived for five days in temperatures of –15 (producing a wind chill factor of –60 degrees). ✈

Edited from FAA GENERAL AVIATION NEWS

PART 3 EN ROUTE   Rules of Thumb

PART 3 - EN ROUTE - RULES OF THUMB

RULE OF THUMB - Increased Takeoff Distance

For each 1,000 feet above sea level, the takeoff run will increase approximately 12 percent. (See page 3-4)

RULE OF THUMB - Increased Landing Speed

The landing speed (true airspeed) will increase about 2 percent for each 1,000 feet above sea level when using the same indicated airspeed for approach as at a sea level airport. (See page 3-4)

RULE OF THUMB - Wind and Cruise Altitude

When the wind exceeds 20 knots at mountaintop level, fly half again as high as the terrain. (See page 3-7)

RULE OF THUMB—Approach all mountains and ridges at a 45-degree angle. (See page 3-24)

RULE OF THUMB—Stall Speed Increase

The stall speed increases as the square root of the wing load factor. For example, in a 60-degree bank the load factor is 2 Gs. The square root of two is 1.41, resulting in a 41 percent increase in stall speed. (See page 3-26)

RULE OF THUMB - Crossing a Ridge

When approaching a ridge and arriving at a position where you could dive, with the power reduced to idle, and hit the top of the ridge, you can commit to crossing the ridge. (See page 3-29)

Mountain Flying Bible   3-183

RULE OF THUMB – Canyon Flying

- Never enter a canyon in which there is not room to turn around (remain in a position to turn toward lowering terrain).
- Never fly beyond the point of no return.
- Fly the side of the canyon (See page 3-33)

RULE OF THUMB – Canyon Turnaround

When you approach a "tight," maintain your composure and slow down because the radius of turn decreases as the airspeed decreases. Do not reduce power to slow down. Trade airspeed in excess of the best angle of climb for altitude by climbing as you make a 180-degree turn at the steepest bank you can comfortably make. (See page 3-43)

RULE OF THUMB—Turn Radius versus Airspeed

The radius of turn varies as the square of the true airspeed. (See page 3-52)

RULE OF THUMB – Minimum Width for any Canyon Operation

Double the turn radius and add 200 feet. Do not enter a canyon that is narrower than this computed width. (See page 3-53)

RULE OF THUMB – Box Canyon Turn

✔ Slow to the minimum maneuver speed. Trade excess airspeed for altitude using back pressure on the elevator control.
✔ Make the steepest bank possible.
✔ Use flaps. (See page 3-56)

RULE OF THUMB – Base of Convective Activity

Subtract the dew point temperature from the surface temperature. Multiply this value by two. This is the altitude in hundreds of feet (add two zeros), of the base of convective activity. (See page 3-69)

PART 3 EN ROUTE   Rules of Thumb

 **RULE OF THUMB – Reduce Turbulence Effects**

When turbulence causes fishtailing, step on the right rudder (one quarter of its travel) and apply left aileron to maintain wings level flight. (See page 3-71)

 **RULE OF THUMB — Change in Weight/Stall Speed**

A two-percent change in weight causes a one-percent change in stall speed. (See page 3-72)

 **RULE OF THUMB — Maneuvering Speed Determination**

Divide the reduced weight by the gross weight. Multiply the square root of this value by V_A to determine the reduced weight V_A. (See page 3-60, 3-72)

 **RULE OF THUMB – Turbulence**

A wind velocity change of 6 knots per 1,000 feet is sufficient to produce wind shear and turbulence. (See page 3-75)

 **RULE OF THUMB Estimating In-flight Visibility**

The approximate visibility in miles will equal the number of thousands of feet above the surface when the surface is just visible over the nose of the airplane. (See page 3-108)

 **RULE OF THUMB – AIRCRAFT ICING**

When you start picking up ice, get out of it. Ice is consistently dangerous. (See page 3-156) ✈

Chapter 10 - Survival and Rescue   PART 3 EN ROUTE

FINAL APPROACH FOR RUNWAY 15 AT ASPEN, COLORADO, ELEVATION 7,674 FEET.

THERE IS A 2-PERCENT UPSLOPE ON RUNWAY 15. NORMAL OPERATIONS SUGGEST LANDING ON RUNWAY 15 AND TAKE OFF ON RUNWAY 33.

NOTE THE HIGHWAY RUNNING FROM WEST-NORTHWEST TO EAST-SOUTHEAST JUST BEFORE THE RUNWAY.

⇨ **Influenced by what is known and what is measured.**

⇨ **There is a lack of reporting stations in the mountains.**

⇨ **PIREPS enhance safety.**

PART 4 ARRIVAL

INTRODUCTION

PART 4
ARRIVAL

- CHAPTER 1 — MEDICAL CONSIDERATIONS 4-3
- CHAPTER 2 — AIRPLANE CONSIDERATIONS 4-7
- CHAPTER 3 — DESCENT RULE 4-11
- CHAPTER 4 — DESTINATION AIRPORTS 4-13

There is more to the arrival phase of flight than just acquiring information beforehand about the destination airport. When going to an unfamiliar mountain strip it is a good idea to talk to an experienced pilot in the area you desire to visit. A stop at a nearby airport will cost very little time and can provide peace of mind.

You also must know how to take care of both the passengers and the airplane while descending to avoid injury to both. The use of a descent rule, an example is given, will allow you to arrive at the destination at the proper altitude without thermal stressing the aircraft engine or hurting the passengers' inner ears.

The destination airport must be studied during the landing approach for the best departure path as well as the most advantageous landing direction. ✈

FINAL APPROACH TO RUNWAY 18 AT BIG CREEK, IDAHO.

Introduction

PART 4 ARRIVAL

FLYING BLIND

FLYING BLIND OCCURS WHEN THE SUN IS AT A LOW ANGLE TO THE HORIZON IN THE EARLY MORNING OR LATE AFTERNOON. FLYING TOWARD THE SUN AFTER TAKEOFF OR DURING APPROACH FOR LANDING CAN CAUSE ALL FORWARD VISUAL REFERENCE TO BE LOST. DURING DEPARTURE, CLIMB 2,000 FEET ABOVE THE TERRAIN BEFORE PROCEEDING ON COURSE. DURING ARRIVAL, FLY 2,000 FEET ABOVE THE TERRAIN UNTIL A SAFE CIRCLING DESCENT CAN BE MADE AT THE DESTINATION.

USE CAUTION FLYING TO A MOUNTAIN STRIP LOCATED IN A VALLEY OR CANYON. THERE MAY BE PLENTY OF DAYLIGHT REMAINING, BUT THE AIRSTRIP MAY BE IN THE DARK.

Mountain Flying Bible

PART 4 ARRIVAL   Chapter 1 - Medical Considerations

CHAPTER 1 — MEDICAL CONSIDERATIONS

- BAROTITIS MEDIA 4-3
- VALSALVA MANEUVER 4-4
- BAROSINUSITIS 4-5

Additional altitude—over that required for flying the flatland—is required for most flying in and over the mountains. The en route terrain on many flights may require maintaining a higher altitude along the entire route from the departure airport to the destination airport.

Once the airplane arrives at a mountain airport whose terrain does not allow an en route descent, you may have to descend for quite some time to arrive at pattern altitude.

Descent involves changing atmospheric pressure. This pressure change may create problems with the inner ear and sinus, especially for young children who cannot communicate the problem.

Usually these problems are just minor annoyances, but they can result in severe pain and temporary deafness.

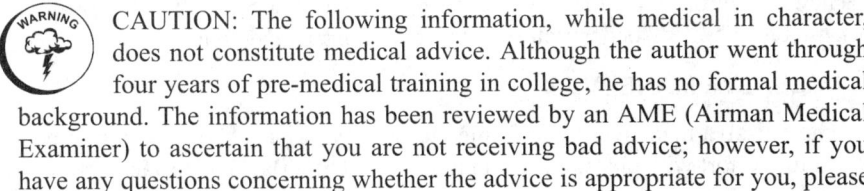

CAUTION: The following information, while medical in character, does not constitute medical advice. Although the author went through four years of pre-medical training in college, he has no formal medical background. The information has been reviewed by an AME (Airman Medical Examiner) to ascertain that you are not receiving bad advice; however, if you have any questions concerning whether the advice is appropriate for you, please contact your doctor.

BAROTITIS MEDIA

Barotitis media (also called *aerotitis media, aviation otitis, aviator's ear*) is an acute or chronic inflammation of the middle ear that is caused by a reduction in pressure in the tympanic cavity in relation to the ambient pressure of the surrounding atmosphere. It is secondary to eustachian tube obstruction.

Aviator's ear is characterized by pain, deafness, tinnitus—temporary deafness that is sometimes accompanied by ringing, buzzing or roaring sounds—and sometimes vertigo.

Mountain Flying Bible   **4-3**

Chapter 1 - Medical Considerations   PART 4 ARRIVAL

Within the middle ear is a bony cavity lined with membrane. It extends from the eardrum to the Eustachian tube. The eustachian tube is normally closed and is similar in function to a flutter valve. A flutter valve only opens in one direction. If there is a flow back, it flaps closed. The eustachian tube is normally closed. As an airplane is climbed, the valve opens to let the reduced pressure into the area of the middle ear. On descent, it is closed until actively opened by muscle effort such as by swallowing, yawning or yelling. That's why it is a good idea to chew gum during a descent.

If a passenger or child is suffering from a large negative pressure the eustachian tube muscles may not have the strength to overcome this pressure difference. It will be necessary to climb back up to altitude, equalizing the pressure and then have the person make muscle effort to open the tube periodically during the descent. Some children will be crying because of the pain and when the airplane is climbed back to the original cruise altitude, the crying will cause the eustachian tube to open relieving the pressure.

The person suffering from a cold or upper respiratory infection will experience an aggravation of this situation. If they wait too long before telling you that they are in pain, climbing back to altitude and opening the eustachian tube may not relieve the entire trauma. The soreness and deafness may last several hours. Severe trauma may last from several days to two weeks before the pain, deafness, vertigo and tinnitus disappear.

TREATMENT

The treatment of choice is to immediately climb back to the original or higher altitude. Have the person try to swallow and perform the Valsalva maneuver. If chewing gum is available, use it during a gradual descent of 300- to 400-feet per minute. Nasal vasoconstrictors like neosynephrine may help.

VALSALVA MANEUVER

The Valsalva maneuver is performed to make your ears "pop." It is a forced expiratory effort with closed nose and mouth used to inflate the eustachian tubes and middle ears.

1. **Close your mouth and keep it closed.**
2. **Pinch your nostrils closed.**
3. **Exhale forcibly through the nose.**

When your ears "pop" the pressure has been equalized. This maneuver should be continued through the descent until after landing.

A common misconception is that using the lungs and diaphragm to create a greater force should not be done because the force may damage the eardrum. This is not true. Physicians have assured me that you can use whatever force you are capable of generating without concern of damaging the eardrum.

PART 4 ARRIVAL   Chapter 1 - Medical Considerations

BAROSINUSITIS

Barosinusitis is the inflammation of the paranasal sinuses caused by a pressure difference relative to the ambient pressure within the sinus. If the condition is painful, see a doctor to obtain analgesics, systemic vasoconstrictors, infraction, or whatever they recommend to overcome this condition. ✈

TURBULENCE PRODUCERS TO WATCH FOR

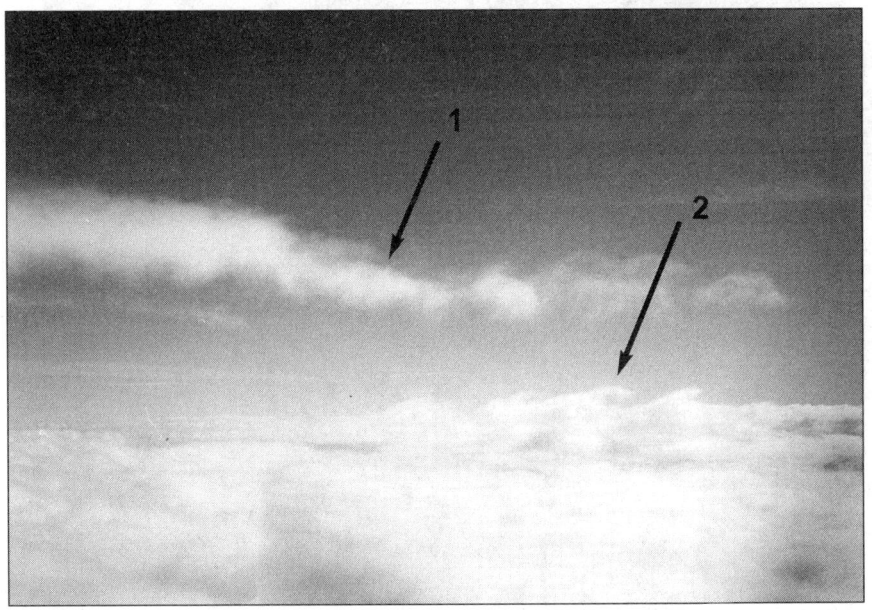

1. ROTOR CLOUDS.
2. KELVIN-HELMHOLTZ BILLOW CLOUDS. LIKE WHITE CAPS IN A LAKE, THE KELVIN-HELMHOLTZ CLOUDS INDICATE TURBULENCE.

Chapter 1 - Medical Considerations   PART 4 ARRIVAL

DESCENDING TO A MOUNTAIN STRIP SHOULD BE ACCOMPLISHED AT MANEUVERING SPEED WHILE CARRYING SUFFICIENT POWER TO PREVENT THERMAL SHOCK OF THE ENGINE.

JOHNSON CREEK, IDAHO

THE POWER-OFF DESCENT MAKES THE ENGINE SUSCEPTIBLE TO CARBURETOR ICING AND THERMAL SHOCK.

Mountain Flying Bible

| PART 4 ARRIVAL | Chapter 2 - Airplane Considerations |

CHAPTER 2 — AIRPLANE CONSIDERATIONS

- ➤ THERMAL SHOCK 4-7
- ➤ DETUNING THE ENGINE 4-8

When descending over mountainous terrain into a valley it is wise to maintain the turbulent air penetration speed or maneuvering speed whenever there is any indication that there may be turbulence. Use caution in making a rapid descent to avoid the two events that can damage the engine, *thermal shock* and *detuning*.

THERMAL SHOCK

When the engine is reduced to idle while descending, the temperature within the engine accessories may cool to below freezing in a matter of minutes. The situation is aggravated during the winter.

Shock cooling induces thermal stress to many parts of the engine such as the valves and exhaust. Warping and distortion can cause failure of certain functions, for example, the turbocharger. The turbocharger operates at temperatures as hot at 1,600 degrees Fahrenheit. If allowed to rapidly cool, it may warp and bind.

Constant-Speed Propeller

Maintain the manifold pressure within or at the bottom of the green arc, around 15 inches.

Fixed-Pitch Propeller

The rpm of a fixed-pitch propeller should be maintained somewhere around 1,500 to 1,700 rpm.

It is best to make a progressive power reduction rather than going from the cruise power setting to the recommended descent setting. Reduce the power about one third to one half of the total to be reduced. For example, if the manifold pressure is 28-30 inches at cruise flight and it is desired to reduce the power to about 12 inches manifold pressure (bottom of the green arc). The first reduction should be to about 18-22 inches of manifold pressure. Wait for about a minute, then reduce the power to the desired setting. "Babying" the engine in this manner will pay off in reliability and reduced maintenance costs.

Mountain Flying Bible

Another technique used to assist the descent is to create drag by extending the flaps and landing gear.

Some pilots disregard the advice about thermal shocking the engine and get away with it. But the cumulative effects are such that some day when needed, the engine will refuse to make power for a go-around maneuver.

DETUNING THE ENGINE

Avco Lycoming Division's Service Bulletin No. 245B provides information about detuning the engine.

Detuning the engine is the result of upsetting the balance between the cylinder pressure loads and the inertial loads of the engine.

All geared-engine models, including those supercharged or turbocharged, are susceptible to detuning. A geared engine is one that incorporates a reduction gear so the propeller turns at a speed less than the engine rpm. Also, direct-drive engines equipped with dynamic counterweights can experience detuning.

The dynamic counterweight system is mounted on the crankshaft where small flyweights move in and out to balance inertia and cylinder pressure loads. Inertia loads are inherent in the operation of the engine and increase as the engine speed increases. Cylinder pressure loads result from the compression forces of the piston, increasing as the manifold pressure increases.

The vibration caused by rotation of the propeller and crankshaft, called torsional vibration, is caused by a difference between the inertial loads and cylinder pressure loads. The purpose of the floating weights of the dynamic counterweight system is to balance any torsional vibration.

Detuning the engine (the dynamic counterweight system of the engine) happens if the engine is operated outside the parameters of normal operation of acceleration and deceleration, or speed. When operated at the low power settings of idle and taxi, both inertial and cylinder pressure loads are minimal. Even during cruise at cruise power setting, the inertial and cylinder pressure loads are in a balanced condition.

The cause of a large differential may be rapid movements of the throttle in applying or reducing power that indices the amplitude of the counterweight swing to attempt to move beyond its limits. Not only are the counterweights damaged, but also their rollers and bushings. The propeller-crankshaft system is exposed to severe torsional stress that may lead to complete engine failure.

- Misfiring of the cylinders at high engine rpm setting can cause detuning. Reduce power if engine roughness occurs.
- Performing a magneto check at a rpm setting higher than recommended by the manufacturer may detune the engine.

Detuning the engine's dynamic counterweight system falls into four operating areas that create possible engine problems.

1. Rapid Throttle Operation

Rapidly advancing or retarding the power level (throttle) is likely to cause detuning the dynamic counterweight system. A procedure that causes unintentional damage occurs during training when the power is suddenly cut to simulate an engine failure. If the power must be rapidly cut, the proper procedure is to leave the power lever in its normal position and move the mixture to the idle cut-off position. This allows the engine to continue breathing air, dampening the deceleration.

2. Propeller Feathering

When your training curriculum calls for practice propeller feathering with engine shutdown and restart, follow the recommendations above for the engine shutdown to allow normal compression forces to cushion the deceleration when the engine is shutdown. On a reciprocating engine, position the power lever to the zero thrust position before restarting to prevent detuning. On turbo prop engines, use caution to properly position the power lever in the flight idle position, not the ground idle position.

Some of my flying experience has been in Brazil. Because of the communication problem between English-speaking and Portuguese-speaking pilots with neither instructor nor trainee-pilot being proficient in the other's language, we developed a problem.

One day in Ji-Paraná, we decided to go on a training flight. There's really nothing else to do in Ji-Paraná, located in northwestern Brazil in the state of Rhondonia. I was really impressed by how my student was progressing and may have become somewhat complacent (with almost catastrophic consequences). I reached down unobserved and turned the fuel selector off on the Cheyenne 400LS. The engine surged and stopped.

The pilot went through the engine securing procedures and like a professional, called for the 'engine restart' checklist. I read the checklist, but didn't notice that the power lever was positioned to ground idle rather than flight idle. When the propeller came out of feather the airplane nearly swapped ends before ending up in a steep, that's very steep, left descending turn. It didn't take long to add power and rectify the problem. It may have been a fatal mistake had I not asked the pilot to make a maximum performance single-engine climb just prior to the engine restart. As a consequence, the airspeed was low, 140 knots, with a rate of climb around 2,000 fpm. At a faster airspeed the airplane may have experienced structural failure.

I'll tell you it scared me, and I'm fearless.

3. High Engine Speed and Low Manifold Pressure

To prevent the occurrence of detuning, avoid making a descent with high engine speed (constant speed propeller set to low pitch/high rpm) and low manifold pressure (fewer than 15 inches).

4. Excessive Speed and Power

A supercharged engine (compressed air to the cylinders is provided by a gear-driven compressor) or a turbocharged engine (compressed air to the cylinders is provided by an exhaust-driven compressor) can easily produce more power than that approved for the engine design. This allows the power lever to be moved forward at higher altitudes, producing sea-level power up to the critical altitude of the engine. Avoid power settings that exceed the limits of the engine. This is especially true during low altitude operations or when the air is much colder than standard.

OVERSPEED/OVERBOOST MAINTENANCE PROCEDURES

Pilot error leading to overboosting the engine can cause the engine to surge or backfire. If the engine is overboosted, more than an inch or two of manifold pressure, check with your mechanic to see if the manufacturer has established an inspection procedure to check for damage that may have occurred. ✈

THERMAL SHOCK
COOLING THE ENGINE TOO FAST CAUSES THERMAL STRESSES TO OCCUR IN THE ENGINE LEADING TO ENGINE FAILURE.

PART 4 ARRIVAL						Chapter 3 - Descent Rule

CHAPTER 3 — DESCENT RULE

If you are anything like me, during your first solo cross-country flights you arrived at the destination airport at cruise altitude and had to circle to lose altitude to land. Since that first flight, most pilots have worked out their own system to determine when to begin a descent to the traffic pattern.

Some pilots use a computer, figuring the time necessary to descend the necessary number of feet from cruise altitude to pattern altitude at a certain rate of descent. Others use DME (or LORAN/GPS) and ground speed. Some compute the ground speed versus their ETA to arrive at what distance out to begin the descent.

Whatever method works for you is the one you should use. Another method exists which involves mental computation rather than computer operation. It compensates for changes of ground speed during the descent.

To use this descent rule we need to define a couple of terms. First, altitude refers to the altitude in thousands of feet (think of it as the altitude divided by 1,000). Second, rate of descent is equal to the ground speed divided by two and multiplied by 10. This might sound more complicated than it is. A few examples should clear it up.

3-DEGREE GLIDE SLOPE DESCENT RULE

The advantage of using this formula is that it provides a constant descent angle with an approximate 3-degree glide path. It does not require complicated mathematical computations and it can be adjusted as the groundspeed increases during the descent. It has been used with satisfactory results in single-engine, twin-engine, turboprop and turbojet airplanes.

Airplanes with a slow groundspeed (normally those without pressurization) make a slow descent that will not hurt the passengers' ears. Airplanes with fast groundspeeds make a faster descent in terms of descent in feet per minute.

3 x ALTITUDE = DESCENT POINT
GROUNDSPEED/2 x 10= RATE OF DESCENT

Suppose you are flying an airplane with a groundspeed of 120 knots at 12,500 feet and you are landing at Jackson, Wyoming, with an elevation of 6,400 feet.

Mountain Flying Bible					4-11

Chapter 3 - Descent Rule

The pattern altitude is 7,200 feet. How far out should you begin the descent? The cruise altitude less the pattern altitude is the total number of feet to descend. Think of altitude in thousands of feet, thus 12.5 minus 7.2 equals 5.3. Round this off to five and the distance out to begin the descent is 3 x 5 = 15 miles.

The rate of descent is the groundspeed divided by two and multiplied by 10. If the groundspeed is 120, 120/2=60x10=600 fpm rate of descent. Suppose that while descending the groundspeed increases to 140 knots. Then, 140/2=70x10=700 fpm. Or, suppose that while descending the groundspeed decreases to 100 knots; then 100/2=50x10=500 fpm.

When the airspeed is increased (decreased if turbulence is limiting) during the descent, due to changes in wind direction and velocity or just the descent, it is a simple matter to recompute "half the groundspeed times ten" to arrive at the required descent rate that compensates for the change.

3 x DISTANCE = ALTITUDE ABOVE CHECKPOINT

To confirm the progress of the descent, multiply the distance from your checkpoint by three. The checkpoint may be an assigned intersection with a crossing restriction or it may be the destination airport. The product of distance times three is the altitude in hundreds of feet that represents the 3-degree glide path. For example, if you are 20 miles from the 'Podunk' intersection, 20 x 3 = 60. The 60 represents hundreds of feet, so add two zeros. To be on the proper glide path, the airplane's altitude should be 6,000 feet above the desired altitude for crossing the intersection (or arriving at the airport traffic pattern). If the altitude is higher, increase the rate of descent; if the altitude is lower, either maintain the present rate of descent or slow the rate of descent, as desired. ✈

An expert is someone who brings confusion to simplicity

PART 4 ARRIVAL   Chapter 4 - Destination Airports

CHAPTER 4 — DESTINATION AIRPORTS

- OVER-FLIGHT OBSERVATION 4-13
- FERRY FLIGHTS 4-15

Operation at a strange mountain airstrip for the first time can create apprehension, a chance of hyperventilation, or an uncomfortable nagging feeling in the back of your mind. Elimination of the unknown, that causes this uneasiness, is a simple matter when you take the time to learn about the strip and its operating characteristics beforehand.

Many times the state aeronautics division will publish an airport directory with all the need-to-know information. Other times you will have to seek out this information from an FSS specialist, Accident Prevention Counselor, or local mountain pilot. These people tend to be very helpful and if they can't answer your questions, they will generally find someone who can.

OVER-FLIGHT OBSERVATION

Operating at an unfamiliar field requires knowledge of the terrain, air currents, runway layout, length, surface condition and irregularities. Operation at any airport, in the mountains or not, should include the determination of a touchdown spot. If touchdown has not occurred by this spot, make a go-around. For an airplane that requires 1,000 feet to land under the current conditions of density altitude and wind, the airplane must touchdown by the halfway point on a 2,000-foot runway. If the runway is 1,500 feet in length, the airplane must be firmly on the ground after one-third of the runway has been flown over.

An over-flight observation of an airstrip, whether it is the first time you have operated at this strip or not, ascertains the runway surface conditions appear safe for operation. In the spring and fall the strip may be muddy enough to prevent operation. During the dry season, you may find ruts that make directional control difficult. If other airplanes are operating to and from the strip, the over-flight may not be necessary.

Another reason for the over-flight is to determine the most suitable direction for takeoff and departure. Often the takeoff direction will be based on the performance limitations of the airplane. For example, look at operating from the Flying B Ranch, located on the Middle Fork of the Salmon River in the Frank

Chapter 4 - Destination Airports   PART 4 ARRIVAL

Church River of No Return Wilderness area of Central Idaho. Takeoff to the north in an airplane with the performance of a Cessna 182 does not cause concern about the narrow canyon area just beyond the Bernard FS strip (forest service). But, while flying a 1946 Fairchild 24 with, at most, 100-fpm rate of climb,

MT. BLACKBURN, WRANGELL MOUNTAINS, ALASKA.

A STANDARD LEFT-TURN DEPARTURE ISN'T ALWAYS FEASIBLE. THE DEPARTURE PATH MUST CONFORM TO THE TERRAIN VAGARIES.

the takeoff was to the south. I just wasn't proficient at knife-edge flight through the narrows.

Exercise great caution when operating to and from one-way strips. As the name implies these are strips with one-way in and one-way out. If the approach is bungled, there is a good chance of crashing, for the terrain does not allow a go-around maneuver. Depending upon your proficiency at slow flight, using the spot landing method with consistency, your ability to plan and execute an approach, and your skill as a pilot, it might be wise to have an experienced pilot accompany you on your first flight into a one-way strip.

In choosing the touchdown spot, perform some quick mental calculations using the performance of the airplane (under the existing density altitude conditions) and the length of the available runway. For example, if your airplane requires 1,000 feet to land and the runway is 2,000 feet long, plan to get the airplane on the ground in the first half of the runway, or perform a go-around. So, too, if the airstrip is 1,500 feet in length, be sure to land in the first one-third of its length, or the airplane will go off the end.

For unfamiliar airstrips located in confined areas you must survey the terrain to determine which direction you will depart and the departure path. You can't always takeoff and make a standard pattern departure.

The landing approach pattern and departure pattern may have little resemblance to what we have grown used to calling the standard pattern. The approach or departure path must conform to the terrain vagaries that exist for the particular airport. If this means flying at low altitude through a canyon with a sharp right turn onto short final, so be it.

FERRY FLIGHTS

When you prepare for departure from a high-elevation strip with a short runway length, you may become concerned about the runway length. Now is the time to dig out the performance data from the airplane manual. If performance data cannot be determined because of a high-density altitude, mark the halfway point on the runway and use the rule of thumb (page 2-39) that 71 percent of the takeoff speed must be obtained by that mark. If not, abort the takeoff and off-load some of the baggage or passengers. Then, make ferry flights, as required, with partial loads to move everyone and everything to a strip that is suitable for takeoff with the total load. The only other option is to wait for the temperature to cool or for the wind to blow down the runway.

Determine by actual flight the takeoff distance at a given weight. The change in gross weight will be the weight of the airplane after loading divided by the weight used to determine the takeoff distance. Square this change in gross weight to determine the takeoff distance factor. Multiply the takeoff distance factor by

Chapter 4 - Destination Airports   PART 4 ARRIVAL

the takeoff distance determined by actual flight and compare this distance to the total usable runway length available. The takeoff distance varies as the square of the gross weight. See page 2-16. ✈

OFTEN THE HARDEST PART OF LANDING AT A MOUNTAIN STRIP IS FINDING THE STRIP. NOTE THE AIRPLANE IS BEING FLOWN TO THE SIDE OF THE CANYON WHILE EN ROUTE TO THE MOUNTAIN STRIP.

Experience is a great teacher, but it gives the test first and the lesson afterwards

PART 4 ARRIVAL   **Chapter 4 - Destination Airports**

MOUNTAIN FLYING BIBLE
SPARKY'S 10 COMMANDMENTS

1. Regardless of the operation-flying over the mountains, flying in canyons, or flying near ridges-**always remain in a position where you can turn to lowering terrain.** This requires a 45-degree angle approach to the terrain.

2. When flying upslope terrain, do not fly beyond the **point of no return.** This is the point where, if the power is reduced to idle, the airplane can still turn around.

3. On a short runway, if **71 percent of the takeoff speed is obtained at the halfway point,** the airplane will takeoff in the space remaining.

4. **Never enter a canyon if there is not room to turn around.**

5. Regardless of altitude, **always fly the approach for landing at the normal sea-level approach indicated airspeed** for the airplane; not slower and not faster. A 10-percent increase in approach speed causes a 21-percent increase in landing distance.

6. Thoroughly **study weather trends and conditions** before takeoff. Delay the flight during marginal weather.

7. **Approach ridges and mountains at a 45-degree angle** to allow an escape route if strong turbulence or downdrafts are encountered.

8. Do not **thermal shock** (power-off descents) or detune (rapid throttle movements) the engine.

9. Prepare an **emergency survival kit** and keep it in the airplane where it is accessible.

10. **Avoid becoming complacent.** Do not fly by rote, ignoring the warning signs of weather, terrain or wind.

Chapter 4 - Destination Airports　　　　　　　PART 4 ARRIVAL

GRAND TETON
JACKSON, WYO.

FLYING ALONG THE LEE SIDE OF THE TETONS CAN PROVE TO BE UNCOMFORTABLE WHEN THE WIND ALOFT EXCEEDS 20 KNOTS. IF A MOUNTAIN WAVE CONDITION EXISTS, PLAN TO FLY ABOUT 5 MILES FROM THE MOUNTAINS, PARALLELING THE SHAPE OF THE MOUNTAINS.

GRAND TETON
JACKSON, WYO.

BEFORE CLIMBING ON TOP OF A CLOUD LAYER, CHECK THE WEATHER FORECAST AND TREND TO DETERMINE THE CLOUDS WILL REMAIN SCATTERED OR BROKEN. NON-INSTRUMENT-RATED PILOTS MUST GUARD AGAINST BECOMING TRAPPED "ON TOP" IN THE MOUNTAINS.

PART 5 - LANDINGS   Introduction

INTRODUCTION

PART 5
LANDINGS

- CHAPTER 1 — DRAG CURVE 5-5
- CHAPTER 2 — FLAPS 5-13
- CHAPTER 3 — LANDING IRREGULARITIES 5-17
- CHAPTER 4 — LANDING CONSIDERATIONS 5-23
- CHAPTER 5 — SPOT METHOD TECHNIQUE. 5-33
- CHAPTER 6 — SOFT-FIELD LANDING 5-41
- CHAPTER 7 — SHORT-FIELD LANDING 5-43
- CHAPTER 8 — CROSSWIND LANDING. 5-49
- CHAPTER 9 — PARKING 5-55

INTRODUCTION

Reminiscing about days past often provides one with insight when analyzing the various flight maneuvers and procedures that do not turn out quite as perfect as one's expectations.

LANDING

Although my logbook shows more than 10,000 landings, not all have been "greasers." It's human nature to make excuses for a botched, or at least a less-than-perfect landing. My favorite justification is to tell myself that I constantly fly different makes and models of planes and the visual perspective changes for each airplane.

Excuses are just that. When I find myself making excuses, it is time to analyze what is happening. Reverting to my primary instructor days helps toward this end. Contemplating how landings are taught usually provides the insight to solve what has gone wrong.

Mountain Flying Bible   5-1

Introduction PART 5 - LANDINGS

 One way to make consistently good landings, especially when changing from airplane to airplane, involves basic attitude flying. That is, looking at the nose in relation to the horizon. Flying the mountains may require that you use the base of the mountains some six to eight miles away as the natural horizon.

To develop the sight picture of the required attitudes for making a perfect landing, climb to a safe altitude. First, determine the attitude for level flight. Look at the horizon line and notice where it intersects the windshield. This will probably be about two to four inches up from the base of the windshield.

Next, learn the attitude for climb at the best rate-of-climb airspeed. The horizon will intersect the side of the cowling below the nose. Memorize the position of the nose with respect to the horizon for these two attitudes. These are the *level attitude* and the *landing attitude*.

To confirm that you have these attitudes in mind, cover the airspeed indicator and make the transition from level attitude to climb attitude. When stabilized, check the airspeed indicator. If the airspeed is not within one knot of the best rate-of-climb speed, practice some more. Transition back to level-flight attitude. Check the vertical speed and altimeter to confirm level flight.

Practice these transitions—from level-flight attitude to climb attitude and back—until the airspeed can be nailed within one knot. It should take fewer than 10 minutes of practice.

Next, go through a pre-landing check and establish the normal approach airspeed. Trim the airplane to maintain the approach airspeed. Practice making the flare from the glide to level-flight attitude, pause, then continue the flare to the climb attitude. This practice should be accomplished with and without flaps.

Move to the traffic pattern. After making the perfect approach for the landing, transition to the level-flight attitude at 5 to 20 feet above the runway. When the airplane begins to sink, make a slow transition to the landing attitude. The transition to the landing attitude must be made at a rate that will not cause a balloon. The landing attitude must be reached before the actual touchdown.

Students who have a hard time developing the perspective on height above the runway will find this technique helps establish the viewpoint necessary for landing. Experienced pilots will find this technique valuable in eliminating the "thumpers" that inevitably sneak up on us all.

APPROACH AIRSPEED

 The most common mistake made by a novice pilot in operating to a high-altitude strip is that of approaching with excessive airspeed. It might be the result of inattention on the part of the pilot, or, more

PART 5 - LANDINGS   **Introduction**

commonly, it may be an intentionally flown airspeed. The pilot fails to realize that the same indicated airspeed at a high altitude results in a true airspeed of approximately 2-percent per 1,000 feet faster than indicated. This results in an automatic compensating factor when using the same indicated airspeed for approach to landing at all altitudes.

RULE OF THUMB – Approach Indicated Airspeed

Regardless of altitude, ALWAYS fly your approach for landing at the normal sea-level approach indicated airspeed for the airplane.

It is true that flight operations at a high altitude airport mean that the wings have less dense air to produce lift, the prop has less dense air to produce thrust and the engine has less air (by weight) to breathe, reducing its output. Because of this the airplane must fly at a faster true airspeed.

When the airplane flies above sea level, its true airspeed increases over the indicated airspeed by about 2 percent per 1,000 feet of altitude gain. This produces an automatic compensation for the reduced aircraft performance that is in the proportion needed for safe flight. ✈

INDIAN CREEK, IDAHO. IT'S A GOOD IDEA TO HAVE EXACT AIRSPEED CONTROL WHEN LANDING AT A SHORT AIRSTRIP.

Mountain Flying Bible

Introduction   PART 5 - LANDINGS

TELLURIDE, COLORADO (TEX)
THE TELLURIDE REGIONAL AIRPORT (VIEWED FROM THE NORTHWEST) IS PERCHED AT 9,062 FEET ON DEEP CREEK MESA, 4½ MILES WEST AND ABOVE THE TOWN OF TELLURIDE. IT IS THE HIGHEST-ALTITUDE COMMERCIAL AIRPORT IN THE U.S.

SINKING AIR CAN BE A PROBLEM DURING LANDING WHEN THE SURFACE WIND REACHES 15 KNOTS OR MORE.

NORMAL OPERATION CALLS FOR LANDING ON RUNWAY 9, TAKE-OFF ON RUNWAY 27. LANDING EITHER RUNWAY IS A DOWNHILL LANDING (RUNWAY DIPS IN THE MIDDLE).

SINKING AIR ON TAKEOFF IS NOT USUALLY A PROBLEM BECAUSE THERE IS A 1,000-FOOT DROP TO THE SAN MIGUEL RIVER.

Mountain Flying Bible

CHAPTER 1 — DRAG CURVE

- ➢ PARASITE DRAG 5-5
- ➢ INDUCED DRAG 5-6
- ➢ DRAG CURVE................................ 5-7
- ➢ AREA OF REVERSED COMMAND OPERATION 5-8

The more serious landing accidents are the result of the pilot's unfamiliarity with the *"back side"* of the drag curve (power curve). Operation on the backside of the drag curve is called operating in the *region of reverse command*.

By developing a basic understanding of drag, we can eliminate any possible problems during low-speed maneuvering in the region of reverse command. This is important because all properly executed landings, whether at sea level or a high-altitude airport, involve flying on the backside of the power curve.

The drag acting on an airplane is a combination of the "high-speed" parasite drag and the "low-speed" induced drag.

PARASITE DRAG

The density of the air causes friction on the airplane. This friction is known as parasite drag. Parasite drag is composed of several elements:

- Form drag—from the basic shape of the airplane
- Skin friction drag—due to the "stickiness" of the air, and
- Interference or Eddy Drag—created by the interference of the airflow between parts of the airplane, such as at the junction of the wing to the fuselage.

The best way to visualize parasite drag is through a demonstration. When driving down the road, roll down the window and stick your hand outside. You can feel the parasite drag. The faster you go, the greater the drag.

In fact, parasite drag increases as the square of the speed. This means that to double the airspeed of the airplane by changing to a higher-horsepower engine, it would require quadrupling the power.

Parasite drag on the airplane is the air resistance created as it moves through the air. Parasite drag is minimal at low speeds, but at high speeds the parasite drag excels and becomes an inhibitor of flight.

INDUCED DRAG

Lift causes induced drag. At cruise speed the angle of attack is at its minimum. As the airplane slows, to maintain level flight, the angle of attack must be increased. As the angle of attack increases, induced drag increases. Induced drag results from the production of lift.

When parasite drag is at a maximum, in high-speed flight, the induced drag is at a minimum. When parasite drag is at a minimum, at slow speeds, the induced drag is at its maximum.

Induced drag varies inversely with the square of the airspeed. For example, when the speed is cut in half, induced drag quadruples. This is just the opposite to the creation of parasite drag.

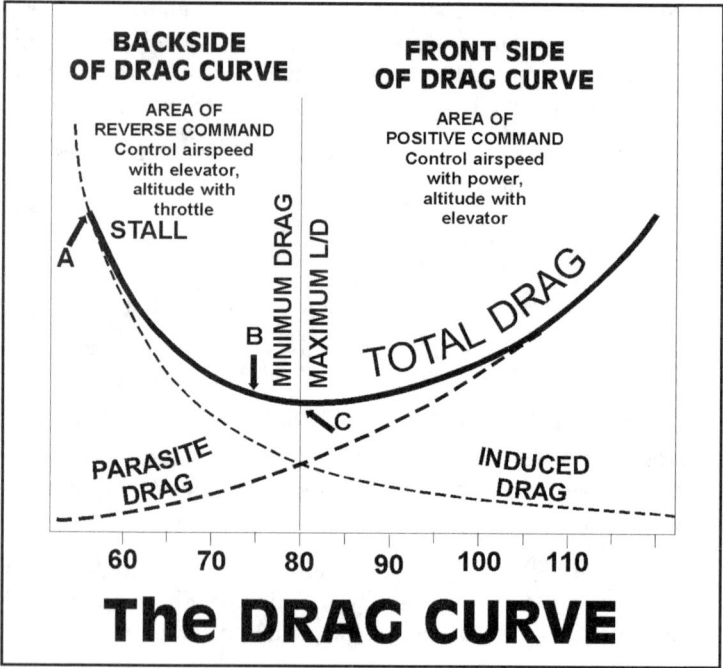

DRAG CURVE

At any particular point in time, an airplane in flight is influenced by both *induced drag*, associated with lift, and *parasite drag*, associated with resistance of the airplane's movement through the air. The combined effect is called the total drag. Looking at a drag curve provides us with information of interest in obtaining specific performance from the airplane.

A – Point A represents the point at which the critical angle of attack is obtained during a slow deceleration of airspeed. The point immediately preceding the stall is known as the *maximum lift coefficient*. Any further increase in angle of attack, reduction in airspeed or turbulence will cause the airfoil to stall.

B – Point B is determined by multiplying the speed of Point C by 75 percent (0.75). It's significance is that it is this speed that provides the *maximum range* for the airplane in a no-wind condition and during an engine failure, it will give the *minimum rate of descent*. With power available, flying this speed results in *maximum endurance*.

C – Point C is called L/D_{MAX} (max lift over drag). It is at this point that parasite drag and induced drag are at their combined minimum. Max L/D is called the *maximum range speed* for flight in a no-wind condition.

It seems strange that glide information cannot be found in the *Performance* section of many Pilot Operating Handbooks. Instead, you must go to the *Emergency Procedures* section and look under *Airspeeds for Safe Operation*. Here you can find the value of the maximum glide that represents the L/D_{MAX} point on the graph (drag curve).

FRONT SIDE OF DRAG CURVE

Examination of the drag curve shows the "backside of drag curve" on the left and "front side of drag curve" on the right. The front side of drag curve is to the right of the max L/D speed where the airplane is said to exhibit speed stability. Flight in this area is relatively efficient, as efficient as the design of the wing allows. Normally, to change altitude, the pilot moves the elevator control; to change speed, the pilot adjust the power level. Although, the pilot may use a combination of pitch change and power change. Operation on the backside of the drag curve is different.

BACKSIDE OF DRAG CURVE

The area to the left of the max L/D point is called the backside of the drag curve. This is the operation area that all pilots should be concerned with and strive to understand.

Primary flight training taught us the basic principle of flight, that attitude plus power equals performance. If the airplane attitude—where the nose is in relation to the horizon—remains constant and the power setting remains constant, the airplane will maintain a constant airspeed.

If the power is changed, either an increase or decrease, the nose (attitude) must be changed to maintain a constant airspeed.

Suppose the nose is in the normal glide attitude and the power has been reduced to maintain the desired approach speed, when the pilot sees the airplane below the desired glide path. Usually the first reaction is to ease back on the control wheel. This should not be done. When the angle of attack is increased, it will increase the induced drag. The increased induced drag increases the rate of descent. There is a point where the drag increases and the rate of descent increases and the pilot is unable to arrest the descent, even with full power. It is necessary to lower the nose to increase the airspeed. Remember, when operating on the backside of the drag curve, control the airspeed with the elevator (angle of attack) and the altitude (rate of climb or rate of descent) with the power control.

When you interpret the various signals on approach and determine the airplane is too high, the first reaction is to lower the nose. This is undesired since the airspeed will increase. The increased speed will cause the airplane to float during the landing. Instead, reduce the power and let the nose of the airplane readjust to maintain a constant airspeed. If the airplane is properly trimmed, this readjustment will occur all by itself.

Proper flight technique involves the following:

- **TOO LOW ON APPROACH** — Increase pitch and power.
- **TOO HIGH ON APPROACH** — Decrease pitch and power.

Rule of Thumb – Landing Flight Path Adjustments

Maintain the airspeed with elevator and altitude with throttle.

BACKSIDE OF DRAG CURVE OPERATION

It is important that the airplane be properly trimmed during the landing approach. It simplifies the matter of airspeed control. Be sure to trim for the approach speed so that you can take your hand from the control wheel and the airspeed remains constant.

With the airplane trimmed, try making power changes. If the power is reduced the nose will lower by itself and maintain the same airspeed. If power is added, the nose will raise and maintain a constant airspeed.

Suppose an approach is made to a mountain strip at a slow speed and high angle of attack. When the flare is attempted, the increased angle of attack may cause an increase in induced drag with a further loss of airspeed that prevents the airplane from reacting to the flare. The result is a higher sink rate. Most general aviation airplanes do not have excess power available to recover or cushion the landing. It is important, then, to maintain the proper approach airspeed, probably a speed that is faster than max L/D (the best glide speed).

BEST GLIDE SPEED

The maximum glide angle through the air is obtained when the airplane is flown at max L/D. Luckily we don't have to be exact within one knot to obtain this performance. A 5-percent deviation in speed from the best glide speed does not cause a significant reduction of the glide ratio. For example, the Cessna 150M, operated at gross weight has a best glide speed of 60 knots. This means that if the airspeed is maintained within 57 to 63 knots, the best glide ratio performance will be realized.

 An airplane, regardless of its weight, can aerodynamically be operated at max L/D. The speed at which max L/D occurs changes, but the performance or glide ratio, remains the same for a heavily loaded airplane or a lightly loaded airplane. It doesn't seem right, but that's the way it works.

GLIDE SPEED AND WEIGHT

Two identical airplanes operated at the same altitude with different weights can obtain the same glide ratio, the difference being that the heavy airplane will maintain a faster speed and greater rate of descent to obtain the optimum glide ratio.

$$\frac{V_2}{V_1} = \frac{W_2}{W_1}$$

The following formula does not require extensive study, it sets up a relationship to make easy calculations of the glide speed with differences in weight.

Where

V_1 = best glide speed at maximum allowable gross weight, W_1

V_2 = best glide speed at reduced gross weight, W_2

The relationship shown means a 10-percent increase in gross weight requires a 5-percent increase in glide speed to obtain max L/D.

EFFECT OF ALTITUDE

Altitude has an insignificant effect on glide performance if the max L/D speed is maintained. Using the same indicated airspeed for max L/D at all altitudes causes the required true airspeed changes to obtain max L/D.

EFFECT OF CONFIGURATION

The application of flaps or extension of the landing gear will have an adverse effect on the glide ratio, causing a large reduction in the glide distance.

EFFECT OF WIND

A headwind (decreases the glide distance) or tailwind (increases the glide distance) has an effect on the glide distance, not the glide ratio. Unless a headwind is greater than 25 percent of the max L/D speed, ignore it. When more than 25 percent of the max L/D speed, increase the glide speed by the amount of headwind over the max L/D speed to obtain the maximum possible distance flown over the ground.

One of the best ways of dealing with wind is to use the spot method for landing. Pick the spot on the ground where you want to flare and see if it moves up or down on the windshield. If it moves up, you will not make it to the spot. If it moves down, flaps (with caution) can be used to adjust the descent rate, but a forward slip is preferred since it can be discontinued without a further penalty of altitude loss.

AREA OF REVERSED COMMAND OPERATION

In no other mountain flying condition or circumstance is improper operation on the back side of the drag curve as dangerous or unforgiving as when the pilot is making an approach for landing at an airstrip.

When operating in the region of reversed command, like flying in the traffic pattern, a reduction in airspeed means that an increase of power must occur to maintain a constant altitude.

Operation in this area—the backside of the drag curve—is done all the time. These warnings are not meant to infer that operation in this region is undesirable. Just be aware that the consequences of operating improperly. Low altitude, slow speed flight creates the potential for dangerous consequences.

The chart on the following page shows power available and power required curves. The *region of reversed command* is the shaded area at the left of the vertical line. Operation in the shaded area occurs during a normal approach for landing.

To reduce confusion in the following discussion the term *thrust* is reserved for turbojet power airplanes. The term *power* is used to define the output of a recip-

PART 5 - LANDINGS   Chapter 1 - Drag Curve

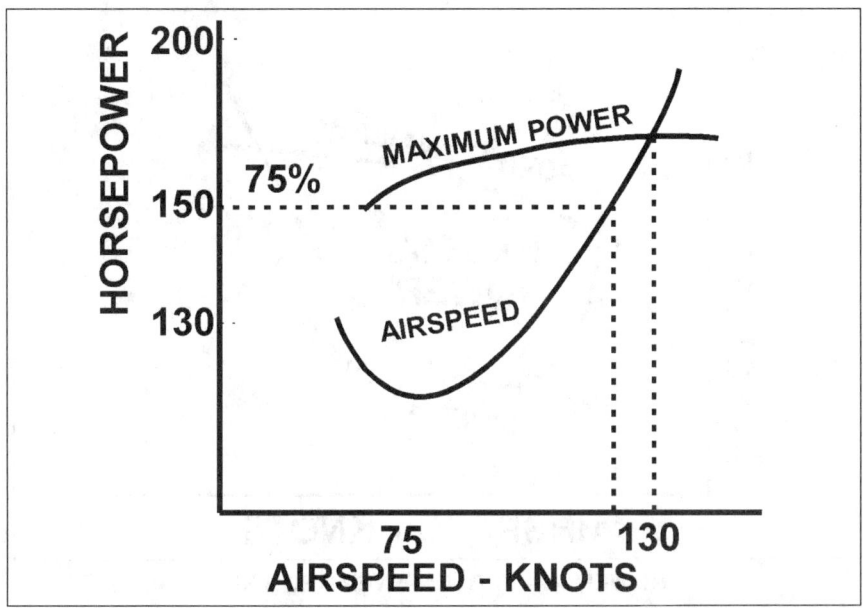

MAXIMUM POWER AVAILABLE AND RESULTANT AIRSPEED

rocating engine. Climb performance is dependent on the distinction between power and thrust. During a steady climb, the rate of climb will depend on excess power while the angle of climb is a function of excess thrust.

The principal flight performance to be expected and to be obtained from an airplane involves both steady-state flight conditions and equilibrium. For an airplane to remain in a particular phase of flight, equilibrium must be obtained between lift and weight and the power must balance the drag. Thus, it is the drag that defines the amount of power required to maintain a steady-state flight condition (in level flight, in a constant rate climb or in a constant airspeed or a constant rate descent).

In the above chart, for cruise flight, the angle of attack is adjusted to balance the weight and maintain a level altitude. The desired airspeed is obtained by adjusting the power. Operation on the high speed side of the power curve is known as flight on the "front side" of the power curve. In this region parasite drag prevails. In level flight, if the airplane is operated at twice as great a speed, the parasite drag is four times greater. But the power required (drag times velocity) to obtain this doubling of airspeed is four times the original value.

The chart (Power Available/Power Required) on the next page demonstrates that when a pilot allows the airspeed to get too slow during the approach, additional power is required to maintain level flight. If that power is not available, the pilot may get into trouble. How does the pilot get into trouble?

Mountain Flying Bible   5-11

Chapter 1 - Drag Curve   PART 5 - LANDINGS

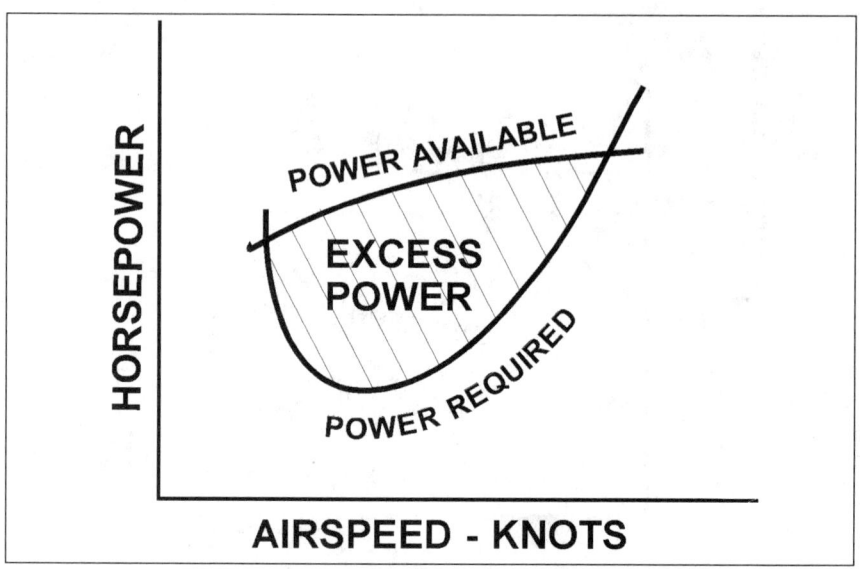

POWER AVAILABLE/POWER REQUIRED

At any speed less than the maximum lift-drag ratio, *(L/D)* $_{max}$ (the low point on the drawing), the power required to maintain a constant airspeed increases. When the airplane is slowed too much and there is no power available to increase or maintain the airspeed, the airspeed will continue to decrease. The pilot still isn't in serious trouble if he lowers the nose to obtain airspeed. The situation turns grave when the airplane is slow and at too low an altitude to be able to trade or convert altitude into airspeed. The pilot can avoid this problem by balancing the kinetic energy (velocity or airspeed) and the potential energy (altitude) through the proper use of the controls—the elevator controls airspeed, the power controls altitude.

In no other flying situation is the association of the region of reverse command as intolerant of mishandling as in the low-altitude, maximum performance operations typical of mountain landing approaches. ✈

PART 5 - LANDINGS   Chapter 2 - Flaps

CHAPTER 2 — FLAPS

> EFFECTS OF FLAPS........................ 5-11
> FLAPS FOR LANDING 5-12

The use and management of flaps is one of the important factors that pilots learn in order to extract the maximum performance from the airplane.

EFFECTS OF FLAPS

Generally speaking, even with those airplanes considered to be underpowered, the application of the first half of the flaps results in gaining more lift than drag. Although lift and drag are directly proportional, using power can offset the additional drag of the first 50 percent of the flaps.

Application of the last half of flaps causes more drag than lift because of the lack of power to overcome the drag.

This means that during an approach for landing, if the pilot decides to make a go-around, the flaps should initially be retracted to 50 percent. The elevator is used to control the airspeed. When a safe speed exists, retract the remainder of the flaps in progressive steps called "milking" the flaps. Milking involves retraction of the flaps in 5- or 10-degree intervals.

The pilot who retracts the flaps totally will find the lift coefficient of the "clean" wing unable to support the weight of the aircraft. The airplane will either set up a high sink rate or it will stall.

During an approach to landing with the flaps extended the airplane is said to be in a "dirty" configuration. To make a go-around involves a transition from "dirty" to "clean" configuration. Three changes will take place:

   (1) When the flaps are retracted, the wing's camber or curvature is reduced, causing a pitching moment that may require trimming the nose down.

   (2) The induced drag will be reduced when the flaps are retracted, allowing the airplane to accelerate better.

   (3) When the flaps are retracted, lift is lost. To maintain the same altitude an increase in the angle of attack is required. When the airplane is low and slow, its acceleration may not be able to cope with the loss of lift and

it will set up a high sink rate. The best procedure involves milking the flaps, that is, retracting them in small increments that allow the airplane to accelerate and compensate for loss of lift.

The pilot should give prior thought to the application of flaps. Flap extension causes the following changes.

(1) Extending (lowering) the flaps will increase the camber and lift of the wing. The increase in lift causes the nose to pitch up, requiring the pilot to trim nose down.

(2) Lift and drag are directly proportional. Increase lift and you increase drag. To maintain a constant altitude and constant airspeed requires a higher power setting.

(3) The same lift coefficient with the application of flaps will require a smaller angle of attack. If the pilot does not ease forward on the control wheel at the same time as the flap application, the airplane will balloon.

(4) Do not extend the flaps when the airspeed is greater than V_{FE}. You run the risk of causing structural damage. If you check the POH, there will be a listing for the design limit load factor with the flaps retracted, probably around 3.6 to 3.8 gs. With the flaps extended, the design limit load factor may be reduced to 2.2 gs, or some such value. This shows that the application of flaps reduces the structural strength of the airplane.

FLAPS FOR LANDING

The FAA created a controversy years ago—that hasn't yet been resolved—when they advocated the use of full flaps for landing, even during crosswind landings. They tried to educate pilots about the benefits of such a landing, but didn't use all their ammunition.

You won't find me trying to convince you one way or the other, but in order for you to make an intelligent decision, facts are presented herein.

Quite a few pilots, especially "tail-dragger" pilots, feel a no-flap landing is easier and more controllable. An experiment will let you determine the controllability of your particular airplane with and without flaps. Slow to the flap operating range and without flaps roll to a 30-degree bank. The airplane may require a slight continued application of the aileron control, depending on its inherent stability, to keep it from rolling back to wings-level flight. Holding the bank constant, apply about one third of the flaps, then one half of the flaps. If the bank becomes steeper, it may indicate that the application of flaps makes the ailerons more effective.

Now the reason why some pilots are hesitant to use flaps during crosswind operations. The airplane has more "air" control with the application of flaps, but it has less "ground" control. With the flaps located behind the main landing gear, the weather vane tendency is greater with flaps extended, than with them retracted.

Proper flap technique calls for retracting the flaps once on the runway, then flying the airplane on the ground by making crosswind corrections with the ailerons.

If the pilot practices this proper technique, flaps may provide a safer crosswind landing because of the decrease in centrifugal force.

Rule of Thumb – Centrifugal Force During a Swerve.

Centrifugal force increases as the square of the speed at which it starts.

Because of the centrifugal force increase, crosswind landings are safer with the use of flaps, if a swerve is encountered. The pilot can more easily control the airplane and the force of any swerve will be reduced.

After landing, when the airplane is firmly on the ground, retract the flaps—but not the gear. This places more weight on the wheels, improving braking, and reducing the effect of the natural weather vane tendency.

A swerve on the ground is to be avoided, especially with excess speed. In a touchdown at 70 KIAS without flaps is compared to a touchdown at 50 KIAS with flaps, we find the result of any swerve to be much more serious at the faster speed. The centrifugal force developed during a swerve increases as the square of the airspeed, meaning that at 70 knots (70 squared) the increase is 4,900, while at 50 knots (50 squared) it is 2,500. A swerve at 70 would be nearly twice as strong as at 50 knots.

Whenever an airplane, either tricycle gear or conventional gear, begins a swerve as the result of a weather vane tendency or a cross wind, it is important to stop the swerve immediately.

It's difficult for the author, or anyone else, to convince someone else to use flaps during crosswind operations. With a little experimentation and practice you can determine what works best for your situation.

CAUTION: Some airplanes are placarded against slips with the flaps extended. The reason for this precaution has to do with the aerodynamics of the airplane. Application of flaps directs airflow down, away from the tail. If the airplane is in a slip, the horizontal stabilizer opposite the slip may not receive a normal airflow since the fuselage blocks a portion of the air. If the airplane is rapidly taken out of the slip, the yaw can cause the horizontal stabilizer that was receiving air to be momentarily blocked as the fuselage moves in the opposite direction.

The tail has a normal down force. If both sides of the horizontal stabilizer have the airflow reduced, the tail stalls momentarily and the nose pitches down. This is difficult to do intentionally in a training situation, but with passengers in the back seat, it occurs easier. The two times I caused this to happen the nose pitched down about 40 to 50 degrees. It seems steeper and if the airplane is close to the ground it will be startling. ✈

TO OBTAIN MAXIMUM LIFT FOR TAKEOFF IN ANY AIRPLANE WITH A PARTICULAR AIRFOIL SECTION (SHAPE AND DESIGN), MAKE FULL AILERON DEFLECTION AND MATCH THE FLAPS TO THE AILERONS.

IF THE AIRCRAFT MANUFACTURER GIVES A RECOMMENDED FLAP SETTING, USE THE MANUFACTURER'S SETTING.

FOR AIRCRAFT WITH EXCESSIVE HORSEPOWER, MORE FLAPS THAN THE "MAXIMUM LIFT" SETTING MAY BE USED.

EXAMPLE: SHORT-FIELD TAKEOFF IN A CESSNA 172. MANUFACTURER'S RECOMMENDATION IS 10-DEGREES FLAPS. "MAXIMUM LIFT" SETTING IS 12-DEGREES FLAPS.

PART 5 - LANDINGS   Chapter 3 - Landing Irregularities

CHAPTER 3 — LANDING IRREGULARITIES

- BALLOONING 5-17
- BOUNCING 5-18
- WHEELBARROWING 5-19
- PORPOISING 5-20
- GROUND LOOP 5-21

It is impossible to make a perfect flare and landing each time you approach an airport. In fact, each and every landing you will ever make is going to be different from the others in some way.

Without knowing the corrective action for porpoising, the nosewheel can be wiped out. Ballooning can cause an unintentional stall and dropping-in that may damage the airplane and the occupants. Whatever the irregularity involved during a landing, it can be fixed.

My parents and I started a fixed base operation at the Jackson Hole Airport in 1968. During the years that followed, I spent many hours flying with my friend, Howard Ballew. Most of the time he taught me bits of wisdom, and occasionally I reciprocated (teaching him basic, intermediate and advanced aerobatics when he was age 78). Anyway, Howard always told me, "It's not your mistakes that get you in aviation, it's how you take care of them." In learning how to take care of landing irregularities, we will discuss ballooning, bouncing, wheelbarrowing and porpoising. Pay particular attention to porpoising.

BALLOONING

When a pilot looks at the ground too closely in front of the airplane the result is a "speed blur." This blur may cause an indication that the ground is rising faster than actuality. During this time it is normal to increase the pitch attitude too fast. This not only stops the descent, but also causes the airplane to start climbing.

The danger of ballooning is that the altitude is increasing and the airspeed is decreasing. If the airplane stalls, there is no pitch control to soften the landing, and both airplane and passengers can be hurt.

Mountain Flying Bible

Chapter 3 - Landing Irregularities   PART 5 - LANDINGS

CORRECTIVE ACTION

Ballooning that causes a small increase in altitude is not serious. By maintaining directional control, moving rapidly to the level-flight attitude, and adding a small amount of power, the airplane will stabilize and a normal landing can be continued.

A moderate balloon effect will require a greater application of power. If you are able to transition immediately to the level flight attitude, the landing may be continued.

If the ballooning is severe, apply full power and lower the nose to the level flight attitude. When the airspeed begins increasing, clean up the airplane by milking the flaps and monitoring the airspeed. As soon as the airplane is able to climb, perform a go-around.

Don't try to salvage a landing when you experience a bad balloon. Make a go-around.

The speed blur can be eliminated by looking down the runway in front of the airplane a distance equal to that used for driving a car at the same speed.

BOUNCING

A bounced landing is similar to ballooning. The difference is the initial causal factor. An airplane touching (or striking) the runway before the normal landing attitude is attained, will bounce into the air. The height of the bounce depends on the rate of descent at the time of touchdown, or if the airplane is stalled, the height where the airplane begins its fall.

Bouncing happens because the airplane strikes the runway before it attains the landing attitude. Because the bounce occurs during the landing, it is invariably accompanied by further back pressure that aggravates the height of the bounce. This is more a matter of startled reaction causing the additional backpressure rather than attempting to establish the landing attitude just as the touchdown occurs.

CORRECTIVE ACTION

Bouncing requires corrective action that is similar to that used for ballooning. If the bounce is slight, there is no particular hazard in making a follow-through landing. Hold a constant pitch attitude (landing attitude) and maintain directional control using the rudders for longitudinal alignment and ailerons for lateral alignment. Add power to cushion the landing and reduce power immediately upon touch down.

If the bounce results in the airplane rebounding 10 to 15 feet above the runway, immediately lower the pitch attitude to level-flight attitude. Add power to cushion the landing and immediately before touchdown, transition to the landing attitude. Reduce the power upon touchdown and maintain the pitch attitude. Several small bounces may follow, but with the elevator control in the landing attitude, these will be minimal.

Remember, once the airplane is on the ground it is important to keep the control wheel back. Too often there is an attempt to continually adjust the flare. This may aggravate the situation and lead to a dangerous porpoise condition.

If the bounce startles or scares you it is a severe bounce. Immediately lower the nose to the level-flight attitude while applying full power. If flaps have been used, retract the flaps to the half-extended position. With flap extension the normal level-flight attitude will be lower than with a clean wing. As the airplane begins to accelerate, milk the flaps and increase the back pressure to stop sink. Continue milking the flaps until the airplane begins to climb, then return for another approach.

I have ridden through bounces with students where the go-around procedure is begun and the airplane bounces again. Even with another bounce, follow through with the go-around procedure.

WHEELBARROWING

Wheelbarrowing is a complication that occurs once the airplane is on the ground. Usually it happens when the pilot tries to hurry the landing and pushes forward on the control wheel. When the airplane is on the ground with a little excess speed and the control wheel is moved forward the wheelbarrow can befall the pilot.

Usually, once the airplane is on the ground there is enough lift being produced for the main wheels to lift off the ground, and there is enough lift for the airplane to become unstable while riding on the nosewheel. The airplane may veer off the runway.

Wheelbarrowing is not too prevalent, but it can sneak up on you. Using forward pressure isn't the normal way of landing. But suppose the weather is marginal with snow showers and reduced visibility. You are approaching a runway from the north with a north wind. The runway is short and narrow and it's cold enough for a slight blanket of snow to cover the surface. Arriving over the runway threshold with excessive speed and a little float makes it look like the airplane will not get down within the confines of the runway. Just a little forward pressure causes the gear to make contact with the ground. With this scenario a wheelbarrowing effect is easy to imagine. When landing with a tail wind, or even a quartering tail wind, just relaxing the backpressure after touchdown may be enough to cause wheelbarrowing.

Chapter 3 - Landing Irregularities   PART 5 - LANDINGS

CORRECTIVE ACTION

Backpressure will correct any wheelbarrowing tendency. With excessive speed, the airplane may begin flying again. Use the same technique to correct for wheelbarrowing that causes the airplane to become airborne again as used for the correction of ballooning.

PORPOISING

The least expected and the most dangerous of the landing irregularities that may cause an accident is the occurrence of porpoising. Some pilots fly for years and years and never experience the porpoise. This is fortunate, but once it happens, it won't be soon forgotten.

Porpoising occurs most often after a bounced landing. The natural tendency to pull back on the control wheel after the bounce causes the airplane to rise higher than it would if the control wheel were left alone. Once the pilot determines the airplane is climbing away from the ground, forward elevator control arrests the climb, but now backpressure is required to prevent another impact. This back elevator control always occurs just a moment too late and the airplane bounces again. This sequence of events continues until:

1. Backpressure is used to obtain and hold the landing attitude allowing the airplane to go through a couple of bounces and then stick to the runway when the airspeed slows.

2. The porpoise continues, getting worse with each contact with the runway until the nosewheel collapses.

We mentioned before that a pilot with excess airspeed—caused by approaching too fast or landing with a tail wind or quartering tail wind—may try to help the airplane land with forward pressure on the control wheel when he sees the runway getting shorter. We said this is the major cause of wheelbarrowing, but when the pilot detects the wheelbarrow beginning, he may use backpressure sufficiently to cause a bounce that allows the porpoise to develop.

CORRECTIVE ACTION

As an instructor, a few students have really scared me during the landing. If they knew what was happening and the consequences, it would probably scare them too. The best recovery technique for the porpoise is backpressure on the elevator control. Immediately raise or lower the nose to the level-flight attitude or slightly above level flight. As the airspeed dissipates, increase the pitch slowly to the landing attitude. The airplane may bounce once or twice more, but that's about it.

 If you try to recover from a porpoise with forward elevator control, beyond the level flight attitude, get ready to spend some money. It's likely the airplane will be damaged.

PART 5 - LANDINGS   Chapter 3 - Landing Irregularities

GROUND LOOP

The ground loop is a rapid and uncontrolled turn occurring on the ground during taxi, take off and the after-landing roll. Conventional-gear airplanes are more susceptible to ground looping, but it can occur with tricycle-gear airplanes. Some of the causes are touchdown while drifting, weather vaning after touchdown, careless use of rudder, a soft spot on the runway that retards one wheel, uneven ground or anything that causes a swerve to begin.

 Centrifugal force increases as the square of the speed at which it begins.

The initial onset of the swerve does not cause the ground loop, it only makes the airplane vulnerable to the ground loop. If the swerve continues, centrifugal force increases and at some point the aircraft controls—brakes, rudder and ailerons—become ineffective in stopping the swerve. It is likely, unless the airplane is going slow, that the swerve's centrifugal force will be sufficient to cause the airplane to tip until one wing strikes the ground. This also places a great deal of stress on the landing gear structure.

What makes the conventional gear airplane more liable to experience the ground loop? If we examine the structure of the conventional gear we find the center of gravity is located behind the main wheels. A swerve allows the centrifugal force to act through the center of gravity, magnifying the effect.

Touchdown speed is important. For example, if the groundspeed is doubled while landing, any swerve will result in quadrupling the centrifugal force involved.

CORRECTIVE ACTION

If a pilot fails to recognize the beginning of a swerve in time to make a normal correction with rudder usage, the application of brakes is also needed to help straighten the airplane.

When a swerve starts, some pilots have frantically reduced the power to idle, determined to straighten and stop the plane. With power on, a blast of air over the rudder makes it more effective. With power off, the rudder may be ineffective in straightening the airplane, especially at slower speeds. Usually, leaving the power on, or adding full power, is the best technique. If full power is used when the other controls are ineffective, it will help straighten the airplane by pulling it along the thrust line and by providing propeller blast on the vertical stabilizer and rudder to make them more effective.

For the taildragger pilot, use the rudder and brakes as necessary to stop the swerve. The important thing is to neutralize the rudder immediately when the

Chapter 3 - Landing Irregularities   PART 5 - LANDINGS

swerve is arrested. Otherwise the plane may swerve in the opposite direction. Do not hesitate to use the brakes when a swerve begins. The wear-and-tear on the brakes and tires may be less than the tear-and-wear on the airplane if a ground loop occurs.

Using everything available—controls, brakes and power—is important. Often the ailerons are forgotten as an aid in controlling the airplane on the ground. If the speed is fast enough for the ailerons to be effective in rolling the airplane, roll the wings level or opposite the swerve. If the speed is too slow for the ailerons to be effective in rolling the airplane, move them toward the swerve. The drag—lift and drag are directly proportional—will have more effect than the lift and will assist in straightening the path. ✈

HOWARD BALLEW'S "GROS VENTRE INTERNATIONAL" DOESN'T LOOK TOO GREAT FROM THE AIR. (PARALLEL TO LOWER SLIDE LAKE, NORTHEAST OF JACKSON, WYO.)

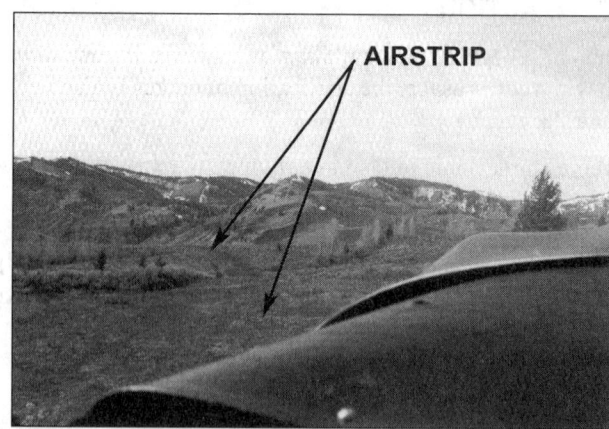

IT DOESN'T LOOK A HECK OF A LOT BETTER FROM THE GROUND.

Mountain Flying Bible

PART 5 - LANDINGS   Chapter 4 - Landing Considerations

CHAPTER 4 — LANDING CONSIDERATIONS

- LANDING UPHILL/DOWNHILL 5-23
- LANDING IN RAIN. 5-25
- STABILIZED LANDING APPROACH. 5-25
- LANDING PRACTICE 5-26
- EYE FOCUS 5-27
- GROUND EFFECT 5-27
- MOUNTAIN STRIP OPERATIONS 5-30

LANDING UPHILL/DOWNHILL

A pilot spends the majority of his time flying from his home-base airport. It is natural to develop a certain perspective of what the runway looks like through the windshield on final approach.

When operating at a strange airport, there is an unconscious tendency to visualize the approach with the same perspective, even if the runway is of a different width and length, or if the runway has slope.

Trying to approach upslope or downslope runway using the developed sight pattern results in a visual illusion—upslope runway, approach too low; downslope runway, approach too high—that can only be properly compensated for by using the spot method for landing.

Rule of Thumb – Upslope Runway Takeoff Distance

Add 10% per degree to the normal takeoff distance to determine the upslope takeoff distance.

Rule of Thumb – Downslope Runway Takeoff Distance

Subtract 5% per degree from the normal takeoff distance to determine the downslope takeoff distance.

Mountain Flying Bible   5-23

Chapter 4 - Landing Considerations — PART 5 - LANDINGS

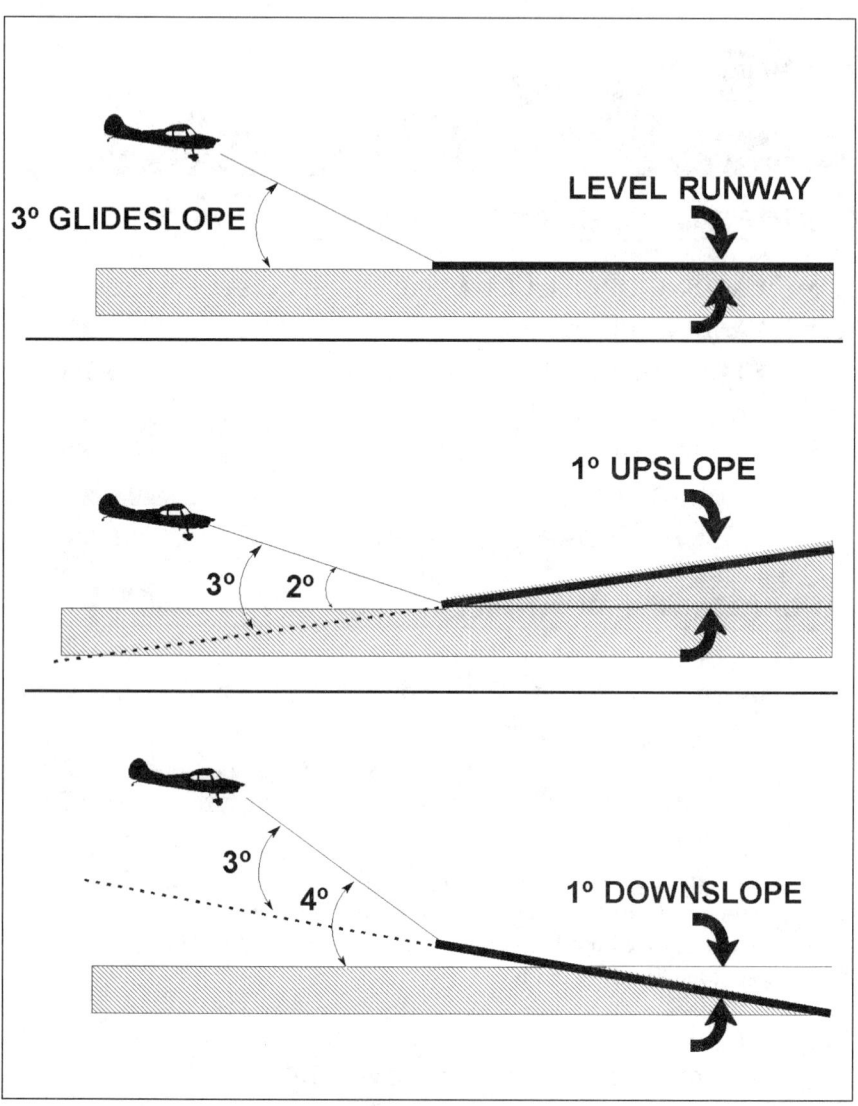

BECAUSE THE RUNWAY FORMS AN OBTUSE ANGLE, AN AIRPLANE APPROACHING AN UPSLOPE RUNWAY WILL COMPENSATE BY APPROACHING TOO LOW. BY THE TIME THE VISUAL MISTAKE IS REALIZED, THE AIRPLANE MAY NOT HAVE ENOUGH POWER TO FLY TO THE RUNWAY.

AN AIRPLANE APPROACHING A DOWNSLOPE RUNWAY WILL COME IN HIGH. LOWERING THE NOSE TO EFFECT THE LANDING CAUSES EXCESS SPEED AND FLOAT.

When landing on upslope terrain, a visual illusion of a very nose-low attitude befalls the pilot to make it appear the airplane is higher than it actually is on the approach.

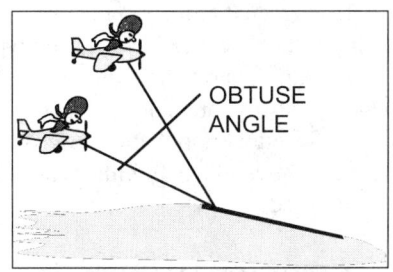

THE DOWNSLOPE RUNWAY CAUSES A HIGH APPROACH

LANDING IN RAIN

Refraction is the culprit that causes light rays to pass obliquely through the air and rain, producing a visual illusion that the airplane is higher than its actual altitude

When approaching to land in heavy rain, the apparent approach must be higher than normal. Using the spot method for landing eliminates this visual illusion.

STABILIZED LANDING APPROACH

Back in the "old days," a landing approach consisted of a reduction of power to idle when opposite the landing point, followed by a glide to the runway. A stabilized approach was developed to prevent thermal shock of the engine and to have the engine in a state of readiness if a go-around was required.

The stabilized approach should be used for landing at all airports including mountain airstrips.

The stabilized approach means reducing the power to a setting that allows 400- to 600-fpm rate of descent when established on the desired approach speed. The stabilized approach provides a method for exact airspeed control—this is highly desired—and precise glide path control.

The airplane equipped with a fixed-pitch propeller uses a power setting of about 1,400 to 1,600 rpm. The constant-speed propeller equipped airplane uses somewhere around 10 to 12 inches of manifold pressure.

Partial power keeps the engine warm. If carburetor heat is needed, it will be more effective.

The stabilized approach avoids thermal shock to the engine. When approaching a runway, time the initial partial power reduction to allow a minute or two for the temperature of the engine to stabilize before making further reductions.

For example, the initial power reduction may be to 20-25 inches. After a minute make another reduction to 17-20 inches. After entering the pattern reduce the power again to about 12-17 inches. Downwind, opposite the point of landing, make the final reduction to about 10-12 inches.

Chapter 4 - Landing Considerations   PART 5 - LANDINGS

This gradual reduction in power lets the engine temperatures cool slowly. This is important because the different types of metal used in the various components of the engine have different cooling rates. Allowing the metals to adjust to the change slowly prevents the engine from self-destruction. Also, the engine is ready for either application of go-around power or a total reduction of power to idle for the landing. In either case, the temperature is such that no damage will be incurred.

LANDING PRACTICE

A pilot who has never operated at a high-altitude mountain airport can get some idea of high-altitude airport operations by simulating a landing. This provides insight into the airplane's performance and flight characteristics to provide confidence in the airplane and yourself.

Landing at a high-elevation airstrip is no more dangerous than landing at a sea-level airstrip. There are, however, differences of which you should be aware.

Begin your experiment to find out the consequences of landing at a high-elevation airstrip by climbing to the anticipated density altitude of the airstrip.

- ✔ At 1,000 feet above the imaginary airstrip, go through the pre-landing cockpit check and establish the same *indicated* approach airspeed and stabilized approach power setting that is used at sea level.

- ✔ Notice the sink rate. Use the same indicated airspeed for approach to landing at this high altitude airport that you use at sea level, but note the same power setting results in a higher sink rate. The airplane requires additional power to create the same rate of descent as at sea level.

- ✔ Continue the approach through the flare and progress to a stall. The indicated airspeed is the same for the airplane regardless of the altitude, but the true airspeed is greater.

- ✔ After you are comfortable with the approach phase, practice the maneuvering phase. Establish slow flight at 1.3 V_{SO}, then 1.2 V_{SO} and execute medium-banked turns to the left and right.

- ✔ Practice a go-around from a full flap configuration. Of importance is the altitude where you initiate the go-around and the altitude when the rate of descent is arrested.

- ✔ One of the most important aspects of high-altitude landings (any elevation) is that of exact airspeed control. A 10 percent increase in approach speed causes a 21 percent increase in landing distance.

VISION

Your vision is important. To gain the best vision, keep your head in a natural straight-ahead position. Use peripheral vision and the movement of the eyes rather than head movement to look at the area to either side of the aircraft's nose.

PART 5 - LANDINGS   Chapter 4 - Landing Considerations

EYE FOCUS

During the approach and landing, do not hold a fixed focus. Instead, look to either side and from close to the nose to the horizon, changing the focus slowly and continually.

By looking at different points, the brain—without you realizing it—will compare and record the relationship of the flight attitude to the various points.

GROUND EFFECT

Ground effect was covered in Part 2 TAKEOFF. See page 2-46.

The phenomenon of ground effect operates on the airplane during landing. Usually an airplane with excess speed flies down from the free air to encounter ground effect.

The reduction of induced drag causes the airplane to float, leading to the classic type of overshoot. Quite often an approach at normal speed requires longer to dissipate the airspeed because of the higher elevation. This will cause some float.

SOME AIRPORTS ALLOW A STANDARD TRAFFIC PATTERN. FLY THE SAME DISTANCE FROM THE RUNWAY EACH TIME. THIS CONSISTENCY IS IMPORTANT IN MAKING A GOOD APPROACH.

AT A FAMILIAR AIRPORT, WHEN YOU ARE ESTABLISHED DOWNWIND AT THE PROPER LATERAL DISTANCE FROM THE RUNWAY, NOTE THE RELATION OF THE WING (OR STRUT) TO THE RUNWAY.

DETERMINE THE POINT WHERE THE WING (OR STRUT) INTERSECTS THE RUNWAY CENTERLINE. THIS POINT CAN BE MARKED WITH TAPE OR BY NOTING A RIVET OR OTHER DISTINGUISHING MARK.

EACH TIME YOU ENTER DOWNWIND, ESTABLISH THE LATERAL DISTANCE FROM THE RUNWAY WITH THIS MARK.

On short fields, approach at the slowest airspeed that is consistent with safety and the ground effect is minimized. If you recognize an overshoot where the far end of the runway is rapidly approaching, go around.

How does one go about determining the proper approach speed? If the airplane is operated at its maximum allowable gross weight, look at the lower limit of the white scale on the airspeed indicator (not on older airplanes). At less than

Mountain Flying Bible

gross weight it is usually sufficient to stall the airplane at the current operating weight and multiply the indicated airspeed by 1.3. Or the Pilot's Operating Handbook can be consulted to obtain the indicated stall speed for different operating weights.

AIRSPEED INDICATOR ERRORS

The airspeed indictors of airplanes manufactured since the mid-1970s are calibrated with standard color coded-markings of *indicated airspeed* values that designate the operating limitations. This is in opposition to the older airplanes that use calibrated airspeed instrument markings.

Airplanes manufactured before the mid-1970s use airspeed indicators with the operating limitations denoted as *calibrated airspeed*.

Use of indicated or calibrated airspeed for determining the approach speed isn't all bad, but you have to understand the limitations of this type of information. At cruise airspeed, indicated airspeed and calibrated airspeed are essentially the same, but at slower speeds there is a difference of as much as 10 knots (or more) due to instrument and position error.

For airplanes using either indicated or calibrated airspeed markings, refer to the airspeed calibration chart to correct for airspeed errors before using 1.3 V_{SO} as the optimum approach speed for executing the spot method for landing.

Airspeed Calibration Chart

KIAS	40	50	60	70	80
KCAS	50	55	62	71	80

AIRSPEED CALIBRATION CHART

If the operating limitations are published as calibrated airspeed (the older airplanes), always use the calibrated airspeed to calculate the proper approach speed at the operating weight being used.

Check the manual to determine the calibrated airspeed/stall speed for the operating weight. Convert the calibrated airspeed to indicated airspeed. Multiply the indicated airspeed by 1.3 to obtain the optimum approach speed.

LANDING FLAPS, MAXIMUM LANDING WEIGHT

The calibrated airspeed table shows that the airplane will stall at 50 knots calibrated airspeed with the landing flaps, and operating at the maximum landing weight. Using this calibrated airspeed, find 1.3 times 50 = 65 KCAS (knots calibrated airspeed, sometimes labeled TIAS, true indicated airspeed on charts). By interpolating, the value of 65 KCAS, find 63 KIAS as the optimum approach speed.

Serious Error

Using an airspeed indicator with the operating limitations given in indicated or calibrated airspeed may lead the unsuspecting pilot into a trap. Using the FAA value for a short-field approach, 1.3 V_{SO}, we multiply the calibrated airspeed by 1.3 to obtain the approach speed.

It's not quite that simple. If the pilot goes out and stalls the airplane, noting the indicated airspeed and multiplies this value by 1.3, there is an error introduced into the equation that will result in the approach being made at too slow an approach speed. During the flare to landing, the change in angle of attack increases the induced drag and the airplane may set up a high sink rate, rather than effect a round-out (flare), causing an arrival instead of a landing.

The Airspeed Correction Table (Airspeed Calibration Chart) on page 5-28 is using borrowed values from the Owner's Manual for a 1972 Cessna Model 182P. Note: Sometimes the speeds are in mph rather than knots.

ERROR COMPUTING APPROACH SPEED

This table can be used to demonstrate the error of using indicated (whether the value is expressed as indicated or calibrated) airspeed in determining the optimum approach speed. We multiply the indicated airspeed, 40, by 1.3 to come up with an indicated approach speed of 52 knots. This is wrong. The calibrated speed for 52 knots indicated is obtained from the table with interpolation as 64.4 knots (52 is 2/10 of the interval value of 6, or 2.4 added to 52). The erroneously determined approach speed of 52 knots is much slower than the calculated 64.4 knots indicated airspeed.

CORRECT METHOD COMPUTING APPROACH SPEED

With older airplanes that use calibrated airspeed as opposed to indicated airspeed, we should have used the calibrated airspeed value. The correctly determined approach speed is 64.4 knots indicated.

Should the unsuspecting pilot use the erroneously determined approach speed of 52 knots indicated airspeed, the actual approach speed is the ratio of 64.4 divided by the stall speed of 52 calibrated or 1.24 V_{SO} (64.4/52=1.239). This is probably too slow for any pilot without extensive experience in operating at this airspeed.

Note: Calibrated airspeed (CAS) may be abbreviated KCAS (knots calibrated airspeed) or TIAS (true indicated airspeed).

Chapter 4 - Landing Considerations   PART 5 - LANDINGS

Reduced Landing Weight

Some older Owner's Manuals may not have a listing that converts indicated airspeed and calibrated airspeed at various operating weights. For these airplanes use the following rule of thumb.

 Rule of Thumb – Reduce the calibrated approach airspeed for the maximum landing weight listed by one-half of the percentage of the weight decrease.

The percentage of weight decrease is the ratio of the maximum allowable gross weight divided by the actual operating weight. In the case of the Cessna 182, the maximum allowable gross weight is 2,950 pounds. If the airplane is being operated at 2,500 pounds, the weight decrease is 450 pounds. The percentage of weight decrease is 450 divided by 2,950 for 0.1525, or a 15.25 percent decrease in gross weight. The maximum allowable gross weight calculated approach speed, 70 mph, should be reduced by half the percentage of weight decrease (7.6 percent). The optimum approach speed at a reduced weight of 2,500 pounds is 65 mph (70–(70*1.076)=65 mph).

GUSTY WIND CONDITIONS

When the steady-state wind is gusty, add one half the gust factor to the computed approach speed to compensate for airspeed changes caused by wind shear.

For example, if the wind is 10 knots gusting to 20 knots, the gust factor is the difference between the two values, or 10 knots. Add half this value, five knots, to the calculated approach speed.

MOUNTAIN STRIP OPERATIONS

If your flight will take you to an airstrip you have never operated at before, consider the following prior to arrival at the strip.

- Research the strip using state aeronautical information to become familiar with the operating procedures. Be able to fly over the strip and figure out the approach. At this time determine also the departure path. Determine if the strip is a one-way airstrip (no chance for a go-around maneuver). Check for drainages nearby that could funnel the wind into a crosswind. What is the surface and condition? Does the strip provide for a go/no-go point? Are there any facilities and services available? What is the surrounding terrain like?
- It is important to know the proper approach, whether the strip allows a normal pattern, non-standard pattern, or no resemblance to any pattern.
- All approaches to a mountain strip consist of the stabilized approach, that is, a power-on approach that results in a descent of about 400-600 feet per minute.

PART 5 - LANDINGS   Chapter 4 - Landing Considerations

- Lean the mixture for the density altitude.
- Always incorporate the spot method for landing technique to insure the airplane will arrive over the runway at the desired point of flare.
- Many mountain strips are located at the confluence of creeks that funnel any wind flow to the airstrip. This may cause downdrafts on short approach. Trying to land at the very end of the strip may result in the airplane landing short of the runway. This is another reason for using the spot method for landing. Encountering a downdraft is immediately discernable, and an adjustment can be made before it is too late.
- Normal flight operations call for all landings to be made upstream and all takeoffs to be made downstream to conform to the upslope/downslope terrain. Using this technique increases the safety of flight. ✈

LENTICULAR CLOUDS STACKED UP ABOVE A HANGAR AT CENTENNIAL AIRPORT, ENGLEWOOD, COLORADO. THIS PICTURE SEEM TO CONTRADICT SOME REPORTS THAT STATE LENTICULARS ONLY FORM STACKS OF THREE OR FOUR CLOUDS.

Chapter 4 - Landing Considerations   PART 5 - LANDINGS

HOWARD BALLEW'S "GROS VENTRE INTERNATIONAL" AIRPORT (NORTHEAST OF THE JACKSON HOLE AIRPORT). CHECK "MOUNTAIN-STRIP OPERATIONS" ABOVE. NOTE THAT THE RUNWAY DIPS AND TURNS TO THE RIGHT.

Trust your instincts.
If a situation feels uncomfortable ...
Get out of it.

PART 5 - LANDINGS   Chapter 5 - Spot Method Technique

CHAPTER 5 — SPOT METHOD LANDING TECHNIQUE

- ➢ OPTIMUM APPROACH SPEED. 5-34
- ➢ STABILIZED APPROACH 5-34
- ➢ LANDING REQUIREMENTS 5-35
- ➢ SPOT METHOD LANDING TECHNIQUE. 5-37
- ➢ GUSTY WIND CONDITIONS 5-38
- ➢ WINDSHEAR AWARENESS 5-38
- ➢ SPOT LANDING USES 5-38
- ➢ SUMMARY. 5-40

Visual illusions are contributing factors in approach and landing accidents. They are not of the chimera-type illusions (illusion of the mind), but rather a perception that causes misinterpretation caused by the convergence of lines, sloping terrain, or heavy rain.

In approaching a runway a pilot customarily adjusts his glide path in accordance with what he sees. He is used to a visual relationship between the altitude and position of his aircraft and the width and length of the runway below. The pilot accustomed to landing on one runway or on runways of similar width may be deceived in his visual approach to a runway of a different width, especially if the length and width proportions appear to be about the same early in the approach.

✓ With a downslope runway, the angle of descent appears more obtuse (shallower) and the pilot flies higher than normal, resulting in a high and hot approach.

✓ With an upslope, even relatively small, the pilot has the illusion of being higher than normal. This misleads him into making a lower than normal approach. Depending upon aircraft performance and density altitude, the airplane may not have enough power to make it to the runway.

Mountain Flying Bible   5-33

Chapter 5 - Spot Method Technique   PART 5 - LANDINGS

These visual illusions and other misleading deceptions can be dealt with effectively by incorporating the spot method for landing into all landing approaches, not just at mountain strips.

✓ Establish and *maintain* the desired approach speed.
✓ Align the nose (windshield mark) with the *spot* on the runway.
✓ Raise or lower the nose position using the throttle to maintain alignment with the spot.

Before delving into the various aspects of the spot method for landing, we will establish a few definitions so we are talking about, and understanding, the same thing.

OPTIMUM APPROACH SPEED

According to the FAA, the optimum approach speed for a short-field approach is the value of 1.3 V_{SO}. Adjustment of this speed must be made if there is gusty wind (add one-half the gust factor). Personally, I find 1.3 V_{SO} too fast. Upon arrival at the *spot* the flare is commenced. If the airplane floats, rather than touches down within about 200-300 feet of the spot, the speed is too fast.

If you recall the previous discussion about airplanes using calibrated airspeed markings for operating limitations, you might ask yourself why would there be any difference between determining the indicated airspeed at which the aircraft stalls when flying one Cessna 172 using an airspeed indicator marked as indicated airspeed and another Cessna 172 using an airspeed indicator marked as calibrated airspeed? Shouldn't you be able to multiply the indicated airspeed for each airplane by 1.3 and be at a value of 30 percent greater than VSO? Absolutely not.

The Cessna incorporating the indicated airspeed dial pretty much reflects the actual aircraft performance (the indicated airspeed would be correct at sea level under standard conditions if there is no position error).

The Cessna using the calibrated airspeed dial would indicate an airspeed less than the calibrated airspeed marking for V_{SO} when the airplane stalls. If this lesser value is multiplied by 1.3, the speed used for the approach will be too slow. You would not be operating with the 30 percent safety factor you thought you had.

STABILIZED APPROACH

The spot method uses a stabilized landing approach. The accuracy of the spot method lies in its ability—while maintaining an exact approach airspeed—to provide an exact glide slope without an electronic aid.

PART 5 - LANDINGS   Chapter 5 - Spot Method Technique

Glide path guidance is provided electronically by the ILS glide slope (instrument landing system), VASI (visual approach slope indicator), or PAR (precision approach radar, sometimes called GCA — ground controlled approach).

It is unlikely that any of these electronic aids will be available for glide slope guidance at a mountain airstrip, yet the knowledgeable pilot is able to fly a pre-determined flight path or glide slope.

GLIDESLOPE	GROUNDSPEED
3 degree	5 X knots
4.5 degree	8 X knots
Stabilized Approach Rate of Descent	

3-DEGREE GLIDE SLOPE

A 3-degree glide slope is the standard for an instrument landing system. To fly a 3-degree glide path without electronic guidance, multiply the ground speed in knots by 5. The result is the rate of descent.

When a pre-determined flight path is followed it results in a stabilized approach. The key to a good landing is the stabilized approach.

As an example, suppose we are approaching an airstrip in a no-wind condition, using an approach speed of 70 knots. What rate of descent is required to fly a 3-degree glide path? Multiply 70 x 5 for a 350 fpm rate of descent.

Don't forget, this rule is applicable when the glide slope factor (5 for the 3° slope and 8 for the 4.5° slope) is multiplied by the *groundspeed,* not the airspeed.

BEST APPROACH ANGLE

The 3-degree glide slope may not be the most favorable approach angle for our small general aviation airplanes. Compare it with the 4.5-degree approach. You may find the 4.5-degree glide slope makes it easier to make glide path corrections on the approach and it provides a better view of the runway. Try both paths and see which one you prefer.

Computation of the 4.5-degree glide path is easy. Multiply the ground speed in knots by 8. For example, 70 x 8 = 560 fpm rate of descent.

LANDING REQUIREMENTS

All pilots should prepare ahead of time for the landing. This preparation should be the same for all airports, performed consistently in the same manner. It doesn't matter if the landing is planned at a sea-level flatland airport or a high

Chapter 5 - Spot Method Technique   PART 5 - LANDINGS

altitude one-way mountain airstrip. The following should be determined for each and every landing.

- ☆ AIMING POINT
- ☆ TOUCHDOWN POINT
- ☆ GO-AROUND POINT

AIMING POINT

The aiming point is the point on the runway where the aircraft would impact if you don't flare. The aiming point is used in conjunction with the windshield mark.

WINDSHIELD MARK

The windshield mark is a point on the windshield used to align the airplane with the aiming point.

To begin with, you will need a crutch to use the windshield mark, but with some practice and experience you will be able to use the windshield mark without conscious thought and without making a mark on the windshield.

Until you have developed this perspective, use a grease pencil (china marker) and make a mark on the windshield in front of your field of view. A grease pencil is used because it can be easily rubbed off with Kleenex. The mark will be about two to four inches up from the dash, depending on your parallax.

Parallax is the apparent change in the direction of an object, caused by a change in observational position that provides a new line of sight. This is why it is important to adjust the seat position to the same place each time you fly. If the position of the seat is moved forward or aft or raised or lowered, it will change your parallax.

To begin with it may be difficult to determine where to make the windshield mark. Until you develop the sight pattern necessary for the spot method, use the following technique to make the windshield mark; it may not be the exact spot, but it will be close enough that you can incorporate the spot method into all of your landings.

While in cruise flight — constant altitude, cruise power setting, and cruise airspeed — look where the horizon intersects the windshield. This is the vertical position on the windshield where you will make your mark. Imagine a horizontal line at this point. Horizontally, the mark should be made directly in front of you. Imagine a vertical line at this point directly in front of you. Where the two lines intersect is where you place the windshield mark. If you have to lean forward to use the grease pencil, your parallax will change so the mark is made too high. Note the position where the mark is to be made before leaning forward.

PART 5 - LANDINGS   Chapter 5 - Spot Method Technique

While making a descent at the desired approach speed, look at the mark on the windshield. If it is properly marked the ground below the mark will be moving down or under the nose. The ground above the mark will be moving up on the windshield. The ground directly in line with the windshield mark will remain in the same position on the windshield. You will most likely have to change the windshield mark to a point approximately one inch lower than that determined while in cruise flight. After revising the windshield mark, make a descent with partial flaps to check the windshield mark. Then try it with full flaps. The mark should remain in the same position on the windshield regardless of flap position.

TOUCHDOWN POINT

The touchdown point, when the proper approach speed is used, will be some 200-300 feet beyond the aiming point.

GO-AROUND POINT

The go-around point is a predetermined point on the runway surface that signals sufficient runway does not remain to stop if the airplane lands.

If we are flying an airplane that requires 1,000 feet to land to a runway with a length of 2,000 feet, the go-around point will be the halfway point of the runway. If the airplane is not firmly on the runway by the halfway point, make a go-around.

SPOT METHOD FOR LANDING TECHNIQUE

As with other landings, on the downwind leg opposite the landing point, perform the pre-landing check. Adjust the trim for flight at the optimum approach speed and the power for the approach path angle.

On final approach use the power to align the windshield mark and the aiming point. Maintain a constant indicated approach speed. The airplane will land exactly where you determined on the downwind leg.

PERFORMANCE

A given in aviation is that a constant power and a constant attitude result in a constant performance. This means that if the attitude and power remain the same during a no-wind approach, the rate of descent will remain constant.

If a power change is required to maintain the windshield mark on the aiming point, the pitch attitude must change to maintain a constant airspeed. If the airplane is too low, adding power will result in an undesired airspeed increase unless the nose is raised. Conversely, if the airplane is too high and power is reduced, the airspeed will bleed off unless the nose is lowered.

Chapter 5 - Spot Method Technique   PART 5 - LANDINGS

The nice thing about these power changes is that if the airplane has been properly trimmed to hold the approach airspeed, a reduction of power (the aiming point is moving down on the windshield) causes the nose to lower by itself to maintain the desired airspeed.

If the airplane is too low (aiming point moves up on the windshield), add power to align the marks. The addition of power will cause the nose to raise by itself, again maintaining a constant airspeed.

PITCH CHANGES

Pitch changes are automatic providing the airplane has been trimmed to maintain a constant indicted airspeed during the pre-landing check. Because of the airplane's built-in inherent stability, power changes will cause pitch changes without the necessity to re-trim. Large power changes may necessitate small trim changes.

GUSTY WIND CONDITIONS

A rule of thumb has evolved over the years to help us compensate for gusty wind conditions that could, if the approach speed is not adjusted, result in an unwanted stall close to the ground. Merely add half the gust factor to the indicated approach speed.

RULE OF THUMB: Gusty Wind Conditions
Add half the gust factor to the indicated approach speed.

WINDSHEAR AWARENESS

If you have DME, Loran or GPS, use them to monitor the groundspeed during the approach. A change of groundspeed will alert you to a headwind or tailwind.

Even without an electronic means of determining the groundspeed, alert pilots will know what is going on. Suppose we are flying a 3-degree glide slope at 70 knots indicated airspeed. A no wind condition will require 350 fpm rate of descent (70 x 5). What if you notice that you require 500 fpm to stay on the desired approach angle? You have experienced a tailwind. The ground speed has increased to 100 knots (X x 5 = 500; X = 100). Conversely, if the rate of descent is 300 fpm, you are experiencing a headwind (X x 5 = 300; X = 60). The groundspeed has decreased to 60 knots.

SPOT LANDING USES

The spot method for landing technique results in very accurate landings. It eliminates visual illusion problems. You should use it for all landing approaches, not just at mountain airstrips.

PART 5 - LANDINGS   **Chapter 5 - Spot Method Technique**

The spot method is functional for landings, yet useful for other flight operations.

- ✓ Cloud Avoidance - A VFR pilot may become trapped on top of an overcast. If a hole is found it is sometimes difficult to get through the hole without becoming trapped in the clouds. Choosing a point on the ground that is aligned with the windshield mark allows flight through the hole without touching the clouds.
- ✓ Descent to Pattern Altitude - When approaching an airport, select an "aiming point" on the ground. Align the windshield mark with the aiming point. It is not necessary to slow to the approach speed. Maintain whatever speed you desire. Level off at the pattern altitude and turn downwind. You will be in the proper position and altitude. This enhances safety since your airplane will not be descending in the traffic pattern.
- ✓ Crossing Ridges - From *level flight* attitude, look at the mountain ridge in relation to the windshield mark. If the ridge is below the windshield mark, the airplane is higher than the ridge. This will not work when climbing. Level off, then check the windshield mark.
- ✓ Forced Landings - If the engine fails, lower the nose for the glide attitude. Look at the windshield mark. Whatever it is aligned with on the ground indicates how far you can glide straight ahead. If a suitable landing area is off to the side, subscribe an arc from the ground aiming point and you have defined the area you can use for landing. The airplane can glide to any point within the area of the arc.

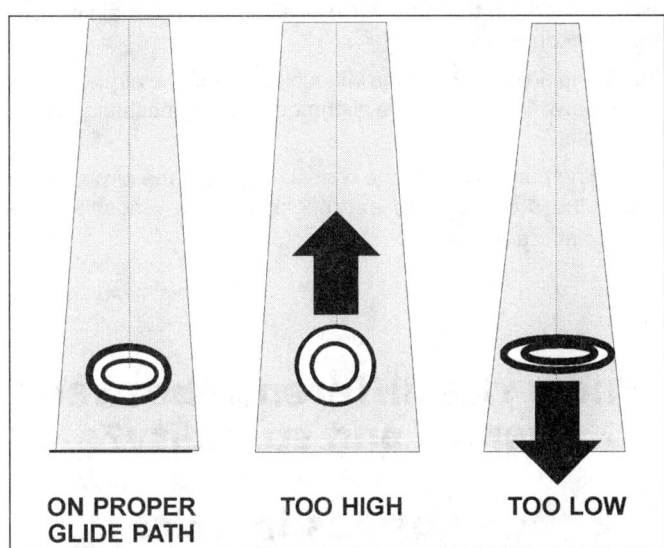

| ON PROPER GLIDE PATH | TOO HIGH | TOO LOW |

AFTER SELECTING AN AIMING POINT ON THE RUNWAY, MAINTAIN ALIGNMENT OF THE WINDSHIELD MARK AND AIMING POINT. IF THE AIMING POINT MOVES UP ON THE WINDSHIELD, REDUCE POWER. IF THE AIMING POINT MOVES DOWN ON THE WINDSHIELD, ADD POWER.

Mountain Flying Bible

Chapter 5 - Spot Method Technique   PART 5 - LANDINGS

SUMMARY

The spot method for landing technique totally eliminates undershoot on upslope runways and overshoot on downslope runways.

- ✓ Make a mark on the windshield with a grease pencil or china marker up about three or four inches from the base, directly in front of your line of vision (about an inch below where the horizon intersects the windshield in level flight at cruise power and cruise airspeed).

- ✓ On the downwind leg of the traffic pattern do a pre-landing check. Reduce throttle to that value that will result in a rate of descent for the desired approach angle. When your airspeed is stabilized at the optimum approach speed, trim the airplane to maintain this speed. Note this power setting and use it for all approaches at this approach angle (glide path) and weight.

- ✓ Determine the aiming point. Choosing an aiming point at the end of the runway will result in touchdown about 200 to 300 feet beyond the end of the runway.

- ✓ For short runways it may be desirable (and necessary) to select the aiming point approximately 150 feet before the end of the runway causing the airplane to touchdown just beyond the approach end of the runway. Do not try this procedure without assistance from an instructor.

- ✓ When the mark on the windshield is aligned with the aiming point, you are on the correct glide path.

- ✓ If the aiming point is below the windshield mark, the airplane is too high. Reduce power and check the alignment of the windshield mark and the aiming point.

- ✓ If the aiming point is above the windshield mark, the airplane is too low. Increase the power slightly and check that the windshield mark and aiming point are aligned. ✈

Know the difference between genius and stupidity?

Genius has it limits

PART 5 - LANDINGS   Chapter 6 - Soft-Field Landing

CHAPTER 6 — SOFT-FIELD LANDING

➤ **SOFT-FIELD LANDING PROCEDURE** 5-42

Mountain airstrips, because of their non-paved surfaces, have the potential of producing a soft-field surface for operation during any season of the year. A soft field is defined as a surface that is soft because of snow, slush, mud, tall grass or sand. Other mountain strips have a rough surface at all times.

The purpose of the soft-field landing is to allow landing on a soft surface or a rough surface at the minimum speed at which the airplane is capable of operating. This will minimize the drag upon touchdown and reduce the stress imposed on the landing gear. This is accomplished by flying the airplane in ground effect at a slower than normal speed.

Although other techniques may work, the most acceptable technique is to perform a normal approach to landing. During the last segment of the approach full flaps are extended. If the flaps are extended too soon and it appears the airplane may undershoot the runway, remember to pitch to airspeed and power to sink. This means that airspeed is maintained with forward and rearward elevator control and the altitude is adjusted with power changes.

During the last segment of the approach the airspeed should be maintained at 1.3 V_{SO}. Somewhere between 15-feet agl and 5-feet agl, the attitude is changed to the level-flight attitude. As the airplane begins to sink, transition to the landing attitude; however, you don't want to land ... yet. Add a small amount of

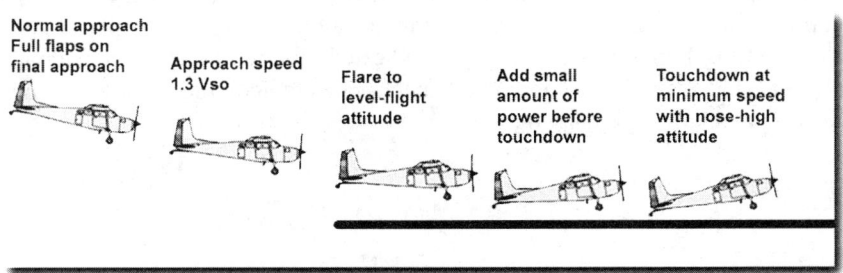

USE THE SOFT-FIELD LANDING TECHNIQUE ON ALL FIELDS THAT HAVE A SOFT OR ROUGH SURFACE.

Mountain Flying Bible

Chapter 6 - Soft-Field Landing   PART 5 - LANDINGS

power (in a fixed-pitch propeller equipped airplane this will be around 1,700 to 2,100 rpm). Continue holding the landing attitude or slightly higher, trying to keep the airplane from touching down while maintaining an altitude of about one foot off the surface. Let the wings support the weight of the aircraft even after touchdown so the wheels do not bog down and flip the airplane onto its back.

By maintaining the small amount of power after touchdown, the nose wheel will lower gently and not dig into the soft surface.

SOFT-FIELD LANDING PROCEDURE

- A normal approach is used for a soft-field landing on a rough or soft surface.
- Apply full flaps on final.
- Airspeed 1.3 VSO.
- Flare to level-flight attitude.
- Add power before touchdown occurs.
- Touchdown at the minimum speed with a nose-high attitude. Reduce the power to idle immediately after the wheels touch the surface.
- Tricycle-gear airplanes - maintain back elevator pressure to aerodynamically keep the nosewheel off the surface as long as possible. Once the nosewheel touches down maintain the backpressure to help in aerodynamic braking and to keep the forces on the nosewheel as light as possible. If maneuvering is required, it may be necessary to lower the nosewheel for more positive steering.
- Conventional-gear airplanes - maintain back elevator pressure throughout the landing roll to reduce the tendency of nose over.
- Low-wing tricycle-gear airplanes - If the surface is muddy or slushy, the flaps may be damaged during the after-landing rollout. Flap retraction just after touchdown is desired, but be careful with a retractable-gear airplane not to retract the gear.

During the flare there should be little or no float. If the airplane floats, the approach speed is too fast. If you are flying an airplane with the airspeed indicator operating limitations expressed as indicated airspeed rather than calibrated airspeed, check out the section on approach speed to determine how to compute the proper approach speed. ✈

Mountain Flying Bible

PART 5 - LANDINGS   Chapter 7 - Short-Field Landing

CHAPTER 7 — SHORT-FIELD LANDING

- ➤ REVIEW OF ATTITUDE FLYING 5-43
- ➤ SHORT-FIELD LANDING - OBSTACLE PRESENT . . 5-44
- ➤ SHORT-FIELD LANDING - WITHOUT OBSTACLE . . 5-47
- ➤ SHORT-FIELD CAUTION 5-47
- ➤ EMERGENCY FORWARD SLIP TO LANDING 5-48
- ➤ TURBULENT AIR 5-48

The most important safety factor for operating at mountain strips is the ability to consistently perform a proper short-field landing approach and touchdown. More times than not, you will not have the textbook 50-foot obstacle at the end of the runway. The real life situation involves non-standard approach to a short field, one that has little or no resemblance to the standard pattern of downwind, base and final.

The approach may involve flight through a canyon or around a mountain where you have to sneak up on the airstrip and you never see it until you are on short final. Because of the surrounding terrain, it may be impossible to execute a go-around maneuver. Because of this, flight proficiency in short-field operations is required before you arrive at the mountain strip.

In *Mountain Flying,* Airguide Publications, I first related that Howard Ballew told me, "Just because you buy a short-field airplane, it doesn't make you a short-field pilot." The short-field landing may turn out to be a disaster because of lack of proficiency, poor planning, poor technique, complacency or over confidence. Again, it is important to practice the short-field landing before the need for its use arises.

Exact airspeed control is essential in performing the short-field landing. Increasing the approach speed as little as 5 knots, may result in the addition of 20 percent more landing distance.

 **RULE OF THUMB – Approach Speed/Landing Distance Relationship**

The landing distance increases by the square of the ratio of the touchdown speed to the normal touchdown speed.

Mountain Flying Bible

For example, a 10 percent increase in approach speed, generally fewer than 7 knots indicated, will result in a 21 percent increase in landing distance. Exact airspeed control is required to keep you from running out of runway before you run out of ideas. At high-altitude strips the same IAS is used as at a sea level strip, but the true airspeed increases about two percent per thousand feet above sea level. This will result in an increase in the landing distance when using the proper approach speed. You certainly don't want to increase the landing distance any more by flying an improper airspeed. Fly the computed airspeed and no other. Even a small increase in approach speed results in a large increase in landing distance.

SHORT-FIELD LANDING – OBSTACLE PRESENT

The short-field landing is a maximum performance operation that provides touchdown on a precise spot on the runway that is either short in length or the landing area is restricted because of an approach over an obstacle. This is a critical operation because the airspeed is flown at the minimum speed for a controlled descent, operating close to the ground.

Use the spot method for landing to provide an exact glide path to the desired spot on the runway surface where the flare will be executed. With proper airspeed control the rest is easy, landing within the confined area without worry.

The variables that make the short-field landing at a mountain strip challenging are wind, updrafts and downdrafts. Again, using the spot method for landing will allow you to compensate for these variables and permit a safe landing.

The airspeed should be the manufacturer's recommended airspeed; otherwise, the maximum airspeed for a short-field landing is 1.3 VSO. The speed is based on the weight of the airplane. If the airspeed is determined to be 62 knots at maximum allowable gross weight and the airplane is being operated 400 pounds under gross weight, the speed must be re-computed.

At any elevation airport, try flying an approach at 1.3 VSO. If the airplane arrives at the position of the flare and lands 200-300 feet beyond this point without float, then you have the proper speed for the operating weight. If the airplane floats, the approach speed is too fast.

Caution: If the approach speed is too slow, there will not be sufficient elevator control to effect a flare and the airplane will make a hard landing. Even at the proper airspeed, if the flare is performed at too high an altitude, the airplane will stall or set up a high sink rate, again impacting the runway with undesired force. If the airplane cannot be flared due to a slow approach speed, add power to make the elevator more effective so the nose can be raised before arrival. Maintain back pressure on the elevator and the airplane will bounce very little, if any,

PART 5 - LANDINGS   **Chapter 7 - Short-Field Landing**

because the speed is too slow in relation to the mass of the airplane to allow much of a bounce.

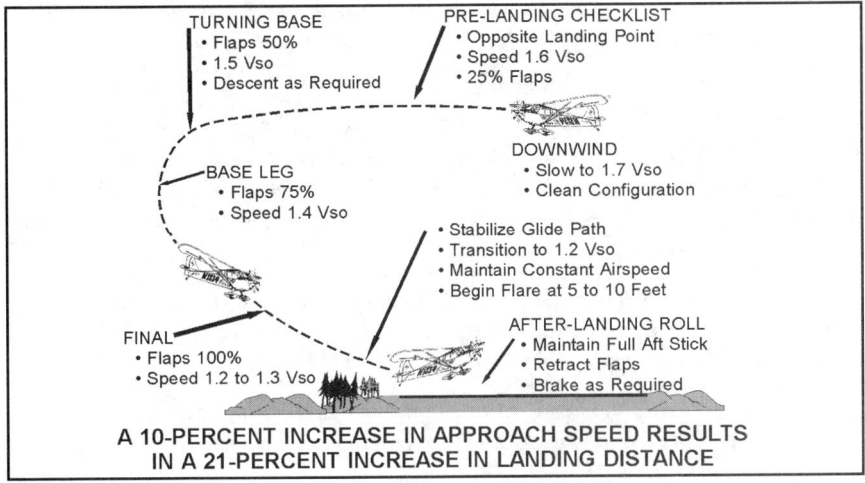

A 10-PERCENT INCREASE IN APPROACH SPEED RESULTS IN A 21-PERCENT INCREASE IN LANDING DISTANCE

THE SHORT-FIELD LANDING

I held the opinion for years that a good short-field landing is not a nice landing. It is an arrival at a particular point on the ground with a firm touchdown. Yet it does not have to damage the airplane.

Then I screwed up a few times, setting up too high a rate of descent. This required adding a burst of power to make the elevator effective in cushioning the landing. The landings were "greasers."

I started contemplating the fact that the "greaser" landing resulted a short-field landing with the same runway distance used as the "arrival" landing. And it is much more acceptable to passengers. You, too, with a little practice can make the short-field landing feel like the arrival of a butterfly with sore feet.

- Use the spot method to arrive over the end of the strip at the slowest speed using full flaps.
- During the flare use enough power to make the elevator effective to cushion the landing.
- Touchdown with the brakes partially on.
- Retract the flaps, pull back for full up-elevator control (aerodynamic braking) and apply brakes as necessary. For taildraggers, if the tail starts to come up, relax the braking slightly.

Mountain Flying Bible

Chapter 7 - Short-Field Landing   PART 5 - LANDINGS

Some mountain airstrips, because of the terrain features, prohibit the use of a standard pattern not only for the approach, but also for the departure. Depending on the pattern used, on the downwind leg opposite the landing point (or a comparable position when the downwind and base legs are not flown), perform the pre-landing cockpit check.

Establish a stabilized approach, transition to 1.3 V_{SO} and adjust the power to result in an approximate 500-fpm rate of descent. Elevator control is used to maintain the airspeed. Maintain an exact airspeed. Generally the flaps are added in increments with 25 percent on downwind, 25 percent on base and the remainder after turning final. Power adjustments are used to adjust the glide path (alignment of the windshield mark and aiming point).

Use the same indicated airspeed at all airports regardless of elevation. At high elevation airports additional power will be required to maintain the same rate of descent as that used at sea-level strips.

Move the eyes, not the head, on final approach and during the flare to enhance the altitude perspective of height and movement of the airplane.

The flare and landing is performed in accordance with attitude flying. At about 10-15 feet above the ground the elevator is used to transition from the glide attitude to the level-flight attitude. The airplane will begin settling fast at the proper approach speed. The flare is continued to the landing attitude. When the wheels touch, reduce the power to idle, maintain backpressure and brake. Short fields require retraction of the flaps immediately after touchdown to place more weight on the tires, increasing the braking effectiveness.

Do not fly over the obstacle and chop the power to drop down to the runway. This technique increases the risk of running out of elevator control and being unable to flare. If the spot method for landing is followed, this will be totally unnecessary, allowing a constant descent angle throughout the approach and flare over the aiming point on the strip.

While you are free to choose the manner that you perform the short-field approach, the author vehemently disagrees with the FAA Flight Training Handbook technique for short-field landings. This book states, "That pitch attitude is adjusted as necessary to establish and maintain the desired rate or angle of descent, and power is adjusted to maintain the desired airspeed."

Try the FAA method and then try the method explained in the spot method for landing. You will probably agree that it is much easier to control the airspeed with elevator and the altitude with throttle. Also, by controlling the airspeed with elevator you will never get into the position where the airspeed is too low. When the airspeed is too slow and additional altitude is needed to fly to the runway, even an increase in pitch and application of full power will not save the day because the airplane's maximum available power will be insufficient to overcome the speed deficit. Maintaining precise airspeed control with the elevator is much easier and much safer.

REVIEW OF ATTITUDE FLYING

The glide attitude is the position of the nose below the horizon that results in a constant performance (constant airspeed) when the power is maintained at a constant setting. If the power is adjusted the pitch attitude must change to maintain a constant airspeed. When power is reduced, the nose is lowered. When power is increased, the nose is raised.

The level-flight attitude is the position of the nose below the horizon during level flight at cruise airspeed and cruise power setting that results in a constant altitude (zero rate of climb and zero rate of descent).

The landing attitude approximates the normal climb attitude of the airplane. During a climb the nose will be above the horizon. Remember this attitude of climbing at V_Y, and note where the horizon intersects the side of the engine cowling. Use this point for transition to the landing attitude.

SHORT-FIELD LANDING - WITHOUT AN OBSTACLE

The short-field landing without an obstacle present is performed in the same manner as the short-field landing with an obstacle present. Instead of using the 4½-degree glide path (8 x ground speed), you might want to use the 3-degree glide path (5 x ground speed).

The only cautionary note is that the approach shouldn't be long and flat with the airplane "hanging" on the prop at a slow airspeed. Make a normal approach and use the spot method for landing to adjust the glide path.

SHORT-FIELD PRECAUTIONS

If the pilot chooses not to use the spot method for landing he may experience an error in judgment concerning the glide path. When this occurs and a go-around maneuver is necessary, remember that some airplanes will require as much as 100 feet of altitude to transition from the descent to a climb after "cleaning up" the flaps and gear.

Suppose you thought everything was going well on the approach, yet you arrive over the runway floating and floating. At this point you could care less what went wrong. You know you have too much airspeed and you need to get on the ground, fast. Do not push the nose forward to get it on the ground. This may complicate the problem. You have two choices, dumping the flaps or a forward slip or a combination of the two.

Assuming the airplane is close to the ground, retract the flaps to reduce the coefficient of lift sufficiently so the airplane can be landed. If maximum braking

Chapter 7 - Short-Field Landing   PART 5 - LANDINGS

is required, maintain some backpressure while applying brake pressure. As the airplane slows, use full backpressure to add aerodynamic braking. Brake pressure to the point of wheel lockup is not desired. If the wheels are locked, the reduced resistance of skidding tires will require a greater stopping distance.

EMERGENCY FORWARD SLIP TO LANDING

The emergency forward slip to a landing requires previous practice, preferably with an experienced flight instructor. Even if you never use this technique it will help make you a better pilot because it will give you a "seat of the pants" feel for the airplane and experience in maneuvering the airplane close to the ground.

The technique is a forward slip to a landing, but it isn't like the normal forward slip to a landing. This forward slip is not initiated until just before or during the flare.

When you discover the far end of the runway rapidly approaching you may consider making a go-around, then think to yourself, "I can't make it." Either the airplane is too heavy, the air's too hot, the elevation is too high, the mountain or power lines are too high. So you decide to land, even if you run off the runway. Running off the runway at slow speed is much less severe than while accelerating and trying to make a go-around.

By stepping on the right rudder, all the way to the floor (if you are strong enough to push the rudder partially through the floor, do it), the nose will swing to the right. Left aileron is applied to maintain the flight path along the runway centerline. Speed will bleed off fast. Before the airplane stalls, relax both aileron and rudder pressure at the same time. The airplane will align itself parallel to the runway and a normal landing can be completed.

Remember if this maneuver is begun before the flare, the flare still has to be executed. You are holding the forward slip while executing the normal landing.

The reason for using the right rudder-left aileron combination is that the pilot normally sits on the left side of the airplane. By doing the forward slip to the left, the pilot has better visibility and can determine the height above the ground more accurately.

TURBULENT AIR

When approaching to land in turbulent air with gusty winds, add one-half the gust factor to the normal approach speed to compensate for any stall tendency. ✈

Mountain Flying Bible

PART 5 - LANDINGS   Chapter 8 - Crosswind Landing

CHAPTER 8 — CROSSWIND LANDING

- CRAB/KICK-OUT METHOD. 5-49
- SIDESLIP TO A LANDING. 5-50
- PREFERRED CROSSWIND LANDING METHOD . . . 5-51
- CURVED-PATH LANDING. 5-53
- CROSSWIND LANDING ERRORS 5-53

Execution of the perfect crosswind landing requires prior thought and practice. The thought involves conditioning yourself against the mechanical slip while the practice develops your flying technique.

There are several techniques for making a crosswind landing. There is the "crab/kick out" method, the "wing-down or side-slip" method, and a combination of both of these. The wing-down method is the most popular, being used by more pilots than any other method because it is easier and requires less judgment.

Crosswind landings are generally more difficult to learn than crosswind take-offs due to the difference in aircraft control while the speed is decreasing instead of increasing. During the acceleration of takeoff the controls become more and more positive; during the deceleration of landing the controls become less and less effective.

CRAB/KICK-OUT METHOD

Crosswind landings allow the airplane to drift away from the extended runway centerline. If the airplane is flown into the wind with a crab sufficient to stop the drift and this crab is continued with no corrective action until the moment of touchdown, the airplane is going to protest the undesirable side force on the landing gear. Once on the ground, the airplane's inherent tendency to weathercock will also try to force it off its desired heading.

If you have never performed and perfected the crab/kick-out method, you would be well advised to obtain a competent instructor to help you practice.

The crab/kick-out method involves flying the airplane in a crab until after the airplane is flared. Just before touchdown, while inches above the runway, lower the upwind wing enough to cause the gear to make contact with the runway. At

Mountain Flying Bible   5-49

Chapter 8 - Crosswind Landing   PART 5 - LANDINGS

the same time, kick downwind rudder sufficiently so the longitudinal axis is aligned parallel to the runway.

This technique is used more by transport category airplanes where the pilot is concerned about hitting the engine or wing tip if he performs a sideslip maneuver.

FORWARD SLIP

The forward slip is a maneuver used to expose a large side profile of the airplane to the relative wind, creating drag, and resulting in a steep descent without an increase in airspeed.

To perform a forward slip, step on one rudder to move the nose sideways. Apply opposite aileron pressure to hold the wing down slightly. For example, if the right rudder is used, left aileron is applied to the extent that the airplane flies along the same flight path as before the slip, maintaining the same track over the ground.

To recover to normal flight, relax both controls, aileron and rudder, at the same time and the airplane will return to the same attitude as before the forward slip.

SIDE SLIP

The side slip is a maneuver used to fly the airplane laterally an amount equal to drift so that it can touch down on the runway with no side loading on the landing gear. The exact same controls are used as with the forward slip; however the ailerons are applied before the rudder.

When the aileron is deflected, the airplane will begin a turn, although it experiences adverse aileron drag. Before the nose begins moving in the direction of the bank, apply sufficient opposite rudder to maintain the longitudinal axis parallel to the runway.

Recovering to normal flight is different than the forward slip recovery. Here the aileron control is relaxed first, then the rudder. The airplane will assume the same attitude as before the side slip maneuver.

SIDE SLIP TO A LANDING

After turning onto final approach, it is preferred that runway alignment along the extended centerline be maintained with a crab, that is, by flying into the wind an amount sufficient to counteract drift. The airplane, while in the crab, is in a wings-level, coordinated flight condition.

Usually the crab is maintained until arriving at an altitude of 400 feet or fewer. Because the wind changes direction and velocity as you approach the ground

PART 5 - LANDINGS   Chapter 8 - Crosswind Landing

(from 2,000-feet agl, the wind usually swings to the left, as much as 45 degrees), if the side slip is initiated too soon the airplane may not have sufficient rudder to maintain the flight path in alignment with the runway. Below 400 feet, if the longitudinal axis cannot be maintained parallel to the runway (while in a slip), the crosswind is probably too strong for a safe landing.

Caution

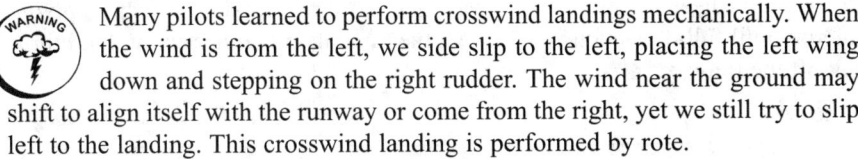 Many pilots learned to perform crosswind landings mechanically. When the wind is from the left, we side slip to the left, placing the left wing down and stepping on the right rudder. The wind near the ground may shift to align itself with the runway or come from the right, yet we still try to slip left to the landing. This crosswind landing is performed by rote.

PREFERRED CROSSWIND LANDING METHOD

A better method involves flying the airplane to the extended runway centerline. Use the ailerons as required to maintain the airplane's position along the extended centerline. Use the rudders as necessary to maintain the longitudinal axis parallel to the runway.

This technique will result in constantly changing aileron positioning to keep aligned with the runway centerline when the wind changes direction or when the wind gusts. There will be constantly changing rudder positioning to keep the longitudinal axis straight. This results in a side slip, but it isn't thought of in terms of a side slip.

Practice this technique. It makes it easier and safer to perform the crosswind landing during gusty conditions when rapid control movement is required to maintain runway centerline alignment and longitudinal axis alignment.

There is no requirement to stop and think, "Gee, the wind switched to the right, I have to make a side slip to the right, and that involves..."

Instead, if the airplane begins drifting to the left, immediate right aileron is applied to stay aligned over the centerline. Adverse aileron drag will yaw the nose right making it necessary to step on the left rudder to align the longitudinal axis parallel to the runway.

You will be surprised at how little practice it will take to become very proficient at crosswind landings using this technique. Your initial practice will be benefited if you make several passes along the runway in slow flight condition, practicing the alignment along the entire length of the runway. Then move on to the actual touchdown.

Mountain Flying Bible   **5-51**

Chapter 8 - Crosswind Landing PART 5 - LANDINGS

When the side slip method is used, there is a continuity of flight control positioning from before touchdown to the end of the landing roll. During the flare the upwind main wheel will contact the runway first. As the airplane decelerates the controls lose effectiveness, first the rudder, followed by the elevator and finally the ailerons. Exercise full attention to keeping the airplane rolling in a straight line, aligned parallel to the runway, to prevent any tendency to ground loop. After touchdown, more and more aileron control is added into the wind until the downwind wheel touches the runway. As the airplane slows, keep applying aileron until full deflection is achieved, then maintain that deflection until turning off the runway.

THE CROSSWIND LANDING

- Fly a crab approach along the extended runway centerline, changing the crab as necessary to maintain runway alignment.
- Switch to a side slip when less than 400-feet above the ground.
- Touch down on the upwind wheel first in a side slip.
- Maintain the side slip until the downwind wheel touches the ground.
- Maintain directional control during the rollout.
- Fly the airplane until it is parked, that is, position the controls for the existing wind condition using the "thumbs up method." See page 2-4.

CURVED-PATH LANDING

When a crosswind landing must be performed at an airport whose only runway alignment allows a wind that exceeds the landing capability of the airplane, the curved path landing may be used. This could occur if there is insufficient fuel to go to another airport or if the weather turns sour and prohibits flight to a more favorable airport.

The technique involves angling across the runway, pointed into the wind with the touchdown near the downwind edge of the runway. A gradual turn is made away from the upwind side of the runway to parallel the upwind edge. This will balance the upsetting force of the wind with the centrifugal force and help keep the upwind wing down. The centrifugal force increases relative to the square of the velocity at which it starts, rather than in a linear manner, so keep the touchdown speed as slow as possible (consistent with safety).

CROSSWIND LANDING ERRORS

The most common crosswind-landing errors include:

- Failure to correct accurately for drift at the moment of touch down. Either too much or too little drift correction will impose side loads on the landing gear.
- Failure to maintain alignment with the ground path results in erratic direction control and increases the probability of a ground loop.
- Failure to apply and maintain aileron control after the initial touchdown.

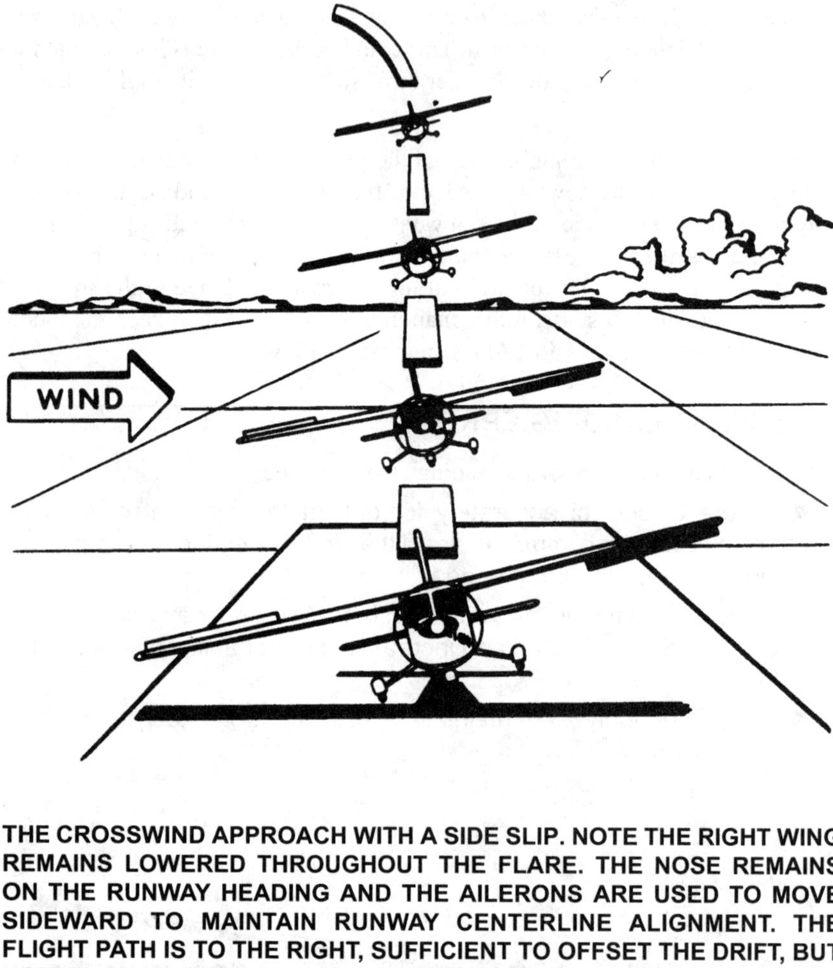

Chapter 8 - Crosswind Landing — PART 5 - LANDINGS

THE CROSSWIND APPROACH WITH A SIDE SLIP. NOTE THE RIGHT WING REMAINS LOWERED THROUGHOUT THE FLARE. THE NOSE REMAINS ON THE RUNWAY HEADING AND THE AILERONS ARE USED TO MOVE SIDEWARD TO MAINTAIN RUNWAY CENTERLINE ALIGNMENT. THE FLIGHT PATH IS TO THE RIGHT, SUFFICIENT TO OFFSET THE DRIFT, BUT NOT ENOUGH TO CHANGE THE RUNWAY CENTERLINE ALIGNMENT. DURING GUSTY WIND CONDITIONS THE AILERONS ARE MOVED BACK AND FORTH TO MAINTAIN THE ALIGNMENT. THE RUDDER IS USED TO MAINTAIN THE LONGITUDINAL AXIS PARALLEL TO THE RUNWAY.

CHAPTER 9 — PARKING

NOSE OVER	5-55
TIE-DOWN	5-55
MOSQUITOES	5-56

NOSE OVER

While owning an FBO, I had the unfortunate opportunity to observe two tail-dragger airplanes park on their noses while maneuvering for a tie-down spot. These incidents occurred when the wind was blowing fewer than 15 knots.

The "locked-wheel turn" technique caused each incident. Conventional-gear airplanes have the capability of turning very sharply when one brake is held and a blast of power is used to swing the tail. If the tail swing is into the wind, the propeller blast may combine with the wind to lift the tail. This occurs very rapidly and the unsuspecting pilot ends up on the nose before he figures out what is happening.

At this point some pilots will smirk and say, "It wouldn't have happened if the pilot had sucked the stick into his gut." This phraseology refers to holding the control wheel or stick all the way back. In at least one of these incidents the stick was all the way back. The prop blast and wind forces combined to lift the tail.

Once the tail starts up the only thing that will correct the situation is to release the brake and add more power to "fly" out of it. If the stick isn't already full back, position it there rapidly, and hope no other airplanes are nearby to block your way.

TIE-DOWN

In mountain areas it is a well-known fact that strong, gusty winds may arise without warning or apparent cause. Many small airstrips do not have adequate tie-down facilities.

For operations at backcountry strips it is a good idea to purchase or make a tie-down kit. Use a screw-type ground anchor rather than pitons. They provide greater security.

Howard Ballew suggested an emergency procedure that will enable the airplane to withstand an unbelievable amount of wind. Dig holes in front of the wheels and roll the airplane into them. Be careful if the airplane is equipped with wheel pants not to damage them. The change in angle of attack helps tremendously in keeping the airplane put.

Another method used by many "tail dragger" pilots is to lock only one brake and let the airplane weathercock into the wind. Be sure to give the airplane "breathing" room to maneuver around.

Tie-Down Caution

If there are cattle near the area where you park the airplane, keep someone around to guard the airplane. Some strips have a fenced enclosure, not to keep the cattle in, but to keep them out. Cows love to eat fabric airplanes. Metal planes are not safe just because they can't be eaten, since the cows will rub against exposed parts and can cause extensive damage.

MOSQUITOES

Mosquitoes can be more than an annoyance at mountain strips, they can downright ruin an otherwise perfect trip. So don't forget to take along the mosquito repellent. I absolutely refuse to practice medicine and suggest that no one take any medications, including vitamins, without the approval of the doctor. So the following is offered with the recommendation that you check with qualified medical personnel to determine the suitability for you.

Years ago I read a publication like *Outdoor Life,* that said if you overdose on Vitamin B-1 (thiamin), the mosquitoes will leave you alone. They suggested taking about 1,000 mg a day for a week before your outdoor exposure, then 500 mg a day to maintain the thiamin body saturation. The thiamin makes you smell bad to mosquitoes. It shouldn't affect your relationship with other people, but it definitely offends mosquitoes.

Vitamin B-1 occurs naturally in the bran coat of grains, in yeast and in meat. It is necessary for carbohydrate metabolism, maintenance of normal neural activity and the prevention of beri-beri. I have tried, unsuccessfully, to eat enough bread and meat to overdose on thiamin. So I tried the pills. Thiamin is a water-soluble vitamin, meaning that any excess that your body requires is expelled through the urine.

There was some controversy a few years ago about whether too much of a water-soluble vitamin can cause the body harm, so don't do this on my recommendation. Check with your physician. (And, yes, it does work.) ✈

PART 5 - LANDINGS   Rules of Thumb

PART 5 — LANDINGS—RULES OF THUMB

 APPROACH INDICATED AIRSPEED

Always fly your approach for landing at the normal sea-level approach indicated airspeed for the airplane. (See page 5-1)

 BACK SIDE OF DRAG CURVE OPERATION

Maintain airspeed with elevator and altitude with throttle. (See page 5-5)

 REDUCED LANDING WEIGHT AIRSPEED

Reduce the calibrated approach airspeed for the maximum landing weight listed, by one-half of the percentage of the weight decreases. (See page 5-19)

NOW THAT'S A SHORT-FIELD LANDING. NOTE THE GOOSE ON THE NATIONAL ELK REFUGE FENCE POST NORTH OF JACKSON, WYO. DON'T TRY THIS AT HOME!

Mountain Flying Bible

The Bowline Knot

The Bowline is considered the only knot to use to secure a rope to a tie-down anchor. It does not slip and it will not jam, making it easy to untie.

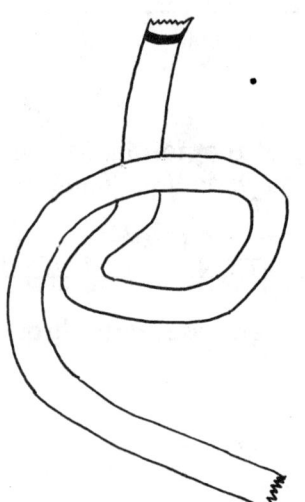

BEGIN WITH THE LONG END OF THE ROPE AT THE TOP (INDICATED BY BLACK RING). COIL A LOOP TOWARD YOU USING THE SHORT END OF THE ROPE.

THE SHORT END OF THE ROPE IS MOVED UP THROUGH THE LOOP AROUND THE LONG END AND BACK DOWN THROUGH THE LOOP. BOY SCOUTS USE THE MEMORY AID: "THE RABBIT COMES OUT OF HIS HOLE, AROUND THE TREE AND BACK DOWN AGAIN."

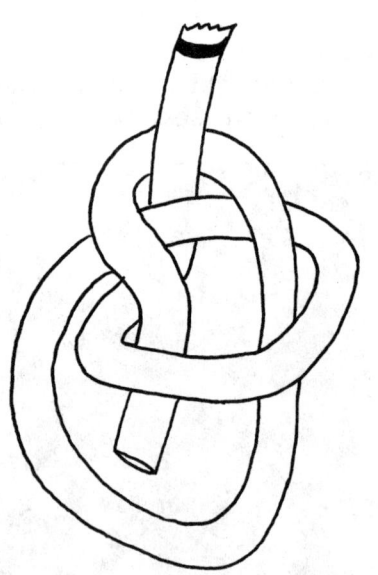

PART 5 - LANDINGS — Possum Creek

POSSUM CREEK AIRSTRIP, COLORADO
OWNER: DAVID FORCE. THE APPROACH END OF POSSUM CREEK IS 9,840-FEET ELEVATION. THE TOP END IS 10,010 FEET (170-FOOT RISE). THE LENGTH IS 1,360 FEET WITH 20-PERCENT UPSLOPE IN THE FIRST 850 FEET AND 10-PERCENT UPSLOPE IN THE LAST 510 FEET. THERE IS A 700-FOOT DROP OFF AT EITHER END. WIND CONDITIONS MUST BE FAVORABLE FOR LANDING UPHILL AND TAKEOFF DOWNHILL. A COMMITMENT TO LAND IS FINAL AS THE TERRAIN PREVENTS A GO-AROUND.

BEFORE COMMITTING TO LAND, AN APPROACH IS FLOWN FROM LEFT TO RIGHT (HIGH TERRAIN TO LOW TERRAIN) TO TEST THE AIR QUALITY (TURBULENCE, UPDRAFTS AND DOWNDRAFTS).

Possum Creek PART 5 - LANDINGS

THE APPROACH IS MADE "FLAT." IF A NORMAL DESCENDING APPROACH IS MADE, EXCESSIVE AIRSPEED IS REQUIRED TO PERFORM A FLARE THAT FIRST PARALLELS THE RUNWAY, THEN CONTINUES AS A NORMAL LANDING.

NOTHING SPECIAL HERE. MAINTAIN EXACT AIRSPEED CONTROL ON FINAL. IF FLOWN AT THE PROPER SPEED, POWER IS REQUIRED TO MAKE IT TO THE TOP OF THE STRIP.

PART 5 - LANDINGS — Possum Creek

AFTER TOUCHDOWN IN THE THREE-POINT LANDING ATTITUDE POWER IS MAINTAINED GOING UP THE SLOPE.

THE TRANSITION FROM 20-DEGREES UPSLOPE TO 10-DEGREES UPSLOPE MAY REQUIRE A SLIGHT POWER REDUCTION. SUFFICIENT POWER IS USED TO MAKE IT TO THE TOP OF THE SLOPE, BUT NOT BEYOND. THERE IS A 700-FOOT DROPOFF.

Possum Creek   **PART 5 - LANDINGS**

AT THE TOP OF "POSSUM CREEK INTERNATIONAL," WHERE THE "INTERNATIONAL" MONIKER IS APPLIED JOKINGLY. IT DOESN'T MUCH RESEMBLE THE U.S. CUSTOMS-MANNED FACILITIES THAT RESERVE THE NAME "INTERNATIONAL."

FIRST APPEARANCES ARE OFTEN DECEIVING. YOU MIGHT THINK THIS STRIP "AIN'T SUCH A MUCH." FROM A DISTANCE IT HAS THE INNOCUOUS LOOK OF A ROTOR CLOUD. JUDGMENT SHOULD BE RESERVED UNTIL MAKING THE ACTUAL APPROACH.

MANY MOUNTAIN STRIPS APPEAR TERRIBLE. HERE THE STRIP LIES BETWEEN TWO RIDGES AND 700-FOOT CLIFFS AT EACH END. THE INCLINE ADDS TO ITS MYSTIQUE. BUT IF THIS STRIP WERE MOVED TO FLATLAND, A STUDENT PILOT COULD SAFELY OPERATE FROM ITS PARAMETERS.

BECAUSE OF THE TERRAIN, IT BECOMES NECESSARY TO PSYCHE YOURSELF UP FOR THE LANDING.

AS ANY SELF-RESPECTING MOUNTAIN PILOT WOULD WANT TO GIVE THIS STRIP A TRY, A WORD OF CAUTION. THE STRIP IS PRIVATELY OWNED BY DAVE FORCE JR. YOU CAN CALL HIM IN GLENWOOD SPRINGS, COLO. HIS STRIP, THE POSSUM CREEK RANCH AND THE BARN STRUCTURE HAS BEEN LISTED FOR SALE. (HE HAS A NEW SUMMER CABIN AND STRIP.)

(Cessna 180)

PART 5 - LANDINGS Possum Creek

THE BEGINNING OF THE TAKEOFF ROLL IS MADE DOWNHILL WITH THE FLAPS RETRACTED.

AT THE TRANSITION FROM 10-PERCENT DOWNSLOPE TO 20-PERCENT DOWNSLOPE, THE "JOHNSON BAR" FLAPS ARE APPLIED AND THE AIRPLANE BECOMES AIRBORNE WITHOUT EFFORT.

Possum Creek   **PART 5 - LANDINGS**

IT DOESN'T REQUIRE MUCH RUNWAY TO BECOME AIRBORNE. ONCE IN THE AIR, THE AIRPLANE IS MANEUVERED TOWARD LOWERING TERRAIN.

USE CAUTION LANDING ON UPSLOPE TERRAIN.

IN A NORMAL APPROACH TO LANDING, THE APPROACH AIRSPEED IS MAINTAINED UNTIL BEGINNING THE FLARE. THE AIRSPEED DISSIPATES AND THE AIRCRAFT BEGINS TO SINK. IDEALLY THE AIRCRAFT REACHES THE STALL AT THE TIME OF TOUCHDOWN.

APPROACHING A SLOPED RUNWAY WITH NORMAL APPROACH SPEED IS HAZARDOUS. IT IS NECESSARY TO TRANSITION FROM THE DESCENT ANGLE OF APPROXIMATELY THREE DEGREES TO PARALLEL THE RUNWAY. THEN THERE MUST BE SUFFICIENT AIRSPEED TO MAKE THE FLARE AND PERFORM A NORMAL LANDING.

WITHOUT THE EXCESS AIRSPEED THE AIRPLANE MAY NOT HAVE ENOUGH ELEVATOR CONTROL TO CHANGE THE ATTITUDE FOR THE LANDING. A HIGH SINK RATE WILL OCCUR AND WITHOUT EXCESS POWER (LOTS AND LOTS OF POWER) THE AIRPLANE WILL PROBABLY BE DAMAGED.

Mountain Flying Bible

Aeronautical Information   APPENDIX

AERONAUTICAL INFORMATION

For information concerning the availability of state-published aeronautical charts and airport directories, contact the following:

California Division of Aeronautics P.O. Box 942874 Sacramento, California 94272-0001 Phone 916-322-3090	Colorado Division of Aeronautics 56 Inverness Drive, East Englewood, Colorado 80112-5114 Phone 303-397-3039
Idaho Transportation Department Division of Aeronautics 3483 Rickenbacker Street Boise, Idaho 83705-1129 Phone 208-334-8789	Montana Aeronautics Commission P.O. Box 5178 Helena, Montana 59604 Phone 406-444-2506 www.mdt.mt.gov/aeronaut/aeronaut.htm
Oregon Aeronautics section 3040 25th Street, S.E. Salem, Oregon 97310 Phone 503-378-4880 Fax: 503-373-1688 E-mail: ODOT.Aero@state.or.us	Utah Department of Transportation Division of Aeronautics Salt Lake International Airport 135 North 2400 West Salt Lake City, Utah 84116 Phone 801-533-5057
Washington Division of Aeronautics 8600 Perimeter Road -Boeing Field Seattle, Washington 98108 Phone 206-764-4131 www.wsdot.wa.gov/aviation	Wyoming DOT/Aeronautics Division 200 East 8th Avenue Cheyenne, Wyoming 82002-0090 Phone 307-777-7481

For states not listed here, you can call or write to obtain information on what may be available and the cost. It is sometimes difficult to determine the name of the aeronautical department. If you can't find it, call the long distance telephone operator at the state's capital and ask for a listing for the state government. Call them and ask for the aeronautics department phone number or address. For searching the internet, try "state dot."

Some states will allow you to register as a "state" pilot. Once you have registered, you will probably be sent the official state aeronautical chart and airport-facility directory (if these are available). Your pilot registration may represent a

Mountain Flying Bible   A-1

APPENDIX — Formulas

fraction of the cost of ordering the chart and directory separately. You may also be placed on the state's mailing list for updates to aeronautical information plus their newsletter.

FORMULAS

Some pilots have no use for formulas and mathematical equations. The charts and graphs provided in Part 3 - EN ROUTE, eliminate the need for computations. For the few who like to play with numbers (or want to check the validity of the charts), the formulas used to make the charts are included:

The following abbreviations are used in the formulas

C = circumference	Cos = Cosine
d = diameter	f = force, pounds
G = load factor	g = acceleration of gravity (32.2 fps)^2
G_b = limit load factor, at θ	$\sqrt{G\theta}$ = square root of limit load factor, at the banked angle, degrees
π = 3.14159	
R = radius, feet	r = turn radius, feet
∅ = bank angle, degrees	ROT = rate of turn, degrees per second
T = time in minutes to complete 180° turn	t = time in seconds
v = speed, feet per second	Tan = Tangent
Vp = minimum maneuver speed	V = velocity, true airspeed, knots
Vsθ = velocity of stall at any bank angle, degrees	Vs = stall speed, knots, at θ
	W = weight, pounds

LOAD FACTOR

To determine the load factor acting upon the airplane at any particular bank angle, the following formula applies:

$$G = \frac{1}{\cos \varnothing}$$

TURN RADIUS

To determine the turn radius in feet, the following formula applies:

$$r = \frac{v^2}{11.26 \tan \varnothing}$$

Formulas   APPENDIX

CENTRIPETAL FORCE

To determine the centripetal force or total horizontal lift required in a turn, the following applies:

$$F = \frac{Wv^2}{gr}$$

MINIMUM MANEUVER SPEED

The minimum maneuver speed, not to be confused with maneuvering speed, is the aerodynamic limit and structural limit of the turn that produces the smallest turn radius. It can be determined as:

$$V_p = V_s \sqrt{G\ limit}$$

Excel format: = $V_{s}*(SQRT(1/COS(\varnothing*PI()/180)))$

CIRCUMFERENCE/DIAMETER OF A CIRCLE

Circumference is the perimeter or border or a circle. Diameter is the chord from the center of the circle to the edge. Either can be determined by:

$$d = \frac{C}{\pi} \qquad C = \pi d$$

TURN RATE (RATE OF TURN)

Rate of turn is expressed in degrees per second. A standard rate turn is 3-degrees per second, taking 120 seconds (2 minutes) to complete a 360 degree turn.

$$ROT = \frac{1{,}091\ Tan.\varnothing}{V}$$

DIAMETER OF TURN

$$d = \frac{0.17762\ V^2}{Tan.\varnothing}$$

STALL SPEED AT ANY GIVEN BANK ANGLE

$$V_s\varnothing = \sqrt{G\varnothing}\ V_{so}$$

Excel format: =$(SQRT(1/COS(\varnothing*PI()/180)))*V_{so}$

Mountain Flying Bible

APPENDIX   Formulas

TIME TO COMPLETE 180-DEGREE TURN

$$T = \frac{0.031022415\ r}{V}$$

TIME TO COMPLETE 180° TURN, RADIUS UNKNOWN

$$T = \frac{0.002755099\ V^2}{V}$$

CAP CLOUD COVERING THE TETON MOUNTAINS, JACKSON HOLE AIRPORT, WYO.

HIGH ALTITUDE AND LOW ALTITUDE LENTICULARS WITH ASSOCIATED ROLL CLOUDS. LENTICULARS MERELY INDICATE AREAS WITH MOISTURE, NOT NECESSARILY THE AREA OF MAXIMUM WAVE ACTIVITY (UPDRAFTS, DOWNDRAFTS AND TURBULENCE).

Lesson Plan APPENDIX

MOUNTAIN FLYING LESSON

This mountain flying lesson has been incorporated into one flight lesson; however, it may require several flights to accomplish the goals. As a suggestion, check off and date each area that has been completed satisfactorily.

OBJECTIVES:
The objective is to gain an understanding of mountain flying activities, procedures, high-altitude operations, mountain flying techniques and operating safety considerations.

The student will develop the aeronautical knowledge and ability to accomplish the various maneuvers and procedures in a safe and orderly manner.

PREFLIGHT DISCUSSION AND ORIENTATION

GROUND INSTRUCTION

1. MOUNTAIN FLYING BASIC PREMISES

☐ Always remain in a position where you can turn toward lowering terrain.

☐ Do not fly beyond the "point of no return."

2. COORDINATION MANEUVERS

☐ Coordination Rolls – Align the airplane's nose on a point on the horizon. Roll the aircraft back and forth, using coordinated aileron and rudder to maintain the nose on the point. Too much rudder causes the nose to yaw in the direction of the turn. Too much aileron causes the nose to veer opposite the turn.

☐ Climbing Turns – To learn the application of right rudder during left and right turns.

☐ Descending Turns – To learn the application of left rudder during left and right turns.

3. FLIGHT MANEUVERS

☐ Flight at Minimum Controllable Airspeed

Mountain Flying Bible

APPENDIX Lesson Plan

☐ Stall Series – Takeoff and approach-to-landing stalls in straight and turning flight.

☐ Cross-control stalls – To teach rudder usage in the prevention of spin entries.

☐ Spins – Only if the aircraft and loading limitations allow, e.g. no spins with passenger/s in the rear seat, or baggage in the rear.

4. TAKEOFFS AND LANDINGS

☐ Soft Field - Set the flap position for maximum lift. Unless the manufacturer specifies otherwise, make full aileron deflection and match the flap setting to this deflection.

☐ Short Field – Airspeed control is most important. Do not maintain a shallow angle, then reduce power to "swoop" down to the landing strip. Instead, maintain a constant descent angle on final all the way to the landing strip.

☐ Takeoff Roll Techniques – For a short, short runway it may be necessary to accelerate during the turn-around to takeoff alignment.

☐ Crosswind Operations – Non-mechanical side slip technique during approach for landing. After liftoff, fly a crab, not a side slip.

5. KINDS OF MOUNTAIN FLYING

☐ Climb to an altitude 2,000 feet above the highest terrain and proceed to the destination. If the destination (or departure) is in the mountains, make a circular descent (or climb).

☐ Betwixt and between the mountains – Visualize lift, sink and turbulence. Determine terrain clearance parameters.

6. ROUTE PLANNING

☐ Select the route of flight based on terrain, altitudes to be flown, aircraft performance, weather, mountain wave conditions, oxygen requirements, and VHF navaids (if Loran or GPS are not available)

☐ For dead reckoning navigation, compute the ground speed. To the flight time for each climb leg, add one minute per 1,000 feet of climb.

☐ File a flight plan to insure peace of mind and search-and-rescue operations. Make periodic position reports.

7. MOUNTAIN FLYING DIFFERENCES

☐ Air is thin – This affects aircraft performance, the lift of the wings, the thrust of the propeller, and the power output of the engine.

Lesson Plan   APPENDIX

☐ Thin air is moving – This creates updrafts, downdrafts and turbulence.

☐ The airplane is in close proximity to terrain – This can be intimidating for the novice pilot.

☐ Wind changes – Due to terrain features, the wind flow patterns are modified and the wind may seem to be coming from all directions at once. And, sometimes they are. Sometimes you will see windsocks along a mountain strip, each showing the wind from a different direction.

☐ Because of these, the safety margins are reduced. To maintain safety, different techniques must be incorporated, e.g. at many mountain strips it is impossible to take off and climb on course; circling is required.

8. MOUNTAIN WAVE

☐ What is a mountain wave? What forms it? Why is it of concern to pilots? (turbulence and downdrafts) What are its distinguishing characteristics? (clouds/dry wave) How do we deal with it? (visualize the wavelength, avoid the rotor).

☐ Visualization – Lenticular and rotor areas.

☐ Clouds generally delineate the area to fly and the area to avoid. During a dry wave condition, where insufficient moisture is available to form lenticulars or rotor clouds, knowledge for visualization will allow you to avoid the areas of downdrafts and turbulence.

9. ENGINE OPERATION

☐ Mountain operations may require a descent of many thousands of feet with the possibility of:

☐ **Thermal Shock** – If the engine is cooled too fast, thermal stresses may cause engine damage. Make progressive power reductions. Use flaps and landing gear to increase drag.

☐ **Detuning Engine** – Operating the engine outside its normal range of inertia loads and cylinder pressure loads can be caused by rapid throttle movements, high engine speed with low manifold pressure, and excess speed and power.

10. MIXTURE CONTROL

☐ Lean the mixture based on the density altitude, not the physical altitude.

☐ Adjust the mixture for takeoff and *landing*.

Mountain Flying Bible

11. WEIGHT AND BALANCE

☐ 10% increase in gross weight will cause (the takeoff distance varies with the square of the gross weight):

☐ 5% increase in rotation speed

☐ 9% decrease in acceleration

☐ 21% increase in takeoff distance

12. PREFLIGHT CHECK

☐ Fuel for the flight plus 50%

☐ Check the weather – Stay out of marginal areas

☐ Study charts – Determine the best route, altitudes to fly, airspace restrictions, and man-made obstructions (especially power lines)

☐ Carry survival gear

☐ File some type flight plan

13. SURVIVAL KIT

☐ Items to be carried (see definitions, page 9)

☐ Don't leave home without it

DEFINITIONS

Crosswind landing – Fluctuating wind direction and velocity at mountain strips makes the mechanical-slip technique for crosswind landing dangerous. To avoid a mechanical slip, maintain runway centerline alignment with ailerons, moving the aileron control back and forth as required. Maintain the aircraft's longitudinal axis parallel to the runway with rudder movement.

Point of NO Return – When flying upslope terrain, the area beyond a place where if the throttle is reduced to idle, there is sufficient altitude to allow a 180-degree turn.

Scud Running – VFR flight in marginal weather (scud running) often results in flight into a visibility condition that prohibits further flight. Scud running is discouraged; however, if you get trapped, circle a prominent landmark at low altitude until the visibility improves.

Spot Method – Used to cope with visual illusions during landing. For example, approaching a downslope runway gives the illusion of being too low, causing the pilot to approach too high. Approaching an upslope runway gives the illusion of being too high, causing the pilot to approach too low with the possibility of insufficient power to make it to the runway. Approaching a brightly-lit runway at night produces the illusion that the runway is closer, causing the pilot to approach too steeply and too fast. Approaching a runway, or even a mountain ridge, in rain tricks the pilot into thinking he is too high.

Make a grease pencil mark on the windshield about one-half inch below where the horizon intersects the windshield at cruise airspeed, cruise-power setting, and level flight. (It may need to be adjusted up or down a little.) For landing, align the windshield mark with the aiming point on the runway (point where the flare is made). Maintain a constant indicated airspeed. Add power if the aiming point moves up from the windscreen mark; reduce power if the aiming point moves down from the windscreen mark.

Survival Equipment – First-aid kit; axe or hatchet; knife; matches in waterproof bag; signaling devices (glass mirror, not metal; strobe light; whistle); tools (screwdriver, pliers); plastic garbage bags; nylon cord; flashlight; candles; space blankets; food as desired (raisins, candy).

FLIGHT

INTRODUCTION AND REVIEW OF MANEUVERS—FLIGHT

1. PRE-FLIGHT / USE OF CHECKLIST

2. EQUIPMENT FAMILIARIZATION

3. COORDINATION MANEUVERS
☐ Coordination Rolls.
☐ Turns, Climbs, Descents, Climbing Turns.

4. WINDSCREEN MARK FOR SPOT METHOD.
☐ Establish level flight with cruise power setting.
☐ Use a grease pencil to mark the windshield one-half inch below the intersection of the horizon with the horizon.
☐ Caution: When leaning forward to make the mark on the windshield, the perspective (parallax) changes. Make the mark in the proper place.

5. SLOW FLIGHT AT MINIMUM CONTROLLABLE AIRSPEED
☐ Practice during straight and turning flight, maintain altitude.
☐ Practice during straight and turning flight while climbing and descending.

6. VISUALIZING LIFT

☐ Study of the wind allows us to develop some generally acceptable rules of thumb:

☐ Surface winds of greater than 20 knots, proceed with caution.

☐ Mountaintop winds of greater than 30 knots, consider delaying or postponing the flight.

☐ The wind velocity may double (or more) over a ridge or between peaks due to a venturi effect.

☐ Cloud shadows show the wind direction and velocity at cloud level. Expect lower level winds to be modified by canyons and peaks.

☐ Visualize the wind as water. Ask yourself what water would do in the same situation.

☐ Visualize orographic lift (mechanical due to mountains) and solar effect (anabatic lift or convection currents).

☐ Strong winds blowing perpendicular to a ridge can create lift on the downwind side above the ridge top.

☐ Winds aloft of less than 20 knots create a laminar flow (depending upon air stability) where there is no downdraft close to the mountain on the downwind side.

☐ Visualize updrafts, down drafts and turbulence.

7. APPROACHING RIDGES

☐ Use the *spot method* to determine adequate terrain clearance.

☐ Look for more and more terrain to appear on the other side.

8. DOWNDRAFTS

☐ Maintain thine airspeed least the ground rise up and smite thee.

☐ The airplane stalls at the same indicated airspeed regardless of altitude (assuming the same weight and configuration).

9. CROSSING RIDGES

☐ Visual aspects of mountainous country can be very deceptive.

☐ Approach ridges (when ½ to ¼ mile away) at 45° angle. This permits a safer retreat with less stress on the aircraft.

☐ If you can see more and more of the terrain on the other side of a ridge, the altitude is sufficient to clear the ridge, if there are no mitigating factors (wind, turbulence, downdrafts).

☐ Pick two spots on the other side of the ridge, if the distance between them increases, the altitude will allow clearing the ridge. Caution: this technique may cause "tunnel vision."

Lesson Plan   APPENDIX

☐ Spot method. In level flight if the ridge line is below the spot, the aircraft is at an altitude that will clear the ridge.

☐ Commitment to cross the ridge can be made when the airplane is in a position to dive with the power off and hit the ridge line. The ridge line is the highest elevation of the ridge in front of the aircraft.

10. FLYING CANYONS

☐ Path through a mountain drainage (mostly level canyon) - fly the updraft side to be in an area of lift.

☐ Fly the sides of a canyon, not the center. The center places the airplane in a poor position to turn around and may expose it to shear turbulence.

☐ How close to sides? Depends on the stability of the air.

☐ Avoid shadows. Shadows are usually indicative of downdrafts (but, not always).

☐ Pick a speed faster than V_X. Rough air requires additional speed to prevent an accidental stall.

☐ If you can't gain altitude on one side of the canyon, try the other.

☐ The preferred method of flying in canyons with sloping terrain is to gain altitude, fly to the head of the canyon, then fly down the canyon.

☐ Caution in unfamiliar areas. Blind canyons may dead end. This shouldn't be a problem with the basic axioms in mind and adhered to.

☐ Never fly up a canyon where there is not adequate room to make a turn around.

☐ Do not fly beyond the *point of no return*.

☐ Downdrafts may exist where an updraft is expected due to a pressure system or inversion.

☐ Narrow canyons - Definition: *turn radius exceeds one-half the canyon width*. Fly downdraft side. If you get into trouble and need to turn around, you are turning into a better-air condition, not worse. Remember the airplane will be subjected to a tail wind while turning around that will increase the radius of turn.

11. CANYON TURN AROUND (COURSE REVERSAL)

☐ Wing over or chandelle – Avoid these maneuvers. If you get into trouble and need to turn around, the airspeed will be too slow to accomplish either maneuver.

☐ Steep bank at slow speed – Preferred method.

Mountain Flying Bible

- ☐ Use flaps if turbulence is not structurally limiting. The load factor tolerance is decreased from 8-57 percent with application of flaps.
- ☐ Turn radius (from chart in book, page 3-100).

12. FLYING BLIND

- ☐ Early morning and late evening flights subject the pilot to the problems of flying blind.
- ☐ Solution - climb 2,000 feet above highest terrain.

13. MOUNTAIN WAVE

- ☐ Fly 50 percent above the highest terrain to avoid destructive turbulence (not all turbulence, only the destructive type).
- ☐ Avoid lenticulars with ragged or irregular edges.
- ☐ Visualize the wavelength to allow flight in an area of updraft.
- ☐ Avoid the rotor area.

14. VISUAL ILLUSIONS

- ☐ The *Spot Method* eliminates visual illusion problems that can be encountered during landings.
- ☐ Maintain a constant airspeed on final.
- ☐ Align the windscreen mark with the runway aiming point.
- ☐ Control the nose position with throttle.

15. TURBULENCE PROCEDURES

- ☐ Reduce to maneuvering speed – Compute this speed if it is not given in the POH or Owner's Manual. Multiply the gross weight maneuvering speed by the square root of the actual weight divided by the maximum allowable gross weight.
- ☐ Visualize what is causing the turbulence and fly away from it.
- ☐ Aircraft control - Fly attitude, not altitude.

16. FORCED LANDINGS

- ☐ Keep the aircraft's vital structure intact.
- ☐ Avoid forceful bodily contact with interior structure. Use padding.
- ☐ Maintain aircraft control until the airplane is parked. This means you should continue to fly the airplane, using whatever controls are available, until the airplane comes to a complete stop.
- ☐ Select an area and plan the approach. This is determined by wind direction and velocity; dimension and slope of the chosen

area; and obstacles in final approach path.

- Upslope landings require extra speed. A descent at 50 knots and 500 fpm results in 6-degree flight path. To transition to an upslope will require extra airspeed, first to parallel the upslope, then to make a normal flare and landing.
- Tree landings – Make a normal approach in the normal landing configuration.

17. RULE OF THUMB TO DETERMINE IF RUNWAY LENGTH IS ADEQUATE FOR TAKEOFF

- 10 x square root of percentage of liftoff distance required = percentage of liftoff speed that should be attained in that distance.
- 50 percent (halfway point of the runway is used as the percentage of liftoff distance required), Then 10 x 7.07 (square root of 50) = 70.7 percent of liftoff speed required at the halfway point to be able to takeoff safely in the remaining distance.

18. TAIL WIND TAKEOFF

- A tailwind requires 110 percent of the normal takeoff distance plus the percentage of tailwind speed divided by the rotation speed.

19. AIRSPEED CONTROL FOR LANDING

- The landing distance will increase by the square of the ratio of the touchdown speed to the normal touchdown speed.
- A 10 percent increase in approach speed = a 21 percent increase in the landing distance.
- Always use the same indicated airspeed for approach to landing at high-altitude airstrips as you do at low-altitude airstrips.

20. FALSE HORIZON ILLUSION

- Caused by visual illusion and not monitoring the aircraft instruments when flying gently upsloping terrain.
- Monitor the aircraft instruments, in addition to the VFR attitude, to avoid assuming a slight, but constant climb (unless intentional) that may lead to a stall situation.

21. DENSITY ALTITUDE

- For each 10°F above (or below) standard temperature, add (or subtract) 600 feet to (from) the field elevation.
- Definition: Pressure altitude corrected for non-standard temperature conditions.

- ☐ Better definition: The altitude the airplane thinks it is at and performs in accordance with.

22. NIGHT FLYING
- ☐ Takeoff and departure
- ☐ Climbout
- ☐ Terrain-clearance techniques
- ☐ Approach for landing

23. CROSSWIND LANDINGS
- ☐ Non-mechanical method for maintaining runway alignment (without consciously thinking of a sideslip). ✈

Index

10 Commandments, Sparky's 4-17
50-foot 2-7–8, 2-64, 5-39

A

Abort . . .i-10, i-12, 2-39, 2-47, 2-54, 2-58, 4-15
Above freezing 3-117, 3-120, 3-123, 3-159
Absolute altitude 1-31, 1-111
Absolute instability 1-64–65
Absolute stability 1-64–65
Acceleration error 1-98, 1-101, 1-103–104, 3-17
Acclimated 1-25, 3-58
Accretion rate . .3-116, 3-123, 3-140, 3-142, 3-144, 3-159
ACSL 3-87, 3-100
Adhesion 3-123, 3-129
Adiabatic lapse rate 1-62–63, 1-65, 3-92
Aerodynamic .i-8, 1-71, 1-76–77, 2-45, 2-47, 3-128, 5-15
Aerotitis 4-3
Aft cg loading 1-94
After effect (Altimeter) 1-112
Agemaster 3-129
Agonic 1-42, 1-99, 1-100
Airflow . . i-3, i-4, 1-76, 1-78–79, 1-88–90, 1-105, 2-5, 2-64, 3-7, 3-24, 3-33, 3-78, 3-91–92, 3-95, 3-118, 3-126, 3-135, 3-139, 3-170, 5-5, 5-15–16
Airmass .3-92, 3-151
Airspace 1-37–38, 1-48, 3-139, A-8
Airstream .3-135–136
Airway i-7, 1-24, 1-46, 1-51, 2-70–71, 3-115, 3-141, 3-145–146, 3-173
Airworthiness 3-59
Alaska(n)   1-12, 1-37, 1-67, 3-86, 3-96, 3-99, 3-111, 3-139, 3-176, 3-178, 4-14
Alcohol 1-14–16, 1-30, 1-33, 2-6, 3-127–128, 3-131–132
Alcor 2-25, 2-31, 2-33
Alkaline .1-10, 1-35
Alternator 1-86, 3-126
Altimeter   1-55, 1-64, 1-79, 1-111–116, 2-8–9, 2-11, 2-69, 2-73, 3-127–128, 5-2
Altitude pressure chart 1-34–35
Altitude sickness 1-30
Altocumulus 3-87
Alveolar 1-28–29, 1-30–31
AME 4-3
Ammeter 3-22
Amplitude 3-93–94, 3-142, 4-8
Anabatic 1-80, 3-10, 3-12, 3-68, A-10

Analgesics 4-5
Anchorage 3-111
Angle of climb   1-22, 1-79–80, 1-108–109, 2-45, 2-49–50, 2-53–55, 2-57–58, 2-66–67, 2-71, 3-11, 3-18, 3-31, 3-35, 3-43, 3-71, 3101, 3-136, 3-167, 3-184, 5-11
Animal(s) 3-19, 3-134
Anoxia 1-30
Antenna 3-118, 3-124, 3-126, 3-146
Anti-ice . .3-127–128, 3-131, 3-133–134, 3-157
Appalachian 3-93, 3-143
Apprehension i-4, 3-69, 3-181, 4-13
Approach to landing   1-88, 1-106, 2-38, 3-85, 5-3, 5-13, 5-26, 5-41, 5-64, A-6, A-13
Approaching ridges . .   i-8, i-10, 1-5, 3-12, 3-23–24, 4-17, A-10
Arcus 3-97
Arkansas 3-39
Arrival   i-2, i-12, 1-47, 1-57, 1-67, 1-93, 2-44, 3-80, 3-112, 3-140–141, 3-169, 3-175, 4-1–6, 5-29–30, 5-34, 5-44–45
ARSA 1-38, 1-48
Arteriolar(es) 3-16
Aspen 2-43, 2-70, 3-23, 3-38–39, 3-186
Asymmetric(al) 1-73, 2-36, 2-51
Atom 2-10
Atomization 2-23
Autokinesis 3-17–18
Available power . . .3-57, 3-148, 5-11–12, 5-46
Avalanche 3-180–181
Avco Lycoming 1-84, 2-25, 4-8
Axe3- 3-176, A-9

B

Backcountry   2-8, 2-16, 2-40–41, 2-44, 3-104, 3-173, 5-55
Back pressure   1-6, 1-90, 2-45, 2-50, 2-56–57, 2-66, 3-44, 3-56, 3-70, 3-184, 5-18–19, 5-44
Backfire(s) 1-21, 2-34, 4-10
Backside i-6, 3-121, 5-5, 5-7–8, 5-10
Backtracking .3-111
Ballew, Howard 2-65, 5-127, 5-22, 5-32, 5-43, 5-56
Balloon(ing)   1-61, 1-62, 1-65, 1-114, 2-55, 3-68, 3-82–84, 3-90, 3-168, 5-2, 5-14, 5-17–18, 5-20
Barosinusitis 4-3, 4-5
Barotitis 4-3
Basic premise - ice 3-144, 3-156
Basic premise mountain flying   i-9, 1-1–9, 1-115, 3-39, 3-45, A-7

Index

Battery 1-10, 1-82, 1-85–87, 3-181
Below freezing   1-19, 2-33, 3-117, 3-119–120, 3-122–123, 3-127, 3-150, 3-178, 4-7
Beriberi 5-56
Bernoulli 1-72
Best angle of climb 1-22, 1-79–80, 1-108–109, 2-49, 2-50, 2-53–55, 2-57–58, 2-66, 3-11, 3-18, 3-31, 3-35, 3-42, 3-71, 3-136, 3-167, 3-184
Best economy mixture 2-27, 2-29
Best power mixture .1-11, 1-16–17, 2-26–27, 2-30
Best rate of climb   1-23, 1-80, 1-108–109, 2-45, 2-48, 2-50, 2-53–55, 2-57, 2-69, 3-11, 3-18, 3-35, 3-49, 3-101, 3-166, 3-167, 5-2
Bikle, Paul 3-94
Billings, Mont. 2-43, 3-43, A-15
Bodrero, Doug 3-180
Boeing 3-58, 3-140, A-1
Bora(l) 1-67
Bounce(s,ed,ing) .   2-62, 3-92–93, 3-178, 5-18–20, 5-44–45
Bourdon 1-105
Bracket(s,ing) 3-111, 3-126, 3-131, 3-154
Breeze i-8, 1-66, 1-68, 2-41, 3-78
Bridger, Fort 3-179–180
Bridging 3-129–130
Briefing format, weather 1-58
Bump(s,ing,iness,y) . . .1-61, 2-69, 3-84, 3-151
Burble(ing) 1-88, 3-135–136

C

Calibrated airspeed 1-110, 5-28–30, 5-34, 5-42
California . .1-67, 3-94, 3-178, 3-181–182, A-1
Camber i-3, 1-88, 2-44, 3-47, 5-13, 5-14
Camp(ing) 3-50, 3-180
Canada(ian) i-12, 1-42, 1-45, 1-99, 1-100, 3-99, 3-139
Canyon downdraft 3-23, 3-63
Canyon(s)   i-6, i-7, i-9–10, 1-5–6, 1-10, 1-39, 1-60, 1-66, 2-41, 2-68, 3-4, 3-8–12, 3-23, 3-27, 3-30—42, 3-57, 3-63, 3-105–106, 3-171, 3-175, 3-178, 3-180, 3-184, 4-2, 4-14—17, 5-43, A-10—11
Canyons, flying . .3-30, 3-33, 3-35, 3-40, 3-184
Cap cloud 3-95–96, A-4
Carbohydrate 5-56
Carburetor heat . . . .   1-20—22, 1-82, 2-3, 2-34–35, 3-161, 3-165, 5-25
Carburetor ice 2-33–34, 3-120
Carolina 3-178
Carrots 3-14
Cattle 3-169, 5-56
Ceiling . . .i-6, 1-1, 1-3, 1-10, 1-28, 1-39–40, 1-54–1-55, 1-59–60, 1-79, 1-89, 1-108, 3-1, 3-5–6, 3-11, 3-105–107, 3-145, 3-149, 3-152–153, 3-158, 3-173, 3-179–181

Centennial 2-9, 2-12, 5-31
Center of gravity 1-91, 1-93, 1-95, 1-101, 2-58, 5-21
Centrifugal force   1-101, 2-53, 2-63–65, 2-67, 3-19, 3-49, 3-54–55, 3-128, 5-15, 5-21, 5-53
Cessna   i-4, 1-4, 1-36, 1-38, 1-76, 1-88–89, 2-13, 2-15–16, 2-45, 3-9, 3-38, 3-46, 3-57, 3-61, 3-118, 3-126, 3-137, 3-140, 3-145, 3-170, 3-179, 4-14, 5-9, 5-16, 5-29, 5-30, 5-34
Chamois .1-10, 1-15
Chandelle i-11, 3-43–44, A-11
Chart   i-7, i-8, 1-34–35, 1-37–40, 1-42–45, 1-48–52, 1-81, 1-95, 1-99–100, 1-110–111, 2-7–8, 2-11, 2-13, 2-19–20, 2-39, 2-59, 2-66, 2-70, 3-8, 3-18–19, 3-35, 3-52–53, 3-55, 3-57–58, 3-80, 3-104, 3-106, 3-110–112, 3-141, 3-150–157, 3-181, 5-10–11, 5-28–29, A-1–2, A-8, A-12
Checklist . .   1-4, 1-57, 2-28, 2-35, 3-165, 3-168–169, 4-9, A-9
Checkout 1-12–13
Checkpoint(s) . .1-42–44, 1-46–50, 3-112, 4-12
Cheyenne 1-76, 3-113, 4-9, A-1
Chicago 3-93
China 3-8, 5-36, 5-40
Chinook wind 1-63, 1-67
Cirriform .3-24, 3-122
Cirrus 3-122
Clear air turbulence 3-79, 3-84
Clear ice 3-118–119, 3-123, 3-125, 3-130, 3-141
Climbout i-11, 1-88, 2-35, 3-7, 3-11–12, 3-18, 3-74, A-14
Cold weather   1-14, 1-82, 1-84–86, 1-109, 2-3, 2-5–6, 2-37, 2-66, 3-178, 3-180
Colorado   1-38, 1-67, 2-38, 2-70, 3-12, 3-64, 3-178, 3-186, 5-4, 5-31, 5-59, A-1
Compass   i-8, 1-1, 1-24, 1-41–44, 1-47–51, 1-97–104, 3-3, 3-28, 3-112–113
Complacent(cy)   . .i-4, 1-7, 2-8, 2-58, 3-38, 3-107, 3-111, 3-150, 4-9, 4-17, 5-43
Compression . .   1-62–63, 1-65–67, 1-82, 2-21–22, 3-95, 3-97, 3-140, 3-165, 4-8–9
Confluence 2-60, 5-31
Continental 1-84, 2-25
Contour(s,ed) . . .   i-7, 1-5, 1-7, 3-226–27, 3-33–34, 3-153–155
Convection   1-23–24, 1-62, 1-80, 2-41, 3-10, 3-32, 3-34, 3-67–68, 3-78–79, 3-88, A-10
Conventional gear   2-50–51, 2-53–54, 2-56, 2-62–65, 5-15, 5-21, 5-42, 5-55
Convergence 5-33
Coriolis force 3-90–91
Corona Pass .1-39
Corkscrewing 3-33–34, 3-153–155
Course reversal procedure   i-11, 2-67–68, 3-23, 3-30, 3-42, 3-44, 3-46, 3-50, 3-52, 3-159, A-11

Critical angle of attack   1-73, 1-75, 1-77, 2-36, 2-52
Cross control 1-76–78, 3-73, A-6
Crossing ridges 3-8, 3-23, 3-28, 3-30, 5-39, A-10
Crosswind component 2-18, 2-59, 2-63–64
Crosswind(s) 2-2, 2-4–5, 2-17–18, 2-34, 2-40, 2-48, 2-58–65, 3-11, 3-104, 3-112, 5-1, 5-14–15, 5-30, 5-49–54, A-6, A-8, A-14
Cruise altitude, optimum   i-9, i-11–12, 1-9–12, 1-35, 1-39, 1-47, 3-7, 3-107, 3-130, 3-183, 4-4, 4-11–12
Cruise performance 1-9, 1-11
Cumuliform .3-084, 3-118, 3-122, 3-138, 3-141
Cumulonimbus 3-118, 3-156
Cumulus clouds   1-56, 1-60, 1-62, 1-96, 2-69, 3-68, 3-82, 3-87, 3-98, 3-101, 3-116, 3-118–123, 3-138–139, 3-156, 3-158
Cyanotic 3-106

D

Dalles, The 3-106
Danger(ous)   i-4–6, 1-10, 1-95, 2-35, 2-47, 3-2, 3-4, 3-10, 3-13, 3-20, 3-30–31, 3-68, 3-71, 3-101, 3-119–120, 3-127–128, 3-146, 3-151, 3-156, 3-176, 3-180, 3-185, 5-10, 5-17, 5-19–20, 5-26, A-8
Dark(ness)   . .i-11, 1-10, 1-32, 1-48, 1-60, 3-13–18, 3-89, 3-98, 3-104, 3-113, 3-180, 4-2
Death Canyon .3-9
Deicer(s) 3-127, 3-133–134
Denalt 2-12, 3-134
Density Altitude .   i-4, i-7, i-9–10, 1-24–25, 1-28, 1-35–36, 1-39, 1-44, 1-79–80, 1-93, 1-106, 1-111, 2-7–9, 2-11–17, 2-19–20, 2-27–30, 2-38–41, 2-43, 2-46, 2-48, 2-50, 2-52, 2-56, 2-63, 2-73–74, 3-9, 3-32, 3-38, 3-47, 3-55, 3-68, 3-177, 4-13, 4-15, 5-26, 5-30, 5-33, A-7, A-13
Denver   1-38–39, 1-56, 1-76, 1-100, 2-9, 2-12, 2-14, 3-23, 3-80, 3-93, 3-99
Depart(ed,ing,ure)   i-8, 1-16, 1-27–28, 1-31, 1-38, 1-42–48, 1-56–57, 1-61, 1-93, 1-113, 2-18, 2-28, 2-38, 2-41–42, 2-45, 2-48–49, 2-52, 2-60, 2-67–69, 3-9, 3-11, 3-13, 3-17, 3-23, 3-26, 3-27, 3-76, 3-80, 3-85, 3-103–104, 3-140, 3-142, 3-145, 3-147, 3-151, 3-157–158, 3-169, 3-176, 3-179, I3-181, 3-182, 4-1–3, 4-13–15, 5-30, 5-46, A-6, A-14
Descend(ing)   1-33, 1-63, 1-65, 1-67, 1-75, 1-85, 2-30, 2-32, 3-9, 3-32, 3-45, 3-63, 3-79, 3-88, 3-92, 3-95, 3-97–98, 3-107, 3-114, 3-119, 3-128, 3-140, 3-143–144, 3-156–159, 3-166, 3-170, 3-174, 4-1, 4-3, 4-6–7, 4-9, 4-11–12, 5-39, 5-60, A-5, A-9
Descent rule 4-1, 4-11
Determining wind direction 3-161, 3-169
Detonation 2-21, 2-23, 2-32–33, 2-52
Detune i-12, 4-8, 4-17

Dew point   1-10, 1-15, 1-18–19, 1-63, 3-69, 3-82, 3-95, 3-106, 3-119, 3-125, 3-153–155, 3-185
Disoriented(tation) 1-27, 3-18
Dissipate   3-69, 3-83, 3-95, 3-97–98, 3-130, 3-135, 3-165, 3-169–170, 5-20, 5-27, 5-64
Downburst 3-63, 3-81–83
Downdrafts   i-3, i-6–11, 1-1, 1-10, 1-18, 1-40, 1-45, 1-61, 1-67–68, 2-2, 2-20, 2-60, 3-3, 3-7, 3-9, 3-23–25, 3-28–34, 3-38–41, 3-53, 3-63–68, 3-70–71, 3-81–84, 3-90, 3-93, 3-95, 3-97–101, 3-138, 3-142, 3-178, 3-179, 3-182, 4-17, 5-31, 5-44, 5-59, A-4, A-7, A-10, A-11
Downhill .1-67–67, 2-42–43, 5-4, 5-23, 5-59, 5-63
Downslope . . .   i-10, 1-66–67, 2-19, 2-37, 2-41–43, 2-74, 3-32, 3-35, 5-23–25, 5-31, 5-33, 5-40, 5-63, A-8
Downstream   i-8, 1-19, 2-41, 3-79, 3-88, 3-93, 3-97, 5-31
Downwash 2-46–47, 3-136, 3-139, 3-144
Downwind   2-3–5, 2-61–64, 3-20, 3-24, 3-33, 3-65, 3-69, 3-77, 3-93, 3-97–100, 3-141, 3-146–147, 3-169, 5-25, 5-27, 5-37, 5-39, 5-40, 5-43, 5-46, 5-50, 5-52–53, A-10
Drag . .   i-7, 1-11–12, 1-73, 1-75, 1-88–89, 2-18–19, 2-44, 2-46, 2-47, 2-50–51
Drainage(s)   1-5, I1-7, 2=3-23, 3-26–27, 3-33, 3-52, 5-30, A-11
Drift(ing,s)   1-42, 1-44, 1-112, 2-62, 2-65, 3-42, 3-75, 3-104, 5-21, 5-49–51, 5-53–54
Dry adiabatic lapse rate . .1-62–63, 1-65, 3-92
Dunoir 3-145

E

Early morning flights 1-19, 1-24, 3-9, 3-68, 4-2, A-12
Economy 1-12, 2-23, 2-26–27, 2-29–30
Eddy(ies)   1-11, 1-89, 3-24, 3-30, 3-68–69, 3-73, 3-75, 3-77, 3-97–98, 5-5
EGME .1-15, 3-131
EGT 2-22, 2-24–33
Eisenhower tunnel 1-39, 364
ELT 3-178, 3-180–131
Embedded 3-127
Emergency landing techniques 3-161–174
Empennage 2-64, 3-73, 8-118, A-16
Emulsifier 3-98
En route   i-2, i-11, 1-1, 1-10, 1-12, 1-23, 1-40, 1-44, 1-47, 1-50, 1-54, 1-57–59, 1-113, 1-115, 2-20, 2-68, 2-70, 3-1–2, 3-7, 3-18, 3-21, 3-104–105, 3-107, 3-115, 3-141, 3-143, 3-145–147, 3-152, 3-157–159, 3-167, 3-175, 3-178–181, 3-183, 4-3, 4-16, A-2, A-15
Endurance 3-104, 5-7
Energy   1-17, 1-62, 2-26, 3-83, 3-135–136, 3-164, 3-167, 5-12

Index

Engine(s)   i-3, i-8, i-10, 1-3, 1-7–8, 1-11–23, 1-34–36, 1-39, 1-71, 1-73–74, 1-79–93, 1-106, 1-109, 2-1–3, 2-6–8, 2-11, 2-14–15, 2-19, 2-21–36, 2-38, 2-47, 2-49, 2-50, 2-52–54, 2-66, 2-68–69, 3-13–14, 3-21, 3-35, 3-43–44, 3-49, 3-54, 3-124, 3-126–128, 3-131, 3-141, 3-147–148, 3-161–162, 3-165–166, 3-168, 3-170, 3-173–174, 3-177, 3-182, 4-1, 4-6–11, 4-17, 5-3, 5-5, 5-7, 5-11, 5-25–26, 5-39, 5-47, 5-50, A-6–7
Enrichment 2-30, 2-49
Equator(ial) . .   1-26, 1-51–52, 1-98, 1-10, 3-88–91, 3-112
Escape   i-4, i-8, 1-5–6, 1-8, 1-14, 1-36, 1-54, 1-68, 2-69, 3-9, 3-24–25, 3-28, 3-31, 3-38–40, 3-44–47, 3-68–69, 3-91, 3-101, 3-123, 3-150, 3-157, 4-17
Eskimo 1-67
Estimating in-flight visibility .3-103, 3-107–108, 3-185
ETA . . . .-1-47, 3-114, 3-175, 4-11
ETE 1-50
Ether 1-9, 1-15, 3-131
Ethylene 1-15, 3-131, 3-133–134
Eugene, Ore. .3-178
Euphoria 1-32–33
Eustachian 4-3–4
Evaporate(ion,s) .1-19, 1-62, 3-82, 3-97, 3-128, 3-131
Evening i-8, 1-54, 1-68, 2-41, A-12
Exhaust(ion) .   1-20, 1-32, 1-39, 1-86, 2-6, 2-21–22, 2-24–25, 2-30, 2-31–32, 2-34, 3-128, 3-148, 3-162, 3-165, 4-7
Experiment(ion,y)   2-20, 2-44, 2-65, 3-63, 3-71, 3-124–125, 3-130, 3-166, 3-170, 5-14–15, 5-26

F

FAA   1-15, 1-17, 1-22, 1-32, 1-40, 1-53–54, 1-76, 1-84, 2-23, 2-26, 2-31, 2-38, 2-43, 2-60, 2-70, 3-35, 3-69, 3-103, 3-124–125, 1-130, 3-166, 3-170, 5-14-15, 5-26
Fall wind 1-66–67
False horizon 2-67, 2-69–70, 3-4, 4-13
FAR 1-25, 1-33, 1-48, 3-59, 3-132
Fatigue 1-25, 1-32, 3-62
Fear(ing) .i-4, 1-71, 1-77, 3-18, 3-62, 3-163, 3-174
Feathered(ing,y) 4-9
Ferry . . . .-1-4, 1-91, 4-13, 4-15
Fire   i-1, i-6, 1-15, 1-71, 1-81–82, 1-84, 2-33, 3-27, 3-168, 3-172, 3-177
first aid .3-176, A-9
Fish i-1, 1-56, 3-27, 3-73
Fixed pitch   1-12, 1-20, 1-22, 2-12–13, 2-15, 2-28, 2-34, 2-45, 2-73, 3-128, 4-7, 5-25, 5-42

Flaps .1-107, 1-109, 2-37, 2-44–46, 2-55, 2-57, 3-51, 3-173, 5-14–16, 5-19, 5-26, 5-37, 5-42, A-6
Flare(d)   1-90, 3-21, 3-37, 3-83, 3-144, 3-146, 3-168, 3-170, 3-172, 5-2, 5-9–10, 5-17, 5-19, 5-26, 5-29, 5-31, 5-34, 5-36, 5-42, 5-44–46, 5-48, 5-52, 5-54, 5-60, 5-64, A-9, A-13
Flashlight . .1-10, 1-44, 3-21, 3-104, 3-177, A-9
Flatland   i-5, 1-10, 1-54–55, 3-2, 3-26–27, 3-68–69, 3-87, 4-3, 5-35, 5-62
Flight load factor 3-23, 3-57–58
Float(ing,s)   i-10, 1-19, 1-21, 1-98–99,1-101, 3-99, 3l-168, 3-173, 5-8, 5-19, 5-24, 5-27, 5-42, 5-44
Flow   i-7, i-11, 1-11, 1-20–22, 1-33–34, 1-55, 1-58, 1-61, 1-63, 1-66–68, 1-72, 1-85–86, 2-20, 2-22–30, 3-17, 3-24, 3-31, 3-39, 3-63, 3-65–66, 3-68–70, 3-75, 3-78–79, 3-87–88, 3-91–93, 3-96, 3-98–99, 3-119, 3-124, 3-127, 3-135–136, 3-153, 3-155–156, 3-169, 4-4, 5-31, A-7, A-10
Flutter 1-84, 1-107, 4-4
Flying blind 1-24, 3-7, 3-9, 4-2, A-12
Flying canyons i-10, 3-23, 3-33, A-11
Flying up canyons 3-23, 3-36–38
Flying up narrow canyons 3-33, 3-35, 3-40
Foehnwall 3-95
Fog(gy)   1-10, 1-53, 1-61, 3-18, 3l-20, 3-35, 3-106, 3-120, 3-128, 3-179–180
Footprints 1-39
Forced landing i-6, 1-24, 1-70, 1-87, 3-161–162, 3-164–174, 3-176, 8-178, 3-181, A-12
Forecasters(ing)   i-7, 1-40, 1-45, 1-47, 1-49, 1-54–59, 1-83, 3-4–6, 3-67–68, 3-72, 3-74, 3-76, 3-80, 3-100, 3-104, 3-107, 3-113, 3-115–3-116, 3-132, 3-137–141, 3-147–152, 3-156–158, 3-179, 3-181, 4-18
Forest 3-48, 3-102, 3-171, 4-14
Fork 1-37, 3-38, 4-13
Fort Bridger 3-179–180
Formula(s)   1-95, 1-106, 2-12, 2-43, 3-17, 3-47, 3-56–57, 4-11, 5-9, A-2–4
Forward slip 3-169–170, 5-10, 5-43, 5-47–48, 5-50
Free air 3-92, 3-120, 5-27
Freezing temperature   1-14–15, 1-85, 3-120, 3-122, 3-124, 3-127, 3-131, 3-147, 3-154, 3-159, 3-178
Friction . .   2-6, 2-18–19, 2-28, 2-51, 3-98, 3-135–136, 3-154, 5-5
Frontal zone 3-74, 3-76, 3-122, 3-151
Frost . . .   i-7, 1-82, 2-48, 3-118–119, 3-131, 3-134–137, 3-178
Frostbite 3-178
Fuel flow 1-21, 2-23, 2-28–30

Fuel injection 1-20, 1-22, 2-26, 2-32
Fuel management 1-9, 1-14
Fuel requirements 1-44, 1-46, 1-50
Fuel . . . .
  i-7–8, 1-4, 1-7, 1-9–24, 1-39–40, 1-44–50,
  1-81–84, 1-91, 1-93, 1-96, 2-3, 2-5–6, 2-
  21–26, 2-28–35, 2-39, 2-53, 3-11, 3-104, 3-
  124, 3-127, 3-131, 3-137, 3-140, 3-148, 3-
  161–162, 3-165, 3-176, 3-181, 4-9, 5-53, A-
  8
Fuel-air mixture/ratio 2-21–24, 2-33
Full power . . . 1-12, 2-27–27, 2-30, 2-35, 2-
  38–39, 2-49–50, 2-52–55, 3-51, 3-82–83, 3-
  85, 3-140, 3-144, 5-8, 5-18–19, 5-21, 5-46
Full rich . . .1-16, 2-23–24, 2-27, 2-30–31, 2-34
Funnel 1-10, 1-67, 2-3, 3-67–68, 5-30–31
Fuselage .1-74, 1-89, 2-58, 2-64, 3-128, 3-163,
  3-170, 5-5, 5-15–16

G

G load   i-8, 1-31, 2-68, 3-25–26, 3-46–47, 3-
  49, 3-51, 3-54, 3-58–59, 3-61, 3-63, 3-136,
  3-148, 3-183, A-2
Gear down 1-109, 3-168
Gear up 1-109, 3-168
Gear, landing   1-105, 1-107–109, 2-49–54, 2-
  56–58, 2-62–65, 2-67, 3-56, 3-118, 3-127, 3-
  140, 3-144, 3-147, 3-163, 3-167–168, 3-
  171, 3-173, 4-8, 5-10, 5-15, 5-19, 5-21, 5-
  41–42, 5-47, 5-49–50, 5-53, 5-55, A-7
Geared engine 2-25, 4-8
Generator 1-86, 3-126
Geostrophic 1-68
Gethomeitis 3-105
Gimbals 1-77
Glide slope . .   3-22, 3-82–83, 3-140, 4-11, 5-
  34–35, 5-38
Glide   i-9–10, 1-5, 1-7, 3-21, 3-29, 3-32, 3-38,
  3-40, 3-45, 3-163, 3-165)166, 3-168–173, 5-
  2, 5-7–5-10, 5-25, 5-39, 5-46–47
Glory 3-120–121
Glycol 1-15, 3-131, 3-133–135
Glypro 3-134
Go around   4-8, 4-13, 4-15, 5-13, 5-18–19, 5-
  25–27, 5-30, 5-36–37, 5-43, 5-48, 5-59
Goodrich 3-129
Gorge 3-106
Governor .1-85, 2-29
GPS   1-10, 1-39, 1-41, 3-82, 3-142, 3-176, 4-
  11, 5-38, A-6
Gradient . . .   1-29, 1-66, 2-15, 2-19, 2-37, 2-
  42–43, 3-73, 3-154
Gravity wind 1-66
Greaser 5-1, 5-45
Greenville 3-178

Ground effect   i-7, 2-37, 2-46–48, 2-50, 2-55,
  2-57–58, 2-66, 2-74, 3-136–137, 3-139, 3-
  146, 3-68, 3-170, 5-23, 5-27, 5-41
Ground loop . .   2-4, 2-65, 5-17, 5-21–22, 5-
  52–53
Ground reference 1-73–74, 3-107, 3-179
Ground speed   1-11, 1-23, 1-41, 1-45–47, 1-
  49–50, 1-115, 2-71–72, 3-32, 3-82, 3-142, 3-
  164, 4-11, 5-35, 5-38, 5-47, A-6
Grumman 3-182
Gs, gravity loading/load factor   1-108, 2-68, 3-
  26, 3-48, 3-54, 3-56, 3-58–62, 3-99, 3-
  164–165, 3-183, 5-14
Gust front 3-78, 3-82
Gust(ing,s,y)   2-37–38, 2-40, 248, 2-65, 2-69,
  3-58–61, 3-69, 3-72, 3-84, 3-104, 3-136, 5-
  30, 5-33–34, 5-38, 5-48, 5-51, 5-54, 5-55
Gyro 1-73, 1-77, 2-36, 2-52

H

Hagerman Pass 3-39
Hail 3-119
Halfway .   i-10, i12, 1-48, 2-40, 2-43, 2-47, 2-
  58, 3-20, 3-46, 3-53, 3-140, 4-13, 4-15, 4-
  17, 5-37, A-13
Hammerhead i-11, 3-43, 3-46
Handbook   i-8, 1-11, 1-14, 1-17, 1-50, 1-80, 1-
  96, 1-107, 2-11, 2-13, 2-18, 2-26, 2-45, 3-48,
  3-55, 5-7, 5-28, 5-46
Hangar   1-13, 1-15, 2-6, 2-21, 2-46, 3-119, 3-
  131, 3-133, 3-137, 3-145–146, 5-31
Harmonic 3-133
Hatchet .3-176, A-9
Hazard(s)(ous)   i-4, i-6, 1-24, 1-66, 1-94, 2-26,
  3-20, 3-35, 3-40, 3-68, 3-75–76, 3-78, 3-87,
  3-121, 3-123–124, 3-126–127, 3-131, 3-
  135, 3-140, 3-157, 3-161–164, 3-166, 3-
  168–169, 5-18, 5-64
Haze 1-65, 3-18, 3-20
Headnet 3-177
Head wind   1-10, 1-23, 2-4–5, 2-17–19, 2-39,
  2-41–43, 2-54, 2-59, 2-74, 3-33, 3-38, 3-40,
  3-74, 3-77, 3-82–84, 3-112, 3-180, 5-10, 5-
  38
Heading   1-24, 1-29, 1-37, 1-41–44, 1-47–48,
  1-98–104, 2-47, 2-58, 2-64, 2-69, 3-25, 3-
  43, 3-46, 3-112–114, 3-167, 3-179, 5-49, 5-
  54
Hemp 3-133
Herrod 1-59
Hexylene 1-15, 3-131
High altitude   i-7, i-10, 1-1, 1-3, 1-17, 1-23, 1-
  31, 1-35–36, 1-96, 1-105–106, 2-8, 2-14, 2-
  23, 2-27–28, 2-38, 2-49, 3-79, 3-82, 3-
  101–102, 3-145, 3-173, 5-2–3, 5-5, 5-26, 5-
  44, A-4–5, A-13
High elevation .   i-10, i-4, 1-25, 1-39, 1-
  67, 1-93, 1-106, 2-50, 4-15, 5-26, 5-46

Index

High performance 2-45
High pressure   1-58–59, 1-65, 1-88, 1-93, 1-112–113, 3-34, 3-39, 3-63, 3-89–91, 3-156
High wing 5-27
Highway(s) 1-10, 1-39, 1-70, 3-106, 3-111–112, 3-186
Hikers 3-178
Hill Air Force Base 3-180
Histotoxic hypoxia 1-30
Horizon, false 2-67, 2-69–70, 3-4, A-13
Horizon, natural   2-48, 2-67, 2-69–70, 3-4, 3-8, 3-11, 3-45, 3-48–49, 5-2
Horse Creek 1-8
Horse latitudes 3-90–91
Horsepower 2-7, 2-45–46, 5-5, 5-16
Horse sense i-8, 3-10–11
Howard Ballew 2-65, 5-127, 5-22, 5-32, 5-43, 5-56
Humidity   1-18–19, 1-63, 1-93, 2-8–9, 2-11, 2-15, 2-18, 2-33, 3-96
Hunch 3-112
Hydraulic 1-93, 3-127, 3-133
Hydrogen 1-26, 2-10
Hypemic 1-31
Hyperventilation 1-33, 1-35, 4-13
Hypoxia -9, 1-25–28, 1-30–33, 1-35, 3-13, 3-16
Hypoxic 1-27, 1-31
Hysteresis 1-112

I

IAS . . . .
3-125, 5-44
Ice free 3-130, 3-138, 3-143–144, 3-159
Iced 1-82, 3-178
Icex 3-129
Icing 1-9, 1-14–15, 1-18–22
Idaho   2-1, 2-35, 3-123, 3-140, 3-145–146, 1-179, 4-1, 4-6, 4-14, 5-3, A-1
IFR   i-6, 1-3, 1-38, 1-57, 1-59, 2-70, 3-3, 3-32, 3-105, 3-115–116, 3-120, 3-129, 3-138, 3-145, 3-147, 3-153, 3-161–162, 3-173, 3-179–181, A-16
Ignition 2-32–33
Illegal 1-25, 1-79
Illusion(s)   1-60, 2-69–70, 3-13, 3-17, 3-22, 3-35, 5-23, 5-25, 5-33, 5-34, 5-38, A-8, A-12–13
ILS 3-2, 3-22, 3-82, 3-123, 3-140, 5-35
Imbedded 3-19
Immune 3-142
Impact(ing) . . . i-9, 1-5, 1-19–20, 1-22, 1-105, 3-32, 3-45, 3-123, 3-128, 3-164, 3-170, 3-171, 3-173, 3-178, 3-182, 5-20, 5-36, 5-44
Inbound 3-140, 3-145
Incapacitation 1-26, 1-30
Independence Pass 3-38–39
Indians 1-67

Indian Creek 5-3
Instability   1-62, 1-64–65, 3-39, 3-66, 3-68, 3-78, 3-91, 3-121, 3-137, 3-147, 3-151
Instinct 1-6–8, 1-77, 3-37, 3-46, 3-63, 3-70
Instructors   1-4, 1-7–8, 1-24, 1-69, 1-71, 1-73, 1-77–78, 2-20, 2-53, 3-9, 3-11, 3-21, 3-28, 3-30, 3-36, 3-44, 3-49, 3-51, 3-103–104, 4-9, 5-1, 5-20, 5-40, 5-48–49
Insulated 1-81
Intermountain 1-10, 1-12, 3-88
Interpolate 2-13, 3-155
Inverse(ly) 1-112, 2-11, 2-18, 3-93, 5-6
Inversion(s)   1-58, 1-65, 2-6, 3-74–75, 3-91–93, 3-119–120, 3-138, 3-157, 3-159, A-11
Iowa 1-67
Iranian 2-26
Irregularities 3-60, 4-13, 5-1, 5-17, 5-20
Isobar(s) 1-113, 3-154, 3-156
Isogonic 1-42, 1-49, 1-99
Isopropyl 1-14–15, 2-6, 3-131
Isotachs 3-154
Isotherm(s) 3-91–92, 3-120, 3-154, 3-159

J

Jackson, Wyo. .   1-8, 1-38, 1-56, 1-59–60, 1-76, 2-7, 2-9, 3-2, 3-9, 3-24, 3-27, 3-36, 3-80, 3-111, 3-137, 3-145–146, 3-173, 4-11, 4-18, 5-17, 5-22, 5-32, 5-57, A-4, A-15
Jet stream   3-75, 3-79, 3-87–89, 3-95, 3-141
Jet .1-48, 3-58, 3-89
Jimmy Mattern 3-111
Judgment   i-2, i-4, 1-9, 1-33, 1-40, 1-54, 1-76, 3-10–11, 3-21–22, 3-33, 3-105, 3-165, 3-169, 5-47, 5-49, 5-62
Juneau 3-111
J-Y ranch 3-9

K

Kansas 1-89, 2-14
KCAS 5-28–29
Kerosene 1-99
Kershner, William 1-76
Ketchup 2-50
KIAS .5-15, 5-28–29
Kick out 5-49
Kinetic 3-83, 3-136, 5-12
Kirol, Vincent 3-145
Kollsman 1-112, 2-8, 2-11
Kremmling 1-39
Krypton 1-26

L

Lags 1-102–103, 1-112
Landing - wind shear   3-67, 3-74, 3-76–77, 3-80, 3-82–83, 3-85, 5-30
Landing considerations 5-1, 5-23–32
Landing in rain 5-23, 5-25

Landing irregularities 5-1, 5-17, 5-20
Landing uphill 5-23, 5-59
Landmark . 1-40, 3-3, 3-107, 3-111–112, A-8
Lapse rate 1-26, 1-58, 1-62–65, 1-80, 2-12, 3-75, 3-88, 3-92, 3-137, 3-147, 3-151
Laramie, Wyo. 1-38, 2-14
Las Vegas, Nev. 3-11
Latitude(s) 1-42, 1-52, 1-80, 1-99, 1-100, 1-103, 3-90–91, 3-97, 3-99, 3-112
Law(s) i-1, 1-27–28, 1-53, 1-58–59, 1-72, 3-27, 3-33, 3-40, 3-45, 3-175–176, 3-181
Layer like .1-65, 3-138
Lead acid 1-85–86
Lead sulfate .1-86–87
Leading edge 1-88, 1-90, 2-3, 3-89, 3-97, 3-118, 3-127–129, 3-135, 3-139, 3-144, 3-146
Leadville 2-38–39
Leaning mixture i-10, 1-17, 1-21–22, 1-80, 2-21, 2-23–30, 2-32, 2-34
Lee wave 3-87, 3-94
Lee 1-67, 3-24–25, 3-63, 3-65, 3-87, 3-92, 3-95, 4-18
Leeward . . .1-40, 3-77, 3-92, 3-97 3-99, 3-141
Left quartering 2-4–5
Leg i-7, 1-46–47, 1-50, 1-70, 1-115, 3-20, 3-104, 5-37, 5-40, 5-46, A-6, A-15
Legal(ity,ly) .1-13, 1-93, 1-112, 3-115, 3-132, 3-152
Lennys 3-96
Lens shaped 3-96
Lenticular 1-96, 3-76, 3-86–87, 3-93, 3-95–102, 3-160, 5-31, A-4, A-7, A-12
Level flight . 1-13, 1-73, 1-79, 1-90, 1-94, 1-104–105, 1-110, 2-69–70, 3-8–9, 3-20, 3-41, 3-46, 3-49–50, 3-54–55, 3-58, 3-61, 3-71, 3-144, 3-159, 3-185, 5-2, 5-6, 5-11, 5-14, 5-18–20, 5-39–42, 5-46–47, A-9, A-11
Leverage 1-95
Lifesaver(ing) 3-103, 3-107
Liftoff speed . .3-39–40, 2-43, 2-45, 2-74, A-13
Light to moderate 2-32, 3-158
Limits(ations) i-1, 1-3–4, 1-14, 1-18, 1-20, 1-24–25, 1-27, 1-59–60, 1-68–69, 1-79–80, 1-91–93, 1-95, 1-101, 1-105–107, 1-109, 2-25, 2-28, 2-44, 2-49, 2-52, 2-58–60, 2-66, 2-68–69, 3-2–5, 3-7, 3-11, 3-20, 3-41, 3-48, 3-54–63, 3-72, 3-88, 3-99, 3-104, 3-122, 3-129–130, 3-132, 3-134, 3-148–149, 3-153, 3-155, 3-166, 4-8, 4-10, 4-12–13, 5-14, 5-27–29, 5-34, 5-42, A-2, A-3, A-6, A-12
Lincoln 3-38
Litigation 2-71
Load factor 1-92, 1-95, 2-68, 3-23, 3-25–26, 3-46–51, 3-54–63, 3-72, 3-99, 3-183, 5-14, A-2, A-12
Locked wheel .5-55
Lockup 5-48
Logan, Utah 3-179–180

Logbook 2-54, 3-145, 5-1
Longitudinal . . 1-73–74, 1-94, 2-47, 2-51, 2-62–63, 3-104–105, 5-18, 5-50–51, 5-54, A-8
Longmont, Colo. 3-178
Loop(ing,s) 1-97, 2-4, 2-65, 3-43, 3-170, 5-17, 5-21–22, 5-52–53, 5-58
LORAN 1-41, 3-82, 3-142, 3-176, 4-11, 5-38, A-6
Lost procedures 3-1, 3-111
Loveland Pass .1-39
Low altitude i-7, 1-10, 1-40, 2-70, 3-9, 3-27, 3-31, 3-33, 3-36, 3-40, 3-68, 3-141, I3-147, 3-161, 3-165–166, 3-169, 3-171, 3-174, 4-10, 4-15, 5-10, 5-12, A-4, A-8, A-13
Low and slow 3-106, 5-13
Low performance i-6, 3-62
Low power 2-33, 2-56–57, 3-17, 4-8
Low speed 1-11, 1-88–89, 2-3, 2-44, 2-46, 3-31, 3-46, 3-51, 3-54, 3-69, 3-106, 5-5–6, 5-9–10m 5-48, A-11
Low wing 3-127, 3-173, 5-27, 5-42
Low-Level temperature inversion 3-75
Lowry, John 2-43
Lows 3-153, 3-155–156
Lubber line 1-99, 1-102
Lubricants 1-84
Lull 2-9, 3-38, 3-69, 3-72, 3-107
Lungs 1-27–29, 4-4
Lycoming, Avco 1-84, 2-25, 4-8

M

Magnetic compass i-8, 1-1, 1-51, 1-97–104, 3-3, 3-113
Magnetic dip 1-97–98, 1-101–103
Magneto 4-8
Maintenance i-3, 1-80, 2-5, 2-31, 3-178, 4-7, 4-10, 5-56
Malad City, Ida. 3-179–180
Mammoth Lakes 3-181
Maneuver speed 1-68, 3-41, 3-53–56, 3-60, 3-184, A-2–3
Maneuvering speed . . 1-108, 3-12, 3-23, 3-41–44, 3-56, 3-60–63, 3-67–68, 3-71–73, 3-185, 4-6–7, A-3, A-12
Manifold . . . 1-18–20, 1-82, 2-22, 2-26, 2-33
Manifold pressure 1-17, 1-20–23, 2-27, 2-32, 2-34, 2-50, 2-66, 4-7–8, 4-10, 5-25, A-7
Manual i-2, i-8, 1-13, 1-15, 1-50, 1-76, 1-80, 1-84, 1-96, 1-107, 2-11, 2-15, 2-18, 2-45, 2-52–53, 2-56, 2-59, 2-70, 3-13, 3-55, 3-57, 3-60–61, 3-87, 3-114, 3-129–132, 4-15, 5-28–30, A-12
Map(s) 1-112, 3-150–151, 3-154, 3-156
Marginal weather 1-10, 1-53, 1-59, 3-23, 3-35, 3-106, 3-109, 3-111, 3-161, 3-165, 4-17, A-8
Mattern, Jimmy 3-111
Maximum power 2-23, 2-27–28, 5-11
MDA 3-131

Index

MEA 2-70–71, 3-115, 3-120, 3-128, 3-145–146, 3-158–159
Mechanical discrepancy (altimeter) 1-112
Mechanical turbulence 1-23,s 3-67–69
Medical 1-25, 1-50, 4-1, 4-3, 5-56
Medicine(tion,s) 3,40, 5-56
Mediterranean 1-67
Membrane 1-29–31, 4-4
Memorize(ation) 1-41–43, 1-105, 2-4, 5-2
Mercury   1-27, 1-79–80, 1-111–112, 3-113, 2-8–9, 2-73
Meridian   1-42–43, 1-48–49, 1-51–52, 1-99, 3-112
Metabolism(ize) 1-27, 1-31, 5-56
METARs 3-82, 3-100, 3-151, 3-157
Meteorology i-9, 1-53–54, 3-4, 3-149
Methanol 1-15, 3-131
METO power 3-140
Mexico 1-45
MH, magnetic heading 1-42, 1-44
Milk(ing)   2-45, 2-55, 2-57, 2-66, 3-14, 3-118, 3-125, 2-144, 5-13–14, 5-18–19
Millivolt 2-31
Milliwatts 3-145
Minimum control speed 1-109, 2-66
Minimum maneuver speed .3-41, 3-53, 3-56, 3-184, A-2-3
Minnesota 1-67
Misconception 2-10, 3-88, 4-4
Misfiring 4-8
Missouri 1-67
Mistake(s)   1-45, 3-3, 3-61, 3-103, 3-113, 4-9, 5-2, 5-17, 5-24
Mixed ice 3-119
Mixture distribution 2-21, 2-26, 2-29
Mnemonic 1-41
MOCA 2-70, 3-145
Moffat Tunnel, Colo. 1-39
Moist adiabatic lapse rate 1-63, 1-65
Monomethyl 1-15, 3-131
Monoxide, carbon 1-30–31, 2-6
Montana 3-45, A-1
Mosquito(es) 3-177, 5-55–56
Mother of pearl 3-95, 3-99
Mountain downdrafts 3-23, 3-30
Mountain sickness 1-30
Mountain wave   1-39, 1-45, 1-56, 1-67, 1-79, 2-69, 3-1, 3-28, 3-30, 3-32, 3-76, 3-79, 3-87´88, 3-90–100, 3-115, 3-124, 3-137–139, 3-141–143, 3-147, 4-18, A-6–7, A-12
Mountain winds 3-65, 3-68
Mountaintop . . i-6, 2-69, 3-7, 3-24, 3-30, 3-63–65, 3-67, 3-70–71, 3-91–32, 3-99, 3-101, 3-139, 3-181, 3-183, A-10
Mountology 1-3, 1-7
Mud(dy) 2-18, 2-56, 2-74, 4-13, 5-41–42
Multiengine 2-66

Multiviscosity 1-71, 1-81–85
MVFR 3-153

N

Narrow canyons   1-5, 2-68, 3-33, 3-35, 3-40, 3-105–106, 3-180, 4-14, A-11
Nasal 1-33, 4-4–5
Natural horizon   2-48, 2-67, 2-69–70, 3-4, 3-8, 3-11, 3-45, 3-48–49, 5-2
Navaids A-6
Navigate(tion,ional) .   1-10, 1-37, 1-40–48, 1-50–51, 1-98, 3-82, 3-105–106, 3-124, 3-145–146, 3-176, A-6
Navigation log 3-20, 3-22
Need to know i-1, 1-46, 4-13
Neon 1-26
Neoprene 3-130
Neosynephrine 4-4
Neural 5-56
Neurons 3-17
Neutralize 5-21
Never exceed 1-107, 1-109, 3-59
Night vision 3-13, 3-14, 3-16
Night flying . . .   1-3, 1-10, 1-48, 3-1, 3-11, 3-13–18, 3-20–22, 3-104, 3-161, 3-173, 3-176, A-8, A-14
Nitrites 1-30–31
Nitrogen 1-25–26, 3-133
No flap 5-14
No wind   1-23, 1-43, 3-7, 3-28–29, 5-7, 5-35, 5-37–38
NOAA 1-38
No-go   1-9, 1-53, 1-55, 2-54, 2-59, 3-150–151, 3-158, 5-30
Noise 1-83, 3-35, 3-127–128, 3-146
Non-paved 5-41
Non-standard pressure 1-111, 1-113
Non-standard temperature   1-28, 1-79, 1-111, 1-114, 2-8, 2-11, A-13
Non-turbo(charged) 1-11, 1-36, 3-147
Normal takeoff   2-16, 2-17–19, 2-37, 2-45–46, 2-48–50, 2-58, 2-62, 2-74, 3-17 5-23, A-13
Normally aspirated   1-11–12, 1-17, 1-36, 2-25–26, 2-29–30, 2-66, 3-147
Northerly turning error 1-98, 1-101–104
Nose down .1-79, 3-31, 3-165, 3-170, 5-13–14
Nose high 3-166, 5-42
Nose low 3-40, 3-165, 3-173, 5-25
Nose up 2-48, 3-37, 3-57, 3-82
Noseover 1-94, 5-42, 5-55
Nosewheel . . .2-56, 2-58, 5-17, 5-19–20, 5-42
Nostrils 4-4
NOTAMS 1-57–58, 3-104
Novice   i-2, i-5, i-9, 1-10, 1-45, 2-8, 2-56, 3-7, 3-27, 3-33, 3-45, 3-52, 3-103, 5-2, A-7
NTSB 1-54, 3-103–105, 3-178
Nylon 1-15, 3-177, A-9

O

Obliterate(d) 3-177
Obscuration .1-54, 1-60, 3-145–146, 3-153, 3-177
Obscure(d,ment,ing)   i-6, 1-48, 1-59–60, 2-6, 2-69, 3-14, 3-145, 3-153, 3-177, 3-179
Obstacle   1-111, 2-7–8, 2-40, 2-42, 2-45, 2-48, 2-52–57, 2-67, 2-69, 3-18, 3-166, 3-168–170, 5-43–44, 5-46–47, A-13
Obstruction to wind flow turbulence . . .3-69–70
Obstruction(s)   1-37, 1-48, 1-66, 1-68, 1-109, 2-19, 2-50, 2-67, 2-70–71, 3-17–18, 3-21, 3-69–70, 3-74, 3-88, 3-145, 3-152–153, 3-158, 3-166, 3-170, 3-173, 4-3, A-8
Obtuse 5-24–25, 5-33
Ocean 1-63, 3-78, 3-88–89
Octane 2-32
Odorless 2-6
Off load   1-91, 1-93, 2-16, 2-39, 3-61, 3-181, 4-15
Offset 1-73, 1-75, 1-100, 5-13, 5-54
Oil(s)   1-13, 1-61, 1-71, 1-81–86, 1-89, 1-93, 1-96, 2-3, 2-26, 2-44, 2-68, 3-35, 3-49
Oklahoma .1-67, 1-76
One way .   i-2, 2-2, 2-18, 2-42, 2-67, 3-14, 3-58, 4-15, 5-2, 5-14, 5-30, 5-36
Opaque 3-125
Optimum cruise altitude 1-9, 1-11–12
Optimum   1-9, 1-11–12, 2-24, 2-31, 2-44, 5-9, 5-28–30, 5-33–34, 5-37, 5-40
Orographic .   3-10, 3-12, 3-34, 3-38, 3-63, 3-126, 3-141, 3-151, A-10
Oscillation(s)   1-91–92, 1-97, 1-99, 1-101, 1-104, 3-71, 3-73, 3-92–93, 3-133
Otitis 4-3
Out of balance 1-91, 3-128
Overload(ed) 1-91, 1-95
Over rotate 2-57
Over stressed 1-94, 3-62, 3-181
Overboost(ing) .4-10
Overcast 1-60, 3-19, 3-153, 5-39
Over flight 4-13
Overhaul 1-36, 1-77, 1-83, 2-8, 2-30
Overheat(ing) 2-6, 2-23, 3-133
Overleaning 2-6, 2-23, 3-133
Overshoot(ing) 3-22, 3-92, 5-27, 5-40
Overspeed 4-10
Oxygen   1-9, 1-24–35, 1-39, 2-10, 3-7, 3-16, 3-101, 3-113, 3-147, 3-180–181, A-6
Oxyhemoglobin 1-31–31

P

Parachute 1-92, 3-44
Parallax 3-8, 3-20, 3-107–108, 5-36, A-9
Paralleled(s)   1-39, 1-50–52, 1-73–74, 1-98, 1-101–102, 2-4–5, 2-47, 2-50, 2-62–64, 3-10, 3-17, 3-29, 3-37, 3-64, 3-88, 3-98, 3-100, 3-112, 3-141, 3-146, 3-154–155, 3-166, 3-169, 3-171–172, 4-18, 5-22, 5-48, 5-50–54, 5-60, 5-64, A-8, A-13
Paranasal 4-5
Parasite 1-11, 2-46–47, 5-5–7, 5-11
Park(ed,ing) .1-13, 1-112, 2-19, 3-97, 3-107, 5-55–56
Partial pressure, oxygen 1-26–31
Pass(age,ageway,es)   i-6, i-12, 1-10, 1-19–21, 1-28, 1-39, 1-42, 1-60–61, 1-67, 1-75, 1-80, 1-82, 1-86, 2-6, 2-22, 2-26, 2-33–34, 2-50, 3-4, 3-6, 3-8, 3-18, 3-23, 3-31, 3-36–39, 3-51, 3-73, 3-76, 3-82, 3-91, 3-101, 3-116, 3-129, 3-134, 3-137, 3-144–146, 3-149, 3-178, 3-182, 5-25, 5-51
Patchy 3-120
Pattern   i-3, i-12, 1-53, 1-55, 2-9, 2-20, 2-30, 2-68, 3-11, 3-18, 3-20–21, 3-34, 3-46, 3-52, 3-88, 3-90–91, 3-96, 3-111, 3-114, 3-136–137, 3-139, 3-142, 3-144, 3-154, 3-156, 3-169, 4-3, 4-11–12, 4-15, 5-2, 5-10, 5-23, 5-25, 5-30, 5-36, 5-39–40, 5-43, 5-46, A-7
Peak(s)   i-5, 1-81, 2-24–27, 2-29–30, 3-69, 3-178
Pennant 3-155
Performance   i-3–4, i-6–9, 1-4, 1-9, 1-11–12, 1-16, 1-40, 1-44, 1-46–47, 1-69, 1-79–81, 1-85, 1-88–94, 1-110–111, 2-1, 2-7–21, 2-24, 2-27, 2-30, 2-37–39, 2-42, 2-45–46, 2-56–57, 2-63, 2-65–66, 2-69, 2-71, 3-2, 3-7, 3-32, 3-34–35, 3-38, 3-44, 3-55, 3-62, 3-67, 3-82, 3-104, 3-115, 3-121, 3-126, 3-128, 3-135, 3-141, 3-147, 3-150, 3-158, 3-171, 3-174, 4-9, 4-13–15, 5-3, 5-7, 5-9–13, 5-26, 5-33–34, 5-37, 5-44, 5-47, A-6
Peripheral 1-32, 3-16, 5-26
Peroxide 1-85
Perspective 5-1–2, 5-23, 5-36, 5-46, A-9
Petroleum 1-84
P-factor 1-74, 1-75, 2-36, 2-51, 2-62
Phenomena   1-37, 1-59–60, 1-67, 3-12, 3-35, 3-44, 3-153
Philippines 3-178
Photosensitive 3-14
Phraseology 5-55
Physician 1-34, 4-4, 5-56
Pilotage 1-40–41, 1-50–51, 3-112
PIREP   1-58, 1-61, 3-67, 3-81, 3-84–85, 3-97, 3-100, 3-125, 3-132, 3-137, 3-145–147, 3-150, 3-152, 3-157–158, 3-179, 3-181
Pistol 3-177
Pitch . . .   1-23, 1-77, 1-92, 2-48, 3-17, 3-46, 3-49–51, 3-57, 3-73, 3-77, 3-84–85, 3-108, 3-144, 3-168, 3-170, 3-172, 4-10, 5-7–8, 5-13–14, 5-16–20, 5-37–38, 5-41, 5-46–47
Pitons 5-55
Pitot static 1-110, 3-127

Placard(s,ed) 1-6, 1-107, 3-170, 5-15
Plains 1-59, 1-67
Plan . . . .
i-6–9, 1-4, 1-24, 1-39, 1-40–46, 1-48, 1-54, 2-6, 2-20, 3-17–19, 3-53, 3-103, 3-112, 3-147, 3-152, 3-159–160, 3-165, 3-169, 3-171, 3-175–176, 3-179, 3-181, 4-15, 4-18, A-6, A-8, A-12
Planning i-4, 1-9–10,1-37–38, 1-40, 1-43–46, 1-50–51, 1-47, 1-79, 1-81, 3-2–3, 3-18, 3-87, 3-100, 3-103–104, 3-111–112, 3-141, 3-150, 3-152, 3-0157, 3-160–162, 3-165, 3-167, 3-173, 5-43, A-6
Plateau 1-66–67, 3-39, 3-179
Pliers 4-12
Pocatello, Ida. 3-179
Podunk 4-12
POH 1-11, 1-35, 1-50, 1-80–81, 1-96, 2-13, 2-26, 2-43, 2-52, 3-48, 3-57, 5-14, A-12
Point of free convection 1-62
Point-to-point i-5, 1-11, 1-46–47
Poisons 1-30
Polar front 3-87, 3-89, 3-91
Polar outbreak 3-87, 3-89, 3-91
Polar region 3-89–91, 3-139
Polar tropopause 3-88–89
Poles 1-48, 1-51, 1-99–101, 3-12, 3-35, 3-88–90, 3-109, 3-171, 3-181
Police 1-56
Polish(ed,ing) 2-48, 3-119, 3-130, 3-137
Pond(s) 3-107
Porpoise(ing) 1-91, 5-17, 5-19–20
Portland, Ore. .3-106
Post flight 5-150
Postpone(d,ing) i-9, 1-24, 1-68, 2-69, 3-67, 3-140–141, 3-158, 3-181, A-10
Power off i-8, 1-90, 1-105, 1-107, 3-35, 3-40, 3-49, 3-146, 4-6, 4-17, 5-21, A-11
Power on i-10, 1-73–74, 5-21, 5-30
Precautionary landing 1-6, 1-70, 3-106, 3-161–162, 3-176
Precautionary i-1
Precaution(s)1-14, 3-1, 3-7, 3-100, 3-147, 5-15, 5-47
Precession 2-36, 2-52
Preflight i-2, i-4, 1-1–2, 1-4, 1-9, 1-13, 1-15, 1-24, 1-37, 1-40, 1-44–46, 1-50, 1-56, 1-81, 1-87, 1-115, 3-18, 3-80, 3-103–104, 3-111–113, 3-141, 3-158, 3-160–161, 3-167, 3-173, 3-179, A-5, A-8
Preheat(ing) 1-20, 1-71, 1-81–83, 2-35
Preignition 3-21, 2-32–33
Prelanding 5-2, 5-26, 5-37–38, 5-40, 5-46
Premix 1-16
Pressure altitude 1-34, 1-79, 1-93, 1-111, 2-8–9, 2-11–13, 3-154, A-13
Prevailing Westerlies . . .1-67, 3-38, 3-64, 3-91

Procedure(s) i-1–4, 1-9, 1-13, 1-15, 1-17, 1-21–22, 1-69–71, 1-76, 1-80, 1-87, 1-93, 2-11, 2-21, 2-26–30, 2-50, 2-57, 2-62, 2-65, 2-67, 2-70, 3-1–2, 3-17, 3-23–24, 3-42, 3-46, 3-49, 3-51, 3-67, 3-71, 3-76, 3-83, 3-85, 3-87, 3-100–101, 3-104, 3-107–108, 3-111, 3-116, 3-131, 3-133–134, 3-140, 3-143, 3-147, 3-157, 3-166, 49–10, 5-1, 5-7, 5-14, 5-19, 5-30, 5-40–42, 5-56, A-5, A-12
Prop(eller,s) . . i-3, i-6–7, i-10, 1-12, 1-20, 1-22–23, 1-73–75, 1-81–82, 1-85, 1-106, 2-3, 2-6–8, 2-12–15, 2-21–22, 2-28–29, 2-33–34, 2-36, 2-38, 2-45, 2-50–55, 2-66, 2-73, 3-124, 3-126–128, 3-133, 3-166, 3-168, 3-176, 4-7–10, 5-3, 5-21, 5-256, 5-42, 5-47, 5=55, A-6
Propeller icing 3-128
Psychological hazards 3-161, 3-163
Psychological 2-55, 3-129
Psychology 1-7

Q

Quartering 2-4–5, 5-19–20

R

Radar 1-48, 3-6, 3-21, 3-79, 3-114, 3-149, 3-157, 3-180, 5-35
Radius of turn i-11, 2-68, 3-41–43, 3-47, 3-51–54, 3-57, 3-110, 3-184, A-11
Radius 3-40, 3-56, 3-124, 3-139, A-2, A-11
Railroad 1-39, 3-106, 3-111, 3-177
Rain 1-19, 1-54, 1-60–62, 2-10, 2-18, 2-33, 3-6, 3-35, 3-81, 3-111, 3-117–118, 3-120, 3-121, 3-123, 3-138–141, 3-149, 3-158, 5-23, 5-25, 5-33, A-9
Rainbow 3-120
Raining 2-3, 2-10, 3-129
Rapid descents 3-170, 4-7
Rapid throttle operation 4-9, 4-17, A-7
Rate of climb i-7, 1-12, 1-23, 1-40, 1-80, 1-95, 1-108–109, 2-9, 2-11–2-12, 2-14–15, 2-19–20, 2-40, 2-44–45, 2-48–50, 2-52–55, 2-57–58, 2-67, 2-69–73, 3-11, 3-18, 3-32, 3-35, 3-48–51, 3-101, 3-113, 3-125, 3-128, 3-158, 3-166–167, 4-9, 4-14, 5-2, 5-8, 5-11, 5-47
Rate of turn 3-54, A-2–3
Ravine 3-10, 3-33–34, 3-178
Recommendation i-1, i-8, i-10, 1-12, 1-15, 1-17, 1-104, 2-23, 2-26–27, 2-29–31, 2-44–46, 2-52–53, 3-24, 3-36, 3-129, 3-131, 3-133, 3-161, 3-170, 3-181, 4-9, 5-16, 5-56
Recommended lean mixture 2-21, 2-26–27, 2-29–30
Recommended 1-14, 1-23, 1-44, 1-48–49, 1-57, 1-82, 2-19, 2-29, 2-31, 2-51–53, 3-3, 3-

7, 3-35, 3-43, 3l-72, 3-105, 3-114, 3-134, 3-166, 3-168, 3-199, 4-7, 4-8, 5-16, 5-44
Refracted .3-120–121
Refreeze 1-84
Region of reverse command 5-5, 5-12
Rerouting 3-141
Rescue(d,s)   i-1, i-7, 1-46, 3-1, 3-27, 3-33, 3-40, 3-175, 3-178, 3-180, 3-182, A-6
Retina(l) 3-16–17
Retractable gear 3-167, 5-42
Return   i-9, 1-5–6, 1-8, 1-23, 1-61, 1-64, 1-98, 1-115, 2-16, 2-34, 2-69, 3-3–4, 3-9, 3-12, 3-16, 3-33, 3-36–39, 3-45–46, l3-61, 3-77, 3-90, 3-121, 3-134, 3-178–179, 3-184, 4-14, 4-17, 5-19, 5-50, A-5, A-8, A-11
Reversal   i-11, 2-67–68, 3-23, 3-30, 3-42, 3-44, 3-46, 3-50, 3-52, 3-75, 3-78, 3-159, A-11
Reversed i-3, 1-44, 2-56, 3-145, 5-5, 5-10
Revolver 8-177
Ridge(s)   i-4, i-6, i-8–10, 1-5, 1-55, 1-64–65, 1-67–68, 1-70, 1-80, 2-69, 3-4,.3-7–10, 3-12, 3-20, 3-23–26, 3-28–31, 3-38–40, 3-46, 3-63–65, 3-68–69, 3-88, 3-92, 3-94, 3-100–101, 3-118, 3-129, 3-141, 3-153, 3-179–180, 3-183, 4-17, 5-39, 5-62, A-9–11
Ridgelinei-10, 1-67, 3-28–29, 3-40, 3-92, 3-101, A-11
Rifle 3-177
Rime ice 3-118–119, 3-125, 3-145–146
Ringing 4-3
Ripple(d) 2-69, 3-118, 3-169
Risk(s)   i-1, 1-3, 1-8, 1-94, 2-5, 2-23, 2-35, 3-163, 5-14, 5-46
River(s)   1-37, 1-44, 1-67–68, 2-40, 3-4, 3-35, 3-38–39, 3-87, 3-106, 3-111–112, 3-170, 3-172–173, 4-13–14, 5-4
Road(s)   1-37, 1-39, 1-55, 3-9, 3-111–112, 3-167, 3-171, 5-5, A-1
Roadblock 1-55, 3-9
Roaring Fork River, Colo. 3-38
Rockies 1-63, 1-67
Rocks . . .   2-3, 2-53–56, 3-167, 3-176, A-16
Rocky 2-18, 2-74, 3-33
Rocky Mountains 3-93, 3-178
Rods 3-14, 3-16
Roll cloud 3-90, 3-97, A-4
Rope 3-133, 5-58
Rotate   1-106, 2-38, 2-48–51, 2-53–54, 2-57
Rotation speed   1-92, 1-109, 2-17–18, 2-41, 2-48, 2-74, A-8, A-13
Rotor cloud 3-95–99, 3-101, 5-62
Rotor(s)   1-83, 3-70, 3-76, 3-80–81, 3-86, 3-95–101, 4-5, 5-62, A-7, A-12
Rough air speed 1-68, 1-108, 3-60, 3-72
Rough field 2-38, 2-56
Roughness   1-22, 1-82, 2-25, 2-28–30, 2-32, 3-49, 3-69, 3-128, 3-136, 4-8

Roulette 3-137
Route   i-2, i-4, i-6–7, i-9, i-11, 1-1, 1-6, 1-8–10, 1-12, 1-14, 1-23–24, 1-37–40, 1-42, 1-44–50, 1-52, 1-54–59, 1-70, 1-113, 1-115, 2-20, 2-68, 2-70, 3-1–2, 3-7, 3-18, 3-21, 3-27, 3-30, 3-32, 3-38, 3-100, 3-104–105, 3-107, 3-111, 3-115, 3-123, 3-141, 3-143, 3-145–147, 3-150–152, 3-155, 3-157–160, 3-167, 3-175, 3-176, 3-178–181, 3-183, 4-3, 4-16–17, A-2, A-6, A-8, A-15
Rudders   1-6, 1-73–79, 1-83, 2-3, 2-36, 2-52, 2-58, 2-61–63, 2-65, 3-37, 3-70–71, 3-73, 3-104–105, 3-133, 3-171–172, l3-185, 5-18, 5-21, 5-48, 5-50–52, 5-54, A-5–6, A-8
Runup 2-3
Runway edge 3-17
Runway gradient 2-37, 2-43
Runway lengthi-6, i-10, 1-3, 1-93, 2-37, 2-39, 2-40, 2-42–43, 2-47–48, 2-54, 2-58, 2-63, 2-74, 3-1, 4-15–16, A-13
Russian 3-137

S

Saccule 3-19
Sailplane 3-10, 3-94, 3-99
Sand 2-3, 2-18, 2-56, 5-41
Saturated air 1-18, 1-63–64
Sea breeze fronts 3-78
Sea level pressure 1-80, 3-156
Search and rescue   i-1, i-7, 1-46, 3-27, 3-33, 3-40, 3-175, 3-178, A-6
Sectional .i-8, 1-37, 1-39, 1-45, 2-70, 3-8, 3-35, 3-111, 3-118, 3-141, 3-181
Self preservation   1-76, 3-31, 3-37, 3-44, 3-49, 3-63, 3-163
Semicircular .3-19
Shadow(ed,s) 1-66, 3-9, 331, 3-34, 3-120
Shallow(er) 1-66, 2-42, 3-94, 3-120, 3-123, A-6
Shear(ing,s)   i-7–8, 2-20, 3-30, 3-33, 3-67–68, 3-73–85, 3-179, 3-185, 5-30, 5-33, 5-38, A-11
Shed 3-140
Sheriff 1-55, 3-9, 3-180
Shock(ing)i-8, i-12, 2-26, 3-92, 3-180, 4-6–8, 4-10, 4-17, 5-25, A-7
Shortcuts 1-50
Short-field landing 5-1, 5-43–47, 5-57
Shotgun 3-177
Shunts 1-20, 1-31, 2-3
Side slip 5-49–52, 5-54, A-6
Sideward 1-73, 2-62, 3-50, 5-54
Sideways .2-64, 5-50
Sierra 1-88, 3-94, 3-182
SIGMETS 3-137, 3-152, 3-157
Signaling .3-177, A-9
Signpost 3-71, 3-96–97
Silicone 3-129

Index

Single channel 2-29, 2-31
Sink(ers,ing) i-11, 1-65, 1-68, 2-45–46, 2-57, 3-21, 3-39, 3-41, 3-63–64, 3-66, 3-77, 3-79, 3-83, 3-92–94, 3-97, 3-146, 3-165–166, 3-170, 3-177, 5-2, 5-4, 5-9, 5-13–14, 5-19, 5-26, 5-29, 5-41, 5-44, 5-64, A-6
Sinus(es) 4-3, 4-5
Skid(ding) 1-73–74, 2-63, 5-48
Skills .i-2, 1-4, 1-50, 2-71, 3-3, 3-100, 3-114, 3-168
Slant range 3-108
Sling(er,s) 2-53, 2-67, 3-124, 3-128
Slip(ping,s) . . . 1-73–74, 2-6, 2-50, 2-65, 3-104–105, 3-169–170, 5-10, 5-15, 5-43, 5-47–52, 5-54, 5-58, A-6, A-8
Slipstream .1-73, 1-75, 2-26, 2-36, 2-52, 3-129, 3-140
Slope(d,s,ing) 1-62–63, 1-65–68, 2-19, 2-41, 2-43, 2-71, 3-4, 3-22, 3-27, 3-29, 3-33, 3-35, 3-38–39, 3-63, 3-65, 3-76–77, 382–83, 3-92, 3-121, 3-126, 3-140–141, 3-155, 3-167–169, 3-171–172, 4-11, 5-23, 5-33–35, 5-38, 5-61, 5-64, A-11–12
Slow moving 3-6, 3-120, 3-149, 3-151
Slow speed   1-89, 2-3, 2-44, 2-46, 3-31, 3-46, 3-51, 3-54, 3-106, 5-6, 5-9–10, 5-48, A-11
Slow(ed,er,est,ing) 3-106, 5-6, 5-9–10, 5-48, A-11
Slung 1-13, 3-128
Slush . . .2-18–19, 2-56, 2-67, 3-134, 3-147, 5-41–42
Smoke(y)   1-131, 1-65, 3-9, 3-18, 3-20, 3-48, 3-102, 3-111, 3-169, 3-176, 3-177
Snag 3-36, 3-170
Snow covered 2-6, 3-14, 3-177
Snowshoes 3-177, 3-180
Soaring 3-32
Soft field . . .2-18, 2-19, 2-48, 2-63, 2-74, 5-41
Soft-field takeoff 2-37, 2-45–46, 2-56–58, 2-68, A-6
Solar 2-41, 3-34, A-10
Solipsism 1-92
Sparsely 3-18–19, 3-179
Spin recovery 1-79
Spin(ning,s)   1-5–7, 1-72, 1-76–79, 1-95, 2-3, 2-36, 2-52, 2-67, 3-37, 3-43, 3-46, 3-70, 3-128, 3-133, 3-171, 3-176, A-6
Spot landing 4-15, 5-33, 5-38
Squall 3-5–6, 3-149
Stabilator 3-181
Stabilized landing approach . .5-23, 5-25, 5-34
Stagnant hypoxia 1-31
Stall speed   1-88, 1-109, 2-44, 2-59, 2-689, 3-25–26, 3-41, 3-44, 3-46–47, 3-49–50, 3-52, 2-54–58, 3-60–61, 3-63, 3-72–73, 3-119, 3-125, 3-136, 3-144, 3-148, 3-168, 3-183, 3-185, 5-28–29, A-2–3

Stall warning 3-72, 3-144
Standard lapse rate 1-26, 1-64, 3-92
Standing lenticular 3-87
Standing wave 3-76, 3-87, 3-90, 3-101
Stationary 3-9, 3-76, 3-88, 3-97–99
Steep turn 3-25, 2-46–47, 3-49–50, 3-52, 3-166
Stoichiometric 1-16–17, 2-24
Stratiform 3-118, 3-120, 3-121–122, 3-138–139
Stratocumulus 3-98
Stratosphere 1-26, 3-88–89, 3-97
Stratus   1-60, 1-62, 3-35, 3-119–120, 3-122, 3-138
Strip(s)   i-6, i-8, i-10–12, 1-17, 1-24, 1-55–56, 1-59, 1-61, 1-93, 1-106, 2-1–2, 2-8, 2-16, 2-18, 2-27–28, 2-37–38, 2-41–42, 2-44, 2-48, 2-54–55, 2-58, 2-67–68, 3-2, 3-11, 3-104, 3-173, 4-1–2, 4-6, 4-13–16, 5-2, 5-9, 5-23, 5-30–32, 5-34, 5-41, 5-43–46, 5-55–56, 5-60, 5-62, A-6–8
Subfreezing .3-123
Sublimate 3-119
Subside(ence,ing) . .1-65, 3-34, 3-38–39, 3-63
Sump 1-13–15, 3-131
Supercharged(er)   i-10, 1-11, 1-17, 2-25–26, 2-29, 2-38, 2-49–50, 2-53, 2-66, 4-8, 4-10
Supercooled water droplets   3-100, 3-117, 3-120, 3-122–125, 3-137–138, 3-142
Supplemental oxygen   1-25, 1-33–35, 1-39, 3-7, 3-16, 3-101, 3-147, 3-180–181
Survival equipment   i-7, 1-24, 1-91, 3-172, 3-175–176, A-9
Swinging the compass 1-99, 1-101

T

Taildragger . .   2-37, 2-53–55, 5-21, 5-45–55
Tail wheel .   1-83, 1-94, 2-50, 2-53, 2-56–37
Tailwind   i-8, 2-4–7, 2-16–18, 2-37, 2-40–43, 2-74, 3-32, 3-38, 3-40, 3-74, 3-77, 3-82–84, 3-112, 3-168, 5-10, 5-38, A-13
Takeoff, cold weather 2-37, 2-66
Takeoff, short-field .   2-37–38, 2-45–46, 2-48, 2-51–54, 2-56, 5-16
Takeoff, soft-field . .   2-37, 2-45–46, 2-56–58
Taku 1-67
Tehachapi 3.94
Teledyne Continental 1-84, 2-71
Temperature-dew point 1-19, 3-125, 3-153–155
TERPS 2-70–71
Teton(s)   3-1, 3-9, 3-24, 3-27, 3-37, 3-71, 3-95, 3-175, 4-18 A-4, A-15
Thermal shock   .i-8, i-12, 4-6–8, 4-10, 4-17, 5-25, A-7
Thiamin 5-56
Thumbs up method 2-5, 5-52
Thumpers 5-2
Tie-down 5-55–56, 5-58
Tioga Pass 3-182

Tire(s) 2-67, 3-16, 3-48, 5-22, 5-46, 5-48
Tools 3-6, A-9
Tornado 1-13, 2-3
Torque 1-73–75, 2-36, 2-50–51, 2-62, 3-43
Touchdown   2-44, 3-161, 3-163–165, 3-168, 1-370–171, 4-13, 4-15, 5-2, 5-15, 5-18–19, 5-21, 5-36–37, 5-40–46, 5-49, 5-51–53, 5-61, 5-64, A-13
Track .1-40, 1-42, 2-62, 2-64, 3-46, 3-111, 5-50
Translucent 3-118, 3-125
Transparent 1-13, 3-118
Trap(ped,s) 1-55, 5-29
Trauma 4-4
Traverse(d,ing) 3-34, 3-68, 3-180
Treetop 3-31, 3-37
Tricycle gear   2-49, 2-51, 2-56–58, 2-63, 2-65, 5-15, 5-21, 5-42
Tropopause 1-26, 3-88–89, 3-94, 3-97
Troubleshoot(ing) 2-32, 3-165
TRSA 1-38, 1-48
Tunnel 1-18, 1-39, 3-28, 3-64, 3-106, A-10
Turbulence penetration 3-71
Turn around   1-5–6, 1-60, 3-4, 3-29–33, 3-36, 3-38, 3-40–41, 3-43–45, 3-48, 3-52–54, 3-57, 3-101, 3-159, 3-184, 4-17, A-6, A-11
Turn radius .   3-40, 3-52–53, 3-56, 3-184, A-2–4, A-11–12
Turn rate 1-101, A-3
TWEB 1-57
Tympanic 4-3

U

Uinta Mountains 1-67, 3-64
Underpowered 5-13
Upwash 2-47, 3-136, 3-139
Updraft(s)   i-3, i-6, i-s11, 1-1, 1-61, 1-67–68, 2-2, 3-23–24, 3-27, 3-29, 3-31, 3-34–35, 3-38, 3-39–41, 3-53, 3-63, 3-65–68, 3-70, 3-90, 3-93, 3-95, 3-99–101, 3-106, 3-121, 3-138, 3-142, 5-44, 5-59, A-4, A-7, A-10–12
Uphill 2-42–43, 5-23, 5-59
Upstream i-8, 2-41, 5-31
Urine 5-56
Utah 1-67, 3-64, 3-179–180, A-1
Utricle 3-19

V

Valley winds 1-53, 1-66
Valsalva maneuver 4-3–4
Vancouver 3-111
Vapor   1-12, 1-18–21, 1-62–63, 1-82, 2-10, 2-23, 2-33, 3-96
VASI 3-22, 5-35
Vasoconstrictors 4-4–5
Venous 1-31
Venturi   i-6, 1-13, 1-20–21, 1-55–56, 1-67, 2-26, 3-67–68, 3-104, A-10

Vertigo 3-13, 3-18–20, 4-3–4
Vestibular 3-19–20
Vibration(s) 3-44, 3-126
Victor 1-46, 3-179
Virga 3-82
V speeds 1-105, 1-108, A-2
VOR   1-10, 1-39, 1-41–43, 1-48, 1-49, 1-51, 3-112–113, 3-115, 3-145–146, 3-179
Vortices 3-136

W

WAC i-8, 1-37, 1-45, 3-35, 3-181
Warm front 3-6, 3-76, 3-121–122, 3-149, 3-151
Warning(s)   i-1, 1-30, 1-48, 1-59, 2-22–23, 2-26, 3-34, 3-69, 3-72, 3-105, 3-107, 3-134, 3-144, 3-170, 4-17, 5-55
Wasatch Range 3-179–180
Washington 3-178, A-1
Wavelength   3-93–94, 3-99–100, 3-142–143, A-7, A-12
Weather accidents 1-53, 1-54
Weather briefing   1-45, 1-54, 2-68, 3-2, 3-100, 3-113, 3-116, 3-150–152, 3-160, 3-179
Weathercock 2-62, 5-49, 5-56
Weight and balance   1-1, 1-14, 1-44, 1-80, 1-83, 1-91, 1-93, 1-95–96, 3-126, A-8
Westerlies(y) .1-68–68, 3-38, 3-64, 3-91, 3-141
Wheelbarrow(ing) 5-17, 5-19–20
Whirlpool 1-13
Whistle(s) 1-105, 3-107, A-9
White Pass 3-178
Whiteout 3-173
Wind shear   2-20, 3-67–68, 3-73–77, 3-79–80, 3-82–85
Windward   1-39, 1-67, 2-4, 2-52, 3-63–64, 3-91–92, 3-95, 3-138, 3-141, 3-147
Wing over 3-43–44, 3-46, 3-50, A-11
Wires across canyons 3-23, 3-35
Wrangell Mountains 4-14
Wyoming .   1-38, 2-14, 3-95, 3-172, 3-175, 3-179, 4-11, A-1

X

Xenon 1-26

Y

Yakima, Wash....................3-178
Yaw 2-36, 2-50–52, 3-71, 3-84, 5-15, 5-51, A-5
Yelling 4-4
Yosemite 3-181–182
Zigzag(ging) 1-40, 3-25, 3-111

APPROACHING ASPEN, COLORADO AIRPORT (KASE) FROM THE SOUTH

FINAL APPROACH RUNWAY 15 ASPEN

Visit us on the web:

http://www.mountainflying.com